The Cambridge Handbook of
American Literature

THE CAMBRIDGE HANDBOOK
OF
AMERICAN
LITERATURE

edited by

Jack Salzman

**Director, Center for American Culture Studies,
Columbia University**

with

CAMERON BARDRICK NANCY NYSTUL
PAUL BONGIORNO JANE REMUS
LAURA HENIGMAN LUCY RINEHART
ERIC LOTT CLARE ROSSINI
PAUL M. McNEIL MARK SHERMAN

J. JORDAN SULLIVAN

The right of the
University of Cambridge
to print and sell
all manner of books
was granted by
Henry VIII in 1534.
The University has printed
and published continuously
since 1584.

CAMBRIDGE UNIVERSITY PRESS
Cambridge
London   New York   New Rochelle
Melbourne   Sydney

Published by the Press Syndicate of the University of Cambridge
The Pitt Building, Trumpington Street, Cambridge CB2 1RP
32 East 57th Street, New York, NY 10022, USA
10 Stamford Road, Oakleigh, Melbourne 3166, Australia

© Cambridge University Press 1986

First published 1986

Printed in Great Britain at the University Press, Cambridge

British Library cataloguing in publication data

The Cambridge handbook of American literature.
1. American literature – Dictionaries
I. Salzman, Jack
810'.3'21   PS21

Library of Congress cataloguing in publication data

The Cambridge handbook of American Literature.
Bibliography.
Includes index.
1 American literature – Dictionaries.
I. Salzman, Jack.
PS21.C36   1986   810'.3   86–2587

ISBN 0 521 30703 1

WV

Preface

The Cambridge Handbook of American Literature was designed from the outset to be more compact than other such reference works. It is intended as much for individuals as for libraries; we hope that its concise form will make it widely accessible as well as affordable, and that it will be carried and consulted with frequency.

It is, above all, a handbook of American *literature*, and the reader will find little that is digressive, anecdotal, or peripheral to this. Entries are designed to be factual and informative, biographical and bibliographical. The length of an entry should not necessarily be taken as an index to its subject's importance in the literary canon. Our guiding concern has been to provide basic information, and it sometimes turns out that the plot of a major novel or the career of a major author can reasonably be outlined in a briefer compass than can that of a lesser work or figure. We have deliberately tried not to be judgmental; such critical comments as there are tend to reflect received historical attitudes rather than our own opinions. Of course, since we are not producing an encyclopedia, we have been obliged to make decisions about what to leave out, and these decisions inevitably involve the exercise of critical judgment. We hope, though, that most readers will agree that the 750 or so entries that follow represent a core list of those writers, works, and movements of which some knowledge is essential to all serious students of American literature.

That said, we appreciate that some readers may still be concerned at certain omissions. We know, too, that despite our efforts to double and triple check facts and dates, it is in the nature of such reference works that there may be some errors. Should that indeed prove the case, we invite readers to write to us at the Center for American Culture Studies at Columbia University, informing us of any mistakes or lacunae they have noticed. When a second edition of the *Handbook* appears we will have an opportunity to correct errors and address the question of omissions.

As the title page indicates, this volume is the work of the staff of Columbia University's Center for American Culture Studies. Numerous members of staff not listed on the title page have also helped in various ways, and their efforts are gratefully acknowledged: Linda Ainsworth, David Cantor, Mary Corcoran, John Davis, Jeanne Gottschalk, Eric Haralson, Kevin Keenan, Donna Kerfoot, John Kilduff, Bette Kirschstein, Francesca Kobylarz, Jeff Levin, Daniel Manheim, Timothy Lubin, Jonathan Margolies, Nathaniel Margolies, Jackie Peters, Mark Rothman, Ellen Salzman, Laurence Sopala, Nancy Stula, Gordon Tapper, Margaret Vandenburg, Karen Ward, Jay Williams, Richard Wollman, Emily Wright, and Steve Wurtzler. Particular thanks are due to Meryl Altman, who, as usual, provided us with exceptional help when we most needed it. Nat Austen, Mary Dearborn, George Economu, Paul Kleinpoppen, Randy Malamud, Tenney Nathanson, and Eric Sandeen helped with various entries. Andrew Brown of Cambridge University Press must be singled out for his efforts to make the book not only more accurate but more readable. For their support, kindness, and generosity of spirit, we offer our thanks to Quentin Anderson, Ann Douglas, Mary Dobbie, Lynn Hieatt, Carl Hovde, Karl Kroeber, and especially to Joseph Ridgely, who read the entire manuscript and saved us from many mistakes.

NOTE

Bold-face type is used through the *Handbook* to indicate a separate entry for the work or writer named.

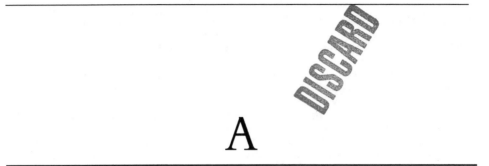

A

Absalom, Absalom! A novel by **William Faulkner**, published in 1936. The story is told by several narrators, but in the main represents the attempt of Quentin Compson to understand at once the history of a family and of the American South. Parts of the story are told to Quentin by his father and by Rosa Coldfield, parts by Quentin himself to his college roommate at Harvard, Shreve McCannon, a Canadian. Pieced together, the story that emerges is as follows:

Thomas Sutpen is born poor in the West Virginia mountains. He runs away at an early age and settles in Haiti, where he marries a planter's daughter, Eulalia Bon. They have a son, Charles, but when Sutpen discovers his wife's partially black ancestry he abandons her and the child. He eventually turns up in Jefferson, Mississippi, with a group of Haitian slaves. By dubious means he acquires a large estate in Mississippi and, unrelenting in his drive for social position, builds a mansion there. He marries the daughter of a respectable family, fathers Judith and Henry, and emerges as the biggest cotton planter in Yoknapatawpha County.

Years later, when Henry comes home from the University of Mississippi, he brings with him his friend – and Sutpen's son by his first marriage – Charles Bon, who becomes engaged to Judith. Sutpen orders Charles from the house. Refusing to believe that Charles is his half-brother, Henry renounces his birthright and follows Charles to New Orleans. They join the Confederate Army (as does their father) at the outbreak of the Civil War. After the war, still angered by Sutpen's refusal to recognize him as his son, Charles determines to marry Judith and returns to the family estate. Henry learns of Charles's mixed ancestry and, to prevent the miscegenation that would result from his marriage, murders him and then disappears.

Sutpen, meanwhile, wants an heir. With the war over, his plantation in ruins, his son gone, his wife dead, and his slaves dispersed, he suggests to his sister-in-law Rosa Coldfield that they try to produce a son; if they are successful he will marry her. Rosa understandably refuses, so he seduces Milly Jones, the granddaughter of a squatter on his land. She bears him not the son he needs to continue the line, but a daughter. When Sutpen repudiates mother and child, Milly's grandfather murders him. Judith Sutpen dies of yellow fever, leaving the mansion to Clytie, Sutpen's mulatto daughter by one of his slaves. Many years later Henry comes home to die. Rosa Coldfield and Quentin Compson (whose grandfather had once befriended Sutpen) find Henry, ill and wasted, hiding in the house. When Rosa sends for an ambulance, Clytie thinks it is a police car come to arrest Henry for Charles's murder. She sets fire to the house, killing herself and Henry, and thus bringing the Sutpen dynasty to an end.

Ada   See **Nabokov, Vladimir**

Adams, Andy 1859–1935 Adams was born in Indiana but spent much of his life in the Texas cattle country and the mining centers of Colorado. He is best known for his authentic, unsentimental depictions of cowboy life in the days of the open range and of the westward expansion of the railroad. His most notable book is *The Log of a Cowboy* (1903). His other works include *The Outlet* (1905), *Cattle Brands* (1906), *Reed Anthony, Cowman* (1907), *Wells Brothers* (1911), and *The Ranch on the Beaver* (1927).

Adams, Brooks 1848–1927 Historian, born in Quincy, Massachusetts, the younger brother of **Henry Brooks Adams**. His first book, *The Emancipation of Massachusetts* (1887), expresses the view that the early colonists were the victims of a repressive theocracy and traces their efforts to move beyond its confines. In *The Law of Civilization and Decay* (1893), generally regarded as his most distinguished work, he argues that any established order always contains the elements of its own decline, since it will eventually be overcome by economic forces that lead to the establishment of another order. In 1919 he wrote a long preface to his brother's *A Letter to American Teachers of History* and published the whole as *The Degradation of the Democratic Dogma*.

Adams, Henry (Brooks) 1838–1918 Historian and man of letters, born in Boston, the grandson of John Quincy Adams, the sixth President of the United States, and the great-grandson of John Adams, the second President. Having been educated at Harvard and in Germany, he served as secretary to his father, Charles Francis Adams, when he became the US minister to England during the Civil War. The author of numerous histories and political essays, his two most important works are *Mont-Saint-Michel and Chartres* (privately printed 1904, published 1913), a study of 12th-century culture, and *The Education of Henry Adams* (privately printed 1907, published 1918), an autobiographical exploration of his heritage and a critical examination of the age in which he lived.

His first publication, an essay on Captain John Smith, appeared in 1867 while he was in England. He continued to write articles and reviews after his return to the US in 1868. From 1870 to 1877 he taught history at Harvard and edited *The North American Review*. During this period he produced *Chapters of Erie and Other Essays* (1871, with his brother Charles Francis Adams) and edited *Essays on Anglo-Saxon Law* (1876) and *Documents Relating to New England Federalism 1800–15* (1877). Discouraged by his experiences as a teacher, he left Harvard and went to Washington to observe the political scene at first hand. In 1879 he wrote *The Life of Albert Gallatin* and *The Writings of Albert Gallatin*, both of which examine the career of the *émigré* Swiss who became a controversial politician, Jefferson's

Secretary of the Treasury, and the author of a pioneering study of the North American Indian. In the following year he anonymously published *Democracy*, a novel about political life in Washington. His biographical study, *John Randolph*, appeared in 1882. In 1884 he published the novel *Esther* under the pseudonym of Frances Snow Compton. The heroine was modeled on his wife, Marian, whose subsequent suicide in 1885 apparently brought to a head the discontent that Adams had been feeling for some time with life in America. He began to travel, first in the Orient with the artist John La Farge and then in the Sierras with the geologist Clarence King.

He returned to Washington to complete his largest-scale historical study, the nine-volume *History of the United States of America during the Administrations of Thomas Jefferson and James Madison* (1889–91). Further travels in the Pacific and in Europe led to *Memoirs of Marau Taaroa, Last Queen of Tahiti* (1893) and *Mont-Saint-Michel and Chartres* (1904). In 1910 he published *A Letter to American Teachers of History*, which was later reprinted in *The Degradation of the Democratic Dogma* (1919) by his brother **Brooks Adams**. In *The Education of Henry Adams* he self-consciously presents himself as being representative of the American mind at a particular historical moment; he has taken his place as such in the literary and critical tradition.

Adding Machine, The A play by **Elmer Rice**, first presented by the **Theatre Guild** in 1923 at the Garrick Theatre in New York City. It was among the earliest and most successful Expressionist experiments in the American theatre. The central character, Mr Zero, is a slave to routine; he works in a department store, where he has been adding columns of figures every day for 25 years. When his boss tells him he has been fired and replaced by an adding machine, he murders the boss with a bill file. Condemned to death and executed, he goes to a pastoral heaven, but is unable to adjust until he is set to work on a giant adding machine. Finally the authorities decide to send him back to earth, where he will operate an even better and more efficient machine.

The point of the play lies not in its plot but in Rice's portrayal of Zero's over-mechanized, joyless existence through carefully chosen, symbolic detail: for example, the dinner party scene in which 12 guests, Mr and Mrs One, Mr and Mrs Two, etc, talk past each other in bigoted clichés while Zero calmly waits for the police to arrive. Even though Zero is not an entirely sympathetic character, the play is a clear indictment of the systematic application of commercial values to crush the soul of the individual.

Ade, George 1866–1944 Born in Kentland, Indiana, Ade began his career as a humorist while writing for the Chicago *Record*. Interested in stories of everyday characters, he achieved success with his extensive use of colloquialism in *Fables in Slang* (1899). This form of fable became his trademark and the substance of several more books, including *Forty Modern Fables* (1901), *People You Know* (1903), and *Hand-Made Fables* (1920). Ade was also a popular playwright of both musical and dramatic comedies, of which the best known are probably *The Sultan of Sulu* (1903) and *The College Widow* (1904).

Adventures of Augie March, The A novel by **Saul Bellow**, first published in book form in 1953, although portions of it had appeared previously in magazines. Augie March is one of three sons born to a feeble-minded Jewish woman on Chicago's West Side. The father has abandoned the family. Augie's older brother – ambitious for himself and for Augie – marries Charlotte Magnus and tries to arrange a match between Augie and Charlotte's sister Lucy. Georgie, Augie's younger brother, is an idiot whom the family put in a home when they can no longer care for him. Augie attends but does not finish college; becomes involved briefly in union organizing; travels to Mexico; returns to the US and joins the navy; marries; and, after leaving the service, goes to Europe to write his "memoir."

In it he records his encounters with the people who have shaped (or tried to shape) his life. The first, and perhaps most important, is his Grandma Lausch, a Machiavellian *grande dame* who lives with the Marches. There are also William Einhorn, the brilliant and wealthy cripple for whom the teenaged Augie works; the wealthy Renlings from Evanston, who want to adopt him; Mini Villar, the tough waitress who becomes pregnant by another man and whom he helps to obtain an abortion; Thea Fenchel, the rich married woman who takes him with her to Mexico, where she plans to divorce her husband; the millionaire Robey, who hires Augie to help him write a masterwork defining the nature of man; Stella Chesney, the USO showgirl he marries; and the lunatic scientist Bateshaw, with whom he shares a lifeboat after their ship has been torpedoed.

Adventures of Huckleberry Finn A novel by **Mark Twain**, published in 1884. Conceived as a sequel to *The Adventures of Tom Sawyer*, it was begun in 1876, the year the earlier book was published, and has far exceeded its predecessor in critical acclaim (if not always in popular attention). Its often harsh satire of life on the banks of the Mississippi, especially concerning the issue of slavery, gives to *Huckleberry Finn* a moral dimension which *Tom Sawyer* generally lacks.

Huck narrates the entire work in his native Missouri dialect, the duplication of which is itself one of Twain's major achievements. The story begins with a summary of *Tom Sawyer* and explains how Huck has fared since being adopted into the home of Widow Douglas and her sister Miss Watson. He is having trouble with being "civilized," but half-heartedly aims to try. Meanwhile his blackguard father threatens his relative security by trying to claim the money that Huck and Tom had recovered from the cave of Injun Joe. Eventually Huck is kidnapped by his father and imprisoned in an isolated cabin. He frees himself by making it appear as if he has been murdered, and then flees to Jackson's Island.

While hiding out on the island Huck meets Jim, Miss Watson's goodhearted slave, who has decided to run away because he has overheard a plan to sell him. When Huck discovers that his own "death" has been blamed on Jim and that a search party may be on its way to Jackson's Island, the two runaways resolve to travel down the Mississippi on a raft. Jim plans to leave the Mississippi at Cairo (the mouth of the Ohio River) and travel up the Ohio to freedom, but they miss Cairo in a dense fog, continue floating downstream, and undergo a series of encounters with feuding clans, murderers, lawless "aristocrats," and numerous mobs, all of which they survive by luck, wit, and determination. The casual cruelty of the river people is often presented, in all its grotesqueness, in an almost offhand manner for satirical effect. Finally, in Arkansas, the two scoundrels who have joined Huck and Jim on their raft, thinking that Jim belongs to Huck and not knowing that there really is a reward on him, tell a local farmer that he is a runaway and offer him to the farmer for a portion of a fictitious reward. By coincidence, this farmer and his wife are Tom Sawyer's Uncle Silas and Aunt Sally Phelps. Huck discovers Jim's whereabouts and tries to free him by posing as Tom. Tom himself happens to arrive and, catching on to Huck's game, poses as his own brother Sid. Tom and Huck free Jim, but only after making him suffer through an absurdly romantic rescue devised by the unsympathetic Tom. All the time Tom knows that Jim is actually a free man, having been freed by Miss Watson (who is now dead) in her will. The rescue goes awry and Tom is shot in the leg. Huck, after fetching a doctor for the injured Tom, becomes separated from him and Jim. Jim gives up his hard-won freedom, or so he thinks, to make sure that Tom receives the attention he needs. Shortly after Jim, Tom, and the doctor return to Silas and Sally's farm, Tom's Aunt Polly arrives and sets matters straight. At the novel's end Huck decides to "light out" for the territories rather than face life with Aunt Sally, who, Huck tells the reader, plans to "sivilize" him.

Adventures of Tom Sawyer, The   A novel by **Mark Twain**, published in 1876. Tom is an intelligent and imaginative boy, who is nevertheless careless and mischievous. In one of the book's most famous episodes he is forced to whitewash the front-yard fence as punishment for playing truant. He evades the task by pretending it is a great privilege, and then allowing other boys to take over from him – for a considerable price.

Tom lives in the respectable home of his Aunt Polly in the Mississippi River town of St Petersburg, Missouri. His preferred world, however, is the outdoor and parentless life of his friend Huck Finn. When Tom is rebuffed by his sweetheart, Becky Thatcher, he and Huck take to the diversion of playing pirates. By coincidence, they are in the graveyard on

the night that Injun Joe murders the town doctor and frames the drunkard, Muff Potter, by placing the knife in his hands. Tom, Huck, and a third boy hide out on a river island in fear of the half-breed murderer, and are believed dead. They finally return to witness their own passionate eulogies, and with much uproar they are discovered in the funeral audience. Later Tom becomes a hero, when at the trial of Muff Potter he stands up and accuses the true murderer. Injun Joe rushes from the room and thus proves his own guilt. Subsequently Tom and Becky abandon a school picnic and get themselves lost for several days in the very cave where Injun Joe is hiding. They make good their escape, and Tom then returns to the cave with Huck. They find Injun Joe dead, and also find his buried treasure. The two boys return to town as heroic as ever, and the riches are divided between them. Their story is continued in ***Adventures of Huckleberry Finn*** (1884).

Agassiz, (Jean) Louis (Rodolphe) 1807–73 Zoologist and geologist, born in Fribourg, Switzerland, Agassiz received a PhD in 1829 from the University of Erlangen and an MD in 1830 from the University of Munich. In the following year he studied under Georges Cuvier, and in 1832 he accepted a position as Professor of Natural History at the University of Neuchâtel, where he published the two works which distinguished him as a pioneer in the classification of fossil fishes and the study of glacial deposits and movements: *Recherches sur les Poissons fossiles* (5 vols., 1833–43), and *Etudes sur les glaciers* (1840).

Agassiz became Professor of Natural History at the Lawrence Scientific School at Harvard University in 1848, two years after coming to America, and founded what was to become the Harvard Museum of Comparative Zoology. Among his colleagues and pupils, who included **William James** and Charles Lyell, he acquired a reputation as a demanding teacher and popular lecturer. When not teaching he undertook numerous and extensive research expeditions throughout North and South America, many of which informed his four-volume *Contributions to the Natural History of the United States of America* (1857–62).

Agee, James 1909–55   Born in Knoxville,

Tennessee, Agee received his BA from Harvard in 1932. He then moved to New York City, where he worked as a staff writer and eventually as a film critic for *Fortune* and *Time* (1932–58), as well as for *The Nation* (1943–8). He also wrote several filmscripts, including *The African Queen* (1951, with John Huston), *The Bride Comes to Yellow Sky* (1953, based on **Stephen Crane**'s short story), and *The Night of the Hunter* (1955).

He is perhaps best known for *Let Us Now Praise Famous Men* (1941). The product of an eight-week collaboration with photographer Walker Evans, the work sympathetically depicts the plight of three rural Alabama families during the Depression. Agee's poems and short stories were collected and edited by Robert Fitzgerald in 1968. His two novels, *The Morning Watch* (1951) and *A Death in the Family*, which was published posthumously in 1957 and won the Pulitzer Prize the following year, are partly autobiographical, the first dealing with religious piety and the second with the effects on a family of a father's early death.

Age of Innocence, The   A novel by **Edith Wharton**, published in 1920 and set in New York during the 1870s. It tells the story of Newland Archer, a lawyer, and his involvement with two women: May Welland, who becomes his wife, and her cousin Ellen Olenska, the wife of a Polish Count. Ellen, having left her husband, appears in New York, where her unconventional behavior displeases society. Newland, on behalf of the Welland family, is called upon to dissuade her from divorcing the Count. Attracted by her foreign exoticism, Newland falls in love with her, but the constraints of society and his impending marriage to May keep them apart. Nevertheless, his interest in Ellen continues after his marriage and prompts May to disclose to her cousin that she is pregnant, whereupon Ellen quickly leaves New York to live in Paris. Thirty years later, Newland, now a widower, visits Paris with his son. As they are about to call on Ellen, Newland decides not to go; he forgoes real contact with her in order to preserve his ideal memories. The novel was dramatized by Margaret Ayer Barnes in 1928.

Age of Reason, The   See **Paine, Thomas**

Aiken, Conrad (Potter) 1889–1973   Born in Savannah, Georgia, Aiken was educated at Harvard, where his contemporaries included **T. S. Eliot** and **Walter Lippmann**. Both his fiction and his poetry reflect his interest in psychology, and his reading of Freud, **William James**, and the French Symbolists, as well as of **Edgar Allan Poe**, his most obvious American antecedent.

His first collection of verse, *Earth Triumphant, and Other Tales in Verse*, was published in 1914, and was followed by *Turns and Movies* and *The Jig of Forslin; A Symphony* (both 1916). His 16 subsequent volumes include *Selected Poems* (1929), for which he won the Pulitzer Prize; *And in the Human Heart* (1940), a sonnet sequence; *Collected Poems* (1952); and *Thee* (1967), a book-length poem. He also published several collections of short stories, including *Bring! Bring!* (1925), *Costumes by Eros* (1928), and *Among the Lost People* (1934); five novels, which appeared together in *The Collected Novels* (1964); and numerous critical essays, collected in *Scepticisms, Notes on Contemporary Poetry* (1919), and *A Reviewer's ABC* (1958). *Ushant*, an autobiographical piece, appeared in 1952.

Albee, Edward (Franklin) 1928–   Born in Washington, DC, Albee was adopted by the owner of a chain of vaudeville theatres. He rose to prominence in the early 1960s with a series of one-act plays: *The Zoo Story* (Berlin, 1959; New York, 1960), *The Death of Bessie Smith* (Berlin, 1960; New York, 1961), *The Sandbox* (1960), and *The American Dream* (1961). All four plays were impressive formal achievements that expressed disenchantment with American middle-class values in a manner reminiscent of the British theatre's Angry Young Men of a few years earlier. In 1962 Albee had his first major success on Broadway with *Who's Afraid of Virginia Woolf?*, a three-act play about a night of drunken verbal conflict between a middle-aged professor and his wife, in which a state of compassion is finally achieved after the "death" of their imaginary son.

Albee next dramatized **Carson McCullers**'s novel, *The Ballad of the Sad Café* (1963). This was followed by *Tiny Alice* (1964), the story of a rich woman who seduces a Catholic lay brother into marriage and then murders him. He dramatized **James Purdy**'s *Malcolm* in 1966, and in the same year he won the

Pulitzer Prize for *A Delicate Balance*, which depicts a family's vain search for happiness and purpose. *Box* and *Quotations from Chairman Mao* were staged in 1968, both works focusing on the banality of human relationships in America. *All Over* appeared in 1971; *Seascape* (1975) won Albee a second Pulitzer Prize. His most recent work has been *Counting the Ways* (1976) and *Listening* (1977), which were both staged in New York in 1979, *The Lady from Dubuque* (1980), and a dramatization of **Vladimir Nabokov**'s *Lolita* (1981).

Alcott, (Amos) Bronson 1799–1888 Born in Connecticut, and perhaps best known as the father of **Louisa May Alcott**, Bronson Alcott was a pioneer of new educational methods in America. Although he himself had little formal schooling, he became a teacher in 1823, and in 1834 founded his own Temple School. At a time when American education consisted mostly of strict discipline, codified moral instruction, and memorization of texts, Alcott was devoted above all to instilling the joy of learning in his students. Adhering to **Transcendentalist** principles that upheld the unlimited potential of every human being, he encouraged his students to look into themselves to realize their individual intellects. After 11 years at the Temple School – during which time he helped establish **Fruitlands** – he became school superintendent of Concord, Massachusetts, in 1859. There his work initiated the Concord School of Philosophy (1879–88), which was run by his disciple William T. Harris. His books are no longer widely read, but his ideas have had a lasting influence on American education. His major works include *Observations on the Principles and Methods of Infant Instruction* (1830), *Record of a School* (with **Elizabeth Peabody**, 1835), *The Doctrine and Discipline of Human Culture* (1836), and *Tablets* (1868). *Sonnets and Canzonets* (1882) was written in memory of his wife, Abigail May.

Alcott, Louisa May 1832–88 Daughter of **Bronson Alcott** and author of *Little Women*, she was born in Germantown, Pennsylvania, and grew up in Boston and Concord, Massachusetts. She completed her first book, *Flower Fables*, when she was 16, though it was not published until 1855. During the Civil War she worked as an army nurse in a Union hospital (1861–3), an experience she documented in *Hospital Sketches* (1863). She visited Europe twice, in 1865 and 1870. From 1867 she edited a children's magazine, *Merry's Museum*.

Although she produced nearly 300 titles in a variety of genres, Alcott generally is remembered as a writer of domestic novels, of which the best known is *Little Women: or, Meg, Jo, Beth, and Amy*. (The novel originally was published in two parts: the first part, *Little Women*, appeared in 1868; the second part, *Good Wives*, came out the following year. In 1871, the two appeared as a single volume entitled *Little Women and Good Wives*.) She drew upon her own life and family experiences in writing this and her other wholesome domestic tales: *Little Men: Life at Plumfield with Jo's Boys* (1871), *Jo's Boys and How They Turned Out* (1886), *Eight Cousins, or, The Aunt-Hill* (1875), *Rose in Bloom* (1876), and others. Under various pseudonyms, she also wrote melodramatic adventure stories. *Work: A Study of Experience* (1873) is a feminist and autobiographical novel. When, as she noted in her journal, she became "tired of providing moral pap for the young," she wrote *A Modern Mephistopheles* (1877), in which an innocent young woman resists seduction by the diabolic genius with whom her poet-husband has made a Faustian pact. This novel was republished posthumously with another, *A Whisper in the Dark* (1889), which has a similar theme. Louisa May Alcott died on March 6, 1888, the day of her father's funeral.

Aldrich, Thomas Bailey 1836–1907 Born in Portsmouth, New Hampshire, Aldrich was a successful journalist who edited the *Illustrated News* during the Civil War. In 1866 he became editor of *Every Saturday* and from 1881 to 1890 edited **The Atlantic Monthly**. His first book, a collection of poems entitled *The Bells*, was published in 1855. His best-known work is *The Story of a Bad Boy* (1870), a novel based on his childhood. Other notable works are *Marjorie Daw and Other People* (1873), a collection of short stories, and *The Stillwater Tragedy* (1880), a detective novel.

Alger, Horatio 1832–99 A popular novelist of boys' books, Alger was born in Massachusetts into a strict Puritan family. He graduated from The Harvard Divinity School (1852) and eventually became a Unitarian minister (1864) after spending some years as a bohemian in Paris. He left the ministry in 1866, following alleged liaisons with choirboys, and moved to New York, where he became chaplain of the Newsboys Lodging House, a position to which he devoted most of his remaining years.

Although he wrote several novels for adults (almost all of which were unsuccessful), he is especially known as the author of well over 100 novels for boys, most of them based on a rags-to-riches theme and the moral that a boy can rise from poverty to wealth if he has a good character. The most popular of these were *Ragged Dick* (1867), *Luck and Pluck* (1869), and *Tattered Tom* (1871), all of which appeared initially in serial form. In addition to fiction, but in the same vein, he wrote several biographies of famous self-made men, under such titles as *From Canal Boy to President* (1881, about Abraham Lincoln), and *From Farm Boy to Senator* (1882, about James Garfield).

Algerine Captive, The A novel by **Royall Tyler**, published in 1797 and providing a satiric commentary on contemporary American life. In the first part, Underhill, the narrator, tells of his inappropriately classical education in New England, his own attempts to teach school, and his study and practice of medicine, exposing along the way various instances of American pretension and quackery. He then travels south, serves as a doctor on a slave ship, and sharply condemns American slavery. Abandoned by the ship in Africa, he is himself taken into slavery by the Algerians. The second part of the novel, interspersed with observations about Muslim life, comments obliquely on American culture, as Underhill recounts his first-hand experience of slavery, his resistance of attempts to convert him to Islam, and his various plans to escape. He finally gains his freedom and returns to America.

Algren, Nelson 1909–81 Algren was born in Detroit, but his work is associated with Chicago, the city where he lived and worked. He graduated from the University of Illinois School of Journalism in 1931 and spent much of the Depression as a migratory worker in the Southwest, an experience which contributed to his earliest fiction. In 1935 he returned to Chicago to a WPA Writers' Project, and in the same year published his first novel, *Somebody in Boots*. He became co-editor of *The New Anvil Magazine* in 1939, and worked on a venereal disease program for the Chicago Board of Health from 1941 to 1942, when his second novel, *Never Come Morning*, was published. He is best known for his novel of narcotic addiction, *The Man With the Golden Arm* (1949), which won the National Book Award. Other books are *The Neon Wilderness* (1947), *Chicago: City on the Make* (1951), *A Walk on the Wild Side* (1956), *Who Lost an American?* (1963), *Notes from a Sea Diary: Hemingway All The Way* (1965), and *The Last Carousel* (1973). His last novel, *The Devil's Stocking*, was published posthumously in 1983.

Allen, James Lane 1849–1925 Allen was born in Kentucky and taught there until he moved to New York City in 1893. His first attempts at writing, mostly for **Harper's New Monthly Magazine**, were the short stories, descriptive articles, and critical essays collected in the volume *Flute and Violin* (1891).

In an 1886 article, "Realism and Romance," which appeared in the New York *Evening Post*, Allen attacked claims for the primacy in American letters of the realist school of **William Dean Howells**, defending the merits of an older romance tradition associated with **Nathaniel Hawthorne** and carried on to some extent by the non-urban, regional writers of his own time. He himself is best known for his romances set in the South, especially *A Kentucky Cardinal* (1894) and its sequel, *Aftermath* (1895). His other works include *Summer in Arcady* (1896), *The Choir Invisible* (1897), *The Mettle of the Pasture* (1903), *The Bride of the Mistletoe* (1909), and *The Kentucky Warbler* (1918). His last collection of short stories, *The Landmark*, was published in the year of his death.

Allen, Paula Gunn 1939– Allen was born in Cubero, New Mexico, of Laguna Pueblo, Sioux, and Chicano parentage. The recipient of an MFA and a PhD, she is currently associated with the Native American Studies program at the University of California at Berkeley. She has published five collections of poems: *The Blind Lion* (1974), *Coyote's Daylight Trip* (1978), *Starchild* (1981), *A Cannon between My Knees* (1981), and *Shadow Country* (1982). Many of her poems attempt a modern transformation of the mythic heritage of her people. She explores the nature of the Native American past, the alienation of the half-breed and the trauma of biculturation, and the influence of contemporary white consumer culture on the Native American. In particular, she focuses on the dual role of Native American women as victims and reformers of their culture. Her novel, *The Woman Who Owned the Shadows: The Autobiography of Ephanie Atencio* (1983), tells the story of one woman's psychological journey toward spiritual rebirth and her attempt to adapt to a biculturated world. Allen has also written numerous critical essays and edited *Studies in American Indian Literature: Critical Essays and Course Designs* (1983).

All My Sons   See **Miller, Arthur**

All The King's Men   See **Warren, Robert Penn**

Ambassadors, The   A novel by **Henry James**, first published in serial form in *The North American Review* in 1903. It was published in volume form later that year, containing two chapters which had not appeared in the magazine version. James himself considered the novel his most "perfect" work of art.

Lambert Strether is sent to Paris by Mrs Newsome, a wealthy widow, to persuade her son Chad to return to Massachusetts and his responsibilities as head of the family business. Strether's success as an ambassador will ensure his marriage to Mrs Newsome when he returns. *En route* to Paris, he meets Maria Gostrey, an expatriate American whose witty and sympathetic observations introduce him to the pleasure of European life. In Paris, he finds Chad an assured and sophisticated young man who is not eager to return to America. Strether is introduced to Madame de Vionnet, a charming French woman who has clearly been the refining influence on Chad's life.

Strether's letters to Mrs Newsome reveal his declining enthusiasm for his embassy, and she sends further ambassadors – her daughter Sarah and Sarah's husband and sister-in-law – to appeal to Chad. They receive little help from Strether, and their lack of success with Chad estranges Strether from Mrs Newsome. In the ensuing action Strether makes two discoveries: that Chad's liaison with Madame de Vionnet is an intimate one, and that his own sympathies rest with Chad. He remains detached, however, content to observe life rather than participate in it, and ultimately returns to his life as a widower in Massachusetts.

American, The   A novel by **Henry James**, published in *The Atlantic Monthly* between June 1876 and May 1877, and as a volume in 1877. Christopher Newman, a bachelor who has become wealthy through shrewd business dealings in America, travels to Paris to find a wife. Though an accomplished businessman, he is naïve about European ways. Mrs Tristram, an expatriate American, serves as a sort of guide and confidante to him, much as Maria Gostrey serves Lambert Strether in *The Ambassadors*.

Newman becomes engaged to Claire de Cintré, a widow, and the daughter of an aristocratic French family, the Bellegardes. But the Bellegardes decide they cannot sacrifice the family pride, even to Newman's wealth, and they terminate the engagement. Meanwhile Newman has introduced Valentin Bellegarde, Claire's brother and his own friend and ally, to Noémie Nioche, a young woman who copies great paintings for a living. Because of his involvement with Noémie, Valentin fights and dies in a duel. Just before dying, however, he provides Newman with the means of compelling the Bellegarde family to allow him to marry Claire: he sends Newman to Mrs Bread, the Dowager Marquise's maid, who reveals that the Marquise had caused her husband's death by withholding his medication. In the end, however, Newman decides not to use this information to force the marriage, and the novel closes with Claire's becoming a Carmelite nun.

American Crisis, The   A series of 16 pamphlets by **Thomas Paine**, published between 1776 and 1783, the first of which begins "These are the times that try men's souls." They made an important contribution to the American Revolutionary cause and influenced the direction of the early nation's political and philosophical ideology. They discuss human nature and the individual's proper relationship to the state, tyranny, the spirit of liberty, and the future of colonialism.

American Dream, An   See **Mailer, Norman**

American Mercury, The A magazine of literary criticism and social commentary founded in 1924 by **H. L. Mencken** and **George Jean Nathan**. When Nathan left the journal in 1925 Mencken assumed sole editorship, a position he retained until his own departure in 1933. Subsequent editors included Henry Hazlitt, Charles Angoff, Paul Palmer, Eugene Lyons, Lawrence Spivak, William Bradford Huie, and John A. Clements. The journal featured fiction, essays, and social and political commentary by such authors as **Vachel Lindsay, Theodore Dreiser, W. E. B. DuBois, Ben Hecht, James T. Farrell, Edgar Lee Masters, William Faulkner, William Saroyan, Lionel Trilling, Mark Van Doren, Thomas Wolfe, Pearl S. Buck, Conrad Aiken, Eugene O'Neill, Dorothy Parker**, and **Sherwood Anderson**. The journal ceased publication in 1975.

American Tragedy, An A novel by **Theodore Dreiser**, published in 1925, and based on an actual New York murder case of 1906, in which a man named Chester Gillette was convicted of the murder of a young woman, Grace Brown.

Clyde Griffiths, anxious to escape his family's dreary life, goes to work as a bellboy in a luxury hotel. He enjoys the lively society of his more sophisticated co-workers until he is involved in a car accident and found to be legally culpable. Fleeing the scene, he meets his uncle Samuel Griffiths, a successful manufacturer in New York State, who gives him a job in his Eastern factory. Clyde falls in love with Sondra Finchley, a rich girl from a nearby town, who represents the elegance and culture to which he has always aspired. Meanwhile, however, he has seduced a young factory worker, Roberta, who becomes pregnant and demands that he marry her. Seeing marriage to Sondra within his grasp, Clyde decides to dispose of the unfortunate Roberta. He takes her to a lake resort, deserted at that time of year, where he plans to murder her. He lacks the resolution to carry out his plan, but when the boat accidentally overturns he swims away and leaves Roberta to drown. He is accused of her murder, and the rest of the novel traces, in relentless detail, the investigation of the case, and Clyde's indictment, trial, conviction, and execution.

Ammons, A[rchie] R[andolph] 1926– Born in North Carolina, Ammons studied at Wake Forest College and the University of California at Berkeley. His first book of poetry, *Ommateum with Doxology*, appeared in 1955 (the title refers to the compound eye of an insect). *Expressions of Sea Level*, the volume which established him as a major poet, was published in 1964; in the same year he accepted a post at Cornell University, where he continues to teach creative writing.

Ammons's work, characterized in particular by its precise descriptions of the natural world, also includes *Corsons Inlet* (1965), *Northfield Poems* (1966), *Uplands* (1970), *Briefings* (1971), *Collected Poems: 1951–1971* (1972), *Diversifications* (1975), *The Snow Poems* (1977), *Highgate Road* (1977), *A Coast of Trees* (1981), *Worldly Hopes: Poems* (1982), and *Lake Effect Country: Poems* (1983). He has published two long poems as books, *Tape for the Turn of the Year* (1965) and *Sphere: The Form of a Motion* (1974). *The Selected Poems 1951–1977* appeared in 1977, and *Selected Longer Poems* in 1980.

Anderson, Maxwell 1888–1959 Born in Atlantic, Pennsylvania, Anderson spent much of his childhood traveling through Pennsylvania, Ohio, Iowa, and North Dakota, following the "call" of his father, a Baptist preacher. He attended the University of North Dakota, and then taught school in North Dakota and California (he was fired twice for his outspoken pacifism) and earned an MA from Stanford with a thesis on Shakespeare. Newspaper work in San Francisco led to the offer of an editorship on *The New Republic*. He moved to New York City, where he soon began writing for the theatre.

His first play, *White Desert* (1923), about struggling North Dakota miners, was a failure, but a second effort, *What Price Glory?* (1924), written in collaboration with Lawrence Stallings, won acclaim for its realistic portrayal of soldiers during wartime. The 1930s were successful years for Anderson; during that decade he wrote and saw produced *Elizabeth the Queen* (1930), a blank-verse tragedy; *Night Over Taos* (1932); *Both Your Houses* (1932); *Mary of Scotland* (1933); *Valley Forge* (1934); *Winterset* (1935), a verse tragedy based on the Sacco and Vanzetti case; *Wingless*

Victory (1937); *High Tor* (1937), a comedy about a struggle over land rights; *The Masque of Kings* (1937); *The Star Wagon* (1937); *Knickerbocker Holiday*, a musical comedy written in collaboration with his close friend **Kurt Weill**; *Key Largo* (1939), another tragedy; and *Journey to Jerusalem* (1940), a retelling of the story of Christ's childhood.

During World War II he produced two anti-Nazi plays, *The Miracle of the Danube* (1941) and *Candle in the Wind* (1941), and two more plays about the lives of soldiers, *The Eve of St Mark* (1942) and *Storm Operation* (1944). 1946 saw the appearance of *Truckline Cafe* and *Joan of Lorraine*; in 1948 he completed his Elizabethan trilogy with *Anne of the Thousand Days*. *Lost in the Stars* (1950), another collaboration with Weill, was an adaptation of Alan Paton's novel of South Africa, *Cry The Beloved Country*. Among his last plays were *Barefoot in Athens* (1951), about the life of Socrates, and *The Bad Seed* (1954).

Anderson, Sherwood 1876–1941 A novelist and short-story writer, Anderson was born in Camden, Ohio, and completed his education at the age of 14. He drifted from job to job, served in the Spanish–American War (1898–9), married, and managed a paint factory in Elyria, Ohio. Then, apparently, he left family and job and went to pursue a literary career in Chicago, where he met **Carl Sandburg**, **Ben Hecht**, **Floyd Dell**, and others.

Anderson's first book, *Windy McPherson's Son*, was published in 1916. Other early works include *Marching Men* (1917), a novel about coal miners in Pennsylvania, and *Mid-American Chants* (1918), a volume of unrhymed verse. He received his greatest recognition following the publication of **Winesburg, Ohio** (1919), a collection of interrelated stories of small-town life, and the novel **Poor White** (1920), which explores the effects of technological change on American culture. His later work includes collections of short stories – *The Triumph of the Egg* (1921), *Horses and Men* (1923), and *Death in the Woods* (1933) – and the novels *Many Marriages* (1923), *Dark Laughter* (1925), *Tar: A Midwest Childhood* (1926), and *Beyond Desire* (1932). His autobiography, *A Story Teller's Story*, was published in 1924. A volume of *Letters* was issued in 1953, and a critical edition of his

Memoirs in 1973. The influence of his flat, minimalist prose style, evocative of a bleaker vision of life than had previously been characteristic of American writing, can be seen in such writers as **Ernest Hemingway** and **William Faulkner**.

Angelou, Maya 1928–   Noted for her varied and international involvement in the arts, Angelou was born Marguerita Johnson in St Louis, Missouri, on April 4, 1928. She attended public schools in Arkansas and California and then studied music, dance, and drama.

Her theatrical career began when she appeared in *Porgy and Bess* on an international tour sponsored by the US State Department (1954–5). Off Broadway, she performed in *Calypso Heatwave* and *The Blacks*, and in *Cabaret for Freedom*, which she wrote and produced in 1960 in collaboration with Godfrey Cambridge. She has since written for both stage and screen: *The Least of These*, a two-act drama first produced in Los Angeles in 1966; *The Clawing Within* (1966, unproduced); *Adjoa Amissah* (1967, unproduced); *Georgia, Georgia*, filmed by Independent Cinerama in 1972; an adaptation of Sophocles' *Ajax*, first produced in 1974 at the Mark Taper Forum; *And Still I Rise*, a one-act musical first produced in 1976 under her direction at the Ensemble Theatre, Oakland, California; *All Day Long*, filmed by the American Film Institute in 1974 and directed by herself.

In 1959 and 1960, she served at the request of Martin Luther King as Northern Coordinator of the Southern Christian Leadership Conference. She has worked as associate editor of the *Arab Observer* in Egypt, and as assistant administrator of the School of Music and Drama at the University of Ghana. She continues to visit numerous American and European universities as a lecturer, visiting professor, and writer-in-residence.

Angelou's more recent work has confirmed her reputation as a telling commentator on black American culture. In her four autobiographical volumes she examines the challenges confronting and the potential awaiting black American women: *I Know Why The Caged Bird Sings* (1969); *Gather Together in My Name* (1974); *Singin' and Swingin' and Gettin' Merry Like Christmas* (1976); and *The Heart of a Woman* (1981). Two collections of poetry –

Just Give Me a Cool Drink of Water 'Fore I Diiie (1971) and *Oh Pray My Wings Are Gonna Fit Me Well* (1975) – and four television documentaries – *Blacks, Blues, Black* (1968), *Assignment America* (1975), *The Legacy* (1976), and *The Inheritors* (1976) – explore the presence of African traditions in American culture.

Another Country See **Baldwin, James**

Armies of the Night See **Mailer, Norman**

Arrowsmith See **Lewis, Sinclair**

Arthur Mervyn A gothic novel by **Charles Brockden Brown**, published in two volumes between 1799 and 1800, and set in Philadelphia during the plague year of 1793. It opens when Dr Stevens, the narrator, finds the 18-year-old Arthur Mervyn, a farmboy who has come to the city, sick with yellow fever in the streets. He takes him home and cares for him. Soon, however, a friend voices the suspicion that Mervyn is not the country innocent he seems, but has been involved in criminal dealings with an embezzler named Thomas Welbeck. Mervyn then tells Stevens his story.

Upon his arrival in Philadelphia Mervyn was employed by Welbeck, but soon began to suspect him of criminal activities. These suspicions were confirmed one night when Welbeck shot a man in his study. At this point Welbeck had told Mervyn *his* story – of how, despite his ideals, he had been guilty of seduction, the theft of $20,000, forgery, and now murder. Welbeck then tried to escape by boat (with Mervyn's help), but jumped into the river, presumably to his death. Mervyn returned to the country, taking with him a manuscript of Welbeck's; he found a new home on the farm of a Mr Hadwin, and fell in love with his daughter Eliza. Later he discovered the stolen $20,000 in the manuscript. Back in Philadelphia on an errand, he found Welbeck still alive and searching frantically for the missing manuscript. As a result of their confrontation Mervyn burned the money. By now ill with yellow fever, he wandered into the streets and was found by Dr Stevens.

Mervyn's account dispels suspicion and, with Stevens's sponsorship, his future looks promising. He returns to the Hadwin farm and finds that only Eliza has escaped the epidemic, thereby becoming the sole inheritor of the farm. When he arrives back in Philadelphia he has a final confrontation with the now dying and repentant Welbeck. Meanwhile, fresh suspicions about Mervyn's character and activities have arisen, and this time his explanations prove somewhat less satisfactory. Indeed, the second part of the book in general casts some doubt on the validity of the version of his life he had given originally. The novel ends when Mervyn, having reevaluated his love for Eliza (she turns out not to have inherited the farm after all), falls in love with Mrs Fielding, a widow of means whom he finally marries.

Ashbery, John (Lawrence) 1927– Ashbery was born in Rochester, New York, and grew up on his father's farm in Sodus, New York. He was educated at Harvard, Columbia, and New York universities. He worked in publishing until 1955, when a Fulbright Scholarship enabled him to study in France. He became an art critic for the European edition of the *New York Herald Tribune*, and returned to the US in 1965. The best-known poet of the **New York School**, he published his first volume, *Turandot and Other Poems*, in 1953. His work is characterized by an essentially sceptical world view, and his poems are generally self-referential and self-enclosed. His other volumes are *Some Trees* (1956). *The Poems* (1960), *The Tennis Court Oath* (1962, Harriet Monroe Memorial Prize), *Rivers and Mountains* (1966), *Sunrise in Suburbia* and *Three Madrigals* (1968), *Fragment* (1969), *The Double Dream of Spring* and *The New Spirit* (1970), *Three Poems* (1972, Shelley Memorial Award), *The Vermont Notebook* (1975, with Joe Brainard), *Self-Portrait in a Convex Mirror* (1975), *Houseboat Days* (1977), *As We Know* (1979), *Shadow Train* (1981), *A Wave* (1984) and *Selected Poems* (1985). He is also the joint author of a novel, *Nest of Ninnies* (1969, with James Schuyler).

As I Lay Dying A novel by **William Faulkner**, published in 1930. Experimental in both subject and narrative structure, it treats the events surrounding the illness, death, and burial of Addie Bundren, wife of Anse and mother of Cash, Darl, Jewel, Dewey Dell, and Vardaman. It is divided into 59 short interior monologues, predominantly in the present tense, spoken both by the seven members of the family and by various other characters, including the Reverend Whitfield, Dr Peabody, and the Bundrens' neighbors, Vernon and Cora Tull.

As the novel opens, Addie lies silently in her bed, watching Cash construct her coffin outside the window. Dewey Dell stands beside her, fanning her and musing about a sexual encounter with Lafe. Jewel, Addie's illegitimate son by the Reverend Whitfield, and Darl, the most devoted son, who is considered "queer" by the townspeople, are hauling a load of lumber to a Northern town. While they are away, Addie dies. Vardaman, the youngest son, is severely traumatized; he confuses his mother with the large trout he has just caught and bores holes in her coffin to allow her to breathe. Addie's dying wish was to be buried in her home town of Jefferson, Mississippi, and Anse is stubbornly insistent that this wish be fulfilled, despite the series of accidents and setbacks which the family encounters during its ten-day journey to Jefferson with the coffin.

They set out for Jefferson in the wagon, with Jewel astride his own horse, and immediately have problems trying to cross a flooded river. They lose control of the team and Cash's leg is badly broken. While resting at the Armstid farm Anse trades Jewel's horse for a new team, and the volatile-tempered Jewel runs away. They set Cash's leg in concrete, which leaves him crippled for life. The corpse has begun to rot and buzzards are circling in the sky above the wagon, but the family continues toward Jefferson, with the crippled but stoic Cash lying on top of the coffin. Jewel rejoins the group and they stop to rest at the Gillespie farm, placing the coffin in the shade inside the barn. Darl, realizing the absurdity of their venture, attempts to cremate his mother's body by setting fire to the barn; Anse decides to turn him over to the authorities once they have buried Addie.

Once in Jefferson, Dewey Dell, who has discovered that she is pregnant, goes into a pharmacy to get a "cure." Skeet MacGowan, one of the assistants, gives her some false medication and then rapes her in the cellar, claiming that she must have a "hair of the dog" that bit her in order to get rid of her trouble. They bury Addie in the family plot. Darl is taken away to an asylum. Anse confiscates the money which Lafe had given to Dewey Dell to get an abortion and buys himself the set of false teeth he has always wanted. As the family prepares to leave for home, Anse appears with a strange woman and introduces her as the new "Mrs Bundren."

Aspern Papers, The   A story by **Henry James**, published in *The Atlantic Monthly* from March to May 1888, and as the title piece of a volume of stories in the same year. The narrator, an American editor, travels to Venice to recover the letters written by Jeffrey Aspern, a Romantic poet of the early 19th century, to his mistress, "Juliana." He rents rooms from Juliana, now the aged Miss Bordereau, who lives with her niece, Tina, an unattractive spinster. After Miss Bordereau dies, Tina says that she could give the letters only to "a relative" of the family. The veiled proposal is plain and the editor balks at it. When they next meet, Tina reveals that she has burned the letters.

Assistant, The   See **Malamud, Bernard**

Atlantic Monthly, The   A magazine devoted to literature and current affairs, founded in Boston in 1857 by **Oliver Wendell Holmes** and **James Russell Lowell**. Its editors have included **James T. Fields**, **William Dean Howells**, **Thomas Bailey Aldrich**, Horace E. Scudder, Walter Hines Page, and Edward A. Weeks. It regularly features the work of America's most prominent writers, and since 1938 has included articles and essays on international as well as national affairs.

Auden, W[ystan] H[ugh] 1907–73   Born in York, England, Auden was educated at private schools and at Oxford University. His first book of verse, *Poems* (1928), was printed privately by his friend Stephen Spender while he was still at Oxford. Auden went on to become the most prominent member of a group of English writers with Marxist sympathies, including Spender, Cecil Day Lewis, and Louis MacNeice. During this period he wrote a number of experimental Marxist plays for the Group Theatre in London; these include *The Dance of Death* (1933), and, in collaboration with Christopher Isherwood, *The Dog Beneath the Skin, or, Where Is Francis?* (1936), *The Ascent of F6* (1936), and *On The Frontier* (1938).

In the early 1930s Auden supported himself by teaching, but after 1935 he turned to writing about his travels, publishing *Letters from*

Iceland (1937, with MacNeice); *Spain* (1937), a pro-Loyalist poem; and *Journey to War* (1939), a collaborative work with Isherwood about the war between China and Japan. His poetry in the 1930s showed the influence of Freud and reflected his left-wing political views. Early volumes include *Poems* (1930, rev. 1933); *The Orators: An English Study* (1932, rev. 1966), a satire in verse and prose; and *Look Stranger* (1936, published in the US as *On This Island* in 1937).

In 1939 Auden left England to settle in the US, and in 1946 he became a US citizen. The move marked a change in his work, which became increasingly religious and personal in tone, reflecting his return to the Anglican faith and to more traditional values. As a result, he dropped or extensively edited many early poems for *The Collected Poetry of W. H. Auden*, issued in 1945. Other volumes of the American period include *Another Time* (1940), *The Double Man* (1941), *For The Time Being: A Christmas Oratorio* (1944), *The Age of Anxiety: A Baroque Eclogue* (1947, Pulitzer Prize), *Nones* (1951), *The Shield of Achilles* (1955), *The Old Man's Road* (1956), and *Homage to Clio* (1960). Despite their thematic differences, these poems resemble the early work in their experimental forms and their attempt to conjure meaning from the fragments of everyday experience.

During his first years in the US, Auden again turned to teaching to support himself. In 1945, however, he began working as a freelance writer; among his more famous projects was his collaboration with Chester Kallman on the libretto of Stravinsky's *The Rake's Progress* (1951). He also published important critical works during this period, including *The Enchafed Flood: The Romantic Iconography of the Sea* (1951), and *The Dyer's Hand* (1962). Most of his final years were divided between his homes in Greenwich Village, New York City, and Kirchstetten, Austria. In 1972 he was invited to return to his college in Oxford, where he remained until his death. His later poetry, which became increasingly meditative, was published in *City Without Walls and Other Poems* (1969), *Academic Graffiti* (1971), and *Epistle to a Godson* (1972).

Audubon, John James 1785–1851 A Haitian-born naturalist and artist, educated in the US and later in France, where he studied with Jacques-Louis David. Audubon came to the US in 1806, and spent much of his life traveling throughout the States and Canada to find material for his wildlife drawings, which became celebrated for their accurate detail and delicate use of watercolor. Many of these were included in his most famous work, *The Birds of America*, which was published in England between 1827 and 1838. Sections of his journals also have been published; these include *Delineations of American Scenery and Character* (1926), *Journal of John James Audubon, Made During his Trip to New Orleans in 1820–21* (1929), and *Audubon's America* (1940).

Autobiography of Alice B. Toklas, The A fictionalized account by **Gertrude Stein** of her life with Alice B. Toklas, the ostensible author-narrator of the book. The complete work was published in 1933, having appeared previously in an abridged version in *The Atlantic Monthly*. Stein adopts the persona and even the manner of her secretary and long-time companion, but the story she tells is essentially about her own life, as seen from Toklas's point of view.

Stein and Toklas were, as the narrator claims, "in the heart of an art movement," and *The Autobiography* catalogs the many famous artists and intellectuals with whom they came into contact. The narrator notes how many wives of geniuses she has had to sit with while Stein – also a genius – has been with their husbands: among them the wives of Picasso, Matisse, Braque, Gris, **Ernest Hemingway**, **Sherwood Anderson**, and Ford Madox Ford. The book also tells of the visit Stein and Toklas made to Alfred North Whitehead's home in England, where they met Lytton Strachey and Bertrand Russell; and of their wartime involvement with the American Fund for the French Wounded, when they visited French hospitals and were decorated by the French government. It also provides an account of their busy life from 1919 to 1932 – the years of "constantly seeing people" such as **Sylvia Beach**, **Ezra Pound**, Tristan Tzara, **T. S. Eliot**, **Djuna Barnes**, Jacques Lipschitz, Jean Cocteau, Marcel Duchamp, and Edith Sitwell.

Autobiography of an Ex-Colored Man See **Johnson, James Weldon**

Autocrat of the Breakfast Table, The   First published (1857–8) in The Atlantic Monthly, and in volume form in 1858, this book is an expanded version of two earlier papers written by **Oliver Wendell Holmes** while studying medicine at Harvard and published in *The New England Magazine* (1831–2). The book consists of essays, poems, and occasional pieces in the form of table talk in a Boston boarding house. Among those present at the breakfast table, besides the "autocrat" himself, are the landlady, her daughter, and a poor relation, a schoolmistress, a divinity student, and an old gentleman. The autocrat is generally seen as a vehicle for Holmes's own wit and social commentary.

Awake and Sing!   A play by **Clifford Odets**, first performed by **The Group Theatre** in New York in 1935. Odets's first play, it depicts "the struggle for life among petty conditions" of an impoverished Jewish family, the Bergers, living in the Bronx during the Depression. Faced by a crisis – Hennie – the family's unmarried daughter, is pregnant – the matriarchal Bessie persuades her to deceive and marry Sam Feinschreiber, a gentle man whom she does not love. Meanwhile Bessie clashes with her father, Jacob (who loves Caruso and Karl Marx and is the moral center of the play), and with her son, Ralph, whom she succeeds in preventing from marrying the girl he loves, and whose desires are generally stifled by poverty and tenement life. Accused of complicity in the family's deception of Feinschreiber, Jacob kills himself; Hennie runs away with a family friend; but we are left with the sense that Ralph will fight the conditions in which he finds himself because of his grandfather's example.

Awakening, The   A novel by **Kate Chopin**, published in 1899. It is a study of the inner life and rebellion of Edna Pontellier, the wife of a successful Creole speculator in Louisiana, and the mother of two small boys. While spending the summer at Grand Isle, she flirts with Robert Lebrun, the son of the resort owner, who awakens her to a new sense of spiritual and physical self-awareness. She begins to question the importance of the traditional roles of wife and mother that she has always fulfilled and that she sees embodied in her friend Adele Ratignolle. On her return to New Orleans, she begins to assert her new sense of identity. She develops her artistic nature by painting and attains some financial independence by selling her work. She moves out of the family house, and has sexual relations with another man. Lebrun returns and their intimacy is renewed, but the consummation of their love is prevented when Edna is called to help Adele through the birth of her child. Profoundly distressed by the birth scene, she returns home to find Lebrun gone. She realizes that a succession of lovers will not lead to fulfillment, and that, though she feels neither loyalty nor guilt toward her husband, she cannot escape from her responsibilities to her sons. In a final desperate assertion of her independence, she returns to Grand Isle, and the novel closes as she swims far out to sea to her death.

Awkward Age, The   A novel by **Henry James**, published serially in *Harper's Weekly* from October 1898 to January 1899, and as a volume in revised form in 1899. It is written almost entirely in the form of dialogue. Its heroine, Nanda Brookenham, is a "knowing" young woman brought up in the permissive and worldly atmosphere of her mother's *salon*. Aggie, a "pure" young lady who has been raised strictly, in the Continental manner, by her aunt, the Duchess, serves as her foil. The action of the novel revolves around the relations between Nanda and Aggie and two men, Mr Vanderbank and Mr Mitchett.

Nanda loves Mr Vanderbank, but he does not return her feeling. Mr Longdon, an elderly gentleman who once cared for Nanda's grandmother, encourages Vanderbank to marry Nanda, even offering to provide her with a dowry. But Nanda, out of the worldly wisdom that has perhaps made her less marriageable than Aggie, realizes Vanderbank does not love her and, in a typically Jamesian renunciation scene, graciously gives him up. Meanwhile, Mr Mitchett, who had hoped to marry Nanda himself, has been sought by the Duchess as a match for Aggie. Accepting that he cannot have Nanda, Mitchett marries Aggie. Nanda leaves the marriage market and retires to Longdon's country house.

B

Babbitt A novel by **Sinclair Lewis**, published in 1922. It depicts the complacency and materialism of George F. Babbitt, a real-estate agent and representative middle-class family man from the midwestern city of Zenith. After his only real friend, the artist-turned-businessman Paul Riesling, shoots his wife and is sent to prison, Babbitt rebels against commonplace values: he begins a love affair with the widow Tanis Judique, refuses to join the Good Citizens' League, and becomes influenced by the socialist lawyer Seneca Doane. But he soon finds the price of nonconformity too great and once again resigns himself to the superficial values of his business culture. His reconciliation with society is completed by his acceptance back into the Booster Club. At the end of the novel, his son (ironically named Theodore Roosevelt Babbitt) himself rebels against the wishes of the family and the town by leaving college and marrying hastily. Babbitt supports him in this rebellion, hoping that, unlike himself, his son will be able to do as he wants and lead a more independent and fulfilled life.

Babbitt, Irving 1865–1933 Scholar and critic. Born in Ohio, Babbitt graduated from Harvard in 1889 and then taught at Williams College (1893–4) and Harvard (1894–1933). With Paul Elmer More he was a leading figure among the New Humanists. His criticism emphasized the ethical component of art, rejecting more romantic ideals which, in his view, tended too much to establish art or science as objects of veneration. His ideas influenced **T. S. Eliot**, who was his student at Harvard. His major works are *Literature and the American College* (1908), *The New Laokoön* (1910), *Masters of Modern French Criticism* (1912), *Rousseau and Romanticism* (1919), *Democracy and Leadership* (1924), *On Being*

Creative (1932), and *The Spanish Character and Other Essays, With a Bibliography of His Publications and an Index to His Collected Works* (1940).

Baldwin, James (Arthur) 1924–   The son of a preacher, Baldwin was born in Harlem, New York City. He left home at 17 and eventually made his way to Paris, where he lived for some years and began to write.

His first novel, *Go Tell It on the Mountain* (1953), was based on his experiences in Harlem, and with it he was welcomed as a black writer of unusual promise. It recounts a young boy's coming to terms with the religious beliefs of his father, a storefront preacher incapable of controlling his desires, and of his stoical mother. The boy is desperately in search of some kind of identity; he does not share the fervent belief of others, and this lack obsesses him. His father's lusts and inability to communicate with his children have kept the Lord away from him, for before kneeling to the Lord he must kneel to his father, something he cannot bring himself to do. After a long series of conflicts, he is finally able to reject his father and turn to the Lord at one stroke, and he feels something die in him as well as come alive. He has achieved faith through struggle.

The promise of this first book was borne out in further novels, plays, short stories, and essays, which have shown Baldwin to be a powerful and articulate enemy of racial discrimination. After *Giovanni's Room* (1956), which is set in Paris, he returned to black America as a setting for his fiction. *Another Country* (1962) is set in New York City and focuses mainly on Harlem society. The death – perhaps the suicide – of the main character, Rufus Scott, is representative of the treatment individuals receive in an environment which is essentially hostile and which erects barriers to their desire for love. Other works of fiction by Baldwin include *Going to Meet the Man* (1965), ***Tell Me How Long the Train's Been Gone*** (1968), *If Beale Street Could Talk* (1974), and *Just Above My Head* (1979). His essays are published in *Notes of a Native Son* (1955), *Nobody Knows My Name: More Notes of a Native Son* (1961, published in England as *No Name in the Streets*, 1972), *The Fire Next Time* (1963), *The Devil Finds Work* (1976), *The Evidence of Things Not Seen: An Essay* (1985), and *The Price of the Ticket: Collected Nonfiction, 1948–1985* (1985). He has also written four plays: *The Amen* (produced 1965, published 1968), *Blues for Mr Charlie* (produced and published 1964), *One Day, When I Was Lost* (produced 1972, published 1973), and *A Deed from the King of Spain* (produced 1974).

Baldwin, Joseph G. 1815–64 Although primarily a jurist, Baldwin is also remembered for his sketches describing his legal career in the Southern backwoods. Born in Virginia, he educated himself in both literature and law, and in 1836 decided to seek work in the comparatively uncivilized region of Mississippi. After spending many years in Mississippi, Alabama, and later in California, he published *The Flush Times of Alabama and Mississippi* in 1853. A hodge-podge collection of sketches and anecdotes about frontier law, *Flush Times* combines serious and moralistic portraits of great men Baldwin admired with comic tales of infamous rascals. The latter pieces remain better known, and include "Ovid Bolus, Esq," about a chronic liar, and "Simon Suggs, Jr, Esq: A Legal Biography," about a lawyer who cleverly cheats his way to success. Encouraged by the volume's favorable reception, he published *Party Leaders* (1855), a more sober work containing studies of **Thomas Jefferson**, Alexander Hamilton, Andrew Jackson, Henry Clay, and John Randolph. The rest of his life was devoted to legal duties, including three years as an associate justice of the Supreme Court (1858–62).

Ballad of the Sad Café, The See **McCullers, Carson**

Bancroft, George 1800–91 Born in Massachusetts, Bancroft graduated from Harvard at the age of 17, and the following year went to Germany, to study history in Berlin under Hegel and in Göttingen under Heeren and Eichhorn. Though trained for the ministry, he held a variety of government positions: Secretary of the Navy (1845–6); Minister to England (1846–9); and Minister to Germany (1867–74). A Jacksonian Democrat, he supported the Manifest Destiny policy in the 1840s.

His life work, the ten-volume *History of the United States* (1834–75), tells the story of the progressive tendency toward liberty exemplified by American history, culminating in the American Revolution. Bancroft's progressivist notions of history, imbibed in Germany, his extensive use of manuscript sources, and his interest in the human characters underlying historical events place him in a class with his major American contemporaries, **William Hickling Prescott**, **John Lothrop Motley**, and **Francis Parkman Jr**, whose historiographical ideas and practices were similar. The *History*, highly nationalistic and characterized by a resounding rhetoric, was a popular work in its own day.

Baraka, (Imamu) Amiri 1934– Born LeRoi Jones in Newark, New Jersey, this poet, playwright, and editor has been a prominent voice in the Black movement since the mid 1950s. He studied at Howard University and then served in the airforce as a gunner; on his discharge in 1956 he began his career as a writer and activist. He established his reputation under his given name of LeRoi Jones; in 1965 he converted to Islam, changed his name to Imamu Amiri Baraka, and moved to a black ghetto in Newark, where he founded the Spirit House Theatre. His other activities have included the founding of Totem Press (1958), which prints the work of contemporary poets, directing of the Black Arts Repertory Theatre in Harlem, and teaching contemporary poetry and creative writing at Columbia, the New School for Social Research, and the State University of New York at Buffalo.

His first published work was a play, *A Good Girl Is Hard To Find* (1958). In 1961 he published *Preface to a Twenty Volume Suicide Note*, a collection of personal and often domestic poems typical of his early period. This was followed by two plays, *The Baptism* (1964) and *The Toilet* (1964), particularly concerned with issues of personal identity. His work then became progressively more radical and more involved with issues of racial and national identity; **Dutchman** (1964), *The Slave* (1964), and *Slave Ship: A Historical Pageant* (1967) all deal with black–white relations and, as works of "revolutionary theatre," demonstrate Baraka's self-awareness as a leader of a black arts movement which seeks to use dramatic presentation as a weapon against American racism. After 1974 his political ideology underwent a change; his separatist fervor gave way to a revolutionary commitment to the overthrow, by blacks and whites alike, of an oppressive capitalist system. Plays like *S-1* (1976) and *The Motion of History* (1977) exemplify this third stage of his literary career. In addition to other volumes of verse, he has also published *Blues People: Negro Music in White America* (1963); *Tales* (1967), a book of short stories; *Raise, Race, Rays, Raze: Essays Since 1965* (1971); *The Autobiography of LeRoi Jones* (1984); and *Daggers + Javelins: Essays* (1984).

Barker, James Nelson 1784–1858 Born in Philadelphia, Barker followed his father's example by becoming mayor of that city in 1819 after a distinguished military career. He later served as Collector of the Port of Philadelphia and then as Comptroller of the United States Treasury. Only five of his ten plays have survived. *Tears and Smiles* (1807), a comedy of manners, was first produced in Philadelphia. His operatic play, *The Indian Princess; or, La Belle Sauvage*, was produced in 1808; the first extant play to deal with American-Indian life, it was mounted in London in 1820 as *Pocahontas; or, The Indian Princess*. Barker's biggest success, *Marmion; or, The Battle of Flodden Field* (1812), was based on Sir Walter Scott's poem. Although he originally advertised the play under the pen name of Thomas Morton, Barker acknowledged his authorship after its implicit criticism of the British stance toward the United States during the War of 1812 was enthusiastically received by the public. His second romantic comedy, adapted from a French novel about medieval Spain, was published as *How to Try a Lover* in 1817, and produced as *The Court of Love* in 1836. *Superstition; or, The Fanatic Father* (1824), a tragedy in verse, deals with a Puritan refugee who leads attacks against the Indians, and deals with religious intolerance and witch-hunting.

Barlow, Joel 1754–1812 Barlow is best remembered as one of **The Connecticut Wits**, though he eventually became politically estranged from the group. Born in Redding, Connecticut, he attended Dartmouth College and in 1774 transferred to Yale, where he met others of the Wits, with whose orthodox Calvinism and aristocratic politics he sympathized. On graduation he worked as a schoolteacher, but became disenchanted after a year and returned to Yale to take an MA in Theology (1778). He enlisted in 1780 as Chaplain for the Third Massachusetts Brigade. At the war's conclusion he founded *The American Mercury* with Elisha Backock (1784), opened a bookstore (1785), studied law, and was admitted to the Bar in 1786. Throughout this period he maintained contact with the Wits and contributed to their most notable production, *The Anarchiad*, a satire in mock-heroic verse which attacked democratic liberalism in favor of federalist conservatism and was published between 1786 and 1787 in *The New Haven Gazette* and *The Connecticut Magazine*. In 1787 Barlow published *The Vision of Columbus*, an epic poem in which he envisions America's glorious future.

In 1788 he went to France, where he lived periodically for 17 years, an experience which changed his political perspective. Contact with prominent European liberals – Horne Tooke, Mary Wollstonecraft, William Godwin – and a reevaluation of the writings of **Thomas Jefferson** and of his friend **Thomas Paine** transformed him into a champion of democracy, a change evident in three pamphlets in the 1790s: *Advice to the Priviledged Orders*; *The Conspiracy of Kings*; and *A Letter to the National Convention of France*, for which he was awarded French citizenship. While in France he was appointed consul to Algiers (1795) and wrote his renowned *Hasty Pudding* (published 1796), a mock epic in three cantos which celebrates a native American dish as well as "simplicity of diet." He returned to the US in 1805 and in 1807 published **The Columbiad**, a revision of *The Vision of Columbus*. Accepting an appointment as US minister to France in 1811, he went back to Europe and died in Poland on his way to negotiate a treaty with Napoleon.

Barnes, Djuna 1892–1982 Born in Cornwall-on-Hudson, New York, Barnes began her career in New York City as a journalist and graphic artist, but spent much of her later life among the post-war Paris expatriates, active as a novelist, playwright, short-story writer, and poet. In her early years in New York she was associated with the experimental Provincetown Players, who produced three of her one-act plays in 1919 and 1920. Her first publication was a collection of poems, *The Book of Repulsive Women* (1915). Her stories and short plays were collected in *A Book* (1923); the stories were revised and reissued subsequently as *A Night Among the Horses* (1929) and later still as *Spillway* (1972). In 1929 she published her first novel, *Ryder*, a satiric chronicle of family history; and *Ladies' Almanack*, a celebration of lesbian life and loves in the form of a quasi-medieval calendar or miscellany.

Her best-known work is the novel *Nightwood* (1936), which concerns the relationships of a group of expatriates in Paris and Berlin, including Felix Volkbein, a German Jew in search of history and a family; Robin Vote, the inexplicable "somnambule" whom he marries; Nora Flood, the American who becomes Robin's lover and who is the emotional center of the book; Jenny Petherbridge, a cultural parasite, who takes Robin away from Nora; and Doctor Matthew O'Connor, an Irish-American unlicensed gynecologist and anatomist of night, war, and modern culture, whose alcoholic, melancholic, and apocalyptic monologues give *Nightwood* its unusual, modernist shape. No plot summary can do justice to the play of language and forms in this book, which **T. S. Eliot** praised in his introduction to the first edition as an example of poetic prose. Barnes went on to write *The Antiphon* (1958), a full-length revenge tragedy in blank verse which again takes up issues of family history. Her *Selected Works* was published in 1962.

Barren Ground A novel by **Ellen Glasgow**, published in 1925, and later singled out by the author as the one of her works she would most wish to achieve immortality.

Barren Ground is the story of Dorinda Oakley, a lower-middle-class country woman who goes to work in Nathan Pedlar's store, hoping the money she earns will restore her father's farm – the barren ground. She falls in love with Jason Greylock, but he is committed to another woman. Dorinda travels from her native rural Virginia to New York City, where, after a street accident, she supports herself by caring for her doctor's children. Another doctor proposes to her, but she refuses him. In her spare time she studies new techniques in agriculture. When her father dies, she returns to Virginia and single-handedly establishes a prosperous dairy farm. After her mother's death, she marries Nathan Pedlar, the man for whom she once worked and a widower with children. After his death, Dorinda, out of kindness, shelters the degenerate Jason Greylock. But she no longer loves him, and in fact plans never to marry again, being thankful "to have finished with all that." The title takes on new significance when one considers that Dorinda, although she nurtures other people's children and restores fertility to her family's farm, has no offspring of her own.

Barry, Philip 1896–1949 Playwright, born in Rochester, New York. He attended both Harvard and Yale, and his first play was produced at Yale in 1919. *You and I* (1923) was his first professional production. A number of his other plays – such as *Holiday* (1929), *Tomorrow and Tomorrow* (1931), and *The Animal Kingdom* (1932) – are comedies that puncture the snobbish pretensions of wealthy society. His other works include *Here Come the Clowns* (1938), *The Philadelphia Story* (1939), *Liberty Jones* (1941), and *The Foolish Notion* (1945). *Second Threshold*, another comedy, unfinished at his death, was completed in 1951 by **Robert Sherwood**.

Barth, John (Simmons) 1930– Barth was born in Cambridge, Maryland, and educated at The Johns Hopkins University, where he now teaches. After publishing short stories in various periodicals, he attracted considerable critical attention with a novel, *The Floating Opera* (1956). This book, about a nihilist who, contemplating suicide, decides not to kill himself after all, is informed by a sense of the absurd that has colored all Barth's work. His other novels are *The End of the Road* (1958), *The Sot-Weed Factor* (1960), *Giles Goat-Boy: or, The Revised New Syllabus* (1966), *Chimera* (1972), which won the National Book Award, *Letters* (1979), and *Sabbatical* (1982). *Lost in The Funhouse* (1968) is a volume of short stories. *The Friday Book*, a collection of non-fiction pieces, was published in 1984.

Barthelme, Donald 1931– Barthelme was born in Philadelphia and grew up in Texas. His first book, *Come Back, Dr Caligari*, a collection of stories, appeared in 1964. *Snow White* (1967), a novel set in Greenwich Village, is a contemporary reworking of the popular fairy tale. The fragmented narrative is made up of word games and random allusions to both literature and popular culture, taking the disintegration of language as a central metaphor for the breakdown of personal relationships. His later collections of stories – *Unspeakable Practices, Unnatural Acts* (1968), *City Life* (1970), *Guilty Pleasures* (1974), and *Amateurs* (1976) – continue his satiric commentary on contemporary American life and language. His second novel, *The Dead Father* (1975), is a humorous story about paternity and the fragmentation of the self. His other publications include *Great Days* (1979), *Sixty Stories* (1981), and *Over Night To Many Distant Cities* (1983).

Bartram, John and William John Bartram (1699–1777) was a Philadelphia Quaker and the first American botanist. In his official capacity as botanist for the American colonies he went on various expeditions, keeping records in his journals, and publishing *Observations on the Inhabitants, Climate, Soil . . . Made by John Bartram in his travels from Pensilvania to Lake Ontario* (1751).

On his later trips he was accompanied by his son William (1729–1823), who made anthropological and ornithological, as well as botanical, contributions, and painted some of the flora and fauna he observed. William is most remembered, though, for his *Travels through North and South Carolina, Georgia, East and West Florida, the Cherokee Country, The Extensive Territories of the Muscogulges, or Creek Confederacy, and the Country of the Chactaws* (1791). The *Travels* are both descriptions of the American landscape and imaginative, romantic reflections on the wilderness and natural man.

Battle Hymn Of The Republic, The This patriotic song was written by **Julia Ward Howe** in December, 1861, after visiting a Union army camp near Washington. The melody was provided by *John Brown's Body*, a song popular with the soldiers. The hymn was given its title by **James T. Fields** and was published in *The Atlantic Monthly* in 1862.

Battle-Pieces And Aspects of the War A book of poems by **Herman Melville**, published in 1866. The 72 poems commemorate the tragedy of the Civil War and its impact on the nation. The sense of Northern victory and celebration is muted; many poems dwell upon the tragic loss of young men cut down in battle. Among the more notable pieces are "The Portent," on the hanging of **John Brown**; "Misgivings," on slavery; and "Shiloh: A Requiem." The volume also contains a prose appendix appealing to Northern readers for a humane rather than vengeful attitude toward the South during Reconstruction.

Bay Psalm Book, The; *or The Whole Book of Psalmes Faithfully Translated into English Meter* The authoritative hymnal of the Massachusetts Bay Colony and the first book published in America (Cambridge, 1640). The translation, by **Richard Mather, John Eliot**, and Thomas Weld, replaced the Sternhold and Hopkins version, which the Bay Puritans rejected because it sacrificed the literal rendering of the Hebrew text to poetic effect. *The Bay Psalm Book*'s motto, "God's Altar needs not our Polishings," makes clear the Puritan translators' insistence on a direct confrontation with the Word of God, unmediated by added ornaments. Following a second printing in 1647, it was revised by Henry Dunster (the president of Harvard) and Richard Lyon, and reprinted in 1651 with the title *The Psalms Hymns and Scriptural Songs of the Old and New Testament*, an edition which was reissued several times over a period of almost a century.

Beach, Sylvia 1887–1962 The daughter of a minister, Sylvia Beach is best remembered as the proprietor of the Paris bookstore, Shakespeare and Company. Founded by Beach in 1919 across the Rue de l'Odéon from Adrienne Monnier's La Maison des Amis de Livres, Shakespeare and Company became the center for the Franco-American literary world of Paris. It provided a meeting-place for writers such as **Ezra Pound, Sherwood Anderson, Ernest Hemingway,** and

Gertrude Stein. In 1922 Beach published James Joyce's *Ulysses*, which had been banned as obscene in the US.

Beats, The A group of writers centered in San Francisco and New York City in the latter half of the 1950s. The term "beat" was first used by **John Clellon Holmes** in his 1952 novel, *Go*, the first literary description of the people of the Beat movement and their milieu. The name "beat" has been variously interpreted as meaning "beaten down" and "beatific"; members of the group shared an antagonism toward middle-class values, commercialism, and conformity, as well as an enthusiasm for the visionary states produced by religious meditation, sexual experience, jazz, or drugs. The poet **Allen Ginsberg** and the novelist **Jack Kerouac** were perhaps the most prominent spokesmen for the group. Ginsberg's *Howl and Other Poems* (1956) was one of the first major publications by a Beat writer, and employs the Whitmanesque, incantatory free verse which is common to Beat poetry. Kerouac's *On The Road* (1957) became a central text of the movement. Other major figures in the movement include the novelist **William S. Burroughs** and the poets **Gregory Corso**, **Gary Snyder**, and **Lawrence Ferlinghetti**, whose City Lights Bookstore, founded in San Francisco in 1953, was a gathering-place for Beat writers. Publications associated with the Beats are the *Pocket Poet Series*, *Beatitudes*, and, to a lesser extent, the *Evergreen Review*.

Beecher, Henry Ward 1813–87 Son of the Congregationalist minister Lyman Beecher, he became one of the most prominent preachers in Victorian America, known, like his father, for his successful revivalist techniques. Many of Lyman's children had prominent public careers; most of Henry's brothers were also ministers, and his sisters Catharine and Isabella became active in the women's movement. The most famous member of the family was his sister **Harriet Beecher Stowe**, the author of *Uncle Tom's Cabin*.

Born in Litchfield, Connecticut, Beecher attended Amherst College and Lane Seminary. After serving as minister to several Indiana churches, in 1847 he was called to the Plymouth Church in Brooklyn, New York,

where he remained for the rest of his life. There he preached a theology of love rather than fear, exploiting the emotional Protestant revival tradition while addressing social issues such as education, temperance, and slavery. His fame grew as he spoke on lecture tours as well as from the pulpit, and wrote weekly columns for *The Independent*, a widely read sectarian newspaper. In the 1850s he emerged as a major moral spokesman on secular issues of national concern, especially slavery; and though a moderate, he became associated in the popular mind with the radical Abolitionists. When he opposed the radical Republicans after the Civil War, he was denounced as a turncoat both by **Horace Greeley**'s *New York Tribune* and by *The Independent*, now under the direction of Beecher's parishioner and long-time associate, Theodore Tilton. The split between Beecher and Tilton became more and more acrimonious, culminating in Tilton's accusation in 1874 that Beecher had had an affair with his wife. The notorious trial that ensued resulted in Beecher's acquittal in 1875.

Despite these public criticisms, Beecher maintained his popularity, engaging in activities which kept him in the public eye. His sermons were published periodically in *The Plymouth Pulpit* throughout the 1860s, and in 1870 he began editing a new journal, *Christian Union*. He was a prominent proponent of votes for women, and became active in the American Woman Suffrage Association. His novel, *Norwood; or, Village Life in New England* (1867), whose characters have long conversations about religious values, sold well. In the 1870s he incorporated many of the new Darwinian ideas to support his old teachings of evangelical liberalism, the community benefits of virtuous self-improvement, and the moral value of material success. He remained a popular and effective spokesman for these ideas until the end of his life.

Behrman, S[amuel] N[athaniel] 1893– 1973 Behrman was born in Worcester, Massachusetts, and was educated at Clark, Harvard, and Columbia universities. He began his theatrical career as an actor but was forced to give up the stage because of ill health, and took to writing – mostly sophisticated social comedies dealing with success, wealth, love, and marriage. His first play,

Bedside Manners, written with J. Kenyon Nicholson, was produced in New York in 1923; in the following year the two of them collaborated on *A Night's Work*. Behrman's third play, *The Man Who Forgot*, written with Owen Davis, appeared in 1926. Others of his plays include *Serena Blandish; or, The Difficulty of Getting Married* (1929, adapted from Enid Bagnold's novel), *Meteor* (1929), *Love Story* (1933), *End of Summer* (1936), *Wine of Choice* (1938), *No Time For Comedy* (1939), *Jacobowsky and the Colonel* (1944; New York Drama Critics Circle Award), *Jane* (1952, adapted from a Somerset Maugham short story), *Fanny* (1954, with Joshua Logan), and his last play, *But For Whom Charlie* (1964). Behrman also wrote more than 25 screenplays between 1930 and 1962. He published several collections of essays which had first appeared in *The New Yorker*, as well as volumes of short stories. *People in a Diary: A Memoir* appeared in 1972.

Belasco, David 1853–1931 Dramatist, theatrical impresario, and director, born and educated in San Francisco. He began his long career as an actor in California, and then in 1882 moved to New York City, where he was to make a major contribution to Broadway theatre, both as author or co-author of over fifty plays and as a deviser of sensational stage effects in the plays he directed at his own Belasco Theatre between 1906 and his death. In 1879 he collaborated with **James A. Herne** on *Hearts of Oak*. The domestic drama *Lord Chumley* (1888) was written with Henry C. DeMille, and *The Girl I Left Behind Me* (1893) with Franklin Fyles. A play set during the Civil War, *The Heart of Maryland*, appeared in 1895. He co-wrote a number of plays with John L. Long, including the one-act tragedy, *Madame Butterfly* (1900); *The Darling of the Gods* (1902); and *Adrea* (1904), which tells of a princess of an Adriatic island in the 5th century. Both *Madame Butterfly* and *The Girl of the Golden West* (1905) were turned into operas by Puccini, first performed as such in 1906 and 1910 respectively. *The Return of Peter Grimm*, based on an idea by Cecil B. DeMille, was produced in 1911.

Bellamy, Edward 1850–98 Born in Massachusetts, Bellamy was a journalist and little-known novelist until 1888 when he wrote *Looking Backward: 2000–1887*, an immensely popular Utopian romance. For the rest of his life he developed and disseminated the political principles set forth in this book. Above all, these involved a government program of strict state capitalism, resulting in non-revolutionary socialist reform. A Nationalist party was established to advocate his ideas; in support Bellamy founded the journal *The New Nation* (1891), and later wrote *Equality* (1897), a more theoretical sequel to *Looking Backward*. His earlier, less political writings include *The Duke of Stockbridge* (1879), about Shay's Rebellion; and *Dr Heidenhoff's Process* (1880) and *Miss Ludington's Sister* (1884), novels dealing with psychic phenomena in the tradition of **Nathaniel Hawthorne**. *The Blind Man's World And Other Stories* (1898) was published just before his death from tuberculosis.

Bellow, Saul 1915– The son of immigrant Russian parents, Bellow was born in Quebec. The family moved to Chicago in 1924, and Bellow was educated at the University of Chicago, Northwestern University, and the University of Wisconsin. He has followed an academic career since 1938. His first novels were *Dangling Man* (1944) and *The Victim* (1947). *The Adventures of Augie March* (1953) won him his first National Book Award. *Seize The Day* (1956), *Henderson The Rain King* (1959), *Herzog* (1964), *Mosby's Memoirs And Other Stories* (1968), *Mr Sammler's Planet* (1970; National Book Award), *Humboldt's Gift* (1975), and *The Dean's December* (1982) further contributed to his reputation as an interpreter of the struggles of urban dwellers to define their roles and responsibilities in the modern world. He was awarded the Nobel Prize for Literature in 1976. Among his other books are *Recent American Fiction: A Lecture* (1963), *The Future of the Moon* (1970), *Technology and The Frontiers Of Knowledge* (1975), and *To Jerusalem and Back: A Personal Account* (1976). He edited *Great Jewish Short Stories* (1963) and has written several plays, including *The Wrecker* (1954), *The Last Analysis* (1965), and *A Wen* (1965). A collection of short stories, *Him With His Foot In His Mouth And Other Short Stories*, was published in 1984.

Benchley, Robert (Charles) 1889–1945 A humorist, drama critic, and actor, Benchley graduated from Harvard in 1912. He began his career as a journalist, working on several New York newspapers and magazines. He was theatre critic for *Life* (1920–9) and then for *The New Yorker* (1929–40). During these years he also wrote and published humorous sketches, based on the daily lives of ordinary people and marked by an ironic appreciation of life in an era of rapid and often confusing change. They were collected in *Of All Things* (1921), *Love Conquers All* (1922), *Pluck and Luck* (1925), *The Early Worm* (1927), *20,000 Leagues Under The Sea; or, David Copperfield* (1928), *The Treasurer's Report* (1930), *My Ten Years in a Quandary* (1936), *After 1903 – What?* (1938), *Inside Benchley* (1942), and *Benchley Beside Himself* (1943). In addition to his writing, Benchley made frequent appearances in motion pictures and on the radio.

Benét, Stephen Vincent 1898–1943   Poet, short-story writer, and novelist born in Bethlehem, Pennsylvania, Benét is best known for his Pulitzer Prize-winning collection of verse about the Civil War, *John Brown's Body* (1928). Another book of poetry, *Western Star* (1943), deals with American roots in 17th-century European migrations; although it was unfinished at his death it was awarded a posthumous Pulitzer Prize. A collection of short stories, *Thirteen O'Clock* (1937), includes the popular "The Devil And Daniel Webster," which has been made into an opera and a film. Benét's other collections of stories include *Tales Before Midnight* (1939) and *The Last Cycle* (1946). He also wrote five novels, and a number of radio scripts which appeared in a posthumous collection, *We Stand United, And Other Radio Scripts* (1945).

Benét, William Rose 1886–1950   The elder brother of **Stephen Vincent Benét**. A poet, critic, and editor, founder and member of the editorial board of the **Saturday Review** (1924), he was also the first editor of *The Reader's Encyclopedia* (1948). He published several books of poetry, including *Merchants from Cathay* (1913), *Moons of Grandeur* (1920), *Days of Deliverance* (1944), and *The Stairway of Surprise* (1947). An experimental verse novel, *Rip Tide*, appeared in 1932. He was awarded a Pulitzer Prize for his autobiography, *The Dust Which Is God* (1941).

Ben-Hur, *A Tale of The Christ*   A novel by **Lew Wallace**, published in 1880. Judah Ben-

Hur and Messala the Roman are apparently devoted friends, but Messala, in search of advancement, accuses Ben-Hur of an attempt on the life of the Roman governor. Ben-Hur is sent to the galleys for life, and his mother and sister are also imprisoned. In the slave train to the coast he is given water by a stranger outside a carpenter's workshop. Years later he returns to Judaea a free man and a Roman officer; soon after, he challenges Messala in the chariot races in Caesarea. His mother and sister, meanwhile, have contracted leprosy. Ben-Hur wins the chariot race; Messala, who has staked everything on the victory, is crippled and ruined. He is later killed by his wife when his evil nature is revealed. Ben-Hur rescues his mother and sister and they return to Jerusalem – on the day of the Crucifixion. The condemned man is the same one who once aided Ben-Hur as a slave; he dies on the cross, but his passing cures the lepers. Ben-Hur and his family embrace the new faith of Christianity.

Berlin, Irving 1888–   The composer and lyricist was born Israel Baline in Temun, Russia, and grew up on New York's Lower East Side, where his family had come to escape persecution. He had almost no formal education – in music or anything else; his father, a cantor, died when he was 9, and he left home to become a street singer, then a song-plugger for a music publisher, then a singing waiter. His first published song, "Marie From Sunny Italy" (1907), earned him nothing, but the next, "Sadie Salome Go Home," a parody of grand opera, was successful and prompted Tin Pan Alley publisher Ted Snyder to hire him as staff lyricist. Then "Alexander's Ragtime Band" (1911), a simplified version of ragtime rhythms, sold a million copies in a few months, and made Berlin famous, as well as contributed to popular enthusiasm for jazz.

His first complete musical, *Watch Your Step: A Syncopated Musical Show* (1914), starred Vernon and Irene Castle and introduced ragtime to the theatre. It was quickly followed by *Stop, Look, and Listen* (1915), *The Century Girl* (1916), and *Dance and Grow Thin* (1916), a midnight revue. Drafted in 1917, he wrote *Yip, Yip, Yaphank*, including the song "Oh, How I Hate To Get Up In The Morning." He contributed songs to the Ziegfeld Follies of

1910, 1911, 1919, and 1920, including "A Pretty Girl Is Like A Melody" (1919). In 1921 he joined producers Sam Harris and Joseph Schenk to build the Music Box Theatre, a small house designed especially for musicals, and contributed music and lyrics for four annual *Music Box Revues*.

The shows of Berlin's middle period include *The Cocoanuts* (1925), written for the Marx Brothers, and *Face the Music* (1932), which dealt with police and political corruption during the Depression and included the song "Let's Have Another Cup of Coffee." *As Thousands Cheer* (1933), a revue based on different sections of a Sunday newspaper, included songs about real people and occurrences, ranging from "Easter Parade" to "Supper Time," a powerful account of a lynching sung by Ethel Waters. *Louisiana Purchase* (1940) satirized political corruption. His longest-running show, *Annie Get Your Gun* (1946), based on the life of sharpshooter Annie Oakley of Buffalo Bill's Wild West Show, included such classics as "There's No Business Like Show Business," "You Can't Get A Man With A Gun," and "Doing What Comes Naturally." *Miss Liberty* (1949), about a search for the woman who posed for the Statue of Liberty, was followed by two more gentle political satires, *Call Me Madam* (1950) and *Mr President* (1962). Berlin is also remembered for his part in many of the great motion picture musicals, including *Top Hat* (1935), *Follow the Fleet* (1936), *Holiday Inn* (1942), and *Blue Skies* (1946). While he never became a sophisticated musician (he could play the piano in only one key, F sharp major), he wrote over 900 songs, including such national classics as "Always," "God Bless America," and "White Christmas."

Berryman, John 1914–72 Born in McAlester, Oklahoma, Berryman was educated at Columbia and Clare College, Cambridge. He taught at Princeton, Harvard, the University of Cincinnati, and, from 1955 until his death, at the University of Minnesota. His poems appeared in small magazines and reviews during the 1930s, and then in 1940 his work was published in *Five American Poets*. His first collected volume was *Poems* (1942), followed in 1948 by *The Dispossessed*. Widespread recognition came with *Homage to Mistress Bradstreet* (1956), and in

1965 he was awarded the Pulitzer Prize for 77 *Dream Songs* (1964). The poems in this latter volume became the first section of the lengthy collection called *The Dream Songs*, which was published in its entirety in 1969. He committed suicide in 1972. A posthumous volume of poems, *Delusions* (1972), shows him looking toward the end of his life, also the subject of his novel, *Recovery* (1973). *The Freedom of the Poet*, a collection of his essays on poets and poetry, appeared in 1976. He also wrote a notable biography, *Stephen Crane* (1950), which was revised and reissued in 1962.

Bierce, Ambrose (Gwinnett) 1842–*c*.1914 Bierce was born in Horse Cave Creek, Ohio. The Civil War gave him the chance to escape from what he saw as a constricting environment, and he reached the rank of major. The war disgusted him, however, and he saw his part as a soldier as little more than that of a paid assassin. This bitterness (his nickname was "Bitter Bierce") later informed his Civil War stories – stories of defeat and disillusionment.

When the war ended Bierce went to California and eventually became a journalist, contributing to the celebrated **Overland Monthly**, which **Bret Harte** had helped to establish. Later he published his own newsletter, and with Harte, **Mark Twain**, and **Joaquin Miller** constituted a Western literary circle. With the departure of Twain and Harte for the East, his position as chief arbiter of the Western literary establishment (and later, chief short-story writer) was unchallenged.

He went to England in 1872, where he lived and wrote until 1876. Although he was a busy contributor to periodicals, his success did not match that of his San Francisco period, and he returned there to write for William Randolph Hearst's *Examiner*. In 1891 he published *Tales of Soldiers and Civilians* (entitled *In The Midst of Life* in England and in the 1898 US edition), and *Can Such Things Be?* in 1893. He moved to Washington in 1897 as the capital correspondent for the Hearst papers. He contributed to *Cosmopolitan* and in 1906 published *The Cynic's Word Book*, a volume of ironic definitions. He also published verse and essays, and in 1909 produced the first volume of his *Collected Works*, which reached 12 volumes in 1912. The following year, estranged from all family connections, Bierce went to Mexico, where civil war was raging, and disappeared. It is not known exactly when or how he died.

Biglow Papers, The Two series of popular satirical verses by **James Russell Lowell**, written in Yankee dialect. The first series (1848) opposes the Mexican War, and the second (1867) attacks the policy of the Confederate states in the Civil War.

Hosea Biglow is a young farmer in New England. In the first series, three of the "papers" are verse letters to him from his friend Birdofredum Sawain, who is serving as a private in the war and becoming increasingly disillusioned with it. The other six papers consist of Hosea's comments on politicians, recruiting officers, and declarations of "principles." The second series includes two letters from Birdofredum, who now lives in the South and is convinced by Confederate propaganda. In the other papers Biglow discusses the war, Southern attitudes, England's selfish involvement because of their interest in the cotton trade, "conciliation," the approaching peace, and Reconstruction.

Big Money, The Published in 1936, the third novel in the trilogy **U.S.A.** by **John Dos Passos.**

Big Sleep, The See **Chandler, Raymond**

Billings, Josh See **Shaw, Henry Wheeler**

Billy Budd, Sailor A short novel by **Herman Melville**, begun in 1886 but left in semifinal draft form at the time of his death in 1891. Discovered among his manuscripts, it was first transcribed and published by Raymond Weaver in 1924; this version was further "improved" by Weaver in 1928, by F. Barron Freeman in 1948, and by Elizabeth Treeman in 1956. Harrison Hayford and Merton M. Sealts, Jr undertook a new transcription and made from it the now standard "reading text" in 1962.

The story is set aboard *HMS Bellipotent* in 1797, a tense period following mutinies in the British Navy when England is at war with France. Billy Budd, the "Handsome Sailor" of sailors' folklore, is impressed from a merchantman, the *Rights-of-Man*, where he has been known as a "peacemaker." He quickly adjusts to life aboard a man-of-war and is a favorite of the crew, but he becomes the target of the envious and brutal master-at-arms, John Claggart. Claggart concocts a plot of a supposed mutiny and accuses Billy of being involved in it before the ship's commander, Captain Vere. The innocent Billy, unable to answer the charge because of a chronic stammer, strikes Claggart on the forehead and kills him. Vere, though recognizing the falsity of Claggart's story and sympathizing with the agonized Billy, fears reaction among the crew if Billy is not punished for assaulting a superior. He calls a drumhead court and in effect instructs it to find Billy guilty of a capital crime. The court, though troubled by the ambiguities of the case and by Vere's precipitate action, condemns Billy, who is hanged from the yardarm after crying out, "God bless Captain Vere!" Some time later Vere is killed during an engagement with the French; his last murmured words are Billy's name.

Melville's story – involving a complex interplay between a Christlike innocent, a devilish antagonist, and a godlike commander, and thereby posing social, moral, and theological enigmas – has received widely differing interpretations. The author's second most popular work (after **Moby-Dick**), *Billy Budd* has furnished the plot for a play, a film, and a notable opera by Benjamin Britten.

Bird, Robert (Montgomery) 1806–54 Bird was born in Delaware and attended the University of Pennsylvania, where he received an MD in 1827. He taught for a short period at Pennsylvania Medical College (1841–3) but left to take up a career as a writer.

He began with romantic plays about Philadelphia life, including *The City Looking Glass* (1828, first published 1933), and historical dramas: *Pelopidas, The Gladiator*, and *Oralloosa* (1830, 1831, and 1832, respectively; all published in 1919), and *The Broker of Bogota* (1834, first published 1917). After revising John Augustus Stone's *Metamora* (1836), tired of faulty financial agreements and increasingly disillusioned with the theatre, he turned to the writing of fiction. His first novel, *Calavar; or the Knight of the Conquest*, was published anonymously in 1834 and its favorable reception prompted him to write a sequel, *The Infidel; or, The Fall of Mexico* (1835). He then turned from tales of Mexican conquest to stories of Pennsylvania society:

The Hawks of Hawk-Hollow (1835), about a well-to-do family's fatal lack of patriotism; and *Sheppard Lee* (1836), a satire on contemporary society, informed by Bird's Whig politics.

Nick of the Woods; or, The Jibbenainosay (1837) is generally considered to be his best novel. Set at the end of the American Revolution, it concerns the abduction of a white woman by Indians who, unlike those of **James Fenimore Cooper**, are not in the least noble. Its leading character is a Quaker known as Bloody Nathan; it is he who is Nick of the Woods, or the Jibbenainosay, the "devil" who kills Indians mercilessly to avenge the murder of his family. Bird published only two other books: *Peter Pilgrim; or, A Rambler's Recollections* (1838, travel sketches); and *The Adventures of Robin Day* (1839, a novel). In 1847 he became literary editor and partial owner of the Philadelphia *North American*, which he helped to edit until his death.

Bishop, Elizabeth 1911–79 Bishop's childhood was troubled by the early death of her father and by her mother's mental illness; she was raised by grandparents in Nova Scotia and in her birthplace of Worcester, Massachusetts. By the time she graduated from Vassar in 1934 she was already writing prose and poetry and had become friends with **Mary McCarthy** and traveling; *Questions of Travel* (1965) contains a number of poems about her experiences in Brazil, where she spent 16 years. *Poems: North and South A Cold Spring* (1955) won her the Pulitzer Prize. Another product of her time in Brazil is her translation, from the Purtugese, of *The Diary of "Helena Morley"* (1957), which reproduces the diary of a young Brazilian girl at the end of the 19th century; when Bishop met her she was an old woman and explained that she wished the diary to be preserved for her granddaughters. *The Complete Poems* (1969) won the National Book Award; *Geography III* appeared in 1976. *The Collected Prose* was published in 1984 and includes autobiographical sketches, travel accounts, a memoir of Marianne Moore, and several short stories.

Blackburn, Paul 1926–71 Born in St Albans, Vermont, the son of the poet Frances Frost, Blackburn graduated from the University of Wisconsin in 1950 and attended the University of Toulouse from 1954 to 1955 on a Fulbright fellowship. A prolific poet, Blackburn's early work appeared in *The Dissolving Fabric* (1955), *Brooklyn–Manhattan Transit* (1960), and *The Nets* (1961). His middle-period poems were collected in *The Cities* (1967) and *In. On. Or About the Premises* (1968). A substantial number of late poems appeared in *Halfway Down the Coast* and *The Journals*, both published in 1975. *The Collected Poems of Paul Blackburn* appeared in 1985. Before his death of cancer at the age of 44, Blackburn had also established a reputation as a translator of the Provençal troubadours and of the works of Julio Cortazar and Antonio Jimenez-Landi.

Black Elk 1863–1950 A Sioux warrior and priest born into the Oglala division of the Teton Dakota. His youth coincided with the last years of territorial freedom for the Plains Indians. He became a prominent leader of the Messianic Movement, a protest movement among American Indians that arose in the late 19th century as the tribes were gradually forced onto reservations and became the victims of increasingly genocidal attacks. Black Elk had been instructed as a child in the ancient tribal religions, and his mission to defend the embattled Indian cultures involved both active resistance of US encroachments – he fought at Little Big Horn and Wounded Knee – and the perpetuation of the spiritual vision and commitment of his forefathers. He was considered a visionary, though he thought himself inadequate to the task of preserving his culture in the face of white oppression and the falling off of spiritual commitment among his own people. His oral autobiography, *Black Elk Speaks* (1932, recorded and edited by John Neihardt), is a moving account of his life and mission. He also delivered an account of the religious rites of the Oglala Sioux, *The Sacred Pipe* (1953, recorded and edited by John Epes Brown).

Black Mask, The A detective magazine, founded in 1920 by **H. L. Mencken** and **George Jean Nathan**. It began by publishing traditional stories with heroes modeled after English characters, but with the introduction of Carroll John Daly's Race Williams, the first of the hardbitten detectives, it began to reflect the realities of post-war America. **Dashiell Hammett**'s Continental Op stories, which began to appear in 1923, and Sam Spade, the hero of *The Maltese Falcon*, mirrored the cynical, detached, and disillusioned times of Prohibition. **Raymond Chandler** also published extensively in *The Black Mask*, and by the time Philip Marlowe made his appearance in 1939 the magazine had fathered a unique American hero – the private eye. Other contributors included Erle Stanley Gardner, George Harmon Coxe, Frederick Nebel, Lester Dent, and Horace McCoy.

Black Mountain School   A group of poets based at Black Mountain College near Asheville, North Carolina, in the early 1950s. A number of poets attended the experimental liberal arts college to study with **Charles Olson**, who was for a time both an instructor and rector of the college. Olson's "projective verse," which described poems as "open fields" conducting energy from the poet to the reader, influenced many of his students, among whom were **Robert Creeley**, **Robert Duncan**, and **Denise Levertov**. The work of these poets appeared in the influential *Black Mountain Review*, which was published from 1954 to 1957.

Blithedale Romance, The   A novel by **Nathaniel Hawthorne** published in 1852, and based on the author's experience at the **Transcendentalist** utopian community at **Brook Farm**.

The narrator, Miles Coverdale, is probably the book's most complex character. He is untrustworthy, often intellectually dispassionate, but also effusive and sentimental; much to the reader's occasional frustration, he is also one's only perspective on the story. He goes to Blithedale, a utopian community, and meets the famous Zenobia, an exotic feminist; Hollingsworth, a blacksmith turned philanthropist; and Priscilla, a mysterious and fragile seamstress. Zenobia passionately loves the egotistic Hollingsworth, who wishes to turn Blithedale into an institution for criminal reform. Priscilla has escaped to Blithedale from the control of the evil Westervelt, who forced her to pose as the mysterious "Veiled Lady," through whom he demonstrated his mesmeric powers to Boston audiences. Westervelt also has a mysterious past connection with Zenobia. Sensing competition for Hollingsworth from Priscilla, Zenobia delivers her back to Westervelt. Hol-lingsworth, however, intervenes to save Priscilla, and pledges himself to her. Meanwhile, it is revealed to all that Priscilla is Zenobia's half-sister, and that apparently she has been chosen to receive the inheritance that Zenobia thought was hers. Hollingsworth has chosen her over Zenobia because he needs the inheritance money to realize his reform scheme. The spurned and impoverished Zenobia drowns herself. Hollingsworth and Priscilla marry, but the egotistical reformer, overcome by guilt for Zenobia's suicide, is a broken man. Coverdale lapses back into a lonely bachelor's life, offering as explanation for his obsession with his three friends that he has all along been in love with Priscilla.

Blitzstein, Marc   1905–64   Composer, librettist, and lyricist, best remembered for his contributions to the theatre of social protest in the 1930s. Blitzstein was a child prodigy as a pianist; he studied piano with Alexander Siloti at the Curtis Institute of Music in Philadelphia, and in 1926 went to Europe to study composition with Nadia Boulanger and Arnold Schoenberg. His early musical works were highly experimental.

His first attempt to use music for purposes of political protest was in the form of oratorio, *The Condemned* (1932), based on the martyrdom of Sacco and Vanzetti. This was followed by *I've Got the Tune* (1937), a radio play. His best-known work is the musical play *The Cradle Will Rock* (1937), which fused elements of opera and popular music to portray the tyranny of a wealthy businessman over all aspects of life in a small city. Another play, *No For an Answer*, was produced in 1941 but was soon censored and shut down by the authorities because of its political content. After World War II, during which he served in the air force, he completed a ballet, *The Guests* (produced by The New York City Ballet in 1949), and an adaptation of the text of **Kurt Weill**'s *The Three Penny Opera*, produced off Broadway in 1954 with Lotte Lenya as Jenny. His musical *Regina*, based on **Lillian Hellman**'s play *The Little Foxes*, was first produced in 1949 and later became part of the repertory at The New York City Opera. Hellman's plot and characterizations allowed Blitzstein to continue his criticism of capitalism in America while focusing, not on trade unionism or judicial corruption, but on the way pure greed can lead members of a family to destroy one another.

Bloudy Tenent of Persecution, The The first in a series of American Puritan tracts which debate the questions of freedom of conscience and the separation of church and state, *The Bloudy Tenent* was written and published by **Roger Williams** in London in 1644. Provoked by **John Cotton**'s defense of persecution to preserve orthodoxy, Williams presents a two-part dialogue between Truth and Peace. The first part constitutes both a point-by-point rebuttal of an argument made by Cotton in a letter addressed to an Anabaptist imprisoned in Newgate, and a defense of freedom of conscience as an inalienable right. On the grounds that civil power derives from the people and not from God, the second part denounces the ministerial intervention in secular affairs sanctioned by the Puritan theocracy of Massachusetts Bay. Thus, *The Bloudy Tenent* subverts the idea of a national church, the basis of New England's theocratic practices.

The work excited violent response. In the midst of the English Civil War, Parliament ordered it burned immediately following publication. Between 1644 and 1649 more than 120 pamphlets were published in London attacking Williams's position. In New England, John Cotton replied at length in *The Bloudy Tenent Washed and Made White in the Bloud of the Lamb* (1647), a tract to which Williams in turn responded with *The Bloudy Tenent Yet More Bloudy by Mr Cotton's Endeavour to Wash it White in the Bloud of the Lamb* (1652).

Bly, Robert 1926–   Bly was born in Madison, Minnesota, and grew up on a nearby farm. After serving for two years in the navy, he earned degrees from Harvard (1950) and the University of Iowa (1956). In 1958 he founded a journal, *The Fifties*, which later became *The Sixties* and then *The Seventies*. Bly's poetry is filled with images of rural Minnesota, where he continues to live and write. The natural world, however, often becomes a figure for the poet's unconscious, and Bly's exploration of interior "landscapes" frequently gives his work a mystical or surreal quality. In this, his own poetry reflects his interest in South American and European poets such as Pablo Neruda, Juan Ramón Jiménez, and George Trakl, whose work he has both translated and published.

His first book, *Silence in the Snowy Fields*, appeared in 1962. Since then he has published numerous other volumes of verse and translations; these include *The Light Around the Body* (1967), *Sleepers Joining Hands* (1973), *Point Reyes Poems* (1974), *Old Man Rubbing His Eyes* (1975), *The Morning Glory* (1975), *This Body Is Made of Camphor and Gopherwood* (1977), *This Tree Will be Here for a Thousand Years* (1979), *The Man in the Black Coat Turns* (1981), *The Eight Stages of Translation* (1983), and *Four Ramages* (1983). *Leaping Poetry* (1975) is a critical work.

Bogan, Louise 1897–1970   Born in Maine, Bogan was educated at Boston University and spent most of her life in New York City. She was the regular poetry reviewer for *The New Yorker* from 1931 to 1968, and in 1951 published the highly regarded *Achievement in American Poetry 1900–1950*.

Her own poetry was strongly influenced by her study of 16th- and 17th-century English verse, and is characterized by dramatic structure and highly refined metrical forms. She published six volumes of poems: *Body of This Death* (1923), *Dark Summer* (1929), *The Sleeping Fury* (1937), *Poems and New Poems* (1941), *Collected Poems 1923–1953* (1954), and *The Blue Estuaries: Poems 1923–1968* (1968). A prose collection, *A Poet's Alphabet*, appeared in 1970. A "mosaic" of autobiographical materials entitled *Journey Around My Room* was edited by Ruth Limmer and published in 1980.

Boker, George Henry 1823–90   Born into a wealthy Pennsylvania family, Boker was educated at the College of New Jersey (later Princeton University) and went on to study law, but he aspired to the life of a poet. He published his first collection of verse, *The Lesson of Life*, in 1848. *Calaynos*, the first of his eleven plays, only six of which were produced professionally, was staged without authorization in London in 1849. He wrote two comedies in verse, *The Betrothal* (1850), set in Renaissance Italy, and *The Widow's Marriage* (1852, unproduced), and one in prose about contemporary London, *The World a Mask* (1851). His two most successful plays were the historical verse tragedies *Leonor de Guzman* (1853), about the rivalry between the mistress of Alfonso XII and his wife Maria, and *Francesca da Rimini* (1855), based on Dante's story of the lovers Paolo and Francesca. The latter play was unsuccessful at first, but its revival in 1882 won great critical acclaim. Boker's last two plays, *Nydia* (1885) and *Glaucus* (1886), were both based on Edward Bulwer Lytton's novel *The Last Days of Pompeii* (1834); both were unproduced. His patriotism during the Civil War was rewarded by his appointment as United States Ambassador to Turkey (1871–5) and to Russia (1875–8).

Bonifacius A pamphlet by **Cotton Mather**, sub-titled *An Essay Upon the Good*, published anonymously in Boston in 1710 and discussing the meaning of true Christian conduct. Invoking the traditional Puritan idea that every person has a social as well as a spiritual calling, he suggests ways in which people of diverse callings – ministers, lawyers, doctors, magistrates, merchants – may translate Christian principles into their daily lives and activities. He stresses that true Christians fulfill their callings for the good of the whole community, and should direct their energies in responsible and cooperative rather than competitive ways. Interested as he is in people working together in groups, he pays particular attention to the nurture of pious principles in the family and to the value of organized church prayers.

Although Mather retains his Puritan orthodoxy in *Bonifacius*, his concern with worldly activity is an attempt to address traditional Puritan teachings to the immediate concerns of his changing society, with its increasingly complex and diversified secular activities. The book went through many printings both during and after Mather's lifetime, and provided something of a programmatic statement of the social vision of the American Protestant sensibility.

Bontemps, Arna (Wendell) 1902–73 A black novelist born in Louisiana, Bontemps was raised in California. He received an MA from the University of Chicago in 1943, and spent much of his professional life working at Fisk University, first as a librarian, then as public relations director. He was also a professor at the University of Illinois at Chicago Circle and at Yale. His writing is dedicated to portraying the life of black people in America.

Black Thunder (1936) and *Drums at Dusk* (1939) are novels about slave revolts in Virginia and in Haiti. *God Sends Sunday* (1931) was dramatized by **Countee Cullen** as *St Louis Woman* (1946). *Sam Patch* (1951) is one of many children's books written with **Jack Conroy**. His non-fiction includes *They Seek a City* (1945, with Conroy), *The Story of the Negro* (1948), and *100 Years of Negro Freedom* (1961). His correspondence with **Langston Hughes** was published in 1980.

Bostonians, The A novel by **Henry James**, serialized in *The Century Magazine* (1885–6) and then published in volume form in 1886. It is a satirical study of the movement for female emancipation in New England. In searching for a tale which would be characteristic of social conditions in the US, James concluded that the most striking aspect of American life at the time was "the situation of women, the decline of the sentiment of sex, and the agitation in their behalf."

The novel recounts the story of a young lawyer from the South, Basil Ransom, who comes to Boston on business. He becomes acquainted with his two cousins, the feminist Olive Chancellor and her sister, the widow Mrs Luna, who soon falls in love with him. Olive takes Basil to a suffragette meeting, where he meets the altruistic philanthropist, Miss Birdseye. At the meeting a beautiful young woman, Verena Tarrant, delivers an eloquent address, and both Olive and Basil are immediately interested in her. Verena is easily persuaded to share Olive's luxurious home, and Olive sets out to make her a leader of the feminist cause, pleading with her to forswear the thought of marriage. Basil, however, increasingly irritated by the attentions of Mrs Luna, falls in love with Verena and attempts to counter Olive's sway over her. As a result, hostility develops between Olive and Basil. Verena is preparing to deliver a course of lectures, but when Miss Birdseye dies she loses confidence in her purpose. She is about to begin her first lecture when Basil's appearance in the hall unnerves her. She finds herself having to choose between Olive and Basil, and to Olive's bitter disappointment she decides to accept Basil's proposal of marriage.

Boucicault, Dion 1820–90 Born in Ireland and educated in England, Boucicault established his reputation as an actor and dramatist in London before moving to the US in 1853. In New York he continued to write musical sketches, melodramas, and dramatizations of Dickens's novels. Among his plays with American themes is *The Poor of New York* (1857), which is set during the panic of 1857. His best-known work is probably *The Octoroon; or, Life in Louisiana* (1859), a melodrama about slavery which he adapted from **Mayne Reid**'s novel, *The Quadroon*. From 1862 to 1872 he lived in London, where he collaborated with Joseph Jefferson on *Rip Van Winkle* (1865), a dramatization of the **Washington Irving** tale. Altogether he wrote over 100 plays, including a series of comedies about Irish life, the most popular of which were *The Colleen Bawn* (1860), *Arrah-na-Pogue* (1864), and *The Shaughraun* (1874).

Bourne, Randolph 1886–1918 Born in Bloomfield, New Jersey, Bourne attended Columbia University from 1909 to 1913. His first articles, on the revolutionary character of youth, were published in *The Atlantic Monthly* and collected in *Youth and Life* (1913). As his reputation as an essayist rose, he found audiences through *The New Republic*, the *Dial*, and the *Seven Arts*. He was an eclectic reader, and his writings reflected broad interests, notably education (*The Gary Schools*, 1916, and *Education and Living*, 1917), the development of socially responsible fiction, and the depreciation of an ethnically diverse American culture ("Trans-National America," 1916). He was also a fervent pacifist, and after Woodrow Wilson's abandonment of neutrality in 1917 he became an eloquent and increasingly isolated advocate of non-intervention (for example in *Untimely Papers*, 1919). His prowess as a conversationalist impressed a generation of writers and critics, including Van Wyck Brooks, Lewis Mumford, and **John Dos Passos**. Among these figures Bourne developed an almost mythic stature. Disfigured – he was a hunchback who had been deformed at birth by an incompetent doctor – but brilliant, he seemed to represent to them the spirit of 1910 which could not outlive the war.

Bowles, Jane 1917–73 Born Jane Sydney Aves in New York City, she married the novelist **Paul Bowles** in 1938. Four years later she wrote her only novel, *Two Serious Ladies* (published 1943), about two women struggling for independence in a hostile, modern society. Her play *In The Summer House*, the story of an alcoholic woman, was produced in New York in 1953. Her short stories, written in the 1940s, appeared in the US as *The Collected Works of Jane Bowles* and in England as *Plain Pleasures* (both in 1966). Another volume of stories, *Feminine Wiles*, was published posthumously in 1976. For the last 15 years of her life, having suffered a cerebral hemorrhage, she was unable to read or write. She died in Malaga, Spain.

Bowles, Paul 1910– Bowles was born in New York City and attended the University of Virginia before going to Paris, where his first poetry was published in the magazine *transitions* during the 1920s. He studied musical composition with Virgil Thompson and Aaron Copland. After some years as a composer and music critic, he published his first novel, *The Sheltering Sky*, in 1949. In subsequent works, notably *The Delicate Prey* (1950, called *A Little Stone* in England), *Let it Come Down* (1952), and *The Spider's House* (1955), he continued to explore the theme of spiritually weary westerners attempting to escape the ennui of their lives only to find themselves displaced in an Orient they find unsatisfying and even frightening.

Resident in Tangier since 1952, Bowles has tape-recorded, transcribed, and translated original accounts of indigenous life, including *A Life Full of Holes* by Driss ben Hamad Charhadi (1964), *For Bread Alone* by Mohammad Chourkil (1973), and several by Mohammad Mrabet: *M'Hashish* (1969), *The Boy Who Set The Fire* (1974), *Harmless Poisons, Blameless Sins* (1976), and *The Beach Café and The Voice* (1980). Among Bowles's other books are *Pages From Cold Point and Other Stories* (1968), *Their Heads Are Green and Their Hands Are Blue* (1963, travel sketches), *Scenes* (1968, poems), and *Collected Stories* (1979). *Without Stopping*, an autobiography, was issued in 1972.

Boyesen, H[jalmar] H[jorth] 1848–95 Born and educated in Norway, Boyesen came to the US in 1869. He was professor of German at Cornell and Columbia, and published two scholarly works – *Goethe and Schiller* (1879) and *Essays on Scandinavian Literature* (1895). He is best known, however, for his many novels. He also wrote children's books and poetry. He was friendly with **William Dean Howells** (and with the Northeastern literary community generally). It was Howells, then editor of *The Atlantic Monthly*, who published his novel *Gunnar* in that magazine (it appeared in book form in 1874). After writing this romantic tale of Norwegian life he changed course somewhat, and most of his later work is informed by a kind of urban realism, represented most clearly in *The Mammon of Unrighteousness* (1891), *The Golden Calf* (1892), and *Social Strugglers* (1893). *Boyhood in Norway* (1892) is one of his many children's books.

Boyle, Kay 1903–   Born in St Paul, Minnesota, Boyle lived in Europe for 30 years before and after World War II. From 1946 to 1954 she was a foreign correspondent for *The New Yorker*. She held appointments as a fellow, lecturer, or writer-in-residence at various US universities between 1962 and 1971.

Among the 24 volumes of fiction she published between 1929 and 1975 were several collections of short stories: *Short Stories* (1929), *Wedding Day and Other Stories* (1930), *The First Lover and Other Stories* (1936), *The White Horse of Vienna and Other Stories* (1936), and *Thirty Stories* (1946). In 1935 and 1941 she was the recipient of the O. Henry Award. Among her novels are *Year Before Last* (1932), *My Next Bride* (1934), *Monday Night* (1938), *The Crazy Hunter: Three Short Novels* (1940), *Avalanche* (1944), and *A Frenchman Must Die* (1946). She often takes as her subject a young and unworldly American who travels to Europe. A vivid depiction of extraordinary instances of brutality or absurdity in life is a particular characteristic of her work. In addition to novels and short stories she has published five books of verse, various works of non-fiction, and books for young people. She made additions to Robert McAlmon's *Being Geniuses Together* (1938) for the 1968 edition of that record of the literary scene in Europe during the 1920s and 1930s. She edited, among other works, *The Autobiography of Emanuel Carnevali* (1967), and translated René Crevel's *Mr Knife, Miss Fork* (1931).

Bracebridge Hall or, *The Humourists: A Medley*   A book of 49 tales and sketches by **Washington Irving**, published in 1822 under Irving's pseudonym, Geoffrey Crayon, Gent. It is a sequel to Irving's popular *The Sketch Book*. English, French, and Spanish settings are intermingled with American; the best-remembered tales, "Dolph Heylinger" and "The Storm-Ship," are set in America.

Brackenridge, Hugh Henry 1748–1816   Brackenridge was born in Scotland; his family emigrated to Pennsylvania when he was 5. He educated himself in the classics while growing up on the frontier, and taught school in Maryland for five years before beginning studies at Princeton in 1768. At Princeton he got to know **Philip Freneau** and James Madison; he and Freneau collaborated on *Father Bembo's Pilgrimage to Mecca* (1770), a fictional prose satire on American manners, and on a patriotic poem, *The Rising Glory of America*, which Brackenridge read at their commencement in 1771. After graduation, Brackenridge taught school, studied theology, and became a military chaplain for the Continental Army. During the Revolutionary War he wrote several patriotic works, including *A Poem On Divine Revelation* (1774) and two plays, *The Battle of Bunkers-Hill* (1776) and *The Death of General Montgomery* (1777). In 1779 he went to Philadelphia and founded the *United States Magazine*, which published patriotic speeches and state constitutions, as well as poetry (including some by Freneau), and his own series of fictional essays on Revolutionary themes "The Cave of Vanhest."

With the folding of the *United States Magazine* in December 1779, Brackenridge became more ambivalent politically, expressing doubts about the prospects for the new country in his last editorial. He left Philadelphia and went to Pittsburgh to practice law. There he became involved in politics, but cultivated an eccentric image and was a true partisan of neither political party. Having founded *The Pittsburgh Gazette* (1786), the first Western newspaper, he frequently contributed satires of both Eastern and Western manners, both Federalist and Republican politics. He acted as mediator during the Whiskey Rebellion (1794), provoked by Alexander Hamilton's excise tax on liquor; his account of the rebellion was published as *Incidents of the Insurrection in the Western Parts of Pennsylvania, in the Year 1794* (1795). Brackenridge served on the Pennsylvania Supreme Court from 1799 to 1814, and wrote a book in which he attempted to adapt Blackstone's *Commentaries* in the context of the American legal system. This volume was published in 1814 as *Law Miscellanies*. During his tenure on the Supreme Court, he continued to publish volumes of *Modern Chivalry*, the novel on which his literary reputation chiefly rests. The first volume was published in 1792, and the complete edition was issued in 1815.

Bradbury, Ray (Douglas) 1920– Born in Waukegan, Illinois, Bradbury became a full-time writer in 1943 and contributed numerous short stories to periodicals before publishing a collection of them as *Dark Carnival* (1947). His reputation as a leading science-fiction writer was established with the publication of *The Martian Chronicles* (1950, entitled *The Silver Locusts* in England), which describes the first attempts of Earth people to conquer and colonize Mars during the years 1999–2026; the constant thwarting of their efforts by the gentle, telepathic Martians; the eventual colonization; and finally the effect on the Martian settlers of a massive nuclear war on Earth. As much a work of social criticism as of science fiction, *The Martian Chronicles* reflects some of the prevailing anxieties of America in the early 1950s: the fear of nuclear war, the longing for a simpler life, and reactions against racism and censorship. Another of Bradbury's best-known works, the novel *Farenheit 451* (1953), is set in a future when the written word is forbidden; resisting a totalitarian state which burns all the books, a group of rebels memorize entire works of literature and philosophy.

The author of more than 500 stories, novels, poems, essays, radio plays, film-scripts, and television scripts, Bradbury is a social critic of the age of technology. He is not against technological expansion in itself, but insists that we must be aware of its social effects, contemporary and future. Among his other works are the novel *Something Wicked This Way Comes* (1962) and numerous collections of short stories: *The Illustrated Man* (1951), *The Golden Apples of the Sun* (1953), *The October Sky* (1955), *A Medicine for Melancholy* (1959, entitled *The Day It Rained Forever* in England), *The Machineries of Joy* (1964), *I Sing The Body Electric!* (1969), *The Last Circus*

and the Electrocution (1980), and *A Memory of Murder* (1984).

Bradford, William 1590–1657 A governor and historian of Plymouth Colony, Bradford was born in Yorkshire, England. At the age of 12, to his family's displeasure, he joined a group of separatists who later (1606) formed a congregation under the minister John Robinson. In 1609 they emigrated first to Amsterdam and then to Leyden, where Bradford was employed as a fustian weaver and day worker. Leaving Robinson in Leyden, the group traveled to America aboard the *Mayflower* in 1620.

At Plymouth, on the death of John Carver, Bradford was elected governor, an office which he held from 1621 to 1656 except for five years (1633, 1634, 1636, 1638, 1644) when he voluntarily stepped down to serve as assistant governor. In 1627, together with seven fellow emigrants and four London merchants, he assumed the colony's debt of £1,800 from the original investors. In his various writings Bradford tells of other transactions that provide insight into the colonial government and economy. His *History of Plimmoth Plantation*, written between 1630 and 1651, chronicles the settlement of the Plymouth colony. His incomplete *Letter Book* (1624–30) and his letters to **John Winthrop** show a leader working out the colony's internal problems as well as negotiating with England, the neighboring Massachusetts Bay Colony, and the Indians.

Bradstreet, Anne 1612–72 America's first published poet, Bradstreet was born and grew up in aristocratic surroundings in England as the daughter of Thomas Dudley, who had been steward to the Earl of Lincoln. She married Simon Bradstreet at 16, and two years later, in 1630, sailed for America with her husband and father on the *Arbella*. Living in Ipswich and then in Andover, she became the mother of eight children. Both her father and her husband eventually became governors of Massachusetts.

Bradstreet's collection of poems, *The Tenth Muse Lately Sprung Up in America*, was published without her knowledge by her brother-in-law in London in 1650. A second edition, with corrections and additional poems, entitled *Several Poems Compiled With a Great Variety of Wit*, appeared in Boston six years after her death. Most modern editions also include further poems and prose pieces found in the so-called Andover manuscripts. The poems generally follow Elizabethan models, and show the influence of Spenser, Sidney, Du Bartas, and Raleigh. There are "quaternions," such as "The Four Elements," "The Four Humours," "The Four Ages of Man," and "The Four Seasons"; "Contemplations," a series of emblematic stanzas on the themes of time and mutability; and elegies on Sidney, Du Bartas, and Queen Elizabeth. Many of the later poems are more personal in subject and less conventional in form, often meditating on domestic topics from a religious point of view. This group includes poems to her husband and elegies on her dead children.

Braithwaite, William Stanley (Beaumont) 1879–1962 A black poet, short-story writer, and editor, born in Boston, the son of West Indian parents. He was educated at the Boston Latin School, and in 1918 received two honorary degrees for his contributions to scholarship, an MA from Atlanta University, and a Litt. D from Talladega College.

He began his literary career with *The Canadian* (1901), a novel which received little attention. His first collection of poetry, *Lyrics of Life and Love*, appeared in 1904, one year after the well-established poet, **Paul Laurence Dunbar**, had published his *Lyrics of Love and Laughter*. His second book of verse, *The House of Falling Leaves*, followed in 1908. He also produced a volume of short stories, *Frost on the Green Tree* (1928); a second novel, *Going over Tindel* (1924); and an autobiography, *The House Under Arcturus* (1941). *Selected Poems* appeared in 1948.

In the first few decades of the century, Braithwaite was influential as an editor and literary critic. For 16 years he published the annual *Anthology of Magazine Verse and Year Book of American Poetry* (1913–29), which served as a major outlet for black writers and poets. He regularly contributed essays and reviews to journals, and served as literary critic on the editorial staff of the *Boston Transcript*. He also became a mentor to the younger generation of black writers. In an article entitled "Some Contemporary Poets of the Negro Race," published in *The Crisis* in 1919,

he wrote about the dawning of a "new movement" in black letters, a flourishing of creative activity which was later termed the **Harlem Renaissance**. When the Depression brought an end to both the *Boston Transcript* and his annual *Anthology*, Braithwaite joined the faculty of the first black graduate school at Atlanta University, where he taught until his retirement. His other critical works include *The Bewitched Parsonage: The Story of the Brontes* (1950), and numerous essays on contemporary literary figures.

Brautigan, Richard 1935–84 Born in Tacoma, Washington, Brautigan came to prominence in the mid 1960s as a leading exponent of a new social order. His poetry, of which the best-known collection is *The Pill Versus the Springhill Mine Disaster* (1968), paid homage to an unconstrained sexuality and to the enrichment derived from personal encounters. His novel *Trout Fishing in America* (1967), which sold over two million copies, describes the narrator's nostalgic search for a morning of good fishing in a crystal-clear stream. His quest takes him through a variety of American landscapes – San Francisco city parks, Oregon forests, Idaho campgrounds, a Filipino laundry, and a wrecking yard that sells used trout streams by the foot. The fact that his idiosyncratic quest is never realized becomes a metaphor for the unpromising and unappealing cultural environment that surrounds his journey. *In Watermelon Sugar* (1968) portrays a mode of life in a commune that shuns all standard American values, the residents defining themselves largely in opposition to the social structure of the outside world.

Many of his novels display a childlike conception of a world in which one can rearrange, ridicule, or ignore elements that are threatening or irrelevant. His other works of fiction include *A Confederate General from Big Sur* (1964), *Revenge of the Lawn: Stories, 1962–1970* (1971), *The Abortion: An Historical Romance 1966* (1971), *The Hawkline Monster: A Gothic Western* (1974), *Willard and His Bowling Trophies: A Perverse Mystery* (1974), *Sombrero Fallout: A Japanese Novel* (1976), *Dreaming of Babylon: A Private Eye Novel, 1942* (1977), *The Tokyo–Montana Express* (1980), and *So The Wind Won't Blow It All Away* (1982). Among his other collections of poetry are *The Galilee Hitch-Hiker* (1958), *The Return of the Rivers* (1958), *Lay the Marble Tea* (1959), *The Octopus Frontier* (1960), *All Watched Over By Machines of Loving Grace* (1967), *Please Plant This Book* (1968, a combination of poems and seed packets), *Rommel Drives Deep Into Egypt* (1970), *Loading Mercury with a Pitchfork* (1976), and *June 30th, June 30th* (1978). Brautigan was found dead from a self-inflicted gunshot wound in 1984.

Breakfast at Tiffany's See **Capote, Truman**

Bridge, The A long poem by **Hart Crane**, published in 1930. Begun in 1923, the poem was Crane's attempt to present an affirmative, epic vision of America; New York City's Brooklyn Bridge is its central image. In his prefatory "Proem" Crane describes the bridge as both "harp and altar" which will "lend a myth to God," and he returns to this affirmative vision in "Atlantis," the final part of the sequence. In the intervening seven sections, however, he explores the negative as well as the positive aspects of the American experience, which are symbolized by literary and historical figures, geographical features and place names, and technological inventions. In the section entitled "Powhatan's Daughter," for example, the Indian princess Pocahontas becomes a figure representing the beauty of the American landscape; in a subsection entitled "The River," the Mississippi River is transformed into a natural force fusing history with eternal time; and in "The Tunnel," the New York City subway becomes a hellish underworld haunted by the ghost of **Edgar Allan Poe**.

Bridge of San Luis Rey, The See **Wilder, Thornton**

Bromfield, Louis 1896–1956 Born in Mansfield, Ohio, Bromfield began studying journalism at Columbia University in 1916 but left shortly thereafter to serve in World War I. Between 1922 and 1925 he worked as foreign editor of *Musical America*. He subsequently wrote columns for *The New Yorker* and *The Bookman* (for which he was also a music and drama critic). His first novel, *The Green Bay Tree*, was published in 1924, and was followed by numerous others, including *Possession* (1925); *Early Autumn* (1926), for which he was awarded the Pulitzer

Prize; *The Farm* (1933); *The Rains Came* (1937); *Night in Bombay* (1940); *Wild is the River* (1941); *Mrs Parkinson* (1943); and *Pleasant Valley* (1945). He also published collections of short stories, including *Awake and Rehearse* (1929), *It Takes All Kinds* (1939), and *The World We Live In* (1944); and such plays as *The House of Women* (1927), and *De Luxe* (1935). Bromfield's fiction often reflects a profound distrust of industrialism and materialism, which he saw as dehumanizing factors in 20th-century American life.

Brook Farm A cooperative reform community, founded in 1841 by **George Ripley** and other **Transcendentalists** on a farm in West Roxbury, Massachusetts, about eight miles from Boston, and set up as a joint stock company. The Brook Farmers' aim was to simplify and purify economic relations by retreating from an increasingly commercial society and working the farm together (other occupations, such as shoemaking, were later introduced) to achieve a simplified, near-subsistence existence which would leave time for intellectual and spiritual self-improvement. Many figures prominent in the Transcendentalist movement either lived on the farm or visited it from time to time. These included **Margaret Fuller**, **Ralph Waldo Emerson**, **William Ellery Channing**, **Theodore Parker**, **Orestes Brownson**, and **Nathaniel Hawthorne**, who based his novel, *The Blithedale Romance*, on his Brook Farm experience. The Brook Farmers produced two periodical publications: *The Phalanx* (1843–5) and *The Harbinger* (1845–9). In 1844 the Farm explicitly embraced the reform principles of Charles Fourier, redrawing its Articles of Association in 1845 to establish a phalanx. In 1846 its nearly completed new phalanstery was burned down, and the Farm was threatened with bankruptcy. It disbanded in 1847.

Brooks, Gwendolyn 1917– Black poet, born in Topeka, Kansas, and raised and educated in Chicago. Her first verse appeared in little magazines, and she won contests sponsored by *Poetry* magazine. Her first volume, *A Street in Bronzeville*, was published in 1945, and she won the Pulitzer Prize for *Annie Allen* (1949). *Selected Poems* appeared in 1963. She succeeded **Carl Sandburg** as Poet Laureate of Illinois, and in 1968 she published the celebratory *For Illinois 1968: A Sesquicenten-nial Poem.* The first volume of her autobiography, *Report From Part One*, was published in 1972, followed by *The Tiger Who Wore White Gloves: Or, What You Are You Are* in 1974.

Brougham, John 1810–80 Born in Dublin and educated there at Trinity College, Brougham made his American acting debut in 1842 at the Park Theatre in New York. He continued to act throughout his long career as a dramatist, during which he also wrote and adapted at least 125 plays. His greatest popularity, both as an actor and as a dramatist, was in the years preceding the Civil War, and he is best known for his two-act musical burlesque of 1855, *Po-ca-hon-tas! or, Ye Gentle Savage.* Also notable are his *A Row at the Lyceum; Or, Green Room Secrets* (1851), an innovative one-act skit in which a rehearsal is interrupted by an objection from a plant in the audience; and *The Game of Love* (1855), a five-act social satire about marriage between upper and lower classes. His other burlesques include *Metamora; Or, The Last of the Pollywoags* (1847), *Columbus* (1857), and *Much Ado About the Merchant of Venice* (1869). He also adapted several contemporary British and American novels for the stage: *Dombey and Son* (1848), *Jane Eyre* (1849), *Vanity Fair* (1849), and *Dred* (1856). His other successes include *Temptation* (1849), *The Irish Immigrant* (1857), and *The Mustard Ball; or, Love at the Academy* (1858).

Brown, Charles Brockden 1771–1810 Often considered America's first professional author, Brown was born in Philadelphia into a family of prosperous Quakers. He studied law and during his brief practice in Philadelphia met Elihu Smith, one of the **Connecticut Wits**, with whom in 1790 he formed the "Society for the Attainment of Useful Knowledge." Contemptuous of the legal profession, he moved to New York City in 1796 and began writing. His first publication, *Alcuin: A Dialogue* (1798), was a treatise on the rights of women which shows the influence of William Godwin. Further stimulated by Godwin's philosophy of rational individualism, and by the novels of Mrs Radcliffe, Brown wrote feverishly for the next two years and produced four novels, all of which translate the English Gothic romance into an American

idiom: *Wieland* (1798); *Arthur Mervyn* (1799–1800); *Ormond* (1799); and *Edgar Huntly* (1799).

Although widely read in America and England, these novels were not commercial successes. Brown invested in an import business, which collapsed in 1806, and simultaneously engaged himself in more lucrative literary ventures. From 1799 he served as editor of *The Monthly Magazine and American Review*, and at the turn of the century produced two more traditional romances which sold well but lacked the artistic innovation of his previous fiction: *Clara Howard* (1801, published in England as *Philip Stanley*) and *Jane Talbot* (1801). *Memoirs of Carwin*, a sequel to *Wieland*, appeared serially (1803–5) in his newly founded and highly successful *The Literary Magazine and American Register* (1803–7), but remained unfinished at his death in 1810.

Brown, John 1800–59 The celebrated Abolitionist leader was born in Torrington, Connecticut. In 1855 he joined his sons in the Ossawatomie settlement in Kansas. The Kansas–Nebraska Bill, which allowed the settlers themselves to determine whether slavery should be permitted in these territories, had been passed the previous year, and the conflict surrounding that local decision provoked Brown's Abolitionist sentiments. God intended him, he decided, to destroy pro-slavery settlers. On May 24, 1856, together with four of his sons and another sympathizer, he murdered five pro-slavery men. Retaliation followed: Brown and the Ossawatomie settlers were attacked and their dwellings burned. Over the next few years Brown gathered arms and money from leading Abolitionists, and on October 16, 1859, staged an attack with 21 men on the US armory at Harper's Ferry, Virginia. His intention was to establish a base from which he could begin to free the slaves by force of arms. He captured the armory, but he and his group were defeated by a force of marines under Robert E. Lee; Brown himself was wounded and taken prisoner.

His trial and subsequent hanging (on December 2, 1859) made him a martyr of the Abolitionist movement. He was celebrated in American literature by such writers as **Henry David Thoreau** (*The Last Days of John*

Brown), **Carl Sandburg** (*Ossawatomie*), **John Greenleaf Whitter** (*John Brown of Ossawatomie*), **W. E. B. Du Bois** (*John Brown*), and **Stephen Vincent Benét** (*John Brown's Body*).

Brown, Rita Mae 1944– Brown was born in Hanover, Pennsylvania, and attended universities in Florida and New York as well as the New York School of Visual Arts. Her first novel, *Rubyfruit Jungle* (1973), established her at the forefront of the feminist and gay-rights movements. Other novels include *In Her Day* (1976), *Six of One* (1978), *Southern Discomfort* (1982), and *Sudden Death* (1983). Her poetry has appeared in collections such as *The Hand That Cradles The Rock* (1971) and *Songs to a Handsome Woman* (1973). A collection of essays, *A Plain Brown Rapper*, was published in 1976.

Brown, Sterling A[llen] 1901– Black poet, editor, and critic, born in Washington DC, the son of a Howard University professor. He was educated at Williams College and at Harvard. His first volume of poetry, *Southern Road* (1932), with its direct style and use of folk material, shows the influence of **Carl Sandburg**. A leading characteristic of Brown's poetry is the appropriation of folk idioms, such as work songs and ballads, which he then transforms into contemporary statements of social protest. Most of his work has appeared in various magazines, with few published volumes. *The Last Ride of Wild Bill, and Eleven Narrative Poems* appeared in 1975, and *Collected Poems* in 1980. An active and prolific critic of black literature in the 1930s, he produced two critical volumes, *The Negro in American Fiction* and *Negro Poetry and Drama*, both in 1937. He was also co-editor, with Arthur P. Davis and Ulysses Lee, of the influential anthology of **Harlem Renaissance** writers, *The Negro Caravan* (1941).

Brown, William Hill 1765–93 Brown was born in Boston; his mother was the great-granddaughter of **Increase Mather**. In 1789 he published his first book, *The Power of Sympathy*, which is generally considered to be the first American novel. He contributed prose and poetry to the *Massachusetts Magazine* and the *New England Palladium*, occasionally using the pseudonym "Pollio." As "The Yankee," he wrote literary and political essays for Boston's *Columbian Sentinel* from September to December 1790. In 1791 he traveled to Murfreesboro, North Carolina, to visit his sister, and while there he published several poems in the *North-Carolina Journal*. He died during an epidemic, probably of malaria, at the age of 28. Several works were published posthumously: a tragedy entitled *West Point Preserved, or the Treason of Arnold* (1797); various poems and prose pieces published in the *Boston Magazine* and the *Emerald* (1805–7); and his second novel, *Ira and Isabella: or The Natural Children* (1807), whose plot is similar to that of *The Power of Sympathy* except that it has a happy ending.

Brown, William Wells *c*.1816–84 The black leader was born into slavery in Kentucky, and raised in St Louis, where he worked at Elijah Lovejoy's press. After gaining his freedom he aided fugitive slaves in Ohio. His autobiographical *Narrative of William W. Brown, a Fugitive Slave* was published in 1847 by the Massachusetts Antislavery Society, and he soon became widely known, both in the US and abroad, as a leading black advocate of abolition. He was considered by many of his contemporaries to be **Frederick Douglass**'s successor after Douglass broke with **William Lloyd Garrison**'s policies in 1851.

Soon after the publication of his *Narrative* Brown turned to other forms of writing. A collection of poems, *The Anti-Slavery Harp*, appeared in 1848, and *Three Years in Europe; or, Places I Have Seen and People I Have Met* in 1852. *Clotel; or, The President's Daughter* was published in London in 1853. Long thought to have been the first novel published by a black American, this story of the mulatta daughter of **Thomas Jefferson**'s black slave was issued in the US in 1864, without reference to the President, as *Clotel: A Tale of the Southern States*. Brown's other works are a play entitled *The Escape; or, A Leap For Freedom* (1858), and the essay *The Black Man: His Antecedents, His Genius, and His Achievements* (1863), which was later expanded into *The Rising Son* (1873).

Browne, Charles Farrar 1834–67 A humorist who wrote under the pseudonym of Artemus Ward, Browne was born in Waterford, Maine, and was for the most part self-educated. From 1857 to 1859 he wrote for the *Cleveland Plain Dealer*, and during this period created Artemus Ward – the writer of mock letters to the editor, letters full of colloquial language and misspellings that result in puns or malapropisms. Browne left Ohio in 1859 to join the staff of New York's *Vanity Fair*, where Browne, eventually its editor, came to be known as the "unofficial dean of American humor."

He was a pioneer in the genre of the comic lecture – a form of entertainment **Mark Twain** would later capitalize on. His targets were Abolitionists, Mormons, Shakers, feminists, temperance movements, and anyone else he considered hypocritical or ineffectual. His publications include *Artemus Ward, His Book* (1862), *Artemus Ward, His Travels* (1865), and *Artemus Ward Among The Ferians* (1866). While on a lecture tour in England (1866–7), during which time he contributed to *Punch*, he died of tuberculosis. *Artemus Ward In London and Other Papers* was published posthumously in 1867.

Brownson, Orestes (Augustus) 1803–76 Born in Stockbridge, Vermont, into an old Connecticut family, Brownson received no formal education. In the course of his life he underwent several changes of faith. In 1824 he left the Presbyterian church and became a Universalist. By 1832 he had joined the Unitarian church, and finally, in 1844, he became a Roman Catholic. Although he was associated with **Transcendentalism** and the **Brook Farm** experiment, and shared the Transcendentalists' belief that moral reform had to be the basis of political change, his own activities were often more radical than those emanating from that movement. He helped organize The Workingmen's Party in the early 1830s; he agitated for the reform of the penal code and inheritance laws; and in 1836 he founded a church for the working classes in Boston called the "Society for Christian Union and Progress."

Brownson provided forums for these ideas in several of the magazines he edited: *Boston Quarterly Review*, *Democratic Review*, and *Brownson's Quarterly Review*. Many of his works put forth his religious and social beliefs and describe his changes of faith. In *New Views of Christianity, Society and the Church* (1836), he attacked organized Christianity; *Charles Elwood; or The Infidel Converted* (1840) is a semi-autobiographical novel about a man's conversion to Unitarianism; *The Medi-*tational Life of Jesus* (1842) outlines his Roman Catholic beliefs; *The Spirit-Rapper: An Autobiography* (1854) is less an autobiography than a novel about the Satanic influences evident in contemporary spiritualism; *The Convert; or, Leaves from My Experiences* (1857) is an account of his personal religious growth. His *Complete Works* appeared in 20 volumes (1882–7).

Bryant, William Cullen 1794–1878 Poet and editor, born in Cummington, Massachusetts. He began writing poetry at the age of 13; his first work, *The Embargo* (1808), satirizes **Thomas Jefferson**'s government. He attended Williams College, then studied law and followed a legal career until he was 31. He was still a young lawyer when the first version of *Thanatopsis*, which he had written when he was 16, appeared in *The North American Review* in 1817. He published a collection, *Poems*, in 1821, and from 1824 to 1825 contributed regularly to the *United States Literary Gazette*. It was during this period that his reputation as a leading American poet was established.

He became an editor of the *New York Review* and *Athenaeum Magazine* in 1825, and chief editor of the *New York Evening Post* in 1829, a position he held for nearly 50 years, during which time he became a vigorous opponent of slavery and an advocate of the new Republican party. His career as a poet continued with the publication of a second collection, *Poems*, in 1832. Late in life he produced blank verse translations of the *Iliad* (1870) and the *Odyssey* (1871–2). Though he was strongly influenced by European Romanticism, and by Wordsworth in particular, his verse reveals a concern with distinctively American political and philosophical issues, and reflects a movement, in mid century, from Federalist politics to the New Republicanism.

Buck, Pearl S[ydenstricker] 1892–1973 Born in Hillsboro, West Virginia, Buck was taken to China as a child by her parents, who went there as missionaries. She was to spend much of her life there, teaching at various universities. Her first husband, John Lossing Buck, was also a missionary. Many of her works of fiction are set in China, including *The Good Earth* (1931), probably her best-known novel, for which she was awarded the

Pulitzer Prize in 1932. An epic story about a peasant's relationship with the soil, it is the first in a trilogy called *The House of Earth*, of which the others are *Sons* (1932) and *A House Divided* (1935). Her first novel about Chinese life was *East Wind, West Wind* (1930). Subsequent novels about China include *The Mother* (1934), *This Proud Heart* (1938), *Dragon Seed* (1941), and *Kinfolk* (1949).

A prolific writer, Buck produced over 100 titles: novels, collections of stories, plays, screenplays, one book of verse, books for juveniles, biographies, two autobiographies, a cookbook, and works of non-fiction about the mentally retarded, her philanthropic activities, Russia, the Kennedy women, and missionaries. She also translated and edited works by various Chinese writers. The biographies of her parents, *The Exile* (1936) and *Fighting Angel: Portrait of A Soul* (1936), are considered classics. In 1938 she became the first American woman to win the Nobel Prize for Literature. In addition to her literary activities, she founded two institutions (Welcome House and the Pearl S. Buck Foundation) dedicated to helping Eurasian children and their Asian mothers.

Bukowski, Charles 1920–   Born in Germany, Bukowski was brought to America by his parents in 1922. He grew up in Los Angeles and attended Los Angeles City College between 1939 and 1941. He wrote some short stories and worked at a variety of odd jobs before beginning to write poetry in the 1950s.

His first volumes of verse, *Flower, Fist and Bestial Wall* (1959), *Longshot Poems for Broke Players* (1961), and *Run with the Hunted* (1962), were not widely noticed, but in 1962 *Outsider* magazine named him "Outsider of the Year" and devoted an issue to his work, bringing him more recognition. Since then he has written some 30 volumes of poetry. These include *Crucifix in a Deathhand: New Poems, 1963–65* (1965), *At Terror Street and Agony Way* (1968), *Poems Written Before Jumping Out of an 8-Story Window* (1968), *The Days Run Away Like Wild Horses over the Hills* (1969), *Burning in Water, Drowning in Flame: Selected Poems 1955–1973* (1974), *Love Is a Dog from Hell* (1977), *Dangling in the Tournefortia* (1981), and *Hot Water Music* (1983). He has also written novels, including *Post Office* (1971), *Factotum* (1975),

Women (1978), and *Ham on Rye* (1982), and other prose pieces, including *Confessions of a Man Insane Enough to Live with Beasts* (1965) and *All the Assholes in the World and Mine* (1966). His correspondence with the poet Al Purdy was collected and published in 1983 by Seamus Cooney for the Paget Press in *The Bukowski/Purdy Letters: A Decade of Dialogue, 1964–1974*.

Bukowski's work circulates in limited editions and magazines published by small presses (his most frequent publisher is the Black Sparrow Press in Los Angeles), among an underground rather than a commercial readership. His poetic ancestors are **The Beats**, and he emphasizes immediate, unprettified experience, writing as an alienated outcast, irreverent, angry, and especially critical of the pretentiousness of the academic and commercial mainstream of contemporary American poetry.

Bullins, Ed 1935–   One of the most prolific playwrights of the black American theatre, Bullins was born in Philadelphia and educated there and in California. His first play, *Clara's Ole Man* (1965), immediately showed his sensitivity to the nature of life in the ghetto; *The Gentleman Caller* (1968), *The Electronic Nigger* (1968), *A Son, Come Home* (1968), and *Goin A Buffalo* (1969) are typical examples of his work's mixture of improvisatory energy and formal discipline. He has planned a cycle of 20 plays to cover the twentieth-century life of Afro-American communities, loosely united around the Dawson family. The cycle includes *In New England Winter* (1967), *In the Wine Time* (1968), *The Duplex* (1970), *The Fabulous Miss Marie* (1970), *Street Sounds* (1970), *Daddy* (1977), and *Leavings* (1980). A collection of works written during a militant phase was published in 1971 as *Four Dynamite Plays*. *The House Party* (1973) and *The Taking of Miss Janie* (1975) look back at the politics of the 1960s. After collaborating on the musicals *Sepia Star* (1977) and *Storyville* (1977), Bullins directed the 1978 New York production of his play *Michael*. *The Hungered One: Early Writings*, a collection of short stories, was published in 1971, and his novel, *The Reluctant Rapist*, in 1973. Since 1967 he has been associated with the New Lafayette Theatre in Harlem, New York, as both playwright and director; he has served as producing director of The Surviving Theatre in New York since 1974.

Burk, John Daly *c.*1775–1808 Born in Ireland, Burk came to America in 1796 and settled there in 1800. He is best known for *Bunker-Hill; or, the Death of General Warren* (1797), the first of his seven plays. He was a fervent patriot whose plays were popular exercises in American chauvinism. *Female Patriotism, or, The Death of Joan d'Arc* (1798) was another such production. In addition to his writing, Burk founded two newspapers, *The Polar Star and Boston Daily Advertiser* and *The Time Piece*, both of which failed after short runs.

Burke, Kenneth 1897– Born in Pittsburgh, Pennsylvania, Burke was educated at Columbia University. He wrote essays, short fiction, and poetry before becoming the music critic of the *Dial* magazine and, later, *The Nation*. He was associated briefly with the American Communist movement. He is best known as a theorist of literary forms, whose studies also encompass history, rhetoric, and philosophy. His most famous books, *A Grammar of Motives* (1945) and *A Rhetoric of Motives* (1950), are inquiries into the ways all human activity is ordered in language.

Apart from his early fiction and poetry, Burke's first works were *Counter-Statement* (1931), *Permanence and Change* (1935), *Attitudes Toward History* (1937), and *The Philosophy of Literary Form* (1941). His fiction and poetry are collected in *The Complete White Oxen* (1968) and *Collected Poems, 1915–1967* (1968). *Towards a Better Life* (1932) is his only novel. His other books include *The Rhetoric of Religion* (1961), *Perspective by Incongruity* (1964), *Terms for Order* (1964), and *Language as Symbolic Action* (1966).

Burnett, Frances (Eliza) Hodgson 1849–1924 A novelist and children's writer, Burnett was born in Manchester, England, and moved to Tennessee in 1865. She established a popular reputation with her first publication, a sentimental novel entitled *That Lass o'Lowrie's* (1877), but she is most famous for her children's books: ***Little Lord Fauntleroy*** (1886), *The Little Princess* (1905), and *The Secret Garden* (1911). Her other works include *Editha's Burglar* (1888), *The White*

People (1917), a novel about the supernatural, and *The One I Knew Best of All* (1893), an autobiography. She was also instrumental in establishing the legal precedent which gave American authors control over the English publication of their works.

Burroughs, William S[eward] 1914– Born in St Louis and educated at Harvard, Burroughs has spent much of his life in Paris and Tangier. Before leaving the US he was friendly with **Jack Kerouac**, **Allen Ginsberg**, and a circle of writers younger than himself who had gathered at Columbia University and who later became known as **The Beats**.

He wrote of his experience of heroin addiction in *Junkie* (1953, under the pseudonym of William Lee) and *Naked Lunch* (1959). The latter became notorious for its frank treatment of the life of the addict, and was banned on grounds of obscenity until writers such as **Norman Mailer** and Ginsberg came to its defense in court. (It was published legally in the US in 1962.) Its bitter rendering not only of the horrors of addiction, but of the far-reaching cultural illusions for which addiction is a metaphor, has made it his most famous book. His subsequent work includes *The Exterminator* (1960, with Brion Gysin), *The Soft Machine* (1961), *The Ticket That Exploded* (1962), *The Yage Letters* (1963, a collection of letters with Allen Ginsberg), *Dead Fingers Talk* (1963), *Nova Express* (1964), *The Job* (1970, an interview), *The Wild Boys* (1971), *Exterminator!* (1973), *Port of Saints* (1973), *The Last Words of Dutch Schultz* (1975), *The Third Mind* (1978), *Ah Pook Is Here and Other Texts* (1979), *Blade Runner: A Movie* (1979), *With William Burroughs: A Report from the Bunker* (1981, interviews), *Cities of the Red Night* (1981), *Letters to Allen Ginsberg 1953–1957* (1982), *The Place of Dead Roads* (1983), and *Queer* (1984).

Bus Stop See **Inge, William**

Butterfield 8 See **O'Hara, John**

By Love Possessed See **Cozzens, James Gould**

Byrd, William 1674–1744 A Virginia aristocrat, Byrd was educated in Europe and was admitted to the Bar in England after studying at the Middle Temple. Throughout his life he lived for long periods in England as well as in Virginia, where he served in various public offices, including, from 1709 to his death, on the Royal Council of Virginia. Under his management Byrd's family estates at Westover increased from 26,000 to 180,000 acres. His English acquaintances included the playwrights Congreve and Wycherley; he was a member of the Royal Society; and he owned one of the largest libraries in the American colonies (4,000 volumes).

Byrd's writings, though not published during his lifetime, provide a vivid picture of his milieu, as well as a satiric commentary on some of his experiences. His journal was discovered in the 20th century, and two portions were published as *The Secret Diary of William Byrd of Westover 1709–1712* (1941) and *Another Secret Diary 1739–1741* (1942). He also wrote important narratives of American travel and exploration. The most famous of these, *The History of the Dividing Line*, is his reworking of the journal he kept while serving on a surveying commission in 1728 to determine the boundary between Virginia and North Carolina. It includes a history of Virginia, satiric digs at North Carolinians, observations on the countryside and Indians, and humorous anecdotes from the surveying expedition. *The Secret History of the Dividing Line*, probably an earlier version, is shorter, and its humor more racy. *A Progress to the Mines in the Year 1732* and *A Journey to the Land of Eden in the Year 1733* are also travel accounts, probably reworked from his journals of the late 1730s. Portions of all four manuscripts were first published in 1841; they were collected in a modern edition by Louis B. Wright in 1966.

C

Cabell, James Branch 1879–1958   Born in Richmond, Virginia, Cabell is best known for his creation of the mythical French province Poictesme, whose "history" from 1234 to 1750 he chronicled in a series of allegorical novels which comment obliquely on American life. He went into great detail about the life, customs, and liberal morality of the people of Poictesme, and one novel in the series, *Jurgen* (1919), was suppressed as being immoral. The case stirred public curiosity, and Cabell enjoyed a large popular following in the 1920s. He published his first novel, *The Eagle's Shadow*, in 1904. *The Soul of Melicent*, the first in the Poictesme series, appeared in 1913; the last, *Straws and Prayer-Books*, in 1924. He also wrote poetry and non-fiction throughout his career.

Cable,   George   Washington   1844–1925   Born in New Orleans, Cable served in the Mississippi Cavalry during the Civil War, and then worked as a surveyor, as a reporter and columnist for the New Orleans *Picayune* (using the pseudonym "Drop Shot"), and as an accountant and clerk. Though he contributed stories of Louisiana life to *Scribner's Monthly* and *Appleton's Journal* between 1873 and 1879, he did not take up writing as a career until the later date. From 1885 he made annual reading tours of the US. He was also involved in publishing two journals – *The Letter* (1892–6) and *Symposium* (1896).

One of the leading local-color writers of the "New South," Cable produced 18 volumes of fiction between 1879 and 1918. The best of these are generally thought to be the collection of short stories entitled **Old Creole Days** (1879) and the novels **The Grandissimes** (1880) and **Madame Delphine** (1881). He moved to Northampton, Massachusetts, in 1885 and several of his novels – *Dr Sevier*

(1884), *Bonaventure* (1888), *John March, Southerner* (1894), and *Bylow Hill* (1902) – treat the collision between Northern and Southern manners and morals. He also wrote a history, *The Creoles of Louisiana* (1884), and a treatise advocating reforms for the improvement of the lives of blacks, *The Silent South* (1885). It was because of the offense these books caused to some of his Southern neighbors that Cable moved to the North. His correspondence with **Mark Twain**, a writer who praised his work, was published in 1960.

Cahan, Abraham 1860–1951   Having emigrated to the US from Russia, in 1897 Cahan founded the *Jewish Daily Forward*, a pioneering Jewish newspaper in New York. He had just published his first novel, *Yekl: A Tale of the New York Ghetto* (1896), which had won the enthusiastic support of **William Dean Howells**. Its realistic treatment of the experience of Jewish immigrants became the hallmark of Cahan's work. *The Imported Bridegroom and Other Stories of the New York Ghetto* (1898) further established him as a leader in Jewish American fiction, a position exemplified by his best-known work, *The Rise of David Levinsky* (1917). His richest and most complex novel, it portrays a rich but dissatisfied garment manufacturer looking back at his rise from poverty in Russia and in the New York ghetto. Cahan also published several books in Yiddish, many of which have yet to be translated, and continued as editor of the *Forward* until his death.

Cain, James M[allahan] 1892–1977   An essayist, journalist, dramatist, and screenwriter, Cain was also a popular novelist and a prominent member of the "tough-guy" school – a later manifestation of the uncompromising naturalism of such writers as

Frank Norris and **Theodore Dreiser**. In most of his novels, characters lust after sex and money and commit crimes in order to satisfy these desires.

Born in Annapolis, Maryland, Cain received his BA in 1910 and his MA in 1917, both from Washington College, in Chestertown, Maryland. Having worked as a coal miner, as a teacher of mathematics, English, and journalism, and as a reporter for the Baltimore *Sun* and Baltimore *American*, as well as having served in France as a private in World War I, in 1924 he began to write editorials for the New York *World* under the supervision of **Walter Lippmann**. In 1931 he became managing editor of *The New Yorker*, a position he held for 10 months, and then moved to Hollywood, where he remained for 17 years writing scripts for motion pictures. During his stay there he continued to write articles and syndicated columns, as well as several novels.

The Postman Always Rings Twice (1934) was adapted for the stage in 1936 and became a movie in 1946. It is the story of Frank Chambers and Cora Papadakis, lovers who murder Cora's wealthy husband for money, making his death look like an accident. Cora then dies in a car crash, and ironically Frank is convicted of murder for her truly accidental death. In *Double Indemnity* (serialized in *Liberty* in 1936, and made into a movie in 1943), an unmarried man and a married woman again plan and execute the husband's "accidental" death, in this case for the insurance money. Cain's other novels include *Serenade* (1937), *Career in C Major* (1938), *The Embezzler* (1940), *Mildred Pierce* (1941), *Love's Lovely Counterfeit* (1942), *The Butterfly* (1947), and *The Root of His Evil* (1951). *Past All Dishonor* (1946) and *Mignon* (1962) are historical novels set during the period following the Civil War.

Caldwell, Erskine 1903–   This Georgia-born writer's best-known fiction depicts the experiences of sharecroppers and poor blacks in the rural deep South. *Tobacco Road* (1932), the novel which first brought him to prominence, is about a family of sharecroppers driven to desperate and degenerate acts by the oppression of a changing economic system. It was successfully dramatized by Jack Kirkland in 1933 and ran for over 3,000 consecutive Broadway performances. In the same year Caldwell published his second novel, *God's Little Acre*, which consolidated his reputation. *Journeyman* (1935), *Trouble in July* (1940), *A House in the Uplands* (1946), and *Jenny by Nature* (1961) are among his many other novels with Southern settings. He also wrote numerous short stories; collections include *American Earth* (1930), *Jackpot* (1940), and *The Courting of Susie Brown* (1952). Among his works of non-fiction is the documentary study of Southern sharecroppers, *You Have Seen Their Faces* (1937), on which he collaborated with his former wife, the photographer Margaret Bourke-White. The two also collaborated on *North of the Danube* (1939) and *Say! Is This the USA?* (1941). *All Out On the Road to Smolensk* (1942) is Caldwell's personal account of his work as a war correspondent in Russia. *Call It Experience* (1951) is his literary autobiography. The essays collected in *Around About America* (1964) and *Afternoons in Mid-America* (1976) tell of his travels throughout the US.

Calef, Robert 1648–1719   A cloth merchant from Boston, Calef was a bitter critic of the reports of witchcraft in New England in the 1690s. His *More Wonders of the Invisible World* (circulated in manuscript in Boston before its publication in London in 1700) was a response to **Cotton Mather**'s *Wonders of the Invisible World* (1693), giving alternative descriptions and interpretations of the Salem witch trials and of some cases of possession in Boston. Hinting at a sexual component in Mather's exorcism of young girls, Calef argued that the ministers, especially Cotton and **Increase Mather**, had manipulated the crisis in a bid for social control. Calef is apparently the originator of the story that Cotton Mather exhorted the crowd at the Salem executions on horseback. The Mathers, in turn, charged Calef with libel.

Calisher, Hortense 1911–   Calisher was born in New York City and graduated from Barnard College in 1932. Her work is wide-ranging in subject and includes studies of family relationships and racial conflict. She began her career with short stories; her early collections include *In the Absence of Angels: Stories* (1952), *Tale for the Mirror: A Novella and Other Stories* (1963), and *Extreme Magic: A Novella and Other Stories* (1964). Her first novel, *False Entry*, was published in 1962, and was followed by *Textures of Life* (1963), *Journal from Ellipsia* (1965), *The Railway Police and The Last Trolley Ride* (1966), *The New Yorkers* (1969), and *Queenie* (1971). Her more recent work includes *Herself* (1972), *Standard Dreaming* (1972), *Eagle Eye* (1973), *The Collected Stories of Hortense Calisher* (1975), *On Keeping Women* (1977), and *Mysteries of Motion* (1983), and *Saratoga Hot* (1985).

Call It Sleep   See **Roth, Henry**

Call of the Wild, The   A novel by **Jack London**, published in 1903. Buck, the "hero," is a dog who is kidnapped from his comfortable existence on a California estate, and sold into service as a sledge dog in the Klondike. He proves himself among the other dogs, but is brutally mistreated by a series of cruel masters before being rescued by John Thornton, a gold prospector who treats him with kindness. Fiercely loyal to Thornton, Buck performs several heroic exploits for him, most notably saving him from drowning and winning a wager by drawing a 1,000-pound sledge. Later, he fends off an Indian attack during which Thornton is nevertheless killed. Masterless, but now at home in the Alaskan wilds, Buck abandons human civilization to become the leader of a wolf pack.

Cane   A book by **Jean Toomer**, published in 1923 and composed of stories, sketches, and poetry. A major work of the **Harlem Renaissance**, it treats black life in the rural South as well as in the more integrated and urban North. Among its recurrent concerns are the effects of racism and materialism, and the problems of relationships between men and women. With its experimental structure and intricate symbolism, it was hailed by many of Toomer's contemporaries, including his friend **Waldo Frank**, as a significant document of the American *avant-garde* in the 1920s.

Cantos, The   The major work of **Ezra Pound**, widely regarded as one of the most influential poetic works of the 20th century. The first cantos were published in *Quia Pauper Amavi* (1919). A total of 117, some of them fragmentary, appeared over the next 50 years. Thematically and stylistically varied, the cantos deal with people and events in ancient, Renaissance, and modern history, employ diverse languages, and comment on various political and moral problems. The effect is often that of a series of evocative fragments; at other times, such as in the *Pisan Cantos* (1948), the focus is on one subject – in this case, Pound's incarceration in an Italian prisoner-of-war camp during World War II. Other volumes include *A Draft of XVI Cantos . . . for the Beginning of a Poem of Some Length* (1925), *A Draft of Cantos XVII to XXVII* (1928), *A Draft of XXX Cantos* (1933), *Eleven New Cantos, XXXI–XLI* (1934), *The Fifth Decad of Cantos* (1937), *Cantos LII–LXXI* (1940), *Section: Rock-Drill: 85–95 de los Cantares* (1956), *Thrones: 96–109 de los Cantares* (1959). A collection, *The Cantos of Ezra Pound*, appeared in 1970.

Cantwell, Robert   1908–78   Born in Little Falls (now Vader), Washington, Cantwell attended the University of Washington. He then served in the coast guard for two years before going to work in a lumber mill. In 1931 he became literary editor of *New Outlook*, and in 1935 literary editor of *Time*. He also worked on the staffs of *Fortune*, *Newsweek*, and *Sports Illustrated*. He is best known as a proletarian writer. His first novel, *Laugh and Lie Down* (1931), describes life in a lumber mill. His second, *The Land of Plenty* (1934), about factory life, is widely considered one of the finest novels to come out of the left-wing movement in the US. I addition to a few uncollected short stories (much admired by **F. Scott Fitzgerald**), Cantwell published *Nathaniel Hawthorne: The American Years* (1948); *Famous American Men of Letters* (1956); *Alexander Wilson* (1961); *The Real McCoy* (1971), a biography of Norman Selby; and *The Hidden Northwest* (1972).

Capote, Truman   1924–84   Born in New Orleans, Capote moved to New York City in 1942. He got a job at *The New Yorker* and also submitted stories to the magazine, but none was accepted. He did publish elsewhere, however, and his short story "Miriam" won the O. Henry Award in 1946. This distinction led to a book contract, and in 1948 *Other Voices, Other Rooms*, his first novel, was published. This study of youthful innocence in a decadent world was followed by *A Tree of Night and Other Stories* (1949) and *The Grass Harp* (1951), both set in the South. In 1956 he published *The Muses Are Heard*, an account of an officially sponsored tour of Russia by an

American company performing *Porgy and Bess*. He turned away from Southern settings with his next novel, *Breakfast at Tiffany's* (1958), a comedy of life in New York City. His next collection of short stories was *A Christmas Memory* (1966). His major publication of that year, however, was **In Cold Blood**, an investigation of the murder of a Kansas family committed by two youths. Capote also worked as a journalist and published collections of his pieces in *Local Color* (1950), *Selected Writings* (1963), *The Dogs Bark* (1973), and *Music for Chameleons* (1981). He was working on a massive project, "Answered Prayers," when he died unexpectedly in August 1984. Excerpts of this work had appeared in *Esquire* starting in 1975, but the rest remains unpublished.

Carver, Raymond 1939–   Born in Clatskanie, Oregon, and raised in eastern Washington, Carver completed college with a BA from Chico State College in 1966. He has taught at the universities of Iowa, Texas, and California as well as at Syracuse University. His poetry, usually focused on a particular object or aspect of daily life, has appeared in four collections: *Near Klamath* (1968), *Winter Insomnia* (1970), *At Night the Salmon Move* (1976), and *Where Water Comes Together with Other Water* (1985). He is best known, however, for his short stories, which, in addition to appearing in magazines, have been collected in *Will You Please Be Quiet, Please?* (1976), *What We Talk About When We Talk About Love* (1981), *Cathedral* (1983), and *Fires: Essays, Stories, Poems* (1983). These stories, which frequently appear in revised form under different titles, have a beguiling surface simplicity. The development of their narratives, however, is accompanied by an intense and dark vision of the contemporary world.

Catcher in the Rye, The   A novel by **J. D. Salinger**, published in 1951. The 16-year-old Holden Caulfield narrates his own story of rebellion against the banality and "phoniness" of middle-class values. Expelled from his Pennsylvania prep school, the caustic but quixotic teenager goes to New York City and checks into a cheap hotel. He spends the evening going to nightclubs, but he misses his young sister Phoebe (the only person he feels really close to) and becomes increasingly depressed. On returning to his hotel he has an unsuccessful encounter with a prostitute, and ends up in a skirmish with her pimp. The next day he meets an old girlfriend, Sally Hayes, and takes her skating. His spirits lifted, he suggests that the two of them escape to the New England countryside. Sally rejects this impractical offer and Holden, completely discouraged, gets drunk and then sneaks home to see his sister, telling her that he plans to "go West." Later that night he has an unsettling reunion with a former schoolteacher, Mr Antolini, who makes homosexual advances to him. The next morning he goes to Phoebe's school to say goodbye, but he is overwhelmed by his love for her and decides to stay. He then has a nervous breakdown, and tells his story as he is recovering.

Cat on a Hot Tin Roof   A play by **Tennessee Williams**, first performed in New York in 1955 and awarded a Pulitzer Prize in the same year. It was revised for a revival in 1974.

The action centers on the wealthy and chaotic Pollitt family in Mississippi, and on the question of the inheritance of Big Daddy Pollitt's 28,000-acre estate. Big Daddy has stipulated that to inherit a share of the estate each of his sons must have children. Brick, the younger son, and his wife Maggie, the "cat" of the title, are childless – in sharp contrast to Gooper Pollitt and his wife Mae, who already have five children and are expecting another. The discovery that Big Daddy is terminally ill forces the family to confront the tensions and hostilities which have developed as a result of his rigid control of their lives. Obsessed with guilt over his homosexuality, and the relationship he had had with a high school friend and teammate, Brick has turned to alcohol. This in turn worsens his relationship with the passionate Maggie, which has already been damaged by the vindictiveness of Gooper and Mae. At the end of the play, though the situation is left unresolved, there is a suggestion that Maggie will be able to seduce Brick and conceive a child.

Catch-22   An anti-war novel by **Joseph Heller**, published in 1961. Its non-chronological plotting technique, intended to emphasize the displacements that war produces, makes for a disjointed, fragmented narrative. The story is set in an air force base hospital on the fictional island of Pinosa during World War II. Captain John Yossarian is determined to survive the war and will use any means at his disposal to do so. He hopes to get a medical discharge by pretending to be insane, but the "catch-22" ruling – that anyone rational enough to want to be grounded could not possibly be insane, and is therefore capable of returning to flight duty – keeps him in the war. Finally, after all his friends are killed or missing, he decides to desert to Sweden.

Cather, Willa (Siebert) 1873–1947 Born in rural Virginia, where she spent the first few years of her life, Cather moved with her family to Red Cloud, Nebraska, in 1883. In an attempt to escape the conservatism of the small town, she moved to Lincoln in 1890 and the following year entered the University of Nebraska. There she became editor of the undergraduate literary periodical, to which she contributed criticism, poetry, and stories. (Much of the material in the stories written in these early years reappears in her later novels.) After graduating, she moved to Pittsburgh to pursue a career in journalism. She spent ten years there, first as a newspaper woman and then as a high-school teacher of English and Latin. *April Twilights*, her only volume of poetry, appeared in 1903. Two years later she published *The Troll Garden*, a collection of short stories which showed the influence of **Henry James**. She later reissued four of these stories and added four more in a collection entitled *Youth and the Bright Medusa* (1920).

When she was 32, Cather moved to New York City and joined the staff of **McClure's Magazine**. Over the next seven years she published stories in **The Century Magazine** and **Harper's Monthly Magazine**, as well as in *McClure's*. In 1912 her first novel, *Alexander's Bridge*, was published. She resigned from *McClure's* and traveled to the Southwest. Her second novel, **O Pioneers!**, appeared in 1913. She returned to the Southwest in the summer of 1915, and her novel of that year, *The Song of the Lark*, is partly set in the ancient cliff-dwellings of Walnut Canyon, Arizona. In her next novel, **My Ántonia** (1918), she returns to the Nebraska of her childhood.

Her first popular success was the Pulitzer-Prize-winning *One of Ours* (1922), the story of a boy from the Western plains who joins the army and is killed in France in World War I. Her next novel, *A Lost Lady* (1923), deals with stages of the moral decline of a woman from a small Nebraska town. *The Professor's House* (1925) is set in a small midwestern college in the post-war years; the story of Professor St Peter's move from his old house to a more modern one is interrupted by the account of the discovery by his former student, Tom Outland, of an ancient cliff-dweller's village in a New Mexico canyon. *My Mortal Enemy* (1926) is set in New York and on the West Coast in the early 1900s. The New Mexico landscapes in **Death Comes for the Archbishop** (1927) reflect Cather's continuing love for the Southwest.

Composed after several visits to Quebec, and set in French Canada at the end of the 17th century, *Shadows on the Rock* (1931) won her the first Prix Femina Américaine in 1933. The three tales that make up *Obscure Destinies* (1932) take place in the Midwest. *Lucy Gayheart* (1935) tells the story of the daughter of a German-born watchmaker who leaves a small Nebraska town to study music in Chicago. *Not Under Forty* (1936) – later renamed *Literary Encounters* – is a volume of critical essays, including one on **Sarah Orne Jewett**. Cather's last novel, *Sapphira and the Slave* (1940), is the only one of her novels to be set in the Virginia of her grandmothers. In 1944, when she was 70, she was awarded the gold medal of the National Institute of Arts and Letters.

Celebrated Jumping Frog of Calaveras County, The This collection of stories was **Mark Twain**'s first published book (1867). The title sketch, which first appeared in the New York *Saturday Press* in 1865, was based on an old California folk tale. Dan'l Webster, the champion jumping frog, is owned by Jim Smiley. A stranger claims that any frog could beat him, and sends Smiley off to catch another one to have a contest. Dan'l is defeated, but only because, as Smiley discovers after the race, the stranger had managed to fill his gullet with quail shot to weigh him down.

Century Magazine, The First published in November 1870 as *Scribner's Monthly, an Illustrated Magazine for the People*, the journal was founded by Roswell Smith, Charles Scribner, and Dr Josiah Gilbert Holland, who served as its editor until his death in 1881. Under Holland's control *Scribner's Monthly* featured essays on politics, religion, and current affairs; serial fiction; and numerous high-quality illustrations. Contributors included George Macdonald, Mrs Oliphant, Jules Verne, Edward Everett Hale, Alice Trafton, George E. Waring, Jr, **H. H. Boyesen**, John Muir, and J. W. Powell. In 1873 the magazine published a series of profusely illustrated articles by Edward King called "The Great South"; it also published Southern stories, including most of the "Nights with Uncle Remus" by **Joel Chandler Harris**.

In 1881 the name was changed to *The Century Illustrated Monthly Magazine*, under the editorship of Richard Watson Gilder. A series of Civil War papers by Generals Grant, McClellan, Longstreet, and Beauregard were published, as were the Civil War experiences of **Mark Twain**. Under Gilder *The Century* displayed an increased concern with public events, but continued to serialize novels, among them **William Dean Howells**'s *A Modern Instance*, *The Rise of Silas Lapham*, and *The Minister's Charge*; **Henry James**'s *The Bostonians*; **Jack London**'s *The Sea Wolf*; and **George Washington Cable**'s *Dr Sevier*. In 1925 the title became *The Century Monthly Magazine*, and from May through August 1929 *The Century Magazine*. In the fall of 1929 it became a quarterly publication called *The Century Quarterly*; it was merged with *Forum* in 1930.

Chandler, Raymond (Thornton) 1888–1959 Chandler was born in Chicago and worked as a journalist and businessman before starting to write fiction at the age of 45. His detective stories were published regularly in *The Black Mask* magazine until 1939. In *The Big Sleep* (1939) he introduced his most famous character, the detective Philip Marlowe, who reappeared in many subsequent novels. Chandler's other novels include *Farewell, My Lovely* (1940), *The High Window* (1942), *The Lady In The Lake* (1943), *The Little Sister* (1949), *The Long Goodbye* (1953), and *Playback* (1958). His stories are collected in *Trouble Is My Business* (1950), *Killer In The Rain* (1964), and *The Smell of Fear* (1965). He discusses his work in *The Simple Art of Murder* (1950) and the posthumous *Raymond Chandler Speaking* (1962).

Channing, William Ellery 1780–1842 Born in Newport, Rhode Island, Channing graduated from The Harvard Divinity School, and was ordained in 1803 as a Congregational minister. His "Baltimore Sermon" (*A Sermon Delivered at the Ordination of the Rev Jared Sparks . . .*, 1819) and *The Moral Argument Against Calvinism* (1820) state plainly his opposition to the dogma and coercion of strict Calvinist theology, and his rejection of the tenet that man is essentially depraved. These revisionist ideas were common among many of Channing's circle, which included such important New England writers as **Ralph Waldo Emerson**, **Henry David Thoreau**, **Margaret Fuller**, and **Bronson Alcott**. He put forth his ideas on pacificism, prison reform, child labor, education, and slavery – which he opposed fiercely – in many pamphlets and sermons. In his time his views were widely discussed, and his influence was considerable. His writings were collected and published in six volumes (1841–3).

Charlotte Temple, *A Tale of Truth* A novel by **Susanna Rowson**, published in England in 1791 and in America in 1794. Modeled on Samuel Richardson's *Clarissa*, it sold poorly in England but was a great success in the US. Rowson's stated intention was to warn against the dangers of seduction, and the book is full of authorial admonitions.

The story recounts the wooing of Charlotte, a 15-year-old pupil at Mme Du Pont's school for young ladies, by Montraville, an army officer. They elope to New York, where Montraville, despite qualms of conscience, soon deserts Charlotte for an heiress, Julia Franklin. Charlotte is now stranded, and pregnant. She looks in vain for help, and is even rebuffed by her former schoolteacher, Mlle La Rue, the woman of moral laxity who had introduced her to Montraville in the first place. Charlotte dies in poverty after giving birth to Montraville's illegitimate child, Lucy. Montraville is conscience-stricken, but returns to Julia. Mlle La Rue dies in ignominy. Charlotte's father adopts Lucy.

Cheever, John 1912–82 Born in Quincy, Massachusetts, Cheever was educated at Thayer Academy and taught creative writing at several universities including Barnard College (1956–7) and Boston University (1974–5). The author of numerous short stories and novels, Cheever writes humorously and compassionately of the spiritually and emotionally impoverished life in materially affluent suburban communities. His first novel, *The Wapshot Chronicle* (1957), won the 1958 National Book Award. In 1965 he received the Howells Medal for Fiction from the National Academy of Arts and Letters. His other novels include *The Wapshot Scandal* (1964), *Bullet Park* (1969), *Falconer* (1977), and *Oh, What a Paradise It Seems* (1982). His short stories, many of which appeared originally in *The New Yorker* and *The New Republic*, were collected in *The Way Some People Live: A Book of Short Stories* (1943), *The Enormous Radio and Other Stories* (1953), *Stories* (1956), *The Housebreaker of Shady Hill and Other Stories* (1958), *Some People, Places, and Things That Will Not Appear in My Next Novel* (1961), *The Brigadier and the Golf Widow* (1964), *Homage to Shakespeare* (1965), *The World of Apples* (1973), and *The Day the Pig Fell into the Well* (1978). *The Stories of John Cheever* was published in 1978 and received a Pulitzer Prize, a National Book Critics Circle Award, and an American Book Award.

Chesnutt, Charles W[addell] 1858–1932 The black novelist, short-story writer, and critic was born in Cleveland, Ohio, to parents who recently had left Fayetteville, North Carolina, to escape the repression of free blacks in the South at the time. After the Civil War, the family returned to Fayetteville, where Chesnutt's education included instruction in German, French, and Greek. By the age of 20, he had taught at schools in North and South Carolina, been a high school principal in Charlotte, and served as assistant principal at a new state Normal School in Fayetteville. In 1883 he went to New York City to work as a reporter, and then moved to Cleveland, where he began his career as a writer.

His work came to the attention of a national audience when his story "The Goophered Grapevine" was published in *The Atlantic Monthly* in 1887. He rapidly mastered the conventions of the short narrative aimed at readers of the popular literary magazines of his day, and this urbane, fluent style is seen in his first two collections of stories, *The Conjure Woman* and *The Wife of His Youth and Other Stories of the Color Line*, both published in

1899. Despite his adoption of prevailing literary forms, Chesnutt is considered a pioneer of black fiction, with his probing exploration of racial themes and his realistic view of slavery and the Reconstruction era. In his later works he focused on the problems of racial and class identity in a changing society. He wrote three novels, *The House Behind the Cedars* (1900), *The Marrow of Tradition* (1901), and *The Colonel's Dream* (1906), and regularly published essays and reviews in various journals.

Child, Lydia M[aria] 1802–80 Born in Medford, Massachusetts, Child was one of the leading humanitarians of the 19th century, known especially for her work as an Abolitionist. She achieved her greatest success with her "Appeal in Favor of that Class of Americans Called Africans" (1833). Her persuasive letters to the governor of Virginia were later published as *Correspondence* (1860), and won many adherents to the anti-slavery cause. She also wrote several novels, including *Hobomok* (1824), a didactic story about the Indians of colonial Massachusetts; *The Rebels: or, Boston Before the Revolution* (1825), about the Stamp Tax agitation; and *Philothea* (1836), a romance set in classical Greece.

Chopin, Kate 1851–1904 Born Kate O'Flaherty in St Louis, Missouri, to an Irish father and French mother, she moved to New Orleans following her marriage to Oscar Chopin. After the death of her mother and husband, she began to devote herself to writing. Her first novel, *At Fault* (1890), showed the influence of Guy de Maupassant. This was followed by two collections of short stories set among Creoles and Acadians in Louisiana, *Bayou Folk* (1894) and *A Night in Acadie* (1897), which helped establish her as a leading exponent of the "local color" school. She also contributed regularly to popular and literary magazines. Her best-known work, *The Awakening*, was published in 1899. Its sympathetic portrayal of a woman who rejects the constraints of marriage and motherhood provoked hostile criticism. The book was banned from the library shelves in Chopin's home town of St Louis, and following a reprint in 1906 went out of print for over 50 years. *The Complete Works of Kate Chopin* (2 vols., 1969) included ten stories unpublished during the author's lifetime.

Civil Disobedience, On the Duty of An essay by **Henry David Thoreau** which was originally printed in 1849 as *Resistance to Civil Government*, it first appeared under its familiar title in a posthumous collection of essays called *A Yankee in Canada, with Anti-Slavery and Reform Papers* (1866). Citing the controversial Mexican War, slavery, and the treatment of Indians, and referring to the night he himself spent in jail for refusing to pay his poll tax, Thoreau argues that an individual may refuse to participate in a government that does not uphold his or her moral standards.

Clarel: A Poem and Pilgrimage in the Holy Land A 7,000-line poem by **Herman Melville** in octosyllabic couplets, published in two volumes in 1876. Inspired by Melville's reflections on his visit to the Holy Land 20 years earlier, the poem is an inquiry into and search for faith. Its various characters represent a range of attitudes: some express religious doubts arising from their personal experience or philosophy; others are comfortably certain of their faith. None, however, is able to assist Clarel, an American theology student visiting Jerusalem, to resolve his own uncertainties.

Clark, William 1770–1838 Born in Caroline County, Virginia, Clark saw active service in the army on campaigns against the Indians, and was then appointed by **Thomas Jefferson** as co-commander of the 1803–6 Lewis and Clark expedition (see **Meriwether Lewis**). He later undertook surveys, notably one of the Yellowstone, and produced numerous maps and drawings which proved indispensable to other explorers. From 1813 to 1821 he served as governor of Missouri Territory and thereafter acted as superintendent of Indian affairs.

Clemens, Samuel Langhorne 1835–1910 Born in Florida, Missouri, he moved with his family to the Mississippi River town of Hannibal when he was 4. Later, as Mark Twain, he would make the scenes of his youth internationally famous in his most popular novels, *The Adventures of Tom Sawyer* and *Adventures of Huckleberry Finn*. Although always associated with the Mississippi River region, he traveled widely. He left school at the age of 12, and later traveled throughout the East and Midwest as a journeyman printer. He served briefly in the Confederate Army during the Civil War, but his division deserted and he spent the remainder of the war out West, some of it prospecting for silver in Nevada with his brother Orion, and then working with **Bret Harte** as a journalist in San Francisco. In 1863 he began using the name Mark Twain, and in 1865 made it famous with his story **"The Celebrated Jumping Frog of Calaveras County."**

Twain's rise to celebrity was impressive. His sparkling personality and his quotable phrases caught on fast and he soon began making lecture tours. His 1867 trip to Europe and the Holy Land produced his first major work, *The Innocents Abroad* (1869). He returned to America to settle in the East, and in 1870 married Olivia Langdon, the wealthy daughter of a New York coal magnate. His popularity continued to grow, through a series of works, including *Roughing It* (1872), a humorous narrative of his early travels out West; *The Gilded Age* (1873), a satirical novel of the post-Civil War era which he co-wrote with **Charles Dudley Warner**; the ever popular *The Adventures of Tom Sawyer* (1876); and *A Tramp Abroad* (1880), another travel narrative. He traveled often in Europe, and especially in England, where he was received with even more enthusiasm than in the US.

The last works of what might be called Twain's optimistic period were *The Prince and the Pauper* (1882) and *Life on the Mississippi* (1883). In 1884 his heavy investment in a badly managed publishing firm and an inefficient typesetting invention drove him into bankruptcy. Ironically, the products of this harsh awakening are among his best works, most notably the renowned *Adventures of Huckleberry Finn* (1884), which has a moral dimension that is lacking in its predecessor *Tom Sawyer*. *A Connecticut Yankee in King Arthur's Court* (1889) and *The Tragedy of Pudd'nhead Wilson* (1894) are both characterized by a deep pessimism, though both were conceived simply as entertainments. In *The American Claimant* (1892), *Tom Sawyer Abroad* (1894), and *Tom Sawyer, Detective* (1896) he sought to recapture the innocent fun of his early works, but he was never quite able to write with his former casual ease.

He gradually overcame his debts, but after his daughter Susy died in 1896 Twain became increasingly alienated from the good-humored wit on which his popularity was based. Books such as *The Man that Corrupted Hadleyburg* (1900) and *What Is Man?* (1906), as well as much of his posthumously published work, reflect a severe pessimism and dissatisfaction. However, when his personal life was devastated (his wife died in 1904 and his second daughter in 1909), his professional life carried him through. He continued to lecture widely, in the US and abroad, though his opinions were often controversial, and he was supremely proud of the honorary doctorate of letters awarded to him by Oxford University in 1907. When he died in 1910 he left a wealth of unpublished material, including *The Mysterious Stranger* (1916) and *Letters From the Earth* (1962). His *Autobiography* was published in 1924, and his letters have appeared in various forms: an initial collection in 1917, love letters in 1949, and his correspondence with **William Dean Howells** in 1960.

Cliff-Dwellers, The A novel by **Henry Blake Fuller**, published in 1893, and one of the earliest American novels to have as its setting the monstrous and impersonal city. A satire on greed and social striving set in Chicago, it depicts the lives of the "cliff-dwellers" – those inhabiting a skyscraper called the Clifton Building. The characters include Arthur Ingles, the rich owner of the Clifton; Erasmus Brainard, an anti-social banker; Eugene H. McDowell, a crooked real estate agent; George Ogden, an ambitious clerk who works in Brainard's bank; and the various women who contribute to their fortunes and misfortunes.

Columbiad, The An epic poem in heroic couplets by **Joel Barlow** published in 1807, 20 years after it first appeared as *The Vision of Columbus*. The two versions, however, have little in common. In nine books, *The Vision* presents a dialogue between an angel and Christopher Columbus, both of whom ascend the Mount of Vision and survey human history. The angel argues that all historical events, particularly Columbus's discovery, lead to the future glory of America. The poem thus reaffirms America's manifest destiny; it offers an essentially conservative vision congenial to Federalists of the new Republic.

By 1807 Barlow had changed his political orientation and had revised the poem accordingly into *The Columbiad*. Now a liberal democrat, he replaced the simple dialogue with a colloquy of different voices, each intended to represent a different political or social interest. He also included further classical allusions, often explained in lengthy scholarly footnotes, and developed the prefaces to each of the nine books into extensive political and philosophical arguments. Ironically, these revisions, which aimed at widening the poem's audience, in fact limited it, and made *The Columbiad* read more like a political treatise than an epic poem.

Come Back, Little Sheba See **Inge, William**

Commentary A monthly magazine founded by the American Jewish Committee at the end of World War II to provide a forum for "significant thought and opinion on Jewish affairs and contemporary issues," its first number came out in November, 1945. It publishes fiction, critical pieces, and social commentary. Elliot E. Cohen served as editor until 1959; Norman Podhoretz took over in 1960. Among the many contributors to *Commentary* have been Hannah Arendt, Lionel Abel, **James Baldwin**, **Saul Bellow**, Leslie Fiedler, Nathan Glazer, **Paul Goodman**, Clement Greenberg, Sidney Hook, Irving Howe, Dan Jacobson, Dwight Macdonald, **Bernard Malamud**, Philip Rahv, **Henry Roth**, **Philip Roth**, Harold Rosenberg, **Lionel Trilling**, and **Edmund Wilson**.

Common Sense Published anonymously in Philadelphia on January 10, 1776, this political pamphlet by **Thomas Paine** was the first public statement to urge immediate and unqualified separation from England.

Paine's argument divides into four parts. The first, entitled "Of The Origin and Design of Government in General; With Concise Remarks on the English Constitution," insists that insofar as governments are established only to protect the freedom and security of citizens, England has violated its mandate by its economic and political enslavement of the colonies. The second part, "Of Monarchy and Hereditary Succession," rejects hereditary succession in favor of democratic election, a process which respects individual talents rather than family lineage in the designation of a ruler. The third and fourth parts, "Thoughts on the Present State of American Affairs" and "Of the Present Ability of America," celebrate both America's economic security and its potential to safeguard, by example, the inalienable rights of all people. The carefully argued pamphlet sold widely at the time (over half-a-million copies) and helped galvanize the forces which only seven months after its publication began to fight the Revolution.

Confessional Poetry A type of verse whose subject matter reveals intimate details of the poet's life, confessional poetry emerged in America in the 1950s. Its chief practitioners included **W. D. Snodgrass**, **Robert Lowell**, **Theodore Roethke**, **John Berryman**, **Sylvia Plath**, **Anne Sexton**, and **Adrienne Rich**. In their confessional verse, these poets focus on particularly painful moments in their lives, which they often relate to more general historical or cultural problems. The intimate and intensely autobiographical approach of the confessional poets remains a major influence on contemporary American verse.

Confidence-Man, The: *His Masquerade* A novel by **Herman Melville**, published in 1857, the last to be published during his lifetime. It is a complex exploration of the dialectic between trust and sincerity on the one hand, and manipulation and violation of trust on the other, a conflict which Melville saw as pervading contemporary American society.

The action takes place on the Mississippi River steamer *Fidèle*, and involves a large number of characters, many of whom are different manifestations of a single figure, the confidence man. He makes his initial appearance as a deaf-mute on the riverboat landing in St Louis. Holding up a chalkboard sign advertising the virtues of charity, he is derided by the crowd, but in his later appearances he proves to be more persuasive. For example, in the guise of an herb doctor, he succeeds in persuading a distrusting miser to buy his worthless tonic; in other disguises he sells phony stock to passengers, petitions for a loan to alleviate alleged hardship, and solicits contributions to Indian missions. In some of his appearances, however, he merely encourages the more disaffected and cynical passengers to keep faith and to trust in the goodness of others.

Throughout the second half of the novel, the confidence man is in the costume of a friendly "cosmopolitan," Frank Goodman, who engages in philosophical conversations with other passengers, occasionally digressing to tell long stories related to the central themes of the book, especially to that of trust in personal relationships. The narrative ends with a discussion between him and an old man about the status of the apocryphal scriptures, thus fusing the book's thematic concern with trust with the literary issue of narrative as a bearer of meaning. The novel offers no resolution of the problem, but instead closes with the nihilistic image of a light being extinguished – a figure for the cessation of communication itself.

Congo and Other Poems, The A collection of poems by **Vachel Lindsay**, published in 1914. The title piece is a celebration of black Americans, characterized by a remarkable use of syncopated rhythms. The volume also includes the famous "Abraham Lincoln Walks at Midnight," in which Lincoln walks once more in Springfield, his shade unable to rest because Europe is on the brink of war, and pain and terror will soon be abroad in the world.

Connecticut Wits, The A group of 18th-century poets, often referred to as the Hartford Wits (because they were centered in Hartford, Connecticut), and drawn together at Yale by shared academic, literary, and political values. They advocated a revision of Yale's curriculum to include the study of American literature, and they sought themselves to produce poetry which would simultaneously proclaim and signify America's literary independence. They also adhered to the orthodox Calvinism and conservative Federalism which had found a home in Connecticut.

The group espoused its causes in numerous publications, three of which stand out in literary history: *The Anarchiad*, 12 papers in mock-heroic verse printed serially between 1786 and 1787 in *The New Haven Gazette* and *The Connecticut Magazine*; *The Echo*, a verse satire against anti-Federalists, as well as against **Thomas Jefferson**, and printed in **The American Mercury** between 1791 and 1805; and *The Practical Greenhouse*, a Federalist satire printed in 1799 in the *Connecticut Courant*. All three represent the collaborative efforts of the group's members: **John Trumbull**, **Timothy Dwight**, **Joel Barlow**, Lemuel Hopkins, David Humphreys, Richard Alsop, Theodore Dwight, E. H. Smith, and Dr Mason F. Cogswell.

Connecticut Yankee in King Arthur's Court, A   A satirical fantasy by **Mark Twain**, published in 1889. It tells the story of Hank Morgan, a master mechanic and chief superintendent at the Colt arms factory in Hartford, Connecticut, who is knocked unconscious during a fight with one of his workmen and awakes to find himself near Camelot in 6th-century England. The Yankee uses his knowledge of history and 19th-century technology to convince King Arthur and the Knights of the Round Table that he has magical powers. Having earned the nickname "The Boss," he then sets himself, in the author's words, to "the task of introducing the great and beneficent civilization of the nineteenth century" into the chivalric order of Camelot.

Originally conceived by Twain as a comic experiment in anachronistic contrast, the novel gradually developed into a darker, more violent story. Hank's introduction to Camelot of 19th-century "enlightenment," with its ideology of progress and its powerful gadgets, leads to civil war in Arthur's England, and to an apocalyptic last battle in which both sides are destroyed by advanced technology.

Connection, The   See **Gelber, Jack**

Connell, Evan (Shelby) Jr 1924–   Connell was born in Kansas City and educated at Dartmouth and the University of Kansas before going on to do graduate work at Stanford, Columbia, and San Francisco State universities. A successful writer of short stories, he published his first collection, *The Anatomy Lesson and Other Stories*, in 1957. He is best known, however, for his novels *Mrs Bridge* (1959) and *Mr Bridge* (1969). Other novels include *The Patriot* (1960), *The Diary of a Rapist* (1966), and *The Connoisseur* (1974). A further collection of short stories, *At The Crossroads*, was published in 1965. His verse includes *Notes From a Bottle Found On A Beach At Carmel* (1963) and *Points From a Compass Rose* (1973). His essays are collected in *A Long Desire* (1979) and *The White Lantern* (1980).

Connelly, Marc[us] (Cook) 1890–1980 Connelly was born in McKeesport, Pennsylvania. His parents were touring actors, and he grew up in the company of theatre people who frequented his father's hotel. As a young man he worked as a reporter and drama critic on the *Pittsburgh Gazette-Times*, and wrote plays and song lyrics for amateur theatre groups. His first full-length effort, a comic opera called *The Amber Princess* (music by Zoel Parmenteau), failed in New York, but Connelly stayed on in the city, working as a reporter and scenario writer and joining the Algonquin Group, a group of young writers – among them **Dorothy Parker**, **Robert Benchley**, **Robert Sherwood**, **Ring Lardner**, Heyward Broun, and Edna Ferber – who contributed humorous pieces to Franklin Pierce Adams's newspaper column, "The Conning Tower," and who habitually lunched together at the Round Table of the Algonquin Hotel.

George S. Kaufman, then drama critic for the *New York Times*, was another member of this group of wits; in 1921 he and Connelly collaborated on *Dulcy*, based on a bird-brained character who had appeared in Adams's column. *Dulcy* was a hit, with Lynn Fontanne in the title role. Subsequent Kaufman–Connelly collaborations include *To The Ladies* (1922), written for Helen Hayes; *Deep Tangled Wildwood* (1922), about the transformation of small-town America by mass culture; *Merton of the Movies* (1922), the story of a Hollywood neophyte; *Helen of Troy, NY* (1923), with music and lyrics by Harry Ruby and **Ira Gershwin**; *Beggar on Horseback* (1924); and *Be Yourself* (1924), another musical. After the collaboration ended, Connelly went on to write several other plays, including his most famous, **The Green Pastures** (1930), a retelling of the Biblical stories after the manner of black folk tales; as well as radio scripts, screenplays, and an autobiography, *Voices Offstage* (1968).

Conquest of Canaan, The   Identified by its author, **Timothy Dwight**, as the first American epic, this poem was written between 1771 and 1773, but not published until 1785. Its 11 books of heroic verse elaborate upon the Biblical account of Joshua's conquest of Canaan and, by allusion to people and events of the 18th century, draw a parallel between the Hebrew invasion of Canaan and the English settlement of New England. The poem thus confirms the Puritan conception of America as the seat of the New Jerusalem and in turn provides theological justification for the American Revolution.

Conroy, Jack 1899– Conroy was born at Monkey Nest coal camp near Moberly, Missouri, and spent several years as a migrant worker in steel mills, rubber factories, and coal mines. When the Depression came, he drew on his experiences to write poems and articles about unemployment, which were published in periodicals such as *Northern Lights, Unrest,* and *The New Masses.* In 1933 his novel *The Disinherited* appeared. A classic of proletarian literature, it explores working-class life in the Depression with unsentimental directness and is widely considered to be Conroy's greatest achievement. He later founded *The Anvil* and *The New Anvil*, important left-wing magazines which published work by writers such as **Richard Wright, Erskine Caldwell, Frank Yerby, James T. Farrell, Michael Gold, Langston Hughes,** and **Meridel Le Sueur.** Conroy's other books include *A World to Win* (1935), *Anyplace But Here* (1966, with **Arna Bontemps**), and *Writers in Revolt: The Anvil Anthology* (1973, with Curt Johnson). He also wrote children's books with Arna Bontemps, among them *The Fast Sooner Hound* (1942) and *Sam Patch* (1951).

Contrast, The A five-act play by **Royall Tyler**, generally considered to be the first American comedy, and written after Tyler had attended a performance of Richard Sheridan's *The School for Scandal* in New York in 1787. It was produced in the same year and published in 1790. Clearly influenced by the 18th-century English comedy of manners, it was an immediate success.

The "contrast" of the title is that between Bill Dimple, the representative of European affectation, and Colonel Manly, the representative of American straightforwardness and honesty. Maria van Rough is to marry Dimple, the match having been arranged by her father. The intensely Anglophilic Dimple is carrying on flirtations with two other women, Letitia and Charlotte. Charlotte's brother, Colonel Manly, is in love with Maria. Dimple gambles away his fortune and

decides to marry the wealthy Letitia. Maria's father discovers his baseness and gives his blessing to Manly's suit. Dimple is finally thwarted in his ambition when Letitia learns of his flirtation with Charlotte. The subplot reproduces the contrast between national manners in the amorous rivalry between Dimple's servant, the devious and conceited Jessamy, and Manly's servant Jonathan, the prototype of the naïve, goodhearted Yankee.

Cooke, John (Esten) 1830–86 A Virginian, Cooke wrote historical novels of colonial Virginia in the manner of **James Fenimore Cooper**: *Leather Stocking and Silk* (1854), *The Virginia Comedians* (1854), and *Henry St John, Gentleman* (1859). While fighting on the side of the Confederates in the Civil War, he wrote *The Life of Stonewall Jackson* (1863), and later a biography of Robert E. Lee (1871). A series of novels about the Civil War appeared in the late 1860s, but he then turned again to the colonial history of Virginia: *Her Majesty The Queen* (1872), about the Cavaliers; *Canolles* (1877), about Virginia during the Revolution; *Virginia, A History of the People* (1883); and *My Lady Pokahontas* (1885).

Coolbrith, Ina Donna 1842–1928 The first published poet from California, Coolbrith wrote verse in a simple lyrical style which marked an important stage in the regional development of Western literature. Her verse appeared in three volumes: *A Perfect Day* (1881), *The Singer of the Sea* (1894), and *Songs From The Golden Gate* (1895). She also shared the editorship of the *Overland Monthly* with **Bret Harte.**

Cooper, James Fenimore 1789–1851 The novelist was born in Burlington, New Jersey, the son of Judge William Cooper, an enterprising and wealthy land agent who founded Cooperstown in upstate New York, a community where Cooper spent much of his childhood. He attended a school in Albany and studied for a time at Yale until he was expelled in 1805. He spent the next five years at sea, first on a merchant ship and then as a midshipman in the US Navy. He left the sea in 1811 to marry Susan Delancy, who was descended from the early governors of New York colony.

The Coopers settled in Scarsdale, where in 1820 he wrote his first novel – *Precaution*, a study of manners in English society in the tradition of Jane Austen – after his wife had challenged him to improve upon an English novel he had criticized. His next novel, *The Spy*, appeared in 1821. They moved to New York City in 1822, and in the following year he published a novel of the sea entitled *The Pilot* and the first of the **Leatherstocking Tales**, *The Pioneers*. Firmly set in his career as a writer, he soon established a popular reputation as one of America's leading authors. He planned a series of novels to celebrate each of the 13 original states, and in 1825 published *Lionel Lincoln*, a story of Boston during the Revolution, but the rest of the series never materialized. His next publications were two more volumes of the Leatherstocking saga, *The Last of the Mohicans* (1826) and *The Prairie* (1827).

In 1826 he took his family to Europe and stayed there for almost seven years. Though he served as US consul at Lyons and traveled a great deal, he continued to write, publishing a sea story, *The Red Rover* (1827); a novel of early American frontier life, *The Wept of Wishton-Wish* (1829); and another naval tale, *The Water Witch* (1830). He became friends with Sir Walter Scott and with the Marquis de Lafayette, who partly inspired his essay *Notions of America* (1828). A historical trilogy, *The Bravo* (1831), *The Heidenmauer* (1832), and *The Headsman* (1833), completed one of his most active periods.

In 1832 he returned to the US, where his conservative political essays made him less popular. Non-fictional works of social commentary such as *The Monikins* (1835) and *The American Democrat* (1838) contain rather sharp criticism of American society and the abuses of democracy. The novels *Homeward Bound* (1838) and *Home as Found* (1838) also dramatize his "aristocratic" social and political beliefs.

In the last decade of his life Cooper published 21 books. The Leatherstocking series was completed with *The Pathfinder* (1840) and *The Deerslayer* (1841), and in 1844 came two sea novels, *Afloat and Ashore* and *Miles Wallingford*, which drew on his own early experiences. *Satanstoe* (1845), the first novel of his trilogy about a New York family (known as the "Littlepage Manuscripts"), explores problems of property rights in America, from the Colonial period to the 1840s. *The Chainbearer* (1845) is set during the

Revolution, and *The Redskins* (1846) tells how the Littlepage family manages, with the help of Indians, to deal with the exploitations of agents and lawyers in developing American society.

Coover, Robert (Lowell) 1932–   Born in Iowa, Coover studied at Southern Illinois, Indiana, and Chicago universities, served in the US Navy from 1953 to 1957, and then taught philosophy at several universities. His novels, with their particular emphasis on cultural patterns and movements, are representative of postmodernist fiction. His first, *The Origin of the Brunists* (1966), which received the William Faulkner Award for best first novel of 1966, concerns the founding of a religious cult by the survivor of a mining disaster. *The Universal Baseball Association, Inc., J. Henry Waugh, Prop.* (1968) is an allegorical novel which uses baseball as its central metaphor to satirize American religious attitudes. His third novel, *The Public Burning* (1977), is set in the 1950s and treats the impulses that lead to dogmatic extremism, an interest that has been integral to most of Coover's fiction. *Spanking the Maid* (1981) is a dark story of the obsessive relationship between a man and his maid which focuses on human enslavement to ritual behavior. Coover has also published short stories which are collected in *Pricksongs and Descants* (1969).

Corso, Gregory (Nunzio) 1930–   The son of poor immigrants, Corso was born and raised in New York City. His youth was difficult and violent, and by the age of 20 he had served three years in prison for attempted robbery. His poetry, which has affinities with that of the **Beats** in its concern with political and social issues, often adopts the stance of a sophisticated child who looks upon a world gone mad. His first volume, *The Vestal Lady of Brattle*, appeared in 1955. Subsequent volumes include *Gasoline* (1958), *Bomb* (1958), *The Happy Birthday of Death* (1960), *Long Live Man* (1962), and *There is Yet Time to Run Back Through Life and Expiate All That's Been Sadly Done* (1965). The title poem of his *Elegiac Feelings American* (1970) is dedicated to **Jack Kerouac**. His recent volumes, which reflect his interest in Egyptology and eastern religions, include *Egyptian Cross* (1971), *Ankh* (1971), *The Night Last Night was at its Nightest. . .* (1972), and *Earth Egg* (1974). He has also written a play, *This Hung-Up Age* (1955), and a novel, *The American Express* (1961).

Cotton, John 1584–1652 Born in Derbyshire, England, Cotton entered Trinity College, Cambridge at the age of 13 and received his BA in 1603 and MA in 1606. Awarded a fellowship at Emmanuel College for his proficiency in Hebrew, he served as a lecturer, dean, and catechist (1608–12), experienced his "genuine" conversion in 1610, and received a BD in 1613. In 1612 he was appointed vicar of St Botolph's Church in Boston, Lincolnshire, a post which he resigned 20 years later when the Court of High Commission summoned him for instituting Puritan reforms in his parish. In July 1633 he emigrated to Massachusetts Bay aboard the *Griffin* and was chosen to be minister of the Boston church, where he remained until his death.

A distinguished preacher, he took up the issues most pressing to the Puritan consciousness in edifying and affective sermons. *A Brief Exposition on the whole Book of Canticles* (1642) reads the history of the Christian church in the Biblical *Song of Solomon*, an interpretation which theologically justifies the Puritan enterprise in Massachusetts. The sermons collected in *Christ the Fountaine of Life: or, Sundry Choyce Sermons on part of the fifth chapter of the first Epistle of St John* (1651) describes Cotton's ideas about religious conversion. They reveal the emphasis he placed throughout his ministry on the irrelevance of good works to salvation, an emphasis which, when misconstrued by **Anne Hutchinson** in 1638 as a denial of preparationist theology, led to her banishment, and prompted Cotton's fellow ministers to examine closely his theological teachings.

He also wrote several widely read theological tracts. *The Keyes of the Kingdom of Heaven* (1644), written to persuade the Westminster Assembly to adopt the New England Way of church governance, and *The Way of Churches of Christ in New England* (1645; composed in the early 40s and first circulated in manuscript), attempt to define Congregational theology and ecclesiology. In 1646 he published *Milk for Babes, Drawn from the Breasts of Both Testaments*, one of the authoritative catechisms which was used widely throughout the 17th century. The following year, he responded to **Roger Williams**'s criticisms of New England church policies in *The Bloudy Tenent Washed and Made White in the Bloud of the Lamb* (see *The Bloudy Tenent*). Having been attacked for the views expressed in *The Way of Churches of Christ in New England*, by Robert Baille, whose critique was published as *A Dissuasive from the Errours of the Time* (1645), Cotton refuted Baille's charges in *The Way of the Congregational Churches Cleared* (1648). That same year he published his most thorough ecclesiastical statement, *A Survey of the Summe of Church Discipline*.

Country of the Pointed Firs, The A novel by **Sarah Orne Jewett**, published in 1896. It concerns an unnamed female narrator's summer vacation in the imaginary town of Dunnet Landing in rural Maine. The townspeople, at first somewhat distant, gradually include the narrator in their daily lives as though she were family. The novel reveals the dramatic depth and intensity in the life of an apparently placid community. It focuses in particular on the characters and abilities of women, and also addresses the issue of aging and its impact on one's life and activities.

Cozzens, James Gould 1903–78 Born in Chicago, Cozzens attended Harvard and began his writing career early, publishing in *The Atlantic Monthly* when he was 16. His novels explore the social order of American life and its potential for stability and hierarchy, by portraying professional men caught in moral and cultural dilemmas: *The Last Adam* (1933) is about the medical profession, *Men and Brethren* (1936) about the ministry, and *The Just and the Unjust* (1942) about the law. *Guard of Honor* (1948), an ambitious novel set during World War II, won Cozzens the Pulitzer Prize. In 1957 he published *By Love Possessed*, about a lawyer, his most controversial and widely read book. Cozzens has long been the object of controversy; his inquiries into the possibilities of social stability have been criticized by some as dangerously right-wing. His last publications were *Children and Others* (1964, children's stories) and *Morning Noon and Night* (1968, a novel).

Cradle Will Rock, The   A musical drama of social protest, with lyrics and music by **Marc Blitzstein**, first produced in 1937. Blitzstein brought techniques of classical opera together with elements of popular music to tell the story of a strike in "Steeltown, USA." The characters are representative types rather than realistic individuals. Mr Mister, who owns the steel mill and everything else in town, is trying to break the strike with the aid of his "Liberty Committee" – Reverend Salvation, Editor Daily, Yasha (a musician), Dauber (an artist), Dr Specialist, and Professor Trixie and President Prexy from the local university. Most of the play takes place in a courtroom to which the Liberty Committee has been taken, mistakenly arrested along with "the man who made the speech" – Larry Foreman, a union organizer and the hero of the piece. Through a series of flashbacks the sympathetic Harry Druggist, a former drugstore owner who has become a bum after the death of his son in an explosion caused by Mr Mister's henchmen, explains to Moll, a poor woman who is being framed for soliciting, how each member of the Liberty Committee came to sell his soul and his profession to Mr Mister and his family. At the end of the play, Mr Mister appears and attempts unsuccessfully to buy off Larry Foreman; we are left with the impression that the union will be successful.

The Cradle Will Rock was originally a production of the **Federal Theatre Project**, produced by John Houseman and directed by Orson Welles, with Will Geer playing Mr Mister. However, in response to political pressure the production was canceled at the last minute, literally while the audience was filing into the theatre. An empty theatre was quickly found, and the premiere took place as scheduled, but without costumes, scenery, or orchestra (Blitzstein himself accompanied the singers at the piano and provided a commentary). Nonetheless the production succeeded and subsequently ran on Broadway for four months; it has since been revived twice.

Crane, (Harold) Hart 1899–1932 Crane was born in Ohio but spent most of his life in New York City. His parents' unhappy marriage deeply troubled him; alcoholism and his inability to support himself in New York further undermined his stability. He committed suicide at the age of 33.

Strongly influenced by the French symbolists and by **T. S. Eliot**, Crane produced in his relatively brief career a body of poetry that has received considerable critical attention and acclaim. Characterized by dramatic rhetoric and exotic diction, his work often drew on images of water and the sea, which provided him with material for his symbolic and psychological speculations. He is best known for his long poem *The Bridge* (1930), written partly in response to the negativism of Eliot's *The Waste Land*. Each section of the poem focuses on a particular aspect of American history or culture, which Crane then unifies in the figure of the Brooklyn Bridge, which he called "a symbol of our constructive future." His first book of poetry, *White Buildings*, was published in 1926, his *Collected Poems* in 1933. Two collections of letters have appeared: *The Letters of Hart Crane, 1916–1932* (1952) and *Letters of Hart Crane and His Family* (1974).

Crane, Stephen 1871–1900 Crane was born in Newark, New Jersey, the son of a Methodist minister. After leaving high school he moved to New York City and worked as a journalist for the *Tribune* and the *Herald* before starting on his first novel, eventually published as *Maggie: A Girl of the Streets* (1893). Though *Maggie* was not widely noticed, Crane was encouraged by the responses of **William Dean Howells** and **Hamlin Garland**. His second novel, *The Red Badge of Courage* (1895), was a critical and popular success. He also published a volume of poetry, *The Black Rider* (1895), stylistically influenced by the poetry of **Emily Dickinson**. In 1896 a collection of short stories, *The Little Regiment*, focusing on the Civil War, was published. In the same year, working-class life in New York City provided material for the novel *George's Mother*. *The Third Violet* (1897) is a short novel about a young artist.

Crane's career as a journalist continued during these years and he traveled to the Southwest, to Mexico, and, in 1896, to Cuba. On this last journey he was shipwrecked, spending nearly three days in an open boat at sea, an experience which formed the basis for one of his most famous stories, the title piece of *The Open Boat and Other Stories* (1898). In 1897 he and his companion Cora Taylor traveled to Greece, where he served as a war correspondent. His poor health forced them to leave and they moved to England, where he met Joseph Conrad and **Henry James**, two of his most distinguished admirers. A novel, *Active Service* (1899), was derived from his experience of the Greco–Turkish War.

In 1899 Crane returned to Cuba as a war correspondent (this time to cover the Spanish–American War) but was again obliged to return to England due to poor health. He died of tuberculosis at the age of 29. Some of his most highly regarded stories appeared in *The Monster* (1898). A second collection of verse, *War is Kind*, appeared in the year of his death. Posthumous publications include the sketches and stories from his life as a correspondent in *Wounds in the Rain* (1900); and *Whilomville Stories* (1900), about a childhood in a small town in New York state. The *Collected Works*, edited by Wilson Follett, were published in 12 volumes (1925–6). His *Letters* were collected in 1960.

Crawford, Francis Marion 1854–1909 Son of the sculptor Thomas Crawford and nephew, on his mother's side, of **Julia Ward Howe**, Crawford was born in Italy. He was educated in the US and at Cambridge and Heidelburg universities. An accomplished linguist, he traveled extensively, sometimes gathering material for his novels.

His first novel, *Mr Isaacs: A Tale of Modern India* (1882), was an immediate success, and he went on to write almost 50 more romances, historical novels, and tales of cosmopolitan adventure which enjoyed a large following. His aim, as he argued in *The Novel: What It Is* (1893), was not to moralize or to paint life in the realistic mode that was then becoming popular, but simply to entertain. Among his other novels are *A Tale of a Lonely Parish* (1886), *Don Orsini* (1891), *Corleone: A Tale of Sicily* (1896), *Via Crucis* (1898), *In the Palace of the King: A Love Story of Old Madrid* (1900), and *The White Sister* (1909). Many of his novels were adapted for the stage. He wrote *Francesca da Rimini* (1902), a play in four acts, for Sarah Bernhardt. His tales of the supernatural, *Wandering Ghosts*, were published posthumously in 1911.

Creeley, Robert 1926– Born in Arlington, Massachusetts, Creeley attended Harvard but did not graduate. In 1954 he joined the faculty at Black Mountain College, where he founded and edited the *Black Moun-*

tain Review (see **Black Mountain School**). When the college closed in 1956 he moved to San Francisco, where he met **Jack Kerouac**, **Allen Ginsberg**, and other writers of the **Beat** movement. He has since taught at the University of New Mexico and the State University of New York at Buffalo.

Creeley's poems, often syntactically compressed and beginning and ending in mid-thought, are collected in *You* (1956), *For Love: Poems 1950–1960* (1962), *Words: Poems* (1967), *Divisions and Other Early Poems* (1968), *St Martin's* (1971), *The Collected Poems of Robert Creeley, 1945–1975* (1982), and *Mirrors* (1983). His prose works include a novel, *The Island* (1963), and a collection of short stories, *The Gold Diggers* (1954), *Was That a Real Poem and Other Essays* (1979), and *The Collected Prose of Robert Creeley: A Story* (1984).

Crèvecoeur, J. Hector St John de 1735–1813 Born in Normandy, Michel-Guillaume Jean de Crèvecoeur was educated in France and England and in 1754 went to Quebec to serve in Montcalm's army. After the war, he traveled around the Great Lakes and the Ohio River Valley, New York, and Pennsylvania, describing his experiences in *Voyage dans la Haute Pennsylvanie et dans l'état de New York* (Paris, 1801). He became naturalized as a Colonial citizen in New York in 1764 and, adopting an anglicized version of his family name, married and settled on a farm in Orange County, New York, in 1769.

The American Revolution forced Crèvecoeur to leave America for France in 1780. In Europe he moved in fashionable circles and published, under the name J. Hector St John, a collection of his impressions of America called **Letters from an American Farmer** (London, 1782); the book was not published in America until 1793. Returning to America after the war in 1783, he found his farm burned, his wife dead, and his children dispersed. He served as French consul and eventually went back to France in 1790. Further letters and essays written during his American period were published in 1925 as *Sketches of Eighteenth Century America*. He also wrote essays on agriculture, and was a member of **Benjamin Franklin**'s Philosophical Society in Philadelphia.

Crockett, Davy 1786–1836 Crockett was born in Tennessee and received little more than basic schooling. In 1814 he served with General Andrew Jackson in holding off the Creek Indian rebellion, and was rewarded by Jackson with an appointment as Justice of the Peace. He ran for Congress in 1826, and was elected to the first of three terms. His backwoods "natural born sense" appealed to many, as did his calm confidence and robust humor.

All of the works attributed to Crockett were produced while he served in Congress. It is not clear, however, whether he had a hand in writing the books that swelled his popularity as a frontier soldier, pioneer, and statesman. *A Narrative of the Life of Davy Crockett* (1834) is accepted by some as an autobiography. Crockett himself claimed to have written *An Account of Colonel Crockett's Tour to the North and Down East* (1835) and *The Life of Martin Van Buren* (1835), but even here authorship is disputed.

Crothers, Rachel 1878–1958 Born in Illinois, the daughter of two physicians, by her early teens Crothers had already written, produced, and acted in her first play. She pursued her studies of acting and elocution at the Illinois State University Normal High School, the New England School of Dramatic Instruction in Boston, and the Stanhope–Wheatcroft School of Acting. After the production of her play *Nora* (1903) she gave up acting and assumed the unusual role of director-playwright. Between 1899 and 1937 she wrote 30 plays for the New York stage. She was also involved in the foundation of the Stage Women's Relief Fund in 1917, the United Theatre Relief Committee during the Depression, and the American Theatre Wing for War Relief which organized the Stage Door Canteen in 1940.

A box-office success throughout her long career, the central thematic concern of her plays – with their realistic characterization, dialogue, and settings – was always the possibility of freedom for the modern woman in a world dominated by men. In her first successful full-length play, *The Three of Us* (1906), she relates the story of a determined spinster's attempt to save her and her brothers' interests in a Nevada mine. In *A Little Journey* (1918), a self-centered young woman's world is changed by the experience of a train wreck. *He and She* (1920) examines the conflicts in a woman's life between her artistic career and her role as wife and mother. *Nice People* (1921) describes the rebellion and reform of three flappers. *Mary the Third* (1923) recounts another flapper's feelings about love and marriage. In one of her more enduring social comedies, *Let Us Be Gay* (1929), she examines a woman's attempt to gain freedom through marital infidelity. Her last successful production, *Susan and God* (1937), is the story of another woman's search for independence through religion. Among her other notable plays are: *A Man's World* (1910), *Young Wisdom* (1914), *Old Lady 31* (1916), *39 East* (1919), *Expressing Willie* (1924), *A Lady's Virtue* (1925), *As Husbands Go* (1931), and *When Ladies Meet* (1932).

Crucible, The A play by **Arthur Miller**, first performed at the Martin Beck Theatre in New York in 1953, at the height of Senator Joseph McCarthy's campaign against Communists and their associates. The play draws a clear analogy between McCarthy's activities and the Salem witch-hunts.

The play is set in Salem in 1692, and follows the unfolding horror of the witch-trials there. Abigail, the niece of Reverend Parris and a mischief-maker, has led some of the girls of Salem in a naked frolic. To protect herself, she claims to be the victim of witchcraft, and frightens the other girls into making the same claim. When the witch-finders are brought to Salem, Abigail and the girls denounce any member of the community who resists them. One by one the weak and the virtuous are brought to trial, condemned, and hanged. The strongest resistance comes from John Proctor, a good-hearted man whom Abigail had seduced when she was working for his wife. His confession of adultery promises to end Abigail's reign of terror, but his wife lovingly denies it, and Proctor goes to his death knowing that society has lost its ability and its right to distinguish between good and evil.

Crying of Lot 49, The See **Pynchon, Thomas**

Cullen, Countee 1903–46 A leading figure of the **Harlem Renaissance**, Cullen was reared by foster parents in Harlem, New York. He graduated from New York University in 1925 and received an MA from Harvard in 1926. His first verse collections were *Color* (1925), *Copper Sun* (1927), and *The*

Ballad of the Brown Girl: An Old Ballad Retold (1927). While in France on a Guggenheim scholarship, he wrote *The Black Christ, and Other Poems* (1929). The title piece recounts the lynching of a black youth for a crime he did not commit. Cullen's only novel, *One Way to Heaven* (1932), is a social comedy of lower-class blacks and the bourgeoisie in New York City. *The Medea and Some Poems* (1935) is a collection of sonnets and short lyrics together with a translation of Euripides' tragedy (in prose, with the choruses in verse). Cullen also edited the magazine *Opportunity* and compiled an anthology of black poetry entitled *Caroling Dusk* (1927). *On These I Stand: An Anthology of the Best Poems of Countee Cullen* was published posthumously in 1947.

Cummings, E[dward] E[stlin] 1894–1962 One of the most technically innovative poets of this century, Cummings was born in Cambridge, Massachusetts, and graduated from Harvard in 1916. He drove an ambulance in France during World War I, and stayed on in Paris after the armistice. His first published work was a novel, *The Enormous Room* (1922), based on his mistaken imprisonment in a French detention center during the war. This was followed by collections of verse, *Tulips and Chimneys* (1923) and *XLI Poems* (1925).

& and *is 5* (both 1925) presented Cummings's new style, which was influenced by jazz and contemporary slang and characterized by an innovative use of typography and punctuation. Features of this poetry include the use of capital letters and punctuation in the middle of single words, phrases split by parentheses, and stanzas arranged to create a visual design on the page. Formal devices were often used as visual manifestations of theme or tone; the poem's typographical dimension itself becomes a new level of meaning.

Cummings's other works include *ViVa* (1931), *No Thanks* (1935), *1/20* (1936), *Collected Poems* (1938), *50 Poems* (1940), *1 × 1* (1944), *Poems 1923–1954* (1954), *Ninety-Five Poems* (1958), *73 Poems* (1963), and *Complete Poems 1913–1962* (1972). He also published two plays, a book of drawings and paintings, a travel book, and *i, six nonlectures* (1953). The *Selected Letters of E. E. Cummings* appeared in 1969.

Cunningham, J[ames] V[incent] 1911–85 Poet, born in Cumberland, Maryland, and educated at Stanford (AB 1934, PhD 1945). He taught at the universities of Hawaii, Chicago, Virginia, and, from 1953 until his retirement, at Brandeis. His first volume of poetry, *The Helmsman*, was published in 1942 and was followed by *The Judge is Fury* (1947) and *Doctor Drink* (1950). The poems in all three volumes are notable for their economy of presentation, and their use of precise meters and traditional verse forms. An accomplished Renaissance scholar, Cunningham was drawn to the form of the epigram, publishing *Trivial, Vulgar, & Exalted: Epigrams* in 1957. His later collections include *The Exclusions of a Rhyme; Poems and Epigrams* (1960), *To What Strangers, What Welcome: A Sequence of Short Poems* (1964), and *Some Salt: Poems and Epigrams* (1967). *The Collected Poems and Epigrams of J. V. Cunningham* and *Selected Poems* were both published in 1971. His *Collected Essays* appeared in 1976.

D

Dahlberg, Edward 1900–77 Dahlberg was born in Boston, the illegitimate son of a lady barber who eventually owned her own shop in Kansas City. At an early age, Dahlberg was sent to an orphanage in Cleveland, Ohio, but ran away and later enrolled at the University of California and then at Columbia University. In 1926 he settled in Europe, where he wrote his first book, *Bottom Dogs* (1929), a semi-autobiographical novel about a childhood in slums and orphanages. This was followed by *From Flushing to Calvary* (1932), about the slums of New York City, and *Those Who Perish* (1934), about the effects of Nazism upon American Jews. Dahlberg's interests were wide ranging: his literary criticism is collected in *Do These Bones Live?* (1941); studies of "classical sensuality" and myth comprise *The Sorrows of Priapus* (1957) and *The Carnal Myth* (1968); and essays on modern society and modern writers are collected in *The Flea of Sodom* (1950), *Truth is More Sacred* (1961), and *Alms for Oblivion* (1964). *Because I Was Flesh* (1964) is his autobiography. Other books include *Cipango's Hinder Door* (1965, poems), *Epitaphs of Our Times* (1967, letters), *The Confessions of Edward Dahlberg* (1971), and *The Olive of Minerva* (1976).

Daisy Miller A short novel by **Henry James**, published in 1879. Daisy Miller is touring Europe with her mother and brother. The expatriate American community interprets her innocence and lack of concern for social convention as immodesty and forwardness, and she is ostracized. One of its number, Frederick Winterbourne, though agreeing with that judgement, is also charmed by her innocence. In Rome Daisy takes up with Giovanelli, a young Italian of no social position. Winterbourne meets them one evening viewing the Coliseum by moonlight without a chaperone, and berates Daisy for her lack of social decorum. Shocked and hurt by his reaction, she returns at once to her hotel, where she contracts malaria and dies after a week.

Daly, (John) Augustin 1838–99 Playwright and theatre manager, born in North Carolina and educated in New York City, where he began his career as a drama critic. He wrote or, more often, adapted more than 100 plays, usually working in collaboration with his brother Joseph. The first of these, *Leah the Forsaken* (1862), was an adaptation of S. H. von Mosenthal's novel *Deborah*. Among his successful and spectacular melodramas were *Under the Gaslight* (1867), *The Flash of Lightning* (1868), and *The Red Scarf* (1868). He also wrote comedies of American high society, including *Divorce* (1871), *Pique* (1875), and *Love on Crutches* (1884). One of his most successful plays, *Horizon* (1871), is a frontier melodrama which treats the settlement of the American West.

In addition to his writing, Daly was an active company manager and director. From 1869 to 1873 he managed the Fifth Avenue Theatre, and then Daly's Theatre from 1879 until his death. During these years he developed the finest ensemble companies in America and took them to London and Paris on the first international tour by a full American theatre company. He also encouraged the careers of **Dion Boucicault** and **Bronson Howard** by producing their plays in his theatres.

Damnation of Theron Ware, The A novel by **Harold Frederic** published in 1896; its British title was *Illumination*. It tells the story of a talented young Methodist minister's growing disillusionment with conservative, small-town life in upstate New York, and his attraction for exotic, sophisticated ideas which in the end prove disastrous for him.

Through his friendships with Dr Ledsmar, a scientist, Father Forbes, a Catholic priest, and Celia Madden, the beautiful Catholic church organist, Theron Ware becomes fascinated with experimental science, Biblical criticism, and aesthetics, which, together with the lifestyles of his new acquaintances, represent for him a new sort of intellectual and personal freedom outside his narrow Methodist experience. He becomes increasingly detached from his wife and congregation, and increasingly drawn to the beautiful and free-spirited Celia; a series of exciting encounters between the two culminate in a kiss at a church picnic. Elated, Theron follows Celia to New York City and calls on her in her hotel room, but she upbraids him for spying on her and taking a prurient interest in her affairs. Devastated by her rejection and by the realization that he has misunderstood her apparent freedom – it rests on a tradition of spirituality and church institutions that are foreign to him – Theron falls ill. When he eventually recovers, he and his wife go west to Seattle, where he will try to go into business and perhaps into politics.

Dana, Richard Henry, Jr 1815–82 The son of a minor poet and journalist of the same name, Dana was born in Cambridge, Massachusetts. He went to Harvard, but at the end of his second year (1834) withdrew because of eye trouble. For the sake of his health he signed on as a seaman for a voyage to California around Cape Horn. He worked on the Pacific coast for a year, collecting and curing hides, and then returned to Boston by sea. He completed his education at Harvard Law School.

Dana's first work, the article "Cruelty to Seamen," published in the *American Jurist* in 1839, expressed a deeply felt anger at what he had seen on his voyages. In 1840, the year he was admitted to the Bar, he published *Two Years Before The Mast*, the book that made him famous and that described the life of the ordinary seaman as it was lived day by day. The following year saw the publication of *The Seaman's Friend*, which among other things explained to sailors exactly what their rights – as well as their duties – were. It was published in England as *The Seaman's Manual*. His account of another voyage, *To Cuba and Back* (1859), was not a success.

A champion of the underprivileged, Dana opposed slavery in word and deed. He freely gave assistance to fugitive slaves and in doing so antagonized the Boston mill-owners, because cheap raw materials from the South boosted their profits. He hoped for a political career, but his edition of Henry Wheaton's *Elements of International Law* (1866) involved him in accusations of plagiarism, and his appointment as ambassador to Great Britain was withdrawn by the Senate. Convinced that his life had been a failure, in 1878 he withdrew to Europe, where he died four years later. *Speeches in Stirring Times* (1910) and *An Autobiographical Sketch* (1953) were published posthumously.

Daring Young Man on the Flying Trapeze, The See **Saroyan, William**

Davidson, Donald (Grady) 1893–1968 Poet, critic, and historian, born in Tennessee, Davidson helped found (1922) and edit (1922–5) *The Fugitive*, the magazine of **The Fugitives**, a group of Southern writers that included **John Crowe Ransom, Allen Tate,** and **Robert Penn Warren**. Of those in the group, Davidson remained the most committed to its aims to preserve both a distinctly Southern literature and the traditional agrarian economy of the South. His poems were published in *An Outland Piper* (1924), *The Tall Men* (1927), *Lee in the Mountains, and Other Poems* (1938), *The Long Street* (1961), and *Poems, 1922–1961* (1966). His other writings include *The Attack on Leviathan; Regionalism and Nationalism in the United States* (1938), *Still Rebels, Still Yankees, and Other Essays* (1957), *Southern Writers in The Modern World* (1958), and *The Spyglass: Views and Reviews, 1924–1930* (1963). He also contributed to *I'll Take My Stand: The South And The Agrarian Tradition* (1930).

Davis, Rebecca (Blane) Harding 1831–1910 Much of Davis's fiction is set in her native Philadelphia, including her best-known story, "Life in the Iron Mills" (published in *The Atlantic Monthly* in 1861), which portrays the frustrated and tragic life of Hugh Wolfe, a furnace-tender in an industrial mill, and his cousin Deborah, who brings herself to ruin when she tries to help him. One of the earliest exponents of the American realist school, Davis again portrayed the bleak lives of industrial workers in her novel *Margaret Howth* (1862), and of blacks in *Waiting for the Verdict* (1868). *John Andross* (1874) is a tale about political corruption.

Davis, Richard Harding 1864–1916 Davis was one of the most prolific and popular writers of his day. Born in Philadelphia, the son of **Rebecca Harding Davis**, he became at a young age one of the leading journalists in the country. In 1890 he was appointed managing editor of *Harper's Weekly*, and his travels in that capacity provided the material for *The West from a Car Window* (1892), *The Rulers of the Mediterranean* (1893), *Our English Cousins* (1894), *About Paris* (1895), and *Three Gringos in Venezuela and Central America* (1896). His subsequent experiences as a war correspondent gave rise to *Cuba in War Time* (1897), *A Year from a Reporter's Note-Book* (1898), *The Cuban and Porto Rican Campaigns* (1898), *With Both Armies in South Africa* (1900), *Notes of a War Correspondent* (1910), *With the Allies* (1914), and *With the French in France and Salonika* (1916).

Davis also published over 80 short stories, 7 novels, and 25 plays. He was successful in all genres, although not much of his work survived his own day. His 11 short-story collections span his career from *Gallegher* (1891), *Van Bibber and Others* (1892), and *Ranson's Folly* (1902) to *The Lost Road (1913)* and *The Boy Scout* (1917). His novels include *Soldiers of Fortune* (1897), *The Bar Sinister* (1903), and *Vera the Medium* (1908). Among his most popular plays are *Ranson's Folly* (1902) and *Miss Civilization* (1905).

Day, Clarence (Shepard) 1874–1935 The son of a stockbroker, Day was born in New York City and educated at Yale. He served in the navy during the Spanish–American War, then worked as a businessman in New York, and eventually became a regular writer for *The New Yorker*. He is best known for his autobiographical writings, which include *God and My Father* (1932), *Life with Father* (1935), *Life with Mother* (1937), and *Father and I* (1940) – all characterized by their humorous examination of upper-class life in 19th-century New York. *Life with Father* was dramatized in 1939 by Howard Lindsay and

Russel Crouse, and became a long-running success. Day's other publications include *This Simian World* (1920), *Thoughts Without Words* (1928), *In the Green Mountain Country* (1934), *Scenes from the Mesozoic and Other Drawings* (1935), and *The Crow's Nest* (1921), which was enlarged in 1936 as *After All*.

Day of Doom, The A didactic poem by **Michael Wigglesworth**, published in 1662. Subtitled "A Poetical Description of the Great and Last Judgement," it describes how God rewards the virtuous sheep with eternal life and condemns the sinful goats to eternal damnation. The poem spoke most clearly to a Puritan audience. Cast in ballad lines of seven feet, it was easily memorized and was soon selected to supplement the catechism in the education of the young Puritan: within a year of the first printing all 1,800 copies had been sold, which suggests that one out of 35 New Englanders owned the poem by 1663. During the next 100 years it was reprinted frequently, and found its way into virtually all Puritan homes.

Day of the Locust, The See **West, Nathanael**

Dead End See **Kingsley, Sidney**

Death Comes for the Archbishop A novel by **Willa Cather**, published in 1927 and based on the careers of two French missionaries, Jean-Baptiste Lamy and Joseph Machebeuf, who worked in the New Mexico territory in the mid 19th century.

Bishop Jean Latour arrives in the New Mexico territory shortly after it has been annexed by the US. With his vicar, Father Joseph Vaillant, who is also his long-time friend, he establishes a new diocese. Latour is withdrawn and ascetic; Vaillant is practical, vigorous, and cheerful. Together they overcome the persistence with which the native Navajo and Hopi Indians cling to their ancient superstitions, and they confront the antagonism of the corrupt Mexican priests already present in the territory. They establish mission schools in remote areas and, after some years, succeed in building a cathedral at Santa Fe.

The cathedral is the outer symbol of the achievement of these two devoted men – of their success in adapting an Old World religion to the New World. Though Latour brings two architects from France to design the cathedral, it is very much inspired by the landscape of the Southwest, a landscape Cather vividly evokes for her readers. Shortly after gold is discovered at Pike's Peak, Vaillant becomes bishop in Colorado, and the two friends part. Later, Latour is made an archbishop. Vaillant is the first to die, and the novel closes with Latour's own death, mourned by all in his diocese – Mexicans, Indians, and Americans alike.

Death of a Salesman A play by **Arthur Miller**, first performed and published in 1949. It won instant critical acclaim, running for 742 performances at the Morosco Theatre in New York City and winning both the Pulitzer Prize and the New York Drama Critics Circle Award.

It relates the tragic story of a salesman named Willy Loman, who is not the great success that he claims to be to his family and friends. After 35 years on the road trying to earn money and recognition, and measuring his own worth by the volume of his sales, Willy has begun to lose his way on trips and to run off the side of the road in his car. His devoted wife Linda and his two grown sons, Biff and Happy, who are home for a visit, worry about him. He is eventually fired because he no longer brings in the business that he used to when he was younger. He begins to hallucinate about significant events from his past: he remembers encouraging his sons to lie if it helped them to be successful and well-liked; he recalls the pathetic scene of being discovered with a prostitute by his older son, who arrives unexpectedly at his hotel room seeking fatherly advice; he has imaginary conversations with his successful brother Ben. Finally, deciding that he is worth more dead than alive (the insurance money will support his family and help Biff get a new start in life), he kills himself in his car on a last trip. Critics have disagreed whether his suicide is meant to be seen as a last desperate and tragic assertion of the American dream or as an act of cowardice and selfishness.

Declaration of Independence, The The document issued by the Second Continental Congress of the American colonies, asserting their severance from Britain. Drawn up chiefly by **Thomas Jefferson**, the paper was revised by Congress and signed on July 4, 1776. First invoking, as its justification, the doctrine of natural rights, the Declaration then lists the colonies' grievances against the king, and concludes that "these United Colonies are, and of right ought to be, Free and Independent States."

Deerslayer, The See **Leatherstocking Tales, The**

De Forest, John W. 1826–1906 Born in Connecticut, De Forest went to live in Syria with his brother when ill health prevented him from attending college. After his return to the US he began to write. His *History of the Indians of Connecticut* (1851) was marked by a strict objectivity which later became a characteristic of his fiction. He served for three years as a Union army captain in the Civil War, and in 1867 published **Miss Ravenel's Conversion from Secession to Loyalty**. A romance set during the Civil War and Reconstruction, it includes some grimly realistic battle scenes which anticipate those of **Stephen Crane**. Among De Forest's later, lesser-known novels are *Kate Beaumont* (1872), about South Carolina plantation society; and *Honest John Vane* (1875), a satire of political corruption. His Civil War memoirs, *A Volunteer's Adventures*, appeared posthumously in 1946; *A Union Officer in the Reconstruction* followed in 1948. Much admired by **William Dean Howells**, De Forest may be seen as a forerunner of the realist movement of which Howells himself was the recognized leader.

Degradation of the Democratic Dogma, The Published in 1919, this volume consists of **Henry Adams**'s *A Letter to American Teachers of History*, with a lengthy preface by his brother **Brooks Adams**. The *Letter*, which had first appeared in 1910, elaborates the dynamic theory of history already set forth in **The Education of Henry Adams**.

DeLillo, Don 1936– Born in New York City and educated at Fordham University, DeLillo is the author of novels concerned with such subjects as sports, television, media-manipulated news events, rock-and-roll, consumer products, and the languages that evolve in these subcultures. *Americana*, his first novel, is a media-age picaresque. This was followed by *End Zone* (1972), in which a college football player's obsession with nuclear warfare leads to his retreat to the safety of the signal system of football and, ultimately, to his nervous breakdown. *Great Jones Street* (1973), a novel that deals with the world of rock-and-roll, was followed by *Ratner's Star* (1976), an encyclopedic novel about the conceptual world of pure mathematics. *Players* (1977) and *Running Dog* (1978) are more modest works, taking as their theme the boredom, narcissism, and paranoia that characterizes our spiritual landscape. *The Names* (1982), set in Greece, where DeLillo lived on a Guggenheim Fellowship, is a mystery whose clues are the intellectual checkpoints that language provides. *White Noise* (1985), a novel about a paranoid professor of Hitler Studies at a Midwestern college, won DeLillo the American Book Award in 1985.

Deliverance See **Dickey, James**

Dell, Floyd 1887–1969 Born in Illinois, Dell settled in New York City in 1913. A radical journalist, he edited *The Masses* (1914–17) and *The Liberator* (1918–24). After the success of his first novel, *Moon-Calf* (1920), about the disillusionment of the post-war generation, he turned most of his energy to fiction. *The Briary-Bush* (1921) is a sequel to *Moon-Calf*, and *Janet March* (1923) and *Runaway* (1925) are also about the confusion and turmoil of life in the jazz age. His other works include *An Old Man's Folly* (1926), *Upton Sinclair* (1927), and *Love in the Machine Age* (1930). Together with Thomas Mitchell, Dell dramatized his novel *An Unmarried Father* (1927) as *Little Accident* (1928). *Homecoming* (1933) is his autobiography.

Deloria, Vine, Jr 1933– One of the most important voices of the Indian literary renaissance, Deloria is a Standing Rock Sioux, born and raised on a South Dakota reservation. He received his degree in divinity from the Lutheran School of Theology in 1963, but did not enter the ministry, as had both his father and grandfather. He studied law instead, and in 1970 became the chairman of The Institute for the Development of Indian Law.

Deloria's writings consistently advocate a separatist political strategy for American Indians. These include the satiric *Custer Died For Your Sins: An Indian Manifesto* (1969); *We Talk, You Listen: New Tribes, New Turf* (1970); *God is Red* (1973), a critique of the Judeo-Christian religious tradition; *Behind The Trail of Broken Treaties: An Indian Declaration of Independence* (1974), an examination of the events which led to the 1973 conflict at Wounded Knee; *Indians of The Pacific Northwest: From the Coming of The Whiteman to The Present Day* (1977); and *The Metaphysics of Modern Existence* (1979).

Democracy in America (*La Démocratie en Amérique*) A classic interpretation of American civilization by Count Alexis de Tocqueville, published in two parts in 1835 and 1840. De Tocqueville's predictions about the course democracy would follow in the US were based not only on what he had read about America but also on his own observations, made while on an official visit to the US to study its penal system.

In the first part he discusses America's geography, political institutions and processes, and society. He argues that Anglo-Americans have been able to take possession of and settle such a large portion of the continent because they have the habit of democratic self-government that he considers essential to civilization, and he predicts that they will continue successfully to expand their territory. Noting that the tendency toward equality is advancing throughout the western world, he declares that – at the time he writes – equality is most advanced in the US. In the second part he analyzes the effect of democracy on intellectual movements, art, religion, taste, and mores. He concludes that democracy and increasing equality will lead to greater mediocrity of individual achievement, even as it makes possible greater general comfort and greater achievements by the State.

Democratic Vistas A prose pamphlet by **Walt Whitman**, first published in 1871. It was later included in *Two Rivulets* (1876), the second volume of the sixth edition of **Leaves of Grass**. Whitman was an ardent democrat and a passionate individualist. *Democratic Vistas* asserts his belief in the compatibility of the two positions and sees their union as the basis for a cultural order in the United States that would be independent from that of Britain.

Desire Under the Elms See **O'Neill, Eugene**

Detective Story See **Kingsley, Sidney**

Dewey, John 1859–1952 Philosopher and educator born in Burlington, Vermont. He graduated from the University of Vermont in 1879 and received his PhD from The Johns Hopkins University in 1884. He taught at the University of Michigan and then at the University of Chicago, where he founded the Laboratory School for experimental education. He was a professor of philosophy at Columbia University from 1905 until his retirement in 1929.

Many of his works are concerned with reforms in education, politics, and religion. His numerous writings greatly influenced the development of educational techniques both in the US and abroad. His publications in this field include *Psychology* (1887), *Moral Principles in Education* (1909), *Interest and Effort in Education* (1913), *Democracy and Education* (1916), *Experience and Education* (1938), *The Public Schools and Spiritual Values* (1944).

Dewey started out as a Hegelian, but his study of Darwin led him to a philosophical pragmatism more in the tradition of **William James**. His philosophy, which he termed "instrumentalism," with its emphasis on the practical problems of social construction, is elaborated in such works as *Outlines of a Critical Theory of Ethics* (1891), *Studies in Logical Theory* (1903), *Reconstruction in Philosophy* (1920), *Human Nature and Conduct* (1922), *Experience and Nature* (1925), *The Quest for Certainty* (1929), *Art as Experience* (1934), and *Freedom and Culture* (1939). A prolific writer, Dewey continued to produce books and essays until his death at the age of 93. A selection of his writings, *Intelligence in the Modern World*, was published in 1939.

Dial, The A New England quarterly magazine started in 1840, and the chief periodical of the **Transcendentalist** movement. It published the literary, philosophical, and religious statements of its founders, who included **Margaret Fuller** and **Ralph Waldo Emerson**, as well as the poetry of **Jones Very** and **William Ellery Channing**. Although it was published for only four years, *The Dial* had a major influence on the intellectual life of 19th-century New England. In addition to Fuller and Emerson, its editors included **Henry David Thoreau**.

Dickey, James (Lafayette) 1923– Born in Atlanta and educated at Vanderbilt Univer-sity, Dickey has taught at various colleges in addition to working in advertising. Much of his work is concerned with the causes and consequences of guilt arising from the personal cruelties of life in the Southern backwoods, and from the collective cruelties of nations.

He published his first volume of poetry, *Into the Stone and Other Poems*, in 1960. Subsequent collections are *Drowning with Others* (1962), *Helmets* (1964), *Two Poems of the Air* (1964), *Buckdancer's Choice* (1965), *Poems 1957–1967* (1968), and *The Eye-Beaters, Blood, Victory, Madness, Buckhead and Mercy* (1970). *Babel to Byzantium*, a collection of criticism, was published in 1968; *Deliverance*, a bestselling novel about a violent Georgia canoe trip, in 1970; and *Stolen Apples*, English versions of the poems of Yevgeny Yevtushenko, in 1971. His most recent publications are *The Zodiac* (1976), *The Strength of Fields* (1979), *The Water-Bug's Mittens: Ezra Pound* (1979), *The Central Motion: Poems 1968–79* (1979), *The Early Motion* (1981), and *Puella* (1982).

Dickinson, Emily 1830–86 One of the three children of Edward Dickinson, a respected lawyer, state legislator, US congressman, and judge, the poet was born and lived all her life in Amherst, Massachusetts. She attended Amherst Academy from 1840 to 1847, and then the Mount Holyoke Female Seminary for a year (1847–8). Although her early years were filled with the normal social activities of the daughter of a prominent citizen, she began to withdraw from the world outside her home. By the age of 30 she had become an almost total recluse, never leaving her father's house and garden, dressing completely in white, receiving very few visitors, and carrying on most of her many friendships, like those with the novelist **Helen Hunt Jackson** and the Reverend Charles Wadsworth, through a regular correspondence.

At the age of 32, at the end of what seems to have been the most intense and prolific period of her creative life, Dickinson sent some of her poems to Thomas Wentworth Higginson, the minister, author, and critic. This marked the beginning of a long and sustained correspondence between the two that only twice (in 1870 and 1873) actually resulted in meetings. Although he encouraged her writing and assumed the role of her mentor, Higginson neither realized the full extent of Dickinson's genius nor sought to get her work published. Only seven of some 1,800 of her poems were published during her lifetime. "Sic transit" (1852), "I taste a liquor never brewed" (1861), "Safe in their Alabaster Chambers" (1862), "Blazing in gold, quenching in purple" (1864), and "A narrow fellow in the grass" (1866) were all published in the *Springfield Republican*, the paper edited by her friend Samuel Bowles. "Some keep the Sabbath going to church" appeared in *Round Table* in 1864, and "Success is counted sweetest" in an anonymous volume entitled *A Masque of Poets* (1878).

After her death in 1886, her sister Lavinia found over a thousand poems in her room, all bound neatly in homemade booklets. Almost all were short lyrics; most were untitled and undated; some appeared in several versions. The first volumes of Dickinson's poetry to be published were edited by Higginson and Mabel L. Todd, an Amherst friend, in 1890 and 1891. Uncertain about public reaction to her work, Higginson and Todd changed meters and rhymes, altered metaphors, and substituted conventional grammar for the original complex syntax. Despite their caution the critical reception was mostly unfavorable. Other volumes, also marred by insensitive and unnecessary editing, were edited by Dickinson's niece, Martha Dickinson Bianchi, and Alfred Leete Hampson, and published in 1914, 1924, 1929, 1930, 1935, and 1937. *Bolts of Melody: New Poems of Emily Dickinson*, edited by Todd and her daughter, Millicent Todd Bingham, was published in 1945; it was more faithful than previous volumes to Dickinson's original texts, and included many poems that had been suppressed by her relatives. In 1955 Thomas H. Johnson prepared a three-volume variorum edition, *The Poems of Emily Dickinson*, containing all 1,775 known poems, and this text is now accepted as the authoritative edition. Johnson and Theodora Ward edited her massive correspondence, *The Letters of Emily Dickinson*, which appeared in 1958.

The subjects of Dickinson's poetry are the traditional ones of love, nature, religion, and mortality, seen through her Puritan eyes, or, as she described it, "New Englandly." Much of the dramatic tension stems from her religious doubt; she was unable to accept the orthodox religious faith of her friends and schoolmates, yet she longed for the comfort and emotional stability that such faith could bring. Many of her lyrics, in their mixture of rebellious and reverent sentiments, illustrate this conflict. Her poetry is also notable for its technical irregularities, which alarmed her early editors and reviewers. Her characteristic stanza is four lines long, and most poems consist of just two stanzas. She often separated her words with dashes, which tend to relieve the density of the poems and introduce into them moments of speculative silence. Other characteristics of her style – sporadic capitalization of nouns; convoluted and ungrammatical phrasing; off-rhymes; broken meters; bold, unconventional, and often startling metaphors; and aphoristic wit – have greatly influenced 20th-century poets and contributed to Dickinson's reputation as one of the greatest and most innovative poets of 19th-century American literature.

di Donato, Pietro 1912–   Born and raised in New York City, di Donato is best known for his books about working-class Italian-Americans. His vision was shaped early: his father was killed on a construction site when di Donato was only 11, and he saw the incident as representative of the plight of the working classes in a land ruled by the wealthy. His most famous book, the semi-autobiographical novel *Christ in Concrete* (1939), takes its place alongside the works of **Jack Conroy** and **Michael Gold** by virtue of its uncompromising portrayal of the hardships and oppressions of working-class immigrant life. His other books include *This Woman* (1958), *Three Circles of Light* (1960), *Immigrant Saint* (1960), and *The Penitent* (1962).

Disinherited, The   See **Conroy, Jack**

Dix,   Dorothea   1802–87   Born   in Hampden, Maine, Dix moved to Boston at the age of 10 and began teaching school four years later. She ran her own school for 19 years, and despite failing health wrote a number of books. The most popular of them, *Conversations on Common Things* (1824), a textbook on a variety of subjects, and *Meditations for Private Hours* (1828), a calendar of devotional passages and poems, were reprinted many times.

Dix is best known, however, for her

philanthropic work on behalf of the insane, which she began after poor health forced her to leave teaching. For close to 50 years she worked tirelessly for the humane treatment of the insane, and for legislation on state-operated asylums. Beginning her crusade in Massachusetts, she soon became active throughout the US and Canada, and in the 1850s extended her investigations to Great Britain and Europe. Much influenced by the Reverend **William Ellery Channing**, whose children were educated at her school, she was devoted to his Unitarian belief in the spiritual potential of every human being – a principle frequently expressed in her many published appeals to state legislatures and reports on institutions.

Doctorow, E[dgar] L[awrence] 1931– Doctorow was born in New York City and educated at Kenyon College and Columbia University. His first novel, *Welcome to Hard Times*, was published in the US in 1960, and in England in 1961 under the title of *Bad Man From Bodie*. In 1971 he published *The Book of Daniel*, the novel which brought him his first public acclaim, a fictional account of the espionage trial of Julius and Ethel Rosenberg and its aftermath. His fiction is typified by its use of historical figures, most notably in *Ragtime* (1975), in which the lives of three fictional families at the beginning of the 20th century are entwined with figures such as Henry Ford, Emma Goldman, Harry Houdini, **Theodore Dreiser**, and Sigmund Freud. His other works are the novels *Big as Life* (1966), *Loon Lake* (1980), and *World's Fair* (1985); the play *Drinks Before Dinner* (1979); and *Lives of the Poet, Six Stories and a Novella* (1984), which addresses the position of the writer as both participant in and observer of society.

Dodsworth A novel by **Sinclair Lewis**, published in 1929. Sam Dodsworth, a successful automobile manufacturer in the midwestern city of Zenith, sells out to a larger company and retires. Still vigorous in his middle age, a dreamer and an idealist, he travels with his wife Fran to Europe.

Fran is spoiled, affected, and easily awed by European manners and titles. Wishing to appear a woman of the world – to become European – she flirts with other men and becomes increasingly impatient with Sam's supposed gaucheness. Eventually they separate and she plans to marry Kurt von Obersdorf, a young Austrian aristocrat. But the marriage does not take place: Kurt's mother disapproves of Fran – a soon-to-be-divorced, middle-aged American. She begs Sam's forgiveness, and though in the meantime he has met Edith Cortright, a refined and understanding American living in Italy, he takes Fran back. Soon, however, her shallowness and petulance make him realize how much he cares for Edith. He divorces Fran and returns to Edith in Europe.

D[oolittle], H[ilda] 1886–1961 Doolittle, who used the pen-name of H.D., was born in Bethlehem, Pennsylvania. After a brief and unsuccessful period of study at Bryn Mawr, in 1911 she went to live in Europe, and soon became part of the social and intellectual group known as the **Imagists**. A leading member of the group was **Ezra Pound**, whom she had known since his student days at the University of Pennsylvania, and to whom she had been briefly engaged. It was Pound who arranged for her first publications – in *Poetry* magazine and then in the anthology *Des Imagistes* (1914). In 1913 she married the English poet and novelist Richard Aldington. Her first collection of verse, *Sea Garden* (1916), drew heavily on her passion for the literature of classical Greece. Indeed, all her early collections include translations from – and many poems inspired by – the works of Sappho, Meleager, and Euripides among others. All reveal her gift for concise and direct visual description; she often uses a natural object (a plant, a rock, a wave, a bee) to stand for a human mood or emotion, a method consistent both with the principles of Imagism and with the practice of the Greek poets she loved.

She stayed in England throughout World War I, which brought many changes to her life, including the dissolution of her marriage, the birth of her daughter, and the beginning of her association with Bryher (Winifred Ellerman), the English novelist and patron of the modernist arts, who became her lifelong companion. More collections of poetry followed. *Hymen* (1921), modeled after Greek wedding masques, and *Heliodora and Other Poems* (1924) were included along with *Sea*

Garden and some other translations in her first *Collected Poems* (1925). *Hippolytus Temporizes* (1927) is a drama in classical form, anticipating her translation of the *Ion* of Euripides, published in 1937. *Red Roses For Bronze* (1929) shows her experimenting with longer series of linked lyrics, a form she would later use on a large scale. In the 1920s she also began to write novels. Her first published prose work, *Palimpsest* (1926), consists of three sections, one set in classical Rome, one in post-war London, and one in the Egypt of the excavators; each is told through the stream of consciousness of a central female figure (each one an artist), and the three are unified by themes of sexual betrayal and the woman's attempt to find personal fulfillment through love and art. *Hedylus* (1928), set in ancient Alexandria, deals with the relationship between a woman poet and courtesan and her son, also a poet. During this period Doolittle also worked on several prose works with explicitly lesbian themes, which she chose not to publish during her lifetime: *Pilate's Wife*, *Asphodel*, and *Her* (published as *Hermione* in 1981).

Her analysis by Freud (1933–4) and her experience of London during the blitz of World War II provided two of the main sources for her long poem *Trilogy*, which was comprised of *The Walls Do Not Fall* (1944), *Tribute To The Angels* (1945), and *The Flowering of the Rod* (1946). H.D.'s poetic technique matured with this work, which manipulates many levels of Christian, classical, and modern symbolism, working toward spiritual rebirth after the horrors of war. This method culminated in *Helen in Egypt* (1961), an epic rewriting of the story of Helen of Troy. Her other works include *The Hedgehog* (1936), a children's story; *By Avon River* (1949), a tribute in verse and prose to Shakespeare and the Elizabethans; another novel, *Bid Me To Live* (1960), treating life in London during World War I; three memoirs: *Tribute to Freud* (1956), *End To Torment: A Memoir of Ezra Pound* (1979), and *The Gift* (1982); and a final set of poetic sequences, *Hermetic Definition* (1972). *Collected Poems 1912–1944* was published in 1983.

Dos Passos, John (Roderigo) 1896– 1970 The illegitimate son of a prominent American attorney, John Randolph Dos Passos, the novelist was born in Chicago, but spent much of his early life living abroad with his mother, Lucy Madison. He returned to the US to attend Harvard, where he received his BA in 1916. After graduation he traveled to Spain in order to study architecture. During World War I he served as an ambulance driver in France and Italy. He drew upon his war experiences for his first two novels, *One Man's Initiation: 1917* (1920) and *Three Soldiers* (1921), both of which portray revolt against mindless discipline. In 1922 he published a collection of essays, *Rosinante to the Road Again*, and a volume of poems, *A Pushcart at the Curb*. *Streets of Night*, a novel he had begun white still a student at Harvard, appeared in 1923.

Dos Passos came to prominence with **Manhattan Transfer** (1925), a novel set in New York City and in which he introduced the stylistic innovations he would develop further in his greatest work, **U.S.A.** During the mid 1920s he also became involved with experimental drama, and in 1926 the New Playwrights Theatre performed his play *The Moon is a Gong* (later renamed *The Garbage Man*). His other plays are *Airways, Inc.* (1928) and *Fortune Heights* (1934). His involvement with the New Playwrights Theatre brought him into contact with political radicals, and he began to publish in **The New Masses**, a left-wing periodical.

Certain public incidents – such as his arrest at protests against the Sacco and Vanzetti death sentence (1927) and his visit to the Harlan County miners' strike as part of the Dreiser Committee (1931) – as well as the publication of *The 42nd Parallel* (1930), enhanced his reputation as a proletarian writer. *The 42nd Parallel* was followed by *1919* (1932) and *The Big Money* (1936); the three together comprise *U.S.A.* The trilogy tells the stories of numerous representative Americans, the narratives intersecting and continuing from one novel to the next. They are interspersed with sections called "The Camera Eye" (stream-of-consciousness passages about the experiences of the unnamed narrator), with "Newsreels" (impressionistic collections of slogans, popular song lyrics, newspaper headlines, and extracts from political speeches), and with brief biographical vignettes of actual figures, such as **Randolph Bourne, Thorstein Veblen,**

Theodore Roosevelt, Henry Ford, and Rudolph Valentino. His admirers on the Left may have chosen to see it differently, but *U.S.A.* – particularly *The Big Money* – makes it clear that Dos Passos considered both communism and capitalism as threats to individual freedom.

He became further disillusioned with communism and broke completely with the Left at the time of the Spanish Civil War, as is made clear in his novel *The Adventures of a Young Man* (1939). This work, together with *Number One* (1943), a novel about the dangers of demagoguery, and *The Grand Design* (1949), about the threat of bureaucracy, make up another trilogy – *District of Columbia*. His later novels include *Chosen Country* (1951) and *Midcentury* (1961). He also wrote numerous works of non-fiction: *The Head and Heart of Thomas Jefferson* (1954), a full-length biography of one of his heroes; *The Best of Times: An Informal Memoir* (1966); and several collections of essays and reportage, which reflect his increasingly conservative political stance. *The Fourteenth Chronicle* (1973) contains selections from his letters and diaries.

Douglass, Frederick 1817–95 The black leader was born into slavery on a plantation in Maryland, and was sent to Baltimore when he was 7 or 8 years old. He received no formal education, but learned to read first by bribing young white schoolchildren to help him, then by studying a copy of the journal *The Columbian Orator*, which he purchased in 1831. He worked in a Baltimore shipyard, learned the trade of caulking, and was then able to hire out his time under the supervision of his owner. Later, he taught school to fellow slaves before escaping in 1838 to Massachusetts, where he was employed as a lecturer by anti-slavery societies.

He became known as one of the most eloquent anti-slavery orators of his day. In 1845 he published the *Narrative of the Life of Frederick Douglass, an American Slave*, which was circulated widely and soon translated into a number of languages. Fearing capture as a fugitive, he spent two years in England and Ireland, where he continued to lecture. He returned to the US to purchase his freedom, and in 1847 established an anti-slavery journal in Rochester, New York. This journal, *The North Star* (1847–64), later called *Frederick Douglass' Paper*, advocated political methods of emancipation, in opposition to the policies of **William Lloyd Garrison**. In 1858 he founded a second journal, *Douglass' Monthly*, which continued until 1863. His editorial essays in these publications comprise a substantial portion of his writing.

Douglass's position as a leading spokesman against slavery was strengthened by the appearance of his enlarged autobiography, *My Bondage and My Freedom* (1855). His influence in American political life at this time was considerable, and he was in personal contact with figures such as Abraham Lincoln and, later, Andrew Johnson. During the Civil War he organized two black regiments for the Union. Afterwards, he served as secretary of the Santo Domingo Commission (1871), and marshal of the district of Columbia (1877–81). In 1881, he published his third autobiographical work, *The Life and Times of Frederick Douglass*, a central text of the slave narrative tradition and of American autobiography in general. He continued in public service late in life as recorder of deeds for the District of Columbia (1881–6), and as US minister to Haiti (1889–91).

Drake, Joseph Rodman 1795–1820 Born in New York City, Drake studied medicine and then ran a drugstore for a year until his death of consumption at the age of 25. He is best remembered as the co-author, with **Fitz-Greene Halleck**, of satirical verses on current affairs called *The Croaker Papers*. Collected and published as a volume in 1860, they originally appeared in the New York *Evening Post* and the *National Advertiser* from 1819 onwards. On his deathbed Drake asked his wife to destroy the manuscripts of his "trifles in verse," but she preserved them and a selection was published in 1835 in *The Culprit Fay and Other Poems*.

Dream Songs, The An open-ended sequence of poems by **John Berryman**, first published in its entirety in 1969 and made up of two earlier volumes entitled *77 Dream Songs* (1964) and *His Toy, His Dream, His Rest* (1968). Through the dreams of a character called Henry, Berryman presents a meditation on American literary and cultural history. Several of the "songs" are dedicated to Berryman's contemporaries, including **John Crowe Ransom, Saul Bellow,**

Robert Lowell, and **Adrienne Rich**. Many of the details of Henry's character and life reflect those of Berryman himself, including the profound impact of a father's suicide and the difficulties of overcoming alcoholism.

Dreiser, Theodore (Herman Albert) 1871–1945 Novelist, known for his naturalistic portrayal of the tragic conditions of early-20th-century life in the US. Dreiser was born in Terre Haute, Indiana, the ninth child of German-speaking parents. The poverty of his childhood and the harsh bigotry of his father are reflected in his fiction. He briefly attended Indiana University, and then obtained a job on the *Chicago Globe* as a reporter. He also worked in St Louis and Pittsburgh before arriving in New York City in 1894.

His first novel, *Sister Carrie* (1900), was accepted by **Frank Norris** for Doubleday Page & Co., but Mrs Doubleday objected to its realistic style and subject matter, and interfered with its publication, with the result that it was not widely distributed. Continuing to work as a journalist, Dreiser managed to earn a fairly comfortable living as an editor for Butterick, a company specializing in women's magazines, and ten years passed before the publication of his next novel, *Jennie Gerhardt* (1911). Like *Sister Carrie*, which was reissued in 1912, this new novel was attacked for its candid depiction of American life and for its unconventional subject matter. *The Financier* (1912) and *The Titan* (1914) were the first two novels of Dreiser's "Cowperwood" trilogy based on the life of the business magnate, Charles T. Yerkes. (The trilogy was completed with the posthumous publication of *The Stoic* in 1947.) In 1915 he published *The Genius*, a partly autobiographical novel examining the artistic temperament, but popular acclaim came only with the publication of *An American Tragedy* (1925), which was based on the Chester Gillette–Grace Brown murder case of 1906. Another novel, *The Bulwark*, was published in 1946, the year after he died.

Apart from his novels, Dreiser wrote an account of a visit to the Soviet Union, *Dreiser Looks at Russia* (1928), and gave further expression to his growing hopes for socialism in *Tragic America* (1931) and *America is Worth Saving* (1941). He also published *Plays of the Natural and Supernatural* (1916), the tragedy *The Hand of the Potter* (1918), and books of verse, short stories, essays, and autobiography. *Twelve Men* (1919) contains a portrait of his brother, Paul Dreiser, who became a well-known song writer. In 1959 a three-volume edition of *Letters* was published; *Theodore Dreiser: A Selection of Uncollected Prose* appeared in 1977. Several volumes based on his unpublished manuscripts have appeared in recent years, including *Notes on Life* (1974), *American Diaries 1902–1926* (1983), and *An Amateur Laborer* (1983).

Du Bois, W[illiam] E[dward] B[urghardt] *c.*1868–1963 The black historian, sociologist, poet, novelist, and editor was born in Great Barrington, Massachusetts. He was educated at Fisk University and at Harvard, where he received his PhD in 1895. His doctoral dissertation on the suppression of the African slave trade became the first volume in the Harvard Historical series.

Du Bois taught economics and history at Atlanta University from 1896 to 1910 and soon became famous for his studies of the status of black people in the US: *John Brown* (1909), *The Negro* (1915), *The Gift of Black Folk* (1924), and *Black Reconstruction* (1935). Sketches and verses about the life of blacks make up *The Souls of Black Folk* (1903) and *Darkwater* (1920). *Color and Democracy: Colonies and Peace* (1945) argues for the rights of small nations and rejects all aspects of imperialism. He also wrote a novel, *Dark Princess* (1928), about a black man who becomes involved in a struggle to unify the "dark peoples" of the world. With Guy Benton Johnson he co-edited the *Encyclopedia of the Negro* (1945). The autobiographical *Dusk of Dawn* (1940) was, he declared, "the autobiography of a concept of race." For 24 years he edited the magazine *Crisis*.

Politics played a large part in Du Bois's life. He was a radical leader in the first decade of the century, demanding full and immediate rights for his race; in this he was in sharp disagreement with **Booker T. Washington**, who advocated gradual development and careful training. He left Atlanta University to help found the National Association for the Advancement of Colored People, but later became impatient with the association's moderation. In 1949 he became director of the

Peace Information Center in New York, and in 1961, at the age of 93, joined the Communist party. He died in Ghana where, as editor of *Encyclopedia Africana*, he had gone to live in 1961. He became a Ghanaian citizen in the year of his death.

Dunbar, Paul (Laurence) 1872–1906   A black poet and novelist, Dunbar was born in Dayton, Ohio, the son of former slaves. He was educated in the public school system, and began writing poetry while working as an elevator operator. His first collection of verse, *Oak and Ivy*, was printed privately in 1893, and was followed by *Majors and Minors* in 1895. **William Dean Howells** became interested in his work and wrote the preface to a third volume, *Lyrics of Lowly Life* (1896). Dunbar soon received national recognition and embarked on a number of lecture tours.

Known in his day primarily as a writer of dialect verse, he has been severely criticized for his nostalgic and sentimental depiction of black life in the South. He himself, however, was dissatisfied with the limited basis of his reputation, and in some of his works he reveals a concern with the troubled social climate of his times. His other collections of poetry include *Lyrics of the Hearthside* (1899), *Lyrics of Love and Laughter* (1903), and *Lyrics of Sunshine and Shadow* (1905). He wrote four novels: *The Uncalled* (1898), *The Love of Landry* (1900), *The Fanatics* (1901), and *The Sport of the Gods* (1902).

Duncan, Robert (Edward) 1919–   Born in Oakland, California, Duncan was orphaned shortly after birth and adopted by Edward Symmes, who named him Robert Edward Symmes. In 1941 he took the name Robert Duncan.

Following his education at the University of California at Berkeley, he began a career as a poet, publishing verse in *Phoenix* and serving as co-editor of *Experimental Review* between 1940 and 1941. His first volume of poetry, *Heavenly City, Earthly City*, was published in 1947. Following the publication of *Medieval Scenes* (1950), *Poems 1948–49* (1950), and *The Song of the Border-Guard* (1951), Duncan taught at Black Mountain College (1956–7) and became associated with the **Black Mountain School** poets. Mysticism and frequent allusion to major literary figures – Dante in particular – which had been hinted at in his earlier work, emerged as the mark of his later writing: *Caesar's Gate: Poems 1949–1950* (1956), *Letters* (1958), *Selected Poems 1942–50* (1959), *The Opening of the Field* (1960), *Roots and Branches* (1964), and *Bending the Bow* (1968). After a self-imposed silence of 15 years, he published *Ground Work: Before the War* in 1984.

Dunlap, William 1766–1839   One of the earliest American playwrights, and the first to make the theatre his profession, Dunlap was born in Perth Amboy, New Jersey. He studied painting in New York and then in London under Benjamin West (1784–6), but abandoned art for the theatre soon after his return to the US. His democratic patriotism is evident in the first of his plays to be produced, *The Father; or, American Shandyism* (1789), and in the military tragedy *André* (1798), which concerns an incident in the Revolutionary War. Dunlap wrote over 65 plays, many of them adaptations from foreign works, particularly the fashionably shocking dramas of the German August von Kotzebue. In 1805 he turned to management but was plagued by financial problems. He left the theatre in 1811, and from 1816 until his death resumed his interrupted career as a painter. His advocacy of native art is voluminously represented in *A History of the American Theatre* (1832) and *A History of the Rise and Progress of the Arts of Design in the United States* (1834).

Dunne, Finley Peter 1867–1936   Born in Chicago, Dunne is best known as the creator of Mr Dooley, a Chicago-Irish barman, who first appeared in *Mr Dooley in Peace and in War* (1898), and whose comments on the events of the day were often in the form of asides to his colleague, Malachi Hennesey. The last of several collections was *Mr Dooley on Making a Will and Other Necessary Evils* (1919).

Dutchman   A one-act play by **Amiri Baraka** first performed in 1964 when the author was still known as LeRoi Jones, *Dutchman* had a successful first New York run of 366 performances and drew attention to the growth of a black American theatre. It won the Obie Award for the best American play of the 1963–4 season.

Set in the New York subway in summer, the play depicts the fatal encounter of Lula, a provocative white woman, and Clay, a somewhat naïve, middle-class black man. Their initially flirtatious conversation becomes more antagonistic as Lula taunts Clay for playing the role which the dominant white society has handed him. He finally responds to her with all the force of the racial hatred that he has suppressed in order to survive, claiming that for the black man repression and conformity are necessary because murder is the only alternative. Furious at losing control of the situation, Lula fatally stabs him and orders the other subway riders to remove his body. As they are doing so, another young black man enters the subway car and Lula begins her act again. The constant references to Adam and Eve, fairy tales, and the Flying Dutchman, as well as the physical setting of the play, make it a more mythic than realistic representation.

Dwight, Timothy 1752–1817 One of the founding members of the **Connecticut Wits** and the grandson of **Jonathan Edwards**, Dwight was born in Massachusetts and matriculated at Yale at the age of 13. At 19 he was made tutor, a position which he filled with such zeal that he suffered a nervous breakdown at 25. To aid his recuperation he undertook extensive walking and horseback journeys, which provided the material for his *Travels in New England and New York* (4 vols., 1821–2).

He eventually returned to Yale, where he and his friend **John Trumbull** promoted the study of contemporary English and American literature, an endeavor which led to the formation of the group known as the Connecticut Wits. During the Revolutionary War he served as an army chaplain and in 1783 became pastor of the Congregational church at Greenfield Hill, Connecticut. While serving there, he wrote his most widely read poems, which attempt to inculcate Calvinist and Federalist values: *The Conquest of Canaan* (1785), *Greenfield Hill* (1794), and *The Triumph of Infidelity* (1788). In 1795 he became president of Yale, in which capacity he successfully advocated the enlargement of the curriculum and published a number of statements of his political views, among them *The True Means of Establishing Public Happiness* (1795) and *The Duty of Americans, at the Present Crisis* (1798). *Theology, Explained and Defended* (1818–19), a five-volume collection of 173 sermons, makes a complete statement of his theology.

E

Eastman, Charles (Alexander) 1858–1939 Born of mixed Santee Sioux and white parentage, Eastman was the best-known Native American writer of the early 20th century. His father, Jacob Eastman, was imprisoned for his involvement in the 1862 Minnesota Sioux uprising, and after his release in 1873 he insisted on removing Charles from their traditional tribal life, and sent him to school. He received his BA from Dartmouth in 1887 and his MD from Boston University Medical School in 1890. He treated the victims of the Wounded Knee Massacre in 1890, and that same year married Elaine Goodale, with whom he collaborated on all his books (though only *Wigwam Evenings* bears both their names). Between 1890 and 1910 he held a number of positions connected with the Bureau of Indian Affairs; he also lectured in America and England, meeting many of the great literary and political figures of his day.

Through his writings Eastman attempted to bridge the gap between Indian and white cultures by describing the life, customs, and legends of his people for a primarily white audience. Four of his books were for children: *Indian Boyhood* (1902), *Red Hunters and the Animal People* (1904), *Old Indian Days* (1907), and *Wigwam Evenings: Sioux Folktales Retold* (1909). In *The Soul of the Indian: An Interpretation* (1911) he describes the Indian system of ethics and Indian attitudes toward nature. *The Indian To-day: The Past and Future of the First Americans* (1915) is an overview of Indian history. *From the Deep Woods to Civilization: Chapters in the Autobiography of an Indian* appeared in 1916. *Indian Heroes and Great Chieftains* (1918) is a collection of short biographies of Sioux leaders.

Eastman, Max 1883–1969 A critic, poet, and essayist from New York City, Eastman came to prominence as the author of *Enjoyment of Poetry* (1913), a critical study which is still his best-known work. He co-founded and edited the left-wing magazines *The Masses* (1913–17) and *The Liberator* (1918–22), and later published *Marx, Lenin, and The Science of Revolution* (1926) and a translation of Trotsky's *History of The Russian Revolution* (3 vols., 1932–3). With the rise of Stalin, however, he turned against the Left, publishing *Artists in Uniform: A Study of Literature and Bureaucratism* (1934), a collection of literary and political essays; *Marxism, Is It Science?* (1940); and *Reflections on the Failure of Socialism* (1955). From 1941 to his death he was an editor for *Reader's Digest*. His memoirs of famous friends, including Eugene Debs, Isadora Duncan, Anatole France, Charlie Chaplin, John Reed, and Leon Trotsky, appeared in *Heroes I Have Known* (1942) and *Great Companions* (1959). His collected poems were published as *Poems of Five Decades* (1954), and his autobiography as *Love and Revolution* (1964).

East of Eden See **Steinbeck, John**

Eberhart, Richard 1904– Born in Minnesota and educated at Harvard, Eberhart has been poet-in-residence at several universities. He has published almost 30 volumes of poetry: the first, *A Bravery of Earth*, appeared in 1930; the most recent, *The Long Reach: New and Uncollected Poems 1948–1984*, in 1984. Among his other volumes are *Reading the Spirit* (1936), *Poems New and Selected* (1944), *Undercliff: Poems 1946–1956* (1956), *The Quarry* (1960), *Selected Poems 1930–1965* (1965; Pulitzer Prize 1966), *Fields of Grace* (1972), and *Collected Poems 1930–1976* (1976; National Book Award 1977). His poetry tends to be contemplative and lyrical. His themes, often expressed in a philosophical idiom, range from confrontations with death to meditations inspired by scenes in nature. Many of his poems, especially those of his later years, are concerned with the nature of the poetic process itself. He is also a playwright; his *Collected Verse Plays* appeared in 1962.

Edgar Huntly See **Brown, Charles Brockden**

Education of Henry Adams, The The autobiography of **Henry Brooks Adams**, privately printed in 1907 and published in 1918. Among other things, Adams describes his experience as both student and teacher at Harvard, his impressions of England during the years of the American Civil War, and the impact on him of Charles Darwin's theories, but he notably omits his marriage and his wife's suicide. Subtitled *A Study of Twentieth-Century Multiplicity*, the book illustrates Adams's "dynamic theory of history" by contrasting the dynamo, the symbol of the accelerating forces of modern life, with the Virgin, the symbol of the 12th century and the subject of his earlier book, **Mont-Saint-Michel and Chartres** (1904).

Edwards, Jonathan 1703–58 The Puritan minister and religious philosopher, known for his role in the Great Awakening in New England, was born in East Windsor, Connecticut, and entered Yale when he was 12 years old. There he studied Calvinist theology as well as the works of Locke and Newton. His writings throughout his life reflect his synthesis of these systems of thought into one harmonious outlook. His youthful essays, including "Of Insects" and "Of Being," already evince some familiarity with these ideas, as well as show a characteristically close observation of nature. His lifelong collection of notebook entries on natural phenomena together with speculations on their spiritual significance were published in the 20th century as *Images and Shadows of Divine Things* (1948).

In 1727 Edwards was ordained minister of the Northampton, Massachusetts, church where he served jointly with his grandfather, **Solomon Stoddard**, until Stoddard's death in 1729. His early sermons include *God Glorified in the Work of Redemption* (1731) and *A Divine and Supernatural Light* (1734), the latter

notable for its emphasis on the aesthetic dimension of religious experience. His preaching helped precipitate the religious revival that swept through western Massachusetts in 1734–5, and later contributed to the Great Awakening (1740), which spread through the colonies in general (see **Sinners in the Hands of an Angry God**). These awakenings prompted Edwards to reflect on the nature of religious experience. His *Faithful Narrative of Surprising Conversions* (1737) and *The Distinguishing Marks* (1741) describe and defend the 1735 revival and the Great Awakening, respectively. *Some Thoughts Concerning the Present Revival* (1743) speculates on the millennial possibilities raised by the Awakening. *A Treatise Concerning Religious Affections* (1746) is his systematic exposition of his understanding of religious psychology, while his diary and *Personal Narrative* (*c.*1740, not intended for publication) tell the story of his own conversion.

Edwards had reversed Stoddard's open communion policy, requiring from communicants in his congregation the older, orthodox practice of a statement of religious conversion rather than mere good behavior. Because of this policy, his Northampton congregation dismissed him in 1750. His *Farewell Sermon* (1750) explains his ideas about the mutual obligations of minister and congregation. He then went to Stockbridge, where he ministered to an Indian mission. During this period he wrote *Freedom of the Will* (published 1754), *The Great Christian Doctrine of Original Sin Defended* (published 1758), *The Nature of True Virtue* (published 1765), and *The Great End for Which God Created the World* (published 1765), works of religious philosophy which expand on his conception of religious experience. Fusing an orthodox Calvinism with Lockean psychology and Newtonian physics, he explains religious conversion in 18th-century rationalist terms as the "cordial consent to 'Being in General.'" In 1757 he was appointed president of the College of New Jersey (later Princeton University), but died from a smallpox innoculation soon after taking office. At the time of his death he was working on his systematic sacred history, *The History of the Work of Redemption*, based on his 1739 series of sermons. The series was published in 1774 and held an important place in American millennial thought.

Eggleston, Edward 1837–1902 Born into a strict Methodist family in rural Indiana, Edward and his brother **George Eggleston** were educated in back-country schools. Edward had a busy career as a Bible agent and then as a Methodist minister on circuit; he also wrote and edited juvenile magazines as an extension of his Sunday-school teaching. He was 37 when he abandoned Methodism and went to New York City, where he founded a Church of Christian Endeavor in Brooklyn. He remained its pastor for five years, then in 1879 retired to devote himself to writing, for which he had already achieved some distinction.

His first success, and the novel for which he is best known, was *The Hoosier Schoolmaster* (1871), a realistic if somewhat pious presentation of rural life in Indiana which made excellent use of local dialect. His next novels were also set in the Midwest during the period of the country's expansion: *The End of the World* (1872, set in Indiana), *The Mystery of Metropolisville* (1873, set in Minnesota), *The Circuit Rider* (1874, set in Ohio), and *Roxy* (1878, set in Indiana).

For a brief period Eggleston devoted his attention to writing history and biography, an enterprise which produced several works, among which the uncompleted *History of Life in the United States* (1888) is the most memorable. Before his death he wrote three more novels: *The Hoosier Schoolboy* (1883), a boy's view of the life described in *The Hoosier Schoolmaster*; *The Graysons: A Story of Illinois* (1888), based on Abraham Lincoln's days as a lawyer in Springfield, Illinois, when he successfully defended a man accused of murder; and *The Faith Doctor* (1891), a satirical view of the wealthy devotees of the then-new Christian Science movement.

Eggleston, George Cary 1839–1911 The younger brother of **Edward Eggleston**, George became a teacher in back-country Indiana at the age of 16. His experiences provided his brother with the material for two novels, *The Hoosier Schoolmaster* (1871) and *The Hoosier Schoolboy* (1883). After serving in the Confederate army during the Civil War, George practiced law for a time before becoming a journalist. He served as editor of the New York *Evening Post* and worked for Joseph Pulitzer on the New York *World* for 11 years. He also wrote a number of books for boys, and several novels set in the South, including *A Man of Honour* (1873), *Dorothy South* (1902), *The Master of Warlock* (1903), and *Evelyn Byrd* (1904). With Dorothy Marbourg he co-wrote the novel *Juggernaut* (1891), which is set in Indiana. His autobiographical volume, *A Rebel's Recollections*, based on his experiences during the Civil War, appeared in 1874.

Eliot, John 1604–90 An English Puritan, Eliot received his BA from Cambridge University in 1622. He assisted the non-conformist minister – and later American immigrant – **Thomas Hooker** at his school in Chelmsford, Essex, and himself emigrated to Massachusetts in 1631. He served the church at Boston for a short time, but in 1632 became minister at the church in Roxbury, where many of his old non-conformist acquaintances from England had settled. Now prominent among the Bay Puritans, he contributed, along with several other New England ministers, to the English translations in the *Bay Psalm Book* (1640).

Over the next decade he learned the language of the Massachusetts Indians and began attempts to Christianize them. His missionary efforts received some support from the Massachusetts General Court, and in 1651 he established the first of a series of "praying Indian Towns," at Natick. His pamphlet *The Christian Commonwealth*, written in 1649 and published in 1659, set forth his notions for the governance of these Indian communities. He also compiled a primer to teach the Indians to read, and translated the Bible into the Algonkian dialect. The first edition of his Algonkian New Testament was printed at Cambridge, Massachusetts, in 1661, and the Old Testament in 1663. A second edition appeared in the 1680s as part of Eliot's effort to rebuild his missionary activities after the devastating effects of King Philip's War (1674–6). Known as the "Apostle to the Indians," Eliot was a venerable figure in the Massachusetts Bay community at the time of his death. A youthful **Cotton Mather**, who knew him in his old age, memorialized him in a biography included in the *Magnalia Christi Americana*.

Eliot, T[homas] S[tearns] 1888–1965 Eliot came from a Unitarian family with ties to Massachusetts, but he was born and brought up in St Louis, Missouri. His family encouraged his interest in poetry and gave him a thorough training in the classics before sending him to Harvard in 1906. **George Santayana** and **Irving Babbitt** were among his teachers there, and the latter in particular influenced his ideas about the dynamic relationship between the past and the present, as well as his bias against Romanticism. At Harvard he also became interested in Dante, Jules Laforgue, and the French Symbolists. His formal studies were in philosophy, and after obtaining his BA and MA he wrote a doctoral dissertation on the English philosopher F. H. Bradley but chose not to take the degree. The dissertation was eventually published in 1965.

In 1914 Eliot went to Europe, and after studying in Germany, Paris, and at Merton College, Oxford, settled in London. He taught at Highgate School for a time, reviewed books for *The Times Literary Supplement* and other journals, and worked at Lloyds Bank from 1919 to 1922. In 1923, after a short term as assistant editor of *The Egoist*, he became editor of a newly founded quarterly review called *The Criterion*; he remained with the magazine until it ceased publication in 1939, and served also as a director of Faber and Faber, its publisher. In 1927 he joined the Church of England and became a British citizen.

Meanwhile he had begun publishing poetry. "The Love Song of J. Alfred Prufrock," written while he was at Harvard, appeared in 1915 in **Poetry** magazine (Chicago) and in 1917 was collected in his first volume, *Prufrock and Other Observations*. This was followed by *Ara vos prec* (1920), which contained "Gerontion." His next major work was **The Waste Land**, on which he received extensive editorial help from Ezra Pound; the poem was published in the first number of *The Criterion* in 1922 and was dedicated to Pound. In 1925 he published *Poems 1909–1925*, which includes "The Hollow Men"; and in 1936 *Collected Poems 1909–1935*, which includes "The Journey of the Magi" and "Ash Wednesday." *Old Possum's Book of Practical Cats*, his collection of humorous poems for children, appeared in 1939. In 1943 he published **Four Quartets**, comprised of "Burnt Norton" (1935), "East Coker"

(1940), "The Dry Salvages" (1941), and "Little Gidding" (1942). *Collected Poems 1909–1962* was published in 1963.

Eliot also wrote verse dramas, which enjoyed a degree of popular success in the 1950s. Most of them, like *Four Quartets*, deal with religious themes. The first play, *The Rock*, appeared in 1934 and was followed by *Murder in the Cathedral* (1935), *The Family Reunion* (1939), *The Cocktail Party* (1950), *The Confidential Clerk* (1954), and *The Elder Statesman* (1959). His first collection of critical essays was *The Sacred Wood* (1920), which reprinted contributions to periodicals and included the influential "Tradition and the Individual Talent." *Homage to John Dryden* (1924) contained his essays on Marvell and the Metaphysical Poets. His next volume, *For Lancelot Andrewes: Essays on Style and Order* (1928), reflects his Anglo-Catholic interests. *Selected Essays 1917–1932* (1932, enlarged 1934 and 1951) contains more literary criticism, including "Hamlet and His Problem" (the exposition of the "objective correlative"). His lectures delivered at Harvard are collected in *The Use of Poetry and the Use of Criticism* (1933). Other critical collections include *After Strange Gods* (1934), *Notes towards a Definition of Culture (1948)*, *On Poetry and Poets* (1957), and *To Criticize the Critic* (1965). A volume of *Selected Prose* appeared in 1975. Among the awards and honors Eliot received were the Nobel Prize for literature and the Order of Merit, both awarded in 1948.

Elkin, Stanley (Lawrence) 1930–   Elkin was born in New York City and educated at the University of Illinois, from which he received a BA in 1952, an MA in 1953, and a PhD in 1961. He served in the US Army from 1957 to 1959. He has taught at several universities; since 1968 he has been on the faculty of the University of Washington.

His novels tend to explore the nature of evil, frequently through a comic examination of both ordinary and extraordinary situations. His first novel, *Boswell* (1964), traces its protagonist's struggle to satisfy the needs of his ego, which culminates in a wrestling match with the Grim Reaper. His second novel, *A Bad Man* (1968), treats a salesman's compulsion to make "the ultimate sale" regardless of its consequences. Other novels include *The*

Dick Gibson Show (1971), *The Franchiser* (1976), *The Living End* (1980), and *The Magic Kingdom* (1985). Elkin has also published short stories in *Criers and Kibitzers, Kibitzers and Criers* (1966) and *The Making of Ashendon* (1972). His collection of novellas, *Searches and Seizures* (1973), has been published in England under two different titles: *Eligible Men* (1974) and *Alex and the Gypsy* (1977). *Stanley Elkin's Greatest Hits*, an omnibus collection, appeared in 1980.

Ellison, Ralph (Waldo) 1914–   Born in Oklahoma City, Ellison attended Tuskegee Institute in Alabama (1933–6), where he studied music and became an accomplished trumpet player. He then moved to New York City to study sculpture, and soon began writing book reviews, essays, and short stories, encouraged by **Richard Wright**. In 1942 he helped to found and edit the magazine *Negro Quarterly*, which had a short run.

After World War II he worked for seven years on the novel that made him famous, *Invisible Man* (1952). This semi-autobiographical account of a black man's gradual self-discovery remains Ellison's only major work of fiction to date. For over two decades he has reportedly been working on a second novel, parts of which have been published, including one entitled "And Hickman Arrives." His short stories have never been collected, though several are widely anthologized, among them "Flying Home" and "King of the Bingo Game." He has, however, collected nearly two dozen of his many essays on black music, literature, and American culture in *Shadow and Act* (1964).

Ellison's reputation as the most important literary heir to Richard Wright – matched only by that of **James Baldwin** – remains strong. *Invisible Man* was attacked by the radical left in the 1950s and by black nationalists in the 1960s, but it has weathered critical controversy and remains one of the central texts of the 20th-century Afro-American experience.

Elmer Gantry   See **Lewis, Sinclair**

Elsie Venner: A Romance of Destiny   A novel by **Oliver Wendell Holmes**, published serially in *The Atlantic Monthly* (as *The Professor's Story*, January 1860–April 1861), and as a volume in 1861. In it Holmes sought to "test the doctrine of 'original sin,'" to ques-

tion the belief that holds individuals responsible for antenatal influences upon them.

Elsie Venner, whose mother was bitten by a rattlesnake three weeks before Elsie's birth, has been infected with the venom and now exhibits peculiar, snake-like qualities: her eyes glitter; she is wild, seemingly insane; she both fascinates and frightens those around her. The professor in the story is a professor of medicine who becomes interested in Elsie's abnormal behavior after he is told of her by Bernard Langdon, one of his students who has temporarily taken a job as a teacher at the school Elsie attends. Elsie falls in love with Bernard; she even saves his life, exerting her snake-like powers to enchant a rattlesnake that is about to strike and kill him. But he does not love her. Rejected by him, Elsie falls ill and, gradually losing her snake-like strangeness, dies. Helen Darley, a schoolteacher whose sympathy is stirred by the strange, motherless girl, attends her to the end. Old Sophy, a faithful servant, dies only days after Elsie, and at *her* death an earthquake buries Rattlesnake Ledge with all its poisonous snakes.

Emerson, Ralph Waldo 1803–82 The prominent essayist, philosopher, and poet was the son of William Emerson, the minister of the First Unitarian Church of his native Boston. After completing his education at Harvard, Emerson himself became a minister in 1829. The orthodoxy of Unitarianism, however, though far removed from the original Calvinism of New England, was something he could not accept. Shortly after the death of his first wife, Ellen Tucker, he became involved in a controversy with his congregation over a sermon on the Lord's Supper. He resigned his ministry and sailed to Europe in 1832, his mind disturbed by personal grief and religious confusion. During the year he spent in Europe, he met Samuel Taylor Coleridge and William Wordsworth, and commenced a lifelong friendship with Thomas Carlyle.

Contact with European thought stimulated his interest and wide reading in religion and philosophy, and back in Boston he drifted away from preaching into the broader field of lecturing. With the growth of the lyceum movement in the Northeast and Middle West in the early 1830s, he found that he could command large audiences who came to hear him expound his natural philosophy. He drew much of his lecture material from his personal journals, which he had begun in 1820 and continued throughout his life. In 1835 he married Lydia Jackson and moved to Concord, Massachusetts, where his ancestors had first settled in the New World and where **Transcendentalism** took form. He became part of the circle which included **Nathaniel Hawthorne**, **Bronson Alcott**, **Henry David Thoreau**, and **Margaret Fuller**.

Emerson's first book, *Nature*, was published in 1836; *The American Scholar*, an oration in which he applied Transcendentalist views to national and cultural questions, followed in 1837. His assertion that human thought and action proceed from Nature was a radical departure from tradition; **Oliver Wendell Holmes** referred to his philosophical position as an "intellectual declaration of independence." In 1838 he delivered the "Divinity School Address" at Harvard. The statement of his belief that the individual's intuitive spiritual experience was of more importance than any formal church ensured his exclusion from that university for almost 30 years. In 1840 he became involved in the publication of the Transcendentalist quarterly magazine, *The Dial*, and two years later became its editor. His reputation, already considerable in the US, became firmly established in Europe, too, with the publication of two volumes of essays in 1841 and 1844. He earned further distinction as a poet with his first collection, *Poems* (1847), and later with *May-Day and Other Pieces* (1867).

He went to England in 1847 and lectured in Oxford and London, where he renewed his friendship with Carlyle and met other English intellectuals. The lectures were published under the title *Representative Men* (1850). *English Traits* (1856) contains his observations on the English character. During this period, as his journals show, he became deeply interested in the issue of slavery and saw its abolition as a matter of paramount importance. Two further volumes of his lectures were published as *The Conduct of Life* (1860) and *Society and Solitude* (1870). In 1866 Harvard conferred on him the degree of Doctor of Law. Edward Waldo Emerson edited his father's *Complete Works* (12 vols., 1903–4) and his *Journals* (10 vols., 1909–14). His *Letters* were edited by R. L. Rusk and published in six volumes in 1939.

Emigrants, The   See **Imlay, Gilbert**

Emperor Jones, The   A play in eight scenes by **Eugene O'Neill**, produced by the Provincetown players in 1920 and published in 1921. It is an early example of O'Neill's symbolic expressionism and of his progressively more experimental use of dramatic devices. Brutus Jones, a black man who has escaped from an American prison, becomes the emperor of a West Indian island. When he learns from his cockney major-domo, Henry Smithers, that his subjects have rebelled, he boasts that he can escape through the forest. He has stored money and food in various places, foreseeing that his reign would be short, and created the legend that he can be killed only by a silver bullet. The reduction of the proud bully to a terrified savage as he is hunted down to the relentless beating of native drums is a theatrical *tour de force*.

Ethan Frome   A novel by **Edith Wharton**, published in 1911. On a poor farm in western Massachusetts Ethan Frome struggles to wrest a living from the soil. His slatternly wife Zeena (Zenobia) is a whining hypochondriac and spends much of Ethan's hard-earned money on quack remedies. Her cousin, Mattie Silver, is left destitute when her parents die and the farm is the only place she can go. Ethan and Mattie are attracted to each other and Zeena's jealousy is aroused. After a year Zeena drives Mattie off the farm to make way for a hired woman, and Ethan takes her to the railroad station through the snow. Realizing that he cannot bear to part from her, he causes an accident that he hopes will kill them, but the pair survive the crash and spend the remainder of their lives as invalids under the care of Zeena.

Europeans, The   A novel by **Henry James**, published serially in *The Atlantic Monthly* (July–October 1878), and as a volume, in slightly revised form, later that same year.

Felix Young, an artist, and his sister Eugenia, the wife of a German nobleman who is about to renounce her for reasons of state, come from Europe to Massachusetts to visit their relatives, the Wentworths. Though concerned about the "peculiar influence" these European cousins may exert on his family, the elder Wentworth establishes Felix and Eugenia in a nearby house. Relations between the cousins become friendly. Wentworth's daughter Gertrude falls in love with Felix, and he with her; his son Clifford becomes infatuated with Eugenia, who is looking for a wealthy husband and welcomes his attentions. Gertrude, however, already has an "understanding" with Mr Brand, the Unitarian minister. Although she does not in fact care for Mr Brand, her sister Charlotte does. Robert and Lizzie Acton further complicate matters: Robert is drawn – but not unreservedly – to Eugenia; Lizzie hopes to win Clifford Wentworth.

At the end of the novel, Mr Wentworth consents to the marriage of Felix and Gertrude; Clifford, having overcome his infatuation for Eugenia, marries Lizzie Acton; Mr Brand discovers that he cares not for Gertrude but for Charlotte, and marries her. Robert Acton and Eugenia do not, however, make a fourth happy couple. Though attracted to her, Acton cannot overcome his scruples about her past and about the calculating way in which she uses her feminine wiles. Eugenia returns to Europe alone.

Evangeline, A Tale of Acadie   A narrative poem by **Henry Wadsworth Longfellow**, published in 1847, and set in Acadia, a province of Canada roughly corresponding to present-day Nova Scotia. Composed in unrhymed hexameter, the poem recounts the frustrated love story of Evangeline Bellefontaine and Gabriel Lajeunesse, whom the French and Indian Wars have separated. Gabriel and his father, a blacksmith, make their way to Louisiana. Evangeline follows them and eventually finds Gabriel's father, but he has become separated from his son. Together they fruitlessly search for Gabriel. After many years, Evangeline, prematurely aged, becomes a Sister of Mercy in Philadelphia. During a pestilence there she recognizes a dying old man as her lover. She dies of grief, and they are buried together.

Executioner's Song, The   See **Mailer, Norman**

F

Fable for Critics, A A verse satire by **James Russell Lowell**, first published anonymously in 1848. At a gathering on Olympus a critic is asked by Apollo to give an account of the state of letters in America. Those who come under his review are **Oliver Wendell Holmes, Ralph Waldo Emerson, Bronson Alcott, Henry Wadsworth Longfellow, William Cullen Bryant, Margaret Fuller, Washington Irving, John Greenleaf Whittier, Edgar Allan Poe, Nathaniel Hawthorne**, and Lowell himself. Among the most acute of the critical portraits are those of Emerson ("A Greek head on right Yankee shoulders, whose range / Has Olympus for one pole, for t'other the Exchange"), Hawthorne ("There is Hawthorne, with genius so shrinking and rare / That you hardly at first see the strength that is there"), and Poe ("There comes Poe, with his raven, like Barnaby Rudge, / Three fifths of him genius and two fifths sheer fudge").

Farewell To Arms, A A novel by **Ernest Hemingway**, published in 1929. Set mainly in war-torn Italy of 1917–18, the story focuses on Frederic Henry, an American ambulance driver for the Italian Army. He meets a young English nurse, Catherine Barkley, at a military hospital and they begin a relationship which gradually becomes passionate. When Frederic is severely wounded in an enemy mortar attack and is sent to Milan for surgery and therapy, Catherine follows him and obtains a nursing position in the hospital where he is being treated. Shortly before he is to return to active duty Catherine informs him that she is pregnant. The two decide not to marry (as their private commitment is deemed bond enough), but look forward to the birth of their first child.

Frederic returns to active duty but, following disastrous engagements with Austrian forces, the Italians are compelled to retreat. Eventually, Frederic deserts and flees to neutral Switzerland with Catherine. In Montreux they enjoy an idyllic autumn and winter, remote from the direct impact of the war. In March 1918 Catherine gives birth, after a difficult labor and emergency surgery, to a stillborn son; she dies from complications soon after the birth. The story of the romance is set alongside a powerful portrayal of the horrors of war and its threat of the total destruction of civilization.

Farrell, James T[homas] 1904–79 Born in Chicago, Farrell was educated at De Pauw and the University of Chicago. In 1931 he went to Paris, and on his return to the US he moved to New York City and became active in left-wing politics. He supported the Communist party from 1932 to 1935, but was one of the first American intellectuals to break with it over the totalitarian character of Stalin's regime.

The work for which he is best known, *The Studs Lonigan Trilogy* began to appear in 1932 with the publication of *Young Lonigan: A Boyhood in Chicago Streets*. Set on the South Side of Chicago, the novel charts the effects of middle-class morality and adult corruption on the young protagonist, the son of an Irish house painter, who soon learns the way of life of the street corner and the pool room. *The Young Manhood of Studs Lonigan* (1934) and *Judgment Day* (1935) continue the story of Studs's violent and dissolute life until his death from a heart attack at the age of 29. The trilogy is a powerful indictment of the American Dream – the belief that it requires only individual initiative to achieve wealth, status, and, above all, happiness – and it registers this indictment through a series of failures: the failure of urban industrialism to provide an adequate moral vision; the failure of the twin mythologies of Church and Nation to sustain an understanding of a hostile world; and the failure of Studs, inculcated with these broken ideals, to develop his potential. Farrell, writing here in the tradition of **Theodore Dreiser** and **Sherwood Anderson**, powerfully describes the ugliness of American urban life and the sadness of blighted human potential.

Farrell's second series of novels was in five volumes: *A World I Never Made* (1936), *No Star is Lost* (1938), *Father and Son* (1940), *My Days of Anger* (1943), and *The Face of Time* (1953). Linked thematically with those of the earlier trilogy, these novels revolve around the contrasted lives of two families, the middle-class O'Flahertys and the working-class O'Neills. A third series, the Bernard Carr trilogy – *Bernard Clare* (1946), *The Road Between* (1949), and *Yet Other Waters* (1952) – chronicles the difficulties faced by radical literary intellectuals after World War II.

Farrell's subsequent work marked a new departure. Though he continued to believe in struggles for freedom, he rejected Marxist-Trotskyite politics. (In the 1950s he became associated with the anti-Communist American Committee for Cultural Freedom, but resigned when he learned that it was funded by the CIA.) The later work reveals a stoicism in sharp contrast with his earlier radicalism. A series from this period, known as *A Universe of Time*, offers an account of an aspiring young writer in the 1920s. Books in the series are *The Silence of History* (1963), *What Time Collects* (1964), *When Time Was Born* (1966), *Lonely for the Future* (1968), *A Brand New Life* (1968), *Judith* (1969), and *Invisible Swords* (1970). Among the other books published by Farrell during his prolific career are *A Note on Literary Criticism* (1936), *Ellen Rogers* (1941), *The League of Frightened Philistines and Other Papers* (1945), *This Man and This Woman* (1951), *An Omnibus of Short Stories* (1956), *Boarding House Blues* (1961), *Selected Essays* (1964), *New Year's Eve/1929* (1967), and *The Dunne Family* (1976).

Fashion A comedy by **Anna Cora Mowatt**, first performed at the Park Theatre in New York City in 1845. Mr and Mrs Tiffany, newly rich, have established themselves in an opulent house in New York, but Mrs Tiffany's remorseless pursuit of fashion outruns her husband's resources. He takes to forgery to cover her expenses, but is discovered and blackmailed by his clerk, Snobson, to whom he is forced to promise his daughter Seraphina, even though her fortune has attracted the affections of Count Jolimaitre. At the last minute Tiffany is saved by his sturdy and honest friend, Adam Trueman, who sees that Snobson is packed off to the remoteness of California and who exposes Jolimaitre as a fraud, the lover of Mrs Tiffany's maid. The play was revived in 1958 in New York.

Fast, Howard 1914– Fast was born in New York City; during the 1940s and 1950s he became known for a series of novels which reflected his left-wing politics. Many of them were set during the American Revolution, and all displayed a strong sense of class consciousness: for example, *Conceived in Liberty* (1930), *The Unvanquished* (1942), *Citizen Tom Paine* (1943), *The Proud and the Free* (1950), and *April Morning* (1961). Other works which focus on particular moments in the history of the US include *The Last Frontier* (1941), about the 1878–79 campaign against the Cheyenne Indians; and *Freedom Road* (1944), dealing with black Southern legislators in the Reconstruction period. *The American* (1946) is about Illinois governor John Peter Altgeld, and *Clarkton* (1947) details the events of a recent strike in a Massachusetts mill town. Fast is also the author of numerous historical novels set in ancient times, including *My Glorious Brothers* (1948), set in ancient Israel; *Spartacus* (1951), about a Roman slave revolt; *Moses, Prince of Egypt* (1958); and *Agrippa's Daughter* (1964). *The Naked God* (1957), a work of non-fiction, tells of Fast's disenchantment with the Communist party during the Stalinist era. His most recent novels include *The Immigrants* (1977), *The Second Generation* (1978), *The Establishment* (1979), *The Outsider* (1984), and *Immigrant's Daughter* (1985). Under the pseudonym E. V. Cunningham he also has written more than a dozen novels of suspense and mystery.

Faulkner, William (Cuthbert) 1897–1962 Faulkner was born in New Albany, Mississippi, into a family which had played a prominent role in the history of the South.

His grandfather had served as a colonel in the Confederate Army, and had come home to pursue a career as a lawyer, politician, railroad builder, and civic benefactor. The strict family code of honor, its sense of white social status, and its often violent exploits would provide a good deal of material for Faulkner's fiction. When he was 5 the family moved to Oxford, Mississippi, which became his permanent home. He left high school in 1915 and took a clerical job at his grandfather's bank. In 1918, after being rejected by the US military because he was too short, he enlisted in the Royal Canadian Air Force, but the war ended while he was still in training, and he returned to Oxford. In 1919 his first published poem, "L'Après-Midi d'un Faune," appeared in *The New Republic*. He then enrolled as a special student at the University of Mississippi, and published poems and drawings in student magazines. His first book, a collection of poems entitled *The Marble Faun*, was published in 1924 with the financial assistance of his friend Phil Stone.

His first novel, *Soldiers' Pay*, was written in New Orleans in 1925 and published in the following year. The story centers on the return of a soldier who has been physically and psychologically disabled in World War I, and whose subsequent illness and death change the lives of his family and friends. Later in 1925 Faulkner left New Orleans and traveled to Europe. While in France he worked on a novel, "Elmer," which he never finished. His second novel, *Mosquitoes* (1927), set in New Orleans, is a satirical tale about a group of Southern artists and intellectuals. His next novel was the first to be set in the fictional Mississippi county of Yoknapatawpha, which was to provide the setting for many of his best-known works. Originally called *Flags in the Dust*, it was rejected for publication but later accepted in an edited version, retitled *Sartoris*, and published in 1929. (The uncut *Flags in the Dust* finally appeared in 1973.)

Faulkner's most productive period began with *The Sound and the Fury* (1929), about another Yoknapatawpha county family, in which he experimented with narrative technique by using multiple points of view. The novel is divided into four sections: one of the Compson brothers narrates each of the first three sections while the fourth is presented by an outside observer who is sympathetic to Dilsey, the family's black servant. Perhaps due to its fragmented, non-chronological structure, it met with only limited success. *As I Lay Dying* (1930) was still more splintered in form, being comprised of 59 monologues by a variety of characters which gradually reveal the intricate ties that bind and frustrate the poor-white Bundren family of Yoknapatawpha county. In an effort to win a popular audience, Faulkner wrote *Sanctuary* (1931), which was in fact an even more controversial work than its predecessors because of its graphic description of a horrific rape. With its more conventional form, however, it sold well amid the scandal it aroused. *Light in August* (1932) differs from his other early novels in that it does not concentrate on a single family, but it involves similar issues of human need, dissatisfaction, crisis, and redemption through endurance. Also set in Yoknapatawpha county, it broadens the social scope of Faulkner's fiction through the attention it pays to the individual's sense of place in a racist society.

In 1929 Faulkner married Estelle Oldham Franklin, and in the following year purchased the traditional pillared house in Oxford which he named Rowan Oak. His fiction, however, enjoyed no more than mediocre sales, and he was frequently in financial straits. To earn money over the next 20 years he worked periodically as a scriptwriter in Hollywood. Among his more notable credits are versions of **Ernest Hemingway**'s *To Have and Have Not* (1945) and **Raymond Chandler**'s *The Big Sleep* (1946). His next novel, *Pylon* (1935), treats another of his strong interests, aviation, focusing on the lives of four adults and a child who travel nomadically from air show to air show to compete in races. He returned to Yoknapatawpha county with *Absalom, Absalom!* (1936), which concerns the frustrated attempts of Thomas Sutpen to found a Southern dynasty in 19th-century Mississippi. Sutpen's story is reconstructed by Quentin Compson, one of the characters in *The Sound and the Fury*, who is obsessed by the way in which the South's guilt in the matter of interracial relationships is embodied in the misfortunes of the Sutpen family.

Following *The Unvanquished* (1938), *The Wild Palms* (1939), and *The Hamlet* (1940) – the first of three novels about the Snopes family –

came *Go Down Moses* (1942), a novel composed of several interrelated stories about Southern blacks. One of these, "The Bear," is among Faulkner's most frequently reprinted pieces. *Intruder in the Dust* (1948) tells the story of Lucas Beauchamp, a black man who is unjustly accused of murder but who is eventually acquitted despite the racial prejudice that permeates society. When Malcolm Cowley edited *The Portable Faulkner* in 1946, he revitalized the author's reputation. Faulkner began to receive widespread attention, and several of his works that had long been out of print were reissued. He was elected to the American Academy of Arts and Letters in 1949, and was awarded the Nobel Prize for literature in the following year. His *Collected Stories* (1950) received a National Book Award in 1951. He began to find himself in demand for lectures and personal appearances at home and abroad, and traveled as far as Tokyo to participate in seminars on his work.

Requiem for a Nun (1951), a sequel to *Sanctuary*, offers a less brutal treatment of sexual themes than its horrifying predecessor. As his Nobel Prize address made clear, Faulkner wanted his new work to be more affirmative, more insistent on the power of humankind to endure and to prevail. The change of tone is reflected in *A Fable* (1954), an allegory of the story of Jesus in a World War I setting which won a Pulitzer Prize in 1955. *The Town* (1957) and *The Mansion* (1959) complete the Snopes family trilogy – a penetrating examination of the social fabric of the South. Faulkner's final novel, *The Reivers* (1962), which also won a Pulitzer Prize, is a mildly comic portrait of some of the characters introduced in his earlier books. He died in the year of its publication in a sanitorium in Byhalia, Mississippi. His other works include *Knight's Gambit* (1949), a collection of detective stories; *Uncollected Stories of William Faulkner* (1979); and a collection of poems originally written for his wife, *Vision in Spring* (1984). This last is one of several books which Faulkner wrote to present as gifts; another is the allegorical story *Mayday* (written 1926, published 1976), about the adventures of a medieval knight. A volume of *Selected Letters* was published in 1977.

Fauset, Jessie R[edmon] 1882–1961 Born in New Jersey and educated at Cornell and the Sorbonne, Fauset was one of the first black women to receive recognition as an intellectual. While editor of **W.E.B. DuBois**'s magazine *Crisis*, she encouraged and published many of the new writers who constituted the **Harlem Renaissance**. She herself wrote four novels, all depicting the experience of black women, and all asserting the need to accept one's heritage rather than to escape it: *There Is Confusion* (1924), *Plum Bun* (1929), *The Chinaberry Tree* (1931), and *Comedy: American Style* (1934).

Fearing, Kenneth (Flexner) 1902–61 Born in Oak Park, Illinois, Fearing received his BA from the University of Wisconsin and then moved to New York City, where he began writing poetry, some of which appeared under pseudonyms (including that of Donald F. Bedford). His first collection, *Angel Arms*, appeared in 1929 and defined the focus of much of his work: an urban and mechanized society lacking in human compassion. Among his other volumes are *Dead Reckoning: A Book of Poetry* (1938), *Afternoon of a Pawnbroker and Other Poems* (1943), *Stranger at Coney Island and Other Poems* (1948), and *New and Selected Poems* (1956). He also wrote several novels, including *The Hospital* (1939) and *The Big Clock* (1946).

Federal Theatre Project Founded in 1935 as a branch of President Franklin Delano Roosevelt's Works Project Administration, the Federal Theatre Project was intended to provide employment for out-of-work actors and theatrical workers, and to create a censorship-free forum for innovative productions. Under the directorship of Hallie Flanagan, the project mounted approximately 1,000 shows in 30 states, varying from children's plays to dance productions to classic plays to a jazz version of Gilbert and Sullivan's *The Mikado* to a Voodoo *Macbeth*. Altogether it employed over 10,000 people, including Will Lee, Estelle Winwood, E. G. Marshall, Burt Lancaster, Orson Welles, John Houseman, and **Langston Hughes**. Some of the most controversial offerings were the **Living Newspapers**, the documentary-style dramas originated by **Elmer Rice** in New York. Censorship in fact plagued many of the Project's productions, such as Welles and Houseman's version of **Marc Blitzstein**'s leftist musical drama, *The Cradle Will Rock* (1937). Continuing conservative opposition to the radical nature of such productions brought about the abolition of the entire Project by Congress in 1939.

Federalist, The   A collection of 85 essays which appeared over the pseudonym "Publius" in the New York press from October 1787 to April 1788. Intended to persuade the New York State special convention to ratify the newly drafted Constitution of the United States, in addition to explaining the structure of the proposed new government, the essays present one of the earliest rationales for the unity of the states and a strong central government, through the elaboration, particularly in essay number 10, of the theory of factions. Actually written by Alexander Hamilton and James Madison, with some contributions from John Jay, the essays were published in two volumes as *The Federalist* in 1788. The authors' identities soon became known and the essays were frequently reissued over the next few decades. Though their influence on the New York convention is doubtful, they were recognized at the time as important legal commentary on the Constitution, and throughout American legal history have continued to influence interpretations and practical implementations of that document.

Ferber, Edna   See **Kern, Jerome**

Ferlinghetti, Lawrence 1919–   Born in New York City and educated at the University of North Carolina, at Columbia, and at the Sorbonne, Ferlinghetti played a major role in the **Beat** movement of the 1950s. With Peter D. Martin he founded City Lights in San Francisco, the country's first all-paperback bookstore. As publishers of City Lights Books and the Pocket Book Series, Martin and Ferlinghetti made available the work of such poets as **Gregory Corso**, **Allen Ginsberg**, and **Denise Levertov**. Ferlinghetti's public readings and distribution of broadsides also contributed to the renewed interest in a public poetic tradition in America.

Ferlinghetti's own work is experimental in form and often light or satiric in tone; underlying it, however, is a clear interest in social and cultural issues, and it frequently attacks American values and political policies. His first book of poetry was *Pictures from the Gone World* (1955); others include *A Coney Island of the Mind* (1958), *Starting from San Francisco* (1961, revised 1967), *The Secret Meaning of Things* (1969), *Open Eye, Open Heart* (1973), and *Landscapes of Living and Dying* (1979). He has also published a novel, *Her* (1960); experimental drama; and translations of the poetry of Jacques Prévert. His recent volumes include *The Populist Manifestos* (1981) and *Endless Life: The Selected Poems* (1981).

Fields, James T[homas] 1817–81   A New Englander by birth, Fields began working in a Boston bookstore as a teenager, and proved so adept a salesman that at the age of 21 he was made a junior partner at the publishing firm of Ticknor & Reed. He later became head of the firm, which from 1854 was known as Ticknor & Fields. Confidant of many of the nation's most prominent writers, as well as an extraordinary promoter, Fields became the foremost publisher in the US. In 1859, *The Atlantic Monthly*, edited by **James Russell Lowell**, came into the hands of Ticknor & Fields. Lowell resigned in 1861, and for the next decade Fields himself served as editor of the magazine. During his tenure he was able to secure as contributors many of the best American and British writers of the mid century. His own writings include *Poems* (1849), *Yesterdays with Authors* (1872), and *Hawthorne* (1876).

Fitch, William Clyde 1865–1909   Born in Elmira, New York, Fitch studied journalism at Amherst College before becoming a journalist in New York City. His first play, *Beau Brummel* (1890), was a vehicle for the popular actor Richard Mansfield. Over the next 20 years he wrote nearly 60 plays, earning for himself a fortune and for Broadway a new status as the home of American drama. His best plays are society melodramas which combine surface realism with emotional excess. They include *A Modern Match* (1892), *Barbara Frietchie* (1899), *The Climbers* (1901), *Captain Jinks of the Horse Marines* (1901), *The Girl with the Green Eyes* (1902), *The Truth* (1906), and *The Woman in the Case* (1909).

Fitzgerald, F[rancis] Scott (Key) 1896–1940   Fitzgerald was born in St Paul, Minnesota, and entered Princeton University in 1913. In 1917 he left before graduating to take up a commission in the US Army. While stationed near Montgomery, Alabama, he courted and became engaged to Zelda Sayre, herself an aspiring writer. After his discharge from the army in 1919, he moved to New York City and worked briefly for an advertising agency. That same year he sold his first story, "Babes in the Wood," which appeared in *The Smart Set*. He returned to St Paul and rewrote a novel he had begun while in the army; originally entitled "The Romantic Egotist," it appeared in 1920 as *This Side of Paradise* and was an almost immediate success. Its hero, Amory Blaine, like Fitzgerald himself, goes to prep school and then to Princeton, where he becomes a member of the literary coterie. He serves in World War I (*unlike* Fitzgerald, he is sent to France and sees action) and then works in advertising. He has several romantic affairs, none of them lasting. At the end of the novel, aged 24, he recognizes that his own egotism has prevented his finding happiness.

Fitzgerald and Zelda Sayre were married in 1920, and in the same year his first collection of short stories, *Flappers and Philosophers*, was published. The couple traveled briefly in Europe during the summer of 1921, and in October their daughter Scottie was born. Fitzgerald's second novel, *The Beautiful and Damned*, appeared in 1922, and was less well received. Its main character, Anthony Patch, is an alcoholic whose goal in life is to inherit and spend his grandfather's money. Though he is eventually successful in contesting the will that has disinherited him, by the end of the novel he and his wife Gloria have declined both physically and spiritually because of their dissolute, alcoholic lifestyle. (For much of his life Fitzgerald was himself an alcoholic.) Another collection of short stories, *Tales of the Jazz Age*, which included "The Diamond as Big as the Ritz," was published in 1922. "The Jazz Age" is Fitzgerald's own descriptive phrase for the 1920s, and his early financial success as a writer enabled him and Zelda to lead the kind of decadent, boisterous existence it suggests.

In October 1922 the couple moved to Great Neck, New York. (Living in this affluent Long Island community provided Fitzgerald with material for his next novel, *The Great Gatsby*.) While there he renewed his acquaintance with **John Dos Passos** and became friendly with **Ring Lardner**. He also revised his play *The Vegetable*, which had an unsuccessful one-week run in 1923, and continued to turn out stories for magazines in order to finance his extravagant lifestyle. Because they could live more cheaply in Europe than in the US, the Fitzgeralds went to France in April 1924. There Fitzgerald met two other expatriate American writers – **Ernest Hemingway**, who became a close friend, and **Gertrude Stein**. In 1925 he published what many consider his best novel, *The Great Gatsby*, and in 1926 a third collection of short stories, entitled *All the Sad Young Men*.

During the next five years the Fitzgeralds traveled back and forth between Europe and America several times. Zelda had the first of her nervous breakdowns in April 1930; she was hospitalized periodically, both in Europe and the US, from then until her death in 1948. Fitzgerald published his fourth novel, *Tender is the Night*, in 1934; pressed for money, he was disappointed that it did not sell better, though it was generally well received by the critics. Another collection of stories, *Taps at Reveille*, followed in 1935. That same year he began to write confessional essays about his broken health and exhaustion as a writer. The essays – "The Crack-Up," "Pasting It Together," and "Handle With Care" – were published in *Esquire* magazine in 1936, and were subsequently included in *The Crack-Up* (1945), a collection of Fitzgerald's essays, notes, and letters edited by his friend **Edmund Wilson**.

For a few months in 1927, and then again in 1931 and 1932, Fitzgerald worked in Hollywood as a screenwriter. In 1937 he returned to accept a lucrative contract with Metro-Goldwyn-Mayer. He worked on various screenplays, but completed only one (*Three Comrades*, 1938), and was eventually fired because of his drinking. Though he occasionally visited Zelda, who by this time was in a hospital in North Carolina, he became involved with another woman, the columnist Sheilah Graham, whom he met in Hollywood in 1937. (In fact, he died in her apartment, of a heart attack, in December 1940.) During his last months Fitzgerald returned to writing fiction, producing several short stories which were collected and published in 1962 as *The Pat Hobby Stories*. He also began a novel about a Hollywood producer, *The Last Tycoon*, which, though unfinished, was published in

1941. *The Letters of F. Scott Fitzgerald*, edited by Andrew Turnbull, appeared in 1963.

Fixer, The   See **Malamud, Bernard**

Fletcher, John Gould 1886–1950   Fletcher was born in Little Rock, Arkansas, and educated at Harvard. In 1908 he traveled to Italy and in the following year went to live in England. Between 1909 and 1913 he studied and wrote poetry steadily, and in 1913, at his own expense, he published his verse in five volumes: *The Book of Nature*, *The Dominant City*, *Fire and Wine*, *Fool's Gold*, and *Visions of the Evening*. Though critical reception was mixed, he did receive favorable notice from **Amy Lowell**, who became his close friend. That same year he also met **Ezra Pound** while visiting Paris, and agreed to contribute to **T. S. Eliot**'s *The Egoist*. In 1914 he became associated with the **Imagists** and contributed to Lowell's anthology *Some Imagist Poets*. He then returned briefly to the US, where he wrote for the *Dial*, *Poetry*, and *The Little Review*.

After the appearance of *Irradiations: Sand and Spray* in 1915, Fletcher went back to England and in the following year published the collection *Goblins and Pagodas*. He remained in Europe until 1933, contributing to *The Criterion* (1923–7) and becoming friends with T. S. Eliot, **Donald Davidson**, and **John Crowe Ransom**. At the request of **Allen Tate** he contributed to *I'll Take My Stand* in 1930. He returned to the US in 1933, and in 1938 his *Selected Poems* received the Pulitzer Prize. Though he is strongly identified with the Imagists, his later works reflect his association with the Southern Agrarians, and his continuing interest in Eastern mysticism (which had been evident in his early verse). His other works include *Japanese Prints* (1918), *The Tree of Life* (1918), *Parables* (1925), *Branches of Adam* (1926), *The Black Rock* (1928), *XXIV Elegies* (1935), and *South Star* (1941). His prose writings include *Paul Gauguin: His Life and Art* (1921), *John Smith – Also Pocahontas* (1928), and *The Two Frontiers: A Study in Historical Psychology* (1930). His autobiography, *Life Is My Song*, appeared in 1937.

Flush Times of Alabama and Mississippi, The   See **Baldwin, Joseph G.**

Fool's Errand, A   See **Tourgée, Albion W.**

42nd Parallel, The   Published in 1930, the first novel in the trilogy *U.S.A.* by **John Dos Passos**

For Whom the Bell Tolls   See **Hemingway, Ernest**

Four Quartets   A group of poems by **T. S. Eliot** written between 1935 and 1942 and collected in a single volume in 1943. Composed of four long, meditative lyrics, *Four Quartets* has the musical structure implied by its title, each section being divided into five movements. The title of each quartet is a place name which has significance for Eliot: "Burnt Norton," the site of an English country house; "East Coker," the English village of Eliot's ancestors; "The Dry Salvages," a group of rocks off the coast of Massachusetts; and "Little Gidding," an Anglican religious community founded in 1625 near Huntingdon, England. Each quartet focuses on one of the four elements of fire, water, air, and earth as a means of explicating the poem's themes, which include the relationship between the individual and time, timelessness, consciousness, and memory.

Francesca da Rimini   See **Boker, George Henry**

Frank, Waldo (David) 1889–1967   Born in Long Branch, New Jersey, Frank graduated from Yale in 1911, traveled abroad for some time, and then co-founded and edited the magazine *Seven Arts* (1916–17). A member of *avant-garde* literary circles, he advocated social and political reform in his novels, which include *City Block* (1922); *Holiday* (1923), an examination of racial problems in the South; *The Death and Birth of David Markand* (1934), about an American businessman's decision to alter his lifestyle radically; and *The Bridegroom Cometh* (England 1938, America 1939), which tells of a woman's discovery of faith while working for social reform. *Chalk Face* (1924) is a horror novel, *New Year's Eve* (1929) an expressionistic play.

He also wrote a good deal of historical and social criticism: *Our America* (1919), *Salvos* (1924), *The Re-Discovery of America* (1929), and *America Hispana* (1931); a study of industrial America, *In the American Jungle* (1937); *Birth of a World* (1951), about Simon Bolivar; a collection of sketches about Israel, *Bridgehead* (1957); and *The Prophetic Island: A Portrait of Cuba* (1961). He is also known as

Hart Crane's first editor, and was an early supporter of **Jean Toomer** and other young writers of the time.

Franklin, Benjamin 1706–90 Born in Boston, Franklin received little formal education. At the age of 12 he was apprenticed to his half-brother, the printer James Franklin, to whose *New England Courant* he contributed the essays that were published anonymously in 1722 as *The Letters of Silence Dogood* and which are notable for their humorous commentary on **Cotton Mather**'s *Bonifacius*. In 1723, having quarreled with James, he moved to Philadelphia and went to work in the printing house of Samuel Keimer. He soon attracted the patronage of Governor Keith, who sent him to England to buy equipment for a press of his own, but while there he was abandoned by Keith and forced to take a job with a London printer. During a stay of two years he also wrote and published *A Dissertation on Liberty and Necessity, Pleasure and Pain* (1725).

He returned to Philadelphia in 1726 and eventually succeeded in setting up his own press. In 1727 he founded the social and debating society called Junto, and in 1729 he published the first issue under his own proprietorship of *The Pennsylvania Gazette*, the newspaper which he managed and contributed to until 1766. Following his common-law marriage to Deborah Read in 1730, he launched the widely read *Poor Richard's Almanac* (1732–58) and *The General Magazine* (1741). He also became actively involved in the public affairs of Philadelphia: he was responsible for drawing up the plans for the lighting and maintenance of the city's streets, for a police force, and for a circulating library; he founded a city hospital, and an Academy for the Education of Youth which later became the University of Pennsylvania. Between 1751 and 1753 he published the results of his celebrated kite experiments in *Experiments and Observations on Electricity*.

In mid century Franklin assumed a number of colonial responsibilities. He became Deputy Postmaster-General in 1753, and in the following year was elected to serve as Pennsylvania's representative at the Albany Congress, where he drafted a Plan of Union. In 1757 he was chosen to represent the colonies in England. Among numerous diplomatic activities there he petitioned in 1764 for the colonies to be made a royal province of England so that his fellow Americans might enjoy the same rights as British citizens. When Parliament refused to grant this petition and instead passed the Townshend Acts, which denied the colonies the right to decide how their imports should be taxed, Franklin worked hard to advance the cause of colonial representation in Parliament. He returned to America from a brief visit to Paris in the fall of 1769 and founded the American Philosophical Society. Later that year he was appointed New Jersey agent in London and went back to Europe again. Finally convinced that his efforts to promote the colonial cause had failed and that war with England was inevitable, he returned to America in 1775.

He served in the Continental Congress and was part of the committee that ordered the drafting of the *Declaration of Independence*. While serving as Postmaster-General he was sent by the Congress to France, where he remained throughout the war and negotiated an economic and military alliance; together with John Jay and John Adams he signed the Treaty of Paris in 1783. When he returned to America in 1785, he was appointed president of the Executive Council of Pennsylvania, a post which he filled for three years, and participated in the Constitutional Convention; he signed the Constitution in 1787 and died three years later in Philadelphia.

Franklin produced numerous tracts on issues such as politics, legal theory, education, language, population control, and business. These, along with a varied and large body of correspondence, constitute a witty and informative history of 18th-century America. His writings of note include *A Scheme for a New Alphabet and Reformed Mode of Spelling* (1768); *Edict of the King of Prussia* (1773) and *Rules By Which a Great Empire may be reduced to a Small One* (1773), both of which oppose the Townshend Acts; *Remarks Concerning the Savages of North America* (1784); "On The Slave Trade" (1790), a memorandum to Congress which advocates the abolition of slavery; and his *Autobiography* (begun in 1771 and never completed).

Frederic, Harold 1856–98 Born in Utica, New York, as a young man Frederic worked as a journalist, first as a reporter and editor of the *Utica Observer*, then as editor of the *Albany Evening Journal*, and eventually as the London correspondent for the *New York Times*. He turned from journalism to fiction after moving to New York City, and became a pioneer of the American realist movement. His first novel, *Seth's Brother's Wife* (1886), portrays life on an American farm, and also examines the worlds of politics and journalism. *The Lawton Girl* (1890) and *The Return of the O'Mahoney* (1892) extended his reputation as a local colorist. *In the Valley* (1890) focuses on the American Revolution; *The Copperhead* (1893) and *Marsena and Other Stories* (1894) deal with the Civil War. His best-known novel, **The Damnation of Theron Ware** (1896), depicts the religious and psychological decline of a Methodist minister. (It was published in England under the title *Illumination*.) His last three novels – *March Hares* (1896), and the posthumously published *Gloria Mundi* (1898) and *The Market Place* (1899) – are historical tales set in England.

Freeman, Mary (Eleanor) Wilkins 1852–1930 Born in Randolph, Massachusetts, Freeman began by writing stories for children, but soon devoted her attention to an adult audience with stories in *Harper's Bazaar* and *Harper's Weekly*. In 1887 she published her first collection, *A Humble Romance and Other Stories*, and followed this in 1891 with *A New England Nun and Other Stories*. Both volumes focus on the lives of women in small New England villages who are placed in situations where they must defend their own values against those of the community.

Freeman continued to write stories throughout her life, and also produced novels, plays, and poems. *Pembroke* (1894), one of her more successful novels, is a fine study of the New England character and of conventional life there. Her other works include *Giles Corey, Yeoman: A Play* (1893), *Madelon* (1896, a novel), *Silence and Other Stories* (1898), *The Heart's Highway: A Romance of Virginia* (1900), and *The Fair Lavinia and Others* (1907). With **William Dean Howells** and **Henry James** among others, she was one of the contributors to *The Whole Family, A Novel by Twelve Authors* (1908).

Freneau, Philip (Morin) 1752–1832 The major American poet of the 18th century. Of Huguenot ancestry, Freneau was born in New York City and grew up in Monmouth, New Jersey. He attended the College of New Jersey (later Princeton University), where he met James Madison and **Hugh Henry Brackenridge**. While a student he started writing poetry, notably "The Power of Fancy" (1770) and, in collaboration with Brackenridge, *The Rising Glory of America*, which was read at their graduation in 1771 and published the following year. He taught for a while and then studied theology. A short collection of poems, *The American Village*, appeared in 1772 and was followed by "Pictures of Columbus" in 1774. When the Revolution began he contributed patriotic poems in support of the American cause to the newspapers, but in 1776 he withdrew from politics, first to the home of an acquaintance in Santa Cruz, and then joining a ship which sailed to the West Indies, possibly as a privateer. On his return to the US in 1778 he was detained briefly by the British, and when released he joined the New Jersey militia.

The exotic settings of the Caribbean had inspired him to write occasional poetry, including "The Jamaica Funeral," "The Beauties of Santa Cruz," and "The House of Night." He published some of these in Brackenridge's *United States Magazine* in 1779, together with poems on more patriotic themes, such as "George the Third's Soliloquy," "The Loyalists," and "America Independent." In 1780 he was captured again by the British and held prisoner on the *Scorpion* in New York harbor. His brief but harsh captivity prompted him to write *The British Prison Ship*, published as a broadside in 1781. In 1781–2 he contributed essays and further Revolutionary War poems to the *Philadelphia Freeman's Journal*, celebrating American heroes and attacking the British. He continued to express a passionate patriotism and hatred for the British in many of his later poems and journalistic writings – in his associations with the New York *Daily Advertiser* (1789–91); with *The Time Piece* (1797–8), which he helped found; with *Aurora* (1799–1800); and, most notably, with the *National Gazette* (1791–3), a Philadelphia journal that he founded and edited at **Thomas Jefferson**'s urging.

Between 1784 and 1790 he spent a good deal of time at sea, as captain of a trader. His poems during this period include *Journies from Philadelphia to New York* (1787), which introduced the humorous persona of Robert Slender, weaver, one of the fictional voices which Freneau would use in later political essays. In the later 1780s his poems tended to explore rather more somber subjects; "The Dying Indian," "A Visit to an Old Indian Burial Ground," and "The Wild Honey Suckle" date from this period. Although intermittently at sea, he published two collections, *Poems* (1786), and *Miscellaneous Works* (1788), which also included revised versions of some of his earlier poems. With the folding of the *National Gazette*, Freneau returned to Monmouth, where he published an almanac, founded and edited the *Jersey Chronicle*, and printed (on his own press) another edition of *Poems* in 1795. *Letters on Various Interesting and Important Subjects*, a collection of some of the pro-Jefferson "Robert Slender" letters that had appeared in the Philadelphia journal *Aurora*, was published in 1799. The "Slender" series ended with Jefferson's election in 1801. Between 1802 and 1807 he made more sea voyages to support himself, but continued to contribute to the press. A new edition of the *Poems* came out in 1809. Another volume, *Poems on American Affairs*, appeared in 1815; this contained new verses occasioned by the War of 1812, as well as poems exploring deistic ideas, among them "On the Universality and Other Attributes of the God of Nature." Freneau spent his last years living in poverty in New Jersey. He died of exposure after being caught in a snowstorm.

From Here to Eternity   See **Jones, James**

Front Page, The   See **MacArthur, Charles**

Frost, Robert (Lee) 1874–1963 The son of a politically ambitious journalist and a strongly religious schoolmistress, Frost was born and raised in San Francisco. His father's death in 1885 forced the family to return to their native New England, where they lived for a time with Frost's paternal grandparents and then in a series of small, cheap apartments in and around Lawrence, Massachusetts. Challenged by his mother to improve his mind, at the age of 14 Frost began to apply himself seriously to his studies. He wrote poetry in high school and also edited a journal

and yearbook. He matriculated at Dartmouth College but withdrew in his first term to return to Lawrence and support his family by teaching. During these years he continued to write poetry, much of it addressed to his future wife, Elinor White, herself a poet. In 1894 he published his first poem, "My Butterfly," in *The Independent*.

Having married White the following year, Frost taught with her in a school set up by his mother. He soon tired of this arrangement, however, and applied to Harvard as a special student; he was accepted into a three-year program but withdrew after two years. While at Harvard he studied the works of **William James** and found himself repelled by the ideas of the poet-philosopher **George Santayana**, who was then teaching there. Following the deaths of his son Elliott, his mother, and his daughter Elinor, he fell into a deep depression and seriously contemplated suicide. In 1912 he and his family moved to England, where he found a publisher for his first book of verse, *A Boy's Will* (1913). The collection was well received and was soon followed by a second, *North of Boston* (1914). These publications, along with his friendship with poets such as **Ezra Pound** and Edward Thomas, increased his exposure in literary magazines. In 1915 he returned to the US and settled on a farm in New Hampshire.

There Frost the poet was nurtured. Like that of many great national poets, his verse relies heavily on the language of the people. Many of his poems take the form of dramatic monologues or dialogues, using and transforming the New Englander's patterns of speech which he heard each day on his farm. His third collection, *Mountain Interval*, appeared in 1916, and he began to attract national attention. Soon in demand as a lecturer and reader of his own verse, he accepted positions on the faculties of Amherst College, the University of Michigan, and Dartmouth College. *New Hampshire* (1923) was awarded a Pulitzer Prize. Following the publication of *West-Running Brook* (1928), his *Collected Poems* (1930) won him a second Pulitzer. The distinction was bestowed twice more, for *A Further Range* (1936) – making Frost the first to win the Pulitzer three times – and for *A Witness Tree* (1942).

His work developed further in the 1940s

with the production of two masques: *A Masque of Reason* (1945) and *A Masque of Mercy* (1947). These dramatic poems in blank verse portray biblical characters, and explore ethical issues and the relation of man to God in the modern world. In 1947 he published *A Steeple Bush*, a collection of lyrics. Despite increasingly poor health, he wrote poetry to the end of his life; his last collection, *In the Clearing*, appeared in 1962. His poetry is among the most accessible of modern writers, given the central theme of all his collections: the quest of the solitary person to make sense of the world. Although the poetry does not make the complicated simple, it does speak to the common person through a narrative voice which often seems as baffled as the reader. His use of traditional forms, everywhere apparent, is undercut by the ambiguity which his sensibility required. The poem, as a finished product, only temporarily forestalls the confusion of the modern world.

Fruitlands A Communitarian reform experiment undertaken by **Bronson Alcott** and Charles Lane on a farm in Harvard, Massachusetts, 1843–4. The small community consisted of Alcott and his family (including his young daughter, **Louisa May Alcott**), Lane and his son, Samuel Larned, Joseph Palmer, Abram Wood, Abraham Everett, Samuel Bower, and Isaac Hecker. Part of the come-outer movement associated with the **Transcendentalists** (Larned and Hecker had spent some time at **Brook Farm**), and imbued with a strong anarchic impulse, the community aimed to avoid worldly activity, especially trade, to minimize labor, and to support itself at a subsistence level by farming.

Fugitives, The See **Ransom, John Crowe**

Fuller, Henry Blake 1857–1929 Fuller was born in Chicago, and except for two years spent touring in Europe (1878–80) lived there all his life. In addition to writing fiction (all of which is set in Italy or Chicago), he contributed to the *Chicago Tribune* (from 1880), the *Chicago Evening Post* (1901–2), and the *Chicago Record-Herald* (1911–13). He was also a member of the advisory committee of *Poetry* magazine from 1912 to 1929.

His best-known novel is probably *The Cliff-Dwellers* (1893), which satirizes the social ambitions of people living in a skyscraper apartment building. *With the Procession* (1895) also deals with social climbers, in this case a middle-class family. *Bertram Cope's Year* (1919) takes up the topic of homosexuality. In all three novels Fuller sought to deal in a realistic manner with social issues of his time. His other novels include *The Chatelaine of La Trinité* (1892), *The Last Refuge: A Sicilian Romance* (1900), *On the Stairs* (1918), *Gardens of This World* (1929), and *Not on the Screen* (1930). Among his collections of short stories are *The Chevalier of Pensieri-Vani* (1890), *Waldo Trench and Others: Stories of Americans in Italy* (1908), and *Lines Long and Short: Biographical Sketches in Various Rhythms* (1917). He also wrote plays, among them *O, That Way Madness Lies: A Play for Marionettes* (1895), and *The Red Carpet* (not published until 1939).

Fuller, (Sarah) Margaret 1810–50 A leading figure of the **Transcendentalist** circle of Concord, Massachusetts, Fuller was born in Cambridgeport. Her early life was dominated by her father, a possessive parent who undertook her education himself. After his death she became **Bronson Alcott**'s assistant, a friend of **Ralph Waldo Emerson**, and head of a school in Providence. She was an early feminist and, as a member of the foremost group of intellectuals in New England, she enjoyed the stimulus of views and discussions that helped prompt her to write the monumental *Woman in the Nineteenth Century* (1845).

She edited *The Dial* from 1840 to 1842, and in 1843 published *Summer on the Lakes* after a visit to Chicago – her first encounter with the expanding West and the frontier. At about the same time she became literary critic of **Horace Greeley**'s New York *Tribune*, by which in 1846 she was sent to Europe; her distinguished letters from "abroad" appeared on the *Tribune's* front page. In Europe she met Wordsworth, Mazzini, George Sand, Chopin, and Carlyle. She particularly admired Mazzini, and began to write a book on the revolutionary events in Rome in 1848, but never completed it. She married the Marquis Angelo Ossoli and in 1850 they sailed for America with their infant son, but their ship was wrecked in a storm off Fire Island. The whole family perished. In addition to her own work Fuller left another impression of her dynamic personality; she was the inspiration for Zenobia in **Nathaniel Hawthornes**'s *The Blithedale Romance* and for the eponymous heroine in **Oliver Wendell Holme**'s *Elsie Venner*. She is also Miranda in **James Russell Lowell**'s *A Fable for Critics*.

G

Gaddis, William 1922–   Gaddis was born in New York City and educated at Harvard, though he left the university in 1945 without taking his degree. His first work was published during his undergraduate years in the Harvard *Lampoon*. He has traveled extensively in the US, Mexico, and Europe, and the experiences of his travels are incorporated into his first novel, *The Recognitions* (1955), which focuses on a group of artists and poets in Greenwich Village during the late 1940s and early 1950s. Its dominant motifs of ruse and forgery are encountered on many levels – social, aesthetic, theological, and sexual. A lengthy and complex work, which derives in part from Gaddis's ambivalence toward post-World War II American society and politics, it was not well received by the critics (though it led to a National Institute of Arts and Letters grant in 1963). His second novel, *JR* (1975), is written entirely in dialogue and takes place mostly at a school on Long Island. It enjoyed a more favorable critical reception, and better sales, than its predecessor, and received the National Book Award in 1976. *Carpenter's Gothic*, published in 1985, examines the impact of the Vietnam war on the lives of those who endured it.

Gaines, Ernest J. 1933–   Novelist and short-story writer, born in Oscar, Louisiana, the son of a plantation worker, Gaines himself began working in the fields at a young age. In 1948 his family moved to Vallejo, California. After spending two years in the army, he attended San Francisco State College, graduating in 1957, and then Stanford University, where he received the Joseph Henry Jackson Literary Award in 1959.

Gaines's fiction mostly treats black life in the bayou region of Louisiana. His first novel, *Catherine Carmier* (1964), tells of the diffi-

culties encountered by a young black college graduate when he returns home to Louisiana. *Of Love and Dust* (1967) is set on a Louisiana plantation in the 1940s. *Bloodline* (1968) is a collection of five stories. His best-known novel, *The Autobiography of Miss Jane Pittman* (1971), consists of the recollections of a 110-year-old black woman, whose experiences range from slavery to the civil rights movements of the 1960s. Gaines's concern with the effects of racism and the possibilities of social change is further revealed in *My Father's House* (1978), a novel which examines the conflict between a black preacher and his more radical son.

Gale, Zona 1874–1938   Born in Wisconsin, Gale first rose to prominence as a writer in the "local color" vein. Among her early works are the novel *Romance Island* (1906) and a collection of short stories entitled *Friendship Village* (1908). After World War I her sentimental tendencies gave way to a sterner realism in novels such as *Birth* (1918), and her best-known book, *Miss Lulu Bett* (1920), a portrayal of bleak midwestern life and the middle-aged woman who suffers it. *Faint Perfume* (1923) also centers on the stifled hopes and empty existence of a midwestern spinster. In her later novels, however, Gale departed from the realism of her most highly acclaimed works. *Preface to a Life* (1926) and *Borgia* (1929) are representative of this later phase, during which she became interested in Eastern mysticism as a possible answer to the kind of suffering portrayed in her earlier novels. Her final works, *Papa La Fleur* (1933), *Light Woman* (1937), and the posthumously published *Magna* (1939), share a concern with the gap between the pre-war and post-war generations. Some of her best short stories are collected in *Yellow Gentians and Blue* (1927) and *Bridal Pond* (1930).

Gardner, John 1933–82 Born in Batavia, New York, Gardner attended public schools there and then worked on his father's farm. Between 1951 and 1953 he studied at DePauw University, and then transferred to Washington University in St Louis, where he received his BA in 1955. He took an MA in 1956 and a PhD in 1958 from Iowa State University. For most of his life he taught medieval literature and creative writing at various American universities.

As noted in the prospectus to his doctoral dissertation, a novel entitled *The Old Men*, Gardner's fiction almost exclusively considers the "nature and ramifications of man's two essential choices, affirmation and denial." *The Wreckage of Agathon* (1970) – published after the critical failure of his first novel, *The Resurrection* (1966) – is set in ancient Sparta and presents a seer, Agathon, and his companion, Demodokos, who have been imprisoned and engage in a dialogue concerning individual freedom and civil restraint. His most highly praised book, *Grendel* (1971), retells the story of Beowulf from the monster's point of view and focuses on the potential meaninglessness of life, a theme also examined in *The Sunlight Dialogues* (1972). In 1973 he published *Nickel Mountain*; set in upstate New York, it records the life of Henry Soames, a middle-aged motel proprietor who searches for a way of living in the face of intense loneliness and fear of a fatal heart attack. Gardner's first collection of short fiction, *The King's Indian Stories and Tales*, was published in 1974. Two years later came the novel *October Light* (1976), an examination of the problems of aging, which was awarded the National Book Critics Circle award in 1976. His other fiction includes the novels *Freddy's Book* (1980) and *Mickelsson's Ghosts* (1982), and a collection of stories entitled *The Art of Living and Other Stories* (1981). He also wrote an epic poem, *Jason and Medeia* (1973); three libretti, *William Wilson, Frankenstein*, and *Rumpelstiltskin* (collected in *Three Libretti*, 1979); and a volume of *Poems* (1978).

In his role as a scholar, Gardner translated, edited, and wrote widely about medieval literature; these works include *The Complete Works of the Gawain-Poet* (1965) and *The Life and Times of Chaucer* (1977). His theories of fiction are developed in *The Forms of Fiction* (1962), *On Moral Fiction* (1978), and the posthumously published *The Art of Fiction: Notes on Craft for Young Writers* (1984). At his death he left two unfinished projects: a novel, *Shadows*, and a translation of *Gilgamesh*.

Garland, (Hannibal) Hamlin 1860–1940 Garland spent his youth on farms in Iowa, South Dakota, and his native Wisconsin. In 1884 he moved to Boston, where he was befriended by **William Dean Howells**, but he returned to the Midwest in 1887 and dedicated himself to depicting the life there and urging reforms to better it. His stories and sketches, written mostly before 1890, won acclaim when collected in **Main-Travelled Roads** (1891). Two other collections – *Prairie Folks* (1892) and *Wayside Courtships* (1897) – were combined in 1910 and published as *Other Main-Travelled Roads*.

His writing often tended toward propaganda, especially in his novels. *Jason Edwards, An Average Man* (1892) is a plea for the single-tax theories of Henry George; *A Spoil of Office* (1892) campaigns for the Populist party. Less political novels include two books about life in Dakota farm country, *A Little Norsk* (1892) and *Rose of Dutcher's Coolly* (1895). *The Captain of the Gray-Horse Troop* (1902) and *Cavanagh, Forest Ranger* (1910) are novels about the Far West. *A Son of the Middle Border* (1917) and *A Daughter of the Middle Border* (1921) are autobiographical narratives. His essays on his theory of realistic fiction, which he called "veritism," appeared as *Crumbling Idols* (1894).

Garrison, William Lloyd 1805–79 The editor, lecturer, and Abolitionist leader was born in Newburyport, Massachusetts. For five years, he edited *The Genius of Universal Emancipation* with the Quaker Benjamin Lundy. Lundy eventually found his approach too radical, and the two parted company. Garrison then founded the Abolitionist newspaper **The Liberator** in 1831, and in the following year launched a vigorous attack on the American Colonization Society. He continued publishing the influential *Liberator* throughout the Civil War. His own books include *Thoughts on African Colonization* (1832), *Sonnets* (1843), and a collection of essays and speeches entitled *Selections* (1852).

Gass, William 1924– Born in Fargo,

North Dakota, Gass received his BA from Kenyon College in 1947 and his PhD from Cornell in 1954. A professor of philosophy at Washington University in St Louis, he also writes fiction that is notable for its experimental use of language. *Omensetter's Luck*, his first novel, was published in 1966. Comprised of three sections, each written in a different rhetorical style, it presents the conflict between Omensetter, who represents physicality and mindlessness, and Jethro Furber, who is intellectual and religious. *Willie Masters' Lonesome Wife*, a novella, appeared in 1971 and is still more experimental, containing unusual typography, parodies, footnotes, and authorial interruptions of the narrative.

Gass has also published collections of short stories: *In the Heart of the Heart of the Country and Other Stories* (1968; revised and republished in 1981), and *The First Winter of My Married Life* (1979). His non-fiction works include *Fiction and the Figures of Life* (1970), *On Being Blue: A Philosophical Inquiry* (1975), *The World Within the Word* (1978), and *Habitations of the Word: Essays* (1985).

Gelber, Jack 1932– Born in Chicago, Gelber received a degree in journalism from the University of Illinois in 1953. Of the dozen or so of his plays that have been produced in New York, the 1959 **Living Theatre** production of *The Connection* has received the greatest critical acclaim. About four heroin addicts waiting in an apartment for a "connection" to bring their drugs, the play uses jazz, poetry, and the improvisation techniques of popular theatre deliberately to collapse the traditional sense of distance between audience and actors. Though also a poet, novelist, and screenwriter, Gelber is best known for this play and for his association in the 1950s and 1960s with the experimental Living Theatre Company. His other plays, all of which employ radical dramatic methods to explore the relationship between performer and audience, include *The Apple* (1961), *Square in the Eye* (1965), *The Cuban Thing* (1968), *Sleep* (1972), and *Jack Gelber's New Play: Rehearsal* (1976). He has also written a screenplay of *The Connection* (1962), translated Francis Xavier Kroetz's play *Farmyard* (1975), adapted **Norman Mailer**'s *Barbary Shore* (1974) for the stage, and written a novel, *On Ice* (1964).

General William Booth Enters into Heaven and Other Poems A collection of poems by **Vachel Lindsay**, published in 1913. The title poem, which won a $100 prize awarded by *Poetry* magazine, was intended for public performance; Lindsay, who himself toured the US giving recitations of his poetry, included notes explaining how the poem should be performed and what instruments should accompany its performance. The collection also includes an elegy on the death of Illinois' liberal governor John Philip Altgeld, "The Eagle that is Forgotten."

George, Henry 1839–97 Born to middle-class Episcopalian parents in Philadelphia, George left school at the age of 13 to help support his family. After moving to California in 1857, he worked variously as a ship's storekeeper, a gold-digger, and a typesetter, before settling down to a career in journalism. Between 1867 and 1875 he edited four California newspapers, including the *San Francisco Chronicle* and the *San Francisco Evening Post*. He later founded, edited, and published the weekly newspaper *Standard* (1887–91). Throughout his career as a journalist he used his position to comment on issues ranging from free trade and railroad monopolies to political corruption and women's rights, as well as to advance his own theories as a political economist.

His first major political statement was an editorial in *Overland Monthly* (October 1868) entitled "What the Railroads Will Bring Us," in which he argued that the present organization of the railroad industry would serve only to make the rich richer and the poor poorer. His first two separate publications, both pamphlets, *The Subsidy Question and the Democratic Party* and *Our Land and Land Policy*, appeared in 1871. The latter contained the first statement of his Single Tax Theory; he developed this in his most important economic treatise, *Progress and Poverty* (published in 1879 at his own expense), arguing that the gap between the rich and the poor could be closed by replacing the various taxes levied on labor and capital with a single tax on the rental value of property. *Progress and Poverty* eventually sold more than two million copies, established George's reputation in the US and abroad, and won him significant labor support in his three campaigns for public office in New York – twice for mayor (1886 and 1897) and once for state secretary (1887). In four subsequent works he applied his Single Tax Theory to a number of social and economic issues: *Social Problems* (1883), *Protection or Free Trade* (1886), *Perplexed Philosopher* (1892), and *Science of Political Economy* (1897). During the last 16 years of his life he made six lecture tours in Europe, where his theories were even more influential than in the US.

Gershwin, George 1898–1937 and **Gershwin, Ira** 1896–1984 The Gershwins, whose family name was originally Gershvin, spent their early lives in Brooklyn and on the Lower East Side of New York City; together and separately, they went on to leave their mark on the American musical theatre, the popular song, and (in George's case) serious classical music.

George, who was also a talented pianist, began his musical career in Tin Pan Alley as a song plugger for a music publisher, and worked as a rehearsal pianist and vaudeville accompanist before his first musical show, a bedroom comedy called *La La Lucille* (1919), was produced on Broadway. His first big song hit was "Swanee," made popular by Al Jolson. He soon teamed up with his older brother, Ira (born Israel), who had already been writing lyrics. Their first song together was called "The Real American Folk Song (Is A Rag)," thus prophetically characterizing their influence on American music. They went on to work on five editions of the *George White Scandals* (1920–4); *Lady Be Good* (1924), a vehicle for Fred and Adele Astaire, which was their first success; *Tip Toes* (1925); *Tell Me More* (1925); *Oh, Kay!* (1926); *Funny Face* (1927); *Treasure Girl* (1928); *Rosalie* (1928); *Show Girl* (1929); *Strike Up The Band* (1930), an anti-war satire written with **George S. Kaufman** and Morrie Ryskind; *Girl Crazy* (1930); *Of Thee I Sing* (1931), another Kaufman and Ryskind satire, this time about presidential elections, which won the Pulitzer Prize; a sequel, *Let 'Em Eat Cake* (1933); and *Pardon My English* (1933). Their last collaboration, and George's last stage work before his death from a brain tumor, was *Porgy and Bess* (1935), a full-fledged opera of Southern black life based on the novel *Porgy* by **DuBose Heyward**.

Ira also worked with the composers **Jerome Kern**, Harold Arlen, and (after George's death) **Kurt Weill**, with whom his most notable collaboration was *Lady in the Dark* (1941). George is also remembered as a composer of more serious music. Alongside the opera *Porgy and Bess*, such symphonic works as *Rhapsody in Blue* (1924) and *An American in Paris* (1928) integrated conventional classical forms with the energy and the innovative harmonies of jazz.

Gilded Age, The: *A Tale of Today* A satirical novel by **Mark Twain** and **Charles Dudley Warner**, published in 1873 and dramatized by Twain and G. S. Densmore in the following year. The novel comments on the greed, exploitation, and economic speculation during the period of post-Civil War Reconstruction (the era itself has been named after the book). Set in Missouri, New York, and Washington, DC, the story tells of various unscrupulous individuals, their personal relationships, and their rather dubious financial enterprises.

Giles Goat-Boy See **Barth, John**

Gillette, William (Hooker) 1855– 1937 An actor and dramatist born in Connecticut, Gillette's early career was advanced by **Mark Twain**, a family friend. He gained a considerable reputation as an actor, writing parts for himself in which his restrained style and fondness for underplaying could be exploited. His career as a dramatist was launched in 1881 with the production of two plays: *The Private Secretary* and *Esmeralda*, the latter written in collaboration with **Frances Hodgson Burnett**. *All the Comforts of Home* (1890) and *Too Much Johnson* (1894) were adaptations of French farces. His best-known works are two original melodramas about the Civil War, *Held by the Enemy* (1886) and *Secret Service* (1895); and *Sherlock Holmes* (1899), a dramatization of Arthur Conan Doyle's stories in which Gillette himself starred for over 30 years. A short comic sequel, *The Painful Predicament of Sherlock Holmes*, and a melodrama entitled *Clarice* were both produced in 1905.

Gilman, Charlotte Perkins 1860– 1935 Born in Hartford, Connecticut, Gilman was educated at home and, briefly, at the Rhode Island School of Design. *In This Our World* (1893) is a collection of poems about 19th-century womanhood. *Women and Economics* (1898) is a strong indictment of patriarchal culture; other reforming works, including *Concerning Children* (1900) and *The Home: Its Work and Influence* (1903), discuss the detrimental effects that restrictions on women have on the family. *The Yellow Wallpaper*, written in 1890 and published in 1899, is a semi-autobiographical treatment of a woman writer's breakdown and the subsequent "rest cure" prescribed by her physician husband; the cure forbids her to write and leads to true madness. Between November 1909 and December 1916 Gilman edited *The Forerunner*, a magazine consisting entirely of her own articles and fiction dealing with women's issues. Two of her novels, *What Diana Did* (1910) and *The Crux* (1911), appeared in this periodical, as did *The Man-Made World*, which, with the independently published *His Religion and Hers* (1923), further developed her ideas about sexual relations and oppression in modern society. Her autobiography was published in 1935.

Ginsberg, Allen 1926–   Ginsberg was born in New Jersey. His father was the poet and teacher Louis Ginsberg; his mother, the subject of one of his most moving poems, "Kaddish," was a Russian immigrant. He attended Columbia University and then held a number of jobs, from dishwashing to book-reviewing for *Newsweek*. During this time he studied Whitman and Blake and experimented with drugs to investigate other states of consciousness. His first collection, *Howl and Other Poems* (1956), established him as a major poet and, with **Jack Kerouac** and **William Burroughs**, as a leader of the **Beats**.

Other collections include *Kaddish and Other Poems* (1961), *Reality Sandwiches* (1963), *Planet News* (1964), *The Fall of America: Poems of these States, 1965–1971* (1972), *First Blues: Rags, Ballads, and Harmonium Songs, 1971–1974* (1975), *Poems All Over The Place: Mostly Seventies* (1978), and *Collected Poems 1947–1980* (1984). Some of his talks on poetry and politics (he has traveled the world to speak out against authoritarianism) are included in *Allen Verbatim* (1974). *Journals, Early Fifties Early Sixties* was published in 1977. *Selected Gay Poems and Correspondence*, a collection of poems and letters exchanged between Ginsberg and Peter Orlovsky, appeared in 1978.

Giovanni, Nikki (Yolande Cornelia) 1943–   Black poet, born in Knoxville, Tennesse. She was educated at Fisk University, and received an honorary doctorate from Wilberforce University in 1972. Her first two collections of poetry, *Black Feeling, Black Talk* (1968) and *Black Judgment* (1969), are set against the background of the civil rights movement and trace the development of a young black woman into a fiery militant. In *Recreation* (1970) and *Spin a Soft Black Song* (1971) Giovanni's voice has softened somewhat, and the expression of personal concerns is balanced with social and political statement. Her examination of the black experience is further developed in *My House* (1972), *Ego-Tripping and Other Poems for Young People* (1974), *The Women and the Men* (1975), *Cotton Candy on a Rainy Day* (1980), and *Those Who Ride the Night Winds* (1983). *Gemini: An Extended Autobiographical Statement on My First Twenty-Five Years of Being a Black Poet* was published in 1971.

Glasgow, Ellen 1874–1945   Born in Richmond, Virginia, Glasgow published her first novel, *The Descendant*, in 1897, and her only volume of poetry, *The Freeman, and Other Poems*, in 1902. The changing economic and social conditions of the old agrarian South form the subject of a series of historical novels, beginning with *The Voice of the People* (1900) and including *The Battle-Ground* (1902), *The Deliverance* (1904), *The Wheel of Life* (1906), *The Ancient Law* (1908), *The Romance of a Plain Man* (1909), and *The Miller of Old Church* (1911). Her next two novels, *Virginia* (1913) and *Life and Gabriella* (1916), examine the position of women in the modernization of the Old South.

She wrote numerous other novels, including *The Builders* (1919), *One Man in His Time* (1922), **Barren Ground** (1925), *The Romantic Comedians* (1926), *They Stooped to Folly* (1929), *The Sheltered Life* (1932), and **Vein of Iron** (1935). In 1941 she was awarded a Pulitzer Prize for *In This Our Life* (1941), a study of the decay of an aristocratic Virginia family. Two volumes of her stories have been issued: *The Shadowy Third* (1923) and *Collected Stories* (1963). A collection of the prefatory essays to her novels, *A Certain Measure*, was published in 1943, and an autobiographical reminiscence, *The Woman Within*, in 1954. Her *Letters* were collected in 1958.

Glaspell, Susan 1882–1948 Playwright and novelist, born and educated in Iowa. With her husband, George Cram Cook, she was a founder of the Provincetown Players, the experimental, non-commercial theatre group which first introduced the plays of **Eugene O'Neill**. *Suppressed Desires* (1915), a satire on popular enthusiasm for psychoanalysis, written in collaboration with Cook, was the first play presented by the group. Glaspell followed it with a number of one-act plays which were the staples of the Provincetown's early seasons: *Trifles* (1916) shows two small-town women joining together to conceal evidence that a woman they know has murdered her husband; *The People* (1917) deals with arguments for and against the demise of a radical newspaper; *Close the Book* (1917) pokes fun at the desire of the young to appear less conventional than they are; *The Outside* (1917) tells of two women's isolation from a New England community; *Woman's Honor* (1918) mocks both conventional and unconventional attitudes towards that concept.

Her full-length plays deal with social justice and the problems of individuals within families and communities. The first, *Bernice* (1919), is an extended meditation on the meaning of one woman's life and death; *Inheritors* (1921) depicts the struggle between progressive and reactionary forces over the destiny of a Midwestern university; *The Verge* (1921) explores the excitements and the excesses of a woman's extreme individualism; *Alison's House* (1930), which won the Pulitzer Prize in 1931, is based on the life of **Emily Dickinson** and, like *Bernice*, shows a woman's surviving family and friends attempting to make sense of her life and work.

Though Glaspell is remembered mostly for her dramatic work, she considered herself primarily a novelist. When she came to Greenwich Village in 1913 she had already published three novels and numerous short stories, mostly in a regionalist or "local color" mode. In 1922 she and Cook left the increasingly successful Provincetown Theatre and moved to Greece; Cook died there in 1924, and, after writing *The Road to the Temple* (1927), a memoir of their life together, Glaspell returned to fiction as a profession. Her late novels deal with life in the Midwest, and include *Brook Evans* (1928), *Fugitive's*

Return (1929), *Ambrose Holt and Family* (1931), *The Morning is Near Us* (1939), *Norma Ashe* (1942), and *Judd Rankin's Daughter* (1945). She also published two collections of short stories, *Lifted Masks* (1912) and *A Jury of Her Peers* (1927).

Glass Menagerie, The A play by **Tennessee Williams**, first produced in 1944, and published in the following year. It won the New York Drama Critics Circle Award.

Described by Williams as a "memory play," it is framed by the recollections of Tom Wingfield, whose impressionistic narratives, accompanied by images projected onto a screen, introduce a number of the scenes. Tom recalls his life in St Louis with his mother Amanda, a faded Southern belle who clings persistently to glamorous illusions about her past, and with his sister Laura, a crippled and painfully shy young woman whose intensely private world is centered on a treasured collection of small glass animals. Amanda, whose husband has long since deserted the family, has transferred her romantic hopes to Laura, continually asking her about her non-existent gentlemen callers. She persuades Tom, who has become a compulsive movie-goer to escape this intolerable situation at home, to invite his friend Jim O'Connor to dinner. Jim turns out to be the same young man with whom Laura was infatuated at high school; for a moment her sensitivity and reserve are eased by his warmth, and she allows him to see her glass collection. While trying to teach her some dance steps, however, he stumbles and knocks her favorite animal, a unicorn, off the table, breaking its horn. Bravely, Laura tells him it is better this way, for now the animal is no longer different from its peers. Jim kisses her, but then, suddenly embarrassed, tells her he is engaged to another girl, and leaves. Amanda is enraged with Tom for what she thinks was a deliberate practical joke. Finally pushed too far, Tom runs out of the house, never to return. The play ends with an image of Amanda comforting Laura, and with Tom's final narration filled with pain for his sister.

Godfrey, Thomas 1736–63 The author of the first American tragic drama, *The Prince of Parthia* (published in 1765, first public performance 1767), Godfrey was born in

Philadelphia. His father, a friend of **Benjamin Franklin**, was a glazier of modest means who, while completely without formal education, became an amateur scientist and is credited with inventing the quadrant. Thomas attended the Academy and Charitable School of Philadelphia, where he became friendly with the young Benjamin West. His poetic talent was recognized by the provost, William Smith, who succeeded in arranging his release from apprenticeship (to a watchmaker) so that he might continue his studies. At the age of 22 he served with the Pennsylvania forces in the expedition against Fort Duquesne; in 1759 he took up a position as a factor in Wilmington, North Carolina, where he remained for three years; he then served briefly as supercargo on a merchant vessel. He returned to Wilmington shortly before his death from a fever at the age of 26. His collected poems, published by his friends after his death, included *The Prince of Parthia*; two long poems, "The Court of Fancy" and "The Assembly of Birds," both modeled on Chaucer; and a quantity of shorter lyrics.

While *The Prince of Parthia* drew on classical history for names and some characterizations, the plot was Godfrey's own invention. The central conflict is a struggle over succession to the throne of Artabanus, King of Parthia, between two of his sons, the virtuous Arsaces, and the evil Vardanes. The brothers are also rivals for the love of Evanthe, an Arabian captive. Artabanus is assassinated by Vardanes's confederate Lysias; Arsaces is imprisoned, but escapes and kills Vardanes in battle. Evanthe, whose servant has mistakenly told her that Arsaces is dead, takes poison and dies; Arsaces falls on his sword, leaving the kingdom to Gotarzes, the youngest brother. The play, in iambic pentameter, apparently was intended for performance.

Go Down, Moses   See **Faulkner, William**

God's Little Acre   See **Caldwell, Erskine**

Gold, Herbert 1924–   Born in Cleveland, Ohio, Gold served in the army during World War II, and then attended Columbia University, receiving his BA in 1946 and his MA in 1948. He spent time in Paris (1949–51) as a Fulbright Scholar at the Sorbonne, and lived briefly in Haiti as a recipient of an Inter-American Cultural Grant. A number of his novels are autobiographical: *Therefore Be Bold* (1960) tells of the experience of a Jewish adolescent growing up in Cleveland; *Fathers: A Novel in the Form of a Memoir* (1967) draws on Gold's experiences as a father to his five children and as a son to his own father; *Family: A Novel in the Form of a Memoir* (1981) is about a Jewish immigrant family. His other novels are *Birth of a Hero* (1951); *The Prospect Before Us* (1954); *The Man Who Was Not With It* (1956), probably his best-known work, the story of a dope-addict carnival barker and his world; *The Optimist* (1959); *Salt* (1963); *The Great American Jackpot* (1971) and *Waiting for Cordelia* (1977), two stories about a sociology student at Berkeley in the 1960s; *Swiftie the Magician* (1974); *He/She* (1980); *True Love* (1982). His most recent novel, *Mister White Eyes* (1984), is about a journalist's search for love and simple human feelings through, or despite, his profession.

Gold's short stories and essays have been collected in *15 × 3* (1957), *Love and Like* (1960), *The Age of Happy Problems* (1962), *The Magic Will: Stories and Essays of a Decade* (1971), and *A Walk on the West Side: California on the Brink* (1981). His autobiography, *My Last Two Thousand Years*, appeared in 1972. He has written one book for children, *The Young Prince and the Magic Cone* (1973), and edited or co-edited three collections: *Fiction of the Fifties: A Decade of American Writing* (1959), *Stories of Modern America* (1961), and *First Person Singular: Essays for the Sixties* (1963).

Gold, Michael 1894–1967   Born Itzok Isaac Granich to Jewish immigrants, Gold was raised on the Lower East Side of New York City. The major themes of his work are derived from this background. His best-known book, *Jews Without Money* (1930), is a fictionalized autobiography which describes Jewish ghetto life and ends with a political rally in Union Square at which the protagonist is converted to the cause of Communist revolution.

During the years of radical ferment before World War I Gold published articles and stories in *The Masses* and in the Socialist *New York Call*, and had three of his one-act plays produced by the Provincetown Players. In 1920, after returning from Mexico, where he had evaded the draft, he became an editor of *The Liberator*, the successor of *The Masses*.

The New Masses, which he founded as a successor to *The Liberator*, espoused under his editorship the cause of proletarian literature which sought to represent the working class as the saving grace of America – its last hope for true democracy. His fiery columns for *The New Masses*, notable for their polemical Communist views, have been collected in *The Mike Gold Reader* (1954) and *Mike Gold: A Literary Anthology* (1972), which also reprints articles from *120 Million* (1929) and *Change the World* (1937), his earlier collections of *New Masses* prose. By the mid 1930s Gold was embroiled in defending a Communist party position which, because of Stalinism, was becoming increasingly controversial. He remained committed to the Party, and in 1941 published the anti-Trotskyite *The Hollow Men*, a collection of *Daily Worker* articles mocking the political errors of such former comrades as **Ernest Hemingway**, **Archibald MacLeish**, Granville Hicks, and **Sherwood Anderson**. He is perhaps the archetypal 20th-century American literary radical.

Golden Bowl, The A novel by **Henry James**, published in 1904. Adam Verver is an American millionaire living in Europe with his daughter Maggie and amassing an art collection. Maggie is of marriageable age, and her friend Fanny Assingham finds her an Italian prince, Amerigo. The beautiful Charlotte Stant comes to London to stay with Fanny, who knows that Charlotte and Amerigo had once been in love but could not marry since they were both penniless. Charlotte has no trouble persuading Amerigo to accompany her when he goes shopping in search of a wedding present for Maggie. At an antique dealer's she wants to give Amerigo a present also, a gilded crystal bowl. The presence of a flaw in the bowl brings it within the range of her purse; Amerigo, however, is disturbed that the bowl is flawed and declines the gift.

A year later, following the birth of a child to Maggie and Amerigo, Adam Verver, now a grandfather but not yet 50, proposes to and marries Charlotte. But Charlotte and Amerigo have not forgotten their original feelings for each other, and they meet in secret. For her father's birthday Maggie buys a gilded crystal bowl. She has not noticed that

it is flawed, but the dealer feels compelled to point it out and calls on her. He recognizes the photographs of Amerigo and Charlotte and tells Maggie that the pair had visited his shop and rejected the bowl during the days of her engagement to Amerigo. Maggie sends for Fanny and makes clear that she knows the whole truth about Charlotte and Amerigo. She smashes the golden bowl just as Amerigo enters the room. Amerigo stops seeing Charlotte; Adam gives no hint to her that he knows of her liaison; Maggie conducts herself with unruffled serenity. Charlotte, wondering at her lover's withdrawal, cannot provoke Maggie to any kind of exchange. Adam finally resolves the situation by deciding to return to America with Charlotte.

Gone With The Wind A novel by Margaret Mitchell (1900–49), published in 1936 and awarded the Pulitzer Prize in the following year. An immediate best seller, to date it has sold more than 25 million copies and been translated into 27 languages. It was made into a celebrated motion picture in 1939.

The novel opens, just before the outbreak of the Civil War, on a Georgia plantation, Tara, the home of Scarlett O'Hara, a spoilt and willful 16-year-old Southern belle. Against the backdrop of the war, the defeat of the South, and Reconstruction, the story follows the life and loves of Scarlett. Ashley Wilkes, with whom she is hopelessly infatuated, marries Melanie Hamilton; Scarlett marries Melanie's brother Charles out of spite, but soon becomes a young war widow. Having survived the siege and burning of Atlanta, she saves the lives of Melanie and her newborn child by leading them through the lines to the O'Hara plantation. Back at Tara, she finds her mother dead, her father demented, the slaves freed, and the plantation in ruins. The novel now focuses on Scarlett's determination to restore Tara. In need of money, she marries Frank Kennedy, her sister's fiancé, because he owns a profitable business. After he too is killed she marries Rhett Butler, a profiteer who has made a fortune from the war. Through him she acquires the wealth and power she craves, but throughout their marriage he struggles against her continuing passion for Ashley, and at the end of the novel, when Scarlett has finally come to realize her love for Rhett, he walks out on her with the famous words "My dear, I don't give a damn."

Good Earth, The   See **Buck, Pearl S.**

Goodman, Paul 1911–72   Goodman was born in New York City and received his BA from the City College of New York and his PhD from the University of Chicago. He wrote numerous books on a wide range of topics including *Utopian Essays and Proposals* (1962), on political theory; *Gestalt Therapy* (1951), on psychology; *Communitas* (1947, with his brother Percival), on city planning; and *Compulsory Mis-Education* (1964), on education. His political radicalism and discontent also inform many of his plays, novels, and short stories. *The Empire City* (1959), a novel set in New York from 1930 to 1950, first appeared as a series of shorter novels: *The Grand Piano*, or the *Almanac of Alienation* (1942), *The State of Nature* (1946), and *The Dead Spring* (1950). In 1960 he published an influential study of youth and delinquency, *Growing Up Absurd*. *Making Do* (1963), an autobiographical novel, was followed in 1966 by a non-fictional work of autobiography, *Five Years: Thoughts During a Useless Time*. He also wrote several volumes of literary criticism, the last of which was *Speaking and Language: Defense of Poetry* (1971). He contributed to *Dissent*, *Commentary*, *Playboy*, **The Nation**, and many other magazines and journals, as well as serving as film editor for **The Partisan Review** and as television critic for **The New Republic**. He was editor of *Liberation* from 1960 until his death in 1972. His *Collected Poems* appeared in 1974.

Gordon, Caroline 1895–1981   A Southern writer of fiction and criticism, Gordon was born in Trenton, Kentucky. After graduating from Bethany College in 1916 she taught high school for three years and then became a journalist on the *Chattanooga News* (1920–4), during which time she reviewed poetry written by the **Fugitives**. Like them, she considered the stability of the Southern past preferable to the chaos of modern, mechanized society. She married **Allen Tate**, one of the Fugitives, in 1925.

In her first novel, *Penhally* (1931), Gordon contrasts the grandeur of the antebellum South with its diminished condition after the Civil War. *Aleck Maury Sportsman* (1934) has a hero based on her own father. *None Shall Look Back* (1937), modeled on Tolstoy's *War and Peace*, has as its hero an actual figure from the Civil War – General Nathan Bedford Forrest. Her other novels are *The Garden of Adonis* (1937), *Green Centuries* (1941), *The Women on the Porch* (1944), *The Strange Children* (1951), *The Malefactors* (1956), and *The Glory of Hera* (1972).

In 1934 she was awarded the O. Henry Prize for her short story "Old Red," which was later published in the collection *The Forest of the South* (1945), again in *Old Red and Other Stories* (1963), and in *The Collected Stories of Caroline Gordon* (1981). Among her critical works, *The House of Fiction: An Anthology of the Short Story* (1950), with commentary by herself and Allen Tate, and *How to Read a Novel* (1957) provide a key to her own theories of fiction. She also wrote *A Good Soldier: A Key to the Novels of Ford Madox Ford* (1963). Between 1946 and 1951 (and occasionally afterwards) she taught a workshop in fiction techniques at Columbia University.

Go Tell It On The Mountain   See **Baldwin, James**

Grandissimes, The: *A Story of Creole Life*   A novel by **George Washington Cable**, published in 1880, and set in New Orleans in the early 19th century. A feud between the Grandissimes and the De Grapions, aristocratic families of Louisiana, leads to a duel in which Mr Nancanou – related by marriage to the De Grapions – is killed. His widow, Aurora, the last survivor of the De Grapion family, goes to live with her daughter Clotilde in New Orleans. Impoverished, they live in seclusion. Through old Dr Keene, Honoré Grandissime meets Joseph Frowenfield, a young apothecary who is in love with Clotilde De Grapion. Through Joseph, Honoré meets Aurora and falls in love with her. Because Aurora is poor, and serves as a reminder of past hostilities between the two families, the Grandissimes oppose Honoré's marriage to her. However, family objections to the union are cleared away in a deathbed scene: Honoré's uncle Agricola is dying from stab wounds inflicted by Honoré's quadroon half-brother. It was the arrogant Agricola who had killed Aurora's husband, but before he dies he reveals that 20 years earlier he had promised Aurora's father to allow the peace-engendering union between Aurora and Honoré. Obsessed with preserving the "race," Agricola now finds the union desirable again because it will continue the French Creole "aristocracy" to which the two families belong.

Grapes of Wrath, The A Pulitzer Prize-winning novel by **John Steinbeck**, published in 1939, that tells the story of Oklahoma farmers who are driven off their land by soil erosion. The Joad family drives to California, hoping to take advantage of what they imagine to be a land of plenty. The grandparents die on the way, and the Joads arrive only to be worn down by the impossibly hard life of migrant fruit-pickers. They find a temporary respite in a government labor camp, but when it closes they are forced to take work at a black-listed orchard. There Tom Joad joins with Jim Casy, a minister turned labor organizer. During ensuing strike violence Casy is killed, and Tom, who had once served time for killing a man in Oklahoma, kills again to avenge Casy's death. In panic, the Joads flee and try to hide Tom, but they are exhausted by struggle and starvation. Finally Ma Joad decides that for the good of all the family Tom must leave. The rest of the family struggles on together, though to what end and in what direction nobody knows. At the controversial end of the novel, the eldest daughter, Rose of Sharon, who has just given birth to a stillborn child, nurses an anonymous starving man with the milk intended for her baby.

Gravity's Rainbow A novel by **Thomas Pynchon**, published in 1973. A lengthy and extremely dense text, it involves more than 400 characters, and concerns itself with the historical trends identifiable in American society since World War II. It defies any summary statements, but can generally be said to treat scientific and technological discoveries as historical events and forces, and to explore the modes of consciousness which they generate. One of its central metaphors is the all-pervasive paranoia which has been crucial in other of Pynchon's works. Its allusions range from classical music theory to film and comic-strip characters. The literary figures evoked include **William Faulkner**, **Emily Dickinson**, Rainer Maria Rilke, Jorge Luis Borges, and James Joyce, to whose *Ulysses* the novel has frequently been compared.

Great Gatsby, The A novel by **F. Scott Fitzgerald**, published in 1925. The narrator, Nick Carraway, rents a cottage in West Egg, Long Island, next door to the mansion of Jay Gatsby and across the water from the home of Tom Buchanan and his wife Daisy, Carraway's cousin. Gatsby's mansion is the scene of extravagant nightly parties, attended by many people who are uninvited and do not know their host. Carraway, both cynical and curious about Gatsby, soon becomes his confidant. He learns that Gatsby had met Daisy while he was in the army during World War I, and that they had fallen in love and planned to marry. Daisy, however, had grown impatient for him to return and had married Tom, a rich though boring man from Yale. Having risen from his lowly origins as Jimmy Gatz through dubious business deals, Gatsby is obsessed with winning Daisy back. He persuades Carraway to arrange a meeting between them, and Daisy, after initial resistance, succumbs to her former lover's generous attentions, impressed by his newly acquired wealth.

Tom, Daisy, Gatsby, Carraway, and Carraway's girlfriend, Jordan Baker, spend a day together in New York City. Tom, who himself has had a longstanding affair with Myrtle Wilson, the wife of a Long Island garage owner, becomes aware of Daisy's attentions to Gatsby. Gatsby tries to convince Daisy to leave Tom. Tom, in turn, tries to discredit Gatsby by revealing that he has made his money from bootlegging. Gatsby and Daisy leave in Tom's automobile, with Daisy driving. Myrtle Wilson, recognizing the car as it passes her husband's garage, runs out into the street and is hit and killed by Daisy, who drives on. Taking revenge on Gatsby, Tom tells Wilson it was Gatsby who killed his wife, and Gatsby, attempting to protect Daisy, lets the blame fall on himself. Wilson murders Gatsby and then commits suicide. Carraway is left to arrange Gatsby's funeral, which hardly anyone attends, and Tom and Daisy retreat "back into their money, or their vast carelessness, or whatever it was that kept them together."

Greeley, Horace 1811–72 Born in New Hampshire, Greeley grew up in Vermont and in 1831 went to New York City, where he worked as a printer before becoming an editor of *The New Yorker* in 1834. In 1841 he founded *The Tribune*, the New York daily that he would edit until his death. His talented staff – including at various times Charles Dana, **Bayard Taylor**, **Margaret Fuller**, and **George Ripley** – together with Greeley's editorials, made *The Tribune* the leading newspaper in New York and indeed, with the publication of the national *Weekly Tribune*, in the US. Though originally a member of the conservative Whig party, Greeley was a consistent exponent of American democratic principles, as was reflected in his editorial support of reform movements, of the new Republican party in the 1850s, of emancipation in the 1860s, and of amnesty and universal suffrage in the period of Reconstruction. An opponent of the more radical Republicans in the 1870s, he was chosen as the Democratic presidential candidate in 1872; he was defeated by Ulysses S. Grant, however, and died within the month.

Colorful, eccentric, independent, often controversial, Greeley's editorials were nevertheless influential throughout his career. Among his other writings were travelogues: *Glances at Europe* (1851), and *An Overland Journey* (1860); *The American Conflict* (2 vols., 1864–6), an important contemporary history of the Civil War; and *Recollections of a Busy Life* (1868), an autobiography.

Green, Paul 1894–1981 Green was born in Lillington, North Carolina, and educated at the University of North Carolina, where he also taught from 1923–4. His prolific dramatic output began with realistic folk-plays which portrayed the lives of blacks and poor whites in North Carolina. Outstanding among these is the one-act *White Dresses* (1923), one of the six plays for the black theatre published under the title *Lonesome Road* (1926). Another piece in the same collection was later expanded into the full-length *In Abraham's Bosom* (1926), for which Green won the Pulitzer Prize in 1927. Staged in New York by the Provincetown Players, it is an angry story of the persecution and lynching of a black teacher. *The House of Connelly: A Drama of the Old South and the New* (1931), the first production of the **Group Theatre**, deals with the deteriorating fortunes of a white

landowning family in the South. *Tread the Green Grass* (1932) is one of a number of "symphonic dramas," combining dance and music with dialogue. *Johnny Johnson* (1936), written for the Group Theatre, is a fiercely anti-war musical play with music written by **Kurt Weill**. Green's hatred of violence is again vividly expressed in *Hymn to the Rising Sun* (1936), which exposes the sadistic practices of state penitentiaries. He also dramatized **Richard Wright**'s novel *Native Son* (1941), produced a new revival version of *Peer Gynt* (1951), and wrote 11 screenplays, among them an adaptation of John Howard Griffith's *Black Like Me* (1964).

After 1937, when he wrote *The Lost Colony* for a large-scale outdoor performance on the site of Sir Walter Raleigh's landing on Roanoke Island in North Carolina, Green devoted most of his attention to the writing and staging of "symphonic" pageant-dramas about American history, usually designed for outdoor performance in their appropriate geographical location. Other such productions include *The Common Glory* (1947) in Williamsburg, Virginia; *Faith of Our Fathers* (1950) in Washington, DC; *The Stephen Foster Story* (1959) in Bardstown, Kentucky; and *We the People* (1976) in Columbia, Maryland.

Green Pastures, The A play by **Marc Connelly**, first produced in 1930 with an all-black cast. Connelly had already been successful on Broadway with a string of stage comedies when he wrote *The Green Pastures*, based on *Ol' Man Adam An' His Chillun*, a collection of folk-tales by Roark Bradford. The play presents incidents of biblical history, from the creation to the crucifixion, in the storytelling mode of a Southern black preacher: representative scenes are the fish fry in Heaven, with which the play begins and ends, and the meeting in a New Orleans nightclub between the High Priest and the King of Babylon. The play was extremely daring for its time, particularly because God was represented as black. Despite Connelly's previous record of successes he had trouble finding a producer; subsequent attempts at a British production were frustrated when the play was banned by the Lord Chamberlain. Nonetheless, *The Green Pastures* enjoyed a long run in New York and on the road and won the Pulitzer Prize for 1930.

Gregory, Horace (Victor) 1898–1982 Born in Milwaukee, Wisconsin, Gregory received a BA from the University of Wisconsin in 1923. In addition, he spent his summers from 1919 to 1923 at the Milwaukee School of Fine Arts. In 1934 he began teaching at Sarah Lawrence College, where he was made professor emeritus in 1960.

His first volume of poetry, *Chelsea Rooming House*, appeared in 1930. His early verse was strongly influenced by Marxist thought, but in 1935 he angered other left-wing writers by asserting that art should be apolitical. Throughout his career, however, he remained concerned with the plight of the poor and dispossessed in America's cities. His other volumes of poetry include *A Wreath for Margery* (1933), *No Retreat* (1933), *Chorus for Survival* (1935), *Poems 1930–1940* (1941), *Selected Poems* (1951), *Medusa in Gramercy Park* (1961), *Alphabet For Joanna: A Poem* (1963), *Collected Poems* (1964), and *Another Look* (1976). He also published translations of Ovid and Catullus and several works of literary and art criticism, including a study of D. H. Lawrence entitled *Pilgrim of the Apocalypse* (1933); a collection of essays, *The Shield of Achilles* (1944); *The World of James McNeill Whistler* (1959); and two more essay collections, *The Dying Gladiators* (1961) and *Spirit of Time and Place* (1973). With his wife, the poet **Marya Zaturenska**, he edited various poetry anthologies, and wrote *A History of American Poetry 1900–1940* (1946).

Grey, (Pearl) Zane 1872–1939 Born in Zanesville, Ohio, Grey graduated from the University of Pennsylvania in 1896 with a degree in dentistry. He practiced in New York City from 1898 to 1904, during which time he began to write fiction. His first novel, a romance entitled *Betty Zane*, was privately published by him in 1903 but received little public attention. He married Lina Elise Roth in 1905, and shortly after closed his dental office and moved to a rural area on the Delaware River, near Lackwaxen, Pennsylvania. In 1907 his wife convinced him to make his first trip to Arizona, in the company of C. J. "Buffalo" Jones, a retired buffalo hunter. The journey proved to be the turning point in his career. He began writing Western novels in the tradition of **Owen Wister**, and developed the conventions of the Western into a formula with enormous popular appeal.

He wrote 60 books, which sold over 15 million copies in his lifetime, making him the single most popular author of the post-World War I era in America. Over 100 Western films were based on his stories. In novels such as *Riders of the Purple Sage* (1912), *To the Last Man* (1922), *Nevada* (1928), *Wild Horse Mesa* (1928), and *Code of the West* (1934), he presents the West as a moral landscape against which his protagonists struggle, and by which they are either destroyed or redeemed, according to their response to its violent code.

Group, The See **McCarthy, Mary**

Group Theatre, The A New York theatrical organization, founded in 1931 by a group formally associated with the **Theatre Guild**, including Lee Strasberg, Harold Clurman, and Cheryl Crawford. In rebellion against the apolitical nature of the Guild's productions, the founders were committed to the stage as a forum for the open discussion of political and social issues. **Paul Green**'s *The House of Connelly* (1931) was their first production. The Group helped to launch the careers of the playwrights **Clifford Odets** and **Marc Blitzstein**, and during its nine-year career produced some of the most enduring plays of the decade, including **Sidney Kingsley**'s *Men in White* (1933), Paul Green and **Kurt Weill**'s *Johnny Johnson* (1936), Irwin Shaw's *The Gentle People* (1939), **William Saroyan**'s *My Heart's in the Highlands* (1939), and many plays by Clifford Odets, among them *Awake and Sing!* (1935), *Waiting for Lefty* (1935), *Golden Boy* (1937), *Rocket to the Moon* (1938), and *Night Music* (1940). Due to personality and financial problems, the Group ceased production in 1940. One of the founders, Harold Clurman, documented the history of the company in *The Fervent Years* (1945).

H

H.D. See **Doolittle, Hilda**

Hairy Ape, The   See **O'Neill, Eugene**

Hale, Sarah 1788–1879   A noted New England humanitarian, Hale edited *Ladies' Magazine* from 1828 to 1837, and *Godey's Lady's Book* for the next 40 years until shortly before her death. Her novel *Northwood: A Tale of New England* (1827) is a didactic condemnation of slavery. Her short stories were collected in *Sketches of American Character* (1829). The later part of her career was dedicated to compiling her massive *Women's Record* (1853; expanded 1855 and 1870), an encyclopedic work that details the achievements of over 1,500 distinguished women. By no means a radical feminist, Hale upheld a traditional view of women as bearers of spiritual and moral virtue. She was, however, a forceful advocate of education for women, as well as for child welfare and the abolition of slavery.

Halleck, Fitz-Greene 1790–1867   A poet and member of the **Knickerbocker Group**, Halleck was born in Guilford, Connecticut. He worked first in banking and then as personal secretary to John Jacob Astor. He collaborated with **Joseph Rodman Drake** on the satirical "Croaker" poems, published anonymously in 1819 in the New York *Evening Post* and collected as *The Croaker Papers* in 1860. His long poem *Fanny* (1819) satirized New York society in the manner of Byron's *Beppo*; it was republished with 50 additional stanzas in 1821. Traveling in Europe in the following year, he wrote "Alnwick Castle," influenced again by Byron, and by Scott; *Alnwick Castle, with Other Poems* was published in 1827. Other notable poems include "Red Jacket" (1827), "The Field of Grounded Arms" (1831), and "Young

America" (1865). His collected *Poetical Works* were published in 1847.

Halper, Albert 1904–   Born in Chicago into a poor family of Jewish immigrants, Halper is best known as a proletarian novelist. His first books were *Union Square* (1933); *On the Shore* (1934); *The Foundry* (1934), which deals with electrotype workers in Chicago just before the 1929 crash; and *The Chute* (1937), about workers in a mail-order house. *Sons of the Fathers* (1940) is the story of a Jewish immigrant. His subsequent work includes *The Little People* (1942, short stories), and the novels *Only an Inch from Glory* (1943), *The Golden Watch* (1953), and *Atlantic Avenue* (1956). *Good-bye, Union Square*, his memoir of the 1930s, appeared in 1970.

Hammerstein, Oscar (Greeley Clendinning II) 1895–1960 and **Rodgers, Richard** 1902–79   Collaborators for the musical stage. Rodgers's music, Hammerstein's lyrics, and the many shows on which they collaborated are often credited with helping to transform the American musical comedy into a truly modern vehicle for serious entertainment. Born in New York City into a theatrical family, Oscar Hammerstein II was named for his grandfather, the opera impresario. He attended Columbia University, where he wrote and appeared in the Varsity Show. He then attended law school for a time and worked as a clerk and process-server, but soon quit to become assistant stage manager in his uncle's theatre. His first play, *The Light* (1919), closed quickly out of town; *Always You* (1920) and *Tickle Me* (1920), with music by Herbert Stothart, had brief Broadway runs. His first real successes were *Wildflower* (1923), with lyrics by himself and Otto Harbach, music by Vincent Youmans and

Herbert Stothart; and *Rose Marie* (1924), lyrics by Hammerstein and Harbach, music by Rudolph Friml. With the composer **Jerome Kern**, he went on to write *Sunny* (1925); *Show Boat* (1927), an adaptation from Edna Ferber's novel; and *Music in the Air* (1932). Other successes included *The Desert Song* (1926) and *New Moon* (1928), both with music by Sigmund Romberg. Even so, Hammerstein was recovering from a long string of failures when Richard Rodgers suggested they collaborate on what would become *Oklahoma!* (1943).

Richard Rodgers was born on Long Island, New York, and published his first songs privately at the age of 14; a year later he wrote the score for a complete amateur musical production. A mutual friend introduced him to **Lorenz Hart** in 1918; their first collaboration, "Any Old Place With You," was performed on Broadway by the comedian Lew Fields. Rodgers entered Columbia University in 1919, and he and Hart promptly wrote two Varsity Shows, *Fly With Me* (1920) and *You'll Never Know* (1921). Some songs from the first of these found their way to Broadway in Lew Fields's *Poor Little Ritz Girl* (1920). After his sophomore year, Rodgers left Columbia for the Institute of Musical Art (now the Juilliard School) and he and Hart continued to collaborate on amateur shows, often with the assistance of Lew Fields's son Herbert. A break came when the **Theatre Guild** asked them to write a benefit revue: *The Garrick Gaities* (1926), which included the song "Manhattan," was a great success. This led to many other productions, including *Dearest Enemy* (1925), set during the American Revolution; *The Girl Friend* (1926), an experiment in dream-projection; *A Connecticut Yankee* (1927), based on the **Mark Twain** novel; three shows in 1928 alone, *She's My Baby*, *Present Arms*, and *Chee-Chee*; and two in 1929, *Spring Is Here* and *Heads Up*. *Simple Simon* (1930) was a vehicle for Ed Wynn; *America's Sweetheart* made fun of Mary Pickford and Hollywood, where both Rodgers and Hart were spending much of their time, writing for films. In 1935 they contributed songs to *Jumbo*, a Billy Rose extravaganza that was half-play and half-circus. *On Your Toes* (1936) included Rodgers's famous "Slaughter on Tenth Avenue Ballet," choreographed by the young George Balanchine. *Babes in Arms* (1937) was performed by and for children; *I'd*

Rather Be Right (1937), written with **George S. Kaufman** and **Moss Hart**, featured George M. Cohan as a caricature of FDR; *The Boys From Syracuse* (1938) was a modern adaptation of Shakespeare's *Comedy of Errors*. Perhaps their most radical departure from the conventions of musical theatre was *Pal Joey* (1940), based on a series of sketches in *The New Yorker* by **John O'Hara**. The central character was a nightclub operator and gigolo; critics and public did not react well to a comedy whose hero was a "heel," but when the play was revived in 1952 it had a long run and won the New York Drama Critics Circle Award. Rodgers and Hart followed this daring show with *Higher and Higher* (1940) and *By Jupiter* (1942), which depicted a war between Amazon women and Greek men. The collaboration came to an end with Hart's death in 1943; the pair had written over a thousand songs together.

Rodgers had known Oscar Hammerstein since 1915, and they had even collaborated on a few songs together for the Varsity Show and other amateur productions. In 1942 the Theatre Guild approached Rodgers to do a musical adaptation of Lynn Riggs's folk-play *Green Grow the Lilacs*; this became the first Rodgers and Hammerstein show, *Oklahoma!* (1943), a smash hit which ran for over five years. *Oklahoma!* was the first musical to use dance (choreographed by Agnes de Mille) as an integral part of plot and characterization rather than simply as decoration. A string of successes followed for the pair: *Carousel* (1945), based on Ferenc Molnar's *Liliom*, dealt with another sympathetic anti-hero, transplanted from Molnar's Hungary to the New England coast; *South Pacific* (1949), based on stories by James Michener, won the second Pulitzer Prize ever awarded to a musical; *The King and I* (1951), based on a true story retold by Margaret Landon in *Anna and the King of Siam*, dealt with conflicts between two cultures and was revolutionary in omitting any "love interest" between hero and heroine. Rodgers and Hammerstein went on to write a film musical, *State Fair* (1945); three less successful experimental musicals, *Allegro* (1947), *Me and Juliet* (1953), and *Pipe Dream* (1955); and a made-for-television musical, *Cinderella* (1957). *Flower Drum Song* (1958), about generational conflicts among Chinese-Americans, and the enormously successful *The*

Sound of Music (1959) were the duo's last successes before Hammerstein's death in 1960. Rodgers went on to write *No Strings* (1962); *Do I Hear A Waltz?* (1965), with lyrics by **Stephen Sondheim**; and *Two by Two* (1970).

Hammett, (Samuel) Dashiell 1894– 1961 Hammett was born in Maryland and briefly attended the Polytechnic Institute of Baltimore. He served in the army during World War I and then went to work for the Pinkerton Agency in San Francisco as a private detective. His experiences served him well when he turned to writing detective stories and published his first novel, *Red Harvest*, in 1929. He used an unadorned realistic style – later christened the "hard-boiled style" – that suited his material perfectly, and soon drew admiring comments from writers as diverse as André Gide, **Sinclair Lewis**, and Robert Graves. He also drew a host of imitators, but not all of them realized how important intelligence and acute observation were to the credibility of Hammett's heroes. They are not merely tough; they often confront violence with full knowledge of its inherently corrupting potential.

Hammett's other books include *The Dain Curse* (1929), *The Maltese Falcon* (1930), *The Glass Key* (1931), and *The Thin Man* (1934). He also published a number of short stories in the magazine **The Black Mask**, which were collected in *The Adventures of Sam Spade* (1944), *The Creeping Siamese and Other Stories* (1950), and *The Continental Op* (1974). His longtime companion, the playwright **Lillian Hellman**, contributed a memoir of him to her selection of his short stories called *The Big Knockover* (1966), which also includes his unfinished autobiographical novel, *Tulip*.

Politically left-wing, he refused in 1951 to testify before the New York State Supreme Court about the funds of the Civil Rights Congress, of which he was a trustee. As a result he was jailed for six months. In 1953 he refused to answer questions about his politics before Senator Joseph McCarthy's Subcommittee on Investigations, and was blacklisted by Hollywood. Suffering from a heart condition, he was cared for by Lillian Hellman from 1951 until his death.

Hammon, Jupiter 1720–1800 A slave in a Long Island household, Hammon became the first published black poet in America when *An Evening Thought* appeared in 1760. He is also known for his essay *An Address to the Negroes of the State of New York* (1787), in which he insisted that his fellow slaves be patient, and urged owners to free slave children. His work helped generate support for the Abolitionist movement growing in the northern states at the time.

Hansberry, Lorraine 1930–65 Born in Chicago and educated at the University of Wisconsin, Hansberry was the first black woman to have a play produced on Broadway. Her best-known play, *A Raisin in the Sun* (1959), is a sympathetic examination of the economic, educational, and racial concerns of a family of black Chicagoans who plan to move into a white neighborhood. It was enormously successful, running for 530 consecutive performances, and winning a New York Drama Critics Circle Award. *The Sign in Sidney Brustein's Window* (1964) is the story of a group of Jews, other whites, and blacks in New York's Greenwich Village. In 1964, the year before her death, Hansberry wrote the captions for the photographs in *The Movement*, a documentary of the Civil Rights Movement. After her death her husband assembled *To Be Young, Gifted and Black* (1969) from her letters, diaries, and other unpublished material. *Raisin*, a musical adaptation of her best-known work, was produced in 1973.

Harland, Henry 1861–1905 Harland was born in New York City and studied at City College. After a visit to Paris and a brief period at The Harvard Divinity School, he embarked on a literary career under the pseudonym of Sidney Luska. Pretending to be Jewish, he wrote several realistic novels about Jewish immigrants in New York: *As It Was Written: A Jewish Musician's Story* (1885), *Mrs Peixada* (1886), *The Yoke of the Thorah* (1887), and *My Uncle Florimund* (1888).

In 1889 he went to Paris, and dropped his assumed character with the publication of the collection *A Latin Quarter Courtship and Other Stories* (1889) and the four novels *Grandison Mather* (1889), *Two Women or One* (1890), *Two Voices* (1890), and *Mea Culpa* (1891). He moved to England in 1890, where he became the first editor of *The Yellow Book*, the activity for which he is best remembered. He then wrote a number of stories and romances, including *Mademoiselle Miss and Other Stories* (1893), *Grey Roses* (1895), and *Comedies and Errors* (1898). His most successful novels were *The Cardinal's Snuff Box* (1900) and *My Friend Prospero* (1904).

Harlem Renaissance Also called the "New Negro" or Black Renaissance, the Harlem Renaissance is a term used to designate a period of cultural activity by black artists from the early 1920s through the early 1930s. As **Alain Locke** noted in his introduction to the anthology *The New Negro* (1925), there was felt to be a new spirit of achievement and opportunity for collective creative expression by black writers, in contrast to the solitary efforts of earlier literary figures. The movement was also marked by an emphasis on the African heritage of American blacks, and was paralleled by a renewed interest in black culture by white writers such as **Eugene O'Neill**, **Carl Van Vechten**, Ridgely Torrence, and others. Although few of the writers who are identified with the Renaissance were actually native New Yorkers, and some, such as **Claude McKay** and **Langston Hughes**, lived in other parts of the US for most of the 1920s, Harlem was nevertheless the center of activity, and so lent its name to the movement.

Four major writers who established their reputation during this period were Claude McKay, **Jean Toomer**, **Countee Cullen**, and Langston Hughes. The publication of *Harlem Shadows* (1922) brought McKay recognition as a poet, and his novels *Home to Harlem* (1928) and *Banjo* (1929) were equally well received. Before going south in 1922 Jean Toomer spent time in Harlem, and he remained in contact with New York intellectuals throughout his life. His *Cane* (1923), with its experimental style and form, and its complex examination of black heritage and culture, is a central text of the Renaissance. No less influential was the work of Countee Cullen and Langston Hughes. Cullen's *Color* (1925) is noted for its disciplined style and form and for its lyrical exploration of the writer's African heritage, and Hughes's *The Weary Blues* (1926) embodies the spirit of the Renaissance with its celebration of black culture and folk traditions.

Other writers who came to prominence at this time were **Zora Neale Hurston**, **Jessie Redmon Fauset**, **Arna Bontemps**, and **Sterling A. Brown**. Lesser figures who contributed to the Renaissance include the novelists Walter White, Nella Larsen, George Schulyer, Wallace Thurman, Eric Walrond, and Rudolf Fisher. Among the other poets connected with the movement were Waring Cuney, Frank Horne, Gwendolyn B. Bennett, and Helene Johnson.

Harper, Frances E. (Watkins) 1825–1911 One of the most popular anti-slavery poets of her day. Harper was a free black born in Baltimore, Maryland. She was educated at schools in Pennsylvania and Ohio, taught for a short time in Pennsylvania, and then worked as a volunteer lecturer for the Anti-slavery Society. Her first volume of verse, *Poems on Miscellaneous Subjects* (most of them expressing anti-slavery sentiments), was published in 1854. It proved extremely popular and by 1874 had gone through 20 editions. Her other works include *Moses, A Story of the Nile* (1869), *Poems* (1871), *Iola Le Roy; or, Shadows Uplifted* (1892), about the tragic life of a young octoroon woman before and during the Civil War, and *Atlanta Offering, Poems* (1895).

Harper's New Monthly Magazine Founded in 1850 under the title *Harper's Monthly Magazine* by Harper and Brothers in New York City with Henry J. Raymond as editor, by 1860 its circulation had reached 200,000. It initially concentrated on publishing established British authors, such as Dickens, Thackeray, Trollope, and Hardy, but under the editorship of Henry M. Alden (1869–1919) it drew regularly on American writers also, among them **John De Forest**, **Hamlin Garland**, **William Dean Howells**, and **Sarah Orne Jewett**. Though fiction remained its main offering, after 1900 (and under its new title of *Harper's New Monthly Magazine*) it devoted more space to political and social issues, and featured articles by well-known public figures such as Woodrow Wilson, Calvin Coolidge, and Theodore Roosevelt. In 1925 the shortened title of *Harper's Magazine* was adopted, and it is now commonly known simply as *Harper's*.

Harris, George Washington 1814–69 Born in Pennsylvania, Harris was a Tennessee River steamboat captain before he turned to writing. His best-known work is *Sut Lovingood: Yarns spun by a "Nat'ral Born Durn'd Fool"* (1867). A collection of tall tales and sketches, full of Southwestern frontier dialect and robust humor, it is a clear forerunner of some of **Mark Twain**'s early writings.

Harris, Joel Chandler 1848–1908   The creator of Uncle Remus was born in Georgia, where from an early age he worked on plantations and imbibed the black folklore that was to inform the style and subject matter of his fiction. The first of the Uncle Remus stories, "The Story of Mr Rabbit and Mr Fox, as Told by Uncle Remus," was published in 1879. *Uncle Remus: His Songs and Sayings* appeared in 1881 and was followed by *Nights With Uncle Remus* (1883), *Uncle Remus and His Friends* (1892), *Mr Rabbit at Home* (1895), *The Tar Baby and Other Short Rhymes of Uncle Remus* (1904), and *Uncle Remus and Br'er Rabbit* (1906). These stories offer traditional black folk-wisdom in what **Mark Twain** considered a flawless duplication of Southern black speech. Moreover, Harris's special interest in the animal mythology of black folklore has brought to American culture such figures as Br'er Rabbit and Br'er Fox. His other works include *Mingo and Other Sketches in Black and White* (1884), and two novels, *Sister Jane: Her Friends and Acquaintances* (1896) and *Gabriel Tolliver: A Story of Reconstruction* (1902). *On the Plantation* (1892) recounts the childhood experiences that inspired so much of his work.

Hart, Lorenz   See **Hammerstein, Oscar**

Hart, Moss 1904–61   A writer of comic dramas, best known for his collaborations with **George S. Kaufman**, Hart was born to a poor family in New York City. He left school in the eighth grade and worked first as a clerk in a fur vault, then as office boy for Augustus Pitou, Jr, a producer of road shows. It was Pitou who produced Hart's first play, a melodrama called *The Beloved Bandit*, which closed out of town and took Hart's job with it. He then worked as a bit player, Little Theatre director, and social director at summer camps in the Catskills, writing a number of unproducible scripts before Kaufman agreed to work with him on *Once in a Lifetime* (1930), the success of which put a permanent end to his financial worries.

Harte, (Francis) Bret[t] 1836–1902   Harte was born in Albany, New York. At the age of 18 he traveled to California, where he worked as a prospector, a teacher, a Wells Fargo expressman, and then as a journalist. In 1860 he settled in San Francisco, and began to contribute to the *Golden Era* and *The Californian*. As editor of the latter he commissioned weekly articles from his friend **Mark Twain**.

He was appointed secretary of the US Mint in San Francisco in 1863. He continued to write, however, and his first book of poems, *The Lost Galleon*, was published in 1867. *Condensed Novels and Other Papers*, parodies of distinguished authors, appeared in the same year. In 1868 he helped to establish *Overland Monthly* as an outlet for Western writers. He edited the journal for two years, and contributed a number of his own stories to it. In 1870 he published a comic ballad, *Plain Language from Truthful James*, as well as the collection of Western stories which made him famous, *The Luck of Roaring Camp and Other Sketches*. The book's success brought him an offer from *The Atlantic Monthly*. He returned to the East, where he lived and wrote until 1878, when he was appointed US consul in Germany. He was consul at Glasgow from 1880 to 1885 and spent the rest of his life in London.

His stories are collected in *Mrs Skaggs's Husbands* (1873), *Tales of the Argonauts* (1875), *An Heiress of Red Dog, and Other Sketches* (1878), *A Sappho of Green Springs, and Other Stories* (1891), and *Colonel Starbottle's Client, and Some Other People* (1892). He also published several novels, including *Gabriel Conroy* (1876) and *Jeff Briggs's Love Story* (1880); and two plays, *Two Men of Sandy Bar* (1876) and *Ah Sin* (1877), the latter of which he wrote with Mark Twain.

Hawkes, John (Clendennin Burne, Jr) 1925–   Hawkes was born in Connecticut and educated at Harvard; he has taught at Brown University since 1958. His first novel, *The Cannibal* (1949), is a bleak and formally complex work about the horrors of World War II. Subsequent novels, such as *The Beetle Leg* (1951), *The Goose on the Grave* (1954), *The Lime Twig* (1961), and *Second Skin* (1964), continued to evoke the extremes of violence he saw as characteristic of the modern world. His more recent work has become more popular, but it remains macabre. He is, with **John Barth**, a leading figure of what has come to be called postmodernist fiction, a position evidenced by the collection of stories, *Lunar Landscapes* (1969), and by the novels *Death, Sleep and the Traveller* (1974), *Travesty* (1976), *The Owl* (1977), *The Passion Artist* (1979), *Virginie: Her Two Lives* (1981), *Innocence in Extremis* (1985), *Adventures in the Alaskan Skin Trade* (1985).

Hawthorne, Nathaniel 1804–64 Hawthorne was born in Salem, Massachusetts, into a prominent family whose ancestors were among the earliest settlers of the colony. Later in life, he was especially preoccupied, and troubled, by his descent from John Hathorne, a judge in the Salem witch trials of 1692. Hawthorne grew up in seclusion with his widowed mother, his father, a sea captain, having died of yellow fever in 1808. When he was 11 they moved to Maine. There he attended Bowdoin College and made a number of important and lasting friends, including **Henry Wadsworth Longfellow** and the future president Franklin Pierce.

After graduating in 1825 he returned to Salem and, determined to become a writer, worked on short stories and historical sketches. In 1828, anonymously and at his own expense, he published *Fanshawe*, a novel based on his college life. While the book itself received only slight critical attention and an ashamed author burned the unsold copies, it did initiate a long, productive friendship between Hawthorne and the publisher Samuel Goodrich. He returned to writing short fiction, and in historical and allegorical tales began to explore the impact of harsh Puritanism on the guilty conscience of New England. Many of these stories were published in Goodrich's *The Token*, an annual gift-book, and were later collected in *Twice-Told Tales* (1837, expanded 1842).

Hawthorne then worked for Goodrich as an editor and hack writer from 1836 to 1839, when he accepted a post as surveyor of the Boston Custom House. After becoming involved with the Boston literary circle, which included his old friend Longfellow, he quit his post at the Custom House in 1841 and invested in the communal experiment at **Brook Farm**. That same year he married Sophia Peabody, herself an active participant in the **Transcendentalist** movement. Soon, however, the retiring Hawthorne was disappointed by communal life; in 1842 he and his wife moved to Concord, where they lived in the Old Manse, a former home of **Ralph Waldo Emerson**. He returned to serious writing, and in 1846 published *Mosses from an Old Manse*, which includes the famous story "Young Goodman Brown." After serving as customs surveyor at Salem for three years (1846–9), at the age of 45 he finally produced his first significant long work of fiction. *The Scarlet Letter* (1850), still considered the most important of his works, won almost immediate acclaim. It was rapidly followed by *The House of the Seven Gables* (1851) and *The Blithedale Romance* (1852), which was based on the Brook Farm experience. Hawthorne was never again to equal the productivity of this three-year period, during which he also published *The Snow Image and Other Tales* (1851), which includes stories such as "Ethan Brand" and "My Kinsman Major Molineux." The publication of *A Wonder Book* (1852), which retells Greek myths for children, and *Tanglewood Tales* (1853) marked the end of his most prolific period.

In 1853 Franklin Pierce became president and Hawthorne, who had written a campaign biography for him, was appointed US consul at Liverpool. He lived in England for four years and in Italy for two, returning to the US in 1860 and publishing his final novel, *The Marble Faun*. He tried to regain his former creative energy, but without success. Four unfinished novels were found among his papers after his death in 1864; they were eventually published as *Septimius Felton; or, the Elixir of Life* (1872), *The Dolliver Romance* (1876), *Dr Grimshawe's Secret* (1882), and *The Ancestral Footstep* (1883). His last publications were *Our Old Home* (1863), a book of essays on England, and various pieces in *The Atlantic Monthly*. After his death his wife edited and published his notebooks, which appeared as *Passages from the American Notebooks* (1868), *Passages from the English Notebooks* (1870), and *Passages from the French and Italian Notebooks* (1871). Modern editions of these works include many of the sections which she cut out or altered.

Hay, John Milton 1838–1905 Born in Salem, Indiana, Hay graduated from Brown

University in 1858. He became one of Abraham Lincoln's private secretaries after Lincoln was elected president in 1860 and soon thereafter served on a legation to Paris. On his return to the US he forsook politics for letters. In 1871 he published *Castilian Days*, a travel book combined with historical comment describing his European experiences, and a volume of dialect poems, *Pike County Ballads*. In 1878 he reentered politics as Assistant Secretary of State to Rutherford B. Hayes, and in 1883 he anonymously published *The Bread Winners*, a satirical attack on labor unions and a defense of economic individualism. His 10-volume biography, *Abraham Lincoln: A History*, appeared in 1890. He was President McKinley's ambassador to Great Britain from 1897 to 1898, and Secretary of State under both McKinley and Theodore Roosevelt from 1899 to 1905, in which latter capacity he was responsible for the treaty which gave the US control of the Panama Canal. He collaborated with John Nicolay on the collection and editing of the Abraham Lincoln papers (12 vols., 1905).

Hayden, Robert (Earl) 1913–   Black poet, born in Detroit, and educated at the Detroit Institute of Musical Art, Detroit City College, and the University of Michigan. He has taught at Fisk University and at the University of Michigan. His first collection of poetry, *Heart-Shape in the Dust* (1940), displays the wide variety of verse forms and styles which characterize his work as a whole. *The Lion and the Archer* was written in collaboration with Myron O'Higgins in 1948, and was followed by *Figures of Time* in 1955. In *A Ballad of Remembrance* (1962) he developed a more complex poetic vision, using frequent historical and literary allusions, and subjects taken from black history and folklore. The volume won the grand prize for poetry in English at the first World Festival of Negro Arts at Dakar, Senegal, in 1966. The tone becomes slightly darker and more disquieting in his later volumes, which include *Words in the Mourning Time* (1970), *The Night-Blooming Cereus* (1972), *American Journal* (1978), and *The Legend of John Brown* (1978). *Selected Poems* was published in 1966, and *Angle of Ascent: New and Selected Poems* in 1975. Hayden is also the editor of *Kaleidoscope: Poems by American Negro Poets* (1967).

Hazard of New Fortunes, A   A novel by **William Dean Howells**, published in 1890. The early chapters, set in Boston, tell how Fulkerson, who is involved in syndicated journalism, convinces Basil March (a character who appears in other novels by Howells) to move to New York City and serve as the literary editor of a new magazine called *Every Other Week*. Basil, his wife Isabel, and their two children make the move – they "hazard" this new enterprise. Describing the Marches' search for a home provides Howells with the opportunity to set before his readers detailed descriptions of New York City – a new and urban wilderness. The Marches soon encounter the Dryfoos family. Jacob Dryfoos, an old farmer who became rich when natural gas was discovered on his Ohio farm and who increased this wealth through real estate and stock-market speculation, has moved his family from Ohio to New York in order to launch his children in society, and has financed *Every Other Week* in order to give his son Conrad something to do. Conrad, however, wishes to become a minister and shows little interest in the magazine, spending much of his time in charity work among the poor. He meets and becomes infatuated with Margaret Vance, a young society woman who also spends her spare time doing charitable work.

Basil March hires Lindau, an elderly socialist of German extraction who had taught Basil German when he was young, to translate pieces for the magazine. The idealistic Lindau interests young Conrad, but Jacob Dryfoos is enraged when he learns that Lindau is a socialist, and orders March to dismiss him. March refuses to do so, but Lindau – morally outraged at having received money (even if indirectly) from Dryfoos, a strike-breaking capitalist – resigns and returns all the money he has earned from the magazine. Near the end of the novel, both Conrad and Lindau appear on the scene of a streetcar-workers' strike. Conrad is killed by a stray bullet from a policeman's gun, and Lindau dies later from injuries inflicted by the police who are breaking the strike. Disheartened by his son's death, Jacob sells the magazine to Fulkerson and March, and travels to Europe with his wife and daughters to try their "fortunes" in European society. Margaret Vance becomes an Episcopalian nun.

Hearn, (Patricio) Lafcadio (Tessima Carlos) 1850–1904 Born in Greece of Irish-Greek parentage, Hearn was educated in France and England. In 1869 he emigrated to the US and attempted a journalistic career, but his progress was hampered by poverty and the scandal caused by his living with a black woman. His first successful newspaper articles were colorful descriptions of Creole life based on his experiences in New Orleans in 1877. *Gombo Zhebes*, published in 1885, was a collection of proverbs in French from Louisiana and the West Indies; this was followed in 1890 by *Two Years in the French West Indies*. Hearn then traveled to Japan to write a series of articles for **Harper's New Monthly Magazine**, and in fact remained there for the rest of his life, becoming a Japanese citizen and adopting the name Yakimo Koizumi. His works describing the Japanese land, people, and customs include *Gleanings in Buddha-Fields* (1897), *In Ghostly Japan* (1899), *A Japanese Miscellany* (1901), and *Japan: An Attempt at Interpretation* (1904). *Chita* (1889) is a novel set on the Gulf Coast of Louisiana. *The Life and Letters of Lafcadio Hearn*, edited by Elizabeth Bisland, was published in 1906.

Heart is a Lonely Hunter, The See **McCullers, Carson**

Hecht, Ben 1894–1964 Hecht was born in New York City but his family later moved to Racine, Wisconsin, where he attended high school. After a brief period at the University of Wisconsin he moved to Chicago, attracted by the city's burgeoning literary renaissance. He worked for many years there as a reporter, first with the *Journal* (1910–14) and then with the *Daily News* (1914–23), establishing a reputation as the most creative and energetic newsman in the city. In the early 1920s he began writing novels, the most successful of which was *Erik Dorn* (1921), a work inspired in part by his years in Germany following World War I as foreign correspondent for the *Daily News*. He did not achieve national prominence, however, until he began writing plays in the mid 1920s. He scored a huge success with *The Front Page* (1928, co-written with **Charles MacArthur**), about Chicago newspapermen. He and MacArthur also co-wrote the popular comedy *Twentieth Century* (1932). From the early 1930s Hecht turned his attention to screenwriting, and he and

MacArthur enjoyed further collaborative success. Their screenplays include *Nothing Sacred* (1937), *Wuthering Heights* (1939), *Spellbound* (1945), and *Notorious* (1946).

Heller, Joseph 1923– Born in Brooklyn, Heller served in the US Army Air Corps in World War II. After receiving his BA from New York University (1948) and MA from Columbia (1949), he studied at Oxford on a Fulbright Scholarship (1949–50). His reputation as a novelist was firmly established by his best-selling anti-war novel *Catch-22* (1961). While teaching literature and working in advertising, he has produced three more novels: *Something Happened* (1974), *Good as Gold* (1979), and *God Knows* (1984). He has also written a play, *We Bombed in New Haven* (1968).

Hellman, Lillian (Florence) 1907–84 Born in New Orleans, Hellman spent her childhood shuttling between the South and New York City. She started work as a publisher's reader while still a student at New York University and already had several years' experience as a reader of plays and filmscripts when she wrote her first play, *The Children's Hour* (1934), which tells of the havoc caused by a malicious schoolgirl's invention of a lesbian relationship between her two teachers. Though controversial, the play was an immediate success. She followed it with *Days To Come* (1936), which was a failure, and with several film scripts. In 1937 her anti-Fascist convictions led her to visit Spain. Her second successful play, *The Little Foxes* (1939), dealt with the breaking up of a Southern family, the Hubbards, through greed, cruelty, and hunger for power; it was followed by two anti-Nazi dramas, *Watch on the Rhine* (1941) and *The Searching Wind* (1944). *Another Part of the Forest* (1946) took a second look at the Hubbard family, some 20 years earlier, revealing the sources of their cruelty and hatred for one another.

About this time Hellman found herself blacklisted, unable to work in Hollywood, because of her earlier political activities. Called to testify in 1952 by the House Un-American Activities Committee, she agreed to talk about her own involvement with radical movements but refused to discuss the involvement of others. She was not sent to jail, but many friends were, including her companion, **Dashiell Hammett**. One of her three autobiographical volumes, *Scoundrel Time* (1976), tells the story of this period of her life. The others, *An Unfinished Woman* (1969) and *Pentimento* (1973), are largely concerned with her childhood experiences and early political and personal involvements. She wrote two other plays, *The Autumn Garden* (1951) and *Toys in The Attic* (1960).

Hemingway, Ernest (Miller) 1898–1961 Born in Oak Park, Illinois, Hemingway spent much of his early life in the Great Lakes region, which provided the settings for his early stories. After graduating from high school he worked as a reporter for *The Kansas City Star*, and then volunteered for service in World War I. He served with an ambulance unit and was wounded in 1918. That experience, as well as his father's suicide, began his preoccupation with human vulnerability and mankind's efforts to confront it. After the war he worked as a journalist in Chicago and Toronto, and in 1921 married Hadley Richardson, seven years his senior. The couple moved to Paris, and made frequent excursions to Spain and to the Austrian Alps.

Hemingway made friends easily; among those who encouraged him in his literary career were **Ezra Pound**, **Gertrude Stein**, **Sylvia Beach**, and Ford Madox Ford. His first collection of stories, *In Our Time* (1925), consists of 15 tales – some of them relating the experiences of the young Nick Adams in the Great Lakes region and in Europe – interspersed with vignettes of World War I and the bullring. Though written when he was only 27, the volume amply demonstrates Hemingway's gifts as a writer of prose fiction: in particular, the spare, controlled, and connotative style. *The Torrents of Spring* (1926), his first novel, satirized the style of **Sherwood Anderson**, whom Hemingway had once admired but whose latest novel, *Dark Laughter* (1925), he regarded as a mere mechanical rendering of what Anderson had written previously. His next novel, and the one which first made him famous, was *The Sun Also Rises* (1926), about the disillusionment of the "lost generation" – young British and American expatriates in France and Spain – in the aftermath of World War I.

In 1927 Hemingway and Hadley Richardson were divorced and he married Pauline Pfeiffer. Later that year he published the collection *Men Without Women*, which contains some of his most popular stories. "The Killers" tells of Ole Andreson, whom two thugs have been hired to kill, and of his surrender to the fact that his death is inescapable. "The Undefeated" depicts the pointless heroism of Garcia, an aging bullfighter facing his last fight. "Fifty Grand" is a brutal and cynical tale of prizefighters, in which Jack Brennan bets money on his own defeat. Hemingway's next novel, *A Farewell to Arms* (1929), is the poignant story of Frederic Henry, an American lieutenant in the Italian ambulance corps during World War I, and Catherine Barkley, an English nurse on duty in Italy. *Death in the Afternoon* (1932), a study of bullfighting, was followed by *Winner Take Nothing* (1933), a collection of short stories including "A Clean Well-Lighted Place," "The Sea Change," and "A Natural History of the Dead." *Green Hills of Africa* (1935) is about big-game hunting. *To Have and Have Not* (1937) is a short novel about smuggling in the Key West–Havana region. The collection *The Fifth Column and the First Forty-Nine Stories* (1938) includes the story "The Snows of Kilimanjaro." *The Fifth Column*, a play about espionage in the Spanish Civil War, was subsequently produced in New York and in wartime England. The conflict in Spain, in which Hemingway was involved as a war reporter, also provided the background for *For Whom the Bell Tolls* (1940), an ambitious novel with the theme (implied in the title, with its quotation from John Donne) that the loss of freedom anywhere is a diminution of it everywhere. Hemingway was at the height of his fame and the book sold well: 270,000 copies in the first year.

In 1940 Hemingway was divorced from his second wife and married Martha Gellhorn. This marriage also ended in divorce, in December 1945, and he married his fourth wife, Mary Welsh, in March 1946. He spent World War II as a war correspondent, and in 1950 he published *Across the River and Into the Trees*, his first novel in a decade. It was poorly received, but he came back with *The Old Man and the Sea* (1952), a parable of inner strength and courage about a Cuban fisherman's struggle to bring home a great marlin he has caught. It was first published in *Life* magazine, and then in book form a week later.

Two years later Hemingway won the Nobel Prize for Literature. In the last years of his life he was troubled by failing artistic and physical powers; he committed suicide on July 2, 1961. *A Moveable Feast*, a memoir of his years in Paris after World War I, was left completed but unrevised at his death. It was published in 1964. *Islands in the Stream*, an unrevised novel, was published in 1970. *By-Line*, a selection of his articles and dispatches, appeared in 1967, and *Selected Letters* in 1981. Hemingway's account of his trip to Spain in 1959, *The Dangerous Summer*, was published in 1985.

Henderson The Rain King See **Bellow, Saul**

Henry, O. See **Porter, William Sidney**

Herbst, Josephine (Frey) 1897–1969 Born in Sioux City, Iowa, Herbst received her BA from the University of California at Berkeley in 1918. During the 1920s she worked as an editorial reader for **H. L. Mencken** and **George Jean Nathan** on the *Smart Set* and *The American Mercury*, and published stories and articles in these and other magazines. In 1925 she married the novelist John Herrman; they were divorced in 1940.

Her first story was published in the *Smart Set* in 1923. Her first two novels were *Nothing is Sacred* (1928) and *Money for Love* (1929). These were followed by *Pity is not Enough* (1933), *The Executioner Waits* (1934), and *Rope of Gold* (1939), a trilogy dealing with the decay of capitalism and the emergence of a revolutionary movement which falters, however, and fails to bring about the new Communist social order it seeks. Like many other writers of her generation, Herbst aligned herself with the political Left. In 1935 she went to Germany as a special correspondent for the *New York Post*. As a special correspondent for various magazines she subsequently traveled to Cuba (1935), to Spain to cover the Civil War (1937), and to South America (1939). Her other publications include two novels, *Satan's Sergeants* (1941) and *Somewhere the Tempest Fell* (1947). *New Green World* (1954) is a biography of the American naturalist John Bartram. At the time of her death she was at work on *The Burning Bush*, a literary and personal history of the 1920s and 1930s, and *Hunter of Doves*, a collection of novelettes.

Herne, James A. 1839–1901 Born in Cohoes, New York, to an immigrant Irish family, Herne (originally Ahearn) decided to defy his father's wishes and pursue a theatrical career after seeing Edwin Forrest perform in 1852 in Albany. When he was 20 he joined a traveling theatre group. Following a series of engagements with various companies in Troy, Washington, Baltimore, Montreal, and New York, he traveled with a troupe to San Francisco where he met **David Belasco**, married the Irish actress Katherine Corcoran in 1878, and embarked upon his career as a dramatist.

Herne and Belasco collaborated on many productions. Their first significant work was *Chums* (1879), later retitled *Hearts of Oak* (1880). This sentimental domestic melodrama about an old sailor who adopts two orphans and falls in love with one of them is notable for its early indication of Herne's tendency toward realism in the subject matter, dialogue, characterization, and staging of his plays. Herne later outlined his convictions about dramatic writing and presentation in the article "Art for Truth's Sake in the Drama" (1896). His next play, *The Minute Men of 1774–75* (1886), was less successful, and in 1888 he wrote and produced the unconventional temperance drama, *Drifting Apart*. The most important of his contributions to American dramatic realism is *Margaret Fleming* (1891), the story of a woman's response to her husband's infidelity. Clearly influenced by Ibsen in both subject and style, the play was acclaimed by **Hamlin Garland** and **William Dean Howells** but relentlessly attacked by the critics. His next play, *Shore Acres* (1892), an equally realistic but happier story of life in New England, was very successful, and broke performance records in Boston. He wrote two more plays: *The Reverend Griffith Davenport* (1899), a Civil War story based on Helen H. Gardner's novel *An Unofficial Patriot* (1894); and *Sag Harbor* (1900), a reworking of the themes of *Hearts of Oak* in which two brothers are rivals for the love of the same woman.

Herrick, Robert 1868–1938 Born in Cambridge, Massachusetts, and educated at Harvard, Herrick taught at Massachusetts Institute of Technology for three years and then at the University of Chicago (1893–1923). Many of his novels depict professionals or businessmen who struggle to achieve worldly success only to find that it leaves them unhappy and unfulfilled. In his first novel, *The Man Who Wins* (1897), the character who comes to this realization is a doctor who has given up research for a lucrative medical practice. *Web of Life* (1900) also has a doctor as its hero; *The Common Lot* (1904), an architect. *The Real World* (1901, republished as *Jock O'Dreams* in 1908), *A Life for a Life* (1910), and *Waste* (1924) all tell the stories of business executives who come to regret their material success. *Memoirs of an American Citizen* (1905), perhaps his best-known novel, is the story of Van Harrington, who makes a fortune and wins a seat in the Senate but, unlike Herrick's other leading characters, exhibits no regret. *Sometime* (1933) is a satirical Utopian novel. Herrick also published several collections of short stories: *Love's Dilemmas* (1898), *Their Child* (1903), *The Master of the Inn* (1908), *The Conscript Mother* (1916), and *Wanderings* (1925). He died in the Virgin Islands, where he had served for three years as secretary to the Governor.

Herzog A novel by **Saul Bellow**, published in 1964. It won the National Book Award for fiction in 1965 and became a best seller. Its leading character is Moses Herzog, a 47-year-old scholar, twice divorced, who undergoes an emotional, intellectual, and moral crisis. As the novel opens, he is tucked away in a house in the Berkshire Mountains. It is summer, and since spring he has been composing letters to various persons – dead or alive, obscure or famous – in an effort "to explain, to have it out, to justify, to put in perspective, to clarify, to make amends." Among those he addresses in these "mental letters" (not all of which he commits to paper) are the women in his life, friends, relatives, his psychiatrist, politicians, philosophers (such as Heidegger and Nietzsche), the public (in letters to the editor), even God. Flashback scenes carry the action of the novel to other settings (Martha's Vineyard, New York City, Chicago), and provide the reader with information about Herzog's relations with his family, his two ex-wives (Daisy and Madeleine), his Japanese mistress Sono, and his current lover, Ramona.

Herzog travels to Chicago, intent on avenging himself on Madeleine and her lover,

Valentine Gersbach, formerly Herzog's friend. He takes his father's gun and goes to the home that Valentine and Madeleine share. Peering through a window, he watches Valentine tenderly bathe his (Herzog's) daughter Junie; his humanity is touched and his homicidal urges subside. While taking Junie on an outing they are involved in a minor auto accident. The police investigating the accident discover the gun, for which Herzog has no permit, and arrest him. His brother posts his bail, and he returns to the Berkshires for a final week of letter-writing. At the end of the novel he rejects his brother's suggestion that he check into a mental hospital; he engages a local couple to help him put his dilapidated summer place to rights again; he makes plans to have his son Marco (his child by Daisy) visit him; and he prepares for a dinner with Ramona. Herzog's excursions – physical and mental – have left him in relative peace, and for the time being he has "no messages for anyone."

Heyward, DuBose 1885–1940 Poet, novelist, and playwright, born in Charleston, South Carolina. While pursuing a career in insurance, he founded a poetry society in Charleston and in 1922 published his first volume of verse, *Carolina Chansons*, with Hervey Allen. Two further collections followed: *Skylines and Horizons* (1924) and *Jasbo Brown* (1931). In 1925 he published *Porgy*, a novel about black life in South Carolina, set in a tenement neighborhood in Charleston called Catfish Row. A dramatic version of the book was written jointly by Heyward and his wife Dorothy in 1927, and was awarded a Pulitzer Prize. The work was adapted by **George Gershwin** into the opera *Porgy and Bess* in 1935. Characterized by a use of regional materials and southern folklore, Heyward's other novels include a chronicle of the Civil War entitled *Peter Ashley* (1932); and *Star Spangled Virgin* (1939), which explores the response of the Virgin Islanders to the New Deal. *Mamba's Daughters* (1929), a novel about the life of a black mother, was dramatized in 1939 by Heyward and his wife.

Hiawatha, The Song of A long narrative poem by **Henry Wadsworth Longfellow**, published in 1855. It was partly based on Longfellow's reading of Henry Rowe Schoolcraft, an American ethnologist and explorer who was the first white man to translate Indian poetry and to study Indian myths and religion.

The poem tells how Hiawatha is reared by Nokomis, daughter of the moon, who helps him acquire the wisdom and power necessary for an Indian hero and leader. Upon reaching manhood, Hiawatha seeks to avenge his mother, Wenonah, against his father, the West Wind. The combat ends in reconciliation, and Hiawatha becomes the leader of his people. Although his rule is marked by peace and prosperity, hard times come to his tribe; his wife, Minnehaha, dies, and he follows her to the land of the North Wind, having first counseled his people to accept the white man, whose coming he has predicted. Longfellow based the meter of his poem on that of the Finnish epic *The Kalevala*; its hypnotic rhythm has often been parodied.

Higginson, Thomas Wentworth 1823–1911 Born in Cambridge, Massachusetts, Higginson graduated from Harvard in 1840 and from The Harvard Divinity School in 1847. Although best remembered as **Emily Dickinson**'s literary mentor, he also produced important work of his own, especially on the subject of abolition. As a Unitarian minister he was passionate in his opposition to slavery, and engaged in numerous missions to help fugitive slaves. He also wrote numerous magazine essays, on literary as well as political topics, and through these popular writings became known to Emily Dickinson. During the Civil War he commanded the first troop of black soldiers in the Union Army, and out of this experience produced his best work, *Army Life in a Black Regiment* (1870). In 1890, after Dickinson's death, he co-edited with Mabel Loomis Todd the first published volume of her poetry – *Poems, by Emily Dickinson*.

Hillyer, Robert (Silliman) 1895–1961 A poet, novelist, and critic, Hillyer was born in East Orange, New Jersey, and educated at Harvard (BA, 1917). He served in World War I, then returned to Harvard, where he taught from 1919 to 1945. His first volume, *Sonnets and Other Lyrics*, was published in 1917. In 1923 some of his poems were included in *Eight More Harvard Poets*. *The Hills Give Promise, a Volume of Lyrics Together with Carmus: A Symphonic Poem* also appeared in 1923. His novel

Riverhead (1932) was followed in 1933 by *The Collected Verse of Robert Hillyer*, for which he won the Pulitzer Prize. Subsequent publications include *First Principles of Verse* (1938, a critical work), *Pattern of a Day* (1940, poetry), *My Heart for Hostage* (1942, a novel), *Poems for Music, 1917–1947* (1947), *The Death of Captain Nemo, a Narrative Poem* (1949), *In Pursuit of Poetry* (1960, a critical work), and *Collected Poems* (1961). He generally wrote in traditional verse forms, most notably the sonnet and the heroic couplet.

Himes, Chester (Bomar) 1909–   Black novelist, born in Jefferson City, Missouri. He graduated from high school in Cleveland, Ohio, and briefly attended Ohio State University until forced to withdraw for disciplinary reasons. In 1928 he was sentenced to 20 years in the Ohio State Penitentiary for armed robbery. There, he witnessed the prison fire of 1930 that killed 320 convicts, an event which became the subject of his first well-known story, "To What Red Hell?" (1934). His novel *Cast the First Stone* (1952) is also based on his experiences in prison. He was paroled in 1936, and returned to Cleveland where he became friends with **Langston Hughes** and **Louis Bromfield**. He participated in the Ohio Writers Project for a time, then moved to Los Angeles where he became involved in the Communist movement, and later worked in the shipyards of San Francisco. He has lived as an expatriate in France and Spain since 1953.

His first novel, *If He Hollers Let Him Go* (1945), is a story about racial conflict in the defense plants of Los Angeles during the war years. *Lonely Crusade* (1947) examines racial discrimination and violence in the wartime labor unions of California. In 1954 he published *The Third Generation*, a study of the middle-class black experience. *The Primitive* (1955) explores interracial sexuality, a topic taken up later in *Pinktoes* (Paris, 1961; New York, 1965). His later work is dominated by a series of books about the experiences of two Harlem detectives. These novels, in which Himes continues to examine the themes of racism and violence, include *The Real Cool Killers* (1959), *All Shot Up* (1960), *Cotton Comes to Harlem* (1965), *The Heat's On* (1966), *Blind Man with a Pistol* (1969), and *A Case of Rape* (1980). His autobiography, *The Quality of Hurt*, was published in 1972, followed by *My Life of Absurdity* in 1976.

History of New York, A   A satirical history by **Washington Irving**, published in 1809 and revised in 1812, 1819, and 1848. In the guise of "Diedrich Knickerbocker" Irving parodies the events surrounding New York's history and burlesques the epic narrative style in which such histories were customarily written. The history begins with an inflated cosmogony, then moves through the discovery of America, the Dutch colonization, the founding of New Amsterdam, early conflicts with the British, the governorship of Peter Stuyvesant, and ends with the Dutch surrender to the English in 1664. One of its most notable passages is a comic caricature of **Thomas Jefferson**. Irving's hilarity often leads him to bend or even change basic facts, but the book still provides important information on the early history of New York.

History of Plimmoth [or Plymouth] Plantation   A history of the pilgrim settlement at Plymouth by **William Bradford**, probably begun in 1630. He worked on it until 1651, during most of which time he served as the colony's governor. After his death the unpublished manuscript passed to his nephew, **Nathaniel Morton**, who consulted it when writing *New Englands Memoriall* (1669). It also served as a major source for Thomas Prince's *Chronological History of New-England in the Form of Annals* (1736) and Thomas Hutchinson's *History of the Colony of Massachusetts Bay* (2 vols., 1764, 1767). Lost during the Revolutionary War, the manuscript turned up in 1855 in the library of the Bishop of London; it was returned to Massachusetts and in 1856 was published in full (chapters I through IX of Book I had been printed from the Plymouth Church Records in 1851).

The first book, most likely written between 1630 and 1633, tells of the origins of the Separatist movement in England, the settlement in Leyden, the plans to emigrate to New England, and the voyage aboard the *Mayflower*. Book II, written between 1646 and 1650, is a collection of annals recording the sacred and secular affairs of the colony for the years 1620–46. Throughout both books Bradford included primary material – laws, letters, charters, a list of passengers on the *Mayflower* – which has proved an important source for subsequent historians.

Hoffman, Charles Fenno 1806–84   A New York City writer and editor, Hoffman held editorial positions on *The Knickerbocker Magazine*, *The New York Mirror*, and the *American Monthly Magazine*. In 1833–4, he made a journey on horseback through the scarcely settled regions of Illinois and Michigan, and published an account of his experiences in *A Winter in the West* (1835). *Wild Scenes in the Forest and Prairie* followed in 1839. *Greyslaer*, a novel published in 1840, deals with a notorious Kentucky murder case and was a popular success. Three books of verse appeared between 1842 and 1847; many of the poems evoke the Hudson River setting of his New York home. A collection, *The Poems of Charles Fenno Hoffman*, was published in 1873.

Hollander, John 1929–   Hollander was born in New York City and educated at Columbia and Indiana universities. He has been a junior fellow at Harvard and has taught at Connecticut College, Hunter College, and Yale University. In 1958 he was chosen for the Yale Series of Younger Poets by **W. H. Auden**. His verse, poignant and witty, formally strict and sometimes esoteric, has earned him a reputation as one of the foremost contemporary poets. His books include *The Untuning of the Sky* (1961, a critical study), *Movie-Going* (1962), *Visions from the Ramble* (1965), *The Quest of the Gole* (1966, a children's book), *The Night Mirror* (1971), *The Head of the Bed* (1974), *Tales Told of the Fathers* (1975), *Spectral Emanations: New and Selected Poems* (1978), *Rhyme's Reason* (1981, a study of poetic forms), and *Powers of Thirteen* (1983).

Holmes, John C[lellon] 1926–   Born in Holyoke, Massachusetts, Holmes was educated at Columbia University and the New School for Social Research. He was a member of the **Beat** generation of artists and writers, though he never became as famous as his friends and contemporaries **Jack Kerouac** and **Allen Ginsberg**. His first novel, *Go* (1952), published in England as *The Beat Boys*, recorded first hand the lifestyle of this circle of friends. In *The Horn* (1958) he describes the jazz scene of the day; *Nothing More to Declare* (1967) is a collection of essays chronicling the Beat movement. He has published two collections of poems, *The Bowling Green Poems*

(1977) and *Death Drag: Selected Poems* (1979). The memoir *Visitor: Jack Kerouac in Old Saybrook* was published in 1980.

Holmes, Oliver Wendell 1809–94 The son of Abiel Holmes, a Congregational clergyman who had compiled *The Annals of America*, Oliver Wendell Holmes was born in Cambridge, Massachusetts. He was educated at Harvard, where he was class poet. After graduating in 1829 he stayed on at Harvard, first studying law, then medicine. During this period he published two pieces entitled "The Autocrat of the Breakfast Table" in the *New England Magazine*. After studying medicine in Paris for two years (1833–5), he received his MD from Harvard in 1836. In the same year he published *Poems*, a collection of occasional and witty verses. He then set aside his literary interests for some time to concentrate on medicine. After serving as a professor of anatomy at Dartmouth from 1838 to 1840, he returned to Boston. He published two considerable medical works, *Homeopathy and Its Kindred Delusions* (1842) and *The Contagiousness of Puerperal Fever* (1843). In 1847 he became Parkman Professor of Anatomy and Physiology at Harvard, a chair he held until his retirement in 1882.

Holmes was extremely popular as a teacher, and was famous also for his humorous essays and poems and his entertaining after-dinner speeches. During the late 1850s *The Atlantic Monthly*, which he co-founded with **James Russell Lowell** in 1857, published many of his essays – which were then collected in the successful *The Autocrat of the Breakfast Table* (1858) – as well as poems such as "The Chambered Nautilus" and "The Deacon's Masterpiece." Among later collections of his essays are *The Professor at the Breakfast Table* (1860), *The Poet at the Breakfast Table* (1872), and *Over the Teacups* (1891). Drawing upon his scientific training, he wrote three novels about characters who are psychologically disturbed. All three explore the biological and psychological factors determining human behavior and reject any theological version of determinism. The first, *Elsie Venner* (1861), was the most successful; it was followed by *The Guardian Angel* (1867), and *A Mortal Antipathy* (1885). A scientific rationalist, Holmes sought in particular to discredit Calvinism and what he saw as its superstitious and stifling doctrine of determinism. In addition to his poems, essays, and novels, he also published numerous medical articles, and a biography of his friend **Ralph Waldo Emerson** (1885).

Holmes, Oliver Wendell [Jr] 1841–1935 The son of **Oliver Wendell Holmes** the doctor, essayist, and novelist, he became a distinguished jurist. He was a professor of law at Harvard, where his father had taught anatomy and physiology. Having served as Chief Justice of the Massachusetts Supreme Court (1899–1902), he was appointed to the US Supreme Court by Theodore Roosevelt. Throughout his tenure (1902–32) he was known as a champion of human rights and free speech. His *The Common Law* (1881) is recognized as a classic treatise on the subject. *Touched With Fire*, which consists of the diary and letters he wrote during the Civil War, was published in 1946.

Hooker, Thomas 1586–1647 A Puritan minister, and one of the first generation of emigrants to New England. Born in Leicestershire, England, Hooker matriculated at Queens' College, Cambridge, but soon moved to Emmanuel College, a Puritan stronghold. He obtained his BA and MA degrees in 1608 and 1611, and stayed on as a tutor until 1618. He served the church at Esher in Surrey, and then moved to Chelmsford, Essex, in 1626. Known for his effective preaching and successful pastoral techniques, but also for his Puritan leanings, he was summoned by Archbishop Laud in 1629 and 1630. Rather than answer for his nonconformism, he fled to the Netherlands and then in 1633 to New England. Called to the church at Newton, he served as pastor there and then in 1636 migrated with his congregation to Hartford, in the Connecticut Valley.

Admired by his contemporaries as one of the most eloquent preachers in New England, Hooker was the most thorough exponent of the theory of preparation, or the set of steps that a Christian goes through during conversion; his *The Soules Preparation for Christ* (1632) and the expanded *Application of Redemption, By the Effectual Work of the Word, and the Spirit of Christ, for the bringing home of Lost Sinners to God* (published posthumously in 1656), are expositions of part of that process. As a prominent minister and expert on preparation, he was called back to Massachusetts Bay in 1637 to help arbitrate in the **Anne Hutchinson** case. His other works include *A Survey of the Summe of Church Discipline* (1648), an exposition of the independent Congregational church polity, and a defense of it against English Presbyterian critics. *The Poore Doubting Christian Drawn Unto Christ* (1629) is a pastoral manual for dealing with religious melancholy or "cases of conscience."

Hoosier Schoolmaster, The See **Eggleston, Edward**

Hopkinson, Francis 1737–91 A Philadelphian, Hopkinson was a member of the first graduating class of the College of Philadelphia, for which he wrote occasional verses and commencement odes. He worked on a psalter for the Dutch Reformed Church of New York and eventually became organist at Philadelphia's St Peter's Church. Active in Philadephia cultural life during the 1760s, he arranged chamber music evenings and published a number of songs. His pamphlet *The Lawfulness of Instrumental Musick* (1763) angered those Christian sects that opposed the use of music in church services and was lampooned in the Philadelphia press. He spent a year in London (1766–7), with letters of introduction from his friend **Benjamin Franklin**.

He is best known for his humorous patriotic essays. In 1774 under the pseudonym of Peter Grievous he published the pamphlet *A Pretty Story*, a propagandistic but humorous allegory of a family of sons (the colonies) wronged by their wicked stepmother (Parliament). During the Revolution he wrote satires for the *Pennsylvania Packet*, the *Pennsylvania Gazette*, and the *Pennsylvania Magazine*, including, for the latter, essays in the persona of "The Old Bachelor." He also served in the Second Continental Congress (he signed the Declaration of Independence) and then in a variety of positions in the revolutionary government. Among his most popular political writings at this time was a ballad, "The Battle of the Kegs" (1778), which ridiculed the British for overreacting to a Colonial military ruse. In December 1781 his *The Temple of Minerva*, a dramatic masque with music celebrating the American cause,

was performed for General Washington in Philadelphia. James Rivington, a leading New York loyalist printer, published a parody, "The Temple of Cloacina," and Hopkinson carried on a mocking exchange with him in the winter of 1781–2. Hopkinson's next notable productions were further satires in support of the Constitution, including "The New Roof" (an allegory referring to the proposed new government), which appeared in the *Pennsylvania Packet* in 1787. He spent his last years as a judge, and also published some volumes of songs. His revised *Miscellaneous Essays* appeared posthumously in 1792.

Horse-Shoe Robinson: *A Tale of the Tory Ascendancy* A historical novel by **John Pendleton Kennedy**, published in 1835 and set in Virginia and the Carolinas during the last months of the Revolutionary War. The characters include Mildred Lindsay, whose father is a Tory; Tyrrel, the British spy Mildred's father wants her to marry; Arthur Butler, a Revolutionary patriot whom Mildred loves; and the title character, Horse-Shoe Robinson, a blacksmith. Mildred and Arthur are secretly married. When Arthur is captured by the British, Horse-Shoe Robinson comes to the aid of Mildred, who undergoes several adventures before being reunited with her husband. Tyrrel is eventually hanged as a spy.

House of Mirth, The A novel by **Edith Wharton** published in 1905. Set in New York society during the first years of the 20th century, it records the disastrous social career of Lily Bart, a penniless orphan who is related to some of the city's prominent families. Supported by her wealthy aunt, she more or less makes a career of being a house guest in the homes of her more fashionable friends. Now that she is 29, she must secure a rich husband to ensure herself a place in society. She nearly captures Percy Gryce, a pious and somewhat stuffy heir to a large fortune, but loses him when she chooses to spend a Sunday with Lawrence Selden rather than go to church with Percy. Although she is attracted to Selden, she does not think of him as a potential husband: he is sufficiently genteel but not sufficiently rich, and has to earn his living as a lawyer. She also rejects Simon Rosedale, who is certainly rich enough but not yet accepted by genteel society. When she is unjustly accused of having an affair with another woman's husband, she is ostracized by society and her chance of finding a husband is ruined. Disinherited by her wealthy aunt, she is forced to take a job as a milliner to support herself. The novel concludes with her death from an overdose of a sedative.

House of the Seven Gables, The A novel by **Nathaniel Hawthorne**, published in 1851 and inspired by the author's own family history. (According to legend, Hawthorne's great-grandfather, a judge at the Salem witch trials, was cursed by one of his victims.)

The story is set in the mid 19th century. Generations earlier, "Wizard" Maule had pronounced a curse on Colonel Pyncheon just prior to being hanged for witchcraft. With Maule dead, Pyncheon was able to take possession of a plot of land, the ownership of which he and Maule had long disputed, and build the House of the Seven Gables on it. The current owner of the house is the hypocritical Judge Pyncheon, who does not live in the decaying house himself but allows his poor cousin Hepzibah and her debilitated brother Clifford to live there. Clifford has just returned after spending 30 years in prison, a sentence he received from his cousin the judge, having been wrongfully convicted of murdering their rich uncle. Clifford and Hepzibah are joined by Phoebe, a young cousin from the country, and Holgrave, a daguerrotypist who takes lodgings in the house. Believing that Clifford knows where the deeds to the "murdered" uncle's property are, Judge Pyncheon threatens to have him put away as a lunatic, but the judge then dies unexpectedly and Hepzibah and Clifford inherit his considerable wealth. Holgrave reveals that he is the last descendant of "Wizard" Maule and explains how both the "murdered" uncle and the judge were victims, not of any human wrongdoing, but of the Maule curse. Holgrave and Phoebe plan to marry, a union which will remove the curse from the house.

Hovey, Richard 1864–1900 Born in Illinois, Hovey published his first volume of poetry at the age of 16. He attended Dartmouth College and then traveled in Europe. In France he was greatly influenced by the Symbolists; he translated Mallarmé and a number of Maeterlinck's plays. Back in the

US he embarked on a collaboration with the Canadian poet Bliss Carman, which resulted in three volumes celebrating life on the open road: *Songs From Vagabondia* (1894), *More Songs From Vagabondia* (1896), and *Last Songs From Vagabondia* (1901). *Along the Trail* (1898) was published in the year of the Spanish–American War. Drawing on the legends in *Le Mort D'Arthur*, Hovey attempted to create a cycle of poetic dramas, but he did not live to complete it; *The Holy Graal* (1907) contains the fragments. A posthumous collection of poems, *To the End of the Trail*, was published in 1908.

Howard, Bronson (Crocker) 1842–1908 Playwright and journalist, born in Detroit, Howard had his first dramatic success with *Saratoga* (1870), a comedy of upper-class life which was produced by **Augustin Daly** and later adapted for the London stage as *Brighton* (1874). *The Banker's Daughter* (1878), a revised version of his *Lillian's Last Love* (1873), and *Young Mrs Winthrop* (1882) confirmed his reputation as a dramatist. In all his plays he was concerned with the shaping power of American society and convention upon human relationships. His epic Civil War drama, *Shenandoah* (1888), was one of the most successful of its kind. Its first staging in 1888 in Boston was a failure but when it reopened in New York the following year it was a huge success, with a first run of 250 performances. His last popular work was *The Henrietta* (1887), a satiric comedy of Wall Street life that ran for 68 weeks and established Howard's reputation as a pioneer in realist drama. Known as the "dean of American drama," in 1891 he organized the American Dramatists Club. A lecture delivered in 1886 was posthumously published as *The Autobiography of a Play* (1914). A valuable illustration of his ideas about his craft, it recounts the evolution of his play *Lillian's Last Love* into *The Banker's Daughter* and finally into the 1879 English production, *The Old Love and the New*.

Howard, Richard 1929– A poet, critic, playwright, and translator, Howard was born in Cleveland, Ohio, and educated at Columbia University and at the Sorbonne. His first volume of poetry, *Quantities*, was published in 1962. His verse is particularly known for its precision and erudition; his forte is the dramatic monologue, examples of which can be found in collections such as *Untitled Subjects: Poems* (1969), which won a Pulitzer Prize, and *Two-Part Inventions* (1974). He has translated more than 150 books, mainly from the French, including works by Robbe-Grillet, Breton, Gide, Genet, and Barthes. He has also published plays and criticism. His more recent volumes of verse include *Fellow Feelings: Poems* (1976), *Misgivings* (1979), and *Lining Up* (1984).

Howard, Sidney (Coe) 1891–1939 Playwright, born in Oakland, California, and educated at the University of California. He was a member of George Pierce Baker's influential Workshop 47 at Harvard in 1915 and 1916, and following war service he became a journalist in New York. He began his career as a playwright in 1923 and had his first success in the following year with *They Knew What They Wanted*, based on the story of Paolo and Francesca. His most experimental play, *Yellow Jack* (1924), written with Paul de Kruif, deals with the research which led to the identification of the cause of yellow fever. Other plays include *Lucky Sam McCarver* (1925), *The Silver Cord* (1926), and *The Late Christopher Bean* (1932).

Howe, E[dgar] W[atson] 1853–1937 Born in Indiana, Howe owned and edited the *Daily Globe* of Atchison, Kansas (1877–1911), and *E. W. Howe's Monthly* (1911–37). He also published novels and collections of editorials and aphorisms. His novel *The Story of a Country Town* (1883), despite its melodramatic plot, is widely regarded as a landmark of developing realism, and drew high praise from **Mark Twain** among others when it first appeared.

Howe, Julia Ward 1819–1910 A poet and humanitarian, Howe was a tireless worker for women's suffrage, prison reform, and the abolition of slavery. With her husband, Samuel Gridley Howe, she edited the Abolitionist newspaper *Commonwealth* in Boston. Although she is probably best remembered as the author of *The Battle Hymn of the Republic* (1861), she published several collections of poetry, including *Passion Flowers* (1854) and *Later Lyrics* (1866). She also wrote *Sex and Education* (1874), *Modern Society* (1881), *Margaret Fuller* (1883), and *Reminiscences* (1899).

Howells, William Dean 1837–1920 A journalist, editor, novelist, poet, playwright, critic, and translator – known in his lifetime as the "dean of American letters" – Howells was born in Martin's Ferry, Ohio. His family moved from town to town in Ohio, and he began to work as a typesetter for his father (a printer) when he was only 9 years old, so he received little formal education. He did read a great deal, however, and study languages, and at the age of 15 was already contributing essays and poems to Ohio newspapers.

Between 1851 and 1861 he worked as a compositor, reporter, news editor of the *Ohio State Journal* (1860), correspondent of the Cincinnati *Gazette*, and contributor to his father's newspaper *The Sentinel*. Beginning in 1860, he had pieces published in various national magazines, including *The Atlantic Monthly*. Also in 1860, he and John J. Piatt published *Poems of Two Friends*. That same year, Howells did two things that greatly affected his life: he wrote a campaign biography of Abraham Lincoln, for which he was rewarded with an appointment as US consul in Venice (1861–5); and he traveled to Boston, where he met **Oliver Wendell Holmes**, **James Russell Lowell**, and **James T. Fields**, the editor of *The Atlantic Monthly* – all of whom were much impressed by him. During his stay in Venice he translated a guide to Venetian art and history written by Adalbert Müller (1864). Drawing upon his experiences in Italy, he also wrote *Venetian Life* (1866) and *Italian Journeys* (1867). On his return to the US he became associated briefly with *The Nation*. He then became assistant editor of *The Atlantic Monthly* (1866–71), and from 1871 to 1881 served as its editor-in-chief. From 1886 to 1892 he wrote an editorial column for *Harper's Monthly Magazine*, and in 1892 he served as co-editor of *Cosmopolitan* magazine. Even during these busy periods as an editor he wrote novels, collections of verse and of short stories, and various works of non-fiction (memoirs, scholarly works, biographical sketches, and travel pieces).

The first of his 40 or so novels, *Their Wedding Journey*, was published in 1872 and was followed by *A Chance Acquaintance* (1873); in both of them he makes use of his travel experiences. *A Foregone Conclusion* (1874) and *The Lady of the Aroostook* (1879) deal with the contrast between Americans and

Europeans. With *The Undiscovered Country* (1880), a novel about spiritualism and the Shakers, *Dr Breen's Practice* (1881), and *A Modern Instance* (1882), Howells moved beyond the comedy of manners to novels dealing with larger social issues. *A Modern Instance*, for example, depicts a society in which traditional religious and family values are disintegrating in the face of commercial influences. *A Woman's Reason* (1883) came next and was followed by *The Rise of Silas Lapham* (1885), which, like *A Modern Instance*, examines critically the effect of material success on the human soul. *Indian Summer* and *The Minister's Charge; or, The Apprenticeship of Lemuel Barker* were both published in 1886, and a scholarly work, *Modern Italian Poets: Essays and Versions*, followed in 1887.

In 1888, after completing *April Hopes* (1888) and *Annie Kilburn* (1889), Howells moved from Boston to New York City. Greatly influenced by Tolstoy (whom he began to read in 1885), fascinated with New York City's contrasts of wealth and poverty, and appalled by the brutal treatment of striking workers (Chicago's Haymarket Riots and Pennsylvania's Homestead Strike), he produced *A Hazard of New Fortunes* in 1890. That same year he published *A Boy's Town*, an autobiographical work. *The Quality of Mercy* (1892), is a novel about embezzlement; *An Imperative Duty* (1892) has a black heroine. *The World of Chance* (1893), like *A Hazard of New Fortunes*, examines the lack of causality in human affairs. His later fiction includes a Utopian novel, *A Traveller from Altruria* (1894), *The Landlord at Lion's Head* (1897), *The Kentons* (1902), *The Son of Royal Langbrith* (1904), *New Leaf Mills* (1913), *The Leatherwood God* (1916), and the posthumous *The Vacation of the Kelwyns: An Idyl of the Middle Eighteen-Seventies* (1920).

Among his notable critical works are *Criticism and Fiction* (1891) and *Life and Literature: Studies* (1902). His reminiscences in *Literary Friends and Acquaintance: A Personal Retrospect of American Authorship* (1900) and *My Mark Twain: Reminiscences and Criticism* (1910) are important documents since his editorial duties brought him into contact with numerous writers. He was a close friend of **Henry James** as well as of **Mark Twain**. Young authors such as **H. H. Boyesen**, **Hamlin Garland**, **Paul Dunbar**, **Stephen Crane**, **Frank Norris**, and **Robert Herrick** all received encouragement from the older Howells, who from 1908 to 1920 was president of the American Academy of Arts and Letters.

Howl and Other Poems See **Ginsberg, Allen**

Hoyt, Charles Hale 1860–1900 Born in Concord, New Hampshire, Hoyt had little formal education. After holding various jobs he joined the staff of the Boston *Post*, first as a reporter, then as musical, sporting, and dramatic editor. His first experiment with dramatic writing was at the request of his friend William Harris for whom he wrote, rehearsed, and produced the successful melodrama *Gifford's Luck* (1881) in the space of a week. His next play, a four-act comedy entitled *Cazalia* (1882), was less successful. Neither manuscript has survived.

Between 1883 and 1899 he wrote and produced 17 farces and one comic opera. His early plays, like *A Bunch of Keys* (1883), the story of an incompetent hotel manager, are pure farce and slapstick comedy; his later works, like the comical melodrama *A Midnight Bell* (1889) and the political satire *A Texas Steer* (1890), are more socially aware. In 1892 he leased the Madison Square Theatre in New York, which later became known as Hoyt's Theatre. Among the plays he wrote and produced are: *A Trip to Chinatown* (1891), about down-and-out characters in the Bowery; *A Temperance Town* (1893), about the local option and the Prohibition movement; *A Milk White Flag* (1894), about home guard companies; *A Runaway Colt* (1895), about corruption in baseball teams; and *A Contented Woman* (1897), about the women's suffrage movement.

Huckleberry Finn See **Adventures of Huckleberry Finn**

Hughes, Langston 1902–67 Black novelist, poet, and playwright born in Joplin, Missouri. He attended Columbia University in 1921, but left to participate in the more lively activity in nearby Harlem. He was celebrated early on as a young poet of the **Harlem Renaissance**; his poetry appeared in *The Crisis* (1923–4) and was included in **Alain Locke**'s important anthology *The New*

Negro (1925). With the support of **Carl Van Vechten**, he published his first volume, *The Weary Blues*, in 1926, and in the same year wrote a critical essay for *The Nation*, "The Negro Artist and the Racial Mountain." With the publication of his second volume of poetry, *Fine Clothes to the Jew* (1927), he embarked on an extensive speaking tour of the South. He returned to New York and lived for a couple of years on grants from a white patron, Mrs Rufus O. Mason. His first novel, *Not Without Laughter*, appeared in 1930 and won the Harmon Gold Award for Literature.

During the 1930s Hughes rejected white patronage and embraced radical politics, publishing a satirical collection of short stories, *The Ways of White Folks* (1934). In two later collections, *Laughing to Keep From Crying* (1952) and *Something In Common* (1963), he again highlights the absurdities inherent in racial prejudice. His play *The Mulatto* was produced on Broadway in 1935, and he founded black theatre groups in Harlem, Chicago, and Los Angeles. His drama is collected in *Five Plays* (1963). Other volumes of his poetry include *Shakespeare In Harlem* (1942), *Fields of Wonder* (1947), *Montage of a Dream Deferred* (1951), and *Ask Your Mama* (1961). He published two autobiographies: *The Big Sea* (1940) and *I Wonder as I Wander* (1956). He also wrote numerous books, essays, and articles on social, historical, and musical subjects, and edited collections of black folklore, poetry, and stories. In the latter part of his life he devoted his creative energies to writing the "Simple Stories," which involve a seemingly slow-witted black character who always outsmarts his antagonists: *Simple Speaks His Mind* (1950), *Simple Takes a Wife* (1953), *Simple Stakes a Claim* (1957), and *Simple's Uncle Sam* (1965). His second novel, *Tambourines To Glory*, was published in 1958.

Human Comedy, The See **Saroyan, William**

Humphrey, William 1924–   Humphrey was born in Clarksville, Texas, and educated at Southern Methodist University and the University of Texas. His novels are set primarily in the Red River country of northeast Texas. His first, *Home from the Hills* (1958), is both *Bildungsroman* and a family tragedy, which emphasizes the continuance of early Southwestern mores and their conflict with modern values. This was followed by *The Ordways* (1965), which stresses the need for a quality of self-reliance tempered by forgiveness and understanding for others. He has published two other novels, *Proud Flesh* (1973) and *Hostages to Fortune* (1984). His two volumes of short stories, *The Last Husband and Other Stories* (1953) and *A Time and a Place: Stories* (1968), were incorporated into *The Collected Stories of William Humphrey* (1985). In addition to his works of fiction, Humphrey has published two books on fishing, *The Spawning Run: A Fable* (1970) and *My Moby Dick* (1978), as well as a memoir, *Farther Off From Heaven* (1977). A volume of criticism, *Ah! Wilderness! The Frontier in American Literature*, appeared in 1977.

Hunter, Evan 1926–   Novelist, born Evan Lombino in New York City, he also writes under the pseudonym of Ed McBain. (During the 1950s he published novels under two other pseudonyms: Hunt Collins and Richard Marsten.) Before turning to writing he taught briefly in two vocational high schools and worked for six months at a literary agency.

His best-known novel is probably *The Blackboard Jungle* (1954), about an urban high school, for which he drew upon his own teaching experiences. The novels he writes as Evan Hunter generally deal with social problems: *Second Ending* (1956) is concerned with drug addiction; *Mothers and Daughters* (1961) with the emptiness of middle-class life; *Sons* (1969) with the Vietnam War; *Love, Dad* (1981) with the "hippie" movement. As Evan Hunter he has also written plays and screenplays. As Ed McBain he has written the popular 87th Precinct stories, among them *Cop Hater* (1956) and *Fuzz* (1968). A prolific writer, since the mid 1950s he has produced approximately one novel per year under each of his two main pseudonyms.

Hurston, Zora Neale 1903–60 Born in Eatonville, Florida, the first incorporated black town in America, Hurston attended Morgan State College and Howard University, and then moved to New York City as secretary to the novelist Fannie Hurst. She won a scholarship to Barnard College and studied with the anthropologist Franz Boas, under whose direction she began an accomplished career as a folklorist. *Mules and Men* (1935) and *Tell My Horse* (1938) gather black traditions of the American South and the Caribbean. Her most renowned novel, *Their Eyes Were Watching God* (1937), portrays the life of Janie Crawford, an independent black woman and folk heroine. She also published *Moses: Man of the Mountain* (1939), a novel which examines the figure of Moses as he appears both in the Old Testament and in black myth, and an autobiography entitled *Dust Tracks on a Road* (1942). Her popularity and critical reputation have grown since her death; in 1979 the black novelist **Alice Walker** edited a collection of her writings, *I Love Myself When I Am Laughing*. A volume of short stories, *Spunk*, appeared in 1984.

Hutchinson, Anne 1591–1643 Born in England to strictly Puritan parents, she married William Hutchinson in 1612. Around 1620 she heard **John Cotton** preach at St Botolph's Church in Boston, Lincolnshire; she was immediately drawn to his brand of Puritanism, which emphasized the indwelling of the Holy Spirit and the unconditional Grace of God manifest in Redemption. In 1634 she emigrated to New England and settled in Cotton's congregation in Boston.

At first admired for her intelligence and kindness, she drew suspicion on herself when it was learned that at the informal and well-attended meetings in her home she criticized the ministers, with the exception of John Cotton, for emphasizing compliance with the moral, ecclesiastical, and civil law as a component of the process of conversion. She emphasized, in contrast, that Christians are saved solely through the inner workings of the Holy Spirit. To combat the popularity of such Antinomian ideas, a Synod was convened in 1637 and condemned 82 Antinomian "errors;" Hutchinson was tried before the General Court during the fall of 1637 and convicted of "traducing the ministers and their ministry." Sentenced to banishment, she stayed at the home of John Cotton throughout the winter, during which time he attempted to convince her of her "errors." Resolute in her beliefs, she was excommunicated and ordered to leave the colony in the spring of 1638. She traveled to Rhode Island and, following her husband's death in 1642, moved to Pelham Bay, where she and her family were massacred by Indians in 1643.

I

Iceman Cometh, The   A play by **Eugene O'Neill**, first performed in New York in 1946. The play was one of O'Neill's personal favorites, in which he attempted to portray man as a "victim of the ironies of life and of himself."

The men who gather in Jimmy-the-Priest's saloon, as well as its òwner Harry Hope, are good natured and trusting in the value of love and honor. When the salesman Hickey tries to persuade them to abandon their illusions and return to reality, the truths they discover and reveal cause them to despair. Only the cynical philosopher Larry Slade can stand up to Hickey, and it is he who eases the desperate Parritt's route to suicide. When, at the end of the play, it is revealed that Hickey too has been living a lie, the discovery gives Slade no pleasure; it merely confirms his belief in the necessity of pipe-dreams.

I'll Take My Stand   See **Ransom, John Crowe**

Imagism   A poetic movement in England and the US from 1909 to 1917. **Ezra Pound** was a leading spokesman for the movement, and with F. S. Flint wrote an Imagist "manifesto" published in **Poetry** magazine in 1913. Among the tenets they put forth were a free choice of subject matter (often focusing on single, concentrated moments of experience), conciseness of diction, clarity of images, and rhythm composed "in sequence of the musical phrase, not in sequence of a metronome." *Des Imagistes*, the first Imagist anthology, was edited by Pound and published in 1914. Among the contributors were Pound himself, Flint, **William Carlos Williams, H.D.**, and **Amy Lowell**. After 1914 Amy Lowell assumed leadership of the movement, helping to publish three further anthologies, all entitled *Some Imagist Poets* (1915, 1916, 1917). Though Imagism as a movement flourished only briefly, it had considerable influence on the development of form and subject matter in modern poetry – in writers, as well as those mentioned above, such as **T. S. Eliot** and **Wallace Stevens**.

Imlay, Gilbert 1754–1828   Born in New Jersey, Imlay served as a captain in the Revolutionary War. Although little is known about his life, he seems to have been forced out of the US in 1785 or 1786 after having become involved in dubious land speculation in Kentucky. During the 1790s he lived in London where he wrote and published two works. *A Topographical Description of the Western Territory of North America* (1792) portrays the post-Revolutionary West in a series of letters written to a friend in England. *The Emigrants* (1793), epistolary in form, is the first novel about the frontier area of Pennsylvania, which at the time extended from Pittsburgh west to the Mississippi; the novel envisions America as a promised land, and champions social reform, the rights of women, and liberal divorce laws. In Europe Imlay frequented the radical circles of his fellow Americans, **Joel Barlow** and **Thomas Paine**, and for a time lived with Mary Wollstonecraft, who bore him a daughter.

In Cold Blood   A "non-fiction novel" by **Truman Capote**, published in 1966. It recounts the apparently motiveless murder of a Kansas farmer and his entire family, and includes conversations Capote had with the convicted killers before their execution. To compile his account of the events surrounding the murder, Capote researched the case carefully, drawing on interviews, trial transcripts, and other documentary evidence.

Indian Summer A novel by **William Dean Howells**, published in 1886. It tells the story of a middle-aged American newspaper publisher, Theodore Colville, who travels to Florence to take up an interest in architecture he had abandoned years before. He encounters a friend from his childhood, Evalina Bowen, now a widow. Imogene Graham, Evalina's young friend and protégée, is attracted to Colville. Mrs Bowen tells her of an unhappy youthful romance of Colville's which had left him broken-hearted, and Imogene, her sympathy stirred, conceives a romantic attachment to him. The relationship comes to an end, however, when she experiences true love for the young clergyman Morton. This clears the way for the marriage of Colville and Evalina, who have secretly loved one another almost from the beginning of the novel.

In Dubious Battle See **Steinbeck, John**

Inge, William 1913–73 Born in Independence, Kansas, Inge was educated at the University of Kansas where he studied drama and toured in the summers with vaudeville shows. He taught English and drama in Missouri before becoming the arts critic of the St Louis *Star-Times* in 1943. His career as a playwright began with *Farther Off From Heaven* (1947), first produced in Dallas, Texas, and was established with *Come Back, Little Sheba* (1950), about a married couple's fruitless battle with alcoholism and fantasies. *Picnic* (1950), the story of a sexually attractive stranger's relationships with several lonely women in a small Kansas town, won both the Pulitzer Prize and the New York Drama Critics Circle Award.

Inge reached the height of his success as a playwright in the 1950s. Continuing his examination of the loneliness and sexual frustration of midwestern life, he wrote *Bus Stop* (1955), the story of a love affair between a nightclub singer and a lonely cowboy; and *The Dark at the Top of the Stairs* (1957, a revised version of his first play), the semi-autobiographical psychological drama of the Flood family. Two studies of modern Oedipal situations, *A Loss of Roses* (1959) and *Natural Affection* (1963), and the domestic comedy *Where's Daddy?* (1966), were less suc-cessful. In 1961 he reworked his one-act play *Glory in the Flower* (1959) into the screenplay for *Splendor in the Grass*. His last play was *The Last Pad* (1970), about three men on death row. After 1970 he turned to writing novels. *Good Luck, Miss Wyckoff* (1971) relates the story of a white schoolteacher whose affair with the black janitor costs her her job and changes her life. His second novel, *My Son is a Splendid Driver* (1972), the first-person narra-tive of a lonely teacher, is clearly autobio-graphical. He committed suicide shortly after publication.

Innocents Abroad, The: *or The New Pilgrim's Progress* A travel book by **Mark Twain**, published in 1869 and based on his visit to Europe and Palestine during the summer and autumn of 1867. It took shape from letters he wrote to the San Francisco *Alta California* and the New York *Herald* and *Tribune* while on his journey. Comprising the often humorous narrative of a shrewd American in the Old World for the first time, the book marked the beginning of the most productive and suc-cessful period of Twain's career.

In Our Time A collection of short stories by **Ernest Hemingway**, published in 1925 and augmented in 1930. The hero of several of the stories is Nick Adams. In "Indian Camp," the first story in the 1925 edition, he is a young boy who goes with his father, a doctor, to help a pregnant Indian woman through a difficult delivery. The story ends in startling fashion with the discovery that during the delivery the woman's husband has slit his own throat. "Big Two-Hearted River," the two-part story with which the collection ends, is set several years later. Nick, now an adult, is psychologically shattered by his experiences in World War I. He goes alone on a trout-fishing trip in the woods of Michigan; fishing allows him to concentrate on doing one thing at a time in an almost ritualistic manner and proves to be a healing experience. Other notable stories in the collection are "The Three-Day Blow," "Mr and Mrs Elliot" (apparently a caricature of **T. S. Eliot** and his wife), "Cross-Country Snow," and "My Old Man." Another story, "On the Quai at Smyrna," was added to the beginning of the 1930 edition. Between the stories are a series of vignettes about World War I and bullfighting which complement the stories and add to the narrative unity of the volume as a whole.

In the Midst of Life   A collection of stories by **Ambrose Bierce**, first published in 1891 under the title *Tales of Soldiers and Civilians*. More than half of the stories are concerned with soldiers' lives during the Civil War, and reflect Bierce's own revulsion for the life he experienced as a Union soldier. Violence – particularly its psychological effect – and the macabre are dominant themes. Among the best-known of the stories are "The Middle Toe of the Right Foot," about a murderer who is haunted to death by his victim; "A Horseman in the Sky," in which a young Union soldier is forced by circumstances to shoot and kill a Confederate officer, who happens to be his father; and "An Occurrence at Owl Creek Bridge," which presents the fantasy that a man who is being hanged experiences in the last seconds of his life.

Intruder in the Dust   See **Faulkner, William**

Invisible Man   A novel by **Ralph Ellison** published in 1952. Widely regarded as one of the major works of recent American fiction, *Invisible Man* combines elements of realism, surrealism, and folklore. Ellison draws on the literary tradition of **Ernest Hemingway**, André Malraux, and Thomas Mann as well as the native tradition of the blues in his *Bildungsroman* about a nameless black narrator in search of an identity. Set in the 1930s, the book details his often incoherent experiences – as a bright high-school student in the South, as a disoriented college student who is eventually expelled from the Southern "negro" college he attends, as a factory worker in New York City, and as a rising figure in left-wing politics. His life is marked by various traumas of racial and individual identity, but it is through these experiences that he eventually achieves self-consciousness. This self-consciousness is inscribed in the title: He realizes that black skin in American society makes one "invisible" to white eyes. The novel's climax recounts a race riot in Harlem, during which the narrator observes both the destructiveness of black nationalism and the failure of Communist attempts to reform society. He retreats, in his invisibility, to an underground

sewer, which he furnishes and lives in while writing his book. At the end of the novel he is better off in one respect than when he began: His consciousness of the social phenomenon of "invisibility" has provided him with the possibility for free personal action.

Iron Heel, The   A novel by **Jack London**, published in 1908. A socialist vision of the historically inevitable demise of capitalism, though written when London was at the height of his popularity, the book was banned in several communities and met with strong objections to its radical political stance.

The story is set in the years 1912–32 and is supposedly a transcription of a manuscript written at the time by Avis Cunningham Everhard and edited 700 years later by Anthony Meredith, who lives in the fourth century of the Brotherhood of Man. London, through his fictitious editor Meredith, provides extensive footnotes which enable him to voice his passionate opposition to capitalism and to project the ultimate success of socialist revolution in the US.

Avis Cunningham tells how she became a revolutionary socialist after meeting the dynamic proletarian philosopher Ernest Everhard (a composite of Eugene Debs, Ernest Untermann, and London himself) and then observing the social conditions of her native city, San Francisco. The two join the revolutionary movement and become leaders in the fight against the Oligarchy, the Iron Heel of the title. The Oligarchy – a defensive, proto-fascist conglomeration of major trusts and their private militias – is formed after socialism has already made a significant impact on capitalist security. Ernest and Avis marry against a background of the Oligarchy's consolidation of power and the dramatic escalation of social and political unrest. Despite the efforts of the Iron Heel, socialism retains some political power and Ernest is elected to Congress. While he is making an inflammatory speech a bomb is thrown from the House balcony. Although innocent, Ernest and 51 other socialist Congressmen are arrested, tried, and convicted of the bombing. (Meredith's footnotes indicate that proof later surfaced that the Oligarchy itself had been responsible for the incident.) Avis is also arrested as a suspect, but is held only three months. After her release she and fellow revolutionaries spend 18 months planning the escape of the jailed leaders, and all but one do indeed escape.

By this time the Oligarchy has cornered world markets and precipitated global violence. In disguise, Ernest and Avis enter its service and plan a massive revolt, which is sabotaged in the novel's climactic scene of city-wide destruction and slaughter in Chicago. The revolution is crushed, but the socialists remain determined. The manuscript ends abruptly on the eve of a second uprising. Ernest has already been executed. Avis's fate is unclear, though the editor assumes that she too is executed. The reader learns that the Iron Heel is finally overthrown 300 years after the events related in the "Everhard Manuscript."

Irving, Washington 1783–1859 One of the first American writers to earn an international reputation, Irving was born in New York City, the youngest of 11 children. He studied law, and in 1802–3 contributed letters to the *Morning Chronicle*, a newspaper edited by his brother Peter. These were published in 1803 as *The Letters of Jonathan Oldstyle, Gent.* In the following year he made the first of many trips abroad and met the artist Washington Allston, as well as Mme de Staël and Baron Alexander von Humboldt. He returned to New York in 1806 and passed the Bar examination, though he was never to make a career of practicing law.

The next year he began to publish *Salmagundi*, a serial that ran through 20 numbers, written in collaboration with his brother William and **James Kirke Paulding**. His *A History of New York* (1809), by the imaginary "Diedrich Knickerbocker," was an instant success. A burlesque of contemporary historical narratives, it also lampooned **Thomas Jefferson** and his policies. The name Knickerbocker was later used to identify the first American school of writers, the **Knickerbocker Group**, of which Irving was a leading member. In 1812, after several years in his family's import business, he became the editor of *Select Reviews* (later the *Analectic Magazine*). When it failed in 1814 he enlisted in the American army, but saw no combat.

In 1815 he went to England to work in the family business there; he remained in Europe for 17 years. He became friends with Sir Walter Scott, visited Coleridge, and met the publisher John Murray, who in 1820 brought out his *The Sketch Book of Geoffrey Crayon, Gent.* A collection of tales and sketches, including "Rip Van Winkle" and "The Legend of Sleepy Hollow," the book was a tremendous success both in England and America. His next collection, *Bracebridge Hall* (1822), was also well received, but *Tales of a Traveller* (1824) was not. Traveling in Germany, France, and Spain (where he was a diplomatic attaché at the American embassy in Madrid), he met and became friends with John Jacob Astor, Mary Wollstonecraft Shelley, and **Henry Wadsworth Longfellow**. While living in Spain he published *Life and Voyages of Columbus* (1828) and *Conquest of Granada* (1829), both based upon careful historical research. He moved to London in 1829 to become secretary to the American Legation under Martin Van Buren. He published *Voyages and Discoveries of the Companions of Columbus* in 1831, and *The Alhambra*, concerning the history and legends of Moorish Spain, in 1832. Returning to America, where he was enthusiastically received, he traveled in the far West. In 1835 he published *The Crayon Miscellany*, which consists of *Abbotsford and Newstead Abbey*, *Legends of the Conquest of Spain*, and *A Tour of the Prairies*. *Astoria* (1836), written at the suggestion of John Jacob Astor, is about the Astor fur-trade empire; it was received well in England but not in America. *Adventures of Captain Bonneville, USA* appeared in 1837.

Irving declined a series of political posts, but accepted an appointment as Minister to Spain in 1842. After three years of delicate diplomacy, he went to London for the negotiation of the Oregon treaty. There he recommended for publication the manuscript of *Typee*, by **Herman Melville**, which had been read to him by the author's brother Gansevoort. He returned to New York in 1846, and spent his last 16 years at Sunnyside, his home on the Hudson River. Friends and visitors during these later years included **John Pendleton Kennedy** and presidents Millard Fillmore and Franklin Pierce. His later publications include *Mahomet and his Successors* (1850), *Wolfert's Roost* (1855), and his five-volume *Life of Washington* (1855–9).

Israel Potter: His Fifty Years of Exile A novel by **Herman Melville** serialized in *Putnam's*

Monthly Magazine in 1854–5 and published separately in 1855. It is loosely based on an obscure tract, *Life and Remarkable Adventures of Israel R. Potter*, which was published anonymously in 1824.

Israel Potter is a young Yankee from the Berkshires in Massachusetts who leaves his home, works as a surveyor, hunter, fur trader, and whale harpooner, and then enlists in the Revolutionary army in 1775. He serves at Bunker Hill, is taken prisoner by the British, and taken to England. After escaping, he adopts a series of disguises and meets George III. Falling in with clandestine friends of America, he is sent to Paris with messages for **Benjamin Franklin** and meets John Paul Jones. Impressed into the British navy on his return to England, Israel contrives his ship's capture by Jones. He serves under Jones aboard the *Bon Homme Richard* in the raids on Scotland and in the capture of the *Serapis*. Separated from the ship, he again adopts a disguise and serves in the British navy. Escaping once more, he sees Ethan Allen imprisoned in England and goes underground, working in a brick factory and making his way to London, where he marries and has a family. Due to his poverty he is unable to return to America until 45 years have passed. Well past 80, he makes the voyage to Boston and revisits the scenes of his youth. Unable to secure a pension from the American government (there is no documented proof of his service during the Revolutionary War), he dictates his memoirs and soon dies.

Many readers have found in the novel signs of Melville's growing cynicism about his country, which grew still more marked in later works. Among the most notable features of the book are its black humor and fascination with disguise, which anticipate his last novel, **The Confidence Man**; and the portraits of Franklin, Jones, and Ethan Allen, historical figures whom Melville presents as representatives, not wholly laudable, of certain aspects of the American character.

J

Jackson, Helen (Maria) Hunt 1830–85 Jackson was born in Amherst, Massachusetts, and in 1863 began to write poetry that was collected in *Verses by H.H.* (1870) and *Sonnets and Lyrics* (1886). Her concern with the US government's unjust treatment of the American Indians prompted her to write *A Century of Dishonor* (1881), a historical study, and *Ramona* (1884), a novel. Among her other publications are works for children, a travel book, and numerous magazine articles, some of which were written under the pseudonym Saxe Holm. She is also known as the friend of **Emily Dickinson** who most vehemently urged her to publish. Her novel *Mercy Philbrick's Choice* (1876) is probably a fictionalized portrait of Dickinson.

Jackson, Laura Riding See **Riding, Laura**

Jackson, Shirley 1919–65 Born in San Francisco, Jackson began writing as a child. After moving with her family to Rochester, New York, in 1933, she enrolled at the University of Rochester but withdrew after a year because of severe depression. In 1937 she began studying at Syracuse University, and in 1940 married the critic Stanley Edgar Hyman, with whom she founded the literary magazine, *The Spectre*.

Her first novel, *The Road Through the Wall*, appeared in 1948, the year in which *The New Yorker* published her best-known short story, "The Lottery." Although the novel escaped critical notice, the story – a depiction of a communal rite in which each year a person chosen by lot is stoned to death – established her reputation. Her next novel, *The Hangsaman* (1951), explores the

schizophrenia of a young girl named Natalie Waite and typifies that portion of Jackson's *oeuvre* concerned with the dark side of human nature. She also produced a quantity of humorous stories and articles, some of which were collected in *Life Among the Savages* (1953) and *Raising Demons* (1957). Her other works include *The Bird's Nest* (1954); *Witchcraft of Salem Village* (1956); *The Bad Children* (1959); *The Sundial* (1958); *The Haunting of Hill House* (1959); *Special Delivery* (1960); *We Have Always Lived in the Castle* (1962); *Nine Magic Wishes* (1963); and two collections edited by her husband, *The Magic of Shirley Jackson* (1966) and *Come Along With Me* (1968).

James, Alice 1848–92 Sister of the novelist **Henry James** and the philosopher **William James**, Alice was born in New York City, the youngest child and only daughter of Mary and **Henry James Sr.** The family's life, and especially Alice's, was disrupted by the separations imposed by the Civil War, and she began to manifest the classic symptoms of neurasthenia. Like many women in the 19th century, and despite her intellectual acumen and curiosity, she was deprived of the formal education given her brothers. Her family, while respecting her abilities, coddled and protected her throughout her many illnesses. She suffered the first of several breakdowns at the age of 19.

Her letters and diary show that she was an astute critic of the work and careers of both her famous brothers and the issues of her time. The diary, which she seems to have intended for publication, was begun in December, 1886, after she and her companion, Katherine Loring Peabody, had settled in England. Written over the next five years, the later portions were dictated to Peabody, as Alice was too ill to write herself. In March 1892 she died of breast cancer following a gradual decline. One of the major themes of her diary is her awareness of her approaching death, and her confrontation of that finality. Because of her brother Henry's belief that it would violate the family's privacy, the diary was not immediately published. He convinced Katherine Loring Peabody to withhold the copies she had made for the younger James brothers, Garth and Robertson, and it was not published until 1934, under the title *Alice James: Her Brothers – Her Journal*. It has since been republished as *The Diary of Alice James* (1964). A selection of her letters, *The Death and Letters of Alice James*, appeared in 1983.

James, Henry [Sr] 1811–82 James was born in Albany, New York, the son of an Irish immigrant who came to the US shortly after the Revolutionary War and amassed a large fortune. He entered Princeton Theological Seminary in 1835, but withdrew after two years when he found he could not accept the Calvinism to which his family adhered. On a visit to Europe in 1837 he became acquainted with the Scotsman Robert Sandeman, whose letters he later edited for publication. In the 1840s he was drawn to the work of the Swedish mystic, Swedenborg. He also became the friend of **Ralph Waldo Emerson** and Thomas Carlyle. After considerable travel between New York and Europe, he settled in Boston in 1864, and began to lecture widely on his own particular philosophy for social reform, a philosophy based on New England **Transcendentalism** and on the ideas put forward by the French social philosopher, Charles Fourier. James's ideas were firmly rooted in the liberal Christianity that he embraced after rejecting Calvinist orthodoxy. His published works, among them *Christianity the Logic of Creation* (1857), *Substance and Shadow; or Morality and Religion in Their Relation to Life* (1863), and *Society the Redeemed Form of Man, and the Earnest of God's Omnipotence in Human Nature* (1879), expound his religious and social philosophy. He was the father of **William James** the philosopher and **Henry James** the novelist, both of whom owed much to their father's thought and to his belief in a wide-ranging education.

James, Henry 1843–1916 The novelist, short-story writer, playwright, critic, and essayist was born in New York City, the son of **Henry James Sr** and the brother of **William James** and **Alice James**. He was educated by private tutors until the age of 12, and then at schools in Boulogne, Paris, Geneva, Bonn, and – when the family returned to the US – at Newport, Rhode Island. He entered Harvard Law School in 1862 but withdrew after a year and, with the encouragement of **Charles Eliot Norton** and **William Dean Howells**, began to concentrate his energies on writing. In the 1860s his early reviews and critical essays were published in *The North American Review* and *The Atlantic Monthly*.

In 1869 he made his first extended visit to Europe as an adult, and in the same year published a farce, *Pyramus and Thisbe*. His first novel, *Watch and Ward*, appeared serially in *The Atlantic Monthly* in 1871 (and in volume form in 1878). He went to Europe again in 1872 and stayed for two years; his experiences during this trip are reflected in *A Passionate Pilgrim and Other Tales* (1875) and *Transatlantic Sketches* (1875). He spent 1875 in Paris in the company of Turgenev, Daudet, Flaubert, the Goncourts, and Zola. The following year he settled in London, where he lived until 1896. *Roderick Hudson* (1876) was the first novel of this period, and was followed by *The American* (1877) and *The Europeans* (1878). The essay *French Poets and Novelists* appeared in 1878, and the novel *Daisy Miller* in 1879. In the same year he produced a study of **Nathaniel Hawthorne** for the English Men of Letters series, a short novel entitled *An International Episode*, and the collection *The Madonna of the Future and Other Tales*. Two more novels, *Confidence* and *Washington Square*, appeared in 1880.

Early in 1880 he visited Florence – one of the cities which serve as the setting for his next novel, *The Portrait of a Lady* (1881). In 1882 he traveled in France, an experience which prompted the travel sketch *A Little Tour in France* (1884). His father died in December, 1882, and as executor of the will he returned to the US for a short period early in 1883. Later that year Macmillan published a collected pocket edition of his works. A collection of short stories, *The Siege of London*, and a travel book, *Portraits of Places*, appeared in the same year. In 1884 he published *Tales of Three*

Cities, and "The Art of Fiction," his well-known essay about his chosen craft. During this period he struck up acquaintances with the painter John Singer Sargent (1884) and with Robert Louis Stevenson (1885). He continued to write prolifically, producing several more novels over the next few years – *The Bostonians* (1886), *The Princess Casamassima* (1886), *The Reverberator* (1888), *The Aspern Papers* (1888), and *The Tragic Muse* (1890). A collection of essays, *Partial Portraits*, appeared in 1888.

He turned his attention to drama in 1890, writing several drawing-room comedies and adapting *The American* for the stage. A collection of short stories, *The Lesson of the Master*, which includes "The Pupil," "The Solution," and "Sir Edmund Orme," appeared in 1892 and was followed by another, *The Real Thing and Other Tales*, in 1893. His play *Guy Domville* opened in London in January 1895, but was not a success. He returned to fiction and produced two more volumes of short stories – *Terminations* (1895), which includes "The Altar of the Dead," and *Embarrassments* (1896), which includes "The Figure in the Carpet" – as well as three short novels – *The Spoils of Poynton* (1897), *What Maisie Knew* (1897), and *In the Cage* (1898).

The range of his literary acquaintance was remarkable: between 1896 and 1901 he met Joseph Conrad, **Stephen Crane**, H. G. Wells, and George Gissing, and received visits from Ford Madox Ford, **William Dean Howells, Oliver Wendell Holmes, Sarah Orne Jewett**, and others.

The Turn of the Screw, his celebrated tale of the uncanny, first appeared in serial form in 1898, and was followed by the novel *The Awkward Age* in the following year. *The Soft Side*, consisting of 12 stories, was published in 1900, and the novel *The Sacred Fount* in 1901. Over the next three years he produced his last three major novels, all of which are commonly regarded as masterpieces: *The Wings of the Dove* (1902), *The Ambassadors* (1903), and *The Golden Bowl* (1904). His famous short story "The Beast in the Jungle" appeared in the collection *The Better Sort* in 1903, the year in which he began his long friendship with **Edith Wharton**.

After a 21-year absence, James returned to the US in August, 1904. While there he lectured, stayed in the home of **Henry Adams**, and met President Theodore Roosevelt. For the New York Edition of his works, which was published between 1907 and 1909, he made revisions to some of his novels and wrote 18 new prefaces. In 1907 he published an account of a journey in the US, *The American Scene*. He visited Italy and France again in 1907–8 and published a collection of essays about his travels, *Italian Hours*, in 1909. In the following year he returned to America. *The Finer Grain*, a volume of short stories, appeared in 1910; *The Outcry*, his last completed novel, in 1911. Before going back to England he received an honorary degree from Harvard (1911); in the following year he received one from Oxford.

Nearing the end of a long and productive career, he published two volumes of autobiography, *A Small Boy and Others* (1913) and *Notes of a Son and Brother* (1914). A third volume, *The Middle Years*, appeared posthumously in 1917. *Notes on Novelists* was published in 1914. During World War I he became involved in war relief work and served as chairman of the American Volunteer Motor Ambulance Corps. Having lived for years in England, he became a British citizen on July 26, 1915. In December of that year he suffered two strokes. King George V awarded him the Order of Merit on New Year's Day 1916. He died on February 28, 1916, leaving two unfinished novels, *The Ivory Tower* and *The Sense of the Past*.

James, William 1842–1910   The eldest son of the philosopher **Henry James Sr** and brother of the celebrated novelist, William James was born in New York City. His father had considerable means and very positive ideas about education; William and his brother Henry were taught in Europe and America by private tutors and encouraged to find their own way to a career. William studied painting first, then science, and then entered Harvard Medical School. He interrupted his studies to accompany **Louis Agassiz** on an expedition to Brazil, finally taking his MD in 1869. A period of bad health followed and halted his as yet incomplete plans for practice or research; but a reading of Charles Renouvier, the French philosopher, helped order his thinking and he became an instructor in physiology at Harvard in 1872. As his interest shifted to psychology, in a pioneering venture he opened a laboratory of psychology at Harvard in 1876.

For the next 12 years he spent his spare time working on *The Principles of Psychology*, which was published in 1890. It remains a classic in its field, even if later investigations – many of which it inspired – have superseded it. He continued to visit Europe regularly and was in close touch with many of the leading minds of his time. In 1897 he published a collection of essays, **The Will to Believe**, in which he defined his position as that of a "radical empiricist." His international reputation increased when he was appointed Gifford Lecturer on Natural Religion at Edinburgh University from 1901 to 1902. His two sets of lectures there were published as **The Varieties of Religious Experience** (1902). In 1907 he published **Pragmatism**, whose thesis that an idea has meaning only in relation to its consequences in feeling and action won him new followers, but was also attacked in some quarters. *The Meaning of Truth* (1909) was his answer to these critics. Though he retired from Harvard in 1907, where he had been professor of psychology (1889–97) and philosophy (1897–1907), he continued to write and lecture; indeed, during this time he was probably the most honored philosopher in America. He explained his metaphysical principles in *A Pluralistic Universe* (1909), a series of lectures he had delivered in Oxford in 1908. Posthumous publications were *Some Problems of Philosophy; A Beginning of an Introduction to Philosophy* (1911), edited by H. M. Kallen; *Memoirs and Studies* (1911), edited by his brother, **Henry James**; and *Essays in Radical Empiricism* (1912), edited by R. B. Perry. His son Henry edited *The Letters of William James* (1920), and R. B. Perry edited the *Collected Essays and Reviews* (1920).

Jarrell, Randall 1914–65 Though born in Nashville, Tennessee, Jarrell spent much of his childhood in southern California. He received his BA from Vanderbilt University in 1935 and his MA in 1938. He served in the US Army Air Corps from 1942 to 1946. He taught English literature and creative writing at Kenyon College (1937–9), the University of Texas (1939–42), Sarah Lawrence College (1946–7), Princeton University (1951–2), and Woman's College of the University of North Carolina (1947–65).

He is best known as a poet and critic. In 1940 he contributed to *Five Young American Poets*. His other volumes of verse are *Blood for a Stranger* (1942); *Little Friend, Little Friend* (1945); *Losses* (1948); *The Seven-League Crutches* (1951); *Selected Poems* (1955); *Uncollected Poems* (1958); *The Woman at the Washington Zoo* (1960), which consists of poems and translations, and for which he received the National Book Award in 1961; a second edition of *Selected Poems* (1964); and *The Lost World* (1965). Published posthumously were *Complete Poems* (1969), and *Jerome: The Biography of a Poem* (1971), which has illustrations by Albrecht Dürer. His verse is characterized by a particular colloquial quality – a modern plainness. It emphasizes the grotesqueness of a reality made more – not less – chaotic by modern science; war is an important theme in several of his poems, including one of his best known – "The Death of the Ball Turret Gunner."

His critical writings include **Poetry and the Age** (1953), *The Third Book of Criticism* (1969), and *Kipling, Auden, & Co.: Essays and Reviews 1935–1964* (1979). *A Sad Heart at the Supermarket* (1962) includes both fables and essays. He held editorial positions on several periodicals: **The Nation** (1946), **The Partisan Review** (1949–51), the *Yale Review* (1955–7), and the *American Scholar* (1957–65). He translated, among other works, Chekhov's short stories, Grimm's fairy tales, and Part I of Goethe's *Faust*. *Pictures from an Institution*, his only novel, was published in 1954. He also wrote books for children. He was killed in an automobile accident. A volume of *Letters: An Autobiographical and Literary Selection*, edited by Mary Jarrell, was published in 1985.

Jeffers, (John) Robinson 1887–1962 Born in Pittsburgh, the son of a theologian and classical scholar, Jeffers spent most of his life in Carmel, on the Monterey coast of California.

He called for a poetry of "dangerous images" which would "reclaim substance and sense, and psychological reality." Many of his poems are based on biblical stories or Greek and Roman myths, and their language has a classical directness and clarity. His first two volumes, *Flagons and Apples* (1912) and *Californians* (1916), were relatively conventional; it was not until the publication of *Tamar and*

Other Poems (1924) that his particular dramatic and rhetorical power became clear. The title poem is based on the Old Testament figure, and exhibits Jeffers's preoccupation with the themes of lust, incest, and the corrupt nature of man. His many other volumes include *Roan Stallion* (1924), *The Woman at Point Sur* (1927), *Cawdor and Other Poems* (1928), *Dear Judas and Other Poems* (1929), *Give Your Heart to the Hawks and Other Poems* (1933), *Be Angry at the Sun* (1941), *The Double Axe* (1948), and *Hungerfield, and Other Poems* (1954). His best-known play, *Medea*, was staged in New York in 1947 and 1965.

Jefferson, Thomas 1743–1826 The third President of the United States was born in Albemarle County, Virginia. Educated at the College of William and Mary, he then studied law and was admitted to the Virginia Bar in 1767. From 1769 to 1776 he served in the Virginia House of Burgesses, during which time he wrote *A Summary View of the Rights of British America* (1774), which marked him as one of the primary exponents of the colonies' grievances against the king. He went on, as a member of the Second Continental Congress, to draft *The Declaration of Independence* (1776).

Jefferson continued his public career during the American Revolution, serving first in the Virginia legislature (1776–9) and then as the state's governor (1779–81). Though a landed and wealthy slaveowner himself, he espoused a vision of an agrarian society based on an independent yeomanry, and defended the principle of individual freedom against entrenched privilege and government encroachments. During the Virginia period, he was the author of "A Bill for Establishing Religious Freedom," "A Bill for the More General Diffusion of Knowledge," and "A Bill Declaring Who Shall Be Deemed Citizens of this Commonwealth" – all important documents in American legal history, intended to separate church and state, to democratize education, and to eliminate property qualifications for citizens' rights. He also supported, at this time and throughout the rest of his life, the gradual abolition of slavery.

During his tenure as governor of Virginia, Jefferson produced the first version of his *Notes on the State of Virginia*, an answer to a series of questions from abroad about his native state. It was published in 1785; an appendix was added to the edition of 1800. In the 1780s he returned to Congress, where he proposed plans for the governance of the western territories and for a new monetary system. He then served as American minister to France, and in 1788 published *Observations on the Whale-Fishery*. He returned to America in 1789, and between 1790 and 1793 served as George Washington's Secretary of State. An agrarian supporter of states' rights, he consistently opposed Secretary of the Treasury Alexander Hamilton's Federalist policies of concentrating power in the national government, promoting strong and active monetary institutions, and ties to Britain rather than France. In the division between the two men and their supporters lay the origins of party opposition in American politics.

Jefferson became Vice President in 1797, coming in second in the balloting to the Federalist John Adams. During the Adams administration, tensions between America and France led to the passage of the Alien and Sedition Acts by the Federalist party. Jefferson opposed the new laws, and in 1798 drafted the Kentucky Resolutions, which declared the national law null and void, for that state's legislature. He became President in 1801, defeating Aaron Burr after ambiguities in the electoral system – subsequently eliminated by a constitutional amendment as a result of this election – led to a prolonged tie which was finally broken by repeated balloting in the House of Representatives. His Inaugural Address of 1801 was intended to smooth over the acrimonious party feelings left by the election. He served two terms as President, during which he approved the 1803 Louisiana Purchase from France, which doubled the size of the US at the cost of four cents per acre, and commissioned the exploratory expedition of **Meriwether Lewis** and **William Clark**. As tensions between America and Britain rose, Congress passed, with Jefferson's support, the Embargo Act (1807) prohibiting all foreign commerce. It was intended as a punitive measure against Britain, but proved to be unpopular in the US. It was repealed just before Jefferson left office.

Jefferson had lifelong interests in science, architecture, and education. He served as president of the American Philosophical Society from 1797 to 1814. He designed his own home, Monticello, in 1769. After leaving the presidency, he founded and helped to draw up plans for the University of Virginia, chartered in 1819. The Library of Congress was begun when he sold his personal library to the national government in 1815. He was also the author of *A Manual of Parliamentary Practice* (1801), and a *Life of Captain [Meriwether] Lewis* (1814). Among the papers unpublished at his death were his *Autobiography*, the *Anas* (political memoirs), and "The Morals of Jesus of Nazareth," extracts from the Bible which reflected his deistic beliefs. He died on July 4, 1826, the 50th anniversary of the signing of the Declaration of Independence.

Jennie Gerhardt A novel by **Theodore Dreiser**, published in 1911. Jennie, pretty but poor, helps her mother scrub floors in a fine hotel in Columbus, Ohio. There she meets Senator George Brander, and when her brother is arrested for stealing coal and Brander arranges his release, she gives herself to him out of gratitude. She becomes pregnant, and her father – a rigidly moral Lutheran – forces her to leave home. Her situation worsens when Brander dies.

After the birth of her daughter, Vesta, Jennie goes to work as a maid for the Bracebridges, a wealthy Cleveland family. She meets Lester Kane, who is attracted to her and, by being kind to her family, eventually persuades her to live with him. His family, socially prominent in Cincinnati, disapproves of the relationship. His father dies and leaves his inheritance in the trust of his brother Robert, stipulating that Lester can have it only if he abandons Jennie. Though he suffers pangs of conscience, he does indeed leave her, and eventually marries Letty Pace Gerald, a widowed socialite. Vesta dies and Jennie fights against despair by adopting two orphans.

Lester falls ill and summons Jennie to his deathbed, declaring that he was wrong to leave her and that he has not found greater happiness by doing so. Jennie is with him when he dies but withdraws before the arrival of his wife, who has been traveling. She attends his funeral, masked behind a heavy veil, and watches his coffin being loaded onto the train for the trip to Cincinnati. In this final scene she is once again the forgotten outsider, cut off from the world of luxury inhabited by Lester's family, who board the Pullman cars to accompany his body to its final resting place.

Jewett, Sarah Orne 1849–1909 A doctor's daughter, born and raised in South Berwick, Maine. Jewett often traveled with her father to outlying farms and fishing towns, and observed at first hand the decay and depopulation that afflicted them. (Deephaven, the harbor town of her early stories, was modeled on that of York, near her own home town.) Her observation of this desolation, coupled with her reading of **Harriet Beecher Stowe**'s stories of New England life, provided the stimulus for her own first efforts at fiction; she decided to record the life of her own state and succeeded in getting a story accepted by *The Atlantic Monthly* when she was 19. A collection of such pieces was published as *Deephaven* in 1877 and established her at once as a writer of considerable talent.

She became the close friend of Annie Fields (the wife of **James T. Fields**, the publisher and editor of *The Atlantic Monthly*) and visited her frequently in Boston, but always returned to South Berwick to write. She published two novels, *A Country Doctor* (1884) and *A Marsh Island* (1885), and further collections of stories – *A White Heron* (1886), *The King of Folly Island* (1888), *A Native of Winby* (1893), and *The Life of Nancy* (1895). In 1896 came the book that gave her a lasting place in American literature, *The Country of the Pointed Firs*. Her later work included two books for children; a historical romance, *The Tory Lover* (1901); and some poems that were posthumously published as *Verses* in 1916. Jewett's writing is crisp and assured, and is full of telling observation of people and places. She was well read, and her friendship with Annie Fields kept her in touch with the world of letters. She encouraged the young **Willa Cather**, who was later to edit a collection of her stories. Annie Fields edited her *Letters*, which were published in 1911.

John Brown's Body See **Benét, Stephen Vincent**

Johnson, Edward 1598–1672 A historian and prominent figure in the Massachusetts Bay Colony, Johnson was born in Canterbury, England. Leaving his wife and seven children, he traveled to New England with

John Winthrop aboard the *Arbella* in 1630, returning home the following year. In 1636 he and his family emigrated to Massachusetts and settled in Charlestown. In 1640 he moved his household to the newly incorporated town of Woburn, immediately north of Charlestown. There he served as a selectman, town clerk, captain of the militia, and representative to the General Court. Between 1645 and 1647 he assisted the Colonial authorities in their attempt to codify laws, and in 1659 the General Court appointed him surveyor-general of the arms and munitions of the colony. For all his numerous and influential civic contributions, however, he is best remembered for his history of New England: *The Wonder-Working Providence of Sion's Saviour in New-England* (1654).

Johnson, James Weldon 1871–1938 Born and educated in Florida, Johnson was one of the most influential black figures of his day. His success in several areas, especially in literature and politics, at a time when blacks in both fields were largely unrecognized, was remarkable. While practicing law in Florida (he was the first black admitted to the state Bar after the Civil War), he collaborated with his brother J[ohn] Rosamund Johnson in writing popular songs and spirituals. One of these, "Lift Every Voice and Sing," became known as the black anthem. In 1912 he anonymously published his first novel, *Autobiography of an Ex-Colored Man*, about a light-skinned black man who poses as a white. It was reissued in his own name in 1927, the year he published *God's Trombones: Seven Negro Sermons in Verse*. While teaching creative literature at Fisk University, he published *Black Manhattan* (1930), a black history of New York City. His autobiography, *Along This Way* (1933), tells of his political activities as US consul in Nicaragua and Venezuela (1906–12), and of his role as a major figure in the NAACP. *Negro Americans, What Now?* (1934) collects his lectures at Fisk University. More of his poetry may be found in *Fifty Years and Other Poems* (1917), *Saint Peter Relates an Incident at the Resurrection Day* (1930), and *Selected Poems* (1935).

Jones, James 1921–77 Born in Robinson, Illinois, Jones served in the US Army in the Pacific from 1939 to 1944. *From Here to Eternity* (1951), his first and best-known novel, is a realistic story of army life in Hawaii on the eve of the attack on Pearl Harbor; it won him the National Book Award and became a best seller. His career continued with *Some Came Running* (1957), *The Pistol* (1959), *The Thin Red Line* (1962), *Go To The Widow-Maker* (1967), and *A Touch of Danger* (1973). His short stories are collected in *The Ice Cream Headache* (1968) and *The Merry Month of May* (1971). *Viet Journal* (1974) is an account of his visit to Vietnam.

Jones, LeRoi See **Baraka, Amiri**

Jong, Erica 1942– Born in New York City and educated at Barnard College, Jong was catapulted to popular success with the publication of her controversial and sexually explicit novel *Fear of Flying* (1973), whose exploration of female sexuality is continued in the sequel, *How To Save Your Own Life* (1977). Jong has also published collections of poetry: *Fruits & Vegetables* (1971), *Half-Lives* (1973), *Loveroot* (1975), *Here Comes, and Other Poems* (1975), and *Witches* (1981). Her third novel, *Fanny: Being the True History of Fanny Hackabout-Jones* (1980), is patterned on the 18th-century pornographic novel by John Cleland. *Parachutes and Kisses* (1984) returns to the characters introduced in *Fear of Flying*.

Jungle, The A novel by **Upton Sinclair**, published serially in the socialist weekly *Appeal to Reason* in 1905, and in book form in 1906. It protests the labor and sanitary conditions in the Chicago stockyards and slums, as seen through the eyes of Jurgis Rudkus, a young Lithuanian immigrant. Sinclair chronicles the exploitation and victimization of Jurgis and his family, who live and work in Packington, the stockyard district. Jurgis experiences successive changes of fortune and employment. He works in the fertilizer plant after being injured in the slaughterhouse, and serves time in jail for attacking a foreman who has taken advantage of his wife, Ona. The Rudkus family is plagued by ill fortune and sickness, culminating in the deaths of Ona and both the children.

After his incarceration, Jurgis is blacklisted in Packington; finds work in a harvester plant and then in the steelworks; escapes from the city briefly to lead the life of a tramp in the open country; survives as a thief upon his return to Chicago; works as a scab during a meat-packer's strike; serves as the tool of a corrupt politician; then ends up back on the street, outcast and unemployable. Finally, Jurgis is introduced to socialist thought at a political meeting which he attends in order to escape the cold. The novel ends with an affirmation of the need for socialist reform by the workers of Chicago. Sinclair's realistic portayal of the squalid and cruel conditions of the meat factory prompted the Pure-Food legislation of 1906.

Jurgen: A Comedy of Justice A romance by **James Branch Cabell** published in 1919, part of his 18-volume "Biography of the Life of Manuel." It was suppressed on grounds of obscenity from 1920 to 1922. Like others in the cycle, it is set in the mythical kingdom of Poictesme. The pawnbroker Jurgen is married to Dame Lisa, a voluble woman who sometimes makes life difficult for him. Jurgen says some sympathetic things about the Devil, who overhears him and rewards him by making Lisa disappear into a dark cave. Feeling obliged to seek his wife, Jurgen also enters the cave and has several adventures – some of them amatory – with various mythical figures. He encounters the Centaur Nessus, Guenevere, Thragnar, Gogyvran Gawr, Yolande, King Smoit, Merlin, Dame Anaïtis (The Lady of the Lake), Queen Helen, and others. He lives for a while in Hell, where he encounters Grandfather Satan. He then goes to Heaven, where he assumes the identity of Pope John XX. Finally he meets Koshchei, a powerful being who tempts him with beautiful women. After Jurgen has rejected them all, Lisa is returned to him and they resume their normal life. His adventures take exactly a year, extending from one Walpurgis Night to the next.

K

Kaufman, George S. 1889–1961 Playwright, director, drama critic, and wit, famous for his collaborations with other writers. Born in Pittsburgh, Kaufman worked as a ribbon salesman and stenographer in Paterson, New Jersey, until his satiric contributions to Franklin Pierce Adams's column, "The Conning Tower," earned him his own humor column in the Washington *Times*. Fired by an anti-semitic editor, he moved to New York, where he eventually became drama critic for the *New York Times*, a position he held for many years. He also joined a group of young writers, including **Dorothy Parker**, **Robert Benchley**, Alexander Woolcott, **Robert Sherwood**, **Ring Lardner**, Edna Ferber, **Marc Connelly**, and Heywood Broun, who developed the custom of lunching together at the Round Table of the Hotel Algonquin.

Kaufman's career as a playwright took off with *Dulcy* (1921), his first collaboration with fellow newspaperman Marc Connelly. During the next five years the two of them wrote seven more satirical comedies, including *Merton of the Movies* (1922) and *Beggar on Horseback* (1924). Kaufman went on to work with other collaborators, including Edna Ferber, with whom he produced six comedies including *The Royal Family* (1927), *Dinner at Eight* (1932), and *Stage Door* (1936). His longest and most successful collaboration, however, was with **Moss Hart**. Their joint efforts began with *Once in A Lifetime* (1930), which poked fun at Hollywood, and included *Merrily We Roll Along* (1934); *You Can't Take It With You* (1936), which won the Pulitzer Prize; *I'd Rather Be Right* (1937), with music and lyrics by **Richard Rogers** and **Lorenz Hart**; *The Fabulous Invalid* (1938); *The American Way* (1939); *The Man Who Came To Dinner*

(1939), a portrait of their eccentric friend, Alexander Woolcott; and *George Washington Slept Here* (1940).

Kaufman's other plays include *Cocoanuts* (1925) and *Animal Crackers* (1928), written with Morrie Ryskind for the Marx Brothers; *June Moon* (1929), written with **Ring Lardner**; and such musicals as *Strike Up the Band* (1930) and *Of Thee I Sing* (1931), written with Morrie Ryskind and the **Gershwins** (the latter was the first musical to win a Pulitzer Prize), and *The Band Wagon* (1931), with Arthur Schwartz and Howard Dietz. All told, Kaufman had 47 plays produced during an active career of 37 years. He was also much in demand as a director, contributing in that capacity to the success of *Guys and Dolls* (1950) and *My Sister Eileen* (1940).

Kees, Weldon 1914–55 Born in Beatrice, Nebraska, Kees spent most of his early life in New York City and then moved to San Francisco in 1951. Before he disappeared, he had talked of either committing suicide or moving to Europe to live under an assumed name; when his car was found abandoned on the Golden Gate Bridge on July 18, 1955, it was assumed that he had chosen the former.

Kees was a painter, jazz pianist, composer, photographer, and film-maker, but he is best known for his poetry. His allusive, often formal verse takes an unrelentingly pessimistic view of the human condition, only occasionally relieved by a compassionate tone. His poems appeared in *The Last Man* (1943), *The Fall of the Magicians* (1947), *Poems 1947–1954* (1954), and *Collected Poems* (1960), edited by Donald Justice.

Kelly, George (Edward) 1887–1974 Born into a prominent Philadelphia family, Kelly was educated at home by his parents and first entered the theatre in a touring production of *The Virginian* in 1912. In 1915 he joined a vaudeville company and began to write his own material. His first successful full-length play was *The Torchbearers* (1922), a satiric account of a stagestruck woman's involvement with a "little theatre" movement. His second play, *The Show-Off* (1924), a comedy about a braggart, was developed from his earlier one-act play *Poor Aubrey* (1922). *Craig's Wife* (1925), which won the Pulitzer Prize in 1926, is a character study of a grasping and self-centered woman that shows the influence of August Strindberg. *Daisy Mayme* (1926) and *Behold the Bridegroom* (1927) are domestic stories of rich and willful women. Kelly's next two plays focused on conflict between generations: the unsuccessful *Maggie, the Magnificent* (1929) tells of a daughter's rebellion against her domineering mother; *Philip Goes Forth* (1931), which was better received, describes a son's conflict with his father over the choice between a theatrical career and a career in the family business. *Reflected Glory* (1936) further examines the conflict between the theatre and family responsibilities. His last two plays, *The Deep Mrs Sykes* (1945) and *The Fatal Weakness* (1946), are about suspicion and self-deception in marriage.

Kennedy, John Pendleton 1795–1870 While practicing law in his native Baltimore, Kennedy took to writing and produced *The Red Book* (1818–19), which – like **Washington Irving**'s *Salmagundi* – included sketches, satirical essays, and poems. Under the pseudonym of Mark Littleton he then published *Swallow Barn* (1832), a collection of sketches set in Virginia. His first and best-known novel, *Horse-Shoe Robinson*, appeared in 1835, and was followed by *Rob of the Bowl* in 1838. He was a friend of Irving and **Oliver Wendell Holmes**, and the American host to William Makepeace Thackeray. He was also one of the first to recognize **Edgar Allan Poe**, to whom he awarded first prize in a short-story contest he judged. Most of his life from 1840 onwards was devoted to politics, but he still found time to write the occasional satiric piece.

Kentucky Cardinal, A A short novel by **James Lane Allen**, published in 1894. Adam Moss is an amiable but reclusive nature lover who prefers his garden and the migrating birds it harbors to human society. The Cobb family moves into the house next door and disturbs his seclusion, but after a while he discovers that he likes them and feels especially drawn to the eldest daughter, Georgiana, who also loves birds. He falls in love with her, but she is hesitant. As proof of his love, she asks him to capture and cage a cardinal, a bird that lives in his garden and whose trust he has slowly gained. He does as she asks, thinking that his gesture will show her that he is ready to put aside animal attachments for human. The bird soon dies in captivity, and Adam and Georgiana quarrel about the meaning of the incident. Eventually, however, they come to an understanding; they forgive each other and plan to marry. *Aftermath* (1895), the sequel, tells of their marriage. Adam tries to become more involved in town life and pays less attention to nature, but he finds only that human behavior, especially with pre-Civil War tensions rising, is violent and foolish. Georgiana dies after giving birth to their first child, and Adam consoles himself by returning his attention to his first love, nature.

Kenyon Review, The Founded in 1939 by **John Crowe Ransom**, the magazine soon became a leading organ for "**New Criticism**." Contributors of non-fiction have included **Allen Tate**, Cleanth Brooks, R. P. Blackmur, **Robert Penn Warren**, William Empson, **Paul Goodman**, **Kenneth Burke**, Benedetto Croce, Leslie Fiedler, Northrop Frye, Frederick J. Hoffman, Marshall McLuhan, Herbert Read, **Lionel Trilling**, Harry Levin, and Stephen Spender. The emphasis shifted from criticism to poetry and fiction when Robie Macauley became editor in 1958. Contributors during this period included **John Barth**, William Eastlake, **Flannery O'Connor**, and **Thomas Pynchon**. George Lanning and Ellington White edited the magazine from 1967 until its suspension of publication in 1970. It was revived in 1979, under the joint editorship of Ronald Sharp and Frederick Turner. Philip D. Church and Galbraith M. Crump have been the editors since 1983.

Kern, Jerome 1885–1945 A composer of songs and show music, Kern was born in New York City. His father, a successful businessman, hoped to see his son follow the same path, but after proving his incompetence as a buyer the young man was permitted to enroll in the New York College of Music, and then to travel to London and the Continent, where he studied theory and composition. In London he found a job with musical producer Charles K. Frohman and became convinced that his talent was for popular, not "serious," music. Returning to New York in 1904, he worked as a song-plugger and salesman for a music publisher in Tin Pan Alley, and also as a rehearsal pianist, occasionally contributing additional songs to the adaptations of European operettas that were popular at the time. His first song hit was "How'd You Like To Spoon With Me?" and his first complete original score was for a Western, *The Red Petticoat* (1912). He then began a collaboration with the English-born lyricist Guy Bolton, which resulted in such light-hearted comedies as *Nobody Home* (1915), *Very Good Eddie* (1915), and (with P. G. Wodehouse also collaborating) *Have A Heart* (1917), *Oh, Boy!* (1917), *Leave It To Jane* (1917), and *Oh, Lady, Lady!* (1918). *Sally* (1920) and *Sunny* (1925), Kern's first collaborations with lyricist **Oscar Hammerstein**, were written for Florenz Ziegfeld as vehicles for dancer Marilyn Miller.

In 1927 Kern and Hammerstein collaborated on *Show Boat*, an adaptation of Edna Ferber's novel, which has been called the first musical for adults. *Show Boat* was revolutionary because it took up serious themes, including miscegenation, without trivializing or decorating them. Such songs as "Ol' Man River," "Can't Help Loving Dat Man," and "Make Believe" grow out of situation and character in a significant way, rather than simply providing an excuse for singing and dancing. *Show Boat* has been adapted for the screen three times, and became part of the repertory of the New York City Opera in 1954. Among Kern's later works are *Sweet Adeline* (1929), *The Cat and the Fiddle* (1931), *Music in the Air* (1932) (including the song "Smoke Gets In Your Eyes"), and *Very Warm For May* (1939). After 1939 he wrote only for films; he won two Academy Awards, for "The Way You Look Tonight" and "The Last Time I Saw Paris."

Kerouac, Jack 1922–69 Jean-Louis Kerouac was born in Lowell, Massachusetts, and attended local Catholic schools before going to Columbia University in 1941. He spent time as a merchant seaman and in wandering around the US before publishing the first of his semi-autobiographical novels, *The Town and the City* (1950), about a family in his home town of Lowell. **On the Road** (1957), his best-known book, is concerned with the lifestyle and the often aimless search for significant experience of what later became known as the Beat Generation (Kerouac was the first to use the term). The book established Kerouac as the novelist of the **Beats** just as *Howl* had identified **Allen Ginsberg** as their poet. *The Subterraneans* and *The Dharma Bums* (both 1958), *Tristessa* (1960), *Big Sur* (1962), and *Desolation Angels* (1965) are all products of the Beat consciousness; *Doctor Sax* and *Maggie Cassidy* (both 1959) and *Visions of Gerard* (1963) are evocations of Kerouac's boyhood. *Satori in Paris* (1966) is an account of his quest for his Breton ancestors. Among his other books are *Lonesome Traveller* (1960, travel sketches), *Mexico City Blues* (1959, verse), and *Book of Dreams* (1961). *Visions of Cody*, written in 1951–2, was published posthumously in 1972.

Kesey, Ken 1935– Born in Colorado, Kesey grew up in Oregon and graduated from the University of Oregon in 1957, later attending creative writing classes at Stanford. In the early 1960s he volunteered for government drug experiments, and subsequently became an aide on a psychiatric ward in a Veteran's hospital. He made use of this experience in his first novel, **One Flew Over the Cuckoo's Nest** (1962), which is set in a mental hospital. His second novel, *Sometimes a Great Notion* (1964), focuses on the lives of a logging family in the Northwest. The same year he took a cross-country bus trip as leader of the Merry Pranksters, which **Tom Wolfe** memorialized in *The Electric Kool-Aid Acid Test* (1968). *Kesey's Garage Sale* (1973) is a collection of essays, letters, interviews, stories, and drawings. He has since published installments of a novel in progress, *Seven Prayers to Grandma Whittier*, in his magazine *Spit in the Ocean*.

Kingsley, Sidney 1906– Born Sidney Kirschner in New York City, he pursued his high-school interest in drama at Cornell, where he wrote and directed one-act plays. His first play, *Men in White* (1933), examines the conflict in a young medical intern's life between dedication to his medical practice and concern for his personal happiness. Produced by the **Group Theatre**, it was a major critical success, and won a Pulitzer Prize in 1934. His second and longest-running play, *Dead End* (1935), is a realistic examination of how crime breeds among the youth of a poor community. His next two plays, *Ten Million Ghosts* (1936) and *The World We Make* (1939), were critical and popular failures. With *The Patriots* (1943) he again received critical acclaim, and won the New York Drama Critics Circle Award. The only play besides *Men in White* that Kingsley himself did not direct, *The Patriots* is a historical drama about the conflict between **Thomas Jefferson** and Alexander Hamilton, and a defense of democracy and call for unity on the eve of World War II. In his next two plays he addressed the problems of the police or totalitarian state: *Detective Story* (1949) is the realistic portrait of a tough New York cop's harsh treatment of two suspects; *Darkness at Noon* (1951) is the award-winning adaptation of Arthur Koestler's novel about conditions in Stalinist Russia. His last two works were *Lunatics and Lovers* (1954), a first attempt at farce; and *Night Life* (1962), a grim portrait of New York night club life.

Kinnell, Galway 1927–   Poet, born in Providence, Rhode Island. Kinnell received a BA from Princeton and an MA from the University of Rochester. After serving in the US Navy, he went to Paris on a Fulbright Fellowship. He later worked for the Congress on Racial Equality as a field worker. Widely traveled, he has lived in France and in the Middle East, and has taught at the University of California at Irvine, the University of Pittsburgh, and Sarah Lawrence College; he now teaches at New York University.

His first books were *What a Kingdom It Was* (1960), *Flower Herding on Mount Monadnock* (1964), and *Body Rags* (1968), which established him with many critics as a contemporary master of free verse. *The Book of Nightmares* (1971) confirmed this judgment, and emphasized the sacramental dimension apparent in all his work: poems approximating a personalized chant that accepts death as part of the primal rhythm. His other collections are *First Poems 1946–54* (1970), *The Shoes of Wandering* (1971), *The Avenue Bearing the Initial of Christ into the New World* (1974), *Three Poems* (1976), *Mortal Acts, Mortal Words* (1980), *Selected Poems* (1982, Pulitzer Prize), and *The Past* (1985). He has also published a novel, *Black Light* (1966); a collection of interviews, *Walking Down the Stairs* (1978); and a number of translations – *Bitter Victory* (1956, a novel by René Hardy), *The Poems of François Villon* (1965), *On the Motion and Immobility of Douve* (1968, poems by Yves Bonnefoy), and *Lackawanna Elegy* (1970, poems by Yvan Goll).

Kizer, Carolyn (Ashley) 1925–   Born in Spokane, Washington, Kizer was educated at Sarah Lawrence College and at the University of Washington, where she studied under **Theodore Roethke**. She has been a lecturer and poet-in-residence at several universities, and from 1966 to 1970 was Director of Literary Programs for the National Endowment for the Arts. In 1959 she founded the magazine *Poetry Northwest*, which she edited until 1965. Her first volume of verse, entitled simply *Poems*, appeared in 1959. She has continued her exploration of feminist issues in subsequent collections such as *The Ungrateful Garden* (1961), *Knock Upon Silence* (1965), and *Midnight Was My City: New and Selected Poems* (1971). In 1984 she published two more volumes, *Mermaids in the Basement* and *Yin*, the latter of which received the Pulitzer Prize.

Knickerbocker Group An early-19th-century school of writers, primarily associated by their common location in New York City. Deriving their name from **Washington Irving**'s pseudonym, Diedrich Knickerbocker, the major figures in the group were Irving himself, **William Cullen Bryant**, and **James Kirke Paulding**. **Joseph Rodman Drake** and **Fitz-Greene Halleck** were also prominent in the school, which tended toward sophistication in style and conservatism in politics. Many of the members were published in *The Knickerbocker Magazine*.

Knickerbocker Magazine, The   A monthly magazine founded in New York in 1833 by Lewis G. and Willis G. Clark. Although dominated by the local writers of the **Knickerbocker Group**, almost every living American writer of distinction was at some time published in the magazine – **Washington Irving, Henry Wadsworth Longfellow, Nathaniel Hawthorne, John Greenleaf Whittier, William Dean Howells, Oliver Wendell Holmes**, and **William Cullen Bryant** among them. The magazine continued until 1865.

Koch, Kenneth 1925– Born in Cincinnati, Ohio, Koch was educated at Harvard (BA, 1948) and Columbia (PhD, 1959). In the 1950s, with **Frank O'Hara** and **John Ashbery**, he became one of the leading poets of the **New York School**, which sought to oppose the academic austerity of mid-century American poetry. Much of his early work in particular was influenced by that of the French surrealist Jacques Prévert, whom he discovered during three years spent in Europe. Like others of the New York School he makes frequent use of urban settings and metaphors. His volumes include *Poems* (1953), *Ko, or a Season on Earth* (1959), *Permanently* (1960), *Thank You and Other Poems* (1962), *Sleeping With Women* (1969), *The Art of Love* (1975), *The Duplications* (1977), *Sleeping on the Wing* (1981), and *Selected Poems* (1985). As well as teaching poetry at Columbia University, he has taught the writing of poetry to children and the elderly, and published two books on the subject: *Rose, Where Did You Get That Red? Teaching Great Poetry to Children* (1973) and *I Never Told Anybody: Teaching Poetry in a Nursing Home* (1977). He has also written several plays which have been produced off-Broadway. A collection entitled *Bertha and Other Plays* appeared in 1969.

Kopit, Arthur L. 1937– Playwright, born in New York City and educated at Harvard. His most renowned work parodies the theatre of the absurd: *Oh Dad, Poor Dad, Mama's Hung You in the Closet and I'm Feelin' So Sad*, subtitled "a pseudo-classical, tragifarce in a bastard French tradition," was published in 1960, but was not produced professionally until 1962. Six other plays are collected in *The Day the Whores Came Out to Play Tennis* (1965). A satirical drama examining myths of the American West, *Indians*, was produced in London in 1968. *An Incident in the Park, or Pardon Me, Sir, But Is My Eye Hurting Your Elbow?* also appeared in 1968. Other

plays include *What's Happened to the Thorne's House* (1972); *Louisiana Territory: or, Lewis and Clark – Lost and Found* (1975); *Secrets of the Rich* (1976); *Wings* (1978); and *Good Help is Hard to Find* (1982).

Kumin, Maxine 1925– Kumin was born in Philadelphia and educated at Radcliffe College. She has taught at several universities including Brandeis, Columbia, and Washington, and currently teaches at Princeton. She has published several volumes of poetry including *Halfway* (1961), *The Privelege* (1965), *The Nightmare Factory* (1970), *Up Country: Poems of New England* (1972, Pulitzer Prize 1973), *House, Bridge, Fountain, Gate* (1975), *The Retrieval System* (1978), *Our Ground Time Here Will Be Brief* (1982), and *The Long Approach* (1985). Among her works of fiction are the novels *Through Dooms of Love* (1965), *The Passions of Uxport* (1968), *The Abduction* (1971), and *The Designated Heir* (1974); and a collection of short stories, *Why Can't We Live Together Like Civilized Human Beings?* (1982). A collection of essays entitled *To Make a Prairie: Essays on Poets, Poetry, and Country Living* appeared in 1979. Her verse focuses in general on themes of loss and survival, and she frequently emphasizes the importance of family bonds. In her most recent works she has stressed the role of the poet and in poetry dealing with the threat of Armageddon that seems to hover over contemporary society. She served as Consultant in Poetry to the Library of Congress for 1981–2.

Kunitz, Stanley 1905– Poet, born in Worcester, Massachusetts, and educated at Harvard, Kunitz has taught at Bennington College, and at Brandeis, Columbia, and Yale universities. His first volumes were *Intellectual Things* (1930) and *Passport to the War: A Selection of Poems* (1944). Acclaim, however, did not come until *Selected Poems: 1928–58* appeared in 1958 and won the Pulitzer Prize. Since then he has published *The Testing Tree* (1971), *The Lincoln Relics* (1978), *The Poems of Stanley Kunitz: 1928–1978* (1979), and *The Wellfleet Whale & Companion Poems* (1983). His poems are particularly distinguished by their careful formal logic and their quiet humor.

Kunitz, who has traveled in Russia and Poland, has also been responsible for various collections of translations of the poems of Andrei Voznesensky and Yevgeny Yevtushenko, and has published, with Max Hayward, the translation *Poems of Akhmatova* (1973). He served as editor of the Yale Series of Younger Poets (1969–76) and as Consultant in Poetry at the Library of Congress (1974–6). A book of essays and interviews, *A Kind of Order, A Kind of Folly: Essays and Conversations*, appeared in 1975.

L

Lanier, Sidney 1842–81 Born in Macon, Georgia, Lanier attended Oglethorpe University, from which he graduated in 1860. During the Civil War he served with the Confederate forces and became a prisoner of war (1864–5). From 1865 to 1873 he worked in his father's law offices, as a hotel clerk, and as a teacher. From an early age he had trained as a musician, and in 1873 became a professional flautist with Baltimore's Peabody Orchestra. His love of music greatly influenced his literary works, particularly his ideas about prosody. After writing his only novel, *Tiger Lilies* (1867), he turned to poetry. He also occasionally lectured on English literature. In 1876, he supplied the lyrics for *The Centennial Meditation of Columbia*; the music was composed by Dudley Buck. Two years after the publication of his first book of poetry, *Poems* (1877), The Johns Hopkins University offered him a position as lecturer. His *The Science of English Verse* (1880) remains an important study of English prosody.

Most of his other works were published posthumously, several of them edited by his wife, Mary Day Lanier. His collected *Poems* appeared in 1884 and was reissued with additions in 1891 and 1916. *Poem Outlines* – also verse – was published in 1908. Among his critical works are *The English Novel and the Principle of its Development* (1883), a collection of lectures he gave at Johns Hopkins; *Music and Poetry: Essays upon Some Aspects and Interrelations of the Two Arts* (1898); and *Shakespeare and His Forerunners: Studies in Elizabethan Poetry and Its Development from Early English* (1902), also a collection of lectures. He also edited four books for boys: *The Boy's Froissart's Chronicles* (1879), *The Boy's King Arthur* (1880), *The Boy's Mabinogion* (1881), and *The Boy's Percy* (1882).

Lardner, Ring[gold] (Wilmer) 1885–1933 Born in Michigan, Lardner got his first job as a reporter in South Bend, Indiana. He worked in Chicago, and then in St Louis editing a baseball weekly. He went on to become a sports reporter for various newspapers and eventually a syndicated columnist. The letters he wrote in the guise of "Jack Keefe," a newcomer to a professional baseball team, made him famous. They first appeared in the *Chicago Tribune* and were collected as *You Know Me, Al: A Busher's Letters* (1914). Lardner had a sharp-edged sense of humor and a remarkable ear for vernacular speech. Americans of every walk of life appeared in his stories, their utterances establishing their characters. He demonstrated his talent for verse in the *Bib Ballads* (1915). *Gullible's Travels* (1917) is a collection of satirical stories, and was followed by more of the same in *Treat 'em Rough* in 1918. His only novel, *The Big Town*, was published in 1921. By the time he published *How to Write Short Stories (With Samples)* (1924), he already had a large and enthusiastic following. His later works are the collections: *What of It?* (1925), *The Love Nest* (1926), *Round Up* (1929), and *First and Last* (1934).

Last of the Mohicans, The See **Leatherstocking Tales**

Last Puritan, The *A Memoir in the Form of a Novel* A novel by George Santayana, published in 1935. It begins with a prologue in which the narrator, a college professor, introduces the story of Oliver Alden – the "Last Puritan" and one of the narrator's students. Oliver is the heir of a wealthy, established New England family. He and his mother are abandoned by his drug-addict father, who has rebelled against the puritanical values of New England and sails about the world in his yacht, employing Jim Darnley to accompany him on his travels. Oliver is raised by his mother, with the assistance of a German governess, Irma Schlote. At the age of 17 he joins his father for a cruise and becomes Jim Darnley's friend. He then enrolls at Williams College where he is both studious and athletic. His father commits suicide. Oliver becomes friendly with a European cousin, Mario, whom his father has supported, and courts another cousin, Edith. After graduation Oliver visits the Darnleys in England, where he meets and falls in love with Jim's sister Rose. But Rose falls in love with Mario (who does not love her in return) when he in turn visits Oliver at the Darnleys. World War I having begun, Oliver follows Mario's example and enters the army. Rose refuses Oliver's proposal of marriage. He leaves for France, and is killed there. His estate goes to the Darnleys.

Last Tycoon, The   See **Fitzgerald, F. Scott**

Lawson, John Howard 1894–1977 Born in New York City and educated at Williams College, Lawson helped shape the theatre of social consciousness in the 1920s and 1930s. His first play, *Processional* (1925), is a protest against the harshness of life during a coal strike in West Virginia. Lawson was among the first playwrights to move to Hollywood, where he became active as a leader of the Communist faction. *Marching Song* (1937) was another leftist play, which showed the triumph of labor's solidarity over the persecutions of an uncaring management. His career was cut short when he was summoned before the House Un-American Activities Committee. As one of the "Hollywood Ten," he served a one-year sentence (1950–1) for contempt of the House. *Parlor Magic* (1963) was the only play he produced after the effective blacklisting of his name. His other plays include *Roger Boomer* (1923), *Nirvana* (1926), *Loudspeaker* (1927), *The International* (1928), *Success Story* (1932), *Gentlewoman* (1934), and *The Pure in Heart* (1937).

Leatherstocking Tales A series of five novels by **James Fenimore Cooper**, set in the early frontier period of American history. They take their name from their central protagonist, Natty Bumppo, who is variously called Leatherstocking, Deerslayer, Hawk-

eye, and Pathfinder. The chronological sequence differs from the dates of composition. *The Pioneers; or the Sources of the Susquehanna* (1823) was the first volume to be written, followed soon after by *The Last of the Mohicans: A Tale of 1757* (1826) and *The Prairie: A Tale* (1827). Cooper later completed the series with *The Pathfinder; or the Inland Sea* (1840) and *The Deerslayer; or the First War Path* (1841).

The first novel in order of events (though the last to be written), *The Deerslayer*, relates Bumppo's experiences as a young man, and takes place in upstate New York in the early 1740s. The action begins as Deerslayer and his friend Hurry Harry approach Lake Glimmerglass, or Oswego, where the trapper Thomas Hutter lives with his daughters, the beautiful Judith and the feeble-minded Hetty. Hutter's floating log fort is attacked by Iroquois Indians, and the two frontiersmen join in the fight. Harry and Hutter are captured. Deerslayer is joined by his Mohican friend, Chingachgook, whose bride Hist is being held by the Iroquois, and they eventually manage to ransom the two men. They then try to rescue Hist, but Hutter is killed and Deerslayer is captured in the attempt. The frontiersman is released on parole so that he may see his friends for the last time and, keeping his word, he returns to the Indian camp to await his death. Judith, however, manages to delay the proceedings long enough for Chingachgook to arrive with a troop of English soldiers and save Deerslayer's life.

The next novel in the series, *The Last of the Mohicans*, presents Bumppo in his maturity, and is set in 1757 during the Seven Years' War between the French and the British. (In this novel he is known as Hawkeye.) Cora and Alice Munro are on their way to Fort William Henry to join their father, the commander. They are accompanied by Major Duncan Heyward and a singing teacher, David Gamut. Their Indian guide, Magua, plans to betray the group to the Iroquois, who are fighting on the side of the French. Magua's plan, however, is frustrated by Hawkeye and his friends Chingachgook and Uncas, who are the last Mohican chieftains. The group arrives at the fort, but Munro is forced to surrender to the French commander Montcalm. Although supposedly given safe conduct, the English are attacked and the girls captured by Delawares and Hurons. The former take Cora; the latter, Alice. Alice and Uncas, also a prisoner, manage to escape. Uncas is then welcomed at the camp of the Delawares and named successor to the old chief. Magua, however, has laid claim to the captive Cora, and he eventually kills both the young woman and Uncas. Hawkeye avenges the death of his friend and kills Magua.

The Pathfinder takes place soon after *The Last of the Mohicans*, in the same conflict between the French and Indians and the British colonials. Mabel Dunham is making her way to Oswego, the British fort on Lake Ontario, to join her father. She is accompanied by a group consisting of her uncle, Charles Cap, a Tuscarora Indian named Arrowhead and his wife Dew-in-June, the scout Pathfinder (Natty Bumppo), Chingachgook the Mohican chief, and Jasper Western the sailor. The party is harassed by Iroquois, and Arrowhead and his wife disappear. The rest of the company arrives safely at the fort, then proceeds with Mabel's father on Jasper Western's boat to relieve a post in the Thousand Islands. But Jasper is suspected of being disloyal to the English and is sent back to Oswego, while Dunham and his force set out to attack French supply boats. Dew-in-June then arrives, with the warning that Arrowhead, at the head of an Iroquois force, is leading an attack on the post. The Iroquois are eventually routed by Pathfinder and Chingachgook, and Jasper is arrested as a traitor, to the despair of Mabel who, in spite of a promise to Pathfinder, is in love with Jasper. Muir – the lieutenant who had accused Jasper – is unmasked as the real traitor, and Arrowhead kills him. Dunham dies and Pathfinder, realizing the truth, relinquishes Mabel to Jasper.

The next novel in the series, *The Pioneers*, is set in 1793 in Otsego County in the recently settled region of New York state. While hunting deer, Judge Temple, one of the principal landowners in the area, wounds Oliver Edwards, the companion of the aging Natty Bumppo, now known as Leatherstocking. The judge and his daughter Elizabeth befriend Edwards, who becomes their overseer, meanwhile maintaining his friendship with Bumppo and with old John Mohegan, whom everyone knows is the Mohican chief Chingachgook. It is suspected that Edwards is the chief's son and soon Elizabeth and her friends are disdaining his company. Bumppo is arrested for shooting deer out of season and spends a short time in prison. Elizabeth goes to visit him upon his release but is caught in a forest fire on her return, and is saved by Edwards. Chingachgook is also caught in the fire, and dies in spite of Bumppo's efforts to save him. A party searching for Elizabeth comes upon a demented old man. It is discovered that he is Major Effingham, the Loyalist who had once owned Judge Temple's estate, but who was lost in the war and had his lands confiscated. It is revealed that Oliver Edwards is his grandson. Temple relinquishes half of his estate to Oliver, and he and Elizabeth are betrothed at the end.

The Prairie is set in 1804 on the frontier of the great plains. Natty Bumppo – now in his 80s and known simply as the trapper – has joined the western movement. He meets a wagon train, gains an unpleasant impression of its leaders, Ishmael Bush and his brother-in-law Abiram White, and is puzzled by the confinement of a woman in a covered wagon. The trapper's wisdom enables the train to evade an Indian raiding party, and he guides it to a safe camp. A young soldier then joins the camp and Bumppo is overjoyed to recognize Duncan Uncas Middleton, a descendant of his friend Duncan Heyward. Duncan is on a mission for the army but is also seeking his betrothed, Inez de Certavallos, who has been kidnapped and is being held for ransom. The trapper remembers the confined woman, who proves to be Inez, and the two proceed to rescue her. The travelers endure a prairie fire, a buffalo stampede, and capture by the Sioux. A Pawnee raid on the Sioux frees them, but Ishmael Bush catches up with them and accuses Bumppo of the murder of one of his men. There has indeed been a murder, but the guilty man proves to be Abiram White. The arrival of Duncan's soldiers finally provides the party with safety, with the trapper's Pawnee friends watching quietly. The end of the tale brings the frontiersman's life to a close. He dies peacefully on the prairie, surrounded by his friends of both races.

Leaves of Grass The major work of **Walt Whitman**, the collection consisted of 12 untitled poems when it was first published in

1855. Over the next 37 years it appeared in five revised editions and three reissues. Whitman added, deleted, or revised poems for each edition.

The first edition of *Leaves of Grass* was privately printed by Whitman, as were some of the other editions that appeared during his lifetime. It included the poems that Whitman eventually titled "Song of Myself," "I Sing the Body Electric," and "The Sleepers." He wrote a now famous preface for it but omitted it from subsequent editions. The second edition appeared in 1856 and contained 20 new poems, among them "Sun Down Poem" (later renamed "Crossing Brooklyn Ferry") and "Poem of the Open Road" (renamed "Song of the Open Road"). In 1860 Whitman published a third edition, adding "Out of the Cradle Endlessly Rocking," one of his most memorable poems; the "Calamus" poems, extolling friendship among men; and "Enfans d'Adam" (later titled "Children of Adam"), a group of poems about heterosexual, procreative love. The fourth edition of *Leaves of Grass* (1867) was bound with *Drum-Taps* (which had been published separately in 1865) and with *Sequel. Drum-Taps* was a series of poems inspired by what Whitman had witnessed while nursing the wounded during the Civil War, and *Sequel* contained his elegy for the assassinated president, Abraham Lincoln, "When Lilacs Last in the Dooryard Bloom'd." (William Rossetti drew on this fourth edition for his English edition of Whitman's works, a volume entitled *Selections*, published in 1868.) For the fifth edition (1871) Whitman incorporated the poems from *Drum-Taps* into the body of *Leaves of Grass*, and also added a new "annex" – "Passage to India" – which he later incorporated into the body of the work for the sixth edition (1881).

In 1876 a reissue of *Leaves of Grass* appeared sometimes referred to as the "Centennial" edition. For the 1889 reissue of the 1881 edition, Whitman added another annex, which included a group of new poems entitled "Sands at Seventy" and a prose piece called "A Backward Glance O'er Travel'd Roads" – both of which had previously appeared in *November Boughs* (1888). The final version of *Leaves of Grass* to appear in Whitman's lifetime, though sometimes called the "Deathbed" edition (1891-2), is simply a reissue of the 1881 edition supplemented with "Sands at Seventy" and "Goodbye My Fancy."

Both the form and content of the poems in *Leaves of Grass* were revolutionary; Whitman's sprawling lines and cataloguing technique, as well as his belief that poetry should include the lowly, the profane, even the obscene, have had enormous influence. His intention in writing *Leaves of Grass*, he said, was to create a truly American poem, one "proportionate to our continent, with its powerful races of men, its tremendous historic events, its great oceans, its mountains, and its illimitable prairies." But the poem goes beyond its specifically American subject to deal with the universal themes of nature, fertility, and mortality.

LeGuin, Ursula 1929– A writer of science fiction, LeGuin was born in Berkeley, California, the daughter of the anthropologist Alfred L. Kroeber. She received her BA from Radcliffe College in 1951 and her MA from Columbia University in 1952. In the following year, while studying in France on a Fulbright Scholarship, she married the historian Charles A. LeGuin.

Her first three novels – *Rocannon's World* (1966), *Planet of Exile* (1966), and *City of Illusions* (1967) – are characteristic of all her work in their rejection of the technological concerns of more traditional science fiction and in their interest in humanism and anthropology. Her most acclaimed work, *The Earthsea Trilogy*, is comprised of *A Wizard of Earthsea* (1968, Boston *Globe* Horn Book Award 1969), *The Tombs of Atuan* (1971), and *The Farthest Shore* (1972, National Book Award for children's literature 1973). While working on the trilogy she also wrote *The Left Hand of Darkness* (1969); set on an imaginary planet populated by "androgynes," the novel reflects LeGuin's interest in Taoist thought. In some of her later works she has been critical of contemporary American political and social values: *The Word for World is Forest* (1972), about Vietnam; *The Dispossessed* (1974), a fantasy set on an anarchist moon colony and its capitalist mother planet; and *The New Atlantis* (1975), which presents a futuristic vision of totalitarianism in the US.

Her other works include *The Lathe of Heaven* (1971), *From Elfland to Poughkeepsie* (1973), *Dreams Must Explain Themselves*

(1975), *Wild Angels* (1975), *The Wind's Twelve Quarters* (1975), *Orisinian Tales* (1976), *Very Far Away From Anywhere Else* (1976), *The Water is Wide* (1976), *Lesse Webster* (1979), *Malafrena* (1979), *The Language of the Night* (1979), *The Beginning Place* (1980), *The Eye of the The Heron and Other Stories* (1980), and *Hard Words and Other Poems* (1981).

Le Sueur, Meridel 1900–   Born in Murray, Iowa, Le Sueur spent her childhood in Texas, Oklahoma, and Kansas, where she was exposed to a midwestern tradition of radical dissent: her father was a socialist lawyer and participated in various reform movements on behalf of farmers and workers. She quit high school and went to New York City, where she studied at the American Academy of Dramatic Art and lived in an anarchist commune with Emma Goldman, among others. She soon moved to Hollywood, where she worked as an actress, a waitress, and in a factory, and then began to write articles and stories for radical publications such as *The Daily Worker* and *The New Masses*. Her first novel, *The Girl* (1939), examines the lives of various women whom she had known and observed in the 1930s. *Salute to Spring* (1940), a high point in her career before the years of neglect that followed, is a collection of short stories describing the struggle of ordinary women's lives during the Depression. *North Star Country* (1945) is a history of the Midwest in which she grew up; *Crusaders* (1955) is a biography of her parents, Marian Wharton and Arthur Le Sueur. She continued to write radical journalism throughout the 1950s and 1960s. A volume of her poetry, *Rites of Ancient Ripening*, was published in 1975. Her other books include *Conquistadors* (1973), *The Mound Builders* (1974), and a series of children's books. *Ripening: Selected Work, 1927–1980* was published in 1982. Her work as a whole helped to establish a tradition of feminist dissent on which the women's movement of today is partly based.

Letters from an American Farmer   A collection of 12 essays by J. Hector St Jean de Crèvecoeur describing rural life in 18th-century America. They were first published in London, under the name John Hector St John, in 1782, though they were probably written

several years earlier. The first American edition appeared in Philadelphia in 1793.

Addressing his letters to a British correspondent, Crèvecoeur, in the person of "Farmer James," writes glowingly of the conditions of American agrarian life and of the virtue, independence, industry, and prosperity of the American farmer. In the third essay, "What Is An American?" he speculates on the roles that the experience of immigration and of working the American land play in the "Americanization" process that produces this singular breed. He also makes observations on the relationship between the geography of different regions and the typical character and activities of the people therein, discussing on the one hand Quaker simplicity and the whale fishery on Nantucket, and on the other the luxuries of Charleston and the slave system Southerners depend upon. Though extolling the virtues of stable, agrarian life throughout, Farmer James's concluding essay, "Distresses of a Frontier Man," describes his realization that the agrarian idyll is not possible in the midst of frontier raids and Revolutionary violence; reluctantly he resolves to join the Indians on the frontier, leaving his farm and the political conflict that white, European–American society imposes upon him.

Letters of Silence Dogood, The   See **Franklin, Benjamin**

Let Us Now Praise Famous Men   Consisting of photographs by Walker Evans and a text by **James Agee**, this book defies categorization. Evans and Agee began their collaboration in the summer of 1936 when they traveled to Alabama to gather material for an article commissioned by *Fortune*, a New York magazine. The article never appeared, and they made other arrangements for the publication of the work, which they agreed to expand. Those arrangements also fell through, with the result that the book was not published until 1941. (Even then Agee and Evans had to agree to delete certain objectionable words.) Three rural, white tenant families living in extreme poverty constitute the book's subject. The stark photographs and Agee's impressionistic prose pieces provide a record of the lives of these farmers – their economic arrangements, homes, clothing, education, food, and work. According to

Agee, the book was not intended as an exposé of misery but as a celebration of dignity – "an independent inquiry into certain normal predicaments of human divinity."

Levertov, Denise 1923–   Levertov was born in Essex, England, where she wrote her first volume of poetry, *The Double Image* (1946). Two years later, after marrying the American writer Mitchell Goodman, she moved to New York City. Her poems are full of sensory detail and often concern the nature of the creative process itself. She writes in the rhythms of speech, using metaphor and allusion sparingly. *Here and Now* (1957) and *Overland to the Islands* (1958) were written in Mexico. The poems in *With Eyes at the Back of Our Heads* (1959) reflect her decision to leave Mexico and return to New York. In 1961 she became poetry editor of **The Nation** and published another collection, *The Jacob's Ladder*. Since then she has concentrated increasingly on political and feminist themes, in volumes such as *O Taste and See* (1964), *A Tree Telling of Orpheus* (1968), *To Stay Alive* (1971), *The Freeing of the Dust* (1975), and *Wanderer's Daysong* (1981). Prose analyses of her own creative process are collected in *The Poet in the World* (1973).

Levine, Philip 1928–   Born and raised in Detroit, Levine was educated at Wayne State University, and in 1957 received an MFA from the University of Iowa. He has held a fellowship in poetry at Stanford, and since 1958 has taught at California State University in Fresno. His first books of poetry, *On the Edge* (1961), *Silent in America: Vivas for Those Who Failed* (1965), and *Not This Pig* (1968), established him as a bitter and ironic chronicler of the working classes of Detroit and southern California. His subsequent volumes of poetry include *5 Detroits* (1970), *Pili's Wall* (1971), *They Feed They Lion* (1972), *The Names of the Lost* (1974), *Ashes: Poems Old & New* (1979), and *One for the Rose* (1981). *Don't Ask*, a collection of essays and interviews, appeared in 1981, and *Selected Poems* in 1983.

Lewis, Meriwether 1774–1809   The celebrated explorer was born in Albemarle, Virginia. He is best known as co-commander, with **William Clark**, of the expedition that explored the Louisiana Territory between 1803 and 1806. The two of them kept detailed journals of their trek through the newly acquired region. A version of their story appeared in 1814 as *The History of the Expedition under the Command of Captains Lewis and Clark*, edited by Nicholas Biddle and Paul Allen. R. G. Thwaites edited *The Original Journals of the Lewis and Clark Expedition*, which appeared in eight volumes (1904–5).

Though both men were involved in producing the journals, Lewis is generally regarded as the authority. The expedition, in fact, was originally his idea. During the period of negotiations with France for the purchase of the Louisiana Territory, Lewis – who was a friend of and private secretary to President **Thomas Jefferson** – proposed to travel through the territory in search of a land route to the Pacific, and Jefferson approved the plan. Clark, who like Lewis had served as a soldier in frontier posts, was appointed commander. After the expedition, Lewis was made governor of the Louisiana Territory. He died mysteriously somewhere in Tennessee in 1809, while on his way to Washington; it is unclear whether he was murdered or committed suicide.

Lewis, (Harry) Sinclair 1885–1951   Born in Sauk Centre, Minnesota, in 1903 Lewis entered Yale, where he began to write and edited the university's literary magazine. In 1906 he left to join **Upton Sinclair**'s socialist colony in Englewood, New Jersey. He then became a free-lance writer and editor in New York City before returning to Yale and graduating in 1908. Four years later he published his first novel, a boy's book entitled *Hike and the Aeroplane* (1912), under the pseudonym of Tom Graham.

In 1914 he published *Our Mr Wrenn*, which was followed by *The Trail of the Hawk* (1915) and three more novels before the successful **Main Street** (1920), a satirical portrayal of small-town life in the Midwest. He continued his critique of provincial American life in **Babbitt** (1922). In 1926 he was awarded the Pulitzer Prize for *Arrowsmith* (1925), the story of an altruistic doctor who struggles to resist the temptations of a fashionable and profitable practice in order to pursue a scientific career, but Lewis refused to accept the honor. His next novel, *Elmer Gantry* (1927), the story of a sham revivalist minister, was a satire on American religion. **Dodsworth** (1929), about a retired automobile manufacturer traveling in Europe, appeared a year before Lewis was awarded the Nobel Prize, the first American to be so honored.

Lewis's commitment to social and political change is evident also in his novels of the 1930s and 1940s. *Ann Vickers* (1933) is about a discontented midwestern girl who goes east to college and becomes a social worker; she becomes involved in the women's movement and works for prison reform. *Work of Art* (1934) is about the American hotel industry. During the late 1930s and the 1940s Lewis began a career as an actor. His novel, *It Can't Happen Here* (1935), a warning about the possibility of fascism in the US, was dramatized and produced by the Federal Theatre Project in cities throughout the country with Lewis himself playing the lead. The revolt of children against their parents is the subject of *The Prodigal Parents* (1938). *Bethel Merriday* (1940) deals with the career of a young actress. *Gideon Planish* (1943) is about a speech professor who marries a student and then finds himself manipulated into the lucrative advertising profession by his wife. Lewis's next three novels return to the Minnesota setting of *Main Street*. *Cass Timberlane* (1945) is another story of a middle-aged man, a judge, who marries a young girl; *Kingsblood Royal* (1947) deals with race relations; *The God-Seeker* (1949) treats the American Indian question. His last novel, *World So Wide*, was published posthumously in 1951. A year after his death a collection of his letters appeared as *From Main Street to Stockholm* (1952). Essays and ephemera were collected in *The Man From Main Street* (1953).

Liberator, The An Abolitionist weekly journal founded by **William Lloyd Garrison** in Boston in 1831 and edited by him for the next 34 years. From its first issue, *The Liberator*'s editorial policy was unequivocally opposed to slavery, calling for immediate emancipation of the slave population. Its circulation was never higher than 3,000, but its radical stance aroused vocal and violent antagonism in South and North alike. A law was passed forbidding its distribution among free blacks, and a reward was offered in South Carolina for information leading to the arrest of anyone who circulated it. The Georgia Senate passed a resolution offering another reward for the arrest of Garrison himself. The last issue was published on December 29, 1865, shortly after the Thirteenth Amendment, abolishing slavery, was ratified.

Life on the Mississippi A book by **Mark Twain** published in 1883, part history, part geography, part memoir, and part travelogue. It opens with a brief history of the Mississippi River from its discovery by Hernando de Soto in 1541 to the early 19th century, which is more or less factual except for a famous passage in chapter 3 in which Twain offers as "historical" an episode experienced by his fictional character Huck Finn (the passage had originally been intended for inclusion in the novel *Adventures of Huckleberry Finn*). Twain then turns to a more personal form of history, and for the next 19 chapters describes his own childhood and youth, and his life as a river pilot. (This section of the book, which vividly depicts life in the region during the antebellum era, had appeared earlier in *The Atlantic Monthly* in 1875, and as a separate volume, *Old Times on the Mississippi*, in 1876.)

Some seven years later, Twain added the second half of *Life on the Mississippi*, which recounts his experiences during a return trip to the scenes of his youth. He travels from St Louis to New Orleans, observing the changes wrought by, among other things, the railroads. He reminisces about friends from that earlier period of his life, and ruminates on the detrimental effects of Southern romanticism, which he links to the historical romances of Sir Walter Scott that were so popular in the antebellum South. In his opinion it was this self-conscious romanticism that prevented social and economic progress in the South and made the Civil War inevitable.

Life with Father See **Day, Clarence**

Light in August A novel by **William Faulkner**, published in 1932. Set in the imaginary Yoknapatawpha County, Mississippi, it has three main characters: Lena Grove, pregnant and unwed, who travels to Jefferson, Mississippi, in search of Lucas Burch, her baby's father; Joe Christmas, a man who is unsure of his racial origins, and who has murdered his lover Joanna Burden; and the Reverend Gail Hightower, a disgraced minister whose wife committed suicide years earlier, and who lives as a recluse, frequently having a fantasy in which he identifies himself with his grandfather, a Confederate officer who died in Jefferson during the Civil War.

The novel opens with Lena's arrival in Jefferson. She finds, not Lucas Burch (who now calls himself Joe Brown), but Byron Bunch – a hardworking, dependable bachelor who immediately falls in love with her. As they meet, Joanna Burden's body is discovered in a blazing house. Hoping for the reward offered for the capture of her killer, Lucas Burch, who has been involved in bootlegging with Joe Christmas since his arrival in Jefferson, accuses Joe of the crime. Meanwhile Byron tends Lena, who is near to giving birth.

Flashback scenes provide the reader with an account of Joe Christmas's life. His mother, Milly Hines, died when he was born; his father, a traveling circus hand, was killed by his grandfather, Eupheus Hines, who was convinced that he had Negro blood in him. Eupheus then left Joe on the steps of a white orphanage on Christmas night (hence his name). At the age of 5, when his racial background was again called into question, he was sent to the home of an unbendingly strict and puritanical farmer, Simon McEachern. As a teenager Joe finally fled the frequent beatings administered by McEachern, took to the road, and after many years arrived in Jefferson, where he carried on an intensely sexual relationship with Joanna Burden. Her request that he pray with her – something McEachern had often demanded – prompted him to slit her throat and set fire to the house.

After eluding capture for nearly a week, he is finally taken. His grandparents, the Hineses, arrive from nearby Mottstown, his grandmother insisting on seeing the grandson her husband had robbed her of. They go to the cabin which Joe and Burch had shared, and where Byron Bunch has installed Lena. Mrs Hines attends the birth of Lena's baby. Bunch, who serves to bring together the stories of the three main characters, takes the Hineses to see the Reverend Hightower to seek his assistance. They ask Hightower to provide Joe with an alibi, but he refuses. When Joe breaks free from his jailers the next day he runs – as if by instinct – to Hightower's home. The National Guard, led by Percy Grimm, pursue him; Grimm shoots and kills him, then castrates him, ignoring Hightower's frantic explanation (a lie) that Joe was with him at the time of the murder. Hightower withdraws once more into his reverie about his grandfather. Lena, now accompanied by her baby and the attentive Byron Bunch, continues her search for Burch, who has once again fled town.

Lindsay, (Nicholas) Vachel 1879–1931 Lindsay was born in Springfield, Illinois. His parents wanted him to become a minister, but instead of completing his education at Hiram College he left in 1901 and spent several years studying art in Chicago and New York City, lecturing when the opportunity arose. He then tramped across much of the US and began to write verse, which he would often barter for food and lodging. His third collection of poetry, and the first to bring him recognition, was *General William Booth Enters Into Heaven and Other Poems* (1913), the title piece of which had originally been published in **Harriet Monroe**'s *Poetry* magazine. He was welcomed as a new poet whose work was dramatic and full of incisive rhythms, and one whose vivid imagery was drawn from a broad American background. *The Congo and Other Poems* appeared in 1914, and *The Chinese Nightingale and Other Poems* in 1917. He published four further volumes, but none of the quality of the early collections.

As a reader of his own poetry Lindsay became a popular figure; indeed, he tried to extend the popularity of poetry in general by presenting it in what he liked to call "the higher vaudeville." The method enjoyed only limited success but he retained the hope that he might become the great singer of everyman; he wanted above all to "reconcile culture and manliness." This idealism is evident in his *Golden Book of Springfield* (1920), in which he depicts a utopia based on the "Gospel of Beauty," a subject on which he used to lecture before he gained recognition as a poet. As his audience dwindled, and he could no longer support himself by his poetry readings, he became depressed, and committed suicide in 1931. His last published work was a book of political essays, *The Litany of Washington Street* (1929). His *Collected Poems* appeared in 1923 and a revised edition in 1925. A volume of *Letters* was published in 1979.

Lippard, George 1822–54 A popular Pennsylvania writer, best known for his sensational novels about the immorality of large cities. The most famous is *The Quaker City; or, The Monks of Monk Hall* (1844), which went through 27 printings in five years and enjoyed lively sales abroad. Like *New York: Its Upper Ten and Lower Million* (1854), it is lurid in plot but reformist in intention, portraying the corruption of the ruling classes and their sexual, political, and financial exploitation of the poor. The success of his work helped to create an American school of "city novelists." Lippard also wrote romantic historical novels, including *Blanche of Brandywine* (1846) and *Legends of Mexico* (1847).

Lippmann, Walter 1889–1974 Born in New York City, Lippmann graduated from Harvard in 1909. He taught philosophy there under **George Santayana**, and was later one of the founders of *The New Republic*. He served as an assistant to the Secretary of War from 1917 to 1919, and influenced Woodrow Wilson's foreign policy. When he returned to *The New Republic*, he found himself an important spokesman for liberalism. He soon became editorial commentator for the New York *World* (1921–31), and then for the *Herald Tribune* (1931–62). It was during these years that his first books began to appear. *A Preface to Politics* (1913), *Drift and Mastery* (1914), *The Stakes of Diplomacy* (1915), *The Political Scene* (1919), *Public Opinion* (1922), *The Phantom Public* (1925), *A Preface to Morals* (1929), *The Method of Freedom* (1934), and *The Good Society* (1937) represent his attempts to promote a mature liberalism that would depend upon public virtue, individual freedom, and *laissez-faire* economics. His later books include *Some Notes on War and Peace* (1940), *US Foreign Policy* (1943), *US War Arms* (1944), *The Cold War* (1947), *Isolation and Alliances* (1952), *The Public Philosophy* (1955), *The Communist World and Ours* (1959), and *The Coming Tests with Russia* (1961). He was awarded Pulitzer prizes for reporting in 1958 and 1962.

Little Foxes, The A play by **Lillian Hellman**, first performed in New York in 1939. Like her later play, *Another Part of the Forest* (1946), it focuses on the complexity of loyalties and rivalries that bind and divide the newly wealthy Hubbard family. Faced with the opportunity of a lucrative business deal, Ben Hubbard, his brother Oscar, and their sister Regina must each put up a portion of capital, and the action of the play consists of Regina's attempt to force her ailing but morally upright husband to put up a third of the money while Ben, Oscar, and Oscar's son Leo attempt to come up with the money by other means, legal and illegal, in order to outmaneuver Regina. Compassionate alternatives to the rapacious Hubbards are presented by Regina's husband, Horace; their daughter, Alexandra; and Birdie, the aristocratic wife Oscar married for her money and then drove to the brink of dissolution. Regina finally wins the struggle, mercilessly watching her husband die, but loses the affection of her daughter.

Little Lord Fauntleroy A novel for children by **Frances Hodgson Burnett**, published in 1886. The son of the Earl of Dorincourt becomes estranged from his father because he has married an American. The Earl refuses to receive his daughter-in-law who, after her husband's death, takes their son to New York. He is called Cedric Errol, has long curls, is generous, affectionate, and loved by all in his modest neighborhood, particularly by Mr Hobbs the grocer and Dick the bootblack. When his uncles die he becomes heir of Dorincourt and returns to England with his mother. The old Earl still refuses to receive Cedric's mother, and she is obliged to live in a house near the Dorincourt seat. But Cedric wins the Earl's love and soon influences him to behave benevolently to his tenants and other poor people. Then a strange American woman appears, claiming that she is the Earl's real daughter-in-law and that her son is heir to the estate. She is eventually unmasked by Dick and Mr Hobbs, who journey all the way to England to discredit the impostor's claims. The Earl receives Cedric's mother and the three generations settle down happily at Dorincourt, which Cedric – Little Lord Fauntleroy – will inherit.

Little Review, The A literary periodical published from 1914 to 1929, edited by Margaret Anderson and Jane Heap. Begun in Chicago, the enterprise was moved to New York City in 1917 and to Paris in 1924. Numerous writers from both sides of the Atlantic were represented in its pages, among them Richard Aldington, **Sherwood Anderson**, Guillaume Apollinaire, **Djuna Barnes**, Witter Bynner, **Hart Crane, T. S. Eliot, Ernest Hemingway**, Wyndham Lewis, **Vachel Lindsay, Amy Lowell, Marianne Moore, Ezra Pound** (who also served as the periodical's foreign editor), **Gertrude Stein, Wallace Stevens**, Tristan Tzara, **William Carlos Williams**, and William Butler Yeats. The periodical gained notoriety when its editors were tried and found guilty of obscenity for publishing a portion of James Joyce's *Ulysses*.

Little Women A novel by **Louisa May Alcott**, originally published in two parts. The first part, *Little Women; or, Meg, Jo, Beth, and Amy*, appeared in 1868; the second, under the title *Good Wives*, in 1869. In 1871 the two appeared as a single volume, *Little Women and Good Wives*. Subsequent editions have generally included both sections and have been entitled simply *Little Women*.

The March sisters, Meg, Jo, Beth, and Amy, are the daughters of an army chaplain in the Civil War who live with their mother (Marmee) in a small town in New England. The story follows the girls' lives and their efforts to increase the family's small income. Jo, the independent and unconventional sister, wants to be a writer and is on the verge of success at the end of the first part. The second part relates the girls' emergence into womanhood. Meg and Amy marry; Beth falls ill and dies. Jo becomes a successful novelist and later marries a professor, Dr Bhaer. Together Jo and Dr Bhaer establish a school for boys, the subject of Alcott's later novels *Little Men* (1871) and *Jo's Boys* (1886).

Living Newspaper Broadly, the term refers to a form of stage production which addresses current social issues using generic characters in familiar settings, announcer figures, and carefully documented facts. The form is based on various German, Russian, and Chinese theatrical traditions, and, most directly, on the Viennese Spontaneity Theatre, founded in 1921. Various modes of communication, such as the radio, the movie, the newsreel, and the daily newspaper, have influenced the form. The term Living Newspaper is most specifically associated with six plays produced by the **Federal Theatre Project** headed by Hallie Flanagan

under the auspices of President Roosevelt's Work Projects Administration between 1936 and 1939. **Elmer Rice**, the original regional director of the New York branch, resigned when the first planned Living Newspaper production, *Ethiopia*, which dealt with the American response to Italy's aggression against that country, was suppressed before its opening. Of the six productions, the three most successful were by Arthur Arent: *Triple-A Plowed Under* (1936) portrayed the plight of farmers during a drought and exposed corrupt practices in food distribution; *Power* (1937) advocated government control of electrical power plants; and *One-Third of a Nation* (1938) addressed the conditions in low-cost urban housing. This last play was produced in eight cities and adapted each time to the particular housing conditions in the city concerned. All six productions were intended to present to the common people the political issues that affected their lives; they expressed a liberal viewpoint that supported strong governmental intervention and yet refrained from openly contradicting the position of the Roosevelt administration. However, the politically and artistically radical nature of the Living Newspapers, which were just six among the approximately one thousand shows mounted by the Federal Theatre Project, was one of the causes of the disbanding of the entire project in 1939.

Living Theatre Company, The A repertory theatre ensemble founded in 1947 by Julian Beck and his wife Judith Malina. It was originally housed in the Cherry Lane Theatre in New York City and then moved to its own theatre on Sixth Avenue in 1951. The Company is notable for mounting plays by unknown, controversial, or leftist writers. Its best known production was **Jack Gelber**'s *The Connection* (1959). Following two successful tours of Europe (1961–2), the Company closed down in 1963 after its politically and artistically radical productions occasioned critical, popular, and legal controversies.

Locke, Alain (Leroy) 1886–1954 Editor, literary critic, philosopher, art historian, and educator, Locke was born in Philadelphia. He graduated from Harvard in 1904, and from 1907 to 1910 attended Oxford University as the first black Rhodes Scholar. He then studied philosophy at the University of

Berlin, and attended a series of lectures by Henri Bergson in Paris. He began teaching at Howard University in 1912, then returned to Harvard (1916–17) to complete his doctorate. From 1918 to 1953 he was professor of philosophy at Howard.

His influential career as critic and editor began with the March 1925 publication of a special illustrated edition of *The Survey* magazine, entitled "Harlem, Mecca of the New Negro." Locke edited the issue and wrote an introductory essay which announced the arrival of the "New Negro" or **Harlem Renaissance**. Contributors to the volume included such young writers and poets as **Claude McKay**, **Jean Toomer**, **Countee Cullen**, and **Langston Hughes**. Late in the same year Locke published *The New Negro*, the first literary anthology of the Renaissance. The volume consisted of material from *The Survey* with additional essays, stories, poems, and extensive bibliographies.

Locke's other publications include a volume edited with Montgomery Gregory, *Plays of Negro Life* (1927), as well as *The Negro and His Music* (1936), *Negro Art: Past and Present* (1936), and *The Negro in Art: A Pictorial Record of the Negro Artist and of the Negro Theme in Art* (1940). He also wrote numerous reviews and essays on black literature and culture, many of which were published in the magazines *Opportunity* and *Phylon* from the 1930s to the early 1950s.

Locke, David Ross 1833–88 Born in New York City, Locke became a successful journalist in Ohio. His earliest work was published in the form of letters from "Petroleum V[esuvius] Nasby" in the Findlay, Ohio *Jeffersonian* in March 1861. The letters, which ridicule the South and the Confederate cause by loudly proclaiming their righteousness in the silliest way possible, drew a large audience throughout the Civil War. (They were also popular with Abraham Lincoln.) A collection appeared in 1864 as *The Nasby Papers*. Locke became editor (in 1865), and later owner, of the Toledo *Blade*, where he continued to publish letters under his pseudonym. A humorist in the style of **Artemus Ward** and **Josh Billings**, he was one of the most successful exponents of the genre of the facetious letter to the editor. He

also wrote a political novel, *The Demagogue* (1881).

Lolita See **Nabokov, Vladimir**

London, Jack 1876–1916 Jack (really John Griffith) London was born in San Francisco and is believed to have been the illegitimate son of William Henry Chaney, an astrologer. Flora Wellman, his mother, married John London soon after Jack's birth. He grew up on the waterfront of Oakland and his schooling was intermittent. Much of his youth was spent on the wrong side of the law. Among other things he was an oyster pirate, and he also spent a month in prison for vagrancy. At the age of 17 he signed on a sealing ship which took him to the Arctic and Japan. Despite his lack of formal education he also became a voracious reader, especially of fiction.

Depression had struck the US when he returned from his first voyage, and he was unable to find work. In 1894 he joined a march on Washington led by Jacob Sechler Coxey to petition for relief for the poor. The petition was not successful, but London, who had just won first prize in a newspaper competition, added the event to his rapidly expanding store of experience. The aspiring writer became also an aspiring reformer. He discovered the "Communist Manifesto," and from then on was an active socialist. He enrolled in the University of California in 1896, but dropped out after one semester. He continued his education on his own, reading sociology and political science intensively. In 1897 he joined the Klondike gold rush, carrying the works of Darwin and Milton in his backpack. He returned to Oakland in 1898 and began to write about his various experiences.

His early stories were accepted by **Overland Monthly** in the West and **The Atlantic Monthly** in the East, and in 1900 were collected in a volume entitled *The Son of the Wolf*. Like his first novel, *A Daughter of the Snows* (1902), they drew on his experiences in the Klondike. Subsequent collections of his short stories include *Love of Life* (1907), *Lost Face* (1910), *South Sea Tales* (1911), and *The Red One* (1918). His second novel, *The Cruise of the Dazzler* (1902), was based on his experiences as an oyster pirate. His next novel, the hugely successful *The Call of the Wild* (1903), is the story of a sledge dog in the Klondike who eventually becomes the leader of a pack of wolves. *The People of the Abyss*, also published in 1903, draws on his observation of the slums of London made during a visit to England in the previous year. *The Sea-Wolf* (1904) chronicles the voyage of a ship run by a ruthless captain. In 1905, London published *The War of the Classes*, a socialist treatise. That same year, *The Game* appeared, which tells of a man's fatal fascination with prizefighting. *Before Adam* (1906) attempts to recreate a prehistoric community, and *White Fang* (1906) deals with the taming of a wild dog in the Klondike. *The Iron Heel* (1908), set in the near future, tells of socialist struggles against the totalitarian consolidation of capitalist power. *Martin Eden* (1909), more directly autobiographical than most of London's work, is concerned with his attempts to become a successful writer, and then to come to terms with that success. *Burning Daylight* (1910) is set in the Klondike, *Smoke Bellew* (1912) in the Yukon. *The Valley of the Moon* (1912), another socialist novel, is about a working-class couple who escape from the harshness of industrial life in Oakland to an idyllic life on the land. *John Barleycorn* (1913), an autobiographical memoir, deals with the debilitating effects of alcohol. *The Star Rover* (1915) is the story of a San Quentin lifer's spiritual struggles.

With the success of his fiction, London was also in demand on the lecture circuit. He visited Korea, Japan, and Mexico as a foreign correspondent and traveled for two years in the South Seas. But for one so celebrated and so rich (he maintained a ranch of nearly 2,000 acres in California and during his career earned over a million dollars) he was an unhappy man who could not reconcile his own success with the things he had seen and endured. He died at the age of 40, perhaps a suicide. *The Human Drift*, a socialist treatise, was published posthumously in 1917.

Long Day's Journey Into Night A semi-autobiographical play in four acts by **Eugene O'Neill**, written in 1940 and first performed in the US in 1956, three years after the author's death. The action takes place during a single day in August 1912 at the summer home of the Tyrone family (which to some extent is a dramatic recreation of O'Neill's own family). The members of the family are the father, James Tyrone, an actor; the drug-addicted mother, Mary; the elder brother, the alcoholic James, Jr; and the younger brother, Edmund (based on O'Neill himself), who is stricken with tuberculosis. The play explores the tragic nature of family relations, and questions the possibility of forgiveness and redemption. It was awarded the Pulitzer Prize in 1957.

Longfellow, Henry Wadsworth 1807–82 Born in Portland, Maine, Longfellow became one of the most popular writers of his time, his work ranging from sentimental pieces such as "The Village Blacksmith" to translations of Dante. He was educated at private schools and at Bowdoin College; after graduating in 1825 he traveled in Europe for three years. On his return he became a professor of languages at Bowdoin and married his first wife, Mary Potter. During this period he published a series of travel sketches called *Outre-Mer: A Pilgrimage Beyond the Sea* (1833–5). On a second trip to Europe his wife died; when he returned he took up a teaching position at Harvard.

His first volume of poems, *Voices of the Night*, and a prose romance, *Hyperion*, were both published in 1839. A second collection of verse, *Ballads and Other Poems*, appeared in 1842. In the following year he married Frances Appleton and settled in Cambridge, where he remained for the rest of his life. His later work reflects his reading of European epics and his interest in establishing an American mythology; it includes *Evangeline* (1847), *The Song of Hiawatha* (1855), *The Courtship of Miles Standish* (1858), *Tales of a Wayside Inn* (1863), and *Christus* (1872).

Longstreet, Augustus Baldwin 1790–1870 Born in Georgia and educated at Yale, Longstreet was at various times a college president, newspaper editor, clergyman, and jurist. He founded and edited the *States Rights Sentinel* in Augusta in 1834. He is most remembered for his *Georgia Scenes, Characters and Incidents, &c., in the First Half Century of the Republic* (1835), a collection of 18 humorous sketches which record Georgian folkways and language. A pioneering regionalist, he also wrote a series of short stories and a novel, *Master William Mitten* (1864).

Look Homeward Angel. A Story of the Buried Life An autobiographical novel by **Thomas Wolfe**, published in 1929. It tells the story of

Eugene Gant, the youngest of six children born to an eccentric stone-cutter from Altamont, Catawba (modeled on Wolfe's home town of Asheville, North Carolina). Eugene grows up surrounded by a tumultuous, colorful family, and has many encounters with the local townspeople. Along the way he acquires a love of literature, and enters the state university at the age of 16. The novel concludes with his decision to break with his family and set out on a life of his own. A sequel, *Of Time and the River*, appeared in 1935.

Looking Backward: 2000–1887 A Utopian novel by **Edward Bellamy**, published in 1888. It is narrated by Julian West, a Bostonian, who falls asleep in 1887 and wakes in the year 2000. He finds himself in a brilliant new society in which the lot of man has been drastically transformed. Dr Leete, who revives Julian and takes him into his home, explains how American society came – through peaceful means – to adopt a rigorous socialist program under which labor is performed according to a system similar to military service. With all basic human needs accounted for and happiness ensured, human ills once thought to be irrevocable have simply vanished. Great political, technological, and sociological achievements are described in vivid detail. At the end of the novel Julian dreams of a nightmarish return to 19th-century Boston but wakes again in the year 2000 to find that Edith Leete, a descendant of his former fiancée, returns his love. The effect of *Looking Backward* was enormous, comparable perhaps only to that of **Uncle Tom's Cabin**. Numerous Bellamy clubs were founded; political journals and even a Nationalist party all advocated the changes represented in the book.

Lowell, Amy 1874–1925 Born in Brookline, Massachusetts, Lowell was descended from a prominent New England intellectual family. She was a champion of modern poetry, introducing **Imagism** to America in what many of her critics felt was a bastardized form. Her first volume of verse, *A Dome of Many-Colored Glass*, appeared in 1912; *The Complete Poetical Works of Amy Lowell* in 1955. She is best remembered for individual poems such as "Lilacs" and "Patterns." Her idiosyncratic masculine appearance and her vigorous sponsorship of modern poetry have invested her with almost legendary status within the American poetic tradition.

Lowell, James Russell 1819–91 Lowell was born in Cambridge, Massachusetts, and graduated from Harvard in 1838. He studied law but found little fulfillment in it; he had written poetry of some distinction at Harvard but was uncertain about the possibility of pursuing a literary career. His doubts were resolved by the influence of Maria White (herself a poet of some ability, whom he married in 1844), and he soon published two books, *A Year's Life* (1841) and *Poems* (1842). His wife also influenced his political beliefs, and through her he became an active Abolitionist, publishing his views in the short-lived *Pioneer* as well as in the *National Anti-Slavery Standard* and the *Pennsylvania Freeman*. A critic, humorist, and political satirist, in a single year (1848) he published *Poems: Second Series*, **A Fable For Critics**, *The Vision of Sir Launfal*, and the first series of **The Biglow Papers**.

Maria Lowell died in 1853. In 1855 Lowell succeeded **Henry Wadsworth Longfellow** as professor of French and Spanish at Harvard. Like Longfellow, he spent some time in Europe before taking up his appointment. He also followed the example of his predecessor in directing his students to a serious consideration of European literature. He remained a professor until 1886, though he taught very little during the last ten years of his tenure. He did, however, publish seven books of essays. During this period he was also editor of **The Atlantic Monthly** (1857–61) – which he co-founded with Oliver Wendell Holmes in 1857 – and, jointly with Charles Eliot Norton, of **The North American Review** (1864). He also produced the second series of *The Biglow Papers* (1867), which criticized England's part in the American Civil War, and a reflective poem called *The Cathedral* (1869). He was the US minister in Spain (1877–80), and then in England (1880–5), where he was received as a cultured and charming man who did much to interpret American aspirations and ideals to the Old World. He retired to Elmwood, his home in Cambridge, in 1885.

Lowell, Robert 1917–77 Born in Boston,

Lowell spent two years at Harvard but completed his formal education at Kenyon College, where he was a student of **John Crowe Ransom**. He was drafted during World War II, but declared himself a conscientious objector and served a prison term (1943–4). He continued to be politically active throughout the Vietnam War era. In 1970 he moved to England, where he spent a good deal of time until his death in 1977.

The great-grandnephew of **James Russell Lowell**, he was considered one of the leading poets of his generation. His early work, which was formal and highly symbolic, often focused on the history of New England and of his own family, subjects which continued to interest him throughout his life. *Land of Unlikeness* (1944), his first book, dealt especially with his temporary conversion to Catholicism; *Lord Weary's Castle* (1946), which included poems from the earlier book, was awarded the Pulitzer Prize. It was not until *Life Studies* (1959), however, that he began to exhibit the loose form and sharp irony which characterize his mature work. The poems and prose pieces in *Life Studies* are highly autobiographical, and the book is usually identified as one of the major works of the **Confessional** school. He did not confine himself to purely personal subjects, however; *Imitations* (1961), for example, included translations of classical poets; and later volumes, such as *For the Union Dead* (1964) and *Near the Ocean* (1967), linked an understanding of the self to an understanding of politics and history.

His other collections are *The Mills of the Kavanaughs* (1951), *The Voyage, and Other Versions of Poems by Baudelaire* (1968), *Notebook 1967–68* (1969), *Notebooks* (1970), *History* (1973), *For Lizzie and Harriet* (1973), and *The Dolphin* (1973). *Selected Poems* was published in 1976, and a final volume, *Day by Day*, in 1977. His other work includes a number of plays: *Phaedra* (1961), a translation; *The Old Glory* (1965); a version of *Prometheus Bound* (1969); and *The Oresteia of Aeschylus* (1978).

Luck of Roaring Camp and Other Sketches, The A collection of stories and sketches by **Bret Harte** published in 1870. The stories originally appeared between 1868 and 1870 in issues of *Overland Monthly*, a journal which Harte himself helped initiate as a forum for Western writers. Harte's popular reputation was established with the appearance of this volume, which is known for its sharply naturalistic depiction of frontier life in the American West. As well as the famous title piece, the collection includes "The Outcasts of Poker Flat," "Tennessee's Partner," and "Miggles." Most of the stories explore the nature of the individual in frontier society, focusing on human relationships in difficult or even tragic circumstances.

Luska, Sidney See **Harland, Henry**

M

MacArthur, Charles 1895–1956 Playwright, born in Scranton, Pennsylvania, the son of a Unitarian clergyman. He studied for two years in a theological seminary, then joined the Hearst Press in Chicago as a journalist, and eventually became a popular feature writer. His first play, *Lulu Belle* (1926), was written with his uncle, Edward Sheldon. In 1927 he collaborated with **Sidney Howard** on *Salvation*, an exposé of a female revivalist, produced in the following year as *Salvation Nell*. His long collaboration with **Ben Hecht** began with *The Front Page* (1928), a play about popular journalism set in a press room in the Criminal Courts Building in Chicago. Other works written with Hecht include *20th Century* (1932), *Jumbo* (1935), *Ladies and Gentlemen* (1939), and *Swan Song* (1946).

McCarthy, Mary 1912–   Born in Seattle, Washington, and orphaned at the age of 6, McCarthy was sent to Catholic schools by relatives; after completing her education at Vassar in 1933, she moved to New York City and wrote book reviews for *The New Republic*, *The Nation*, and *The Partisan Review*.

At the urging of her second husband, **Edmund Wilson**, whom she married in 1938, she began to write fiction, and her first collection of stories, *The Company She Keeps*, appeared in 1942. Since then she has transformed much of her life into fiction. Her experiences of teaching at Bard and Sarah Lawrence provide much of the material for her novel *The Groves of Academe* (1952); she describes her childhood in *Memories of a Catholic Girlhood* (1957); her best-selling novel *The Group* (1963) follows the lives of eight Vassar women of the class of 1933 for seven years after their graduation. A social critic and moralist, she was active in the American Left during the 1930s. Her political interests are evident in all her writing, including her travel books (*Venice Observed*, 1956; *The Stones of Florence*, 1959). After a visit to Vietnam in the 1960s, she published critical accounts of the war in *Vietnam* (1967) and *Hanoi* (1968). She has also produced works of literary criticism (*The Writing on the Wall*, 1970; *Ideas and the Novel*, 1981) and many more novels, short stories, and essays, including *Birds of America* (1971), *The Mask of State: Watergate Portrait* (1974), *Cannibals and Missionaries* (1979), *The Hounds of Summer and Other Stories* (1981), and *Occasional Prose: Essays* (1985).

McClure's Magazine Samuel Sydney McClure and John Sanborn Phillips started *McClure's* in June, 1893; its last issue appeared in March, 1929, after which it merged with *New Smart Set*. In its first period it ranked as one of the three great illustrated ten-cent monthlies. In its second period, beginning in 1902, it pioneered reformist non-fiction, which was later called muckraking journalism. The January 1903 issue contained three famous exposés: "The History of the Standard Oil Company" by Ida Tarbell, "The Shame of Minneapolis" by Lincoln Steffens, and "The Right to Work" by Ray Stannard Baker. After 1919 the magazine declined, and despite efforts by people such as William Randolph Hearst to infuse new life and money into it, it lost its prestige. In its heyday it was highly regarded on five counts in particular: the liveliness and freshness of its fiction, its attacks upon the railroads, its non-fiction pieces on wild animals and exploration, its emphasis on science, and the number of interesting personalities it both published and published articles about. Contributors of fiction included Rudyard Kipling, **O. Henry, Willa Cather**, and **Jack London**.

McCullers, Carson (Smith) 1917–67 Born and raised in Georgia, McCullers studied at Columbia and the Juilliard School of Music. Her first novel, *The Heart is a Lonely Hunter* (1940), won her immediate recognition. Her work often focuses on the spiritual isolation of the individual, and on the attempt to overcome this through love. She was also one of the first American writers to deal openly with homosexual relationships. Her second novel, *Reflections in a Golden Eye* (1941), was followed by *The Ballad of the Sad Café* in 1951. She herself dramatized her novel *The Member of the Wedding* (1946), which ran successfully on Broadway. Other works include the play *The Square Root of Wonderful* (1958), the novel *Clock Without Hands* (1961), and *The Mortgaged Heart* (1971), a collection of stories.

McGuane, Thomas (Francis) 1939– McGuane was born in Michigan and received his BA from Michigan State University. His fiction, written with a comic energy, concerns the attempts of individuals to find workable sets of values in the modern world. His books include *The Sporting Club* (1969), *The Bushwacked Piano* (1971), *Panama* (1978), *Nobody's Angel* (1979), and *Something to be Desired* (1984). *An Outside Chance* (1980) is a collection of short essays dealing with sports. *Ninety-Two in the Shade*, written in 1973, was filmed in 1975. McGuane has also written the scripts for the films "Rancho Deluxe" (1973), "The Missouri Breaks" (1976), 'and "Tom Horn" (1980).

McKay, Claude 1890–1948 Poet and novelist, born in Jamaica. He emigrated to the US in 1912, and later became an editor of **Max Eastman**'s *The Liberator* (1921–2) and served as liaison between Harlem and Greenwich Village intellectuals. He is often considered the precursor of the post-World War II generation of West Indian writers.

His first two collections of poetry, *Songs of Jamaica* (1912) and *Spring in New Hampshire and Other Poems* (1920), attracted favorable critical attention, but it was not until the appearance of *Harlem Shadows* in 1922 that his popular reputation was established. His first novel, *Home to Harlem* (1928), tells of a black soldier's return to the US after serving in France. *Banjo: A Story Without a Plot* (1929) is about a vagabond's life on the Marseilles waterfront. *Banana Bottom* (1933) examines the dilemma of a young black woman who has returned to Jamaica after an education in England, and explores the racial traditions and attitudes which make her readjustment a painful process. McKay's other publications include a collection of stories, *Gingertown* (1932); an autobiography, *A Long Way From Home* (1937); and a study of the black community, *Harlem* (1940). *Trial by Lynching: Stories About Negro Life in North America* was written in English but first appeared in Russian in 1925, and had to be translated back into English by Robert Winter in 1975.

MacKaye, (James Morrison) Steele 1842–94 Born in Buffalo, New York, MacKaye studied painting with George Inness in America and Jean Gérôme at the Ecole des Beaux Arts in Paris. He made a second trip to Paris after serving in the Civil War, and studied acting with Francis Delsarte. On his return to the US he opened an acting school in New York City to teach Delsarte's methods of acting and elocution. His first play, *Monaldi*, adapted from a Washington Allston novel, opened in 1872; the popular comedy *Won At Last* followed in 1877. He had a major success with *Hazel Kirke* (1880), mounted in the new Madison Square Theatre, which ran for 486 performances. In 1885 he opened the Lyceum Theatre, which housed a second acting school (later to become the American Academy of Dramatic Art). He scored another success with *Paul Kauvar; or Anarchy* (1887), about the French Revolution.

MacKaye's contributions to the theatre were diverse. His acting methods and schools were popular and influential; his stage innovations included overhead and indirect lighting, the orchestra pit, and moveable stages. He also designed a huge auditorium for the Chicago World's Fair of 1892–3. His son **Percy MacKaye** wrote his biography, *Epoch* (1927).

MacKaye, Percy [Wallace] 1875– 1956 The son of **Steele MacKaye**, he was born in New York City and educated at Harvard and Leipzig. He taught at a private school in New York before turning to the writing of poetry and drama. *The Canterbury Pilgrims* (1903) was his first play, a blank verse drama about the wife of Bath's amorous pursuit of Chaucer. His later work includes

Jeanne d'Arc (1906) and *Sappho and Phaon* (1907). His most successful play, *The Scarecrow*, was based on **Nathaniel Hawthorne**'s story "Feathertop." It was published in 1908, produced at the Harvard Dramatist's Club in 1909, and then opened at Garrick's Theatre in New York in 1911. MacKaye also wrote about the theatre. *The Playhouse and the Play* (1909), *The Civic Theatre* (1912), and *Community Drama* (1917) all emphasize the communal functions of theatrical production. He wrote one community masque called *St Louis* (1914) for 7,500 actors, and on the occasion of Shakespeare's Tercentenary wrote another, entitled *Caliban, By the Yellow Sands* (1916). His later work included a biography of his father, *Epoch* (1927); and an ambitious tetralogy of verse plays, *The Mystery of Hamlet, King of Denmark – or, What We Will* (1949), which depicts the major characters in *Hamlet* prior to that play's beginning.

MacLeish, Archibald 1892–1982 Born in Glencoe, Illinois, MacLeish graduated from Yale in 1915 and published his first book of poems, *Tower of Ivory*, in 1917. After serving in World War I he enrolled at Harvard and took a law degree. He practiced briefly, but from 1923 to 1928 joined the group of Americans who had settled in Paris.

His early poetry was highly subjective and owed much to that of **T. S. Eliot** and **Ezra Pound**: *The Happy Marriage* (1924), *The Pot of Earth* (1925), *Streets in the Moon* (1926), and *The Hamlet of A. MacLeish* (1928). *New Found Land* (1930), which contains his well-known "You, Andrew Marvell," was written after his return to the US. *Conquistador* (1932), an epic about the conquest of Mexico, was awarded the Pulitzer Prize in 1933. *Frescoes for Mr Rockerfeller's City* appeared in 1933. He also wrote skillful and fluent verse plays: *Nobodaddy* (1926), and *Panic* (1935), which dealt with the Wall Street crash. *The Fall of the City* (1937), a denunciation of totalitarianism, was written for radio and reached a wide audience in the US and England. *Air Raid* (1938) was also written for radio. His *Collected Poems* (1952) won him a second Pulitzer in 1953. Among his later works are three more verse plays: *The Trojan Horse* (1952, for radio), reflecting the contemporary fear of Communist infiltration; *J.B.* (1958), about a

modern Job, which brought him a third Pulitzer Prize in 1959; and *Herakles* (1967), which explores the conflict between human needs and reason and science. *A Continuing Journey* (1968) is a collection of essays on the American scene since World War II. A volume of letters covering the period 1907–82 was issued posthumously in 1983.

Parallel with his career in letters, MacLeish led an active public and academic life. After editing *Fortune* from 1929 to 1938 he became Librarian of Congress (1939–44), Assistant Secretary of State (1944–5), and Boylston Professor of Rhetoric and Oratory at Harvard (1949–62). He also represented the US in UNESCO.

McNickle, D'Arcy 1904–77 A half-blood American Indian of the Flathead (or Salish) tribe, McNickle was educated at the University of Montana, and then at Oxford and Grenoble. He was the first director of the Newberry Library Center for History of the American Indian and co-founder of the National Congress of American Indians. His first novel, *The Surrounded* (1936), is about a youth facing an identity crisis: half Flathead Indian and half Spanish, he is torn between the two cultures. *Runner in the Sun: A Story of Indian Maize* (1954) is a novel for young people. His last novel, *Wind From an Enemy Sky*, published the year after his death, deals with the conflicts between Indian and non-Indian cultures. He also wrote *Indian Man: A Life of Oliver LaFarge* (1971), as well as several histories: *They Came Here First* (1949), *The Indian Tribes of the United States* (1962), *Native American Tribalism* (1973), and – with Harold E. Fey – *Indians and Other Americans* (1970).

McTeague: A Story of San Francisco A novel by **Frank Norris**, published in 1899. McTeague (Mac) practices dentistry, though he has never attended dental college or obtained a license. He is a bear-like man who appreciates little beyond the physical pleasures of eating, drinking, and smoking. When his friend Marcus Schouler brings Trina Sieppe to have her tooth fixed, Mac experiences another physical desire – the sexual – which he accommodates by courting and marrying Trina.

Shortly before the wedding Trina learns that she has won $5,000 in a lottery. Marcus, who had previously entertained notions of marrying Trina himself, now becomes jealous of Mac's good fortune. The newlyweds live happily enough for a while, though Trina becomes miserly. The tension between Mac and Marcus erupts at a picnic; they wrestle like animals, and Mac breaks Marcus's arm. Marcus takes his revenge by informing that Mac is practicing dentistry without a license. Forced to give up his trade, Mac works for a while making dental instruments. When he loses that job also, he has to get money for tobacco, beer, and food from Trina, who jealously guards her hoard. Theirs is now a sado-masochistic relationship: Mac beats Trina or bites her fingers to get her to give him the money, and she takes a perverse pleasure in this treatment. Eventually, he beats her to death and runs off with her hoard of gold coins.

He flees to the gold mines in the hills where he grew up, but is easily recognizable because he takes his canary and its gold cage with him. Having abandoned his job in a mine, he encounters a prospector and together they discover a rich vein of gold, but he senses that he is being pursued and moves on toward Death Valley. Marcus, who has joined the posse searching for him, tracks him down there. They fight, and Mac kills him, but not before Marcus has handcuffed himself to Mac. The novel ends with Mac (who still has his canary, but no water) handcuffed to the corpse in the middle of Death Valley.

Madame Delphine A short novel by **George Washington Cable**, published in 1881, which tells the story of Delphine Carraze, a quadroon, who lives in 19th-century New Orleans with her daughter Olive. Olive's father, who was white, had left his wife and daughter his property when he died, which was against Louisiana law. Olive falls in love with the banker Ursin Lemaitre, a white man who associates with the pirate Jean Lafitte. A marriage is arranged through Père Jerome, but Lemaitre's affairs come under investigation and he goes into hiding. His friends seize the opportunity to break off what they regard as his disastrous commitment to the daughter of the quadroon. Madame Delphine then declares that Olive is not her daughter, but rather a white woman's child she was given to foster. The marriage takes place. The story ends as Madame Delphine confesses to Père Jerome that she lied for her daughter's sake; she dies as the priest grants her absolution.

Maggie: A Girl of the Streets A novel by **Stephen Crane**, privately printed in 1893 under the pseudonym Johnston Smith and entitled simply *A Girl of the Streets*. Set in the Bowery area of New York City, it describes the sordid and almost hopeless existence of Maggie Johnson. As children she and her brothers are alternately neglected and abused by their drunkard parents, and her baby brother Tommie dies as a result of this mistreatment. Her other brother, Jimmie, grows up to be a truck driver, but like his parents he is coarse, cynical and drinks too much. Her father dies and her mother becomes known to the police for her frequent bouts of drunkenness. Maggie, who dreams of a better life, works in a collar-and-cuff factory and falls in love with a bartender friend of her brother's called Pete. After he seduces and abandons her, her mother and brother disown her. She tries to survive by becoming a prostitute, but eventually drowns herself.

Magnalia Christi Americana **Cotton Mather**'s ecclesiastical history of New England, *The Great Works of Christ in America*, was published in London in 1702. Mather began planning his history in 1693 and worked on it throughout the 1690s, during which time some chapters were published separately. It is divided into seven parts: a history of New England's settlement; biographies of governors; biographies of ministers; a history of Harvard College, including biographies of eminent graduates; a description of New England church practices; a collection of instances of special providences in New England; and an account of New England's "Wars of the Lord," or conflicts with heretics, Indians, and other "subversives." Mather's General Introduction, with its Virgilian echoes, announces his epic subject: the work is intended to be a comprehensive and (especially for its European audience) celebratory account, a vision of a providentially guided, Christian New England. Mather consulted and cited numerous original documents for he had access to the papers of many of the actors in his history; as such, the *Magnalia* is a doubly valuable historical document.

Magnificent Ambersons, The See **Tarkington, Booth**

Mailer, Norman 1923– Born in Long Branch, New Jersey, Mailer grew up in Brooklyn and graduated from Harvard in 1943. He served in the Pacific during World War II and drew upon this experience for *The Naked and the Dead* (1948), an uncompromisingly harsh war novel which is also a bitter commentary on American society. The book made Mailer famous on both sides of the Atlantic. His critical view of society also informed *Barbary Shore* (1951) and *The Deer Park* (1955, dramatized in 1967). *Advertisements for Myself* (1959) is a collection of stories, essays, and extracts from work formerly "in progress," all linked by autobiographical sketches. He excels at what has been called "the new journalism," a form which he helped to create, which takes actual events and submits them to imaginative transformation. In this mode he registered the transformation of American sensibility in *An American Dream* (1965), *Why Are We in Vietnam?* (1967), and *Armies of the Night* (1968). The last of these, subtitled "History as a Novel, The Novel as History," has as its subject the 1967 protest march on the Pentagon; it won both a National Book Award and a Pulitzer Prize in 1969. Mailer's subsequent work includes *Miami and the Siege of Chicago* (1969); *The Prisoner of Sex* (1971); *Marilyn: A Biography* (1973), a study of Marilyn Monroe; *The Executioner's Song* (1979, Pulitzer Prize), a recreation of the events surrounding the execution of convicted killer Gary Gilmore; *Ancient Evenings* (1983); and *Tough Guys Don't Dance* (1984).

Main Street A novel by **Sinclair Lewis**, published in 1920, and his first great success. Carol Milford, after working as a librarian in St Paul for three years, marries Dr Will Kennicott and moves to the small town of Gopher Prairie, Minnesota. She attempts to start an experimental theatre and a discussion group on the appreciation of poetry, but meets only resistance and is finally ostracized by the residents. Her growing sense of discontent is exacerbated by her unsophisticated husband. The story ends with her abandonment of her progressive aspirations and her submission to the complacent values of the small midwestern town.

Main-Travelled Roads A collection of short stories by **Hamlin Garland**, it comprised just six stories when it first appeared in 1891. Three more were added to the 1899 edition, and a further two to the final edition of 1922. All of them depict life in the rural Midwest as something drab and monotonous which crushes the spirit out of many of those who live it. "Under the Lion's Paw," one of the original six stories, is a naturalistic tale about the economic survival of the fittest, or (as the narrator makes clear) of the most ruthless. In "Up the Coulee" an actor returns to the midwestern farm where he grew up, and sees with fresh eyes the brutality of the life his family leads. Contrasted with the harshness and squalid poverty are the "silent heroism" of some of the characters and the panoramic beauty of the prairies.

Malamud, Bernard 1914–86 Born and educated in New York City, the son of immigrant Russian parents, Malamud was one of the foremost contemporary Jewish-American writers. His first novel, *The Natural* (1952), deals with baseball as a realm of American heroism and myth. *The Assistant* (1957) is about a poor New York Jewish shopkeeper who takes on a delinquent Italian-American youth as a helper; the young man comes to look on his employer as a father, but the powerful emotional bonds between them are complicated by cultural barriers. Malamud's interest in the Jewish experience as a metaphor for the human condition has become one of the permanent features of his work. His next novels, *A New Life* (1961), *The Fixer* (1966), and *Pictures of Fidelman* (1969), all explore aspects of the personal struggle involved in the Jewish experience. *The Fixer*, the story of a Russian Jew falsely accused of murder, won the National Book Award and the Pulitzer Prize. Later novels are *The Tenants* (1971), *Dubin's Lives* (1979), and *God's Grace* (1982). Malamud's short stories are collected in *The Magic Barrel* (1958), *Idiots First* (1963), and *Rembrandt's Hat* (1973). *The Stories of Bernard Malamud* is a selection of the author's own favorites.

Maltese Falcon, The See **Hammett, Dashiell**

Maltz, Albert 1908–85 Perhaps best known as one of "The Hollywood Ten" and the author of two short stories of social protest – "Man on a Road" and "The Happiest Man in the World" – Maltz was born in Brooklyn, New York. After graduating from Columbia in 1930 he attended Yale's School of Drama, where one of his fellow students was George Sklar. They collaborated on two plays, *Merry Go Round*, which was produced in 1932, and *Peace on Earth*, which was the first production of the newly formed Theatre Union in 1933. Maltz followed this with another play, *Black Pit* (1935). In addition to drama, he has written a number of short stories and novels, including *The Way Things Are* (stories, 1938), *The Cross and the Arrow* (1944), *The Journey of Simon McKeever* (1949), *A Long Day in a Short Life* (1956), *A Tale of One January* (1966), and *Afternoon in the Jungle* (stories, 1971). He has also written numerous screenplays, of which perhaps the best known are *This Gun for Hire* (1942), *Destination Tokyo* (1943), *The House I Live In* (1945), and, with Marvin Wald, *The Naked City* (1948).

Mamet, David 1947– Dramatist, born in Flossmoor, Illinois, and educated at Goddard College, where he received a BA in English in 1969. His first play, *Lakeboat*, was performed in 1970 and was followed by several others treating the social and sexual mores of post-Vietnam America, including *Duck Variations* (1972), *Squirrels* (1974) and *Sexual Perversity in Chicago* (1974). He is best known for *American Buffalo* (1975), which focuses on the aftermath of the Vietnam War from a veteran's perspective. His other plays include *The Woods* (1977), *All Men Are Whores* (1977), *Dark Pony* (1977), *Shoeshine* (1979), and *Glengarry Glen Ross* (1983, Pulitzer Prize 1984).

Manhattan Transfer A novel by **John Dos Passos**, published in 1925, generally considered to be his first artistically mature work – the novel in which he first employed the themes and techniques that came to characterize his fiction. It tells the stories of numerous characters who have in common only their status as New Yorkers, and who come together randomly, impersonally. Each chapter begins with passages of almost poetic prose comprising observations of city life, slogans, snatches of dialogue, phrases from advertisements, and newspaper headlines. These passages make even clearer that *Manhattan Transfer* is a "collective" novel about the city of New York – about the shallowness, immorality, and mechanization of urban life – not simply the story of a few characters' lives.

The two most prominent figures are Ellen Thatcher and Jimmy Herf. The novel opens with Ellen's birth; it ends with a scene in which Jimmy, having left his job with the *Times* (a job that never fulfilled him) and having left Ellen (whom he married and with whom he has had a child), hitches a ride out of New York and thus makes his escape. Ellen, who begins as a stage-struck young woman, is made cold and brittle by life in New York: at 18 she marries John Oglethorpe, a bisexual whom she eventually divorces. She then falls in love with Stanwood Emery, an alcoholic playboy who marries someone else while drunk (he eventually dies in a fire); pregnant with Emery's child, she has an abortion. She then achieves success on the stage and marries Jimmy Herf. At the end of the novel she agrees to marry the self-serving lawyer George Baldwin, even though she does not love him.

Man with the Golden Arm, The See **Algren, Nelson**

Marble Faun, The; or, The Romance of Monte Beni A novel by **Nathaniel Hawthorne**, published in 1860 (in England under the title of *Transformation*). Kenyon and Hilda are two Americans studying art in Rome. With their friend Miriam, an artist, they meet an Italian nobleman named Donatello and notice that he resembles the Marble Faun sculpted by Praxiteles. Handsome, innocent, and warmhearted, Donatello falls in love with Miriam, but realizes that she is troubled by some secret from the past. There are several rumors circulating about Miriam, though none is proven: she may be the heiress of a Jewish banker fleeing from an unwanted marriage; she may be a German princess; she may be the mulatta daughter of a South American planter; or she may be the mistress of an English nobleman come to Italy to pursue her interest in art. Whichever, she is tormented by a mysterious Capuchin monk who has some connection with her past. One night the four friends take a walk among the hills of Rome; Donatello is enraged to find the Capuchin following them, and, perhaps encouraged by a gesture from Miriam, pushes him off a precipice. Unknown to Miriam and Donatello, Hilda witnesses the scene.

Donatello, horrified by what he has done, flees to his ancestral estate of Monte Beni. Miriam, sharing his guilt, follows him; they agree that they must both bear the consequences. He returns to Rome, gives himself up, and goes to prison; she embarks on a penitential pilgrimage. Hilda also remains troubled, feeling tainted by what she has witnessed; setting aside her Puritan training, she finds relief in a Catholic confessional and marries Kenyon. The secret of Miriam's past is never revealed. In the "Postscript" to the novel, the narrator claims that to seek to know whether Donatello really is a faun, and who Miriam really is, would destroy the poetry and beauty of the story.

Mardi: and a Voyage Thither A novel by **Herman Melville**, published in 1849. A complex political and religious allegory, the book was not well received, and provoked new attacks by critics who had objected to the earlier *Typee* (1846) and *Omoo* (1847).

The narrator, Taji, and Jarl, an older seaman, desert their ship in a whaleboat. They encounter the brigantine *Parki*, which has been abandoned by all except a Polynesian couple, Samoa and Annatoo. The four live a contented life on board until the ship sinks during a storm and Annatoo is drowned. The three survivors take to the whaleboat and soon sight land on the horizon – the islands of Mardi. At this point the adventure tale gives way to something of an experimental allegory. The islands of Mardi repesent a mythical or transcendental realm where Taji lives happily for a while with Yillah, a young woman he and his companions rescue from a priest who had intended to sacrifice her. In saving her Taji killed the priest, whose sons take their revenge by kidnapping her again. Taji sets out to find his lost love, accompanied by a king, a historian, a philosopher, and a poet. Their search takes them to many lands, whose societies are closely observed and discussed. The voyage is now generally seen as an allegorical exploration of the world of 1848, in which Dominora stands for Great Britain, Porpheero for Europe, and Vivenza for the US. The travelers eventually reach the land of Serenia, which is ruled by Alma (Christ). The philosopher declares that Alma's doctrine of love is the ultimate wisdom, but Taji observes that man ignores the doctrine. Although his companions try to convince him to give it up, Taji continues his voyage – alone, still in search of what he has lost, still pursued by the priest's sons.

Markham, Edwin 1852–1940 Born in Oregon City, Oregon, Markham moved with his family to California in 1857. Although he had little formal education he became a schoolteacher and, inspired by the poets he read, began to write verse himself. His first poem, "The Gulf of Night," appeared in 1880. His most famous piece, the title poem of his 1899 volume, *The Man With The Hoe and Other Poems*, was inspired by a painting by Millet. Both this collection and *Lincoln and Other Poems* (1901) are largely concerned with the degrading conditions of the American working classes. His other collections, which were less popular, include *California the Wonderful* (1915), *Gates of Paradise* (1920), *Ballad of the Gallows Bird* (1926), *New Poems: Eighty Poems at Eighty* (1932), and *Collected Poems* (1940).

Martian Chronicles, The See **Bradbury, Ray**

Martin Eden A novel by **Jack London**, published in 1909. Martin Eden, a laborer who was once a sailor, has a questioning mind and has undertaken a program of self-education. He aspires to a higher sort of life, such as that personified by Ruth Morse, a college graduate and the daughter of a wealthy family. He works hard to succeed as a writer, and his work reflects the influence of Herbert Spencer's ethical theories. Although his friend Russ Brissenden, a socialist poet, believes in his work, he has no success. When a newspaper calls him a socialist Ruth deserts him. Then one of his books brings him both fame and money. Ruth seeks him out, but he realizes her true nature and turns away from her. He becomes depressed, and Russ's suicide makes matters worse. He grows to despise the society that has finally honored him, and he commits suicide on a sea voyage.

Masters, Edgar Lee 1868–1950 Born in Kansas, Masters practiced law in Chicago from 1891 to 1920. His first publications were *A Book of Verses* (1898) and a blank-verse drama entitled *Maximilian* (1902). He became famous in 1915 with the publication of *Spoon River Anthology*, a book of epitaphs in free verse about the lives of those buried in a cemetery in rural Illinois. He was never to repeat its success, perhaps because he never again found a subject so perfectly suited to his free-verse style and his vein of irony. He did command attention, however, and published several more collections; three dramatic poems, *Lee* (1926), *Jack Kelso* (1928), and *Godbey* (1931); three novels based on his own youth, *Mitch Miller* (1920), *Skeeters Kirby* (1923), and *Mirage* (1924); and a biographical study of Abraham Lincoln, *Lincoln the Man* (1931), which is hostile and belittling. In 1924 he returned to the scene of his initial success with *The New Spoon River*, in which he applied the same technique as in the original volume but this time to the urban life that was beginning to prevail in America. *Across Spoon River*, an autobiography, appeared in 1924.

Mather, Cotton 1663–1728   A third-generation New England Puritan minister, the eldest son of **Increase Mather**, and grandson of **John Cotton** and **Richard Mather**. A prodigy, he entered Harvard at the age of 12 and prepared for the ministry. He was ordained in 1685 and soon after became co-minister with his father of the Second Church of Boston, serving alone from 1688 to 1692 during Increase's mission to England to obtain a new charter for Massachusetts. Cotton's role, on the American side, in the "Glorious Revolution" of 1688, was to contribute in some capacity to the writing of the *Declaration of the Gentlemen, Merchants, and Inhabitants of Boston* (1689), a denunciation of Royal Governor Andros which helped spur the Boston crowd to their eventual seizure of Andros and a fort. When Increase returned with the new governor, Sir William Phips, whom the Mathers supported, the Salem witch trials had begun. Three years earlier Cotton had taken some possessed Boston girls into his home to observe and treat them, and then had written about the cases in *Memorable Providences, Relating to Witchcrafts and Possessions* (1689). He also published an account of the trials and other instances of what he believed to be the operation of evil spirits in *The Wonders of the Invisible World* (1693), which **Robert Calef** ridiculed in *More Wonders of the Invisible World*.

During the 1690s Mather worked on his history of New England, *Magnalia Christi Americana* (published in London in 1702), and continued his ministerial duties. Distinguished for his piety and learning, known as a forceful preacher and an effective pastor, he preached and published many sermons expounding Puritan doctrine and was regarded by many as the pre-eminent spokesman for Puritan culture. *Bonifacius*, published anonymously in 1710, was an attempt to give Puritan piety a social component, explaining how a true Christian acts in an increasingly secular world of complex business and family relations. Like his father, Mather was interested in science, and he was elected to the Royal Society in 1714. *The Christian Philosopher* (1721) includes scientific observations of the natural world with suggestions of their spiritual significance. *The Angel of Bethesda* (1722) was a medical work.

With his prominent family and his own political activism and intense religious involvement, in many ways Cotton Mather epitomized his culture; his extensive diary is a massive record of the American Puritan experience. He continued his ministry to the Second Church and his international correspondence, becoming influenced by German pietism in his later years. Although his political position and influence declined in the latter part of his life, he retained his pre-eminence among Boston ministers, who eulogized him generously at his death. Among his other works were *Parentator* (1724), a biography of his father; "Paterna," an unpublished autobiography written for his children; *Psalterium Americanum* (1718); and *Manuductio ad Ministerium* (1726), a handbook for ministers. His lifelong project, *Biblia Americana*, a systematic commentary on the Bible, remained unpublished at his death.

Mather, Increase 1639–1723   The son of **Richard Mather**, born in Dorchester, Massachusetts, and educated at Harvard and later at Trinity College, Dublin. From 1657 to 1661 he was in England, preaching in various Congregational churches, but with the Restoration he was forced to return to Massachusetts. There he married the daughter of **John Cotton**, the prominent Puritan minister, and himself became the minister of the Second Church of Boston, which he served for the rest of his life, latterly with his son, **Cotton Mather**. He also became a Fellow of Harvard and eventually its president.

A leading figure in the affairs of Massachusetts, Mather frequently wrote on matters of public import. His election sermon, *The Day of Trouble is Near* (1674), was sometimes interpreted as a prophecy of the Indian wars that followed. *A Relation of the Troubles which have happened in New England, by reason of the Indians there* (1677), is a narrative of Indian relations starting with the first Massachusetts settlements, and *A Brief History of the Warr with the Indians* (1676) is about King Philip's War (1674–6). Both histories interpret the Indian wars as contests between the saints and the forces of the devil; the Indian attacks are seen as judgments on the colonists for apostasy, colonial victories as signs of God's providence.

Mather also wrote frequently on scientific subjects, though his curiosity about natural phenomena was motivated less by an empirical scientific spirit than by a desire to see the glory of God's works in the world. His *Kometographia* (1683) and other works on comets, as well as his *Essay for the Recording of Illustrious Providences* (1685), include detailed observations which point to the mysterious ways of God rather than to rational understanding. No stranger to physical explanations (albeit they were of secondary importance), he was an early champion of inoculation against smallpox, writing in defense of the practice during the epidemic of 1721.

In 1688, he headed a mission to England that obtained a new charter for the colony, and a new governor in the person of Sir William Phips. Mather and Phips returned to Massachusetts, just as the Salem witch trials were beginning. Although Mather believed in the possibility of witches and witchcraft, he later censured the court in his *Cases of Conscience Concerning Evil Spirits* (1693) for basing convictions on "spectral evidence," which he said could be deceptive. His other writings, which exemplify the Puritan mentality of his time, include sermons on conversion and church membership policy (he was the chief opponent of **Solomon Stoddard**, who had instituted an open communion policy), speculations on the millenium, and his "Autobiography."

Mather, Richard 1596–1669 A Puritan minister, and one of the founders of the Massachusetts Bay colony. Born in Lancashire, England, he lived with a Puritan family while he was a schoolmaster at Toxteth Park, and experienced a Puritan conversion in 1614. He spent a year at Oxford before being ordained in 1619. Due to his nonconformity, he was suspended by the Anglican Archbishop Laud in 1633, and emigrated to New England in 1635. There he was called by the Dorchester church, which he served from 1636 to the end of his life. He became one of the leading ministers in the Bay Colony, contributing to the translations of the Psalms in the **Bay Psalm Book** (1640).

In the 1630s and 1640s he produced a series of treatises defending the New England congregational system against Presbyterian opponents, the most significant of which is *Church Government and Church Covenant Discussed* (1643). He took part in the two major synods of his time in 1648 and in 1662. He was one of the main architects of the 1648 Cambridge Synod's *Platform of Church Discipline* (1649), which set out the main principles of New England church polity. He had long been an advocate of extending the sacrament of baptism to children of church members who had not yet been admitted to full communion. The Synod of 1662 allowed the children of these so-called "half-way" members to be baptized, but the "Half-Way Covenant" continued to provoke opposition. Mather's own church at Dorchester rejected it, and his son, **Increase Mather**, remained a vocal opponent of his father's policy for years. Richard Mather wrote one of the most important defenses of the synod, *A Defense of the Answer*, in 1664. Many of his sermons remain in manuscript. His *Journal*, which includes an account of the Atlantic crossing, was published for the first time in the 19th century.

Mathews, John Joseph c.1894–1979 An Osage Indian born in Pawhuska, Oklahoma, and known for his historical and biographical accounts of the American Indian experience. After obtaining a BA from the University of Oklahoma in 1920 and another from Oxford in 1923, he began writing in 1928. His first work, *Wah 'Kon-Tah: The Osage and the White Man's Road*, a historical study of the Osage

Indians from 1878 to 1931, appeared in 1932. His other books include *Sundown* (1934), a novel; and *The Osages: Children of the Middle Waters* (1961).

Melville, Herman 1819–91 One of American literature's greatest figures, Melville was born in New York City into an established merchant family. His father became bankrupt and then insane, and died when Melville was 12. At the age of 15 he left school and began working to support his family, first as a bank clerk, then as a teacher, and also as a farm laborer. At the age of 19 he sailed on a merchant ship to Liverpool. This was followed by several other sea voyages, one of them a whaling trip during which he jumped ship with a friend and lived briefly among the Typee cannibals in the Marquesas.

Although he had no early designs as a writer, he was encouraged to set down some of his more exotic experiences, and the result was *Typee* (1846), loosely based on his encounter with the cannibals. *Omoo* (1847), *Mardi* (1849), *Redburn* (1849), and *White-Jacket* (1850) also treat themes involving life on the sea. These early works won Melville a good deal of popular acclaim; they also stirred controversy because of their sympathy with pagan societies, sometimes to the point of contempt for Western attitudes and practices. During this time Melville began to read widely, acquainting himself with a broad range of writers and philosophers. In 1850 he and his wife moved to Pittsfield, Massachusetts, where they became neighbors and friends of Sophia and **Nathaniel Hawthorne**. Inspired by Hawthorne and by his reading, Melville entered into his most ambitious phase. In 1851 he published *Moby-Dick*, the whaling adventure dedicated to Hawthorne that is considered by many to be the greatest work of American fiction. To his intense disappointment the novel was not well received, and from relative popularity he began to fade into obscurity. *Pierre* (1852), a psychological and moral study based on his childhood, and thus removed from the ocean setting of most of his other fiction, was hardly read at all in the 19th century. At odds with his public, and deprived of the company of Hawthorne, who had moved to Concord, Melville turned increasingly to shorter fiction. After the short novel *Israel Potter* (1855) he published *The Piazza Tales* (1856), a collection of stories which includes "Bartleby the Scrivener," "Benito Cereno," and "The Encantadas." His last novel, *The Confidence Man* (1857), a harsh satire of American life set on a Mississippi River steamboat, represented his most radical innovation in narrative form since *Mardi*.

At the age of 40 he turned almost exclusively to poetry. *Battle-Pieces and Aspects of the War* was issued in 1866, *John Marr and Other Sailors* in 1888, and *Timoleon* in 1891. *Clarel* (1876) is a long poem about religious crisis, based on Melville's trip to the Holy Land in 1857. *Clarel* was the last of his published works; the later volumes were privately printed and distributed among a very small circle of acquaintances. Additional material was published from manuscript long after his death, when his reputation was beginning to revive. Most notably, the unfinished tale *Billy Budd* appeared in 1924. *Journal Up the Straits* (1935), *Journal of a Visit to London and the Continent* (1948), and *Journal of a Visit to Europe and the Levant* (1955), all record his travels in the 1850s. *Weeds and Wildings* (1924) is a collection of previously unpublished poetry; his letters were published in 1960.

Member of the Wedding, The See **McCullers, Carson**

Mencken H[enry] L[ouis] 1880–1956 Mencken was born in Baltimore, Maryland, and lived there for most of his life. His formal education ended with high school. In 1899 he began his journalistic career with a job on a local newspaper. He became editor of the *Evening Herald* (1905–6), and then moved on to become a staff member of the *Evening Sun*. His career as a literary critic started in 1908 on *Smart Set*, a New York periodical which he edited with **George Jean Nathan** from 1914 to 1923. He and Nathan founded the detective magazine *The Black Mask* in 1920, and in 1924 *The American Mercury*, which Mencken edited until 1933.

He became famous with the publication of *The American Language* (1919), a study of English as developed and used in the US. It went through three revised editions, and supplementary volumes were also added, the last in 1948. His essays, with their characteristically caustic and often vulgar tone, were collected in six volumes called *Prejudices*, the first published in 1919 and the last in 1927. Though known primarily as entertainments for middle-class America, they were often sharply critical of what Mencken himself termed the "booboisie." He also published plays; several critical works, including books on Shaw and Nietzsche; and three volumes of autobiography, *Happy Days* (1940), *Newspaper Days* (1941), and *Heathen Days* (1943). A collection of his letters was issued in 1961.

Merrill, James 1926–   Born in New York City, Merrill graduated from Amherst in 1947. He divides his time between homes in Greece and Connecticut. His poetry has received four *Poetry* Magazine awards, two National Book Awards, a Pulitzer Prize, and a Bollingen Prize.

His early poetry, noted for its accomplished tone and careful construction, was published in *Jim's Book* (1942); *The Black Swan* (1946); *First Poems* (1951); *Short Stories* (1954), which despite its title consists of poetry; and *The Country of a Thousand Years of Peace* (1959, revised in 1970). *Selected Poems* was published in 1961, and the collection *Water Street* in the following year. In *Nights and Days* (1966) and *The Fire Screen* (1969) he became increasingly concerned with the visionary and esoteric. *The Divine Comedies* (1976) begins his attempt to mythologize the self in relation to a cosmic order, justifying his homosexuality by arguing that by avoiding procreation he is more like the angels. In *Mirabell* (1978) and *The Changing Light at Sandover* (1982) he again creates "sacred" books, turning to the ouija board as a source of divine intervention. *From the First Nine*, a volume of selected poems, appeared in 1983. He has also written two novels, *The Seraglio* (1957) and *The (Diblos) Notebook* (1965).

Merwin, W[illiam] S[tanley] 1927–
Poet and translator, born in New York City and educated at Princeton. He has spent much of his life abroad, both in England, where he has written radio scripts for the BBC, and in France. His poetry, which shows the influence of the **New York School** in its interest in unconscious forces and use of surrealist modes, reflects his concern with the effects of the contemporary loss of belief in traditional myths, frequently exploring the sense of emptiness which follows that loss.

His first volume, *A Mask for Janus* (1952), won the Yale Series of Younger Poets Award. Among his other works are *Green With Beasts* (1956), *The Drunk in the Furnace* (1960), *The Moving Target* (1963), *The Lice* (1967), *The Carrier of Ladders* (1970, Pulitzer Prize), *The Compass Flower* (1977), and *Feathers From the Hill* (1978). He has also published several translations, including *The Poem of the Cid* (1959), *Spanish Ballads* (1960), *The Satires of Persius* (1961), and *Pablo Neruda, Twenty Love Poems and a Song of Despair* (1969).

Millay, Edna St Vincent 1892–1950   Born in Rockland, Maine, she published her first poem, "Renascence," at the age of 20. It later became the title poem of her first collection, *Renascence and Other Poems* (1917), which comprises pieces she had written as an undergraduate at Vassar. After graduating, she moved to Greenwich Village in New York City and published a second volume, *A Few Figs from Thistles* (1920). The poems in this book established her as a representative voice of her generation in their freshness, gaiety, and implied rebellion against established moral standards. Her popularity continued to grow with the publication of her third volume, *The Harp-Weaver and Other Poems* (1923), which exhibited her mature style and mastery of traditional verse forms; it received the Pulitzer Prize in 1923.

After her marriage in 1923, Millay settled in the Berkshires. She wrote less as time went on, but her later works showed a new political and social consciousness. They include *Distressing Dialogues* (1924), a book of satirical sketches written under the pseudonym of Nancy Boyd; *Three Plays* (1926); *The King's Henchman* (1927), a libretto; *The Buck in the Snow and Other Poems* (1928); and *Fatal Interview* (1931), a sonnet sequence. Subsequent volumes of verse are *Wine from these Grapes* (1934); *Conversation at Midnight* (1937); *Huntsman, What Quarry?* (1939); and *Make Bright the Arrow* (1940). Her *Collected Poems* was published in 1956.

Miller, Arthur 1915–   Born in New York City, the son of a Jewish manufacturer whose business failed during the Depression, Miller studied journalism at the University of Michigan. He wrote plays as a student, and upon graduation he worked for the **Federal Theatre Project** and for American radio. His first Broadway play, *The Man Who Had All the Luck* (1944), closed after only four performances.

His next four plays, however, were enthusiastically received by the critics. His concern with the disruptive and inevitable conflict between successive generations was first shown in *All My Sons* (1947, New York Drama Critics Circle Award), the story of a veteran who discovers that his father sold faulty airplane parts to the government. His celebrated modern tragedy *Death of a Salesman* (1949), which received both the Pulitzer Prize and the New York Drama Critics Circle Award, examined similar issues in its portrait of the unsuccessful salesman Willy Loman. Like Ibsen, whose *An Enemy of the People* he translated in 1950, Miller often explores the origins and consequences of shameful actions. *The Crucible* (1953) clearly relates the issues of the 1692 Salem witch trials to those of the era of McCarthyism in the US. (Miller himself was one of the many who refused to give names when summoned before the House Un-American Activities Committee in 1956 because of his left-wing politics.) *A View from the Bridge* (1955, revised 1956), which also won a New York Drama Critics Circle Award, is an examination of the tragic consequences of Sicilian-American longshoreman Eddie Carbone's forbidden passion for his niece Catherine. Originally produced together with *A View from the Bridge* was the one-act play *A Memory of Two Mondays* (1955), about a young man's resolve to extricate himself from the drudgery of life in a Manhattan automobile parts warehouse and go to college.

After an eight-year absence from the New York stage, Miller returned with *After the Fall* (1964), a semi-autobiographical play with obvious references to his marriage to Marilyn Monroe; and *Incident at Vichy* (1964), which deals directly with the Nazi persecution of the Jews – an undercurrent in much of his other work. *The Price* (1968), his last international success, again examines the issues of family conflict and filial disloyalty. Subsequent plays include *The Creation of the World and Other Business* (1972), *Up from Paradise* (1974), *The Archbishop's Ceiling* (1977), and *The American Clock* (1980). *Theatre Essays* (1973), edited by Robert A. Martin, is a collection of Miller's writings about his own work, and includes the well-known essay "Tragedy and the Common Man" (1949). He has also written a novel about anti-semitism, *Focus* (1945), and the screenplay for *The Misfits* (1961). *I Don't Need You Anymore* (1967) is a collection of short stories; *In Russia* (1969) is a travel journal written with his wife, the photographer Inge Morand.

Miller, Henry (Valentine) 1891–1980 Born in New York City, Miller attended college for just two months in 1909. He then took various jobs and ended up working for Western Union from 1920 to 1924. He left the telegraph company to pursue his writing, selling poems door-to-door and then opening a speakeasy in order to support himself. In 1930 he moved to Paris, where he lived until 1939. There he wrote his most famous work, *Tropic of Cancer* (1934), an autobiographical narrative describing the promiscuous lifestyle he witnessed in Paris. Because of its sexual frankness, the book was considered pornographic and was suppressed in both the US and England. (It was not in fact published in the US until 1961.) *Black Spring* (1936), which consists of ten autobiographical stories, and *Tropic of Capricorn* (1939), an account of his years with the telegraph company, were also suppressed.

Following a trip to Greece in 1939, Miller produced what some consider his best work, *The Colossus of Maroussi* (1941), a travel book which is more about people than places. He returned to the US in 1940 and toured the country by car. Drawing upon this experience, he wrote *The Air-Conditioned Nightmare* (1945), a book of sketches in which he decries the materialism – the spiritual and cultural desolation – of life in his native land. He expresses similar sentiments in *Remember to Remember* (1947). His concern with the role of the artist within society is evident in both these works, and in his earlier *The Plight of the Creative Artist in the United States of America* (1944). Miller was also a painter, and with Hilaire Hiler and **William Saroyan** he wrote *Why Abstract?* (1945), a discussion of modern painting. Among his other notable works are *The World of Sex* (1940), *Books in My Life* (1951), *The Time of the Assassins: A Study of Rimbaud* (1956), and a trilogy – *Sexus* (1949), *Plexus* (1953, first published in French in 1952), and *Nexus* (1960) – collectively titled

The Rosy Crucifixion. A heavily illustrated volume entitled *My Life and Times* was published in 1971.

Miller, Joaquin 1839–1913   The pen-name of Cincinnatus Hiner (or Heine) Miller. Born in Liberty, Indiana, as a young man Miller moved to the Oregon frontier and later lived with Digger Indians in northern California. He published his first collection of poems, *Specimens*, in 1868. In the following year came *Joaquin et al.*, a defense of the Mexican bandit, Joaquin Murieta, from whom he derived his nickname. In 1870 he went to London and there published *Pacific Poems* (1871), which won acclaim from the Pre-Raphaelites, especially Dante Gabriel Rossetti, who took an active interest in this "Byron of Oregon" and helped him revise his next book of poetry, *Songs of the Sierras* (1871), which made him famous. He produced numerous other volumes of poetry; novels; plays, including the successful *The Danites of the Sierras* (1877), about the Mormons; and an autobiography, *Life amongst the Modocs* (1873).

Miss Lonelyhearts See **West, Nathanael**

Miss Ravenel's Conversion From Secession to Loyalty A novel by **John De Forest**, published in 1867. Dr Ravenel is a New Orleans physician who is forced to move north because of his Abolitionist beliefs. The sympathies of his daughter Lillie, however, are with the Confederates. Her conversion begins when she and her father settle in New Boston (based on New Haven, where De Forest lived). There she is wooed by two Union officers, Colbourne and Carter. The more dashing and aristocratic Carter better suits Lillie's Southern sensibility. She marries him and for his sake supports the Northern cause. Although his habits of drinking and womanizing seem to have abated, he begins a secret affair with Lillie's young aunt, Mrs Larue. He breaks off the affair after Lillie gives birth to a child, but Dr Ravenel learns of it and informs his daughter. Lillie eventually leaves her husband and later he is killed in battle; she returns to New Boston and finally marries the virtuous Colbourne. Her conversion to Abolitionism is by now complete. In spite of his preference for the Union cause, De Forest – with his customary harshness – satirizes New England society as well as that of New Orleans. The novel is also memorable for its grimly realistic battle scenes, which anticipate those of **Stephen Crane**.

Mitchell, Langdon (Elwyn) 1862–1935   Born in Philadelphia, the son of the novelist S. Weir Mitchell, he began his career as a dramatist with the romantic tragedy *Sylvian* (1885). His best-known production is *The New York Idea*, which examines contemporary attitudes towards love and marriage. He also wrote stage adaptations of novels, including *The Adventures of François* (1900), from his father's novel of 1898; and *Becky Sharp* (1899) and *Major Pendennis* (1916), both based on famous novels by Thackeray. A collection of essays, *Understanding America*, was published in 1927.

Mitchell, Margaret *See Gone With the Wind*

Moby-Dick; or, The Whale The acknowledged masterpiece of **Herman Melville**, published in New York in 1851 and in London, titled simply *The Whale*, in the same year.

The highly complex story begins with the narrator Ishmael's decision to go to sea. On his way to Nantucket he meets and befriends Queequeg, a harpooner from the South Sea Islands who is the image of the noble savage – a "George Washington cannibalistically developed." The two friends sign aboard the whaler *Pequod*, named for the first Indian tribe exterminated by white Americans. Before they set sail, a man named Elijah delivers mysterious warnings about a disastrous voyage and Father Mapple delivers a symbolic sermon about the prophet Jonah who was swallowed by a whale. The *Pequod's* mysterious Captain Ahab appears after several days at sea. He reveals to the crew the purpose (as he conceives it) of the voyage: to hunt and kill the white sperm whale, known among whalers as Moby Dick, a whale that on Ahab's previous voyage had cost him his leg. Ahab's eloquence convinces the crew to pledge themselves to his monomaniacal plan for vengeance. Only Starbuck, the first mate, demurs, feeling that Ahab's mission is a sacrilege and a threat to the financial investment the ship's owners have made. Stubb, the second mate, and Flask, the third, are easily drawn into Ahab's plan. The crew, the castoffs and refugees of all races and lands, are in their own way a microcosm of humanity. The harpooners are Queequeg, Tashtego (a Gay

Head Indian), and Daggoo (an African). On the first encounter with whales, they find that Ahab has kept hidden his own boat's crew, which is led by Fedallah, a Parsee and fortune-teller.

The narrative is sometimes naturalistic, sometimes fantastic and shaped into obscure parables. Large sections dwell upon the science of whales or upon the intricacies of the whaling business and its history. Amid the often turbulent complexity of the narrative form, the dramatic events unfold slowly. As the men of the *Pequod* sail the open sea in search of a single whale, they still occupy themselves with the regular business of whale hunting. Occasional chases after whales, storms, or meetings with other ships punctuate the long voyage. The crew captures and processes a sperm whale; Pip, a young black cabin boy, becomes caught in a harpoon line and is nearly drowned, whereupon he becomes insane; the *Pequod* nearly founders when Ishmael drowses at the helm; a meeting with the British whaler, the *Samuel Enderby*, provides Ahab with news that Moby Dick has been sighted recently; and Queequeg has a coffin made when he nearly dies of fever.

When a lightning storm sets the mastheads ablaze with St Elmo's fire, Ahab delivers a speech to his crew that confirms his mad devotion to the quest; the crew is panic-stricken and Starbuck warns Ahab that God is against him. These ominous events lead up to the eventual sighting of Moby Dick and the three-day chase with which the novel culminates. On the first day the great whale crushes one of the boats and nearly kills Fedallah. On the second day it drags Fedallah down in Ahab's harpoon line, and Ahab's artificial leg is snapped off as the whaleboat is wrecked. Finally, on the third day, a stricken Moby Dick charges the *Pequod* and smashes her sides. Ahab, in the whaling boat, manages to strike a final blow but is himself caught in the harpoon line and drowned, tied to the whale. The *Pequod* sinks, taking all of the whaling boats and their crews down in the suction. The only survivor is Ishmael, who is shot back up, clinging to the coffin that had been made for Queequeg.

Largely unrecognized in its time, *Moby-Dick* was rediscovered in the 1920s and established Melville's modern reputation as a classic American writer.

Modern Chivalry A novel in seven volumes by **Hugh Henry Brackenridge**, published in installments between 1792 and 1815. Captain John Farrago and his Irish servant, Teague O'Regan, American versions of Don Quixote and Sancho Panza, travel around the Pennsylvania countryside, their adventures providing the occasion for satirical observations about post-Revolutionary American life and manners.

Farrago is a stuffy, aristocratic landowner; Teague, a stereotypical Irishman – irresponsible, untrained, uneducated, one of the men who have been newly placed in positions of power by the Revolution and the institution of democracy. Much of the book consists of a series of incidents in which Teague is given opportunities – as preacher, Indian treaty maker, potential husband for a well-bred young lady, pupil to a French dancing master – for which, according to an earlier set of values, he is socially unqualified. (He is, in fact, unqualified by any standard.) Farrago's unprincipled attempts to discourage and prevent him from exploiting these opportunities derive from his own desire to keep the old aristocratic system in place, thereby retaining Teague as his servant and preserving his own class's exclusive prerogative to fill these roles. The tensions between them thus dramatize the problem of authority and leadership in a democracy. At one point Teague becomes an excise officer and is tarred and feathered by reluctant taxpayers (a reference to the Whiskey Rebellion of 1794, which Brackenridge helped mediate). He is then put on display as a rare specimen by the American Philosophical Society, an incident which typifies the book's satire on American institutions and pretensions, as well as locating it in the genre of humorous frontier writing.

Modern Instance, A A novel by **William Dean Howells**, published in volume form in 1882, and structured around the twin themes of divorce and journalism. Howells was the first to focus on journalism in an American novel, and developed the idea of the divorce theme after seeing a performance of *Medea*. During the composition of the novel, he referred to it as his "New Medea," a "modern instance" of what would happen to a gradually estranged couple.

Bartley Hubbard, a young Boston journalist, is married to Marcia Gaylord. The marriage quickly deteriorates, however, because of his unscrupulous business practices and moral decline. Despite her love for her husband, Marcia leaves him. Hubbard sues for divorce but his suit is defeated and the divorce is granted to Marcia. After the divorce he moves to Arizona where he is killed by someone about whom he has published personal details in his newspaper. Marcia, meanwhile, is courted by Ben Halleck, a highly principled man who cannot decide whether or not to leave the ministry for her. The novel ends without giving his final decision. Howells's close observation of the business world and vivid characterization of Hubbard in his moral decline enhanced the radical themes of the novel, and it was a success from its initial serialization in Scribner's *Century Magazine* (1881). It is a prime example of Howells's concept of realism in fiction and of his exploration of the moral slackness of the Gilded Age.

Momaday, N[atachee or Navarre] Scott 1934– Born on a Kiowa reservation in Oklahoma, Momaday was educated in part through the Bureau of Indian Affairs, and later received a PhD from Stanford University. He first became known as an **Emily Dickinson** scholar and as editor of the poems of **Frederick Goddard Tuckerman**. His first novel, *House Made of Dawn* (1968), which was awarded the Pulitzer Prize, is the story of an Indian named Abel who leaves the reservation when he is drafted, and is forced to confront the non-Indian world and its values. Momaday's next publications were a collection of Kiowa folk-tales, *The Way to Rainy Mountain* (1969), and a volume of poetry, *Angle of Geese and Other Poems* (1974). One of the foremost American Indian writers, his other books include *The Gourd Dancer* (1976) and *The Names: A Memoir* (1976).

Monroe, Harriet 1860–1936 Born in Chicago, Monroe first attracted attention with her *Columbian Ode*, a poem written for the dedication ceremony of the World's Columbian Exposition, held in Chicago in 1892. When the New York *World* published the *Ode* without her permission, she successfully sued the paper in a case which established a legal precedent regarding the rights of authors to control their unpublished works. Her published works include *Valeria and Other Poems* (1891), *You and I* (1914), *The Difference* (1924), and *Chosen Poems* (1935). She also wrote several verse dramas, five of which were published in 1903 as *The Passing Show*. Though her earlier work is more traditional in form, meter, and rhyme scheme than her later, all her poetry is characterized by a sense of "modernity." She tended to deal with contemporary subjects, and many of her poems celebrate modern technology.

In 1912 she founded **Poetry:** *A Magazine of Verse* to encourage and publish the "new poetry." The magazine, which she edited until her death, played a prominent role in the Chicago Renaissance in literature. **Ezra Pound**, who served as *Poetry*'s foreign correspondent for the first six years of its existence, brought **T. S. Eliot**'s early work to Monroe's attention, and she published it in the magazine. Other poets she published include Pound himself, **H. D.**, **Carl Sandburg, Vachel Lindsay, Edgar Lee Masters, Hart Crane, Robert Frost, Edwin Arlington Robinson, Wallace Stevens, Edna St Vincent Millay**, and **Marianne Moore**. Monroe's autobiography, *A Poet's Life: Seventy Years in a Changing World* (1937), provides an informative account of the changes in the American literary scene during the late 19th and early 20th centuries. *Poets and Their Art*, a collection of her critical essays, appeared in 1932.

Mont-Saint-Michel and Chartres A historical study of medievalism by **Henry Adams**, subtitled "A Study of Thirteenth-Century Unity." Printed privately in 1904 for distribution among family and friends, and then published by the American Institute of Architects in 1913, it is complemented by his later study of modernity, **The Education of Henry Adams**, itself subtitled "A Study of Twentieth-Century Multiplicity." Adams identifies the dominant cultural power of the Middle Ages as the Catholic faith which informed and unified all artistic and intellectual endeavor, as well as religious and moral thought. In particular, he sees the unifying symbolic "force" of the Virgin as having provided the spiritual impulse for the arts of the time, which he discusses in separate chapters devoted to architecture, sculpture, stained-glass windows, literature, and historical and religious figures.

Moody, William Vaughn 1869–1910 Playwright and poet, born and raised in Indiana, and educated at Harvard. From 1894 to 1907 he taught English at Harvard, Radcliffe, and the University of Chicago, publishing a number of scholarly editions of prose and poetry and *A History of English Literature* (with Robert Morss Lovett, 1902). His first published work was *Class Poem* (1894). *The Masque of Judgment* (1900) was the first part of a verse drama trilogy continued by *The Fire Bringer* (1904) and the uncompleted *The Death of Eve* (1912). *Poems* (1901) contains the often-anthologized pieces "Gloucester Moors" and "An Ode in Time of Hesitation."

Although only two of his plays were produced during his lifetime, Moody's brief career as a dramatist was of considerable importance to the development of the American theatre. Unlike many dramatists of his time, he chose distinctively American subjects for his plays. His enormously popular *A Sabine Woman* (1906), which was later produced and published under the title *The Great Divide* (1909), treats the conflict between the values of established Eastern culture and the realities of free-spirited frontier life, describing the abduction of a woman from Massachusetts by a man from Arizona, and the events that lead to their eventual marriage. Its realism challenged the melodramatic conventions of the contemporary American stage. Moody's final play, *The Faith Healer*, appeared in 1909. A posthumous volume, *Selected Poems* (1931), is a representative collection of his poetry.

Moore, Julia A. 1847–1920 Moore was known as "The Sweet Singer of Michigan" from the title of her first volume of poetry, *The Sweet Singer of Michigan Salutes the Public* (1876), which was subsequently retitled *The Sentimental Song Book*. Two years later *A Few Choice Words to the Public with New and Original Poems* appeared. She is also the author of a romance about the American Revolution, *Sunshine and Shadow; or Paul Burton's Surprise* (1915). Ironically Moore's verse achieved its reputation not for its intrinsic merits but because it typified certain unfavorable trends of contemporary poetry, such as simplistic syntax and facile rhyme schemes.

Moore, Marianne (Craig) 1887–1972 Born near St Louis, Missouri, Moore graduated from Bryn Mawr College in 1909. Her first book, *Poems*, was published in 1921 by her friends Hilda Dolittle (**H.D.**) and Robert McAlmon. A second volume, *Observations* (1924), won her the *Dial* Magazine Award. She then was appointed to the *Dial*'s staff and served as acting editor from 1925 to 1929. Her poetry is marked by an unconventional but disciplined use of metrics, and a witty, often ironic tone. Known for their eclectic subject matter, her poems contain references to scientific and historical works and to current affairs, and many are written about exotic animals. They also reveal an abiding interest in aesthetic and philosophical issues.

Moore's other volumes of poetry include *Selected Poems* (1935), *The Pangolin and Other Verse* (1936), *What Are Years* (1941), *Nevertheless* (1944), *A Face* (1949), the Pulitzer Prize-winning *Collected Poems* (1951), *Like a Bulwark* (1956), *O, to Be a Dragon* (1959), and *Tell Me, Tell Me: Granite, Steel, and Other Topics* (1966). Other works include a volume of critical essays, *Predilections* (1955), and two volumes of translations, *The Fables of La Fontaine* (1954), and *Selected Fables of La Fontaine* (1955). *The Complete Poems of Marianne Moore* was published in 1967.

Morris, Wright 1910– Morris was born in Central City, Nebraska, a town which figures prominently in his fiction. He graduated from Pomona College in 1933 and then went to live in Paris, where he decided to become a writer. He taught creative writing at San Francisco State University from 1962 to 1975.

His principal concerns have always been with a definition of the American character, with the American Edenic myth, and with the uses and influences of American history. His narratives are often fragmented and his novels many-voiced and subtly ironic. *Plains Song* (1980), for example, has been compared to **William Faulkner**'s *As I Lay Dying*. His other novels include *My Uncle Dudley* (1942); *The Man Who Was There* (1945); *The World in the Attic* (1949); *The Works of Love* (1952); *A Field of Vision* (1956), which was based on his experiences while living in Mexico in 1954 and which received a National Book Award;

Love Among the Cannibals (1957); *Ceremony in Lone Tree* (1960); *Cause for Wonder* (1963); *In Orbit* (1967); *Fire Sermon* (1971); *A Life* (1973); and *The Fork River Space Project* (1977).

He has also published volumes which combine text and photographs and which share affinities with the work of Eugene Atget and Walker Evans: *The Inhabitants* (1946), *The Home Place* (1948), and *Picture America* (1982). He has published three volumes of memoirs: *Will's Boy: A Memoir* (1981), *Solo: An American Dreamer in Europe, 1933–34* (1983), and *A Cloak of Light: Writing My Life* (1985). His literary criticism includes *The Territory Ahead* (1958), *About Fiction* (1975), and a study of American writers entitled *Earthly Delights, Unearthly Adornments* (1978).

Morrison, Toni 1931–   Born in Ohio to working-class parents and educated at Howard and Cornell, Morrison is widely considered to be one of America's leading black novelists. Her first novel, *The Bluest Eye* (1970), is the story of a year in the life of Pecola Breedlove, a young black girl in Ohio who comes to believe that she has blue eyes. In the course of the year Pecola endures a series of degradations, including incest with her father and subsequent pregnancy, until her fixation with the blue eyes of a friend's doll develops into complete insanity. *Sula* (1973), also set in Ohio, focuses on the friendship between two black women, Sula Peace and Nel Wright Greene, as they mature during the 1920s and 1930s. Their friendship is based on a shared sense of alienation from community and family values, and a similar experience of emptiness in their other relationships – especially with men. *Song of Solomon* (1977) is an intricate narrative about Milkman Dead's exploration of his family history, his quest for a place as an individual within a heritage of slavery and violence. *Tar Baby* (1981) is about motherhood and the relationships between black and white cultures in the Caribbean and America.

Morton, Nathaniel 1612–85   Born in the pilgrim community in Leyden, Holland, Morton emigrated to Plymouth Colony in July, 1623 with his father George Morton, a non-conformist and separatist. When his father died in the following year, he was sent to live with his uncle, Governor **William Bradford**.

Morton influenced colonial culture both as a historian and civil servant. In 1647 he was appointed secretary of Plymouth Colony, a post which he occupied until his death and which gave him responsibility for keeping the colony's official records. While serving in this capacity, as well as in that of town clerk, he contributed to the drafting of legislation and the running of the government, and also gained exposure to the civil servants and affairs whose history he eventually told in *New Englands Memoriall: or, A Brief Relation of the Most Memorable Passages of the Providences of God, Manifested to the Planters of New England, in America: With Special Reference to the First Colony Thereof, Called New Plymouth* (1669). The book relied and elaborated upon Bradford's **History of Plimmoth Plantation**, and provided a source for **Cotton Mather**'s *Magnalia Christi Americana*.

Motley, John Lathrop *c.*1814–77   Motley was born in Dorchester, Massachusetts into a prosperous New England family. He graduated from Harvard in 1831 and then studied for two years in Germany. After touring on the Continent he returned to America to marry and to study law in Boston. He published two novels, *Morton's Hope: or, The Memoirs of a Young Provincial* (1839) and *Merry-Mount: A Romance of the Massachusetts Colony* (1849). He also spent time in the diplomatic service in Russia, Austria, and England. *The Rise of the Dutch Republic: A History* was published in three volumes in 1856 after ten year's work in the US, Holland, and Germany. The history, which ends with the death of William of Orange, was well received and soon translated into the principal European languages. Motley followed it with *The History of the United Netherlands*, which examines the years up to the truce of 1609; two volumes were published in 1861 and a further two in 1867. Another history, *The Life and Death of John of Barneveld, Advocate of Holland* (2 vols., 1874), spans the period from 1609 to the Thirty Years War. Motley planned another installment, which would carry the history to the year 1848, but died before the project was realized.

Motley, Willard 1912–65   Born in Chicago, Motley had a diverse career, which included working as a ranch hand, cook, migrant laborer, and photographer. His observation of the slums of Chicago in the 1940s served as material for his first novel, *Knock on any Door* (1947). His next novels, *We Fished all Night* (1951) and *Let No Man Write My Epitaph* (1958), are also critical examinations of the urban environment. In the naturalistic tradition of **Theodore Dreiser** and **James T. Farrell**, these novels stress the tragedy of human existence. He lived in Mexico for the last 12 years of his life; *Let Noon be Fair*, published posthumously in 1966, traces the gradual corruption and cultural decline of a Mexican tourist town.

Mourning Becomes Electra A trilogy of plays by **Eugene O'Neill**, based on the *Oresteia* of Aeschylus, and first produced in New York in 1931. The 13-act trilogy is set in a small New England coastal town at the close of the Civil War. During General Mannon's absence in the war his wife Christine takes Captain Adam Brant as her lover. The grim Mannon house, built in the style of a Greek temple, becomes the setting for the first death, that of General Mannon, poisoned by Christine. Their daughter Lavinia hates her mother as fervently as she loved her father, and finding the remains of the poison, she urges her brother Orin to exact revenge. Orin kills Brant and Christine commits suicide. Driven towards madness by the consciousness of his crime, Orin is taken on a voyage by the unrepentant Lavinia. On their return to the Mannon house, he is still ill but she is transformed into a beauty exactly like her mother (the play was originally intended for performance with masks). Orin's passionate attachment to his mother is now incestuously transferred to Lavinia, and remorse leads him to suicide. Lavinia accepts the punishment of shutting herself away in the decaying mansion of the doomed Mannons.

Moveable Feast, A See **Hemingway, Ernest**

Mowatt, Anna Cora 1819–70 Dramatist, novelist, and actress, Anna Ogden was the ninth of 16 children born in a wealthy American family living in Bordeaux, France, where she spent her early years before the family returned to settle in New York City. She was 15 when she married James Mowatt, a respected lawyer much older than herself. He encouraged her to write, and she published a verse romance, *Pelayo* (1836), and a verse satire, *Reviewers Reviewed* (1837), before turning her hand to novels of New York social life, including *The Fortune Hunter* (1844) and *Evelyn; or, A Heart Unmasked* (1845).

As a figure in New York society, she risked ridicule for her literary aspirations. To turn to the theatre was considered even worse, but when her comic social satire, **Fashion**, opened in 1845 and became widely popular, she was encouraged to take to the stage herself. For nine years she toured as an actress, retiring in 1854 to live in Richmond, Virginia, and after 1861 in Florence, Italy. She spent the rest of her life writing romantic narratives of life in the theatre, *Mimic Life* (1856) and *Twin Roses* (1857); her own *Autobiography of an Actress* (1854); and various historical sketches.

My Ántonia A novel by **Willa Cather**, published in 1918, and set on the Nebraska frontier among Scandinavian, Bohemian, and French immigrants. It takes the form of a memoir by Jim Burden, recounting the life of his childhood friend Ántonia Shimerda. The story opens as Jim, whose parents have recently died, travels West to live on his grandparents' farm outside Black Hawk, Nebraska. On the train he encounters an immigrant Bohemian family and their eldest daughter, Ántonia. The meeting is the beginning of a lifelong friendship.

During their first year in Nebraska the Shimerdas are assisted by Jim's grandparents, who offer food and advice on how to operate a frontier farm. However, the stresses of farm life, poverty, and chronic homesickness depress Ántonia's father and he commits suicide. Ántonia's life changes drastically and she is forced to work in the fields like a man although she is still in her early teens. Then Jim and his grandparents, who have left their farm to live in Black Hawk, arrange for her to work as a hired girl for the Harling family. She remains in this position for some years, leaving only when she refuses to accede to Mr Harling's demand that she cease attending the town's Saturday night dances lest she lose her reputation. She takes up a similar position with Wick Cutter and his wife, but Wick's amorous attentions drive her away and she goes to stay with Jim's grandparents while looking for another job.

As Ántonia learns the skills of homemaking, Jim prepares for and enters college in Lincoln, Nebraska. After two years there he moves East to attend Harvard. Two years later, when he returns to Black Hawk after completing his education, he learns that Ántonia has been duped by Larry Donovan, a flashy railroad man she had sporadically dated years before, and who had pretended he wanted to marry her. Abandoned by him in Denver, Colorado, pregnant and unwed, she returns to her mother's farm outside Black Hawk and resumes her hardworking routine.

In due course she gives birth to a daughter. After a reunion with Ántonia Jim goes East again to attend Harvard Law School. While he is away Ántonia marries a fellow Bohemian, Anton Cuzak, and has a large family. When Jim comes home 20 years later he visits Ántonia and her husband on the farm they have built. He finds her worn down but thoroughly satisfied with her lot. As the novel ends Jim is once again leaving Black Hawk, but this time with the promise of many future vacations with Ántonia and her family.

N

Nabokov, Vladimir 1899–1977 Born into a wealthy and prominent family in St Petersburg, Russia, as a youth Nabokov traveled extensively throughout Europe, indulged his interest in tennis and lepidopterology at his family's country home, and attended the progressive Tenishev School. His father, a member of the Russian Constituent Assembly, moved the family to Yalta in 1919 at the start of the Bolshevik Revolution, and following the White army's defeat in the Crimea they went into exile in Western Europe. Between 1919 and 1922 Nabokov studied modern languages and literature at Trinity College, Cambridge.

Upon graduation he joined his family in Berlin to begin work as a professional writer, but was immediately distracted by the responsibilities acquired and the pain suffered following his father's assassination. Eventually he did write, and while living in Berlin and Paris during the 1920s and 1930s, produced a critically acclaimed canon of poems, short stories, and novels written in Russian and published under the pseudonym of V. Sirin: *Mashen'ka* (1926), *Korol', Dama, Valet* (1928), *Zashchita Luzhina* (1930), *Soglyadatay* (1930), *Podvig* (1932), *Kamera Obskura* (1932–3), *Otchayanie* (1936), *Priglashenie na Kazn'* (1938), and *Dar* (1937–8).

The second phase of his career began in 1940 when he emigrated to America and settled in Boston. While teaching Russian literature at Wellesley College, he published his first novel in English, *The Real Life of Sebastian Knight* (1941), and wrote many of his short stories and poems which appeared in periodicals such as **The New Yorker**. His second novel was *Bend Sinister* (1947). In 1948 he accepted a position as professor of Russian literature at Cornell and during his tenure

there published his first memoir, *Conclusive Evidence* (1951, later retitled *Speak, Memory* and under this title expanded and revised in 1966). It was also at Cornell that he wrote his most famous novel, *Lolita* (1955). Humbert Humbert, the speaker in this first-person narrative, writes from jail a confession and explanation of his socially unacceptable lust for adolescent girls, whom he calls "nymphets." Humbert details the seduction of his step-daughter, Lolita, and their journey westward. The relationship is broken off when Lolita runs off with the actor Quilty, who abandons her and whom Humbert murders. The humorously portrayed address satirizes society's sexual mores and probes the nature of artistic creation. The critical and financial success of *Lolita* enabled Nabokov to resign his post at Cornell and engage exclusively in literary enterprises. While working steadily on his translation of Pushkin's *Eugene Onegin* (published in four volumes in 1964), he wrote three more novels – *Pnin* (1957), *Pale Fire* (1962), and *Ada, or Ardor: A Family Chronicle* (1969) – and two collections of short stories – *Nabokov's Dozen* (1958) and *Nabokov's Quartet* (1966). He also supervised the translation of his Russian novels, a project undertaken by his son Dimitri.

Naked and the Dead, The The first novel by **Norman Mailer**, published in 1948 when the author was 25. Set on a Pacific island during World War II, the story reflects in numerous brutally naturalistic combat scenes Mailer's own army experiences; it won quick acclaim as one of the best personal accounts to emerge from the war. But the major concern of the book centers not on the campaign against the Japanese but on the disparate and often desperate political and moral philosophies of the fighting men – on the problems of the pluralistic American society from which they have emerged. Mailer focuses on 13 characters, whose civilian lives are recalled through an experimental flashback device, "The Time Machine." The men are thus characterized as carrying not only the weapons of war but also the weight of their pasts – of economic, radical, and religious tensions. Mailer's cynicism about America's past and his doubts about its post-war future are expressed largely through the clash between the proto-fascist General Cummings, who holds that the enlisted men must be made into automatons within the power structure, and Lieutenant Hearn, a rich, educated, and confused liberal, who finds that he cannot argue with true conviction his hope for the survival of a democratic spirit. Rough in language, violent in action, and hostile towards mainstream American values, the novel foreshadows much of Mailer's later writings.

Naked Lunch   See **Burroughs, William S.**

Nasby, Petroleum V.   See **Locke, David Ross**

Nash, Ogden 1902–71   Born in Rye, New York, and educated at Harvard, Nash is best known as a writer of light, humorous verse, though he also wrote plays and stories. His first books, *Cricket of Cavador* (1925), *Free Wheeling* (1931), and *The Bad Parents' Garden of Verse* (1936), are early examples of his comical and irreverent vision. A master of irony, he often questions the commonplace in American life, the objects of his humor ranging from the more general assumptions of society, to problems of domestic life, to grammar and prosody itself. His later books include *I'm a Stranger Here Myself* (1938), *Good Intentions* (1942), *Versus* (1949), *Family Reunion* (1950), *Everyone But Thee and Me* (1962), *Marriage Lines* (1964), *Merrill Lynch We Roll Along* (1965), *Bed Riddance: A Posy for the Indisposed* (1970), and the posthumous *A Penny Saved Is Impossible* (1981). He also edited a collection of stories, *I Couldn't Help Laughing* (1957).

Nathan, George Jean 1882–1958   Born in Fort Wayne, Indiana, Nathan graduated from Cornell in 1904. An uncle helped him to obtain a job on the *New York Herald* in 1905, and in the following year he was hired by two national magazines – *Bohemian* and *Outing* – as a reviewer. In 1908 he began contributing to *Smart Set*, and in 1914 became its editor in partnership with **H. L. Mencken**, with whom in 1920 he founded the detective magazine *The Black Mask*. He founded *The American Mercury* with Mencken in 1924 and contributed to it from 1924 to 1930 and from 1940 to 1951. In 1934 he helped to found the New York Drama Critics Circle, and was president of the group from 1937 to 1939. His works include the plays *The Eternal Mystery* (1913), *Heliogabalus* (1920, with Mencken), *The Avon Flows* (1937), and the annual record of the New York stage, *The Theatre Book of the Year* (1943–51).

Nation, The   The first issue of *The Nation*, "a weekly journal devoted to Politics, Literature, Science and Art," appeared on July 6, 1865. Those who sponsored the new journal were concerned with securing full rights for the newly freed American Negroes – a concern recorded prominently in the early issues. Indeed, the National Association for the Advancement of Colored People (NAACP) was first housed in *The Nation's* office in New York. Although in its early years it consisted almost entirely of comment on politics and literature, by the 1920s it came to include original works of literature. The first editor of *The Nation* (which has been published continuously since 1865) was E. L. Godkin, an Anglo-Irish journalist who modeled it on British periodicals of the era. Subsequent editors have included **William Lloyd Garrison**, Paul Elmer More, Oswald Garrison Villard, Freda Kirchway, Carey McWilliams, and Victor Navasky.

Native Son   A novel by **Richard Wright**, published in 1940. It recounts the story of Bigger Thomas, a black ghetto dweller on the South Side of Chicago, who is hired by a wealthy family as their chauffeur. The family's spoiled, liberal-leaning daughter, Mary, and her Communist boyfriend, Jan, befriend him. One night, after Mary has had too much to drink, and while Bigger with the best of intentions is getting her back to her room, he accidentally smothers her with a pillow. A black man with a white woman's death on his hands, he knows that it matters little that his act was not intended, and tries to escape. He goes to his girlfriend for help, but realizing that she is too distraught by the murder to trust him, he kills her too and is soon caught. Waiting in jail for his trial, he feels for the first time a sense of freedom in having successfully carried out an act he was impelled to do by the social conditions from which he arose. In prison he comes to realize what real emotional connection with a white person can be – through his lawyer, Max, also a Communist. Max tries to get him to articulate the harshness of the conditions which have led to his acts, but he cannot: he is not privy to white society's conditions of articulation; he has too much pride to do anything more than affirm that "what I killed for, I am!"

Natural, The See **Malamud, Bernard**

Nature **Ralph Waldo Emerson**'s first book, developed from his early lectures, and published in 1836. In it he sets forth the main principles of **Transcendentalism**, postulating the need for "an original relation to the universe" and rejecting timeworn attitudes to God and Nature. He elaborates on his conception of Nature as the expression of a divine will, and examines Nature's value as commodity as well as its beauty and its expression in language. He asserts the need for man to establish a relationship with Nature that will allow him to take advantage of its spiritual self-governance, and to reunite himself with his spiritual source. An expanded second edition was published in 1849.

Nemerov, Howard 1920– Nemerov was born in New York City and educated at Harvard. He was an associate editor of the magazine *Furioso* from 1946 to 1951, and has taught at Hamilton and Bennington colleges. His first volumes of poetry, *The Image and the Law* (1947), *Guide to the Ruins* (1950), and *The Salt Garden* (1955), demonstrate something of the range of tone and style that characterizes his later verse. His subject matter varies from broad philosophical questions to more immediate and contemporary issues. Other collections are *New and Selected Poems* (1960), *The Blue Swallows* (1967), *Gnomes and Occasions* (1973), and *The Western Approaches: Poems 1973–1975* (1975). His prose fiction, which often explores moral problems in modern society, includes *Commodity of Dreams and Other Stories* (1959), and three novels: *The Melodramatist* (1949), *Federigo, or*

The Power of Love (1954), and *The Homecoming Game* (1957). His criticism is published in *Poetry and Fiction: Essays* (1963), *Reflexions on Poetry and Poetics* (1972), *Figures of Thought: Speculations on the Meaning of Poetry and Other Essays* (1978), and *New and Selected Essays* (1985). He has also written plays, two of which are included in *The Next Room of the Dream: Poems and Two Plays* (1962).

New Criticism An influential movement in American literary criticism from the late 1930s to the 1950s which grew out of the Southern Agrarian Movement. (See **Ransom, John Crowe**.) Stressing the formal features of poetry, the New Critics saw the poem as an autonomous whole and subscribed to a method of close textual analysis, concentrating on the interior relationship of the parts of the poem. The textual emphasis of the New Critics insisted that neither the author's intentions nor the emotional responses of readers were immediately relevant to the interpretation of the poem. John Crowe Ransom's *The New Criticism* (1941) gave the movement its name. His student Cleanth Brooks in *The Well Wrought Urn: Studies in the Structure of Poetry* (1947), and later W. K. Wimsatt in *The Verbal Icon: Studies in the Meaning of Poetry* (1954), continued Ransom's neo-Kantian critique of positivism by converting the poem into a self-enclosed object. Other New Criticis include R. P. Blackmur, **Allen Tate**, and **Yvor Winters**.

New England Nun and Other Stories, A See **Freeman, Mary Wilkins**

New Englands Memoriall See **Morton, Nathaniel**

New Masses, The A journal founded in 1926 in New York City. The original editors were Egmont Arens, Joseph Freeman, Hugo Gellert, **Michael Gold**, James Rorty, and John Sloan. Gold became its sole editor in 1928. *The New Masses* was one of the central forums for those writers and intellectuals involved with radical left-wing politics and the Communist party in America. Among its contributing editors were **Sherwood Anderson**, Van Wyck Brooks, **Max Eastman**, **Waldo Frank**, Lewis Mumford, **Eugene O'Neill**, Lola Ridge, and **Carl Sandburg**. Contributors of fiction, poetry, and critical essays included **Robinson Jef-**

fers, Eugene Jolas, **Horace Gregory**, Whit Burnett, Genevieve Taggard, and **Kenneth Fearing**. The journal ceased publication in 1948.

New Negro, The   An anthology of essays, stories, a play, and extensive bibliographies of black writers, edited by **Alain Locke** and published in 1925. It served as a manifesto which marked the crystallization of the concept of the "New Negro" or **Harlem Renaissance**. In his preface to the volume Locke argued that blacks were making progress in combating prejudice, and that they possessed a new spirit of "group expression and self-determination" which would in turn enrich American culture as a whole.

New Republic, The   A literary and political journal, founded by Herbert Croly in 1914. Its literary editors have included **Edmund Wilson**, Malcolm Cowley, Richard Gilman, and Reed Whittemore. Though markedly liberal in its politics, it has published literary and critical pieces by writers of various political orientations, including **Robert Frost**, **George Santayana**, **H. L. Mencken**, **John Dos Passos**, **John Crowe Ransom**, **Allen Tate**, **Archibald MacLeish**, **Willa Cather**, **Ernest Hemingway**, **Eudora Welty**, **Michael Gold**, and **Walter Lippman**. From the 1950s the magazine began to print more political commentary and less fiction and poetry.

New Yorker, The   Founded in 1925 and edited by Harold Ross until 1951, this weekly magazine is aimed at a cosmopolitan audience, and has traditionally published a variety of materials, including poetry and short stories, and articles on literature, art, theatre, cinema, music, and dance. William Shawn has been editor since 1951. Notable contributors over the years include **E. B. White**, Alexander Woollcott, Robert Benchley, Clifton Fadiman, Wolcott Gibbs, **Ogden Nash**, **John Updike**, **J. D. Salinger**, **S. J. Perelman**, **Truman Capote**, **John O'Hara**, **John Cheever**, **James Thurber**, **Edmund Wilson**, **Donald Barthelme**, and John McPhee.

New York School, The   A group of poets, mostly living in New York City, whose works reflect similar reactions against modernism. The most notable members of the group are **Frank O'Hara**, **Kenneth Koch**, and **John Ashbery**. The urban environment is crucial to their poetic visions, and many of their poems are deliberately surrealistic. A classic example of the work of the school is O'Hara's "Second Avenue."

Nick of the Woods   See **Bird, Robert**

Nicolay, John George   See **Hay, John Milton**

Night Rider   See **Warren, Robert Penn**

Nightwood   See **Barnes, Djuna**

Nin, Anaïs 1903–77   Nin was born in Neuilly, just outside Paris. Her father was a Spanish composer, her mother half-French and half-Danish. In 1914 she moved with her mother to New York, where she lived until returning to Paris in 1923. In her early life she was a model, dancer, teacher, and lecturer, and she later became a practicing psychoanalyst under the tutelage of Otto Rank. She began writing her renowned *Diary* (10 vols., 1966–83) in 1931; her first publication was an essay entitled *D. H. Lawrence: An Unprofessional Study* (Paris, 1932). She turned to fiction with the novel *House of Incest* (Paris, 1936; US publication, 1947). Prominent in Paris literary circles, she became the friend of **Henry Miller** and Lawrence Durrell. At the beginning of World War II she returned to the US.

All of her subsequent work in some way depends on the lyrical reflections of her diaries, and includes a collection of three novelettes, *The Winter of Artifice* (Paris, 1939; US publication, 1942); a volume of short stories, *Under a Glass Bell* (1944); and the novels *Ladders to Fire* (1946), *Children of the Albatross* (1947), *The Four-Chambered Heart* (1950), *A Spy in the House of Love* (1954), *Solar Baroque* (1958), and *Collages* (1964). Her volumes of erotica include *Delta of Venus: Erotica* (1977) and *Little Birds* (1979). Her critical studies are *Realism and Reality* (1946), *On Writing* (1947), and *The Novel of the Future* (1968).

1919   Published in 1932, the second novel in the trilogy *U.S.A.* by **John Dos Passos**.

Noah, Mordecai Manuel 1785–1851   Born in Philadelphia into a Portuguese-Jewish family, Noah later moved to Charlestown where he studied law and, as editor of the *City*

Gazette, wrote controversial editorials under the name of "Muley Molack." His anti-British and vehemently patriotic political sentiments brought him to the attention of President James Monroe, who appointed him consul to Tunis (1813–15). The first of his plays to be produced was *Paul and Alexis; or, The Orphans of the Rhine* (1812), a melodrama later retitled *The Wandering Boys* and based on Pixerecourt's *Le Pelerin Blanc, ou Les Orphelins du Hameau*. This was followed by his best-known work, *She Would Be a Soldier; or, The Plains of Chippewa* (1819), a patriotic comedy about a young woman who disguises herself as a soldier in order to follow her lover who is fighting in the War of 1812. Noah's other plays include *The Siege of Tripoli* (1820), *Marion; or, The Hero of Lake George* (1821), *The Grecian Captive; or, The Fall of Athens* (1822), and *The Siege of Yorktown* (1824). Whether his subject was ancient or contemporary, Noah always wrote what he himself termed "national plays," plays that self-consciously recalled and represented the course of the nation's history.

Norris, Frank 1870–1902 Born Benjamin Franklin Norris in Chicago, at the age of 14 he moved with his family to San Francisco. He studied in Paris and then attended the University of California from 1890 to 1894. In 1895 he visited South Africa, hoping to find material for travel sketches; instead he reported the conflict between the English and the Boers for the San Francisco *Chronicle*. After being captured by the Boer forces he was deported, and returned to San Francisco where he joined the staff of a magazine called *The Wave*. *Moran of the Lady Letty*, a sea story set off the California coast, was serialized in the magazine and published in 1898. *A Man's Woman*, a romantic adventure story, appeared in 1900. Other contributions to *The Wave* were published in later years, such as *The Joyous Miracle* (1906, a novelette), and the short-story collections *A Deal in Wheat* (1903) and *The Third Circle* (1909).

In 1898 Norris went to Cuba to report on the Spanish–American War for *McClure's Magazine*, and on his return took a job with the publishers Doubleday, who in 1899 published the love story *Blix* and *McTeague: A Story of San Francisco*. Strongly influenced by Emile Zola, *McTeague* tells of the descent of a man of limited intelligence into primitivism when his precariously assembled world is brought down by greed and spite. Norris next concentrated his energies on a trilogy, *The Epic of the Wheat*. The first book, *The Octopus* (1901), describes the struggle between farming and railroad interests in California. Norris died in the following year after an appendix operation, and the second novel, *The Pit*, was published posthumously in 1903. The third part, to be entitled *The Wolf*, was never written. *The Pit* concerns the manipulation of the wheat market in Chicago, and *The Wolf* was to tell of a wheat famine in Europe. Also published posthumously were *The Responsibilities of the Novelist* (1903), in which he describes the type of naturalistic writing, based on actual experience and observation, which he had derived from Zola; and the novel *Vandover and the Brute* (1914), which he had started in 1895.

North American Review, The A New England quarterly first published in Boston in 1815 under the editorship of William Tudor. Later, as a monthly publication, its editors included **Charles Eliot Norton, James Russell Lowell, Henry Adams,** and Henry Cabot Lodge. Although founded as a literary journal, it began to publish articles on political and social matters when it was moved to New York City in 1878. After World War I it reverted to quarterly publication and continued until 1940. Writers published in *Review* include **Ralph Waldo Emerson, Washington Irving, Henry Wadsworth Longfellow, Francis Parkman, Walt Whitman, Mark Twain, Henry James,** Leo Tolstoy, Gabriele D'Annunzio, H. G. Wells, Maurice Maeterlinck, and **Alan Seeger.**

Norton, Charles Eliot 1827–1908 The son of the biblical scholar Andrews Norton, he was professor of the history of fine art at Harvard from 1874 to 1898. A regular contributor to *The Atlantic Monthly* and co-editor of *The North American Review*, he also helped to found *The Nation* in 1865. He was a frequent visitor to Europe and had a wide range of friends among writers and artists on both sides of the Atlantic. His *Letters*, published in 1913, are a valuable document of intellectual life in Massachusetts in the latter half of the 19th century. His books include a prose translation of Dante's *The*

Divine Comedy (1891–2), editions of John Donne's poetry (1895) and the early letters of Thomas Carlyle (1886), and *Notes of Travel and Study in Italy* (1859).

Notes on the State of Virginia This book by **Thomas Jefferson** is a collection of answers to a set of questions about America circulated among American statesmen by François Marbois, a French representative in Philadelphia during the Revolutionary War. Jefferson, then governor of Virginia, worked on it in 1780 and 1781, gathering data from his own research and from queries to others. After sending his answers on to Marbois, he continued to revise and expand the manuscript, and carried it with him on his diplomatic mission to France in 1784. There he commissioned a small private printing, which appeared in 1785 without his name. Despite his efforts to restrict the circulation of the *Notes*, plans for a pirated French translation soon forced him to supervise an official translation, which was completed in early 1787. He then authorized an English edition, which was published in London by John Stockdale and appeared later in 1787, this time with the author's name.

Perhaps the best single expression of Jefferson's ideas, the *Notes* goes beyond its rubric of answering questions from a foreign government about American landscape, customs, and institutions, and advocates a specifically Jeffersonian program: religious toleration, emancipation of slaves, an agrarian ideal. Jefferson also describes the legal history of the colonies, especially Virginia, including an account of the events leading up to the *Declaration of Independence*. One of his recurrent concerns in the *Notes* is the nature of and possibilities for civilization in the new world. He devotes a long section, complete with tables, to disproving the assertion of the French naturalist Buffon that American animal species – including human beings – are smaller and fewer than the European. He also defends America against the charge that it has not yet produced any literary masters, reminding critics that it is still too young and sparsely populated. As part of his defense, Jefferson discusses both American black slaves and American Indians, with an eye to distinguishing innate elements of character from the influences of environment on cultural achievement. Although his purpose is to show that many of the differences between these two groups and European whites are appropriate to each group's surroundings, his attitude is a mixture of condescension and regard.

Part of his evidence in support of Indians is a narration of the murders by the Cresap party of the family of John Logan, an Indian previously friendly to whites, and of Logan's subsequent revenge and eloquent speech of protest. This section in particular prompted controversy and criticism, especially on the part of Jefferson's enemies, who defended Cresap's innocence and sometimes accused Jefferson of writing Logan's speech himself. These criticisms prompted Jefferson to research the matter more thoroughly, and in the 1800 edition of *Notes* he added an appendix which printed documents showing that although Cresap's party might not have been responsible for those particular murders, he and other whites had certainly been guilty of Indian killings at that time.

O

Oates, Joyce Carol 1938–   A novelist, poet, short-story writer, and critic, Oates was born in Lockport, New York, in the "Eden County" of many of her novels. She received a BA from Syracuse University in 1960 and an MA from the University of Wisconsin in 1961. She has taught English at the University of Detroit, the University of Windsor, Ontario, and at Princeton.

Her intense, often violent vision is perhaps most powerfully expressed in the novel *Wonderland* (1971), which is structured around Lewis Carroll's Alice stories, and in the loosely arranged trilogy, *A Garden of Earthly Delights* (1967), *Expensive People* (1968), and *them* (1969, National Book Award). Her other novels are *With Shuddering Fall* (1964), *The Assassins: A Book of Hours* (1975), *Bellefleur* (1980), *Angel of Light* (1981), *A Bloodsmoor Romance* (1982), *Mysteries of Winterthurn* (1984), and *Solstice* (1985). Her short-story collections are *By the North Gate* (1963); *The Wheel of Love* (1970), which includes the often anthologized "Where are You Going, Where have You Been" and "The Region of Ice"; *The Goddess and Other Women* (1974); *The Seduction and Other Stories* (1975); and *Last Days* (1984). Her essays and criticism have appeared in several volumes, including *The Edge of Impossibility: Tragic Forms in Literature* (1972), *The Hostile Sun: The Poetry of D. H. Lawrence* (1973), and *Contraries: Essays* (1981). Her volumes of poetry include *Women in Love, and Other Poems* (1968) and *Anonymous Sins, and Other Poems* (1969).

Objectivism   The Objectivist movement grew up in reaction against that of **Imagism**. The poets concerned – **George Oppen**, **Louis Zukofsky, Charles Reznikoff**, and **William Carlos Williams** – believed that the principles of Imagism were too vague, being applicable to almost any conceivable idea. Instead, they emphasized the importance of the poem as a physical object, and this led to an increased attention to typography as well as to the use of more conventional poetic devices. *An "Objectivists" Anthology* appeared in 1932, but the movement was not popular, and it disbanded soon after this publication.

O'Brien, Fitz-James *c.*1828–62   Born in Ireland, O'Brien was already an experienced journalist when he emigrated to the US in 1852. There he established a popular reputation as a writer of short stories in the fantastic vein, of which his most famous, "The Diamond Lens," was published in *The Atlantic Monthly* in 1858. It tells of an inventor who creates a powerful microscope, becomes obsessed with the vision of a human-like figure in a drop of liquid, and goes mad when the creature dies. O'Brien also published a play, *A Gentleman from Ireland* (1858). He fought in the Civil War and died at the battle of Bloomery Gap. The posthumous collection *Poems and Stories* appeared in 1881.

O'Connor, Flannery 1925–64   Born in Savannah, Georgia, O'Connor was educated at Georgia State College for Women and also studied at the Writers' Workshop at the University of Iowa. She suffered from a terminal illness, lupus, for much of her adult life and was frequently hospitalized and in great pain until her death at the age of 39.

Despite the brevity of her career, however, she made a strong impression on the American literary scene, and exerted considerable influence on the development of the American short story. Her own Southern origins and devout Roman Catholic faith are evident throughout her fiction, in which she often uses poor, disabled, or socially marginal characters involved in absurd and violent situations to convey the spiritual poverty and crippled intellect of the modern world. Her vision of violent spiritual struggle in the rural South is marked by a grotesque humor and unnerving irony. Her first novel, *Wise Blood* (1952), tells the story of Hazel Motes, the lonely prophet of a "church without Christ, where the blind stay blind, the lame stay lame, and them that's dead stays that way." Another novel, *The Violent Bear It Away*, was published in 1960. Her short stories are collected in *A Good Man is Hard to Find* (1955, published in England in 1959 as *The Artificial Nigger and Other Stories*) and the posthumously published *Everything That Rises Must Converge* (1965). *Mystery and Manners: Occasional Prose* appeared in 1969, her *Complete Stories* in 1971, and a collection of her letters, *The Habit of Being*, in 1979.

Octopus, The: *A Story of California* A novel by **Frank Norris**, published in 1901, the first part of his uncompleted trilogy *The Epic of the Wheat*.

The octopus of the title is the Pacific and Southwestern Railroad, which in the course of the story economically strangles the wheat farmers of California, who are led by Magnus Derrick, the owner of a large ranch near the town of Bonneville. The railroad is the most powerful vested interest in the state; it dominates the government, gains total control of Bonneville, and is behind the movement of all prices and interest rates. Many of the farmers hold their land on option from the railroad, and it dispossesses them at will; it also manipulates freight charges to lower the price of wheat and thereby ruin other farmers when it wants their land too. Derrick's direct opponent is the railroad agent Behrman, who is eventually suffocated when he falls into the wheat he has plundered from the ruined and dispossessed farmers, wheat that he was intending to sell at a huge profit. Derrick himself is ruined when the railroad succeeds in bribing his son Lyman, a lawyer on the state commission, to act against the farmers' interests. Other leading characters are Dyke, the railroad engineer who wants to be a farmer, and Shelgrim, the railroad president, who blandly tells the protesting poet, Presley, that what has happened has nothing to do with the people – it is all a matter of economic forces and the law of supply and demand.

Octoroon, The See **Boucicault, Dion**

Odets, Clifford 1906–63 Born in Philadelphia, the son of middle-class Jewish immigrants, Odets grew up rather unhappily in the Bronx. He left school at the age of 17 to become an actor, working in radio and playing small parts in stock companies and then in **Theatre Guild** productions. In 1931 he was one of the younger Theatre Guild members, along with Harold Clurman, Lee Strasberg, and Stella and Luther Adler, who formed the **Group Theatre**. As the name indicates, they were committed to the idea of collaborative production, rather than the more common "star system"; they were also interested in Marxist approaches to drama and devoted to Stanislavsky's theories of acting.

At first, Odets participated in the Group Theatre simply as an actor, taking small parts; one act of his play *Awake and Sing!* was given a trial reading in 1933 but rejected for production. Then in 1935 he wrote *Waiting for Lefty* in response to a New Theatre League contest for one-act plays. He won the contest and was rewarded with a production. It was an instant success; the Group Theatre reconsidered and produced *Awake and Sing!* (1935), followed by a double bill of *Waiting for Lefty* and *Till The Day I Die*, a short anti-Nazi play Odets wrote quickly for the purpose. His career as playwright and champion of the underprivileged was launched.

He joined the Communist party in 1934, but soon resigned; he later told the House Un-American Activities Committee that he had found it impossible to write in line with a party program, and that his sympathy for the working classes was due to family experience rather than party ideology. His second full-length play, *Paradise Lost* (1935), dealt with the disintegration of a middle-class family as a result of the Depression. He then accepted a lucrative offer to become a Hollywood screenwriter, but returned to New York to see a new play, *Golden Boy* (1937), through production by the Group Theatre. This play, which was to be his greatest commercial success, is the story of Joe Bonaparte, a talented young Italian violinist who chooses to become a prizefighter, thereby destroying his talent, his integrity, and finally himself and the woman he loves. Of Odets's later plays, *Rocket to the Moon* (1938) explores a dentist's mid-life crisis; *Night Music* (1940) is a story of distrustful love between alienated people in Hollywood; *Clash By Night* (1941) depicts a love triangle which ends in murder. *The Big Knife* (1949) concerns Charlie Castle, a Hollywood actor who has compromised his ideals; in *The Country Girl* (1950), another love triangle centers on a self-pitying, alcoholic actor struggling to make a comeback. Odets's last play, *The Flowering Peach* (1954), retells the story of Noah's ark.

Of Mice and Men See **Steinbeck, John**

O'Hara, Frank 1926–66 Poet, playwright, and art critic, born in Baltimore, Maryland, and educated at Harvard and the University of Michigan. He was associated with the **New York School** of poets, much of his poetry dealing with specifically urban themes. He was also associate curator of exhibitions of painting and sculpture at the Museum of Modern Art in New York City.

His first book of verse, *A City Winter and Other Poems*, was published in 1952. His other volumes are *Meditations in an Emergency* (1957), *Odes* (1960), *Lunch Poems* (1964), and *Love Poems* (1965). His plays are *Try, Try!* (produced in 1951), *Changing Your Bedding* (produced in 1952), *Awake in Spain* (1960), *Love's Labor* (produced 1960, published 1964), and *The General Returns From One Place to Another* (1964). *Collected Poems* (1971), *Poems Retrieved* (1977), and *Selected Plays* (1978) were published posthumously.

O'Hara, John 1905–70 A novelist, short-story writer, and screenwriter, O'Hara was born in Pottsville, Pennsylvania, a town which later figured as the "Gibbsville" of his fiction. He planned to attend Yale University, but was prevented by his father's death in 1925. In 1927 he went to Montana, then worked briefly in Chicago, and finally settled in New York City, where he became a journalist for the *Daily Mirror* and *Herald Tribune*, and had pieces published in *The New Yorker* in 1928.

His first novel, *Appointment in Samarra* (1934), is set in Gibbsville and is a naturalistic account of three days that culminate in the suicide of Julian English, the victim of a stratified society and of his own reckless sexual appetite. The book was well received, and in the same year O'Hara embarked on a career as a screenwriter in Hollywood which lasted

until the mid 1940s. *Butterfield 8* (1935) is a novel about the experiences of a Manhattan newspaperman. *Pal Joey*, published in 1940 and adapted as a musical in the same year, consists of a comic series of letters from a nightclub entertainer to a friend. O'Hara's other novels include *A Rage to Live* (1949), *Ten North Frederick* (1955, National Book Award), *From the Terrace* (1959), *Ourselves to Know* (1960), *The Big Laugh* (1962), and *The Lockwood Concern* (1965). *Sermons and Soda Water*, a collection of three novellas, was published in 1960.

O'Hara's short stories, like his novels, often focus on questions of class and social privilege. His collections include *The Doctor's Son* (1935), *Files on Parade* (1939), *Pipe Night* (1945), *Hellbox* (1947), *Assembly* (1961), *The Cape Cod Lighter* (1962), *The Horse Knows the Way* (1964), and *Waiting for Winter* (1967). His drama was published in *Five Plays* (1961). He received the American Academy of Arts and Letters Award of Merit in 1964. Two volumes appeared posthumously: *Selected Letters of John O'Hara* (1978), and an edition of previously uncollected essays entitled *"An Artist is His Own Fault": John O'Hara on Writers and Writing* (1977).

Oh Dad, Poor Dad, . . . See **Kopit, Arthur L.**

Old Creole Days A collection of seven stories of life in 19th-century Louisiana by **George Washington Cable**, published in 1879. (A short novel, **Madame Delphine**, was added in later editions.) The chief setting is the old French section of New Orleans populated by Creoles, Cubans, Spaniards, and Santo Domingan refugees, as well as by incoming groups of Germans, Irish, and Sicilians. Cable was especially adept in transcribing the varied dialects of the region, but his plots often take a sentimental or melodramatic turn. A typical tale, "Jean-ah Poquelin," set in the first decade of the century, deals with a once wealthy indigo planter, who now lives a secluded life on his decayed estate near the edge of the burgeoning settlement. Because of the unexplained disappearance of his half-brother and his militant refusal to let anyone trespass on his property, he has gained a reputation as an evil man who has some great wickedness to hide. After combatting the efforts of an "improvement company" to take over his house and land, he dies; it is then discovered that he has for many years concealed and cared for his half-brother, now an aged and helpless leper. The collection ends with a rather more domestic tale, "Madame Délicieuse." It concerns a long-standing quarrel between Madame Délicieuse's fiancé, Dr Mossy, a forward-looking young man who champions scientific advances, and his father, General Villivicencio, who is waging a campaign for public office to restore old Bourbon values and to purge New Orleans of Yankee ideals. Madame Délicieuse, a Creole beauty, engineers a reconciliation between father and son, thus making her marriage possible. The other stories in the volume are "Café des Exiles," "Belle Demoiselle Plantation," "Posson Jone'," "Tite Poulette," and "Sieur George."

Old Man and the Sea, The   See **Hemingway, Ernest**

Oldtown Folks   A novel by **Harriet Beecher Stowe**, published in 1869, and set in the fictional Oldtown, Massachusetts, during the post-Revolutionary period. The young Horace Holyoke narrates the rather conventional romance plot about two runaway children who find happiness in spite of their oppressive upbringing in a leading Oldtown family. Holyoke's spiritual turn of mind makes him particularly attentive to the town's religious life. Both children are adopted into clerical families. The boy, Henry, becomes an Anglican minister. Tina marries Davenport, a dashing aristocratic officer, who resembles Aaron Burr. But when Davenport is killed in a duel she eventually marries Holyoke. Other memorable citizens are Parson and "Lady" Lothrop; and Sam Lawson, whose offhanded commentary provides the novel's comic perspective.

Olsen, Tillie 1913–   Olsen did not publish her first book, a collection of stories entitled *Tell Me A Riddle* (1962), until she was nearly 50. Most of her work draws on her experiences as a working-class wife, mother, wage-earner, and labor activist in San Francisco – experiences which provided the emotional sources and raw material for her writing, but which also, as she explains in *Silences* (1978), deprived her of the undivided time, space, and energy necessary to write. The title story of *Tell Me A Riddle*, an often-anthologized feminist classic, portrays a working-class grandmother at the end of her life retrospectively reviewing her early political and personal aspirations and their gradual fragmentation and frustration by the competing claims of her role as wife and mother. Of the other stories, "I Stand Here Ironing" presents, through an interior monologue, a working-class mother's mingled anxiety and pride about her "problem" daughter; "Hey Sailor, What Ship?" shows the disintegration through disillusion and drink of a sailor's dreams; and "Oh, Yes" anatomizes the cultural implantation of racism in children through a story of two small girls, one white and one black, and their mothers. All the stories draw the reader into an understanding of oppression by presenting it through the eyes of the oppressed.

In 1974 Olsen published a novel, *Yonnondio: From The Thirties*, reconstructed from a manuscript begun some 40 years earlier but abandoned and then lost. *Yonnondio* is of the 1930s in both its material and its approach. It is the story, seen through the eyes of a young girl, of a poor family's journey from a mining town to a tenant farm to the slums of an industrial city in an unsuccessful search for a way out of poverty and despair, an unrelenting analysis of the economic roots of oppression. Olsen's collection of essays, *Silences* (1978), draws on both personal and literary sources to explain how social and economic pressures prevent members of oppressed groups from becoming writers, and why the proportion of women writers in the 20th century is still, in her formulation, only "One Out of Twelve." Since emerging from her own silence, in addition to writing she has taught in women's studies programs around the country.

Olson, Charles 1910–70   Born in Worcester, Massachusetts, Olson attended both Harvard and Yale, and finally received a BA (1932) and MA (1933) from Wesleyan. He taught at Clark University in Worcester, and at Harvard from 1936 to 1939. His first book, *Call Me Ishmael*, was published in 1947; a study of **Herman Melville**, and particularly of *Moby-Dick*, it was fiercely unacademic in structure – more of a prose poem than a piece of criticism.

In 1948 he took a position at the experimental **Black Mountain** College in North Carolina, and from 1951 to 1956 was rector there. Early in his tenure he published an essay entitled "Projective Verse" (1950), in which he advocated the use of "open forms" and "composition by field," arguing that the structure of lines should not be determined by metrical feet but by the breath of the poet. The essay was widely influential and attracted a number of poets to Black Mountain, including **Robert Creeley**, **Denise Levertov**, **Robert Duncan**. The criticism and verse of these writers was published in *Black Mountain Review*.

Olson's major poetic achievements were the Maximus Poems, the first of which he published in 1953, signalling the start of a project which would last until 1968. The mosaic structure of **Ezra Pound**'s *Cantos* provided a formal model, and **William Carlos Williams**'s *Paterson* provided a theme. Like *Paterson*, the Maximus Poems focused on a single town – in this case, Gloucester, Massachusetts – in which the central figure, Maximus, attempts to discover the energies which shape both personal and social history. The various volumes of the project are *The Maximus Poems 1–10* (1953); *The Maximus Poems 11–22* (1956); a single edition containing poems 1–22 simply entitled *The Maximus Poems* (1960); *Maximus, from Dogtown I* (1961); *Maximus Poems IV, V, VI* (1968); and the posthumously published *The Maximus Poems: Volume Three* (1975). The first complete edition of the series, *The Maximus Poems*, was published in 1983.

Olson's other books of verse include *To Corrado Cagli* (1947), *y & x* (1948), *Letter for Melville* (1951), *This* (1952), *In Cold Hell, in Thicket* (1953), *O'Ryan 1 2 3 4 5 6 7 8 9 10* (1965), *Selected Writings* (1967), *Archaeologist of Morning: The Collected Poems Outside the Maximus Series* (1970). His prose works include *Mayan Letters* (1953), *Human Universe and Other Essays* (1965), *Causal Mythology* (1969), and *The Special View of History* (1970). *Projective Verse* (1959) and *Poetry and Truth: The Beloit Lectures and Poems* (1971) are books of criticism. *Charles Olson and Robert Creeley: The Complete Correspondence* was published in 1980.

Omoo; a Narrative of Adventures in the South Seas A novel by **Herman Melville**, published in 1847, and inspired by the author's second whaling voyage, which was beset by a dry whaling season, a sick captain, and an unsuccessful mutiny. A sequel to the controversial *Typee*, and accepted only reluctantly by the publisher, it incited new attacks by critics who objected to Melville's depiction of the failure of missionary work in Tahiti.

The nameless narrator is rescued from the sea after his flight from the Marquesas and signs on the crew of the *Julia*, the ship whose boat has picked him up. The *Julia* proves to be unseaworthy, and her captain ill and unstable, but the narrator makes friends with the mate, Jermin, and with the worldly and cheerful Dr Long Ghost. In Tahiti the crew members refuse to take the ship to sea again and are imprisoned. The narrator and the doctor are released and manage to find work on a plantation in Imeeo. Finding that fieldwork is not to their liking, they resort to beachcombing, at the same time exploring the island and observing the people. At the end the doctor stays on in Tahiti while the narrator ships out on the whaler *Leviathan*.

One Flew Over the Cuckoo's Nest A novel by **Ken Kesey**, published in 1962, that inquires into the dehumanizing effects of modern society by examining the lives of inmates in a psychiatric ward. The story is told from the viewpoint of an ex-reservation Indian named Bromden, who pretends to be deaf and dumb in order to remain as far from the center of activity as possible. The inmates are kept in place by their dread of Big Nurse, the authority figure who rules their lives. Into this scene comes the reckless, ingenious, and defiant McMurphy. The novel describes how under his leadership the inmates rebel against Big Nurse, the climax – and McMurphy's triumph – coming when they sneak out for a trip on a yacht. Soon after this incident, however, McMurphy – who is increasingly seen as a troublemaker the institution can do without – has a lobotomy performed on him by the doctors. Bromden, who has grown immeasurably under McMurphy's influence, cannot bear to see him in this state. He smothers him out of rage and pity, and then heaves a panel of medical equipment through a window to make his escape.

O'Neill, Eugene (Gladstone) 1888–1953 Dramatist, born in New York City, the younger son of James O'Neill, a popular actor. As a child he toured with his father, and attended a Catholic boarding school and a preparatory school in Connecticut. He enrolled at Princeton University for one year (1906–7), then held a series of jobs including prospecting for gold, several months as a seaman on a Norwegian freighter, and a brief spell as a journalist in Connecticut. He then spent time in a tuberculosis sanatorium (1912–13), and his early one-act plays date from this period of confinement. His involvement with the Provincetown Players brought him, and the company, to the attention of the New York public, initially with a sequence of plays about the S.S. *Glencairn* and its crew: *Bound East for Cardiff* (1916), *In the Zone* (1917), *The Long Voyage Home* (1917), and *The Moon of the Caribees* (1918). Two other plays, not in the Glencairn cycle but drawing on his memories of life at sea, won Pulitzer Prizes in 1920 and 1922 – *Beyond the Horizon* (1920) and *Anna Christie* (1921, first produced as *Chris* in 1920).

O'Neill went on to become a major influence on the development of the modern American theatre, exploring difficult subjects and experimenting with a variety of dramatic styles. Black Americans made up the cast of *The Dreamy Kid* (1919); an interracial marriage is the subject of *All God's Chillun Got Wings* (1924); and in *The Emperor Jones* (1920) a black actor dominates the stage in the central role. The expressionism of *The Emperor Jones* is further developed in *The Hairy Ape* (1922), in which a ship's stoker's alienation from his peers causes him to embrace his own animality, and in the mask-drama *The Great God Brown* (1926). *Strange Interlude* (1928), which won O'Neill a third Pulitzer Prize, portrays the life of its central character, Nina Leeds, through the juxtaposition of conventional dialogue with stylized internal monologue. O'Neill's interest in the familial patterns of Greek tragedy and in Nietzsche's opposition of the Apollonian and the Dionysian is evident in the grim New England tragedy *Desire Under the Elms* (1924), and is the motive force behind *Mourning Becomes Electra* (1931), a reworking of Aeschylus' *Oresteia* in the context of the American Civil War.

After the failure of *Days Without End* (1934), O'Neill, suffering from increasing ill-health

which was eventually diagnosed as Parkinson's disease, maintained a long theatrical silence, unbroken by the award of the Nobel Prize in 1936. *The Iceman Cometh* (1946), his first new play to be performed for 12 years, is set in a Bowery bar. *Long Day's Journey Into Night* (first performed 1956, Pulitzer Prize 1957) is a tortured but compassionate portrait of his own family, a subject he had treated more lightly and with nostalgia in the comedy *Ah, Wilderness!* (1933). *A Moon for the Misbegotten* (first performed 1957) continues the story of the alcoholic elder brother of *Long Day's Journey Into Night*, describing the process of his self-destruction on a Connecticut farm following his mother's death. Of a projected 11-play cycle which was to trace the fortunes of an American family from the 18th to the 20th centuries, only *A Touch of the Poet* (first performed 1957) and the incomplete *More Stately Mansions* (first performed 1962) were actually written. *Hughie*, the single play of another projected series, was first performed in 1958.

One-Third of a Nation See **Living Newspaper**

On the Road A semi-autobiographical novel by **Jack Kerouac**, published in 1957. One of the most fundamental and popular statements of the **Beat** movement, it tells of a group of friends traveling around America in search of new and intense experiences. The chaos, exhilaration, and despair of the quest is conveyed by the headlong style of Sal Paradise's narration. Sal accompanies his friends on four separate trips as they travel the country, spending time in Colorado, California, Virginia, New York, and Mexico. Several of the characters are modeled on Kerouac's friends: Dean Moriarty, the guiding spirit of the group, is Neal Cassady; Carlo Marx is **Allen Ginsberg**. Sal's view of Dean as an inspired genius suffers as Dean mistreats his wife and lovers, is deceitful, and finally abandons Sal in Mexico. Nothing substantial seems to have been gained; by the end of the novel Dean is mad and Sal is back in New York.

O Pioneers! A novel by **Willa Cather**, published in 1913, the story of Alexandra Bergson, the eldest daughter of Swedish immigrants who live on the Nebraska Divide. After her father dies, Alexandra, in her early

20s, manages the Bergson farm and homestead. Her innovative farming ideas meet resistance from her conservative brothers Oscar and Lou, but after the division of the land upon their marriages, Alexandra's fields flourish, and she becomes rich enough to send her youngest brother Emil to college. She develops a close relationship with a young Bohemian woman, Marie Tovesky, who lives with her husband on a neighboring farm, once the home of Alexandra's childhood sweetheart, Carl Linstrum. Carl, who had left the Divide years ago when he moved east with his parents, returns to visit Alexandra and then travels west to California. Emil graduates from the University of Nebraska and decides to visit Mexico. Back from his travels, he becomes romantically involved with Marie Tovesky. One day Marie's husband finds the two lovers together in a field, and shoots them in a rage. Hearing of the tragedy, Carl returns and marries Alexandra.

Oppen, George 1908–84 Born in New Rochelle, New York, Oppen was educated in California. His first volume of poems, *Discrete Series*, was published in 1934; his second, *The Materials*, not until 1962. During the intervening years he was involved in political activity; he became a member of the Communist party in 1935, and in 1950 he moved to Mexico to escape pressure from the US government to inform on friends in the Party.

He was closely associated with the **Objectivist** School, and was instrumental in providing a forum for new poets through the publishing house (called "To Publishers") which he founded and operated with his wife from 1930 to 1933. He was also a member of the Objectivist Press Co-op in New York from 1934 to 1936. During the next 15 years he worked in a factory in Detroit and as a cabinet maker in Los Angeles, and was a member of the Workers' Alliance in Brooklyn and Utica, New York.

He was particularly concerned with how poetry should communicate the realization of concrete objects without drawing attention to itself, formally, as poetry – as artifact. His own verse is characterized by its clarity of images and its lean and precise diction. His other volumes include *This in Which* (1965), *Of Being Numerous* (1968, Pulitzer Prize),

Alpine (1969), *Seascape: Needle's Eye* (1972), and *Primitive* (1978). *The Collected Poems of George Oppen, 1929–1975* was published in 1975. In 1980 he received the American Academy and Institute of Arts and Letters award.

Oregon Trail, The The record of a journey by **Francis Parkman** and his cousin Quincy Adams Shaw in 1846, published serially in *The Knickerbocker Magazine* from 1847 to 1849. It appeared in volume form as *The California and Oregon Trail* in 1849, but the 1872 edition restored the original title. The 1872 edition also contains Parkman's corrections of the original, which – being too ill at the time to write himself – he had dictated to Shaw.

Parkman and Shaw set out from St Louis in April, 1846. Accompanied by a guide, Henry Chatillon, and a muleteer named Deslauriers, they explored portions of the northern Great Plains and Rocky Mountains. Traveling along both the Mormon and Oregon trails, the group encountered wagon trains of emigrants, Indians, Mormons, hunters, trappers, traders, and buffalo. They traveled as far west as Fort Laramie, Wyoming. Excited by rumors that a Sioux chief, "The Whirlwind" (Tunica), was planning to make war against the Snake Indians, Parkman planned to witness the event and was disappointed when the attack was called off. Leaving Shaw behind, he joined a band of "Ogillallah" (Oglala) Sioux for a hunting excursion and lived among them for several weeks. Early in August he rejoined Shaw at Fort Laramie and they began their return trip. They traveled south through Colorado, crossing below Pike's Peak and heading toward the Arkansas River, then journeyed eastward along the Arkansas to Missouri, arriving in St Louis in late September.

Ormond See **Brown, Charles Brockden**

Ortiz, Simon 1941– Born in Albuquerque, New Mexico, Ortiz was raised in the Acoma Pueblo community. He was educated through the Bureau of Indian Affairs and, later, Catholic school systems. He attended Ft Lewis College, the University of New Mexico at Albuquerque, and the University of Iowa, where he was a fellow in the International Writing Program. He is widely recognized as one of the leading

American Indian poets and fiction writers, and his work reflects a strong concern for Indian civil rights. His volumes of poetry include *Naked in the Wind* (1970), *Going for the Rain* (1976), *Fight Back: For the Sake of the People, For the Sake of the Land* (1980), and *From Sand Creek* (1981). His volumes of stories include *Howbah Indians* (1977).

Other Voices, Other Rooms   See **Capote, Truman**

Our Town   A Pulitzer Prize-winning play by **Thornton Wilder**, first performed in New York in 1938. Its three acts treat Daily Life, Love and Marriage, and Death, respectively, in the small New Hampshire town of Grover's Corners and focus on two families in particular: the Gibbses and the Webbs. Each act is played without curtain or scenery and is introduced by the Stage Manager in a direct address to the audience.

The first act takes place on May 7, 1901; as it begins the Stage Manager describes the town, and introduces the first characters as they appear on stage and go about the business of starting a new day in Grover's Corners. Act Two, set three years later, traces the courtship and marriage of George Gibbs and Emily Webb and the reaction to this of the older generation. By the third act, which is set in the town cemetery, a further nine years have passed, and the Stage Manager begins by describing the changes they have brought to the town. The central event of the act is Emily's funeral, which is followed by the reactions of both the living and the dead. The occupants of the cemetery are present on stage but remain invisible to the living characters. The voices of the dead are the last heard, as they comment on man's foolishness, his inability to understand the events which

structure his life, and his ignorance of the nature and meaning of death.

Overland Monthly   Founded in 1868 and published in San Francisco, *Overland Monthly* was intended to give California and the West a serious magazine and review of the quality of those of New England and the Atlantic states. For the first two-and-a-half years it was edited by **Bret Harte**. It continued in its original form until 1875; then after a hiatus was revived in 1883, absorbing *The Californian* at the same time. It published the work of writers such as **Jack London**, **Edwin Markham**, and **Frank Norris**, and lasted until 1935.

Ozick, Cynthia 1928–   Born in New York City, Ozick received her BA from New York University in 1949 and her MA from Ohio State University in 1950. Her first novel, *Trust*, was published in 1966. Written in the first person, it is the story of the unnamed daughter of Allegra Vand, who searches for the father whom her mother has prevented her from knowing; she no sooner finds him than he dies. *The Pagan Rabbi and Other Stories* followed in 1971. Both this volume and *Bloodshed and Three Novellas* (1976) reflect Ozick's interest in mysticism and the supernatural. In 1981 she published another collection of short works, *Levitation: Five Fictions*. She is perhaps best known as a writer of short stories, and has twice received the O. Henry Award (1975 and 1980). Her most recent publications, however, are *Art and Ardor: Essays* (1983) and a novel entitled *The Cannibal Galaxy* (1983). Her fiction explores the dilemmas of being Jewish in a Christian world. She often expresses her ambivalence about writing in English (which, as she notes, is a Christian language) and her fear that creating fictions is itself an act of idolatry.

P

Page, Thomas Nelson 1853–1922 Page began his career as a lawyer in Virginia, but soon turned to literature. His work is characterized by its preoccupation with the Old South, whose aristocratic ideals he sentimentalized in much of his writing. *In Ole Virginia; or, Marse Chan and Other Stories*, a collection of short stories, was published in 1887. It was followed by two novels, *On Newfound River* (1891) and *Red Rock; A Chronicle of Reconstruction* (1898). The latter focused on the hardship the Reconstruction period caused to southerners, and became a best seller. Others of his works are *Two Little Confederates* (1888), a children's story; *The Old South: Essays, Social and Political* (1892); *Social Life in Old Virginia Before the War* (1897), essays; *Gordon Keith* (1902) and *John Marvel, Assistant* (1909), two novels; and *Robert E. Lee, Man and Soldier* (1911), a biography. Page became the US ambassador to Italy in 1913. His last works were *The Land of Spirit* (1913), *Life of Thomas Jefferson* (1918), and *Italy and the World War* (1920).

Paine, Thomas 1737–1809 Born in Thetford, Norfolk, England, to an Anglican mother and a Quaker father who ran a small farm and made corsets, Paine attended school until the age of 13, when he became an apprentice in his father's shop. Following an unsuccessful attempt to run away to sea in 1756, he began work as a staymaker in 1757 and two years later opened his own shop in Sandwich, Kent. He became a customs officer in 1764, but was dismissed in the following year because of his attempts to organize workers. He then moved to London and taught school until 1768, when he was reappointed to excise service in the district of Lewes, Sussex. The publication of his first pamphlet, *The Case of the Officers of Excise* (1772), and his continued activity as a labor agitator led to his dismissal from the post in 1774. He returned to London immediately, and there met **Benjamin Franklin**, who in the same year sent him to America with letters of introduction.

Paine arrived in Philadelphia as a confirmed radical. As editor of *The Pennsylvania Magazine* he attacked the institution of slavery and advocated independence. *Common Sense* (1776), his most influential pamphlet, demanded an immediate declaration of independence. During the Revolutionary War he served in Washington's army and continued his political writing; *The American Crisis*, a series of pamphlets in defense of the war, appeared between December, 1776 and April, 1783. He became secretary to the Congressional Committee on Foreign Affairs in 1777, but was forced to resign in 1779 after erroneously charging Silas Deane with corruption in his negotiations with France. In 1780 he published *Public Good*, a reiteration of the case for federal union made in *Common Sense* and an objection to the Virginia Plan. After successfully executing a diplomatic mission to France in 1781, he withdrew to his farm in New Rochelle (which the State of New York had given him), where he prepared plans for an iron bridge and wrote *Dissertations on Government*, an attack on paper money and a warning on the dangers of inflation.

When he returned to England in 1787 to promote his iron bridge, he found himself inspired by the impending French Revolution. He replied to Edmund Burke's *Reflections on the Revolution in France* with *The Rights of Man*, a widely circulated tract published in two parts in 1791 and 1792, which attacked hereditary succession. It was labeled seditious; Paine, who had fled to France, was convicted of treason in his absence and sentenced to banishment. In Paris the revolutionary Assembly made him a citizen of France (1792) and a member of the Convention; but he was a moderate republican – a Girondist, not a Jacobin – and when he opposed the King's execution he nearly went to the guillotine himself. Instead, he was deprived of citizenship and arrested. Assuming that he was safer in prison, Gouverneur Morris, the American minister, did not assist him – a decision which Paine viewed as a plot against him and criticized in *A Letter to George Washington* (1796). Following the Reign of Terror, James Monroe secured his release. The years he spent in prison (1793–5) saw the completion of his most famous work, *The Age of Reason* (1794–6). A stark critique of accepted religious beliefs and practices, the work divides into two parts: the first argues that a rational knowledge of God does not accord with traditional conceptions of the Deity; the second illuminates various inconsistencies in the Bible in order to invalidate both literal and figurative readings of the text.

Paine, the patriot in 1776, returned to the US an infidel in 1802. Former friends such as John Quincy Adams ostracized him for his "atheism," and when he died in 1809 he was refused burial in consecrated ground. Interred on his farm at New Rochelle at a funeral which no one of note attended, his body was exhumed ten years later by William Cobbett and transported to England. Cobbett, however, was not allowed to bury the coffin, and after his own death the body disappeared.

Pale Fire See **Nabokov, Vladimir**

Paley, Grace 1922– Born and educated in New York City, Paley began writing the compressed and often highly ironic stories for which she is best known in the 1950s. Earlier, she had written poetry and studied with **W. H. Auden** at the New School for Social Research in New York. Founder of the Greenwich Village Peace Center in 1961, she was a vocal opponent of the Vietnam War, and continues to be active in international movements for peace and social justice. Her volumes of short fiction are *The Little Disturbances of Man* (1959), *Enormous Changes At The Last Minute* (1974), and *Later the Same Day*

(1985). Her stories have also appeared in such periodicals as *The New Yorker*, The *Atlantic Monthly*, *Accent*, *New American Review*, and *Esquire*.

Parable of the Ten Virgins Open'd and Applied See **Shepard, Thomas**

Parker, Dorothy 1893–1967 Born Dorothy Rothschild in West End, New Jersey, she was raised in New York City, where she was educated at a convent, later moving to an exclusive girls' school in Morristown, New Jersey. She married Edwin Parker in 1917 and retained his name after their divorce in 1928. Her first poetry appeared in *Vogue* magazine in 1916. That same year she went to work for *Vogue*, and in 1917 moved on to *Vanity Fair*, where she later served as drama critic (1919–20). In an active career she contributed reviews, articles, columns, poems, and short stories to magazines such as *Esquire*, **The New Yorker, The Nation, The New Republic**, *Cosmopolitan*, *The Saturday Evening Post*, and **The American Mercury**. Her writings are characterized above all by a sardonic wit and irreverent sophistication.

Her first collection of poems, *Enough Rope* (1926), was a best seller. It was followed by two other books of verse, *Sunset Gun* (1928) and *Death and Taxes* (1931). Her collected poems, *Not So Deep As a Well*, were published in 1936. *Laments for the Living* (1930) and *After Such Pleasure* (1933) are collections of short stories. *Here Lies*, published in 1939, contains all her fiction written up to that time. She collaborated with **Elmer Rice** on the play *Close Harmony* (1929) and with Arnaud d'Usseau on *Ladies of the Corridor* (1953). *The Portable Dorothy Parker*, first published in 1944 with an introduction by W. Somerset Maugham, was supplemented by previously unpublished reviews, stories, and articles selected by her friend and executrix **Lillian Hellman** and reissued in 1973. This revised edition was published in England as *The Collected Dorothy Parker* (1973).

Parker, Theodore (1810–60) A Unitarian theologian, pastor, and social reformer, Parker overcame childhood poverty and little early education to become one of the leading figures of the generation prior to the Civil War. Born in Lexington, Massachusetts, he passed the entrance requirement to Harvard in 1830 largely on the basis of his self-acquired learning, but had no money to attend. He was allowed to take courses without enrolling, however, and in 1840 he was awarded an honorary Master of Arts. From 1834 to 1836 he studied at The Harvard Divinity School, and in 1837 he became pastor of the West Roxbury Unitarian Church. During these formative years he steadily drifted from Unitarian orthodoxy, focusing more and more on a personal, intuitive knowledge of God derived from self-knowledge and one's experience of nature. His sermon *The Transient and Permanent in Christianity*, delivered in 1841, denied the authority of the Bible and the supernatural origin of Christ. Christian theological dogma was transient, Christian moral truths permanent. These beliefs were more fully elucidated in *A Discourse of Matters Pertaining to Religion* (1842). Opposition to Parker's liberalism grew, and though he was never formally expelled from the church he resigned his pastorate in 1845 at a meeting of the new Twenty-Eighth Congregational Society of Boston, which was founded by his supporters as a place where "Rev. Parker shall have a chance to be heard." He was installed as pastor there, and for the next 14 years he sought to apply Christian morality to contemporary problems, championing before large crowds such causes as prison reform, temperance, and women's education. His great passion, though, was the abolition of slavery. He delivered strident and moving denunciations of slavery; he was part of the secret committee supporting John Brown; he sheltered and encouraged fugitive slaves. His views on the matter were detailed in *A Letter to the People of the United States Touching the Matter of Slavery* (1848). Probably suffering from tuberculosis, he sailed to Europe, where he died in Florence in 1860.

Parkman,   Francis   (Jr)   1823–93 Descended from established New England families on both sides, Parkman was born in Boston. He graduated from Harvard in 1844 and received his law degree in 1846. Instead of pursuing a legal career, however, he became a historian. In spite of a chronic nervous disorder he traveled extensively in the wilds of America, the information gathered during these excursions providing him with material for his historical works. During vacations from college he journeyed through parts of Canada, Maine, New Hampshire, and upstate New York. He also traveled in Europe (November 1843–June 1844), visiting Italy, Switzerland, France, England, and Scotland.

In 1845 *The Knickerbocker Magazine* printed five short pieces by him about his New England camping trips, all published anonymously or under pseudonyms. He spent the summer of that year researching the uprising led by the Ottawa chief Pontiac. During the summer of 1846 he and his cousin Quincy Adams Shaw undertook a 1,700-mile trek over the prairies and into the Rocky Mountains of the American West. He recorded the experiences of this journey in *The Oregon Trail*, which – owing to his extreme ill health at the end of the journey – he had to dictate to Shaw. The book appeared serially in 1847 and as a volume in 1849. Parkman revised and corrected subsequent editions (1872 and 1892).

In 1851, his *History of the Conspiracy of Pontiac* appeared. It was revised and retitled *The Conspiracy of Pontiac and the Indian War After the Conquest of Canada* in 1870. *Vassall Morton* (1856) is Parkman's only novel. After the death of his son in February, 1857 and of his wife in September, 1858, he traveled to Paris to consult a physician about his own health. He remained there for a year and became interested in horticulture, particularly in growing roses. He continued to cultivate roses after his return to the US, and in 1866 published *The Book of Roses*, a horticultural manual.

Having recovered his strength somewhat, he returned to writing his histories of the North American continent, which are now known under the collective title *France and England in North America*. The individual titles in the series are *Pioneers of France in the New World* (1865), *Jesuits in North America in the Seventeenth Century* (1867), *The Discovery of the Great West* (1869, revised and published as *LaSalle and the Discovery of the Great West* in 1878), *The Old Regime in Canada* (1874), *Count Frontenac and New France under Louis XIV* (1877), *Montcalm and Wolfe* (1884), and *A Half-Century of Conflict* (1892). To write these accounts of the French and English presence in America – of the men and policies involved – Parkman researched his subject scrupulously, traveling to the scenes of the events he described whenever possible. However much he admired the courage and stamina of the French, his works are not entirely free of a bias toward what he perceived as Protestant democracy (represented by the English) and against Catholic despotism (represented by the French). *The Journals of Francis Parkman*, edited by Mason Wade, were published in 1947; his letters, edited by Wilbur R. Jacobs, in 1960.

Partisan, The See **Simms, William Gilmore**

Partisan Review, The A literary and political journal, founded in 1934. Originally published independently in New York City, it was affiliated with Rutgers University from 1963 to 1978, since which time it has been affiliated with Boston University. Although politically radical, the founders of the journal wished to maintain an independent Marxist position, and not to make it a party organ. Philip Rahv and William Phillips were the original co-editors. Rahv served until 1969; Phillips still edits the journal. Others who have served on the editorial board at various times include F. W. Dupee, **Mary McCarthy**, George L. K. Morris, Dwight Macdonald, William Barrett, and **Delmore Schwartz**. Linked to its Marxist tendency has been its encouragement of *avant-garde* art. Indeed, it championed "difficult," Modernist art even when other American Marxist publications decried it as decadent. Among the many distinguished contributors to the journal have been André Gide, Leon Trotsky, **W. H. Auden**, **Wallace Stevens**, **William Carlos Williams**, Dylan Thomas, **T. S. Eliot**, George Orwell, **Vladimir Nabokov**, Albert Camus, André Malraux, Stephen Spender, **Robert Penn Warren**, **Saul Bellow**, F. R. Leavis, and Jorge Luis Borges.

Patchen, Kenneth 1911–72 Born in Niles, Ohio, Patchen attended Alexander Meiklejohn's Experimental College at the University of Wisconsin for one year and Commonwealth College in Arkansas for one semester. He published his first volume of poetry, *Before the Brave*, in 1936. His work is not limited to any one type, but includes love poetry, satire, fantasy, and social criticism. He illustrated many of his books himself. Among his subsequent volumes of poetry are *First Will and Testament* (1939), *The Teeth of the Lion* (1942), *Cloth of the Tempest* (1943), *Pictures of Life and Death* (1946), *To Say if You Love Someone* (1948), *Hurrah for Anything* (1957), and *Because It Is* (1960). His prose works include the surrealist allegory *The Journal of Albion Moonlight* (1941), the satirical novel *Memoirs of a Shy Pornographer* (1945), and the novels *Sleepers Awake* (1946) and *See You in the Morning* (1948). His prose poems are collected as *Panels for the Walls of Heaven* (1947) and *The Famous Boating Party* (1954). In 1950 he had to undergo major spinal surgery and was incapacitated for the last two decades of his life, but he continued to write poetry until his death in 1972. His later works are *Collected Poems* (1968), *Aflame and Afun of Walking Faces: Fables and Drawings* (1970), *There's Love All Day: Poems* (1970), *Wonderings* (1971), and *In Quest of Candlelighters* (1972).

Paterson A long poem by **William Carlos Williams**, published in five volumes from 1946 to 1958. The name refers both to a city on the Passaic River near Williams's home town of Rutherford, New Jersey, and to a character in the poem who merges the details of the poet's private life with the public history of the region. Williams said that "all art begins in the local," and in *Paterson* he combines historical documents, newspaper stories, geological surveys, and personal letters in an attempt to localize his material. The dominant image of the poem is that of the Passaic River, which in its fluid, continual movement unites the particulars of human experience with time. *Paterson* is written in free verse using the colloquial rhythms of Williams's "variable foot." Fragments of a sixth book were published posthumously in 1963 as an appendix to the poem.

Pathfinder, The See **Leatherstocking Tales**

Paulding, James Kirke 1778–1860 Paulding grew up in Tarrytown, New York, where his contemporary **Washington Irving** also lived. His sister Julia married William Irving, Washington's brother. Paulding traveled to New York City when he was about 18 years old and lived there for several years with his sister and brother-in-law. He was a co-founder and major contributor to the literary periodical series *Salmagundi* (1807–8), with Washington and William Irving, and went on to write *The Diverting History of John Bull and Brother Jonathan* (1812). An active participant in the Anglo-American literary dispute over the relative merits of the two nations, he staunchly defended the United States. His *The Lay of the Scottish Fiddle* (1813) parodies Sir Walter Scott's narrative poems; *The United States and England* (1815) is a vigorous defense of the younger nation; and *The Backwoodsman* (1818), a long poem written in couplets, celebrates the American frontier spirit.

Appointed by President Madison, Paulding served on the Board of Navy Commissioners (1815–23); under President Van Buren he was Secretary of the Navy (1838–41). In spite of official duties, however, he continued to write. He produced over 70 tales as well as five novels: *Konigsmarke* (1823), *The Dutchman's Fireside* (1831), *Westward Ho!* (1832), *The Old Continental* (1846), and *The Puritan and His Daughter* (1849).

Payne, John Howard 1791–1852   Born in New York City and educated in Boston and at Union College, Schenectady, Payne's precocity was displayed both in his writing – *Julia; or The Wanderer* (1806) was staged in New York when Payne was 14 – and in his acting. However, after a much-praised debut on the New York stage in 1809, following which he played Hamlet, Romeo, and other leading roles with great success, he found it increasingly hard to sustain his reputation as an actor, and in 1813 he embarked for England.

His version of August von Kotzebue's *Lover's Vows* (1809) had been successful, so he continued to write and adapt plays in addition to acting. *Trial Without Jury* (1815), an adaptation from the French, better known by its alternative title *The Maid and the Magpie*, was followed by several other adaptations and then by *Brutus; or, The Fall of Tarquin* (1818), a clever compilation from several sources, which provided Edmund Kean with one of his more notable roles. In 1820, having failed as manager of Sadler's Wells Theatre, Payne was imprisoned for debt. The successful production of *Thérèse, the Orphan of Geneva* (1821), which he wrote in prison, bought his release, and he settled in Paris. The success of *Clari; or The Maid of Milan* (1823), which contained the famous "Home Sweet Home," set to music by Henry Bishop, encouraged him to return to London, where he collaborated on a number of plays with **Washington Irving**, including *Charles the Second* (1824).

After his return to New York in 1832, Payne wrote little for the theatre, becoming increasingly embittered about the lack of opportunity for writers on the American stage. He collected voluminous notes on the Cherokee Indians, but published none of them during his lifetime. (Grant Foreman edited *Indian Justice: A Cherokee Murder Trial* in 1934.) His service to American letters was recognized by his appointment as US consul in Tunis, 1842–5 and 1851–2.

Peabody, Elizabeth 1804–94   An educator and writer, Peabody was among the leading literary women of her day. Born and raised in Massachusetts, she began teaching school when she was 16. At 18 she opened a school in Boston and began to meet many of the influential New England literati, including **Ralph Waldo Emerson** and **William Ellery Channing**. After serving for many years as Channing's close assistant, in 1834 she began to assist **Bronson Alcott** at his experimental Temple School. The following year she anonymously published *Record of a School*. In 1839 she opened the bookshop in Boston that established her as an important member of the **Transcendentalist** movement; the only source of foreign books in the city, her shop became a center of Boston intellectual life. From 1839 to 1844 she hosted **Margaret Fuller**'s famous conversational classes. The planning of the **Brook Farm** experiment also took place there. At about the same time she introduced **Nathaniel Hawthorne** to her sister Sophia, with the result that Hawthorne soon became a brother-in-law. Another sister later married Horace Mann. Meanwhile, from the printing press in the back of her shop, she published three of Hawthorne's books, several of Margaret Fuller's translations of German works, and from 1842 to 1843 the Transcendentalist journal *The Dial*. She contributed several articles to *The Dial*, but devoted most of her writing to textbooks of grammar and history, including her *Chronological History of the United States* (1856). In 1860 she opened the first American kindergarten, and later published the *Kindergarten Messenger* (1873–7). From 1879 to 1894 she was a member and lecturer at

Bronson Alcott's Concord School of Philosophy. Her final days were spent in support of Indian education, and in putting together *A Last Evening with Allston* (1886), which combines memoirs with her early articles for *The Dial*. Her impact on the Boston literary community is reflected in **Henry James**'s characterization of her as Miss Birdseye in *The Bostonians*.

Percy, Walker 1916–   Born in Alabama, Percy attended the University of North Carolina, received an MD from Columbia, and then embarked on a literary career. Most of his novels are about Southerners, usually alienated individuals in search of fulfillment. His first book, *The Moviegoer* (1961), portrays a New Orleans stockbroker who insulates himself from the real world by going to movies until eventually, during Mardi Gras, a complicated involvement with his neurotic cousin Kate restores him to real life. *The Last Gentleman* (1966) is about a transplanted Southerner who returns home for a visit; in the sequel, *Second Coming* (1980), the same character seeks to affirm the value of his own life in a world which he sees as disintegrating. Percy's novels are often comic, even as they deal with fundamental problems of human experience. *Love in the Ruins* (1971) is a satire about a scientist who seeks to redeem America's mechanistic culture. *Lancelot* (1977) is a darker work, about a man whose quest for self-fulfillment leads him to a murderous arson. Percy's essays on language are collected in *The Message in the Bottle* (1975).

Perelman, S[idney] J[oseph] 1904–79 Perelman was born in Brooklyn and graduated from Brown University in 1925. He soon began writing for *Judge*, and in 1931 published the first of hundreds of articles for *The New Yorker*. The success of his first book, *Dawn Ginsbergh's Revenge* (1929), a collection of prose and cartoons, introduced him to Hollywood, where he wrote comic material for the Marx brothers. He also wrote screenplays for 11 films, notably *Ambush* (1939) and *The Golden Fleecing* (1940) – both with his wife Laura Weinstein, the sister of his friend **Nathanael West**. A sharp and humorous observer and critic of contemporary American society, Perelman published some 20 books, mostly collections of his journalistic pieces. *The Most of S. J. Perelman*

(1958) is a sample of his writing over a 30-year period. He also wrote travel books, including *Westward Ha! or Around the World in Eighty Clichés* (1948) and *Eastward Ha!* (1977).

Piazza Tales, The   A volume of six pieces of short fiction by **Herman Melville**, published in 1856. Except for the title piece, they had all previously been published individually in *Putnam's Monthly* or in *Harper's New Monthly* in the early 1850s.

The volume is introduced by "The Piazza," Melville's descriptive recollection of his Massachusetts farmhouse, to the north side of which he added a piazza; he also recounts a journey to a lonely cottage on a mountain top, which appeared to resemble a fairy land when viewed from the piazza below.

"The Bell Tower" is about an ambitious artist named Bannadonna, who attempts to rival God by creating a mechanical man, and is destroyed by his own creation. "The Lightning-Rod Man" is the story of a man who refuses an insistent lightning-rod salesman because he believes that man should not fear the acts of God.

"The Encantadas; or, Enchanted Isles" contains 10 separate sketches, all concerning the Galapagos Islands. Seven of them are mainly descriptions of the islands, and three are stories of people who live there: a Cuban Creole who acquires the title to Charles's Isle and tyrannizes its inhabitants; a Chola Indian woman who is marooned on Norfolk Island and then rescued by an American ship; and a hermit on Hood's Isle who enslaves deserting sailors until he is himself captured.

"Benito Cereno" is set in 1799. The narrator, Amasa Delano, is a sea captain who puts in to an uninhabited island off the coast of Chile to take on water, and encounters a Spanish ship commanded by a seriously ill Benito Cereno. He listens to Cereno's story of the ship's recent misfortunes at Cape Horn, but suspects something amiss in the unruly and insubordinate behavior of the crew, Cereno's strange relationship with his Senegalese valet Babo, and his ingratitude when Delano offers him aid. As Delano prepares to return to his ship, Cereno suddenly follows him. The crew attack them, but the two captains escape. Cereno then confesses that the apparent crew were in fact slaves, who, led by Babo, had mutinied and demanded that

Cereno take them to Africa. When Cereno had succumbed to fever, the mutineers had planned to seize Delano's ship instead. Delano later succeeds in capturing the slave ship, and takes it to Lima, where Babo is executed. Cereno enters a monastery and dies soon after.

The last of the *Piazza Tales* is "Bartleby." A Wall Street lawyer hires Bartleby as a copyist. Bartleby is pale, quiet, and strange, but extremely diligent in his single task of copying legal documents. To the lawyer's consternation, when Bartleby is asked to do anything other than copy, he replies only, "I would prefer not to." Soon, he would prefer not to leave, and begins to live in the office. Baffled, the lawyer moves his office to another building. The new tenant has Bartleby arrested as a vagrant. He dies in prison within days, resisting the attempts of his former employer to help him. The lawyer later hears that Bartleby had previously worked in the Dead Letter Office in Washington, and ponders on the relevance of this fact to his strange behavior.

Picnic   See **Inge, William**

Piercy, Marge 1937–   Born and raised in Detroit, Piercy has lived in Chicago, Paris, Boston, San Francisco, and New York City, and now lives on Cape Cod, Massachusetts. She has been active in the women's movement for many years, and most of her poetry and fiction reflects the consciousness of women's assigned place in a male-dominated society, and the form that relationships take as a result. Her novels include *Going Down Fast* (1969), *Dance the Eagle to Sleep* (1970), *Small Changes* (1973), *Woman on the Edge of Time* (1976), *Vida* (1979), *Braided Lives* (1982), and *Fly Away Home* (1984). Among her volumes of poetry are *Breaking Camp* (1968), *Hard Loving* (1969), *4-Telling* (1971), *To Be Of Use* (1973), *Living in the Open* (1976), *The Twelve-Spoked Wheel Flashing* (1978), *The Moon is Always Female* (1980), *Circles on the Water: Selected Poems* (1982), and *Stone, Paper, Knife* (1983).

Pierre; or, The Ambiguities   A novel by **Herman Melville**, published in 1852. An exploration of man's psychological complexities and of the moral ambiguities of his existence, *Pierre* was poorly received. Critics were outraged by its depiction of an incestuous relationship and objected to its elaborate prose style.

The novel's protagonist, Pierre Glendinning, is the 19-year-old son of a wealthy widow in upstate New York. He is engaged to Lucy Tartan, a young woman from a prominent family, but he then meets Isabel, who claims to be his illegitimate half-sister. He knows that his mother will never accept a girl whose very existence exposes her husband's immoral behavior. To give Isabel some measure of protection, he takes her to New York, allowing everyone to believe that he has married her. He confides in his cousin, Glen, who rejects his boyhood companion on hearing the truth. Impoverished, Pierre turns to writing to earn a living, but the novel which results from his exhaustive efforts is turned down for publication. Lucy, meanwhile, has followed Pierre to New York. Isabel shows jealousy at her appearance, and Pierre begins to realize his true feelings about his half-sister. During a confrontation with Glen and Lucy's brother, Pierre kills his cousin. He is arrested, and Lucy and his mother die of grief. Tormented by conflicting emotions about their forbidden love, Pierre and Isabel commit suicide in his prison cell.

Pins and Needles   A two-act revue, with music and lyrics by Harold Rome and sketches by various authors, first performed at the Labor Stage in New York in 1937 by members of the International Ladies Garment Workers Union. Though the revue was orginally intended simply as an entertainment for union members, it was an immediate success and had a run of 1,108 consecutive performances. With a mixture of humor, ridicule, and propaganda, the various sketches treat the lives of common people and workers and their relationship to management. The revue included the songs, "Sing Me a Song With Social Significance" and "Sunday in the Park."

Pioneers, The   See **Leatherstocking Tales**

Pit, The; A Story of Chicago   A novel by **Frank Norris**, published in 1903, the year after the author's death. It is the second part of his uncompleted trilogy *The Epic of the Wheat*. The "pit" of the title is the Chicago stock exchange, where the protagonist of the novel, Curtis Jadwin, is a leading speculator who hopes to gain a corner in the wheat market. Much of the novel is devoted to the subtle manipulations necessary to work within the law of supply and demand. By the time he gains a monopoly of the wheat stocks, Jadwin's obsession with money and the operations of the pit has driven him almost to madness. In the meantime, however, the growth of farming in the West has increased the supply of grain, and this results in a sharp devaluation of his investment. With a glut of wheat on the market, Jadwin, already in poor health, loses all his money.

His rise in the wheat market is paralleled by the decline of his marriage to the attractive Laura Dearborn. Neglected by her husband, she begins to return to the flirtations which had characterized her behavior prior to their marriage. In fact, in order to win her hand Jadwin had had to pursue her amid a field of strong competition from rival suitors whom she encouraged. His neglect finally leads her to resume her relationship with the aesthete Sheldon Corthell. At the end of the novel, however, Laura returns to Jadwin; they renew their commitment to each other and are able to look toward the future with hope.

Plath, Sylvia 1932–63   Plath was born in Boston and attended Smith College. After graduation she won a Fulbright to Cambridge, receiving her MA in 1957. In the same year she married the English poet Ted Hughes.

She studied with **Robert Lowell** and has clear affinities with the **Confessional** school of poetry. However, she often distances herself from her personal subject matter by assuming a sharply ironic tone. Whether writing about tulips and elm trees, her experiences as a daughter and a wife, or her suicide attempts, there is an undercurrent of terror in her poems. *The Colossus and Other Poems* (England 1960, US publication 1962) was the only one of her books of poetry to be published before her suicide. Posthumous volumes include *Ariel* (1965), *Crossing the Water* (England 1971, US publication 1972), and *Winter Trees* (England 1971, US publication 1972). A partly autobiographical novel, *The Bell Jar*, was published in 1963 (US publication 1971). Her prose is collected in *Johnny Panic and the Bible of Dreams: Short Stories, Prose, and Diary Excerpts* (1979).

Po-ca-hon-tas!   See **Brougham, John**

Poe, Edgar Allan 1809–49   Born in Boston, Poe was raised by the Richmond merchant, John Allan, after the early death of his parents. Later, by choice, he took Allan as his middle name. The Allans moved to England, where Poe was educated at a private school from 1815 to 20. He completed his schooling in the US, and entered the University of Virginia in 1826. During this time his relationship with his foster-father became increasingly strained. Allan wanted the young man to prepare for a legal career. Instead, Poe left the university and went to Boston, where he began his literary career with *Tamerlane and Other Poems* (1827), which he published anonymously and at his own expense. The book went unnoticed. He then enlisted in the army under an assumed name and incorrect age. He was admitted to West Point in 1830, but in the following year was dismissed for neglecting his duty.

During a brief stay in New York City, he published a volume entitled *Poems* (1831), and then went to Baltimore, where he lived with his aunt, Maria Clemm, until 1835. He began to publish short fiction in magazines, and the story "MS Found in a Bottle" (1833) was awarded the first prize in a contest judged by **John Pendleton Kennedy**, who later found Poe an editorial position on the *Southern Literary Messenger* (1835). In 1836 Poe married his 13-year-old cousin, Virginia. He was fired, then rehired, by the *Messenger*, and moved to Richmond, Virginia. During this period, the unfinished tragedy *Politian* (1835–6) was serialized in the *Messenger*, which also published Poe's numerous reviews, essays, poems and stories. He moved to New York in 1837, published *The Narrative of A Gordon Pym* in 1838, then went to Philadelphia, where he served as assistant editor of *Burton's Gentleman's Magazine* from 1839 to 1840. He contributed a number of stories to this magazine, including "The Fall of the House of Usher" (1839). His first collection of short stories, *Tales of the Grotesque and Arabesque*, appeared in 1840. In the same year he left *Burton's* to begin his own journal, *The Penn*, but when the project failed he became literary editor of *Graham's Magazine* (1841–2), to which he contributed the stories, "Murders in the Rue Morgue," "The Masque of the Red

Death" and "The Imp of the Perverse," and an essay entitled "The Philosophy of Composition."

The year 1843 saw the free-lance publication of "The Tell-Tale Heart," "The Black Cat," "The Pit and the Pendulum," and the prize-winning story, "The Gold Bug." He returned to New York City in 1844 and began working for the *New York Mirror*. He purchased the *Broadway Journal* in 1845, and in the same year published *Tales* and *The Raven and Other Poems*. The *Journal* folded in 1846, and his young wife died in 1847. His later work includes the ambitious philosophical poem, "Eureka," a poem entitled "Ulalume," and the story "The Domain of Arnheim," all published in 1848. He began a three-month lecture tour in 1849 to raise funds for a proposed magazine, but the strain led to a nervous breakdown. He returned to Richmond, where he produced the poem "Annabel Lee" and delivered a lecture entitled "The Poetic Principle." He died in Baltimore later that year.

Poems on Various Subjects   See **Wheatley, Phillis**

Poetry: A Magazine of Verse   A journal that prints reviews as well as verse, *Poetry* has been published monthly since its founding in 1912. Virtually every major American poet of the 20th century has published in it at some point. It has also published poetry by British, Irish, French, Italian, Greek, Indian, Israeli, Japanese, and Soviet dissident poets. **Harriet Monroe**, its founder, served as editor from 1912 to 1936. Subsequent editors have been Morton Dauwen Zabel (1936–7), George Dillon (1937–42 and 1946–9), Peter DeVries (1942–6), Jessica Nelson North (1942–3), Marion Strobel (1943–9), Margedant Peters (1946–7), John Frederick Nims (1946–8), Hayden Carruth (1949–50), **Karl Shapiro** (1950–5), Henry Rago (1955–69), and Daryl Hine (1969–77). The current editor is John Frederick Nims, who returned to the magazine in 1978.

Poor Richard's Almanack   Published by **Benjamin Franklin** under the pseudonym of Richard Saunders, *Poor Richard's Almanack* first appeared in 1732. From 1747 to 1758 it was entitled *Poor Richard Improved*. As well as containing a calendar and astronomical data, it included many of Franklin's well-known maxims dictating homely wisdom, virtue, and frugality. Its fictional author, Richard, and his wife Bridget became popular literary characters. Franklin sold the almanac in 1758, but it continued publication until 1796.

Poor White   A novel by **Sherwood Anderson**, published in 1920. It tells how late-19th-century technology changes the lives of the inhabitants of Bidwell, Ohio, and particularly that of Hugh McVey, a telegraph operator, who at the beginning of the novel is the shy, inhibited "poor white" of the title, and whom Anderson conceived of as a "Lincolnian type from Missouri," whose belief in mechanical and industrial progress is shaken by his experiences.

McVey invents a mechanical planter which he hopes will improve the life of the local farmers. He is exploited by the enterprising speculator Steve Hunter, who convinces the townspeople to invest in a company which, like the invention, is a failure. Hugh's next inventions, however, a corn-cutter and a device to help load coal onto train cars, are extremely profitable. Hunter becomes a millionaire and Bidwell gradually changes into a bustling industrial town. McVey too becomes rich and famous, but is lonely and isolated in his prosperity, staving off madness by menial tasks, counting the trees along a street or gathering twigs to make baskets alone in his room. He then marries Clara Butterworth, the daughter of a wealthy Bidwell agriculturalist. Clara has had troubled relationships with both men and women, but she responds to Hugh's gentleness and though their marriage is unhappy initially they are reconciled at the end of the novel.

Anderson traces Bidwell's economic development from a craftsman's town to an industrial center and the troubles faced by the inhabitants as a result. Social distinctions based on wealth emerge, and the town's former peaceful existence is marred by outbreaks of violence, labor strikes, and company lock-outs. Disillusioned, McVey finally realizes the negative effects of industrial progress.

Porgy   See **Heyward, DuBose**

Porter, Cole (Albert) 1892–1964   Writer of such popular show tunes as "Night and Day," "Let's Do It," "Under My Skin," "It's De-Lovely," "In the Still of the Night,"

"Don't Fence Me In," "You're The Top," and "Anything Goes," Cole Porter was born to an extremely wealthy family in Peru, Indiana, and studied both violin and piano from an early age. He soon went east to attend Worcester Academy and then Yale, where he distinguished himself by writing songs and shows for the Glee Club and other amateur performing groups. He yielded to family pressure and enrolled at Harvard Law School, but switched to the School of Music after one semester. His first Broadway production, *See America First* (1916), a parody of patriotic revues, was not a success. He then went to Europe, where he may have served in the French army (reports differ). After marrying the wealthy divorcée Linda Lee Thomas, Porter became a symbol of an extravagant expatriate way of life.

Despite the absence of financial need, he continued writing for Broadway, contributing songs to revues like *Hitchy-Koo* (1919) and the *Greenwich Village Follies* (1924), and also collaborated with Gerald Murphy on a ballet, *Within The Quota* (1923). His second show, *Paris* (1928), was a hit, and was followed by *Fifty Million Frenchmen* (1929), *The New Yorkers* (1930), *The Gay Divorcée* (1932), *Anything Goes* (1934), *Jubilee* (1935), and *Red, Hot and Blue* (1936). In 1937 Porter was severely injured in a horseback riding accident; he continued to work, however, producing *DuBarry Was A Lady* (1939), *Panama Hattie* (1942), *Kiss Me Kate* (1948), *Can-Can* (1953), *Silk Stockings* (1955), and numerous film scores, including *Born to Dance* (1936), *High Society* (1956), and *Les Girls* (1957). His right leg had to be amputated in 1958, and from then on he lived in semi-seclusion until his death.

Porter, Katherine Anne 1890–1980 Born in Indian Creek, Texas, Porter worked on a newspaper in Denver, Colorado, and then lived in Mexico and Europe for a number of years. Her first collection of stories, *Flowering Judas, and Other Stories*, was published in 1930. *Hacienda: A Story of Mexico* appeared in 1934. She received widespread critical acclaim for the volume *Pale Horse, Pale Rider* (1939), which consists of three short novels: "Old Mortality"; "Noon Wine," which is set on a Texan ranch and had previously been published as a volume in 1937; and the title

piece, which tells of a short-lived love affair between a soldier and a young Southern newspaperwoman during the influenza epidemic of World War I.

Porter published two further collections of stories, *The Leaning Tower, and Other Stories* (1944) and *The Old Order: Stories of the South* (1944), as well as two volumes of essays, *The Days Before* (1952) and *A Defense of Circe* (1954). Her best-known work, *Ship of Fools*, appeared in 1962 after 20 years in the writing. A bitterly ironic novel, it is set on a German passenger ship sailing from Mexico to Germany in 1931, and explores the origin and potential of human evil through the allegorical use of characters as almost one-dimensional representatives of various national and moral types. *The Collected Stories of Katherine Anne Porter* (1965) received both the Pulitzer Prize and the National Book Award. *Collected Essays and Occasional Writings* appeared in 1970. *The Never-Ending Wrong* (1977) is an account of the infamous Sacco–Vanzetti trial and execution. Her other works include *The Itching Parrot* (1942), *Holiday* (1962), and *A Christmas Story* (1967).

Porter, William Sidney 1862–1910 Born in North Carolina, Porter founded *The Rolling Stone*, a comic weekly magazine, in 1894. Five years later, while serving a three-year prison sentence for alleged embezzlement in Columbus, Ohio, he began to write short stories published under the pseudonym of O. Henry. After his release from prison in 1902 he went to New York City, where he became a popular and prolific writer of short stories for magazines. His stories are characteristically marked by a twist of plot which turns on an ironic or coincidental circumstance. He is a master of the surprise ending. His first collection, *Cabbages and Kings* (1904), is set in South America; his second, *The Four Million* (1906), in New York City. His other volumes are *Heart of the West* (1907), *The Trimmed Lamp* (1907), *The Gentle Grafter* (1908), *The Voice of the City* (1908), *Options* (1909), *Roads of Destiny* (1909), *Whirligigs* (1910), *Strictly Business* (1910). Four more volumes were published posthumously: *Sixes and Sevens* (1911), *Rolling Stones* (1912), *Waifs and Strays* (1917), and *Postscripts* (1923).

Portnoy's Complaint A novel by **Philip Roth**, published in 1969, which takes the form of an account by Alexander Portnoy to his analyst. The analyst himself is not heard until the very end of the novel, and the narration proceeds by a rather manic, free-associative rhythm as Portnoy describes his relationship with his suburban Jewish family: his domineering, guilt-inducing mother who dotes on him and yet waves a knife over his head when he won't eat; his perpetually constipated, weak-spirited insurance salesman father; and his pathetic, conformist sister. Portnoy's guilty responses to his family's needs alternate with self-conscious rebellions against them: as an adolescent he performs brilliantly in school, but he seeks relief and revenge through constant masturbation; as an adult he has a respected job as the Assistant Commissioner for the City of New York Commission on Human Opportunity, but he refuses to get married and instead has affairs with gentile women. Toward the end of the novel, having abandoned his latest lover in Greece, he travels to Israel and meets an Israeli girl. For the first time in his life he is impotent. The girl confronts him with the contradictions of his existence, and embodies for him a noble, self-sacrificing model of Jewishness. At the end of the novel Portnoy is emotionally and psychologically exhausted.

Portrait of a Lady, The　A novel by **Henry James**, first published in serial form in *The Atlantic Monthly* (1880–1), and then in volume form in 1881.

Isabel Archer, of Albany, New York, a penniless orphan, becomes the protégée of her wealthy aunt, Lydia Touchett. She goes to England to stay with her aunt and uncle, a retired American banker, and their tubercular son, Ralph, who persuades his father to provide for Isabel in his will. When Mr Touchett dies, Isabel finds herself rich and goes to the Continent with Mrs Touchett and her friend, Madame Merle. In Florence, Madame Merle introduces her to Gilbert Osmond, a middle-aged widower with a young daughter, Pansy. To preserve her freedom, Isabel has previously turned down proposals of marriage from Casper Goodwood, a rich young American, and from Lord Warburton, an English neighbor of the Touchetts. Now, however, impressed with Osmond's taste and intellectual detachment, she accepts his proposal, only to discover him to be a selfish and

sterile dilettante who has married her for her money. When she hears that Ralph is dying she prepares to depart for England to be with him, but Osmond forbids her to go. It is at this point that she discovers that Madame Merle is Pansy's mother, and she at last understands the woman's part in her marriage to Osmond. She goes to England after a final confrontation with Madame Merle and is at Ralph's side when he dies. Casper Goodwood makes a last attempt to gain Isabel, but though she feels an attraction for him she rejects him and returns to Osmond and Pansy in Italy.

Pound, Ezra (Weston Loomis) 1885–1972　Pound was born in Hailey, Idaho. His family moved to Pennsylvania when he was 4 years old and settled in Wyncote, near Philadelphia. He enrolled at the University of Pennsylvania at the age of 16, and in 1903 went to Hamilton College in New York State, where he studied Anglo-Saxon, Romance languages, and medieval history. In 1906 he took up a fellowship at the University of Pennsylvania, and then taught briefly at Wabash College in Crawfordsville, Indiana. His academic career, however, was shortlived; he sailed for Europe in February 1908 and went to live in Venice.

His first volume of poetry, *A Lume Spento* (With Tapers Quenched) was published in Venice in June 1908. In September of that year he traveled to London, where he renewed his acquaintance with W. B. Yeats, whom he had first met during Yeats's visit to the US in 1903. While in London he also became friendly with Ford Madox Ford, T. E. Hulme, James Joyce, and Wyndham Lewis. Ford published Pound's "Sestina Altaforte" in *The English Review* in 1909. Two collections of his poems, *Personae* and *Exultations*, appeared in the same year. *The Spirit of Romance* (1910), a volume of critical essays adapted from lectures he gave in London, further demonstrated the literary erudition that had been evident in his early poetry. His next two collections of poems, *Provença* (1910) and *Canzoni* (1911), again showed the influence of medieval and Victorian literature, of Provençal poets, troubador ballads, and Robert Browning.

His translation of *The Sonnets and Ballate of Guido Cavalcanti* and his volume of poems entitled *Ripostes* (both 1912) marked the beginning of his association with the movement known as **Imagism**, which encouraged experimentation with verse forms, the economic use of language, brevity of treatment, and concreteness of detail. The movement, with Pound as its central figure, was at its peak between 1912 and 1914. During these years he also established his association with **Harriet Monroe**, and through her magazine *Poetry* promoted the work of fellow Imagists, as well as that of **T. S. Eliot** and **Robert Frost**. In 1914 he published an anthology of Imagist poetry, *Des Imagistes*, which included contributions by **H. D.**, Richard Aldington, James Joyce, **Amy Lowell**, and **William Carlos Williams**, as well as by Pound himself. Another influence on him at this time was the sculptor Henri Gaudier-Brzeska, and from their association came the shortlived movement called Vorticism, which opposed representational art in favor of abstract forms and structures. The movement's journal, *Blast*, to which Pound contributed, survived for just two issues (1914–15).

Pound's next volumes of poetry were *Lustra* (1916) and *Quia Pauper Amavi* (1919). During the course of World War I he became increasingly disillusioned with what he saw as a decayed civilization, and this sense of living in a world of false values found its clearest expression in his 1920 volume, *Hugh Selwyn Mauberly*. Late that year he and his wife Dorothy, whom he had married in 1914, went to live in Paris; there he worked through the first draft of **The Waste Land** with T. S. Eliot. He moved from Paris to Italy in 1924, and made a home in Rapallo. An epic poem had been one of his ambitions since his student days, but the form had taken 10 years to evolve. He had begun the **Cantos** before the Vorticist period and had worked on them intermittently. The first collection, *A Draft of XVI Cantos*, was published in 1925. He continued to work on this, his modern epic, for the rest of his life; eventually it consisted of 117 Cantos.

Personae: The Collected Poems of Ezra Pound was published in 1926; *Selected Poems*, edited by T. S. Eliot, appeared in 1928. *A Draft of XXX Cantos* (1930) continued the sequence, which was further extended by *Eleven New Cantos* (1934), *The Fifth Decad of Cantos* (1937), and *Cantos LII–LXXI* (1940). In 1933 Pound had met Mussolini and been impressed

by the dictator's imposition of order on Italy. In 1939 he visited the US, where his new political beliefs and his anti-semitism alienated many of his friends. When he wanted to return in 1941 he was denied permission. In the same year he began to broadcast for the Axis in Rome. In April, 1945 he was arrested by partisans and handed over to the American authorities. He was held under harsh conditions in an American disciplinary center at Pisa and then transferred to the US; in November, 1945, in Washington, he was declared unfit to stand trial for treason on grounds of insanity, and was confined to St Elizabeth's hospital. While incarcerated at Pisa he had begun an additional volume of Cantos; *The Pisan Cantos* were completed at St Elizabeth's in January, 1946 and published in 1948. (Their receipt of the Bollingen Prize for poetry in 1948 caused an uproar which led to the Library of Congress's relinquishing the administration of the prize, which thereafter passed to Yale University.) Pound added to the Cantos with the publication of *Section: Rock-Drill: 85–95 de los Cantares* (1956) and *Thrones: 96–109 de los Cantares* (1959). *The Cantos of Ezra Pound (I–CXVII)* appeared in 1970. *Collected Early Poems* was published posthumously in 1976.

Pound's confinement in St Elizabeth's finally came to an end in 1958, and he returned to Italy. He died in Venice at the age of 87. He himself was uncertain of his achievements, but he is widely recognized as one of the makers of modern poetry. Among his volumes of criticism are *Pavannes and Division* (1918), *Instigations* (1920), *Indiscretions* (1923), *How to Read* (1931), *ABC of Reading* (1934), *Polite Essays* (1937), and *A Guide to Kulchur* (1938). *Gaudier-Brzeska: A Memoir* was published in 1916; his adaptation from the Chinese, *The Classic Anthology Defined by Confucius*, in 1954; and his translation of Sophocles' *The Women of Trachis* in 1956.

Power of Sympathy, The A novel by **William Hill Brown**, published anonymously in 1789. It was originally attributed to Sarah Wentworth Apthorp Morton, and Brown was not finally recognized as its author until 1894. It is written in epistolary form and relates the tragic tale of an attempted seduction which, if it had been successful, would also have been incestuous. Based in part on an actual scandal in Boston society, it warns young women of the danger posed by would-be seducers.

A young man, Harrington, is determined to win a young woman, Harriot Fawcet. Unbeknownst to either of them, they are brother and sister. Harriot is the illegitimate child of the elder Harrington and an unfortunate woman named Maria. Harrington confides his plans – which to start with are simply to seduce Harriot, but change quickly to marrying her without his father's permission – to his friend Mr Worthy, who sensibly counsels against this course. When the truth of Harriot's parentage is revealed, she collapses and soon after dies. Grief-stricken, Harrington becomes increasingly unstable and eventually commits suicide.

Pragmatism: A New Name for Some Old Ways of Thinking An approximate transcript of the Lowell lectures **William James** delivered in Boston (1906) and repeated at Columbia University (1907), *Pragmatism* was first published in 1907 and is considered by some to be the most significant work of American philosophy. As James describes it, pragmatism is not so much a theory as a method of choosing among theories – a means of mediating between rationalist absolutism and empiricist materialism. Although James distrusts the abstract manipulation of words (rationalism), he does not reject abstraction altogether (as perhaps a rigid empiricist would); rather, he accepts abstractions insofar as they redirect one profitably into experience. Ideals are "real" because they have results. James argues that truth, an abstraction, does not reside innately within any proposition; rather, one can call a proposition truthful if it has practical consequences. For the pragmatist, therefore, truth is relative.

James was not the first to formulate the philosophical principle of pragmatism, and in fact he acknowledges his debts to others: C. S. Peirce, who first coined the term; Giovanni Papini, the Italian pragmatist; Friedrich Schiller; and **John Dewey**, who would develop pragmatism further. In 1907 James published *The Meaning of Truth*, a response to the critics of *Pragmatism* in which he amplifies and reasserts his original argument.

Prairie, The **Leatherstocking Tales**.

Prescott, William Hickling 1796–1859

Prescott was born to wealthy parents in Salem, Massachusetts, and educated at Harvard. While there he suffered severe damage to his sight, but went on to take his MA and was determined to follow a literary career. His parents sent him to Europe (1815–17), where his interests became focused on historical studies – particularly on the initiative of the Spaniards in America. He published some essays, and in 1829 began the preparation of his first history.

History of the Reign of Ferdinand and Isabella, the Catholic was published in three volumes in 1838. Prescott was encouraged by its reception and in the following year began to prepare *History of the Conquest of Mexico*, which was published in three volumes in 1843 and brought him widespread acclaim Prescott was careful to indicate the tragedy inherent in the advance of the conquistadors; his careful examination of sources and his adventurous narrative method provided a mode for a younger generation of historians. *History of the Conquest of Peru* followed in 1847, and the cycle was completed with the publication of three volumes of *History of the Reign of Philip the Second* (1855–8) (Prescott had in fact planned to write four volumes, but died before the project was finished).

Prince and the Pauper, The. A Tale for Young People of All Ages A novel by **Mark Twain**, published in England in 1881 and in the US in 1882. It is set during the last years of Henry VIII's reign and tells how Prince Edward and a pauper boy exchange places by mistake.

The Prince encounters the poor Tom Canty, and is fascinated to see that they appear to be exact twins. They exchange clothes, and the Prince is chased from the palace by guards. He is abused by Tom's family, and then wanders through London in rags until a disinherited knight, Miles Hendon, takes pity on the boy, whom he believes – from his repeated claim to royal birth – to be unbalanced. In Miles's company Edward sees at first hand the wretchedness of the poor and the cruelty of the law. Meanwhile, Tom has been treated as a prince, and when the king dies he is prepared for coronation. Edward makes his way to Westminster Abbey and manages to establish his identity by revealing the whereabouts of the Great Seal. The Prince becomes King Edward VI, and during his brief reign does his best to keep in mind the lessons of his own days as a pauper.

Princess Casamassima, The A novel by **Henry James**, published serially in *The Atlantic Monthly* from September 1885 to October 1886, and then in volume form in 1886.

Set in London in the 1880s, the novel portrays a range of characters from all social classes. Its hero is an orphan boy, Hyacinth Robinson, who has been brought up by Miss Pynsent, a quiet little spinster who makes a living as a dressmaker and lives in a lower-class district of London. Hyacinth has seen his mother only once, when she was dying in prison, condemned for the murder of his father, "Lord Frederick." He becomes apprenticed to the book-binder Eustache Poupin, a French Communist in exile. While learning his trade he meets Paul Muniment, a proletarian revolutionary, joins a secret society, and commits himself to the movement. He also comes into contact with Christina, the Princess Casamassima, who, separated from her Italian husband (see *Roderick Hudson*), finds the revolutionary movement an outlet for her energies. After Miss Pynsent dies, Hyacinth travels to Europe and returns with a somewhat altered social vision. Though he no longer supports the society, he receives a summons from it to carry out the assassination of a duke. The Princess Casamassima goes to his apartment, planning to offer to substitute for him, but she arrives too late. He has given up in despair and killed himself.

Principles of Psychology, The A book by **William James**, published in 1890. The text, 12 years in the making, was based in part on James's observations at the psychological laboratory he established at Harvard in 1876. In this laboratory, the first of its kind in the US, James developed his functional approach to psychology. His findings indicated that the mind operates as a part of the body, and that an individual's mental adjustments are in fact environmental responses. In *Principles* he defines the mind as an instrument which, by controlling choice, effort, and will, makes adjustments which are modified by deterministic factors such as heredity and biology.

Pudd'nhead Wilson, The Tragedy of A novel by **Mark Twain**, published in 1894 and dramatized in the following year by Frank Mayo. A story of confused identities, the title character is a lawyer, David Wilson, who is called "Pudd'nhead" by a community which ridicules his eccentric ideas and practices.

The story takes place in the Missouri town of Dawson's Landing in the 1830s. Tom, the son of the prosperous slave owner Percy Driscoll, is born on the same day as Chambers, the son of one of Driscoll's slaves, a light-skinned woman named Roxana, and a Virginian gentleman. The children closely resemble each other. Roxy is afraid that Chambers might eventually be sold down the river, so she switches the two babies to protect her son. When Percy Driscoll dies, his brother Judge Driscoll adopts Chambers, thinking him to be Tom. The boy grows up to be a bully, a gambler, and an arrogant coward. To pay his gambling debts, he decides to sell Roxy, but she escapes from her new owners and blackmails him with the secret of his true birth. He resorts to stealing to help pay his various debts, and, during a robbery attempt, murders the Judge with a knife he had stolen from Luigi, one of the aristocratic Italian twins who have recently arrived in town. Although the twins were initially well received, the false Tom had caused a series of disturbances which led to enmity between them and Judge Driscoll. It is therefore supposed by all that Luigi committed the murder.

The unpracticed attorney "Pudd'nhead" Wilson successfully proves Luigi's innocence by showing that the fingerprints on the knife belong to the false Tom. He also establishes the true identities of Tom and Chambers. Wilson becomes a town celebrity; the disgraced Chambers is sold down the river as a slave; and Roxy is supported by her surrogate son, the true Tom.

Purdy, James 1923–   Purdy was born in Ohio and educated at the universities of Chicago and Puebla, Mexico. He began his full-time writing career in 1953; his first book, a collection of short stories entitled *Color of Darkness*, appeared in 1957. Much of his fiction focuses on small-town provincial America; sometimes a character from a small town is transplanted to a large urban setting and the values of each are juxtaposed. His first novel, *Malcolm*, was published in 1959. Other books are *The Nephew* (1960), *Cabot Wright Begins* (1964), *Eustace Chisholm and the Works* (1967), *I Am Elijah Thrush* (1972); and a trilogy, *Sleepers in Moon-Crowned Valleys*, comprising *Jeremy's Version* (1970), *The House of the Solitary Maggot* (1974), and *Mourners Below* (1981). He has also published collections of poetry, including *The Running Sun* (1971); some plays are included with short stories in the volume *Children is All* (1962).

Pynchon, Thomas 1937–   Pynchon was born in Glen Cove, New York, and graduated from Cornell in 1958. He worked for a time at the Boeing Aircraft Corporation in Seattle, but little else is known about his life – he avoids interviews – beyond his liking for Mexico. His first novel, *V.* (1963, Faulkner Award), is a long, dark-toned fantasy – his preferred medium for depicting American life in the latter half of the 20th century. In *The Crying of Lot 49* (1966, Rosenthal Memorial Award), he explores the attempts of the modern mind to organize an apparently chaotic universe, and juxtaposes various systems and ideologies that exist in contemporary society. His third novel, ***Gravity's Rainbow***, appeared in 1973, and received the National Book Award. He has also published a collection of his early short stories, *Slow Learner* (1984), which includes "Lowlands" and "Entropy."

R

Rabbit Run   See **Updike, John**

Rabe, David (William) 1940–   Rabe was born in Dubuque, Iowa, and educated at Loras College and Villanova University. His first play, *Sticks and Bones*, the first part of what is known as his "Vietnam trilogy," was produced at Villanova in 1969, and deals with the effects of the Vietnam conflict on American family life. The second play in the trilogy, *The Basic Training of Pavlo Hummel* (1971), treats the disruptive and destructive effects of the war upon the participants' personalities, and the third, *Streamers* (1978), concerns a group of soldiers forced to deal with a fellow soldier's homosexuality. Rabe's other plays include *The Orphan* (1973), *Boom Boom Room* (1973), revised as *In the Boom Boom Room* in 1974), *Burning* (1974), and *Hurlyburly* (1984).

Raisin in the Sun, A   See **Hansberry, Lorraine**

Rand, Ayn 1905–82 Novelist and social critic, born and educated in Leningrad, Rand emigrated to the US in 1926, and married the writer Frank O'Connor in 1929. Her first publication was a mystery play, *The Night of January 16th* (1935). The novel *We the Living* appeared in 1936, and was followed by *Anthem* (England 1938, US 1946), a short novel which depicts the plight of an individual in the face of an oppressive, totalitarian society. With the publication of *The Fountainhead* in 1943, Rand attracted a substantial popular audience. Her credo that humans are rational, self-interested, and pledged to individualism was advocated in *The Objectivist*, a journal she founded in 1962, and in *The Ayn Rand Letter* (1971–82). The novel *Atlas Shrugged* (1957) portrays what she considered to be the inevitable results of altruism – socialism or, worse, anarchy. Later in her career she

lectured widely at universities in the US. Her critical works include *For the New Intellectual* (1961), *The Virtue of Selfishness* (1965), and *The New Left: The Anti-Industrial Revolution* (1971).

Ransom, John Crowe 1888–1974 A native of Tennessee, Ransom attended Vanderbilt University in Nashville, was a Rhodes Scholar at Oxford (1913), and then taught at Vanderbilt from 1914 until 1937. His first collections of verse were *Poems About God* (1919), *Chills and Fever* (1924), *Grace After Meat* (1924), and *Two Gentlemen in Bonds* (1927). While at Vanderbilt he became a member of the group known as the "Fugitives," from their contributions to the poetry magazine *The Fugitive*, published from 1922 to 1925. This group, which also included **Allen Tate**, Donald Davidson, **Laura Riding**, and **Robert Penn Warren**, was comprised of Southern conservative writers who stood for traditional agrarian values in an age of industrialism.

In 1930 Ransom edited *I'll Take My Stand: The South and the Agrarian Tradition*, a collection of essays by 12 Southern writers of the Fugitive group: the poets Davidson, Tate, Warren, John Gould Fletcher, and Ransom himself; the scholars Stark Young, John Donald Wade, and Andrew Lytle; the historian Frank Owsley; the political scientist Herman Clarence Nixon; the psychologist Lyle Lanier; and the economist and journalist Henry Blue Kline. This Agrarian manifesto included a "Statement of Principles" written mainly by Ransom, which maintained that the industrial way of life was causing unhappiness and unemployment among the work force and destroying the very roots of religion, culture, and art. Although they differed considerably in their political affiliations and suggested strategies, the essayists advocated a return to the traditional Southern agrarian way of life as the best antidote to the encroachment of Northern industrialist values and problems.

After leaving Vanderbilt, Ransom taught at Kenyon College, Ohio, where in 1939 he founded the **Kenyon Review**, which became one of the most influential academic journals in America. Two years later he gave currency to the principles of the **New Criticism** in a book by that title. His other critical writings include *God Without Thunder; an Orthodox Defense of Orthodoxy* (1930), *The World's Body* (1938), and *Poems and Essays* (1955). His *Selected Poems* appeared in 1945, with a revised and enlarged edition in 1963.

Rechy, John (Francisco) 1934–   Born in El Paso, Texas, Rechy was educated there at the University of Texas and at the New School for Social Research in New York City. He has taught creative writing at various universities. His work usually concerns a search for love and identity in socially marginal settings; his leading characters tend to be homosexual or bisexual and are frequently associated with danger and violence. His first novel, *City of Night*, appeared in 1963 and was followed by *Numbers* (1967), *This Day's Death* (1969), *The Vampires* (1971), *The Fourth Angel* (1973), *Rushes* (1979), and *Bodies and Souls* (1983). His representations of urban lifestyles are generally based on the homosexual communities of major cities such as New York and Los Angeles, and are additionally developed to incorporate the crime and violence of the urban underworld. He has also published a study of urban homosexual lifestyles, *The Sexual Outlaw* (1977).

Recognitions, The   See **Gaddis, William**

Red Badge of Courage, The   A novel by **Stephen Crane**, published in 1895. In preparation for publication, the story was subject to considerable emendations and deletions. An edition of the original manuscript was published in 1982.

The Red Badge of Courage, though only his second novel, established Crane's reputation in critical and literary circles. Set during the Civil War, the frightening realities of battle are violently contrasted with the heroic ideals of conventional war narrative. A youth, who is later identified as Henry Fleming, proudly enrolls as a soldier in the Union army. He is anxious to participate in the glory of the fight, but his expectations are disappointed by his first encounter with the enemy. He witnesses a mass retreat of his fellow soldiers, and receives a head wound from the butt of a gun when he grabs a deserter to ask for an explanation of the disjointed sequence of events. He then sees his friend Jim Conklin die. He is temporarily proud of his own bravery, but during the second encounter he is overcome by fear and flees from the battle into the forest. There he attempts to find solace in Nature, but fails to justify his desertion in his own eyes. After coming across the spectral figure of a dying soldier, he becomes enraged by the injustices of war. He returns to the lines with the wounded, marked by the "red badge" of a soldier who has fought, but does not tell anyone how he received his wound. Back with his regiment, in the heat of battle he automatically picks up the regiment's colors when they fall from another's hands. But he can no longer be proud of his own heroics. He is filled with guilt and haunted by the memory of the "tattered" soldier, a wounded man who was deserted on the field.

Redburn: His First Voyage   A novel by **Herman Melville**, published in 1849. He wrote the book in about ten weeks, drawing on the experiences of his first voyage as an apprentice seaman.

The son of an impoverished New York family, Wellingborough Redburn ships as a "boy" on the *Highlander*, a trader bound for Liverpool. On this his first voyage, he must learn slowly and painfully not only the sailor's strenuous trade but also that he is the lowest in social standing among the crew. Captain Riga seems to treat him kindly at first, but then ignores him contemptuously; his attempts to approach crew members alternate with their rebuffs and his similarly contemptuous withdrawal. Feeling isolated and receiving few kindnesses, he is disturbed by the deaths of some of the seamen and still more by the torments of the evil and tubercular sailor Jackson.

When the ship reaches Liverpool, Redburn finds that a guidebook belonging to his dead father (who had made business trips abroad) is no longer accurate or useful; feeling dislocated and disillusioned, he explores the city and sees the appalling conditions among the poor. He encounters a spendthrift aristocrat, Harry Bolton, and the two go off to London together. London's glitter, however, only thinly disguises its corruption. Harry, who has run up a gambling debt, is obliged to run away and ship on the *Highlander* with Redburn for the trip home. Emigrants to America accompany them on this return voyage, and the unhealthy conditions lead to an epidemic and more deaths. Jackson's treacheries continue, though he dies as they near New York; Captain Riga cheats Harry and Redburn out of their wages; but Redburn is happy to be home with his family.

Redeemed Captive, Returning to Zion, The An account by John Williams, published in 1707, of his two-year captivity among the Mohawk Indians and French Jesuits in Quebec. Williams (1664–1729) was a minister in the frontier town of Deerfield, Massachusetts, and was taken prisoner during a raid (part of the French and Indian Wars) in 1704. He describes how he saw his wife and two of his children killed, and how he himself was constantly threatened with death during the march with the Indians to Canada. He and the party were delivered to the Jesuits in Quebec and their physical hardships lessened, but the Jesuits tried to convert them to Catholicism, an experience which Williams found almost as harrowing as physical deprivation. The latter part of the narrative contains his exchange of letters with his son, also a captive, who had been separated from him and successfully converted by the Jesuits, but who soon reverted to Protestantism and, together with his father, was released from captivity in 1706. Williams's youngest daughter, however, was not released; in fact she later married an Indian, joined the Roman church, and refused to return to New England. Williams stresses that the afflictions of Indian raids and captivities have been visited on the colony for its sins. The work saw many printings, some of them with an appended sermon by Williams, "Reports of Divine Kindness, or Remarkable Mercies Should be Faithfully Published for the Praise of God the Giver."

Reed, Ishmael (Scott) 1938– Born in Chattanooga, Tennessee and raised in Buffalo, New York, Reed began to make his reputation as a poet in the early 1960s in New York City, where he co-founded the *East Village Other* (1965), an experimental newspaper that printed work by new writers. In 1967 he moved to Berkeley and became involved in the Afro-American cultural movement at the University of California. He began to develop a system of world history according to which human civilization is seen as a cyclical battle between oppressors and oppressed. With their combination of radical surrealism and angry social satire, Reed's novels illuminate these historical patterns and aspire to break the cycle of oppression of American minorities. The first of these experimental works, *The Free-Lance Pallbearers* (1967), represents a parodic departure from the autobiographical style of earlier black American narratives. *Yellow Back Radio Broke-Down* (1969) portrays the remarkable adventures of a black cowboy. *Mumbo-Jumbo* (1972) sets forth a pseudo-history of racial oppression. *The Last Days of Louisiana Red* (1974) is loosely based on the racial violence in Berkeley in the 1960s. *Flight to Canada* (1976) surrealistically merges the Civil War period with modern America. *The Terrible Twos* (1982) is a fantastic satire of corruption in present and future American society. Reed's volumes of poetry include *Catechism of D Neo-American HooDoo Church* (1970), *Chattanooga* (1973), and *A Secretary to the Spirits* (1978). *Shrovetide in New Orleans* (1978) and *God Made Alaska for the Indians* (1982) are collections of essays.

Reflections in a Golden Eye See **McCullers, Carson**

Reid, (Thomas) Mayne 1818–83 Reid was born in Ireland and went to the US in 1840. After a varied and adventurous career, which included service with the US Army in the Mexican War and extensive travel throughout America, he returned to live in England in 1850. In the same year he published *The Rifle Rangers; or, Adventures in Southern Mexico*, the first of his approximately 50 books, most of which were concerned with American frontier life and/or were tales of adventure for boys. Other notable titles are *The Scalp Hunters; or, Romantic Adventures in Northern Mexico* (1851); *The Boy Hunters* (1853); *The Quadroon; or, A Lover's Adventure in Louisiana* (1856), which was adapted by

Dion Boucicault in the play *The Octoroon; or, Life in Louisiana* (1859); *The Maroon* (1862); *The Cliff-Climbers* (1864); *Afloat in the Forest* (1865); *The Castaways* (1870), and *Gwen-Wynne* (1877). A 15-volume collected edition of his works was published in 1868. He spent a further three years in the US from 1867 to 1870.

Representative Men A book by **Ralph Waldo Emerson**, published in 1850 and consisting of seven essays that were originally delivered as lectures in Boston between December 11, 1845 and January 22, 1846. The series was given again shortly afterwards in Concord, Massachusetts, and again, with various revisions, in England between May 1847 and November 1848. In the opening essay Emerson suggests that truly great men are representative of their time and place: the genius is not aloof from his society, but is the earliest and finest manifestation of that society's possibilities. The six representative men he discusses in the other essays are Plato, Swedenborg, Montaigne, Shakespeare, Napoleon, and Goethe.

Rexroth, Kenneth 1905–82 Born in South Bend, Indiana, Rexroth spent much of his childhood in the Midwest and was largely self-educated. He led a Bohemian lifestyle in Chicago in the 1920s, and then moved to San Francisco, where he became active in leftist and union movements and eventually established himself as a central figure in the literary community. His work variously consists of elegiac, erotic, and political verse, and is often surreal and experimental in style. His early volumes of poetry are *In What Hour* (1940), *The Phoenix and the Tortoise* (1944), *The Art of Worldly Wisdom* (1949), and *The Signature of All Things* (1949).

Although he later distanced himself from the movement, Rexroth was briefly associated with the **Beats**: he organized the San Francisco Poetry Center with **Lawrence Ferlinghetti** and **Allen Ginsberg**, and participated in the group's "Six Gallery" reading in 1955. His other volumes of verse are *Poems* (1955), *Natural Numbers* (1963), *The Collected Shorter Poems* (1967), *The Collected Longer Poems* (1968), *New Poems* (1974), *The Silver Swan* (1976), and *The Morning Star: Poems and Translations* (1979). He also published a collection of four plays in verse entitled *Beyond the Mountains* (1951), and numerous translations, including *100 Poems from the Japanese* (1954), *100 Poems from the Chinese* (1956), and *100 Poems from the Greek and Latin* (1959). His critical essays are collected in *The Bird in the Bush* (1959) and *Assays* (1961). *An Autobiographical Novel* appeared in 1966.

Reznikoff, Charles 1894–1976 Born in Brooklyn, Reznikoff was educated at the University of Missouri, and received a law degree from New York University. He is generally identified with the **Objectivist** school, and much of his work emphasizes the role of Judaism in his life. His first publication was a volume of poetry, *Rhythms* (1918). Other volumes, many privately printed, include *Poems* (1920), *Uriel Acosta: A Play and A Fourth Group of Verse* (1921), *Chatterton, The Black Death, and Meriwether Lewis: Three Plays* (1922), *Coral and Captive Israel: Two Plays* (1923), *Five Groups of Verse* (1927), *Nine Plays* (1927), *Jerusalem the Golden* (1934), and *Inscriptions: 1944–1956* (1959). By the Waters of Manhattan: Selected Verse appeared in 1962. A poetic meditation on US history, *Testimony: The United States, 1885–1890*, appeared in 1965; its sequel, *Testimony: The United States, 1891–1900*, in 1968. *Poems 1918–1936: Volume One of the Complete Poems* was published in 1976 and was followed the next year by *Poems 1937–1975: Volume Two of the Complete Poems*. Reznikoff also wrote a historical novel, *The Lionhearted* (1944), and, with Uriah Engleman, a history entitled *The Jews of Charleston* (1950).

Rice, Elmer 1892–1967 Born Elmer Leopold Reizenstein in New York City to German-Jewish immigrant parents, Rice left school at the age of 14. He worked for a time as a clerk in his cousin's law office, then studied law, and was admitted to the Bar in 1913, but shortly thereafter gave up this career to become a playwright. His first play, *On Trial* (1914), was a financial and critical success and effectively launched his career. He is often credited with inventing the technique later called flashback: in *On Trial*, a courtroom drama, the action switches between testimony and flashbacks initiated by the testimony, moving progressively further back in time to exonerate the accused man. Despite its revolutionary construction, it deals with relatively conventional themes of honesty, infidelity, and the preying of the immoral rich upon female innocence. In the course of the long and active career that followed, Rice wrote over 50 plays, of which the best known are *The Adding Machine* (1923) and *Street Scene* (1929), which won him the Pulitzer Prize.

Though his drama ranges from Expressionism to Naturalism to light-hearted comedy, Rice's devotion to social justice and liberal causes is apparent throughout his work. Two early plays, *The Home of the Free* (1917) and *The Iron Cross* (1917), took up pacifist themes at an unpopular time; *The Subway* (1929) told the story of a young working girl victimized by lecherous men; *See Naples and Die* (1929) and *The Left Bank* (1931) were light-hearted critiques of expatriate morality, for which Rice gathered material on trips abroad. Other plays include *We, The People* (1933), a vehement indictment of conditions during the Depression, including an attack on racial prejudice; *Judgement Day* (1934), a thinly fictionalized account of the trial which followed the Reichstag fire; *Between Two Worlds* (1934), in which characters on a transatlantic voyage debate and play out the contradictions between the American system and the Soviet, which Rice had observed on a long visit to Russia; *Dream Girl* (1945); *Love Among the Ruins* (1963); and *Close Harmony* (also produced as *The Lady Next Door*) (1929), written in collaboration with **Dorothy Parker**.

Rice wrote several novels; Hollywood screenplays; an autobiography, *Minority Report* (1963); and a history of the theatre. He also worked as a producer and director; and in 1937, three years after a widely publicized "retirement from the theatre" prompted by a battle with the critics, formed the Playwrights Company with **Maxwell Anderson**, **Robert Sherwood**, **Sidney Howard**, and **S. N. Behrman**. He was a founding member of the American Civil Liberties Union and later of the **Federal Theatre Project**, which employed out-of-work actors, playwrights, and other theatre workers, during the Depression. He resigned from the Project when the State Department censored the first **Living Newspaper** production.

Rich, Adrienne Cecile 1929–   Born in Baltimore, Maryland, Rich graduated from Radcliffe College in 1951. Her first book of poems, *A Change of World* (1951), was published in the Yale Series of Younger Poets. A second volume, *The Diamond Cutters*, appeared in 1955. In the 1960s she turned to increasingly innovative forms and a startlingly frank idiom to explore feminist themes. *Snapshots of a Daughter-in-Law* appeared in 1963. Subsequent volumes were *The Necessities of Life* (1966), *Selected Poems* (England 1966, US 1967), *Leaflets: Poems, 1965–1968* (1969), *The Will to Change: Poems, 1968–70* (1971), *Diving Into the Wreck: Poems, 1971–72* (1973), *Poems: Selected and New, 1950–1974* (1975), and *The Dream of a Common Language: Poems 1974–1977* (1978). A prose work, *Of Woman Born: Motherhood as Experience and Institution* (1976), established Rich as an influential radical feminist critic. A collection of essays, *On Lies, Secrets, and Silence: Selected Prose 1966–1978*, was published in 1979. Her most recent collections of poems include *A Wild Patience Has Taken Me This Far: Poems, 1978–81* (1981), *Sources* (1983), and *The Fact of A Doorframe: Poems Selected and New, 1950–1984* (1984).

Ridge, Lola 1871–1941   Born in Dublin, Ridge spent her childhood in Australia and New Zealand, emigrated to San Francisco in 1907, and moved to New York City in 1908. She then began to contribute short fiction and poetry to various journals, and helped establish the Ferrer Association Modern School. In 1918 she published *The Ghetto and Other Poems*, a collection which focuses on immigrant life in New York City and shows the influence of **Imagism** on her work. The publication of this volume brought Ridge a good deal of attention in literary circles; she then edited several issues of the journal *Others* and became the American editor of *Broom*. Her next publication, *Sun-Up* (1920), contains poems which explore both the nature of artistic vision and the realities of working-class experience. The collection *Red Flag* (1927) includes tributes to those who lost their lives in revolutionary struggles, as does *Firehead* (1929), which was written in response to the executions of Sacco and Vanzetti in 1927. Her last volume of verse, *Dance of Fire* (1935), reflects her lifelong concern with the exploitation and martyrdom of the working class.

Riding, Laura (Jackson) 1901– Born Laura Reichenthal in New York City, Riding was educated at Cornell. Her early work was mostly produced during her 15-year residence in Europe following her divorce from Louis Gottschalk in 1925. During this period she traveled widely and wrote several books in collaboration with Robert Graves. Her first collection of verse, *The Close Chaplet* (1926), was followed by *Love as Love, Death as Death* (1928), *Poems: A Joking Word* (1930), *Twenty Poems Less* (1930), *Poet: A Lying Word* (1933), and by several other volumes including *Collected Poems* (1938). A critical work entitled *A Survey of Modernist Poetry* (1927; US publication 1928) was written with Robert Graves, as was a novel called *No Decency Left* (1932), which they published under the single pseudonym of Barbara Rich. Riding writes in free verse with frequent use of assonance and repetition, and focuses on transformations in life and death, the nature of love, and the duality of mind and body. In 1939 she published a critically acclaimed collection of biographical sketches of famous women entitled *Lives of Wives*. Two years later she married the writer Schuyler Jackson and they began work on the ambitious *Dictionary of Exact Meaning*, which remains unpublished. Riding has not published any new poetry since 1939; as she explains in *The Telling* (1972), she renounced poetry in the 1940s because she sensed that it presented irremovable obstacles to the full potential of language itself. Despite this rejection, the volume *Selected Poems: In Five Sets* appeared in 1970.

Rights of Man, The   See **Paine, Thomas**

Riley, James Whitcomb 1849–1916 A poet, lecturer, and newspaperman, Riley began his career in 1877 as a writer for the Indianapolis *Journal*. The poems he published in the paper established him as a regional writer of light and sentimental verse. He became known especially for his dialect poems, which include "Little Orphant Annie," "The Raggedy Man," and "When the Frost is on the Punkin." His great popularity as a poet and lecturer made him one of the wealthiest writers of his time. His most famous collection was *The Old Swimmin'-Hole and 'Leven More Poems* (1883). Other volumes include *Afterwhiles* (1888),

Pipes o' Pan at Zekesbury (1889), and *Poems Here at Home* (1893).

Ripley, George 1802–80 A New England religious thinker and writer who became a **Transcendentalist**, Ripley was born in Greenfield, Massachusetts, and educated at Harvard. In 1826, after graduating from The Harvard Divinity School, he was ordained as pastor of the Purchase Street Church in Boston where he served for nearly 15 years.

Fascinated by contemporary German transcendental thought, Ripley published ten highly controversial articles in the *Christian Examiner* between 1830 and 1837. More conservative Unitarians (among them Andrews Norton) were outraged by the philosophy he espoused. His sermon, "Jesus Christ, the Same Yesterday, Today, and Forever," delivered on May 14, 1834 at the ordination of fellow Transcendentalist **Orestes Brownson**, is considered an exemplary pronouncement of the Transcendentalist doctrine. In 1836 he helped to found the Transcendental Club and also published *Discourses on the Philosophy of Religion Addressed to Doubters Who Wish to Believe*. This was followed by *The Temptations of the Times* (1837) and *Philosophical Miscellanies* (1838). He then edited 14 volumes of translations of European idealistic philosophy, *Specimens of Foreign Standard Literature* (1838–42). In 1839, after he had published the first two volumes of *Specimens*, Andrews Norton charged him with "infidelity." Ripley responded with three lengthy essays, collected in "*The Latest Form of Infidelity" Examined: A First, Second and Third Letter Addressed to Mr Andrews Norton* (1839–40).

He handled the business affairs of the Transcendentalist magazine **The Dial** (1840–4) and also assisted **Margaret Fuller** in editing it. He left the ministry in 1841 and established **Brook Farm**, a Transcendentalist experiment in communal living which continued until 1847. From 1845 to 1849 he edited *The Harbinger*, a socialist weekly published by the Brook Farm Community. He became literary critic for the *New York Tribune* in 1849, and continued as critic, philosopher, and political commentator for the *Tribune* and other periodicals until his death. In 1850 he helped to found ***Harper's New Monthly Magazine***. He and Bayard Taylor edited *A Hand-*

book of *Literature and the Fine Arts* (1852). With Charles A. Dana he edited a 16-volume work entitled *The New American Cyclopedia* (1858–63). He began another project, "Books and Men: A Series of Critical and Biographical Sketches," in 1862, but it was never completed.

Rip Van Winkle A play by the actor Joseph Jefferson and the playwright **Dion Boucicault**, produced in 1865 in London and the following year in New York. Jefferson had played in earlier adaptations of the story, and asked Boucicault to write another for him. Boucicault's first version was unsuccessful and Jefferson assisted him in the minor changes; the product of their collaboration is now the standard theatrical version of **Washington Irving**'s famous story. In 1828 the English actor John Kerr had adapted the story for the stage; another version, based on Kerr's, was written by William Bayle Bernard in 1832. Subsequent versions resulted in G. F. Bristow's opera (1855) from which Boucicault and Jefferson derived their own dramatization.

The story, which takes place in the years before the American Revolution, describes how Rip wanders with his dog Wolf into the Catskill Mountains, where he meets a group of dwarfish people playing nine-pins. He sips from their liquor and falls asleep for 20 years. When he awakens, his beard is long, his nagging wife is dead, and his country is changed: America is no longer part of Britain. Rip adapts to the changes and lives to an old age.

Rise of Silas Lapham, The A novel by **William Dean Howells**, serialized in *Century Magazine* in 1884–5, and published in volume form in 1885.

Colonel Silas Lapham, originally a Vermont farmer, has risen to wealth through his successful paint manufacturing business. He moves his family to Boston, begins to build a house on Beacon Hill, and urges his wife and daughters to enter fashionable society. He looks forward to a new life, but thinks back on his old business practices with increasing moral discomfort. The family does not fit in well with the high-class Boston set, though one of this set's representatives, Tom Corey, falls in love with the older Lapham daughter, Penelope. The younger daughter, Irene, convinces herself and Penelope that Tom is really in love with her; Penelope refuses his proposal and does not attend the Coreys' dinner party. Her father does, however, and gets drunk, revealing himself as a misfit in genteel Boston society. Meanwhile his business speculations have been unsuccessful and he is threatened with bankruptcy. His partner urges him to save himself by selling some mill property to a British firm, even though he knows it to be worthless. After a struggle with himself, he decides not to make the sale. Economically bankrupt, socially disgraced, but morally restored, he returns to Vermont. Penelope and Tom run away to Mexico to escape the rigid social barriers that have created such unhappiness for them in New England.

Robinson, Edwin Arlington 1869–1935 The New England poet was born in Head Tide, Maine. His childhood in Gardiner, Maine, provided the background for "Tilbury Town," the fictional location of many of his poems. He studied at Harvard for a time, but the death of his father and other family difficulties forced him to leave in 1893. He published his first collection of poems, *The Torrent and the Night Before* (1896), at his own expense. In 1897 this volume was revised, expanded, and reissued as *The Children of the Night*. His third book, *Captain Craig* (1902), proved to be the turning point in his career. Theodore Roosevelt became interested in his work, and secured him a job at the Custom House in New York City. The president later wrote an article for *Outlook* in praise of Robinson and persuaded Scribner's to publish his work. *The Town Down the River* (1910) was successful enough to allow him to give up his job and devote his energies to writing. *The Man Against The Sky* appeared in 1916, and was followed in 1917 by the first part of his Arthurian trilogy, *Merlin*. The volumes *Lancelot* (1920) and *Tristram* (1927) completed his reworking of the medieval legend.

Robinson's mature poetry reveals strong counter-romantic tendencies and is concerned with some of the questions raised by the crisis of World War I. His shorter works in particular are characterized by their direct style and often ironic treatment of subject matter, as in the frequently anthologized "Richard Cory" and "Miniver Cheevy." The 1920s and 1930s were the poet's most productive years. He published *The Three Taverns* in 1920 and *Avon's Harvest* in 1921. His *Collected Poems* (1921) and *The Man Who Died Twice* (1924) were both awarded Pulitzer Prizes. His other publications include *Roman Bartholow* (1923), *Dionysus in Doubt* (1925), *Cavender's House* (1929), *The Glory of the Nightingales* (1930), *Matthias at the Door* (1931), *Nicodemus* (1932), *Talifer* (1933), *Amaranth* (1934), and *King Jasper* (1935). The volume *Sonnets 1889–1927* was published in 1928.

Roderick Hudson A novel by **Henry James**, first published as a serial in *The Atlantic Monthly* in 1875, and then in volume form in 1876. The author revised it for publication in England in 1879.

Roderick Hudson, an amateur sculptor, is taken to Europe by Rowland Mallet, a wealthy connoisseur who is impressed by his talent. In Rome he introduces Roderick to his circle, which includes the French sculptor, Gloriani, who is certain that the young American's talent will never develop. Roderick meets Christina Light, the daughter of an expatriate American widow; he is fascinated by her and deserts his work. In order to force him back into reality, Rowland brings his mother and fiancée, Mary Garland, from New England. Their arrival seems to have its desired effect, and Roderick executes a fine bust of his mother. But then Christina, urged on by her ambitious mother, marries Prince Casamassima (see **The Princess Casamassima**), and Roderick's work comes to a complete halt.

Once again Rowland attempts to rekindle Roderick's interest by arranging a visit to Switzerland for Mary, Mrs Hudson, Roderick, and himself. Unfortunately Christina is there too and Roderick borrows money from Mary so that he can follow her. This provokes Rowland to a furious outburst and he condemns Roderick as an ungrateful egoist. Roderick walks off into the mountains where he is caught in a thunderstorm. He is found dead, and it is unclear whether or not he committed suicide.

Rodgers, Richard See **Hammerstein, Oscar**

Roethke, Theodore (Huebner) 1908–63 Roethke was born in Saginaw, Michigan, and educated at the University of Michigan and at Harvard. He subsequently taught

English at various universities, including Pennsylvania State, Bennington, and Washington. His first volume of poetry, *Open House*, was published in 1941. In it, as in much of his early work, he returns to the landscapes of his childhood as a means of reconstructing transcendent moments of "waking." His second volume, *The Lost Son and Other Poems*, appeared in 1948. In 1954 he received the Pulitzer Prize for *The Waking: Poems, 1933–1953* (1953). *Words for the Wind: The Collected Verse of Theodore Roethke* (1957) won him the 1958 Bollingen Prize and the 1959 National Book Award. His later volumes, which include a good deal of love poetry, are *I am! Says the Lamb* (1961), *Sequence, Sometimes Metaphysical, Poems* (1963), and *The Far Field* (1964). Two collections of prose pieces appeared posthumously: *The Contemporary Poet as Artist and Critic* (1964) and *On the Poet and His Craft: Selected Prose* (1965). *The Collected Poems of Theodore Roethke* was published in 1966, and *Selected Letters of Theodore Roethke* in 1968.

Rogers, Robert 1731–95 Born in Massachusetts, Rogers was an explorer and soldier who turned to the theatre in the 1760s. His many encounters with Indians provided him with material for his best-known play, *Ponteach, or, The Savages of America* (1766), a blank-verse tragedy about an Indian chief whose rebellion Rogers himself had helped to put down but whose fortitude he admired. He also published *A Concise Account of North America* and his *Journals* in 1765; both reflect his extensive experience of Northwest explorations and wars with the Indians.

Rogers, Will 1879–1935 Actor, humorist, and writer, Rogers was born William Penn Adair, of Cherokee ancestry, in Oologh Indian territory, in what is now Oklahoma. As a young man he traveled the world, and during the Boer War worked as a horsebreaker for the British in South Africa. On his return to the US he worked as a rodeo cowboy in vaudeville shows, and for several years, starting in 1913, performed in the Ziegfeld Follies. In 1919 he became an actor, first in silent films and later in the "talkies." In 1926 he began writing newspaper articles which commented humorously on American politics and society; eventually his column was syndicated and reached an estimated 40 million readers. His books include *The Cowboy Philosopher on Prohibition* (1919), *The Illiterate Digest* (1924), *Letters of a Self-Made Diplomat to His President* (1927), and *There's Not a Bathing Suit in Russia* (1927). He died in a plane crash in Alaska. *The Autobiography of Will Rogers* appeared in 1949, and a collection of his newspaper pieces, *Sanity is Where You Find It*, in 1955.

Rölvag, O[le] E[dvart] 1876–1931 Born in Norway, Rölvag emigrated to the US in 1896 and studied at St Olaf College in Minnesota, where he became professor of Norwegian (1907–31). He wrote all his books in Norwegian and participated in their translation into English. *Letters from America* (1912) is a semi-autobiographical account of adjustment to American life and anticipates his later work in its concern for the Scandinavian immigrant's experience in the US. His most famous novel, *Giants in the Earth* (1927), the first volume of a trilogy, realistically describes the austere life of Norwegian immigrants on the Northwestern frontier. The trilogy was completed by *Peder Victorious* (1929) and *Their Father's God* (1931). His other books include *On Forgotten Paths* (1914), *Pure Gold* (1930), and *The Boat of Longing* (published posthumously in 1933).

Rose Tattoo, The See **Williams, Tennessee**

Roth, Henry 1906– Born in Austria-Hungary to Jewish parents who emigrated to the US when he was an infant, Roth attended the City College of New York and then began writing in 1929. He has lived in Maine since 1945.

His reputation is based primarily on the novel *Call It Sleep*. Though it went relatively unnoticed at its initial publication in 1934, it was reissued in 1960 and received widespread critical acclaim. Autobiographical in nature, *Call It Sleep* portrays the mind of David Schearl, the only child of Jewish immigrants who settle in New York City, and centers on his relationship with his family and his experiences in the streets of New York between the ages of 6 and 8. David has a troubled relationship with his stern father, who sees his son as soft and pampered, and the boy's only security lies in his affection for his sympathetic but socially isolated mother. At the climax of the book he slips a milk ladle

into a slot in the live rail of a trolley car line and almost electrocutes himself, causing a blinding flash and a blackout in the neighborhood. He awakens to a new sense of self-knowledge. Roth's use of dialect and ethnic speech patterns in the book, his vivid descriptions of the diverse streets of New York, and his sensitivity to the processes of David's growth, combine into a powerfully illuminating story.

Roth's literary output since *Call It Sleep* has been modest. He destroyed the manuscript of a second novel, and though he started work on a third it has never been released. He has, however, contributed to various magazines, and published his memoirs, *Nature's First Green*, in 1979.

Roth, Philip 1933– Born in Newark, New Jersey, Roth was educated at Bucknell and at the University of Chicago. His first book, *Goodbye, Columbus* (1959), consisted of a novella and five short stories and won him the National Book Award in 1960. Jewish-American life in particular, and modern American society in general, are the subjects of his subsequent comedies of manners, which include *Letting Go* (1962), *When She Was Good* (1967), ***Portnoy's Complaint*** (1969), *The Breast* (1972), *The Great American Novel* (1973), *My Life as a Man* (1974), and *The Professor of Desire* (1977). *Our Gang* (1971) is a satire on the Nixon administration. *Reading Myself and Others* (1975) is a collection of essays. His most recent work consists of a semi-autobiographical trilogy of novels about the education, sudden fame, and subsequent disillusion of a writer: *The Ghost Writer* (1979), *Zuckerman Unbound* (1981), and *The Anatomy Lesson* (1983). He is also editor of "Writers from the Other Europe," a series of books by authors from Eastern bloc countries.

Rothenberg, Jerome 1931– Born in New York City, Rothenberg was educated at City College in New York and at the University of Michigan. He has since taught at colleges in New York, California, and Wisconsin. The author of numerous collections of verse, he is best known for *The Seven Hells of Jigoku Zoshi* (1962) and the series of poems *Poland/1931* (1969, complete edition 1974). He has also edited poetry anthologies which reflect his interest in both traditional and contemporary ethnic poetry. *Technicians of the Sacred* (1968) includes tribal and oral poetry from Africa, Asia, and America. *Shaking the Pumpkin* (1972) is an anthology of traditional American Indian poetry. A selection of his own verse, *Poems for the Game of Silence 1960–1970*, appeared in 1971. Since the late 1950s he has been involved with various aspects of poetry performance, notably with the production of his chanted composition *6 Horse Songs for 4 Voices* (1978). He has also edited several small magazines. His most recent work includes *Vienna Blood and Other Poems* (1980); *That Dada Strain* (1983), a collection of verse; and *Symposium of the Whole* (1983), an anthology of writings on ethnopolitics. *Pre-Faces*, a collection of his writings on poetics, appeared in 1982.

Roughing It An early book of autobiographical episodes by **Mark Twain**, published in 1872, telling the story of his journey from St Louis to Nevada, including visits to a Mormon community in Utah and to Virginia City. He also describes his stay in San Francisco and his visit to the Sandwich Islands (Hawaii).

At the outset Twain portrays himself as an Eastern greenhorn, amused and comically befuddled by strange Western ways. As the story progresses, however, the narrator begins to adjust to the lifestyle he portrays, and even begins to speak from a Western perspective. The work has been criticized for unevenness, which is partly due to Twain's inclusion in it of several previously written journalistic pieces, but if the end result is not exactly a coherent picture of life in the American West in the 1860s, the book is held together by the vivid personality and wit of its author.

Rowlandson, Mary White *c.*1635–*c.*1678 The wife of a minister, Rowlandson lived in the frontier town of Lancaster, Massachusetts. During King Philip's War (1674–6), the Narragansetts raided the town, killed some of her family, and took her and two children captive; she was ransomed three months later (May, 1676) through the efforts of her husband. Her account of her experiences, *The Soveraignty and Goodness of God, Together with the Faithfulness of His Promises Displayed; Being a Narrative of the Captivity and Restauration of Mrs Mary Rowlandson*, was published in 1682 in Cambridge, Massachusetts. She tells how she was taken around the countryside by the Indians in their strategic "removes," how she gradually learned how to survive with them and even met their leader, King Philip. Throughout, she likens the captivity to a spiritual affliction. The book went through many editions, becoming a classic of the American captivity genre.

Rowson, Susanna Haswell *c.*1762–1824 Rowson was born in England and came to America with her family as a child; her father was a naval lieutenant stationed in Massachusetts. She returned with her family to England in 1777 and later began to write, producing several sentimental novels and books of verse, including *Victoria* (1786), *The Inquisitor; or Invisible Rambler* (1788; US publication 1793), *Poems on Various Subjects* (1788), a collection of poems entitled *A Trip to Parnassus* (1788), and *Mary; or, The Test of Honour* (1789). ***Charlotte Temple: a Tale of Truth*** (1791; US publication 1794), became the first American best seller. Rowson and her husband returned to the US in 1793 to pursue careers in the theatre. Following *Mentoria; or, The Young Lady's Friend* (1791), a collection of essays and tales on education, and *Rebecca; or, The Fille de Chambre* (1792; US publication 1794), Rowson wrote social comedies and romances for the stage: *Slaves in Algiers* (1794), *The Volunteers* (1795), *The Female Patriot* (1794), *Americans in England* (1796), *A Kick for a Bite* (1795), and *Trials of the Human Heart* (1795). She founded a girls' boarding school and left the stage in 1797, devoting her time to more didactic works for youth, including *Reuben and Rachel; or, Tales of Old Times* (1798), *Miscellaneous Poems* (1804), *Sarah; or, The Exemplary Wife* (1813), and *Charlotte's Daughter; or, The Three Orphans* (1828), the sequel to *Charlotte Temple*.

Rukeyser, Muriel 1913–80 Born in New York City, Rukeyser is best known for her political poetry. Her concern with the Spanish Civil War, women's rights, and the Vietnam War are evident in her numerous volumes of verse, the first of which, *Theory of Flight*, was published in 1935. Other volumes include *U.S. 1.* (1938), *The Turning Wind* (1939), *The*

Green Wave (1948), *Body of Waking* (1958), and *The Gates* (1976). *The Collected Poems of Muriel Rukeyser* appeared in 1979. She also produced one work of fiction, *The Orgy* (1965), translated such authors as Octavio Paz and Bertoldt Brecht, and wrote two biographies – *One Life* (1957), about Wendell Wilkie, and *Willard Gibbs* (1942).

Runyon, (Alfred) Damon 1884– 1946 Born in Manhattan, Kansas, Runyon grew up in Pueblo, Colorado. He began contributing pieces to local newspapers while still in school. He enlisted for the Spanish–American War at the age of 14 and then returned to journalism. His first New York job was as a sports writer on *The American* in 1911. During World War I he became a war correspondent for the Hearst papers, and stayed on there as a columnist after the war. The New York scene provided the material for his unique vernacular humor: athletes, show people, gamblers, hustlers, crooks and their women are transformed into recognizable types. His volumes of stories include *Guys and Dolls* (1931), *Blue Plate Special* (1934), *Take It Easy* (1938), *Furthermore* (England 1938; US 1941), *Runyon a la Carte* (1944), *Short Takes* (1946), and *Runyon on Broadway* (1950). In collaboration with Howard Lindsay, he wrote a farce, *A Slight Case of Murder* (1940), which had a successful run on Broadway.

S

Sacred Fount, The   A short novel by **Henry James**, published in 1901. The story takes place at a weekend party at Newmarch, an English country house. The nameless narrator develops the theory of the "sacred fount" when he observes that his hostess, Grace Brissenden, is much older than her husband, Guy, yet after a few years of marriage seems to be the more youthful and energetic of the two. The narrator speculates that Guy is the "fount" from which his wife draws her new vitality, and that he is correspondingly devitalized. He then applies this theory to another pair of guests, Gilbert Long and May Server. He posits the passage of vital force from May, who appears to be emotionally disturbed, to Gilbert, who once seemed dull but is now a witty man of the world. He further decides that Gilbert and Grace, the dominant partners of their respective marriages, are drawing closer together, and that so are May and Guy, the weaker partners. But Grace, whom the narrator has taken into his confidence, eventually tells him that he has imagined the whole thing. The reader is left uncertain whether Grace is lying or the narrator has merely invented the idea.

Salinger, J[erome] D[avid] 1919–
Salinger was born in New York City and educated at Valley Forge Military Academy, and at New York and Columbia universities. He published short stories in *The Saturday Evening Post* and other magazines during the early 1940s and served in the US infantry during World War II. His only novel has been the highly successful **The Catcher in the Rye** (1951), narrated by a teenaged schoolboy in rebellion against the dubious values of the adult world. In 1953 he published the collection *Nine Stories* (called *For Esmé – With Love and Squalor* in England), in which he introdu-

ces the Glass family, characters who reappear in his later works. *Franny and Zooey* (1961) contains two stories about a brother and sister in the family. Buddy Glass is the narrator of two additional collections, *Raise High the Roofbeam, Carpenters* and *Seymour: An Introduction*, both published in 1963.

Salmagundi; or, The Whim-Whams of Opinions of Launcelot Langstaff, Esq. and Others   A series of satirical essays and poems by **Washington Irving**, his brother William, and **James Kirke Paulding**, *Salmagundi* was first published in 20 periodical pamphlets between January 24, 1807 and January 25, 1808, and then issued in two volumes in 1807 and 1808. The authors used a variety of pseudonyms in the manner of *The Spectator* in 18th-century London, representing members of an imaginary club. The essays cover aspects of life in contemporary New York, their political stance favoring aristocratic federalism in opposition to Jeffersonian democracy. A further series of *Salmagundi* papers, of which Paulding was the sole author, was published between May, 1819 and September, 1820.

Sanctuary   See **Faulkner, William**

Sandburg, Carl 1878–1967   The son of Swedish immigrants, Sandburg was born in Galesburg, Illinois. He left school at the age of 13 and worked as an itinerant laborer, then served in the Spanish–American War, and later worked his way through Lombard College in his native town, graduating in 1902. He then found work as a journalist and advertising copywriter. His career as a poet began in 1904 with the privately printed *In Reckless Ecstasy* (1904), which failed to attract critical attention. The following year he married the daughter of the photographer

Edward Steichen. He continued to work as a journalist, became an organizer in the Social-Democratic party, and served as secretary to the socialist mayor of Milwaukee, Wisconsin, from 1910 to 1912.

In 1914 some of his work was published by **Harriet Monroe** in *Poetry* magazine, and his reputation as a major poet of the Midwest was finally established in 1916 with the publication of *Chicago Poems*, a volume of free-verse poems on 20th-century urban themes. Other collections of poetry followed: *Cornhuskers* (1918), *Smoke and Steel* (1920), *Slabs of the Sunburnt West* (1922), *Good Morning, America* (1928), and *The People, Yes* (1936). His *Complete Poems* (1950) was awarded the Pulitzer Prize. His later verse reveals a rather darker poetic vision, tempered by the experience of the Depression, but throughout his career he retained his optimism regarding the enduring qualities of ordinary working people.

In addition to his poetry, Sandburg is known for his two-part biography of Abraham Lincoln: *Abraham Lincoln: The Prairie Years* (2 vols., 1926), and *Abraham Lincoln: The War Years* (4 vols., 1939). The biography was awarded the Pulitzer Prize, and was abridged in one volume by the author in 1954. Selections from it are also included in Sandburg's picture of the Civil War, *Storm Over the Land* (1942). He also published a collection of folk songs and ballads, *The American Songbag* (1927); several books for children, including *Rootabaga Stories* (1922), *Rootabaga Pigeons* (1923), and *Potato Face* (1930); a study entitled *Steichen the Photographer* (1929); a novel, *Remembrance Rock* (1948); and an autobiography, *Always the Young Strangers* (1952). A volume of *Letters* was issued in 1968.

Santayana, George 1863–1952 Santayana was born in Madrid and taken to the US by his family in 1871. The original form of his name was Jorge Ruiz de Santayana y Borrais. He was brought up in Boston and educated at Harvard. After further study in Germany and England he was awarded his PhD from Harvard in 1889 and became professor of philosophy there in the same year. He stayed until 1912, when he returned to live in Europe.

Santayana published poetry and one novel, *The Last Puritan* (1935), but the main body of his work consists of his philosophical writings. *The Life of Reason* (1905–6) is a five-volume study of reason in everyday life, science, art, and literature. He offers the conclusion that the only reality is matter itself and that all else arises from man's experience of, and response to, matter. He took this idea further in *The Realms of Being*, which began with the introductory volume *Scepticism and Animal Faith* in 1923, and was eventually published in four volumes (1927–40).

His work also includes three studies dealing with American life: *Philosophical Opinion in America* (1918); *Character and Opinion in the United States* (1920), on the conflict of idealism and materialism; and *The Genteel Tradition at Bay* (1931), a criticism of the "new humanism." Among his other works are *Three Philosophical Poets* (1910), which studies the work of Lucretius, Dante, and Goethe; *Egotism in German Philosophy* (1916), a criticism of German idealism and romantic willfulness (he published a revised edition in 1939); and *Soliloquies in England* (1922), an examination of the Anglo-Saxon character. *The Idea of Christ in the Gospels* (1946) is both an interpretation of the Gospels and an examination of the idea of God in man. His memoirs, *Persons and Places*, were published in three volumes: *The Backgrounds of My Life* (1944), *The Middle Span* (1945), and *My Host the World* (1953).

Saroyan, William 1908–1981 Born in Fresno, California, of Armenian parents, Saroyan spent most of his youth in San Francisco. He left school at 15, worked for a telegraph company, and began writing short stories in the late 1920s. His first collection of short stories, *The Daring Young Man on the Flying Trapeze* (1934), which attracted considerable critical and popular attention, typifies the rather genial vision which characterized his work as a whole. Other volumes of short fiction include *Inhale and Exhale* (1936), *Three Times Three* (1936), *The Trouble with Tigers* (1938), *My Name is Aram* (1940), and *Dear Baby* (1944). His first novel, *The Human Comedy*, appeared in 1943, and was followed by *The Adventures of Wesley Jackson* (1946), *Rock Wagram* (1951), *Mama, I Love You* (1956), *Papa, You're Crazy* (1957), and a story about an aging author, *One Day in the Afternoon of the World* (1964).

Saroyan perhaps achieved his greatest fame as a playwright. The one-act play, *My Heart's in the Highlands*, was produced in 1939 and published in 1941. *The Time of Your Life* (1939), set in a San Francisco waterfront saloon, was awarded the Pulitzer Prize, but Saroyan rejected it. His other plays include *Love's Old Sweet Song* (1941), *The Beautiful People* (1942), *Across the Board on Tomorrow Morning* (1942), *Hello, Out There* (1943), *Don't Go Away Mad* (1949), and *The Cave Dwellers* (1957). He published three autobiographical works: *The Bicycle Rider in Beverly Hills* (1952), *Here Comes, There Goes, You Know Who* (1961), and *Obituaries* (1979).

Sarton, May 1912–   Born in Belgium, Sarton emigrated to the US in 1916 and became a citizen in 1924. Her first publication was a collection of lyrics entitled *Encounter in April* (1937). Other volumes of verse include *Inner Landscape* (1939), *The Lion and the Rose* (1948), *The Land of Silence* (1953), *In Time Like Air* (1957), and *Cloud, Stone, Sun, Vine* (1961). *Collected Poems* appeared in 1974.

Her novels and poetry address moral and political issues in a controlled and crafted manner, using a distinct and localized idiom. Her novels include *The Single Hound* (1938), about a young English poet; *The Birth of Grandfather* (1957); *The Small Room* (1961), about a young female teacher and a student at a New England college; *Mrs Stevens Hears the Mermaids Singing* (1965); *Kinds of Love* (1970); *As We Are Now* (1973); and *Anger* (1982). Her autobiographical writings include *I Knew a Phoenix* (1959), *Plant Dreaming Deep* (1968), *Journal of Solitude* (1973), and *Recovering* (1980).

Sartoris   See **Faulkner, William**

Saturday Review, The   Originally called *The Saturday Review of Literature*, the magazine was founded in 1924 by Henry Seidel Canby, C. Morley, Amy Loveman, and **William Rose Benét**. The title was shortened in 1952. Its editors have included Canby (1924–36), Bernard de Voto (1936–8), George Stevens (1938–40), Norman Cousins (1970–1, 1973–9), Carl Tucker (1979–83), and Bruce Van Wyngouden (1983–   ). Cousins encouraged the expansion of the magazine's format, as well as its involvement in social and political issues. In addition to its literary material, it now includes commentary on world events, art, television, recordings, cinema, education, science, and travel. "Letters to the Editor" present opposing views from readers in accordance with the magazine's policy of promoting a dialogue on current and controversial topics.

Scarlet Letter, The   A novel by **Nathaniel Hawthorne**, published in 1850 and developed from an incident described by him in the story, "Endicott and the Red Cross" (1837). In the lengthy introductory section called "The Custom House," Hawthorne describes his work at the custom house in Salem, offers some thoughts on the nature of fiction, and finally tells how he discovered the cloth scarlet letter along with some documents recounting the story he is about to tell.

The novel is set in 17th-century Boston, and opens as a young woman named Hester Prynne emerges from prison with her illegitimate baby in her arms. Charged with adultery, she must stand exposed on the public scaffold for three hours, and must thereafter wear the scarlet "A" on her breast as a lifelong sign of her sin. Her husband is an elderly English scholar who two years earlier had sent her to Boston to prepare a home for them, but had failed to follow her at the appointed time. Unknown to Hester, he had been captured by Indians, and in fact arrives just in time to see his wife publicly condemned. Hester will not reveal the identity of her lover, try as the community does to draw out the secret. Ironically, the guilty man is one of that community's most respected figures, the young minister, Arthur Dimmesdale. A highly conscientious man, he escapes outward condemnation, but is inwardly tormented by his sin.

Years pass and Hester settles into her new life. She proves to be a strongminded and capable woman and, in spite of her humiliation, finds a place in Boston society by helping other unfortunates and outcasts. Her daughter, Pearl, has developed into a mischievous, "elfin" child who reminds Hester of her guilt by asking rather acute questions about the minister and the letter. Meanwhile, Hester's husband has taken the name Roger Chillingworth and has settled in Boston as a doctor. He makes Hester swear to keep his identity secret, and indulges his private obsession with finding the identity of her lover. Happening upon Hester, Pearl, and Dimmesdale speaking together one midnight, he guesses correctly at Dimmesdale's guilt. Aware that the minister's failing health is related to his unconfessed sin, Chillingworth pretends to help him medically, while torturing him spiritually with veiled allusions to his crime. When Hester discovers what he is doing she pleads with him to stop, but he is intoxicated by his power over Dimmesdale and puts aside everything but his continuing revenge. Hester intercepts Arthur one day on a walk through the forest and begs him to escape with her to Europe. He would like to do so, and Hester even removes the letter from her breast, but he sees flight as a yielding to further temptation. He returns to town, his mind filled with evil thoughts, to finish writing his Election Day Sermon. Hester learns that Chillingworth has blocked her plan of escape by booking passage on the same ship. Having delivered a powerful sermon, Dimmesdale leaves the church and bids Hester and Pearl to join him on the pillory, where at last he publicly confesses his sin. As Dimmesdale dies in his lover's arms, Chillingworth cries out in agony at having lost the sole object of his perverse life. Hester and Pearl, now free from the restraints of the mortified community, leave Boston. The book ends with Hester's return to Boston and her voluntary decision to resume wearing the scarlet letter. While Pearl settles in Europe, Hester continues her life of penance, a model of endurance, goodness, and victory over sin.

Schwartz, Delmore 1913–66 Schwartz was born in Brooklyn and graduated from New York University as a philosophy major in 1935. The chief preoccupation of much of his fiction and verse is the complex relationship between the private self and the outside world. The intellectual energy of his writing was reflected also in his career as a teacher at Harvard, Princeton, New York, and Syracuse universities, and in his influential position in the group of Jewish writers that emerged after World War II – particularly as a member of the editorial board of *The Partisan Review* from 1943 to 1955. For the last two decades of his life, however, he was plagued by emotional problems and broke off from family and friends.

His first book of stories and poems, *In Dreams Begin Responsibilities*, was published in 1938. Other collections which combine prose and poetry are *Genesis, Book One* (1943) and *Vaudeville for a Princess, and Other Poems* (1950). He translated Rimbaud's *A Season in Hell* in 1939, and in 1941 he published a verse-play, *Shenandoah*, and a collection of essays, *The Imitation of Life*. His collection of short stories *The World is a Wedding* (1948) deals with the problems of Jewish life in America. *Summer Knowledge: New and Selected Poems 1938–58* appeared in 1959, and *Successful Love, and Other Stories* in 1961. A volume of *Selected Essays* was published posthumously in 1970.

Sea Wolf, The A novel by **Jack London**, published in 1904. In the fog on San Francisco Bay, two ferry boats collide, and Humphrey Van Weyden is thrown overboard. He is saved by a sealing schooner, the *Ghost*, whose captain, Wolf Larsen, presses him into service. He is at once fascinated by Larsen's brute power and repelled by his ruthlessness. They reach the sealing grounds off Japan, where Maude Brewster, a castaway from a shipwreck, is rescued by the *Ghost* and almost at once becomes the object of Larsen's attentions. She finds a sympathetic response in Van Weyden, but the struggle between the two men is hopelessly unequal and she and Van Weyden flee from the ship. They reach a deserted island, but the *Ghost* is driven ashore there. Larsen has been deserted by his crew, and, suffering from cerebral cancer, is blind. Van Weyden and Miss Brewster manage to make the *Ghost* seaworthy again and set out for civilization; Larsen, defiant to the last, dies on the island.

Secret Service A melodrama by **William Gillette**, first performed in Philadelphia in 1895. In its New York production the following year, Gillette himself replaced Maurice Barrymore in the leading role. In a series of fast-moving scenes, the play describes the ruses and eventual unmasking of a gallant Union spy, Captain Thorne, in the Confederate city of Richmond, Virginia. At the last moment his death sentence is commuted, and the audience is left with the prospect of a post-war marriage between him and Edith Varney, the daughter of a Confederate general, for love of whom Thorne had failed to carry out a crucial act of espionage.

Sedgwick, Catharine Maria 1789–1867 Sedgwick was born in Stockbridge,

Massachusetts, into a wealthy and politically active Calvinist family. In 1820 she followed her father's lead and converted to the Unitarianism espoused by **William Ellery Channing**.

Her first novel, *A New England Tale* (1822), became one of America's first best sellers. It tells the story of the orphaned Jane Elton who, after a difficult adolescence of restrictions imposed by poverty, dependence on others, and Calvinist orthodoxy, finally achieves the emotional maturity to assume the responsibilities of marriage and a family. Sedgwick's second novel, *Redwood* (1824), brought its author a popularity equal to that of her contemporaries **James Fenimore Cooper** and **Washington Irving**. It tells the story of Ellen Bruce, another orphan, who competes with Caroline Redwood for the attentions of Charles Westall. Eventually, Caroline reveals her petty nature and Charles marries Ellen. It is then revealed that Ellen is in fact Caroline's half-sister by their father's secret first marriage, and is thus entitled to a share of the family fortune. The novel envisions a society in which women's influence will produce an age of virtue, family harmony, and love.

Sedgwick's third novel, *Hope Leslie* (1827), concerns relations between whites and Indians. Set in 17th-century New England, it introduces the theme of miscegenation that was common in subsequent American fiction. Her other works include *Clarence* (1830), *The Linwoods* (1835), and a trilogy consisting of *Home* (1835), *The Poor Man and the Rich Man* (1836), and *Live and Let Live* (1837). Her last novel, *Married or Single?* (1857), reflects her awareness of the social difficulties faced by unmarried women.

Seeger, Alan 1888–1916 Born in New York City into an old New England family, Seeger graduated from Harvard in 1910. He wrote poetry while at college and some of his verse appeared in *The Harvard Monthly*. He apparently found life in America unsatisfying, and two years after completing his education he departed for Paris. France became his home, and at the outbreak of World War I he enlisted in her defense, joining the Foreign Legion. He served with distinction and was killed in 1916 at Belloy-en-Santerre during the Battle of the Somme. He was posthumously awarded the Croix de Guerre and the

Médaille Militaire. His volume entitled *Poems* was published in the year of his death, with an introduction by William Archer. His famous "I Have a Rendezvous with Death" was first published in *The North American Review* in October 1916. Many of his other poems, such as "Ode to Antares," Sonnet VIII ("Oh, love of woman, you are known to be"), and "Ode to Natural Beauty," are strongly Romantic in tone. His *Letters and Diary* was published in 1917.

Selby, Hubert Jr 1928– Born and educated in New York City, Selby drew upon personal experiences for his stories of life in the lowest circles of society. His best-known work, the collection of stories entitled *Last Exit to Brooklyn* (1964), was the subject of a much-publicized obscenity trial in England. It deals with homosexuality, prostitution, and brutality, while exploring human isolation in an urban environment. Selby followed it with three novels: *The Room* (1971), the story of a nameless psychopath awaiting trial; *The Demon* (1976), about a man possessed by lust, ambition, and violence; and *Requiem for a Dream* (1978), an examination of drug addiction.

Sewall, Samuel 1652–1730 The son of New England settlers, Sewall was born in England and returned with his family to Boston in 1661. In 1671 he received his BA from Harvard, where he remained as a tutor and in 1676 married the daughter of John Hull, a man whose wealth allowed Sewall to enter public life. In 1679 he assumed his first public office as manager of the colony's printing press and soon became deputy to the General Court. Between 1684 and 1686 he served as a member of the Council. In England in 1688–9, he helped **Increase Mather** recover the Massachusetts Charter from William III. While a councilor in Boston (1691–1725), he served as special commissioner at the witchcraft trials in 1692. He soon regretted those proceedings and, in fact, was the only one of the nine judges to make a public confession of error (Old South Church, Boston, 1709).

Sewall distinguished himself as a humane and liberal jurist, most notably while he was chief justice of the Superior Judicature (1718–28). His writings testify to that reputation. *The Revolution in New-England Justified* (1691), written in conjunction with Edward Rawson, justifies the uprising of 1689 which deposed Royal Governor Andros. Having produced a text which typically conceives of New England as the eventual seat of the New Jerusalem, *Phaenomena quaedam apocalyptica* (1697), Sewall went on to write one of the earliest published arguments against slavery, *The Selling of Joseph* (1700). In 1713 he produced another theological treatise, *Proposals Touching the Accomplishment of Prophesies* (1713). Finally came two tracts that most clearly reveal his kind heart and innovative judgment: *A Memorial Relating to the Kennebeck Indians* (1721), an argument for the humane treatment of the Indians; and "*Talitha Cumi*" (Massachusetts Historical Society, 1873), a rebuttal of a theological position which denied the resurrection to women (the work's Arabic title translates as "maiden arise" and is taken from Mark 5:41). As a historical document, Sewall's *Diary* is his greatest contribution to colonial literature. Published 1878–82 by the Massachusetts Historical Society, it covers the years 1674–7 and 1685–1729, and offers an intimate and detailed account of day-to-day life in Puritan New England.

Sewanee Review, The Affiliated with the University of the South (Sewanee, Tennessee), *The Sewanee Review* has been published continuously since 1892. Although essentially a critical journal (concentrating in particular on modern English and American literature), it also publishes some poetry and fiction. It has exerted great influence as a journal of the **New Criticism**, particularly under the editorship of **Allen Tate** (1944–6).

Sexton, Anne 1928–74 Born in Newton, Massachusetts, Sexton grew up in nearby Wellesley, and briefly attended Garland Junior College before marrying in 1948. Her poetry, like that of **Robert Lowell**, with whom she studied, is **Confessional** in its use of the ordinary events of the poet's daily life to explore the self and its relation to the world. Among her main subjects were her struggles with depression and mental illness; her experiences as a daughter, wife, and mother; and the natural world, specifically that of the Massachusetts coastline and Maine. Her depression and loneliness finally led to her suicide in 1974.

Her first volume was *To Bedlam and Part Way Back* (1960). Subsequent books include *All My Pretty Ones* (1962), *Selected Poems* (1964), *Live or Die* (1966), *Love Poems* (1969), *Transformations* (1971), *The Book of Folly* (1972), *The Death Notebooks* (1974), and *The Awful Rowing Towards God* (1975). Two posthumous collections were edited by Linda Gray Sexton: *45 Mercy Street* (1976) and *Words for Dr Y: Uncollected Poems with Three Stories* (1978).

Shapiro, Karl 1913– Born in Baltimore, Maryland, Shapiro attended the University of Virginia and The Johns Hopkins University. His poetry was first recognized when it appeared in an anthology entitled *Five Young American Poets* (1941). His first volume was *Person, Place, and Thing* (1942), a collection of love poems in blank verse. He served in the US Army from 1941 to 1945; *V-Letter and Other Poems* (1944), which won him the 1945 Pulitzer Prize, contains war poetry. Later volumes, such as *Poems 1940–1953* (1953), *The House* (1957), and *Poems of a Jew* (1958), are often caustic and iconoclastic in tone and are written in tight, disciplined verse. *The Bourgeois Poet* (1964) marked a distinct change in form, the poems being composed in Whitmanesque prose paragraphs. Subsequent collections, which include *White-Haired Lover* (1968) and *Adult Bookstore* (1976), have tended to return to more traditional forms, notably the sonnet.

Shapiro has been an influential figure in contemporary American poetry, serving as poetry consultant to the Library of Congress (1946–7), editing *Poetry* magazine (1950–6) and *The Prairie Schooner* (1956–66), and teaching young poets at various colleges, including the universities of Nebraska and Illinois. He has written a number of critical works, among them *Beyond Criticism* (1953, reissued in 1965 as *A Primer for Poets*), *In Defense of Ignorance* (1960), *Randall Jarrell* (1967), and *The Poetry Wreck: Selected Essays 1950–1970* (1975).

Shaw, Henry Wheeler 1818–85 A comic writer who published under the pseudonym of Josh Billings, Shaw was born in Lanesboro, Massachusetts. He worked in a variety of occupations and spent some time in the West. Like **Artemus Ward**, **Petroleum V. Nasby**, and **Mark Twain**, Shaw began his career as a humorist with contributions to local newspapers. These early pieces attracted the attention of Artemus Ward, who helped him publish his first collection, *Josh Billings: Hiz Sayings* in 1865. Thereafter he became a favorite exponent of agrarian folk wisdom and reached an immense public with his comments on government, fashionable pretension, and political corruption. His publications include *Josh Billings on Ice, and Other Things* (1868), *Everybody's Friend* (1874), *Josh Billings' Trump Kards* (1877), and *Josh Billings' Spice Box* (1881). From 1869 to 1880 he published a parody annual called *Farmer's Allminax*. In the tradition of the vernacular humorists of his day, he lectured widely in his Josh Billings persona and commanded a large popular audience.

Shepard, Sam 1943–   Born Samuel Shepard Rogers in Sheridan, Illinois and raised and educated in California. He moved to New York City in 1963 and began writing plays, the first of which, *Cowboys*, was performed in 1964. He has been a leader of the *avant-garde* in contemporary American theatre since his earliest work; to date he has produced more than forty plays as well as several screenplays. His work resists easy categorization but may be said to deal with the vagaries of American mythologies, his plays often focusing on the problems of the individual trying to adjust to historical realities.

His plays include *Icarus's Mother* (1965); *La Turista* (1966); *Melodrama Play* (1967); *Operation Sidewinder* (1970); *Mad Dog Blues* (1971); *The Tooth of Crime* (1972); *Geography of a Horse Dreamer* (1974); and *Angel City* (1976). *Curse of the Starving Class* (1976) was the first play in a trilogy exploring the relationship of Americans to their land, their family, and their history. The trilogy continued in 1978 with *Buried Child* (Pulitzer Prize, 1979) and concluded with *True West* (1980). This group of plays, especially, places Shepard in the tradition of **Eugene O'Neill**, with its treatment of a tragic America mired in sin and immorality. Shepard is the only playwright to have received more than two Obie awards (for Off-Broadway productions); he received his tenth in 1979 for *Buried Child*. His plays have appeared in several collections, including *Five Plays* (1967), *Action and The Unseen Hand: Two Plays* (1975), *Four Two-Act Plays* (1980), *Buried Child and Other Plays* (1979), *Seven Plays* (1981), and *Fool For Love and Other Plays* (1984).

Shepard, Thomas 1605–49   Born in Towcester, England, the youngest of nine children, Shepard was orphaned as a child and raised by his brother. He entered Emmanuel College, Cambridge, as a pensioner in 1620, receiving his BA in 1624 and MA in 1627. Following his ordination he served as occasional lecturer at Earles-Colne in Essex until 1630, when he was silenced by Archbishop Laud for his Puritan leanings and accepted a position as private tutor and chaplain for Sir Richard Darley of Buttercrambe. He married Margaret Tauteville in 1632 and moved to Hedden, where Bishop Morton of Durham denied him the privilege of public preaching, a denial which enforced Laud's prior silencing and drove Shepard to Massachusetts Bay in 1635.

Although Shepard lived only 14 years in New England, he exerted a powerful influence on the Puritan experiment. Between 1636 and 1637 alone, he was appointed pastor of the prestigious Church at Newton (Cambridge), convinced his friend John Harvard to locate the college at Newton, suffered the death of his wife Margaret, married Joanna Hooker, the daughter of **Thomas Hooker**, and played a key role in the Cambridge Synod of 1637 which condemned Antinomianism. His exploration of the stages leading to conversion, *The Sincere Convert* (1641), soon became the most widely read formulation of the theory of preparation. Two of his other tracts, *Theses Sabbaticae* (1649) and *Church Membership of Children and Their Right to Baptism* (1663), demonstrate his contribution to the central ecclesiastical debates of American Congregationalism. Although known as a rigorous theologian and ardent pastor, Shepard tempered his religious conviction with empathy for the common Puritan's struggle with spiritual truths, as is testified to by his sermons, most notably those collected in *The Parable of the Ten Virgins Opened and Applied* (1660) and by his autobiography (first published in 1747 as *Three Valuable Pieces, Viz., Select Cases Resolved; First Principles of the Oracles of God; . . .; And a Private Diary; Containing Meditations and Experiences Never Before Published*; it was republished in 1832 as

The Autobiography of Thomas Shepard; the authoritative text appeared in 1972 as *God's Plot*, edited by Michael McGiffert).

Sherlock Holmes   A melodrama by **William Gillette**, written with full agreement and some assistance from Arthur Conan Doyle. The plot is based on elements from three stories, "A Scandal in Bohemia," "The Final Problem," and "A Study in Scarlet." Its resolution depends almost as much on the incompetence of Professor Moriarty and his criminal associates as it does on the resourcefulness of Sherlock Holmes. The play's immense popularity was partly due to the author's studied playing of the title role. Frederic Dorr Steele, who illustrated the Conan Doyle stories, based his portraits of Holmes on Gillette, so that actor and character became identified in the public mind, both in England and the US, during the 30 or more years that Gillette toured in the play after its first performance in Buffalo in 1899.

Sherwood, Robert E[mmet] 1896–1955 Sherwood was born in New Rochelle, New York, and educated at Harvard. Following his graduation he joined the Canadian army and was wounded in action in 1918. His war experiences led him to adopt an outspoken pacifist stance, which is evident in his first play, *The Road to Rome* (1927), a comedy about Hannibal's deferred march on Rome. His 1936 play, *Idiot's Delight*, was awarded a Pulitzer Prize, the first of four he was to receive. The advocacy of participation in a virtuous war in the late play, *There Shall Be No Night* (1940, Pulitzer Prize 1941), marked a celebrated change of heart in a man who was by then serving as Special Assistant to the Secretary of War as well as writing many of President Roosevelt's speeches. His other plays include *The Queen's Husband* (1928), *Reunion in Vienna* (1931), *The Petrified Forest* (1935), *Abe Lincoln in Illinois* (1938, Pulitzer Prize, 1939), *The Rugged Path* (1945), and *Small War on Murray Hill* (1957). He also wrote screenplays and was awarded an Academy Award for his screenplay for *The Best Years of Our Lives* in 1946. His political memoir, *Roosevelt and Hopkins: An Intimate History* (1948), received the Pulitzer Prize in 1949.

She Would Be a Soldier   See **Noah, Mordecai Manuel**

Ship of Fools   See **Porter, Katherine Anne**

Silko, Leslie Marmon 1948–   Silko belongs to the generation of Native American writers conscious of the need both to preserve a vanishing traditional culture and to confront the social and political pressures which threaten the survival of the Native American. Born of mixed ancestry – Laguna Pueblo, Mexican, and Anglo-American – and raised in traditional Laguna ways but educated in white schools, she has written poetry and fiction which incorporate material and techniques from the traditional sources of her Laguna people to explore contemporary issues and dilemmas. Since her first publication in 1969, a story entitled "The Man To Send Rain Clouds," she has published three books: a collection of poems, *Laguna Woman* (1974); a novel, *Ceremony* (1977); and a collection of poetry and short fiction, *Storyteller* (1981). Her short pieces have been widely anthologized and appear frequently in journals and collections associated with the Native American movement. She has taught English at the University of Arizona, and has received numerous grants and awards, including the MacArthur Foundation Award in 1981.

Her best-known work, *Ceremony*, is the story of Tayo, a half-breed Laguna World War II veteran, shattered by his experience in the Pacific and his inability to save his half-brother, Rocky, a more Americanized, more successful soldier who was killed by the Japanese. Tayo is gradually able to heal himself and reorder his world by reenacting a traditional ceremony with the help of a medicine man, Betonie, and a part-Mexican woman, T'seh, who embodies the female life-giving principle and wholeness of mother earth. The form of the novel is a mixture of modern, graphic realism with traditional Indian ways of seeing and telling, incorporating story, song, and legend. In much the same way, Silko's poems have their roots in ritual but express themselves in the measures of contemporary free verse.

Simms, William Gilmore 1806–70 Born in Charleston, South Carolina, Simms was raised by his maternal grandmother, his mother having died in 1808 and his father having moved to Mississippi to become a planter. In 1825 he published his first book of verse and began contributing to *The Album*, a Charleston periodical. In 1827 he was admitted to the Bar. Between 1827 and 1830, in addition to practicing law, he published four more volumes of poetry.

From 1830 to 1832 he edited the Charleston *City Gazette*. His sixth book of verse, *Atalantis: A Story of the Sea*, appeared in 1832, the same year that he traveled to the North and met various literary figures, among them **William Cullen Bryant**. In 1833 he published his first novel, *Martin Faber*, a study of a murderer, and a collection of short stories entitled *The Book of My Lady: A Melange*. *Guy Rivers: A Tale of Georgia* (1834) is a romance of the Southern frontier. It was followed by his best-known novel, ***The Yemassee: A Romance of Carolina*** (1835), the fictional account of an actual uprising by the Yemassee Indians against British colonists. In the same year he published *The Partisan: A Tale of the Revolution*. A second Revolutionary War romance, *Mellichampe: A Legend of the Santee*, followed in 1836.

Simms continued to write historical romances – another 22 novels published in book form between 1838 and 1859, plus at least three more published serially (appearing in volume form only after his death). Perhaps the most notable of these later novels is *Woodcraft; or, Hawks about the Dovecote* (1854), which originally appeared in 1852 under the title of *The Sword and the Distaff; or "Fair, Fat, and Forty."* During this period he also published three collections of short stories and 12 books of verse. His non-fiction works include the essay "Slavery in America" (1837), *The History of South Carolina* (1840), *The Geography of South Carolina* (1843), and *The Life of Francis Marion* (1844). He was also connected with several periodicals, among them the *Southern Quarterly Review*, which he edited from 1849 to 1854. From 1844 to 1846 he served as a member of South Carolina's legislature. The Civil War broke him financially and spiritually. An extremely successful novelist in his own lifetime, Simms not only depicted the Old South in its essence but also helped to propagate the Southern myth of perfectibility – the myth that God had given the land to the Southern whites so that they could form an ideal society which would include benevolent enslavement of the blacks.

Simon, (Marvin) Neil 1927–   Born in the Bronx, New York, Simon's prolific career in the American theatre began with revue sketches written with his brother Daniel. *Catch a Star!*, his first Broadway show, opened in 1955; *Come Blow Your Horn*, his first play, was written with his brother in 1961. A series of long-running successes followed in the 1960s: *Barefoot in the Park* (1963), *The Odd Couple* (1965), *The Star Spangled Girl* (1966), *Plaza Suite* (1968), and *The Last of the Red Hot Lovers* (1969). His later work includes *The Prisoner of Second Avenue* (1971), *The Sunshine Boys* (1972), *California Suite* (1976), the semi-autobiographical *Chapter Two* (1977), and *Brighton Beach Memoirs* (1983).

Simple Cobler of Aggawam, The   A satire by **Nathaniel Ward**, written in America in 1645 and published in London in 1647. It is an appeal, in the midst of the English Civil War, for an end to hostilities and a return to national stability. Ward chides the king for having overreached his authority, and clearly supports the Parliamentary cause against the Royalists; but he warns the radical Independents that their decentralizing, tolerationist policies will bring instability to England. He takes the side of the Presbyterians, urging the Parliamentarians to end the war and, in the interest of national unity, "rather to compose than to tolerate differences in Religion."

Although orthodox, Ward's *Cobler* is unusual among Puritan texts for its ebullient style. Theodore de la Guard, the pseudonymous cobbler, belongs to a tradition of such working-class personae commenting on ecclesiastical matters of note and seriousness; in this case, Ward develops the "simplicity" of his persona in terms of his living on the American frontier (Aggawam was the Indian name for Ipswich), quite removed from the London scene. Mixing a colloquial style with elaborate wordplay, puns and analogies and doggerel verses, *The Simple Cobler* is perhaps more reminiscent of Elizabethan than of Puritan literature.

Simpson, Louis 1923–   Born in Jamaica, Simpson came to the US in 1940; he attended Columbia University for three years before leaving to serve in the US Army. After the war he completed his doctorate at Columbia, and since then has taught at several universities, including the University of California at Berkeley and the State University of New York at Stony Brook.

Although he has written criticism, a novel, and two plays, he is best known for his poetry, which is characterized by its mythical and dream-like subject matter and its colloquial, often ironic tone. His first volume was *The Arrivistes: Poems 1940–49*, which was published in Paris in 1949. Subsequent publications include *The Father Out of the Machine: A Masque* (1951); *Good News of Death and Other Poems* (1955); *Andromeda* (1956), a play; *A Dream of Governors* (1959); *Riverside Drive* (1962), a novel; and *James Hogg: A Critical Study* (1962). He was awarded the Pulitzer Prize in 1963 for *At The End of The Open Road: Poems*. Recent volumes of poetry include *Adventures of the Letter I* (1971), *Searching for the Ox* (1976), *Caviare at the Funeral: Poems* (1980), and *The Best Hour of the Night* (1983). Simpson is also the author of *An Introduction to Poetry* (1967); *Three on the Tower* (1975), essays on **Ezra Pound**, **T. S. Eliot**, and **William Carlos Williams**; *A Revolution in Taste: Studies of Dylan Thomas, Allen Ginsberg, Sylvia Plath and Robert Lowell* (1978); and *A Company of Poets* (1981), published as part of a "poets on poetry" series.

Sincere Convert, The See **Shepard, Thomas**

Sinclair, Upton 1878–1968 Born in Baltimore, Maryland, Sinclair attended the City College of New York and then did graduate work at Columbia University from 1901 to 1906. He had begun writing dime novels at the age of 15, and in 1906 he won international reputation with the publication of *The Jungle*. An exposé of the meat-packing industry in Chicago, and perhaps the most famous of all "muckraking novels," it remains his best-known book. A prolific writer, he produced more than 100 works in all, among them a series of pamphlets on aspects of American life, including *The Profits of Religion* (1918); *The Brass Check* (1919), on journalism; *The Goslings* (1924), on education; *Money Writes!* (1927), on art and literature; and *The Flivver King* (1937), on the automobile industry.

By 1953 Sinclair had completed 11 volumes of his immense *roman fleuve*, *World's End*. Its hero, Lanny Budd, the illegitimate son of a munitions tycoon, travels the world and becomes involved in international political intrigues. The first novel in the series, also entitled *World's End*, was published in 1940 and narrates the events of Budd's life between 1913 and 1919; *Between Two Worlds* (1941) covers the period from the Treaty of Versailles to the 1929 stock-market crash; *Dragon's Teeth* (1942), which won the Pulitzer Prize, concerns Budd's encounters with anti-Nazi sentiment in Europe in the early 1930s; *Wide is the Gate* (1943) also deals with anti-Nazi sentiment, in Spain and France; *The Presidential Agent* (1944) recounts Budd's relationship with President Roosevelt; *Dragon Harvest* (1945) carries his history through to the fall of Paris; *A World to Win* (1946) and *A Presidential Mission* (1947) cover his experiences in Europe, North Africa, and the Orient during the early years of World War II; *One Clear Call* (1948) and *O Shepherd, Speak!* (1949) recount the last years of the war and the subsequent peace plans; the final novel in the series, *The Return of Lanny Budd* (1953) deals with hostile sentiment in the US toward postwar Soviet Russia. Sinclair published his own selection from his correspondence, *My Lifetime in Letters*, in 1960, and his *Autobiography* in 1962.

Sinners in the Hands of an Angry God A sermon preached by **Jonathan Edwards** at Enfield, Connecticut, on July 8, 1741, at the height of the Great Awakening. Its fire and brimstone style is not characteristic of Edwards's preaching, but it had a great effect on its audience (a congregation he was visiting) and was printed several times soon after its delivery. Edwards follows the Puritan sermon form, explicating the doctrine and application of the biblical text "Their foot shall slide in due time." Developing the theme of the precariousness of the sinner's position and the imagery of the fire of damnation (invoking the famous image of the spider held over the fire by a slender thread), Edwards tries to move his hearers to feel the force of the Calvinist doctrine and to experience the first stirrings of a religious conversion.

Sister Carrie A novel by **Theodore Dreiser**, published in 1900 by the firm of Doubleday but not widely distributed at the time. (Mrs Frank Doubleday in fact disliked the manuscript so intensely that she sought to prevent its publication.) In 1901 it appeared in the Dollar Library series in England, Dreiser having condensed the first 200 pages into 80 to make it conform to the other volumes in the series. Its favorable reception by English reviewers was responsible for its reissue in the US in 1907.

The novel tells the story of Carrie Meeber, a midwestern country girl who moves to Chicago. She meets a salesman called Charles Drouet, and after a period of unemployment becomes his mistress. Soon, however, she becomes disillusioned with him and takes up with his friend George Hurstwood, a middle-aged, married restaurant manager. He embezzles money and elopes with Carrie to New York City, where he opens a saloon which proves a failure. Their liaison continues for some three years, until Carrie is forced by their impoverishment to work as a chorus girl to support them. Though she makes an impression in a small part and begins what is to become a successful career, she fails to find happiness. She deserts Hurstwood, who ends up a drunken beggar on Skid Row. Eventually, and unknown to Carrie, he commits suicide.

Sketch Book, The A book of essays and tales by **Washington Irving**, published serially from 1819 to 1820 under the pseudonym of Geoffrey Crayon, Gent. (In 1820 the work was published in book form in England.) Most of the pieces are descriptive and thoughtful essays on England, where Irving had been living for some years. Six sketches are set in America, among them Irving's most celebrated tales, "The Legend of Sleepy Hollow" and "Rip Van Winkle." In fact he derived most of the stories from European folk-tales which he probably came across while traveling in England and northern Europe. In its own day *The Sketch Book* brought great fame to Irving, both in England and America, making him the first American author to receive international recognition.

Skin of Our Teeth, The See **Wilder, Thornton**

Slaughterhouse Five See **Vonnegut, Kurt, Jr**

Smith, Logan Pearsall 1865–1946 A member of a Philadelphia Quaker family, Smith was born in Millville, New Jersey, and educated at Harvard and Oxford. He had

independent means and decided to settle in England, where he earned a reputation as a lexicographer, a bibliographer, and an essayist with an elegant and witty style. He prepared editions of various authors, including John Donne, and published a biography of Sir Henry Wotton in 1907. His most notable work of criticism is *Milton and His Modern Critics* (1940), in which he takes issue with **T. S. Eliot** and **Ezra Pound** for their attacks on Milton's reputation. *Unforgotten Years* (1938), his autobiography, describes his Quaker boyhood, his experiences as an expatriate American, with some interesting observations on American letters, and his acquaintance with **Walt Whitman**. His aphorisms and essays were collected in *All Trivia* (1933; revised edition 1945) and *Reperusals and Re-Collections* (1936). He also published poems and short stories.

Snodgrass, W[illiam] D[eWitt] 1926– Snodgrass was born in Pennsylvania and educated at the University of Iowa. As a graduate student in the Writers' Workshop there he studied with **Robert Lowell** (his highly personal poems spurred the development of Lowell's own **Confessional** verse). He has since taught at the University of Rochester and at Syracuse University.

Snodgrass's work is characterized by its autobiographical subject matter, its use of traditional verse forms, and its sensitive, often delicate tone. His first volume, *Heart's Needle* (1959), centers on his divorce from his first wife and his subsequent separation from his daughter; it was awarded the Pulitzer Prize in 1960. His other volumes include *Gallows Songs of Christian Morgenstern* (1967); *After Experience: Poems and Translations* (1968), which includes his translations of Rilke; *The Führer Bunker: A Cycle of Poems in Progress* (1977); *Six Troubador Songs* (1977), a book of translations; and *Six Minnesinger Songs* (1983). His lectures and essays on poetry are collected in *In Radical Pursuit* (1975).

Snowbound See **Whittier, John Greenleaf**

Snyder, Gary 1930– Born in San Francisco, Snyder grew up in Oregon and Washington. After graduating from Reed College, he moved to Berkeley to study oriental languages at the University of California, during which time he met **Jack Kerouac**, **Allen Ginsberg**, and other members of the **Beat** movement. He came to share many of the Beats' social and aesthetic views, including their rejection of mainstream American values and their use of experimental poetic forms.

Snyder's poetry reflects his interest in Buddhism – he received formal Zen training in Japan – as well as his experiences as a seaman, logger, and Forest Service trailman. His work often presents his views of nature, religion, and Western culture, and is meditative or philosophical in tone. His first book, *Riprap*, was published in 1959. Among his many other volumes are *Myths and Texts* (1960), *Six Sections from Mountains and Rivers Without End* (1965, revised 1970), *A Range of Poems* (1966), *The Back Country* (1968), *Regarding Wave* (1969), and *Axe Handles* (1983). *Turtle Island* (1974) includes both prose and poetry; *Earth House Hold* (1969) and *The Old Ways: Six Essays* (1977) are prose collections.

Sondheim, Stephen 1930– Composer and lyricist, born in New York City and educated at Williams College. He wrote his first theatrical work, *Saturday Night*, in 1954, and in 1957 established himself as a major lyricist with *West Side Story*. He also wrote the lyrics for the 1959 play *Gypsy*. His other works, for which he often wrote both lyrics and music, include *A Funny Thing Happened on the Way to the Forum* (1962), *Anyone Can Whistle* (1964), *Company* (1970), *Sweeney Todd* (1979), *Marry Me A Little* (1981), *Merrily We Roll Along* (1981), and *Sunday in the Park With George* (1984, Pulitzer Prize). He has also provided the music for several plays, including *Follies* (1971), *A Little Night Music* (1973), and *Pacific Overtures* (1976).

Song of Myself The celebrated poem by **Walt Whitman** which introduced the first edition of *Leaves of Grass* in 1855. Over 1,300 lines long in its final version (1891–2), it set forth the major themes of Whitman's early work: the poet's celebration of the self and of its relation to the common men and women for whom "leaves of grass" is a metaphor; the beauty and spiritual inheritance of the natural world; and the omnipresence and immortality of the cosmic "I" who "sings" the poem. The poem displays the influence of Emerson's thought, and Emerson himself hailed it as "the most extraordinary piece of wit and wisdom that America has yet contributed." It

is written in the long, free-verse lines that Whitman used for most of his poetry, and its endless catalogues – "I will not have a single person slighted or left away, / The kept-woman, sponger, thief, are hereby invited" – attempt to take up into the poem the multiplicity of American life.

Sontag, Susan 1933– Born in New York City, Sontag graduated from the University of Chicago when she was 18, a year after she married the sociologist Philip Rieff. She received her MA and PhD in philosophy from Harvard. She has written two novels, *The Benefactor* (1963) and *Death Kit* (1967), and a collection of short fiction, *I, etcetera* (1978), all of which share an intense preoccupation with dreams and the unconscious. She is probably best known, however, for her essays on *avant-garde* film and for her literary criticism, much of which was first published in **The Partisan Review** and *New York Review of Books*, and later collected in *Against Interpretation* (1966). Another collection of essays, *Styles of Radical Will* (1969), also includes the autobiographical "Trip to Hanoi." She has written two film-scripts, *Duet for Cannibals* (1969) and *Brother Carl* (1971). When she contracted cancer she wrote *Illness as Metaphor* (1977), a study of the stereotypical thinking that surrounds disease in general, and cancer in particular. Another collection of essays, *Under the Sign of Saturn*, appeared in 1980. She received the National Book Critics Circle Award for Criticism for *On Photography* (1977). In 1982 she edited *A Roland Barthes Reader*.

Sot-Weed Factor, The See **Barth, John**

Souls of Black Folk, The A collection of sketches and poems by **W. E. B. Du Bois** on various aspects of the life of blacks in America, published in 1903, and including the author's famous criticism of **Booker T. Washington**'s policies. DuBois attacked Washington's optimistic predictions of economic progress for Southern blacks, as well as his advocacy of "vocational training," because the basic rights of citizenship continued to be withheld. The publication of the book initiated the most bitter phase of the conflict between the two black leaders.

Sound and the Fury, The A novel by **William Faulkner**, published in 1929. An exploration of the American South's legacy of oppression, both its structural and narrative emphasis fall on the subtle relationship between past and present.

A complex account of the history of the Compson family, the novel is divided into four sections, each under a different controlling perspective. The first section (April 7, 1928) is narrated by Benjy Compson, the youngest member of the family, and an "idiot." His section ("a tale told by an idiot, full of sound and fury") blends present and past events into a single present-day narrative. Like those of his brothers Quentin and Jason, Benjy's main focus is on his relationship with his sister Caddy. Indeed, much of the grief, anguish, guilt, and anger expressed in the first three sections is prompted by Caddy's disappearance, which for Benjy amounts to the loss of the center of his universe. The second section of the novel (June 2, 1910) is told by Quentin Compson, a freshman at Harvard. He is oppressed by his incestuous desire for Caddy and by the guilt this feeling evokes, and eventually he is driven to suicide. In the third section (April 6, 1928) Jason, the eldest of the Compson children, reveals his bitterness and anger at the opportunities he has lost because of the irresponsibility and selfishness which he feels predominate in his family. He is most enraged by the fact that Caddy, by leaving home, has evaded the family entrapment which he believes has ruined his life. The final section (April 8, 1928 – Easter Sunday) operates primarily as a commentary on the preceding three. In it the Compson's black servant, Dilsey, and her grandson, Luster, expose the degeneration of the white family and the distortion of its values. In 1946 Faulkner added an appendix which reviews the history of the Compson family from 1699 to 1945. It concludes with Faulkner's assessment of the black people who have served the Compsons: "They endured."

Southern Literary Messenger The longest-lived of the antebellum Southern Literary magazines, founded in Richmond in 1834 by T. W. White, and intended to publish and promote Southern letters. Until it folded in 1864 it printed fiction, poetry, travel accounts, and sketches of Southern life and manners by such writers as Beverley Tucker, **John Esten Cooke**, Philip Pendelton Cooke,

William Gilmore Simms, Joseph G. Baldwin, and **Augustus Baldwin Longstreet**. Largely to increase nationwide subscriptions, it also included pieces by Northerners, such as Lydia H. Sigourney, Elizabeth Oakes Smith, and H. T. Tuckerman. One of its most prominent contributors was **Edgar Allan Poe**, many of whose tales and poems appeared for the first time in the *Messenger's* pages; Poe also served as editor from December 1835 to January 1837, during which period his criticism and book reviews often sparked controversy. In 1845, under Benjamin Blake Minor, the *Messenger* merged with William Gilmore Simms's *Southern and Western Monthly Magazine and Review*, becoming *The Southern and Western Literary Messenger and Review*.

White wanted his magazine to promote Southern regional pride and achievement, and in the first few years of its existence he attempted to remain neutral on the question of slavery. But he and his successors were to adopt an increasingly defensive and sectional tone in their editorial statements as the Civil War approached, eventually identifying Southern literary regionalism with a defense of slavery.

Spencer, Elizabeth 1921–   Spencer was born in rural Mississippi, and her Southern experience is evident in many of her short stories, as well as in her first three novels – *Fire in The Morning* (1948), *This Crooked Way* (1952), and *The Voice At The Back Door* (1956) – in which she shows how the effort to preserve the ways of the antebellum South can sometimes overwhelm the sensitive members of the Mississippian upper-middle class.

She left the South in 1953, and has since lived in Italy and Canada. Her other novels include two set in Italy, *The Light in the Piazza* (1960) and *Knights and Dragons* (1965); and two set in New Orleans, *No Place For An Angel* (1968) and *The Snare* (1972). Her stories have appeared in a number of periodicals, including **The New Yorker**, **The Atlantic Monthly**, *Southern Review*, and *McCalls*, and have been partially collected in two volumes: *Ship Island and Other Stories* (1968) and *The Stories of Elizabeth Spencer* (1981).

Spoils of Poynton, The   A short novel by **Henry James**, serialized in **The Atlantic**

Monthly from April to June, 1896 under the title of *The Old Things*, and published in volume form as *The Spoils of Poynton* in the following year.

Poynton Park is the home of Owen Gereth, and the "spoils" are the antiques and *objets d'art* with which his mother has filled it. When Mrs Gereth discovers that Owen has decided to marry the tasteless Mona Brigstock, she tries to interest him instead in Fleda Vetch, a kindred spirit who shares her own aesthetic taste. As Fleda secretly falls in love with Owen, he enlists her help in persuading his mother to vacate Poynton, which will now be the home of his bride. Mrs Gereth moves out, but takes the most prized possessions with her. Mona threatens to break off the engagement unless the spoils are returned. All the while Owen is becoming more and more attracted to Fleda; Mrs Gereth, certain that he has now transferred his affections to Fleda and will not marry Mona, returns the spoils to Poynton. Owen attempts to break his engagement with Mona, but, hearing of the replenishment of Poynton, she forces him to marry her. Fleda receives a letter from Owen, traveling abroad with Mona, asking her to choose from Poynton whatever object she would like to possess. She arrives at Poynton Park just as the house and its contents inexplicably go up in flames.

Spoon River Anthology A collection of 245 verse epitaphs, published in 1915, and generally recognized as **Edgar Lee Masters**'s best work. The speakers of the epitaphs are the former residents of the fictional Spoon River, a small town in rural Illinois. Speaking from beyond the grave, they reveal the secret ambitions, transgressions, and misery – as well as the interconnectedness – of their lives. The volume was extremely popular and somewhat scandalous at the time, exploding as it did the myth of small-town respectability and morality. The epitaphs, often starkly realistic, are written in free verse.

Spy, The, *A Tale of the Neutral Ground* A novel by **James Fenimore Cooper**, published in 1821, and his first successful book. It is set during the American Revolution and concerns Harvey Birch, a supposed loyalist who is actually a spy for George Washington. The complicated story involves Birch's activities in the "neutral ground" of Westchester County, New York, and his friendship with the Whartons, a family whose loyalties in the conflict are divided: the father and son are loyalists (the son is in the British Army); the daughter, Frances, supports the rebel cause. General Washington appears several times disguised as "Mr Harper."

Stafford, Jean 1915–79 Born in Covina, California, Stafford published her first novel, *Boston Adventure*, in 1944. It deals with the social and economic barriers in Boston society in the early 20th century. Her second novel, *The Mountain Lion*, appeared in 1947, and her third, *The Catherine Wheel*, in 1952. She was associated with the literary circle which included **Robert Lowell** (her former husband), R. P. Blackmur, **Delmore Schwartz**, and **Randall Jarrell**. She also published volumes of highly crafted short stories, including *Children Are Bored on Sunday* (1953) and *Bad Characters* (1964). *The Collected Stories of Jean Stafford* appeared in 1969 and received the 1970 Pulitzer Prize for literature.

Standing Bear, Luther 1868–1939 An American Indian of Sioux extraction, Luther Standing Bear is a representative figure of the transition between the old life and the new for the American Indian. Unhappy with reservation life, he joined Buffalo Bill's Wild West Show. After one tour, he returned to the reservation but decided to sell his allotment and become a US citizen. He then moved to California and became active in Indian affairs. In 1928 he published his autobiography, *My People, My Sioux* (with E. A. Brininstool). His next book was *My Indian Boyhood* (1931), which was written for children. This was followed by *The Land of the Spotted Eagle* (1933), with help from Melvin Gilmore and Warcaziwin. His last book was *Stories of the Sioux* (1934). His writings deal with Sioux customs and beliefs as well as the life of adjustment in white America, and are often critical of government Indian policy.

Stanton, Elizabeth Cady 1815–1902 Born in Johnstown, New York, Stanton was tutored in Greek, Latin, and mathematics as a child and graduated from the Troy Female Seminary in 1832. She married Henry Brewster Stanton, an anti-slavery lecturer, in 1842. Her own reform activities centered on women's rights, and in 1848 she and Lucretia

Mott organized the Seneca Falls Convention for women's rights and suffrage. (Stanton wrote the Declaration of Principles for the convention.) In 1851 she began her association with Susan B. Anthony. In 1868 they started a magazine, *Revolution*, in which they advocated suffrage for women and legal divorce. The following year they formed the National Woman Suffrage Association, and Stanton served as its president for two decades. In addition to these activities Stanton lectured and contributed to newspapers on these issues. She and Anthony edited the first three volumes of *The History of Women's Suffrage* (1881–6), which included many documents from the period 1848–85. *The Women's Bible* (2 vols., 1895–8) included notes by Stanton reflecting her view that the present state of Christianity and the Bible was degrading to women. Her autobiography, *Eighty Years and More*, was published in 1898.

Stein, Gertrude 1874–1946 Born in Allegheny, Pennsylvania, Stein spent her early childhood in Vienna and Paris and then moved with her family to Oakland, California. She was educated at Radcliffe College (1893–7), where she studied philosophy with **William James**, and then enrolled at The Johns Hopkins Medical School (1897–1901), but failed several courses in her fourth year and did not take a degree. From 1903 until her death she lived in France, remaining in Paris except for the period of Nazi occupation, when she moved to the south. A lesbian, she lived with another expatriate American, Alice B. Toklas, from 1907 onwards. Friends of painters such as Picasso, Braque, Matisse, and Juan Gris, Stein and Toklas found themselves at the center of an art movement. During the 1920s Stein became a famous literary figure; her salon was a gathering place for both European artists and expatriate Americans such as **Ernest Hemingway**, **Sherwood Anderson**, and **F. Scott Fitzgerald**.

Her first books – *Fernhurst* and *Q.E.D.* (later retitled *Things as They Are: A Novel in Three Parts*) – were written during the period 1903–5 but were not published until much later. Her first published work, which she claimed to have written under the influence of Flaubert's *Trois Contes* and Cézanne's painting, was *Three Lives: Stories of the Good Anna, Melanctha, and the Gentle Lena* (1909). Its prose

style is highly unconventional: she periodically repeats phrases, sentences, even whole paragraphs, and more or less dispenses with normal punctuation. Her subsequent works, which were even more experimental, were considered exciting by some and merely eccentric by others. In *Tender Buttons* (1914) she uses words so idiosyncratically that many of her sentences literally make no sense. *The Making of Americans, Being a History of a Family's Progress* (1925) is an extremely long novel in which she again employs her technique of repetition.

Altogether, Stein produced over 500 titles – novels, poems, plays, articles, portraits of famous people, and memoirs. Among the most notable of them are *Composition as Explanation* (1926), a critical work; *Lucy Church Amiably* (1930), a novel; *Four Saints in Three Acts* (1929), a lyric drama staged as an opera (with music by Virgil Thompson) in 1934; *Lectures in America* (1935); *Everybody's Autobiography* (1937), which is her own autobiography; *Wars I Have Seen* (1945), a memoir; and *Brewsie and Willie* (1946), a novel about the lives of American soldiers in France during and immediately after World War II. One of her best-known works from the later period is ***The Autobiography of Alice B. Toklas*** (1933), a fictionalized account of her own life from her companion's point of view. Toklas published her own autobiography, *What Is Remembered*, in 1963. Stein's influence on younger writers, particularly Anderson and Hemingway, is widely acknowledged.

Steinbeck, John 1902–68 Born in Salinas, California, Steinbeck studied marine biology at Stanford. He did not take a degree, however, and worked at various jobs before deciding to become a writer. His literary career began in 1929 with a romantic novel, *Cup of Gold*, about the buccaneer Sir Henry Morgan. His next book was a collection of short stories portraying the people in a farm community, *The Pastures of Heaven* (1932). *To a God Unknown* (1933), his second novel, is about a California farmer whose religion is a pagan belief in fertility and who sacrifices himself on a primitive altar to bring an end to drought. It was *Tortilla Flat* (1935), however, with its vivid picture of life among the *paisanos* in Monterey, that brought Steinbeck to prominence. The tone of his work changed with *In Dubious Battle* (1936), a powerful novel about a strike among migratory workers in the California fruit orchards, and with *Of Mice and Men* (1937), the story of two itinerant farm workers who yearn for some sort of home. Steinbeck became the novelist of the rural proletariat, which in the grim years of the 1930s often existed just on the edge of survival.

The *Long Valley* (1938), which consists of 13 stories set in Salinas Valley, was followed by *The Grapes of Wrath* (1939), his best-known work and the high point of his career. This novel of a family fleeing from the dust bowl of Oklahoma to what they hope will be a better life in California was awarded the Pulitzer Prize in 1940 and became a classic American film in the same year. It was followed by *The Moon is Down* (1942), a short novel about Norwegian resistance to the Nazi occupation; *Cannery Row* (1945), in which he returned to the *paisanos* of Monterey; and *The Wayward Bus* (1947), in which the passengers on a stranded bus in California become a microcosm of contemporary American frustrations.

His non-fiction includes *Bombs Away: The Story of a Bomber Team* (1942); *The Log of the Sea of Cortez* (1951); a selection of his dispatches as a war correspondent, *Once There Was a War* (1958); and his book about rediscovering his own country, *Travels with Charley* (1962). Among his other novels are *The Pearl* (1947), *East of Eden* (1952), *Sweet Thursday* (1954), and *The Winter of Our Discontent* (1961). He was awarded the Nobel Prize for literature in 1962. A collection of letters, *Steinbeck: A Life in Letters*, was published in 1975.

Stevens, Wallace 1879–1955 Stevens was born in Reading, Pennsylvania. In 1897 he enrolled at Harvard as a special student (not a degree candidate), and there he published his first poems in the *Harvard Advocate* and the *Harvard Monthly*. One of these poems elicited a sonnet in response from **George Santayana** ("Cathedrals By the Sea"). After graduating from the three-year course in English in 1900, he got a job on the editorial staff of *The New York Tribune* and then on the periodical *The World's Work*. He was unhappy with journalism, though, and in 1901 he entered New York Law School. He was admitted to the Bar

in New York in 1904. In 1909 he married Elsie Viola Kachel, also of Reading, Pennsylvania.

His first poetry since his undergraduate years appeared in 1914 in *Trend* and in **Harriet Monroe**'s magazine *Poetry*. This work, published when he was 35 years old, marked his beginnings as a major American poet. In 1915 one of his most famous poems, "Sunday Morning," appeared in *Poetry*. At this time he was also becoming acquainted with artists and writers such as **Carl Van Vechten**, Mina Loy, **William Carlos Williams**, Carl Zigrosser, and Marcel Duchamp. In 1916 he joined the legal staff of the Hartford Accident and Indemnity Company, and remained with the firm until his death. In the same year he published "Three Travelers Watch a Sunrise," which won the *Poetry* magazine prize for a verse play. It was produced in the following year at New York's Provincetown Playhouse. His first collection of verse, *Harmonium*, appeared in 1923, and though it sold fewer than 100 copies it was well received by reviewers such as **Marianne Moore**. For the next few years he wrote very little, concentrating on his career in the business world (he became vice president of his company in 1934). The second edition of *Harmonium* was published in 1931; for it he dropped three poems from the original and added 14 new ones.

His second volume of poetry, *Ideas of Order*, appeared in 1935 and was followed in 1936 by *Owl's Clover*. This latter collection included poems written in response to charges that he was unconcerned with social issues. Another of his most famous poems provided the title piece of his fourth collection, *The Man With The Blue Guitar and Other Poems* (1937). Two further collections, *Parts of a World* and *Notes Toward a Supreme Fiction*, appeared in 1942, *Esthétique du Mal* in 1945, and *Transport to Summer* in 1947. *The Auroras of Autumn* was published in 1950, the year after he was awarded the Bollingen Prize. *The Necessary Angel: Essays on Reality and the Imagination* (1951), a collection of essays and addresses on poetry and art, received the National Book Award. *Selected Poems*, chosen by himself, was published in England in 1953. *Collected Poems* appeared in the following year. In 1955, the year of his death, he received the Pulitzer Prize as well as his second National Book Award. *Opus Posthumous* (1957) contains poems, essays, and plays, many hitherto unpublished. *The Letters of Wallace Stevens* appeared in 1966, and a selection of his poems edited by his daughter Holly, *The Palm at the End of the Mind*, in 1971.

Poetry for Stevens was "a part of the structure of reality." Throughout his poetic career he worked with the joint awareness of his Romantic heritage and his distinctively modern sensibility. His poetry reveals, on the one hand, an effort to reconcile the product of his imagination with fundamental reality, and on the other his disbelief in the possibility of any such reconciliation. His use of language is meticulous and frequently exotic; his habitual use of extended metaphors makes his poetry distinctly difficult at times.

Stickney, (Joseph) Trumbull 1874–1904 Born in Switzerland, Stickney came to New England at the age of 5 and graduated from Harvard in 1895. Known during his lifetime as a classical scholar, he also published a verse drama, *Prometheus Pyrphoros* (1900), and *Dramatic Verses* (1902). He was a close friend and associate of **William Vaughn Moody**, whose interests in Greek literature often paralleled his own. After Stickney died of a brain tumor at the age of 30, Moody and others published a collection of his verses, *Poems* (1905), which brought him posthumous recognition as a poet.

Stillwater Tragedy, The See **Aldrich, Thomas Bailey**

Stoddard, R[ichard] H[enry] 1825–1903 Born into a poor Massachusetts family, Stoddard educated himself while working as an iron moulder. He received early encouragement from **Nathaniel Hawthorne** after publishing a volume of romantic verses, *Poems*, in 1852. While working at the customs post Hawthorne obtained for him, Stoddard contributed regular reviews over a 20-year period to the *New York World*. He also published poetry in *Songs of Summer* (1857), *Abraham Lincoln: An Horatian Ode* (1865), and *Poems* (1880). *The Lion's Cub: With Other Verse* (1890) was published when he was working as editor for the New York *Mail and Express* (1880–1903). He published his *Recollections, Personal and Literary* in 1903.

Stoddard, Solomon 1643–1729 Born in Boston to wealthy parents, Stoddard studied at Elijah Corlet's grammar school in Cambridge and then entered Harvard in 1658. He received his BA in 1662 and MA in 1665. Following brief service as a fellow and librarian at Harvard (1666–7), he worked as a Chaplain in Barbados and on his return in 1669 was asked to preach at Northampton. The church formally called him to be pastor in 1670, and he moved to Northampton and married the widow of Eleazar Mather, his predecessor.

His appointment marked a major turning point in colonial American history. At first a proponent of the Half-Way Covenant, which granted partial church membership to children of regenerate parents, in 1677 he ceased to distinguish between full and Half-Way church members because of his conviction that the sacraments were vehicles for God's grace and thus should be available to all seeking Christian salvation. This view, referred to as "Stoddardeanism," secured for him not only the title of "Pope" but also the wrath of the orthodox Ministry of Massachusetts Bay. At the synod held in 1679 he defended his theory and practice in "Nine Arguments against Examinations Concerning a Work of Grace before Admission to the Lord's Supper," a paper attacked by **Increase Mather**. The exchange initiated a pamphlet war with the Mathers in which Stoddard defended himself with *The Doctrine of Instituted Churches* (1700), *The Inexcusableness of Neglecting the Worship of God, under the Pretence of Being in an Unconverted Condition* (1708), and *An Appeal to the Learned* (1709).

Most of the churches throughout western Massachusetts accepted Stoddard's admission policy, which occasioned a series of revivals (1679, 1683, 1712, and 1718), and laid the theological groundwork for the Great Awakening. His grandson, **Jonathan Edwards**, who assumed the Northampton pulpit on his death, ultimately rejected the view and was consequently dismissed in 1750, an event which testifies to the support for Stoddard's ecclesiastical position.

Story of a Country Town, The A novel by **E. W. Howe**, published in 1883. The story is told by Ned Westlock, the son of a stern, Bible-quoting minister-farmer. John Westlock's religious gatherings each Sunday are the only social occasions for the neighbors in the midwestern farming community, and their severity of doctrine is commonly accepted. The important people in young Ned's life are Jo Erring, his mother's younger brother, who works on the Westlock farm, the young schoolteacher Agnes Deming, and the miller Damon Barker, to whom Jo is later apprenticed. It is Damon who makes Ned aware that there is a rich and varied world outside.

Jo falls in love with Mateel Shepherd and develops an increasing dislike for Clinton Bragg, a friend of the Shepherd family. Then, to everyone's surprise, John Westlock leaves the land and moves his family to the country town of Twin Mounds. He trades in land and buys the local newspaper, which Ned helps him to edit. Jo builds a mill and a home of his own and is accepted by Mateel Shepherd. John Westlock elopes with Damon's sister; Ned's mother becomes ill with worry, and Ned keeps the paper going on his own. Damon himself turns out to be the father whom Agnes Deming never knew and she goes to live with him at the mill. Ned's mother dies just before his father comes back, alone. The return is brief; John Westlock is now a man without resolution or purpose and he soon disappears again.

Jo has been prospering but now he discovers that Mateel and the hated Clinton Bragg were once lovers. His insane jealousy leads to Mateel's death, and he then murders Bragg. He surrenders to the police but commits suicide. Ned and Agnes marry and settle down happily. Thus the life of the country town continues. Howe's novel successfully captures the tone of a tired old man looking back on life, though the author had not reached 30 when he wrote it. The note of bitterness and disillusion is strong; life in this country town is presented as close, stifling, and arid. Ned Westlock knows that there is more to life but he has never achieved more; and he notes wryly how many of the people who come to the West are those without hopes in the places they have left.

Stowe, Harriet Beecher 1811–96 Stowe was born in Litchfield, Connecticut, where her father, the influential and controversial Calvinist preacher Lyman Beecher, was rector of the First Church. Her mother, Roxana Foote, the first of Lyman's three wives, bore nine children, of whom Harriet was the seventh, and died when Harriet was still a child. Harriet attended dame school and the Litchfield Academy; then in 1824 she went to Hartford, where her sister Catharine – later a prominent writer and ideologue of domesticity, feminine education, and woman's separate sphere – had founded the Hartford Female Seminary. Harriet was a student and then a teacher there until 1832, when the whole family accompanied Lyman to Cincinnati, where he became president of the new Lane Theological Seminary and took up the mission of converting the West.

Harriet Beecher Stowe's life and work were unquestionably shaped by the Calvinist rigor with which she was raised, but her earliest experiences of a feeling of conversion by natural grace did not stand up to Lyman's scrutiny, and, like Catharine, she came to reject his insistence on constant self-searching and his sense of damnation in favor of a gentler gospel, based on an awareness of Christ's love and on the virtue embodied in feminine piety and motherhood. (Late in life she became an Episcopalian.) Nonetheless, just as all Lyman's seven sons went on to become ministers, she remained essentially a religious writer: politics and art were for her always framed by standards of moral purity and questions of salvation.

In Cincinnati she collaborated with her sister on a geography book for children, and in 1834 began to write sketches and short fiction for the *Western Monthly* and other, mostly evangelical, periodicals. Her first book, *The Mayflower: Sketches and Scenes and Characters Among the Descendants of the Puritans*, appeared in 1843. In 1836 she married the widower Calvin E. Stowe, a professor at Lane, with whom she would eventually have seven children. He was a Bible scholar and, in her words, "rich in Greek and Hebrew, Latin and Arabic, and alas! in nothing else." The Cincinnati years were marked by poverty, isolation, and a cholera epidemic in which the Stowes lost a young son. In 1850 Calvin Stowe was offered a professorship at Bowdoin, and they moved to Brunswick, Maine.

There, amid household cares, Harriet wrote her first novel, **Uncle Tom's Cabin**, prompted by the passage of the Fugitive Slave Law. Like most of her subsequent novels, it was written as a serial, and began appearing in the *National Era* magazine in 1851. It was an immediate and scandalous best seller, both in the US and abroad. Stowe made three triumphal tours of Europe (1853, 1856, and 1859), where she formed important friendships with George Eliot, Elizabeth Barrett Browning, and Lady Byron, among others, and gathered material for *Sunny Memories of Foreign Lands* (1854). Meanwhile, attacks on the veracity of her portrayal of the South led her to publish *The Key to Uncle Tom's Cabin* (1853), a book of source material. A second anti-slavery novel, *Dred: A Tale of the Great Dismal Swamp* (1856), told the story of a dramatic attempt at a slave rebellion, while attacking ministers who had failed to take a strong anti-slavery stand and demonstrating again the redemptive powers of Christian womanhood, white and black.

After this, however, Stowe turned away from the political sphere. *The Minister's Wooing* (1859), set in New England, is a novel of love and marriage in the context of Calvinist uncertainty about salvation and the dread of seeing a loved one die unconverted. (She drew on the experiences of her sister, whose fiancé had been lost at sea, and of her own grief at the drowning of her son Henry in 1837.) *Agnes of Sorrento* (1862) took up similar theological themes but was set in the Catholic Italy of Savonarola. *The Pearl of Orr's Island* (1862), another treatment of the redemption of wayward youth by female piety and example, drew heavily on the local color of the New England shore; **Sarah Orne Jewett** credited this book with inspiring her own career. Stowe wrote three more works in a similar vein: **Oldtown Folks** (1869) and *Oldtown Fireside Stories* (1871) drew on her husband's childhood memories, and *Poganuc People* (1878), her last novel, on her own. She also wrote three novels of New York society: *Pink and White Tyranny* (1871), which attacks female frivolity, the French, and divorce; and *My Wife and I* (1871) and its sequel, *We And Our Neighbours* (1875), in which she shows how rural values can be brought to the city. During this time she was also preoccupied by the scandalous and highly public trial of her brother, the charismatic preacher **Henry Ward Beecher**, for adultery – a charge she never believed and of which he was eventually acquitted.

She was a remarkably prolific writer of both books and articles in many genres and styles. She wrote children's books; travelogues; purely theological works, such as *In The Footsteps of the Master* (1877) and *Bible Heroines* (1878); temperance tracts; and practical articles about housekeeping, decoration, and the "servant problem," including the highly influential *The American Woman's Home* (1869, co-written with her sister Catharine). Throughout her career she was both celebrated and financially successful. She lived in Hartford, sometimes wintering in Florida, from 1864 until her death in 1896.

Strange Interlude A play in nine acts by **Eugene O'Neill**, first performed in New York in 1928. Its extreme length is largely the result of O'Neill's decision to have his characters articulate the sub-text of their speeches as well as the text, to say what they are thinking as well as what they actually voice. With this rather daring and unconventional use of dramatic "asides," the play received a mixed critical reception, but won a Pulitzer Prize.

Nina Leeds, the daughter of a New England professor, has been prevented by her father from marrying the man she loves before he goes to war. His death in the war turns her against her father, and she leaves home to become a nurse. In homage to her dead lover, she offers herself as mistress to any war-wounded man who wants her, and is saved from this promiscuity by a fond but loveless marriage to Sam Evans, motivated by her wish for a child. When she discovers that there is madness in her husband's family she obtains a secret abortion and asks her husband's friend, Dr Edmund Darrell, to impregnate her. Darrell's life is destroyed by his love for her, and Nina's possessiveness for their son almost leads her to destroy that son's own hopes of marriage.

Streetcar Named Desire, A A play by **Tennessee Williams**, first performed in New York in 1947. It ran for 855 performances and received both a New York Drama Critics Circle Award and a Pulitzer Prize.

The action revolves around the visit of Blanche Du Bois to her sister Stella, who lives in New Orleans, near the stop of the streetcar named Desire, with her brutish husband Stanley Kowalski. Blanche has an appearance of ladylike grace, and constantly refers to her early life at the family estate of Belle Reve.

Bewildered by her new environment and by the antagonism of her brother-in-law, she turns to his friend Mitch for consolation and company. Stanley, however, learns that Blanche is not the Southern belle she purports to be, and tells Mitch that she is in fact a lonely alcoholic who has been forced into bankruptcy and who has lost her job because of an affair with a young boy who reminded her of her dead husband. Blanche's antagonistic relationship with Stanley culminates in his raping her. She tells Stella but Stella does not believe her, and at the end of the play she is taken into psychiatric care.

Street Scene A three-act play by **Elmer Rice**, first presented in 1929. It was a critical and popular success, running for 601 performances and winning a Pulitzer Prize. In 1947 Rice worked with **Langston Hughes** and the composer **Kurt Weill** on a successful musical adaptation.

Despite many previous successes in the theatre, Rice had difficulty finding a producer for this ground-breaking drama, which required over 50 actors and an innovative and elaborate set to present a day in the life of a New York City tenement. In the course of one extremely hot day, the tenants, drawn from many ethnic groups, converse, complain, quarrel, and gossip, mostly about one of their number, Mrs Maurrant. A baby is born; a poor family is evicted after a visit from an unsympathetic social worker; the relative merits of socialism and capitalism are discussed; Mr Maurrant comes home to find his wife in bed with another man, shoots them both, and is captured by the police; and Rose Maurrant, the heroine, rejects the attentions both of her boss, the flashy Harry Easter, and of Sam Kaplan, the earnest young law student who lives in the building, and strikes out on her own.

Studs Lonigan Trilogy, The See **Farrell, James**

Styron, William 1925– Born in Newport News, Virginia, and educated at Davidson College and Duke University, Styron subsequently studied writing at the New School for Social Research in New York City. His first novel, *Lie Down in Darkness*, was published in 1951. Other novels include *The Long March* (1952), *Set This House on Fire*

(1960), *The Confessions of Nat Turner* (1967), and *Sophie's Choice* (1979). His work generally concerns forms of oppression, ranging from that of the family to the wider social issues of racism and politics. His account of Nat Turner's rebellion met with considerable protest from the black community; *William Styron's Nat Turner: Ten Black Writers Respond* (1968) contains essays which reflect the animosity toward his "white" approach to race relations. In *Sophie's Choice*, his most commercially successful novel to date, he deals with the horrors of the Holocaust as it affects the lives of those who survived the concentration camps and Nazi persecution. *This Quiet Dust* (1982) is a collection of essays.

Suddenly Last Summer See **Williams, Tennessee**

Sun Also Rises, The A novel by **Ernest Hemingway**, published in 1926. Set in the mid 1920s, it deals with the "lost generation" of American and British expatriates who have settled in Paris, depicted here as a moral wasteland of drunkenness and promiscuity.

The story is narrated by Jake Barnes, an American journalist, who has been rendered sexually impotent by a wound suffered during World War I. Jake is in love with the queen of the pleasure-seekers, Lady Brett Ashley. Brett returns his love but, knowing that consummation is impossible, agrees to marry Mike Campbell, another wastelander. Jake lives according to a self-taught emotional pragmatism, which is contrasted with the self-pitying sentimentalism of his acquaintance Robert Cohn. Robert, under Brett's spell, joins her, Mike, and Jake on a jaunt to Spain to witness the fiesta and bullfights at Pamplona. At the bullring Jake finds meaning and hope in the ritual which pits man against beast, and life against death; he especially admires the young matador Pedro Romero, whose skill, bravery, and moral earnestness characterize him as a true Hemingway hero. The others in his group, however, remain true to form, and the fiesta degenerates into a series of brawls. Angered by Brett's seduction of the matador, Cohn beats up both Romero and Jake, and the party disintegrates. Brett runs off with Romero. Jake retreats to a seaside resort in an effort to regain moral stability, but his recovery is interrupted by a telegram from Brett pleading that he come to her aid in Madrid. There she tells him that she has sent Romero away because she does not want to corrupt him further. In a last taxi ride around the city, Brett and Jake face the hopelessness of their situation. Brett clings to the notion that they "could have had such a damned good time together," but Jake responds ironically that it would be "pretty" to think so – his word for his final rejection of a world of false hopes.

T

Tarkington, (Newton) Booth 1869–1946 Born in Indianapolis, Indiana, Tarkington was educated at Philips Exeter Academy and then at Purdue and Princeton, though he left college without taking a degree. His first two novels, *The Gentleman From Indiana* (1899) and *Monsieur Beaucaire* (1900), were accepted for publication on the advice of **Hamlin Garland**; the former is an example of literary realism in the manner of **William Dean Howells**, the latter a historical romance.

In all, Tarkington went on to write over 40 volumes of fiction. Among his nostalgic novels of boyhood and adolescence for juvenile readers are *Penrod* (1914), *Seventeen* (1916), *Penrod and Sam* (1916), and *Penrod Jashber* (1929). His novels for adults include three – *The Turmoil* (1915), *The Magnificent Ambersons* (1918, Pulitzer Prize), and *The Midlander* (1924) – which in 1927 were published as a trilogy entitled *Growth*, and which treat the effects on society of the rise in social prominence of the *nouveau riche* businessman. *Alice Adams*, published in 1921 and awarded the Pulitzer Prize in the following year, is an ironic novel of manners about a middle-class American girl who seeks but fails to marry a rich man.

Tarkington's plays include an adaptation of his novel *Monsieur Beaucaire* (1901), *The Man From Home* (1908), *The Country Cousin* (1921), *The Intimate Strangers* (1921), *The Wren* (1922), and *Bimbo, The Pirate* (1926). In 1928 he published a volume of reminiscences, *The World Does Move*. He continued to write prolifically until his death at the age of 76; among his notable later works are the novels *The Heritage of Hatcher Ide* (1941), *Kate Fennigate* (1943), and *The Image of Josephine* (1945).

Tate, (John Orley) Allen 1899–1979 Born in Winchester, Kentucky, Tate graduated from Vanderbilt University in 1922. While there he became involved in a literary discussion group that included Donald Davidson and **John Crowe Ransom**. In 1923 he assumed some editorial responsibilities for *The Fugitive*, a magazine published by the group at Vanderbilt from 1922 to 1925. Though known primarily as a critic, and particularly as a proponent of the **New Criticism**, Tate was also a poet, biographer, and novelist. He married **Caroline Gordon** in 1924.

His first publication was the privately printed volume *The Golden Mean and Other Poems* (1923, with Ridley Wills). In 1928 he contributed several poems to *Fugitives: an Anthology of Verse*, among them "Ode to the Confederate Dead," one of his most famous pieces. In the same year he published *Mr Pope and Other Poems* and a biography, *Stonewall Jackson: The Good Soldier*. Another Civil War biography, *Jefferson Davis: His Rise and Fall*, followed in 1929. He contributed to *I'll Take My Stand* (1930), a founding document of the Southern Agrarian movement. The volumes of poetry that followed include *Poems: 1928–1931* (1932), *The Mediterranean and Other Poems* (1936), *Selected Poems* (1937), *Poems: 1922–1947* (1948), *Poems* (1960), and *Collected Poems* (1977). He often took the history of the South as his subject and, especially in his later poetry, lamented the decline of Christianity in an increasingly mechanized and atheistic society. He received the Bollingen Prize for poetry in 1956.

His critical works include *Reactionary Essays on Poetry and Ideas* (1936), *Reason in Madness, Critical Essays* (1941), *On the Limits of Poetry, Selected Essays 1928–1948* (1948), *The Forlorn Demon: Didactic and Critical Essays* (1953), *Col-*

lected Essays (1959), and *Essays of Four Decades* (1968). Tate also served as the editor of *Hound and Horn* (1931–4), *The Kenyon Review* (1938), and *The Sewanee Review* (1944–6). His only novel, *The Fathers* (1938), is a first-person narrative in which the 65-year-old Lacy Buchan recalls his past – a past which spans the demise of the Old South and of the stability that it represented.

Taylor, Bayard 1825–78 Born to Quaker parents in Kennett Square, Pennsylvania, Taylor published his first collection of verse, *Ximena*, in 1844. That same year he traveled to Europe, and his experiences there furnished material for his second book, *Views A-Foot* (1846), and for a series of letters published in the *New York Tribune*. When he returned to America, the *Tribune*, impressed by these letters, appointed him manager of their literary section and sent him to California to cover the Gold Rush of 1849. He subsequently published an account of the Gold Rush, *Eldorado: or Adventures in the Path of Empire* (2 vols., 1850). The following year he set off on an extensive journey which took him to Egypt, Abyssinia, Turkey, India, and China, before he joined Commodore Perry in the Pacific. On his return to New York in 1853, Taylor began a series of lectures and wrote several accounts of travels and adventures, including *A Journey to Central Africa* (1854), *The Lands of the Saracen* (1855), and *A Visit to India, China and Japan in the Year 1853* (1855). In 1856 he traveled extensively in Europe and Russia and again published several accounts of the journey: *Northern Travel* (1857), *Travels in Greece and Russia* (1859), and *At Home and Abroad* (1860).

He also wrote several novels, all of which are set in America and comment upon various aspects of Victorian American culture. They include: *Hannah Thurston* (1863), *John Godfrey's Fortunes* (1864), *Joseph and His Friend* (1870), and *Beauty and the Beast and Tales of Home* (1872). Throughout his life, he published numerous volumes of verse, a body of work which reflects his wide, international experience and varied tastes: *Rhymes of Travel, Ballads and Poems* (1849), *Lars, A Pastoral of Norway* (1873), and *The Echo Club and Other Literary Diversions* (1876). Perhaps his most distinguished work was a translation of Goethe's *Faust* rendered in the original meters

(1870–1), which earned him a non-resident professorship in German at Cornell University and a diplomatic post in Germany.

Taylor, Edward *c.*1645–1729 Born in Leicestershire, England, Taylor emigrated to Massachusetts in 1668 under pressure of religious conformity. He graduated from Harvard in 1671 and served as minister to the church in the frontier town of Westfield, Massachusetts, for the rest of his life. A friend of the **Mathers** and of **Samuel Sewall**, he was a conservative in matters of church polity; he corresponded with **Solomon Stoddard**, his frontier neighbor, on the subject of the latter's open communion policy.

Today Taylor is considered the preeminent poet of early New England, but his poetry was not known in his own day; his manuscripts remained undiscovered in the Yale University library until 1937. Thomas H. Johnson edited the *Poetical Works* in 1939. In addition to a few occasional poems, including "Huswifery" and "Upon a Spider Catching a Fly," he wrote the long series *Gods Determinations Touching His Elect; and the Elects Combat in Their Conversion, and coming Up to God in Christ: Together with the Comfortable Effects Thereof*, a poetic treatment of Puritan dogma; and the devotional *Meditations*, each exploring the imagery of a biblical text. He also left manuscripts of various sermons and theological tracts, some of which have been published in the 20th century.

Taylor, Peter 1917– Born in Trenton, Tennessee, he spent his youth in Nashville, St Louis, and Memphis. These cities, as well as the fictional town of Thornton, Tennessee, are the setting of many of Taylor's works, which frequently center on the conflict between the values of small-town Southern life and those of an urban culture. Although he has published one novella, *A Woman of Means* (1950), Taylor has devoted himself primarily to short stories, which have appeared in the following collections: *A Long Fourth and Other Stories* (1948), *The Widows of Thornton* (1954), *Happy Families Are All Alike* (1959), *Miss Leonora When Last Seen* (1963), *The Collected Stories of Peter Taylor* (1969), *In the Miro District and Other Stories* (1977), and *The Old Forest and Other Stories* (1985).

Tender is the Night A novel by **F. Scott Fitzgerald**, published in 1934. Adverse criticism led Fitzgerald to believe that the story's time scheme was faulty, and a revised edition (based on his notes), which reorganized the action into chronological order, was published posthumously in 1948. However, most modern editions follow the original version.

Tender is the Night is a novel about the squandering of creative promise. It is the story of Dick Diver, a young American psychiatrist studying in Zurich in 1917. He becomes interested in the case of Nicole Warren, a beautiful and wealthy American suffering from schizophrenia. As she recovers, she comes to depend on Dick, and eventually they marry. The doctor–patient relationship, however, carries over to their marriage; caring for Nicole prevents Dick both from loving her and from pursuing his intellectual career. They have two children and lead a leisurely life on the Riviera. Their friends include Abe North, a composer who has become an alcoholic and who, like Dick, has failed to fulfill the creative promise of his youth. His failure is consummated when he is killed in a Paris bar. Dick's life as the impeccable host on the Riviera gradually deteriorates. He becomes infatuated with Rosemary Hoyt, an American actress much younger than himself; he begins to drink heavily; he is involved in a brawl in Rome; and his medical career is on the verge of ruin. Nicole falls in love with Tommy Barban, a French mercenary and member of their Riviera circle, and eventually divorces Dick, whose own failure is finalized when he returns to America to a small-town medical practice.

Theatre Guild, The Founded in 1919 by former members of the Washington Square Players, including Lawrence Langner, Rollo Peters, Philip Moeller, Lee Simonson, and Helen Westley, this group specialized in producing works by contemporary American and European dramatists. Most of its productions before 1923 were of foreign works; thereafter it concentrated on American plays, including *The Garrick Gaieties* (1925), **DuBose Heyward**'s *Porgy* (1925), **Eugene O'Neill**'s *Strange Interlude* (1928), *Mourning Becomes Electra* (1931), *Ah, Wilderness!* (1933), and *The Iceman Cometh* (1946), **Philip Barry**'s *The Philadelphia Story* (1939), **William Saroyan**'s *The Time of Your Life* (1939), and **Richard Rodgers** and **Oscar**

Hammerstein's *Oklahoma!* (1943) and *Carousel* (1945). Although originally founded as a little theatre group, the company expanded rapidly due to skillful production and timely play selection. The Theatre Guild helped to promote the careers of many playwrights, including Eugene O'Neill, **Maxwell Anderson**, and **Robert Sherwood**; and of actors such as Alfred Lunt and Lynn Fontane. During the 1930s some members of the Guild left to establish two rival companies, the **Group Theatre** and the Playwrights' Company.

Their Eyes Were Watching God A novel by **Zora Neale Hurston**, published in 1937. The story centers on Janie Crawford, a strong-willed seeker of beauty who is unwilling to lead an existence of drudgery and deprivation like that of the grandmother who raised her. She suffers through a marriage of convenience, finally leaving her husband for the smooth-talking and handsome visionary, Joe Starks. Janie and Joe establish Florida's first all-black town and Joe becomes its mayor. Following Joe's death Janie is left financially secure, fortyish, and sexually, romantically, and spiritually oppressed. Rather than settle into comfortable widowhood, she falls passionately in love with Vergible Woods (known to everyone as Tea Cake), who is several years younger and penniless.

Against friends' advice, she goes off with Tea Cake and marries him. Their marriage provides her with the idyllic love she had dreamed of but it ends tragically. Following a violent hurricane, Tea Cake is bitten by a rabid dog and contracts the disease. When, in his frenzy, he attacks Janie, she is forced to shoot him in self defense. She is charged with murder, but quickly exonerated. She returns, saddened but victorious, to the town she and Joe Starks had founded. The novel openly confronts the issues of civil and social rights in both a racial and feminist context.

Thin Man, The See **Hammett, Dashiell**

Thomas, Augustus 1857–1934 Thomas was born in St Louis, Missouri and was entirely self-educated. His early plays include *Alone* (1875) and *Alabama* (1891). The success of the latter allowed him to give up his job as an adapter of foreign works and to devote his time to his own plays, many of which depend on a specific American locality for their effect:

In Mizzoura (1893), *Arizona* (1899), *Colorado* (1901), and *Rio Grande* (1916). He did, however, continue to adapt the work of others for the stage, notably F. H. Smith's *Colonel Carter of Cartersville* (1892); **Frances Hodgson Burnett**'s *Editha's Burglar* (first as a one-act play, then in a four-act adaptation entitled *The Burglar*, 1899); and **Richard Harding Davis**'s *Soldiers of Fortune*, dramatized in 1902 with the collaboration of the author. *The Witching Hour* (1907) and *The Harvest Moon* (1909) reflected Thomas's interest in mind-reading and hypnotism. His greatest success was *The Copperhead* (1918). His autobiography, *The Print of My Remembrance*, was published in 1922.

Thoreau, Henry David 1817–62 Born in Concord, Massachusetts, Thoreau spent most of his life in the area as a writer, teacher, essayist, and orator, earning extra income by working as a gardener, pencil-maker, and surveyor.

While attending Concord Academy and Harvard, he became known as an individualist who was often scornful of authority. Nevertheless, he was much influenced by many of the men he encountered during those years: **Edward Channing, Orestes Brownson**, and especially **Ralph Waldo Emerson**. Shortly after his graduation from Harvard in 1837, he and his brother John opened their own school in Concord, and operated it according to the **Transcendentalist** principles of Emerson, **Bronson Alcott**, and Brownson. When John became fatally ill in 1841, Henry was unable to find another position, whereupon he lived in Emerson's home as a handyman. It was Emerson who encouraged him to keep the journals which form the basis of most of his major writings.

By this time Thoreau had already contributed several pieces to the Transcendentalist journal, **The Dial**; and he was also an occasional speaker at the Concord Lyceum, which he had started in 1838. His mature writing, however, dates from the two-year period (1845–7) when he lived at Walden Pond. There he put into final form **A Week on the Concord and Merrimack Rivers** (1849), based on a trip he took with his brother John in 1839. The experience at Walden itself, and the journal he kept there, became the source of his celebrated book **Walden** (1854), which

takes the form of a lengthy autobiographical essay in which he sets forth many of his ideas on how the individual should live life to the best advantage of his nature and principles. Another of his well-known works, **On the Duty of Civil Disobedience** (1849), comes from the same period and reflects similar values: he was arrested in the summer of 1846 for refusing to pay his poll tax, and the night he spent in jail prompted his reflections on a man's moral right passively to resist an unjust law. Another influential political essay on a similar theme is "Life Without Principle," published posthumously in 1863. The Abolitionist essay "Slavery in Massachusetts" appeared in 1854. Much of Thoreau's later Abolitionist writing was about John Brown, whom he met in 1857. The best of these essays, "A Plea for Captain John Brown," was published in 1860, three years after Brown was executed.

The majority of Thoreau's work was published after his death. Aware that he was dying of tuberculosis, he cut short his therapeutic travels and returned to Concord, where he prepared some of his journals for publication. Selections from his manuscripts were edited and posthumously published as *The Maine Woods* (1864), *Cape Cod* (1865), and *A Yankee in Canada* (1866), all based on his various journeys. *Excursions* (1863) is a collection of pieces previously published in magazines. His letters were edited by his lifelong friend Emerson and published in 1865 (enlarged 1894). *Poems of Nature* appeared in 1895, *Collected Poems* in 1943. Finally, Thoreau's immense collection of journals was published in 1906 in 14 volumes.

Three Lives See **Stein, Gertrude**

Three Penny Opera, The See **Weill, Kurt**

Thurber, James (Grover) 1894–1961 Born in Columbus, Ohio, Thurber was educated at Ohio State University. After working as a government clerk in Washington, he joined the embassy staff in Paris, and then became foreign correspondent for a Chicago newspaper. On his return to the US he worked on the staff of **The New Yorker** (1927–33) and continued after that as a regular contributor. Both as a cartoonist and as a writer Thurber expressed the dilemma of the moral innocent in a complex modern world. A direct and disarming humorist, he frequently satirized such subjects as psychoanalysis, sexual awareness, the search for identity, and the problem of communication.

Among his collections of stories and sketches are *The Owl in the Attic, and Other Perplexities* (1931), *The Seal in My Bedroom, and Other Predicaments* (1932), *Let Your Mind Alone* (1937), *My World – And Welcome To It!* (1942), and *The Beast in Me, and Other Animals* (1948). With **E. B. White**, his colleague on *The New Yorker*, he wrote *Is Sex Necessary?* (1929), and in collaboration with Elliot Nugent he produced a successful dramatic comedy, *The Male Animal* (1940). *My Life and Hard Times* (1933) is autobiographical, and *The Years With Ross* (1959) a memoir of his years on the staff of *The New Yorker*. He also wrote several books for children, including *The Thirteen Clocks* (1950). *Selected Letters*, edited by Helen Thurber and Edward Weeks, appeared in 1981.

Timrod, Henry 1828–67 The "Laureate of the Confederacy" was born in Charleston, South Carolina, and educated at Franklin College (now the University of Georgia). With **William Gilmore Simms**, Basil Gildersleeve, and his friend Paul Hamilton Hayne, he founded *Russell's Magazine* in Charleston in 1867, modeling it on the British journal *Blackwood's*. Some of his own poetry was published in the magazine. A volume entitled *Poems* had already appeared in 1860. He suffered from tuberculosis and was unable to serve in the Confederate Army in the Civil War, but he did manage to earn his living as an editor, and it was during these years that he wrote his best-known poems. They remained uncollected, however, until after his death, when Hayne published *The Poems of Henry Timrod* in 1872. *Katie*, a love poem addressed to his wife, was published in 1884 and *Complete Poems of Henry Timrod* in 1899.

Tobacco Road See **Caldwell, Erskine**

Tocqueville, Comte Alexis de 1805–59 See *Democracy in America*

To Have and Have Not See **Hemingway, Ernest**

Tom Sawyer See *Adventures of Tom Sawyer, The*

Toole, John Kennedy 1937–69 Born in New Orleans and educated at Tulane and at Columbia, Toole wrote just one novel, *A Confederacy of Dunces*, which was not published until after his death; he committed suicide 11 years before his mother persuaded **Walker Percy** to read the manuscript. A finely composed satirical comedy on a depraved and depressed New Orleans society, *A Confederacy of Dunces* quickly won acclaim and was awarded a Pulitzer Prize in 1980, the year of its publication.

Toomer, Jean (Nathan Eugene) 1894–1967 A central figure of the **Harlem Renaissance**, Toomer was born in Washington, DC, the grandson of a part-black acting governor of Louisiana during the Reconstruction era. He attended the University of Wisconsin and the City College of New York. In 1921 he worked as superintendent of a black rural school in Sparta, Georgia, an experience which provided the source for some of the material in his most widely read work, *Cane* (1923). During the 1920s he contributed poetry to the black journals *Opportunity* and *Crisis*, as well as to *avant-garde* magazines such as *Broom* and *The Little Review*. With the publication of *Cane*, a work composed of stories and poems, he attracted the attention of a number of prominent editors, critics, and authors, including **Waldo Frank** and **William Stanley Braithwaite**. In 1924 he studied in France under the mystic Georges Gurdjieff, whose influence is apparent in Toomer's later work. *Essentials*, a collection of aphorisms on philosophical subjects, appeared in 1931. He experimented with dramatic conventions in two unpublished plays, "Natalie Mann" (1922) and "The Sacred Factory" (1927). He also wrote numerous poems, stories, and autobiographical sketches which remained unpublished in his lifetime and were subsequently collected in *The Wayward and the Seeking* (1980), edited by Darwin T. Turner.

Tourgée, Albion W[inegar] 1838–1905 Born in Williamsfield, Ohio, Tourgée attended the University of Rochester, receiving his BA in 1862. He served with the Union forces during the Civil War and was seriously wounded. In 1864 he was admitted to the Bar and in the following year he and his wife moved to North Carolina. A transplanted Northerner who disapproved of all the Old

South stood for, he was labeled a carpetbagger. In 1867 he briefly edited a Republican newspaper, *The Union Register*, and in 1868 he was elected a judge of North Carolina's Supreme Court, in which capacity he served for six years.

Tourgée's commitment to Reconstruction ideology and to the reform of the South is reflected in the novels he wrote there. *'Toinette: A Novel* (1874, republished as *A Royal Gentleman* in 1881) is the story of a near-white slave girl who is freed but left in a tragic position when her lover, a white Southerner who has fathered her child, refuses to marry her. *A Fool's Errand* (1879) portrays the conflict between a former Confederate general and a former Union colonel who sides with the freed blacks and fights both the Ku Klux Klan and the carpetbaggers. Eventually the two men are reconciled, which enables the colonel's daughter and the general's son to marry. The novel was republished in 1880 incorporating *The Invisible Empire*, a factual inquiry into the history of the Ku Klux Klan. *Bricks Without Straw* (1880) tells of a black's struggle to establish himself as a free and independent man; terrorized by the Klan, he is forced to move with his family to the North.

After leaving the South in 1879, Tourgée continued to write fiction, producing a further 17 novels, among which are *Hot Plowshares* (1882); *Black Ice* (1888); and *Eighty-Nine, or The Grand Master's Story* (1891), in which he returned to the theme of Republican reform of the South after the Civil War. From 1882 to 1884 he edited *Our Continent*, a weekly publication in which he continued to champion the rights of blacks and to expose the evil of the Ku Klux Klan. He served as US consul in Bordeaux from 1897 to his death in 1905.

Transcendentalism A literary and philosophical movement in New England in the early and middle part of the 19th century. It gave expression to several strains of thought: the weakening of Calvinistic views about the corruption of human nature; the rise of Romantic attitudes toward the pervasiveness of the divine and the inherent power of the individual imagination; and the frustration with what was seen as the polite and unemotional rationalism of Unitarian thought. Once considered to have derived from European movements, it is now generally seen as a development of native tendencies.

Centered on Boston and Concord, some of its most notable voices were those of **Ralph Waldo Emerson**, **Henry David Thoreau**, **Margaret Fuller**, and **Bronson Alcott**. Transcendentalism was opposed to the idea that man needed an intercessor through which to reach the divine, and was critical of formalized religion. Like the physical universe itself, all constructive practical activity, all great literature, all forms of spiritual awareness were viewed as an expression of the divine spirit. The often-expressed ambition was to achieve vivid perception of the divine as it operates in common life, an awareness seen as leading at once to personal cultivation and to a sense of history as an at least potentially progressive movement.

Traubel, Horace Logo 1858–1919 A journalist from Camden, New Jersey, Traubel founded the *Conservator* (1890–1919), a monthly magazine published in Philadelphia. He is primarily known, however, for his long association with **Walt Whitman**, with whom he became friends when the poet moved to Camden in 1873. From 1888 he kept a detailed diary of his visits with Whitman, recording conversations and daily impressions. This record of the last four years of the poet's life was published in five volumes as *With Walt Whitman in Camden* (1906–15). Traubel was also one of his friend's literary executors and an editor of *In Re Walt Whitman* (1893) and *The Complete Writings of Walt Whitman* (1902).

Trilling, Lionel 1905–75 Born and raised in New York City, Trilling received his BA from Columbia in 1925 and his PhD in 1938. He taught at Columbia for most of his life. One of this century's most influential critics, his publications include studies of *Matthew Arnold* (1939) and *E. M. Forster* (1943); and essays collected in *The Liberal Imagination* (1950), *The Opposing Self* (1955), *A Gathering of Fugitives* (1956), *Beyond Culture: Essays on Literature and Learning* (1965), and *Sincerity and Authenticity* (1972). Trilling addressed the broadest cultural questions: the relation of morality to politics, and the aesthetic as well as the political meaning of liberalism. His single novel, *The Middle of the Journey* (1947), also reflects these concerns. Since his death his widow, Diana, has edited several collections of his essays and a volume of his short stories – *Of This Time, Of That Place and Other Stories* (1979).

Tropic of Cancer See **Miller, Henry**

Trout Fishing in America See **Brautigan, Richard**

Trumbull, John 1750–1831 Born in Connecticut, Trumbull entered Yale University at the age of 13. He received his BA in 1767 and MA in 1770. His valedictory poem, *An Essay on the Uses and Advantages of the Fine Arts* (1770), condemns neoclassical aesthetics, and in its closing verses, entitled "Prospect of the Future Glory of America," celebrates the potential of American literature. While teaching at Yale (1770–3), Trumbull also wrote a satire on college education, *The Progress of Dulness; or, the Adventures of Tom Brainless* (1772), and published some elegant verse and essays.

He left Yale to study law in Boston with John Adams, who inspired his patriotic poem *An Elegy on the Times* (1774). Practicing law in New Haven and Hartford (1774–1825), he became associated with the **Connecticut Wits** and with them fought to broaden Yale's curriculum to include the study of contemporary American literature, and to defend Federalist politics. After publishing *M'Fingal* (Cantos I–II, 1775–6; Cantos I–IV, 1782), a mock epic which satirizes British conduct during the American Revolution, he collaborated with others of the Connecticut Wits on *The Anarchiad* (1786–7) and *The Echo* (1791–1805).

Tuckerman, Frederick Goddard 1821–73 Born in Boston and educated at Harvard, Tuckerman graduated with a law degree but only practiced for a few years (1844–7), having sufficient means to retire to Greenfield, Massachusetts, where he lived for the rest of his life. He is best known for his sonnets, which are personal and often melancholy in tone. His only volume, *Poems*, appeared in 1860 (two further editions were published during his lifetime). **Nathaniel Hawthorne**, **Ralph Waldo Emerson**, and **Henry Wadsworth Longfellow** all praised his work, as did Tennyson in England. He was generally forgotten, however, until the poet Witter Bynner published a selection from

Poems in 1931 along with three previously unpublished sonnets. All of his work was later collected, edited, and introduced by **N. Scott Momaday** in *The Complete Poems of Frederick Tuckerman* (1965).

Turner, Frederick Jackson 1861–1932 The historian who formulated the "Turner thesis" on the role of the frontier in American history, Turner was born in Portage, Wisconsin. He received his BA from the University of Wisconsin in 1884 and his MA in 1888. In 1890 he was awarded his doctorate from The Johns Hopkins University. He taught at the University of Wisconsin and at Harvard, turning down offers from various other American universities.

Turner read his famous essay, "The Significance of the Frontier in American History," to the American Historical Association in Chicago in 1893. In it he advanced the notion that the continual challenge presented by the frontier was the primary factor in American development, more important than the European influences of ancestry and culture. American life and values, he argued, were shaped above all by the waves of western movement. "The Significance of the Frontier" was published with some of his other essays as *The Frontier in American History* (1920). His earlier publications include *The Character and Influence of the Indian Trade in Wisconsin* (1891), which had been his doctoral dissertation; and *Rise of the New West, 1819– 1829* (1906), which appeared as the 14th volume in the American Nation series edited by Albert Bushnell Hart. For *The Significance of Sections in American History* (1932), Jackson was posthumously awarded the Pulitzer Prize for history. He won a second posthumous Pulitzer for *The United States, 1830–1850, The Nation and Its Sections* (1935), a continuation of *Rise of the New West*, edited from Turner's incomplete manuscript by Avery O. Craven, his friend and former student.

Turn of the Screw, The A short novel by **Henry James**, first published in *Collier's Weekly*, and then with another story, "Covering End," in a volume entitled *The Two Magics*, in 1898. It was dramatized by William Archibald in 1950 as *The Innocents*; four years later Benjamin Britten wrote an opera version under the original title.

The story is about a governess who takes

charge of two children at Bly, a lonely estate in England. Her employer, the children's uncle, has given her strict orders not to bother him with any of the details of their education or behavior. The children, Flora and Miles, are attractive and intelligent, but also seem strained and secretive. Shortly after her arrival, the governess sees two former members of the household, the steward Peter Quint and the previous governess Miss Jessel; later she learns that both of them are dead. She is convinced that the children see the ghosts, too. But they display a remarkable talent for evading questions about them, and she becomes increasingly certain that they are under the maleficent influence of the pair. One day she challenges Flora directly; the little girl's reaction is explosive and hysterical and she falls ill. Miles is confronted next, and during this scene the governess sees Peter Quint at the window. She is determined to exorcise his influence, but while attempting to shield Miles from the apparition, the boy, frantic and terrified, dies in her arms.

The story, told entirely from the point of view of the governess, raises doubts in the reader about her reliability as narrator, and about whether her visions are of real "ghosts" or merely hallucinations.

Twain, Mark　See **Clemens, Samuel Langhorne**

Twice-Told Tales　See **Hawthorne, Nathaniel**

Two Years Before the Mast　A personal narrative, by **Richard Henry Dana**, of life at sea in the 1830s, published in 1840. After leaving Harvard University, Dana sailed on the brig *Pilgrim* on a voyage of 150 days. In his clear-sighted, detailed, and unsparing account of the voyage from Boston around Cape Horn to California, he draws vivid portraits of his shipmates, telling how they were completely at the mercy of the captain, who ordered two of them to be flogged. His return trip, on the *Alert*, lasted 135 days, during which time he determined to quit the sea. Another chapter was added to the book 24 years later, telling of his return to California in 1859 and of the fortunes of some of the men described in the original narrative.

Tyler, Royall　1757–1826　Born in Boston and educated at Harvard, Tyler was admitted to the Massachusetts Bar in 1780. A distinguished legal career culminated in his appointments as chief justice of the Supreme Court in Vermont (1807–13), and as professor of jurisprudence at the University of Vermont (1811–14).

His literary reputation is based largely on his first play, *The Contrast* (1787), said to have been written in the three weeks following his attendance at a performance of Sheridan's *The School for Scandal* in New York. *The Contrast* was the first comedy by a native American writer to be professionally produced. Tyler's second and less successful play was *May Day in Town; or, New York in an Uproar* (1787), a comic opera of which the manuscript has not survived. Two other plays of which no copy exists are *The Farm House; or, The Female Duellists* (1796), possibly an adaptation of J. P. Kemble's *The Farm House* (1789); and *The Georgia Spec; or, Land in the Moon* (1797), a satire of land speculation in Georgia. Tyler may have also written an adaptation of Molière's *The Doctor in Spite of Himself* and a play for children titled *Five Pumpkins*, but evidence in both cases is inconclusive. The texts of four other plays have survived; none has been produced on stage but all were published in the *America's Lost Plays* series (1941): *The Island of Barrataria* is a three-act farce based on an episode from Cervantes' *Don Quixote*; *The Judgment of Solomon, The Origin of the Feast of Purim*, and *Joseph and his Brethren* are all sacred verse dramas. Jointly responsible for the "Colon & Spondee" column with his friend Joseph Dennie, Tyler contributed satirical verse and essays to various periodicals after 1794. The flavor of these pieces can be gathered from the essays and sketches published in *The Yankey in London* (1809). *The Algerine Captive* (1797) was his only novel.

Typee: A Peep at Polynesian Life. During a Four Months' Residence in a Valley of the Marquesas　**Herman Melville**'s first novel, published in 1846, and based on his own experiences in the South Seas.

Two seamen on a whaler, Tom and Toby, jump ship in the Marquesas Islands and make their way to an inland valley. They have heard that the Typee tribe is particularly savage, and hope instead to fall in with the peace-loving Happars. They meet the Typees first, however, and find them fairly friendly. Tommo, as the natives call him, has injured his foot, and Toby is allowed to go and get medicine, planning also to try to get them rescued. But he never returns (Tommo finds out later that through the treachery of an old sailor "guide," he was shipped aboard a whaler in need of hands), and Tommo is left alone among the Typees. The natives are kind and generous, and he enjoys his island paradise in the company of Fayaway, a beautiful native girl. A sympathetic though not always comprehending observer of island culture, he criticizes white missionary efforts and their destructive effects on the islanders, as well as the facile dichotomy between "civilization" and "savagery" by which the whites justify their actions. However, some native customs are strange to him – he has heard uncomfortable rumors about cannibalism – and he becomes more and more homesick for the Western world. He sees evidence of ritual cannibalism among the Typees and begins to fear that he will be their next victim. He decides to flee the valley, and though the tribe pursues him into the sea he is rescued by the boat of an Australian whaler.

Typee was first published in London. An American edition appeared the same year (1846) with some minor revisions. The book, though popular (more than any other of Melville's would be during his lifetime), was considered by some reviewers to be objectionable on account of its sexual content and its condemnation of Christian missions, and Melville edited out the more explicit passages for the revised American edition. Modern editions usually restore the text to its original version.

U

Uncle Remus: *His Songs and His Sayings* The first collection of **Joel Chandler Harris**'s verse and tales based on black folklore, published in 1881. Uncle Remus, once a slave, is a valued family servant; the son of the house is a fascinated audience to whom he recounts the traditional stories of his people. Harris attempts to reproduce the speech of plantation blacks, and endows the animals in his fables with human qualities. Among the characters are Br'er Rabbit, Br'er Fox, and Br'er Wolf. The famous "Tar-Baby" story is included in this collection.

Uncle Tom's Cabin, *or Life among the Lowly* An anti-slavery novel by **Harriet Beecher Stowe**, published serially in the *National Era* (1851–2) and in book form in 1852. It became the best-selling novel of the 19th century. Abraham Lincoln, in the midst of the Civil War, is reported to have remarked that Mrs Stowe was "the little lady who wrote the book that made this great war."

Uncle Tom is a saintly and faithful slave owned by the Shelby family. When the Shelbys find themselves in financial straits, Tom is separated from his wife and children and sold to a slave trader. Young George Shelby sympathizes with Tom and vows to redeem him some day. Tom is taken South, and on the voyage down the Mississippi he saves the life of Eva St Clare (known as little Eva) with the result that her father buys him out of gratitude. They go to the St Clare home in New Orleans, where Tom is happy and grows close to Eva and her black friend Topsy. After two years little Eva dies from a weakened constitution in an attenuated and highly sentimental death scene. Her father is then killed in an accident and Tom is sold at auction to the villainous Simon Legree, a cruel

and drunken Yankee. Legree is bewildered by Tom's ever-patient nature, and two of his female slaves capitalize on this by pretending to escape and going into hiding. Tom will not reveal their whereabouts, and Legree has him brutally whipped to death. As he is dying, George Shelby arrives to rescue him but it is too late. In despair, Shelby pledges to fight for the Abolitionist cause. "God wrote the book," Mrs Stowe once said, "I took His dictation."

In the years following the publication of *Uncle Tom's Cabin*, 12 unauthorized stage versions of the novel were written and produced. Stowe, a woman of strong Christian principles, believed that theatrical performances were immoral, and had failed to reserve to herself the dramatic rights to the novel. Playwrights, however, recognized the book as perfect material for the stage, particularly the characters of Little Eva and Topsy. The first recorded production was Charles Taylor's in Albany, New York, less than six months after the publication of the novel. Of all the adaptations, however, the most famous was by George L. Aiken (1830–76), an actor and author of many sentimental dramas. The first version of his adaptation, which focused primarily upon the character of Little Eva, was written expressly for Cordelia Howard, the daughter of the director of the Troy Museum, and opened in Troy on September 2, 1852, less than a month after Taylor's play appeared in Albany. Realizing the inadequacies of this first version, Aiken promptly wrote a second, entitled *The Death of Uncle Tom; or, The Religion of the Lowly*. He combined the two adaptations into one production on November 15, 1852. It ran for 100 nights in Troy and then moved to New York City on July 18, 1853, where it ran for 325 performances at Purdy's National Theater. Although it significantly reworked the original plot structure, Aiken's dramatization is generally considered to be the most faithful to the sentimentality, religious fervor, and polemical purpose of Stowe's novel.

Under the Gaslight See **Daly, Augustin**

Updike, John (Hoyer) 1932– Updike was born in Shillington, Pennsylvania, and graduated from Harvard in 1954. He worked on the staff of *The New Yorker* for two years and his first work appeared in that magazine. In 1958 he published a volume of verse, *The Carpentered Hen* (it was called *Hoping for a Hoopoe* in England); his first novel, *The Poorhouse Fair*, came in the following year.

Updike established a reputation as a keen observer of modern American life with the short stories in *The Same Door* (1959), and enjoyed major success with the novel *Rabbit Run* (1960, Rosenthal Award), whose central character, Harry Angstrom, appears also in the sequels, *Rabbit Redux* (1971) and *Rabbit is Rich* (1981). *Pigeon Feathers and Other Stories* (1962) and *The Magic Flute* (1962, a children's book) were followed by *The Centaur* (1963, National Book Award), in which the life of a small-town teacher is linked to that of Chiron, the wise centaur of mythology. Updike's other works include the verse collections *Telephone Poles* (1963), *Seventy Poems* (1963), *Midpoint and Other Poems* (1969), *The Dance of the Solids* (1969), and *Tossing and Turning* (1977). Among his other novels are *Bech: A Book* (1970), *Bech is Back* (1982), and *The Witches of Eastwick* (1984). His collections of short stories include *The Ring* (1964, called *Olinger Stories* in England), *The Music School* (1966, O Henry Award), *Museums and Women* (1972), *A Month of Sundays* (1975), *Marry Me* (1976), and *Problems and Other Stories* (1979). *Hugging the Shore*, a collection of essays, was published in 1983.

Up From Slavery Published in 1901, **Booker T. Washington**'s autobiography attributes the author's success as a self-made man to hard work and Christian virtue. He presents a picture of improving racial relations and an improving economic status for blacks, and stresses the need for gradual progress in education and civil rights. These views were vigorously criticized by **W.E.B. DuBois** in a debate which continued until Washington's death in 1915.

U.S.A. A trilogy of novels by **John Dos Passos** consisting of *The 42nd Parallel* (1930), *1919* (1932), and *The Big Money* (1936). In all three novels Dos Passos interweaves the stories of fictional characters with biographies of real people and accounts of historical events. The trilogy begins roughly with the Spanish–American War (1898) and documents an era in America's history marked by rising tension between capitalists and labor unions, technological advances, involvement in World War I, and the Jazz Age; it ends in the early 1930s with the aftermath of the 1929 stock market crash.

Dos Passos's narrative technique is distinctly unconventional. His characters, types rather than fully developed individuals, lead lives that are interconnected in an almost random way. Although several of them appear in all three novels, their activities do not constitute a unified plot. But their lives have a common pattern: all are destroyed – either physically or spiritually – by a society that is becoming increasingly materialistic and inimical to individual freedom.

The characters come from all strata of society. J. Ward Moorehouse is from a fairly poor family; ambitious, he marries for money, sets aside his dream of being a songwriter, and becomes instead a successful public relations man. His success, however, does not bring him happiness. At the trilogy's end he is tired, ill, and cynical. His young business associate, Richard Ellsworth Savage, repeats the pattern of his own life in several ways. A promising young poet from a relatively affluent family, Savage gives up writing poetry for the "big money" in public relations. He leads a dissolute life, which puts him in debt. As his story comes to a close, he plans to court Myra Bingham, the homely daughter of one of his wealthy clients.

Joe Williams, a seaman, fights, drinks, and womanizes whenever he is ashore. He never gets ahead, and eventually dies in a brawl in a bar in France where he had been celebrating the end of World War I. Charley Anderson, a likeable young aviator and inventor, becomes wealthy but is used by other people, most notably by Margo Dowling, an unscrupulous, greedy, and ambitious actress. He dies from injuries sustained in an automobile accident.

Two female characters, Eleanor Stoddard and Eveline Hutchins, begin as friends. Stoddard is from a poor family, Hutchins from a wealthy one. They establish their own interior decorating firm in their native Chicago and later travel to New York to design the costumes and scenery for a friend's play. Though sexually frigid, Eleanor has an affair with J. Ward Moorehouse to advance herself socially. She becomes brittle and calculating and begins to snub her former friend Eveline, who now strikes her as unsophisticated. Eveline becomes pregnant, makes an unhappy marriage, becomes an alcoholic, and eventually commits suicide.

Other characters attempt, not to advance themselves within America's capitalist society, but to change that society. Ben Compton, an organizer for the Communist party, is eventually sentenced to a ten-year term in a federal prison for his radical activities. And because he refuses to be a "yes man," he is abandoned by the Party he has served. Mary French, who for a while is Compton's lover, becomes a Party automaton. Initially a sensitive, bookish young woman who wants to help the downtrodden, she becomes so caught up in Party work – organizing marches, distributing leaflets, sheltering homeless Party members – that she no longer has a clear sense of what purpose, if any, it all serves.

Dos Passos does not rely only on his fictional characters to depict American life in the 20th century. In fact he makes use of four different kinds of narrative throughout the trilogy. He interrupts the stories of his fictional characters with brief biographies of politicians, inventors, intellectuals, labor leaders, businessmen, and artists (people such as Eugene V. Debs, **Randolph Bourne**, **Thorstein Veblen**, Thomas Edison, Frank Lloyd Wright, Theodore Roosevelt, Woodrow Wilson, Henry Ford, Isadora Duncan, and Rudolph Valentino). Impressionistic passages called "Newsreels," in which he juxtaposes slogans, newspaper headlines, lyrics from popular songs, and parts of political speeches, give the reader a sense of the social and historical context in which the fictional characters move. The "Camera Eye" sections, written in stream-of-consciousness form, present a subjective view of American life as experienced by a young boy who grows to manhood during the period covered by the trilogy.

V

Vanity Fair A magazine published weekly in New York City from 1859 to 1863, offering humorous commentary on contemporary social and political issues. Edited by C. G. Leland and then by C. F. Brown, its contributors included **Thomas Aldrich**, George Arnold, **William Dean Howells**, **Fitz-James O'Brien**, and **Richard Henry Stoddard**.

It was revived in 1868, under the editorship of Frank Harris. In 1913 it was purchased by Condé Nast and became a sophisticated review of literature, art, and fashion. Frank Crowinshield was editor from 1914 to 1936, at which time it was absorbed by *Vogue*. It reappeared in 1983 under the editorship of Richard Locke, and is currently edited by Tina Brown. Though it remains a magazine of high fashion and living, it has also printed the work of such literary figures as Gabriel Garcia Marquez, Joseph Brodsky, Italo Calvino, and **Norman Mailer**.

Van Vechten, Carl 1880–1966 Born in Cedar Rapids, Iowa, Van Vechten is best known for a series of novels which deal with the cultural life of New York City in the 1920s. They include *Peter Whiffle* (1922), *The Blind Bow-Boy* (1923), *Firecrackers* (1925), and *Parties* (1930). His most highly acclaimed work is *Nigger Heaven* (1926), which takes place in the exotic world of Harlem's nightclubs and soirées, and which is often seen as epitomizing the renewed interest in black life shown by white writers during this period.

His other novels include a satire of Hollywood entitled *Spider Boy* (1928), and *The Tattooed Countess* (1924), which is set in his home state of Iowa. He was also active as a music and drama critic and wrote several memoirs, the most notable of which are *Sacred and Profane Memoirs* (1932) and an account of his friendship with **Gertrude Stein**, published as an introduction to an edition of her *Three Lives* (1909). He edited *Selected Writings of Gertrude Stein* in 1946.

Varieties of Religious Experience, The A book by **William James**, published in 1902, the compilation of two courses of lectures which he delivered at Edinburgh University in 1901–2. He focuses on a personal instead of an organized religion, which he found to be a matter of "ritual acts" rather than of private importance. His argument, based on scientific analysis of a number of examples of the conversion process, asserts that the particulars of religious faith are true insofar as they provide the believer with emotional fulfillment. The book was especially influential in stimulating the study of the psychology of religion.

Veblen, Thorstein (Bunde) 1857–1929 The son of Norwegian immigrant farmers, Veblen was born in Cato Township, Wisconsin. He studied mostly philosophy at Carleton College and The Johns Hopkins University, and received a doctorate from Yale in 1884. Failing to obtain a teaching post, he then enrolled at Cornell to study economics. In 1892 he became a lecturer in economics at the newly founded University of Chicago. He later taught at Stanford and the University of Missouri. From 1918 to 1919 he edited *The Dial*, which was published in New York City, and then accepted a teaching post at the New School for Social Research, also in New York City.

His first and most famous book, *The Theory of the Leisure Class: An Economic Study in the Evolution of Institutions* (1899), was popular among radicals because it attacked the caste system that grew out of the pursuit of wealth. *The Instinct of Workmanship* (1914) considers two opposing tendencies within men – the disposition to workmanship which survives in the modern capitalist system and the predatory impulse which thrives in it. *The Place of Science in Modern Civilization* (1919) is a study of the two main sources of science – disorderly knowledge of a utilitarian character and disinterested interpretation of this knowledge. Both books employ anthropological, biological, and psychological, as well as economic approaches to their topics. Veblen's abiding interest in the economic determinants of modern society – in particular his concern with the disjunction between those who actually produce goods and those who control the production process and the distribution of products – is evident in several of his other works: *The Theory of Business Enterprise* (1904), *The Vested Interests and the State of the Industrial Arts* (1919), *The Engineers and the Price System* (1921), and his last book, *Absentee Ownership* (1923).

Vein of Iron   A novel by **Ellen Glasgow**, published in 1935, which tells the story of the Scottish-Irish Fincastle family, who have been ministers and leaders in Shut-In Valley in the Virginia mountains since Colonial times. The story focuses on a daughter of the family, Ada, and follows her from her childhood through the years of the Depression. John, Ada's father, has lost his position in the church because of his unorthodox ideas, and has started teaching school. Ada is in love with her father's student, Ralph McBride, and is jealous when he marries the beautiful Janet Rowan. When Janet divorces Ralph to marry a richer man, he and Ada become lovers. He goes to fight in World War I, unknowingly leaving Ada pregnant. Rejected by the community after the death of her grandmother, whose good reputation has helped sustain the family, Ada moves to Queenborough to give birth to her son, Rannie. Ralph returns and they are married. Their happy reunion is upset, however, when Ralph is temporarily paralyzed in a car accident. Ada, with her "vein of iron," her undaunted pride and courage, goes back to work to support her husband, son, and ailing father. After John Fincastle's death, the family uses the insurance money to buy back the family home in Shut-In Valley.

Very, Jones 1813–80   Born in Salem, Mas-

sachusetts, and educated at Harvard, this New England poet was associated with the **Transcendentalists**. His first book, *Essays and Poems* (1839), was edited and published by **Ralph Waldo Emerson**. A licensed Unitarian minister, he briefly held pastorates in New England, but soon retired and lived the remainder of his life with his sisters in Salem. A mystic who believed in the absolute surrender of the will to God, he wrote devotional verse in the vein of the 17th-century English metaphysical poets. His work was highly praised by **William Cullen Bryant** and **William Ellery Channing** as well as by Emerson. Two volumes were published posthumously: *Poems* (1883) and *Poems and Essays* (1886).

Vidal, Gore 1925–   Born in West Point, New York, and educated at the University of New Hampshire, Vidal served on army transports in the Aleutian Islands in World War II and then made use of his war experiences in his early novels, *Williwaw* (1946) and *In a Yellow Wood* (1947). The novel *The City and the Pillar* (1948, revised 1965) dealt frankly with homosexual life in America and became a best seller. He followed this with the novels *The Season of Comfort* (1949), *A Search for the King* (1950), *The Judgement of Paris* (1952), *Messiah* (1954, revised 1965), and the collection of short stories *The Thirsty Evil* (1956). He became a playwright, first for television, with *Visit to a Small Planet* (published with others in 1957), and then for the theatre with *The Best Man* (1960), about an election campaign – based on his own experience of running for Congress that same year. However, it is probably as an essayist and satirist that he is most highly regarded; *Rocking the Boat* (1962) was his first book of essays, *Washington DC* (1964) was his first satire on American politics. The novels *Myra Breckenridge* (1968), *Two Sisters* (1970), *Burr: A Novel* (1973), *Creation* (1982), *Duluth* (1983), and *Lincoln* (1984), and the essay collections *Reflections on a Sinking Ship* (1969), *An Evening With Richard Nixon* (1972), *Matters of Fact and Matters of Fiction: Essays, 1973–1976* (1977), and *The Second American Revolution* (1982), all, in their different ways, present his tart, penetrating view of American life. Vidal also writes detective stories under the name of Edgar Box.

View from the Bridge, A See **Miller, Arthur**

Virginian, The: A Horseman of the Plains A romantic novel of the old West by **Owen Wister**, published in 1902. Extremely popular in its day and widely read ever since, it is the prototype for the whole genre of Western novels and the source of much Western lore. Perhaps the most celebrated episode is the first confrontation between the hero, known only as "The Virginian," and his sworn enemy, Trampas. Trampas calls the Virginian a "son-of-a- " and accuses him of cheating in a poker game, whereupon the bold but gentle hero lays his pistol on the table and replies, "When you call me that, smile!"

Set mostly in the Wyoming cattle country of the 1870s, the novel portrays the unrefined manly life of the cowboys. Civilization is on the move, however, and appears in the form of the pretty Vermont schoolteacher, Miss Molly Wood. The plot builds toward the marriage day of Miss Wood and the Virginian, when the hero is forced to kill Trampas in a showdown duel (probably the first portrayed in literature). Molly, who detests violence, has sworn to break the engagement if such an event were to occur, but she decides to accept the Virginian anyway. Thus the bond between the civilized and pioneer America is closed, but not without some bittersweet undertones on a way of life that will be forever lost.

Vizenor, Gerald 1934– An Ojibwa Indian and currently a member of the Minnesota Chippewa tribe, Vizenor was born in Minneapolis. He attended the University of Minnesota, where he now teaches American Indian Studies. His first collection of poetry, *Born in the Wind*, was privately printed in 1960. He has since published several volumes of English haiku poetry, including *Raising the Moon* (1964), *Seventeen Chirps* (1964), *Two Wings the Butterfly* (1967), and *Matsushima: Haiku* (1984). He also has edited several collections of American Indian writings, including *Ojibwa Lyric Poems and Tribal Stories* (1981), *Earthdivers: Tribal Narratives on Mixed Descent* (1981), and *The People Named the Chippewa: Narrative Histories* (1984).

Vonnegut, Kurt, Jr 1922– Born in Indianapolis, Indiana, Vonnegut was educated at Cornell and the University of Chicago. While serving in the infantry during World War II he was captured by the Germans, and his subsequent experiences as a prisoner of war in Dresden were to influence much of his work. *Slaughterhouse Five* (1969), his most famous novel, is specifically concerned with the bombing of Dresden by the Allies, and offers ironic commentary on both our inhumanity and the appalling opportunity for destruction provided by 20th-century technology.

After the war Vonnegut completed his education at the universities of Tennessee and Chicago, and began publishing short stories in various magazines. His first novel, *Player Piano*, appeared in 1952. *The Sirens of Titan* (1959) and *Cat's Cradle* (1963) developed his use of science fiction as a medium for social and political satire; *Mother Night* (1961), a black comedy about war crimes and anti-Semitism, was republished in 1966 when his reputation was secure. His other books are *Canary in a Cathouse* (1961), *God Bless You, Mr Rosewater* (1965), *Welcome to the Monkey House* (1968), *Happy Birthday, Wanda June* (1971), *Between Time and Timbuktu* (1972), *Breakfast of Champions* (1973), *Wampeters, Foma and Granfallons* (1974, essays), *Slapstick* (1976), *Jailbird* (1979), *Sun Moon Star* (1980, a children's book, illustrated by Ivan Chermayeff), *Palm Sunday* (1981), and *Deadeye Dick* (1982).

W

Waiting for Lefty   A one-act play by **Clifford Odets**, first produced in New York City in 1935, dealing with the oppression of the working class and the need for unions to take strong action. Odets wrote it in three days after hearing of a contest run by the New Theatre League for a politically radical one-act play. The production that was his reward for winning the contest brought him immediate recognition.

The play is framed by a union meeting, at which corrupt bosses are attempting to persuade the membership that the time is not right for a strike. Through flashbacks the audience is shown the hardships undergone by various members at the hands of their employers. Periodically members wonder where Lefty, one of their leaders, is; at the end of the play the news that he has been found murdered provides the impetus for the strike to begin.

Wakoski, Diane 1937–   Wakoski was born in Whittier, California, and received her bachelor's degree from the University of California at Berkeley in 1959. She taught junior high school in New York City between 1963 and 1966, and has since been poet-in-residence at several colleges and has also taught at the New School for Social Research. In 1976 she joined the faculty of Michigan State University.

Her first volume of poetry, *Coins and Coffins*, was published in 1962 and has been followed by over 30 more. With its frequent use of autobiographical material, much of her work resembles that of the **Confessional** poets. In particular, she focuses on her unhappy childhood and, in poems concerned with adult life, on her painful experiences with men (many of these latter poems are marked by a rage against male dominance).

Her other volumes include *Discrepancies and Apparitions* (1966), *The George Washington Poems* (1967), *Greed Parts One and Two* (1968), *Thanking My Mother For Piano Lessons* (1969), *The Lament of the Lady Bank Dick* (1970), *The Pumpkin Pie: or, Reassurances Are Always False, Tho We Love Them, Only Physics Counts . . .* (1972), *Dancing on the Grave of a Son of a Bitch* (1973), *Looking For The King of Spain* (1974), *Waiting For The King of Spain* (1976), *The Lady Who Drove Me to the Airport* (1982), and *The Collected Greed, Parts 1–13* (1984). She has also published three volumes of prose: *Form Is an Extension of Content* (1972), *Creating a Personal Mythology* (1975), and *Towards a New Poetry* (1979).

Walden, *or Life in the Woods*   An autobiographical narrative by **Henry David Thoreau**, published in 1854. It describes a two-year period from March 1845 to September 1847 during which the author retired from the town of Concord to live alone at nearby Walden Pond. This was Thoreau's own **Transcendentalist** experiment, equivalent in many ways to that of **Brook Farm**: he sought to put into action a program of self-reliance, whereby the individual spirit might thrive in its detachment from the fractured world of mass society.

Much of the book was derived from the journals Thoreau kept during his stay. Comprised of 18 essays, it effectively recreates a sense of the multiple dimensions of the author's self. His prose can be complex and poetically evocative, but also lucid, even scientifically direct; at times he engages in allegory and parable. Other passages catalogue the various animals and plants in the area. The narrative often digresses into lengthy discussions of philosophy and poetry; famous sections involve Thoreau's visits with a Canadian woodcutter and with an Irish family, a trip to Concord, and a description of his bean field. His prose powerfully depicts both the solitude of nature and the man-made sounds of the railroad and the wind whistling through the nearby telegraph wires. *Walden* is widely considered to be among the greatest achievements of American autobiography.

Walker, Alice 1944–   Novelist and poet, born in Eatonton, Georgia, the eighth child of a family of sharecroppers. Educated at Spelman College and Sarah Lawrence College, she soon became committed to the civil rights movement. She worked for voter registration in Georgia, welfare rights and Head Start in Mississippi, and the Welfare Department in New York City. She taught for a time in Mississippi, first at Jackson State University (1968–9) and then at Tougaloo College (1969–70).

Her first publications were two collections of poetry: *Once: Poems* (1968), which reflects her experience of the civil rights movement and her travels in Africa; *Revolutionary Petunias and Other Poems* (1973), which is a tribute to those who struggle against racism and oppression. Her first novel, *The Third Life of Grange Copeland* (1970), is the story of three generations of black tenant farmers from 1900 to the 1960s. A book of short stories, *In Love and Trouble: Stories of Black Women* (1973), explores the experience and heritage of black women, a theme to which Walker returns in a second collection, *You Can't Keep a Good Woman Down* (1981). The epistolary novel, *The Color Purple* (1982), which won a Pulitzer Prize, centers on the life of Celie, a black woman who has been raped by the man she believed to be her father. She bears his children, and then is forced to marry an older man whom she despises. The novel is made up of Celie's despairing letters to God and to her sister Nettie who has gone to Africa as a missionary, and of Nettie's letters to Celie. Walker's other publications include a biography for children, *Langston Hughes, American Poet* (1974); *Meridian* (1977), a novel about the lives of civil rights workers in the South during the 1960s; and two collections of poems, *Good Night, Willie Lee, I'll See You in the Morning* (1979) and *Horses Make a Landscape Look More Beautiful: Poems* (1984). A

volume of essays appeared in 1983 entitled *In Search of My Mother's Garden: Womanist Prose*.

Wallace, Lew[is] 1827–1905 Born in Indiana, Wallace spent much of his life as a soldier. He served in the Mexican War and earned distinction in the Civil War, reaching the rank of major general. He lived for a time in Mexico, becoming interested in the country's history and in the attempts of Juarez to establish the people's right to their own land. He returned to Indiana to practice law and to write. *The Fair God* (1873) tells of the Spanish conquest of Mexico. His next book, *Ben-Hur* (1880), was an enormous success, selling over two million copies. His third book was a work of non-fiction, *The Boyhood of Christ* (1888). He served as governor of New Mexico and in 1881 became the US minister to Turkey. He also wrote other works of fiction; a tragic poem, *The Wooing of Malkatoon* (1897); and an autobiography.

Wallant, Edward (Lewis) 1926–62 Born in New Haven, Connecticut, Wallant served in the US Navy during World War II, graduated from Pratt Institute in 1950, and worked in New York City advertising agencies until his death. His first story was published in 1955; *The Human Season*, his first novel, which appeared in 1960, is the story of a middle-aged immigrant Jew following the death of his wife. *The Pawnbroker* (1961), Wallant's most acclaimed work, is one of the first American novels to consider the atrocities that occurred during World War II. Sol Nazerman, a Polish Jew, is the sole member of his family to have survived a Nazi concentration camp; he is now living in Harlem, New York City, where he owns a pawnshop and relives the horrors he endured in his nightmares and in flashbacks. Wallant's early death cut short a brief yet accomplished career. Two works were published posthumously: *The Tenants of Moonbloom* (1963) and *The Children at the Gate* (1965).

Wapshot Chronicle, The See **Cheever, John**

Ward, Artemus See **Browne, Charles Farrar**

Ward, Nathaniel 1578–1652 Born in Essex, England, Ward trained for the law and the ministry; excommunicated by Archbishop Laud for nonconformity, he emigrated to Massachusetts in 1634. He served as minister to Ipswich from 1634 to 1636, and became influential in Massachusetts politics, drafting *The Body of Liberties* in 1638 (published 1641), a set of laws, important in American constitutional history, which restricted the power of the magistrates.

Ward's literary reputation rests on his *The Simple Cobler of Aggawam*, a humorous satire and defense of Parliament, written in 1645 and published in London in 1647. He returned to England in 1646. Orthodox in his Puritanism, he leaned to the side of the Presbyterians rather than the Independents in Parliament. His Fast Day Sermon before Parliament in June, 1647, urged the establishment of a uniform national church polity, with no toleration of independent sects, even more strongly than had the *Simple Cobler*. It brought him the disapprobation of the more radical – and by then more powerful – Independents, but he published another anti-toleration pamphlet, *A Religious Retreat Sounded to a Religious Army*, in August of that same year. Though he remained in England for the rest of his life, he retained his ties with his American friends, and wrote a poem commending **Anne Bradstreet**'s collection, *The Tenth Muse*, which was included in the first edition (1650).

Warner, Charles Dudley 1829–1900   Born in Massachusetts, Warner received his BA in 1851 from Hamilton College and, following brief employment as a railroad surveyor in Missouri, studied law at the University of Pennsylvania, receiving his LLB in 1858. He practiced law in Chicago until 1860, when he turned to writing professionally. He moved to Hartford, Connecticut, in 1861 and became editor of the *Courant*. He is best remembered for *The Gilded Age* (1873), his first published novel, which was written in collaboration with **Mark Twain**. He also produced several collections of essays, including *Summer in a Garden* (1870), *Being a Boy* (1878), and *The Relation of Literature to Life* (1896). He devoted his later years to writing a trilogy of novels: *A Little Journey in the World* (1889), *The Golden House* (1894), and *That Fortune* (1899).

Warner, Susan B[ogert] 1819–85   (pseudonym: Elizabeth Wetherell) Warner's family suffered economic setbacks which in 1837 forced them to move from New York City to a small island off West Point in the Hudson River. At the age of 30 Warner began to write in order to assist the family's finances. Her first novel, *The Wide Wide World* (1850), describes the moral and religious development of a 13-year-old orphan. It was a best seller, as was her second novel, *Queechy* (1852). She followed these with numerous other novels and children's books, some written with her sister, Anna B. Warner. The two sisters continued to live in the family home and were frequent visitors to West Point, where Susan conducted Bible classes. Among her other novels are *Mrs Rutherford's Children* (1853–5), *The Old Helmet* (1863), *Melbourne House* (1864), *Daisy* (1868), *Wych Hazel* (1876), *My Desire* (1879), *Nobody* (1882), and *Stephan, MD* (1883). She is buried in the government cemetery at West Point.

Warren, Mercy Otis 1728–1814   The sister of James Otis, a Colonial political leader, and the wife of James Warren, the president of the Provincial Congress of Massachusetts, Mercy Warren was at the center of Revolutionary politics and in frequent correspondence with Revolutionary leaders. She is best known for her satiric political dramas such as *The Adulateur* (1773) and *The Group* (1775), in which she attacked Governor Hutchinson and other Loyalists, though it is not certain if either was performed. Other plays have been attributed to her, most notably *The Blockheads* (1776) and *The Motley Assembly* (1779). She also published a collection of dramatic verse, *Poems Dramatic and Miscellaneous* (1790), which contains two verse tragedies, "The Sack of Rome" and "The Ladies of Castille," and a three-volume *History of the Rise, Progress and Termination of the American Revolution* (1805), which serves as an important contemporary record of the Revolutionary years.

Warren, Robert Penn 1905–   Born in Guthrie, Kentucky, Warren received his BA from Vanderbilt University in 1925 and his MA from the University of California at Berkeley in 1927. He then attended Yale and, as a Rhodes Scholar, Oxford, from which he received a degree in 1930. A member of the group of poets known as the "Fugitives," he helped to found and edit the group's magazine, *The Fugitive* (1922–5). (See **Ransom, John Crowe**.) His first work, a biography entitled *John Brown, the Making of a*

Martyr, was published in 1929. The following year he contributed to the Southern Agrarian manifesto, *I'll Take My Stand* (1930). He published his first book of verse, *Thirty-Six Poems*, in 1935. It has been followed by many others, including *Brother to Dragons: A Tale in Verse and Voices* (1953); *Promises: Poems 1954–1956* (1957), for which he was awarded a Pulitzer Prize; *Now and Then: Poems 1976–1978* (1978), for which he won a second Pulitzer; and most recently *Chief Joseph of the Nez Perce* (1983). In addition to poetry, he has written nine novels and two collections of short stories. His fiction often deals with Southern history and generally has Southern settings. *Night Rider* (1939), his first novel, is about the Kentucky tobacco wars; its protagonist, Percy Munn, helps to organize a group of "night riders" to combat the tobacco buyers' ring and becomes a hunted outlaw. *All the King's Men* (1946), perhaps his most famous novel, is the story of Willie Stark, who enters the political arena, engages in corrupt politics, becomes governor of a Southern state, and then dies a tragic death. It was awarded the Pulitzer Prize for fiction in 1947 and was made into a movie in 1949. It was also the basis for an opera composed by Carlisle Floyd. The story of *World Enough and Time* (1950) is based on an 1826 murder trial in Kentucky. *Band of Angels* (1955), a tragedy of miscegenation, was followed by *Wilderness: A Tale of the Civil War* (1961), and *Flood: A Romance of Our Times* (1964), the story of a town about to be inundated as a part of a Tennessee Valley Authority dam project. Warren's most recent novel is *A Place to Come To* (1977).

His numerous works of non-fictional prose include *Segregation: The Inner Conflict in the South* (1956), *Remember the Alamo!* (1958), *Who Speaks for the Negro?* (1965), *Homage to Dreiser* (1971), *Democracy and Poetry* (1975), and *Jefferson Davis Gets His Citizenship Back* (1980). He has also written or edited several volumes with Cleanth Brooks, including *Understanding Poetry: An Anthology for College Students* (1938, revised in 1950 and 1960), *Understanding Fiction* (1943, revised in 1958), and *Modern Rhetoric: With Readings* (1949, revised in 1958). Together, he and Brooks founded and edited *Southern Review* (1935–42). He has taught at several universities in the US: Southwestern College, Vanderbilt, Louisiana State, the University of Minnesota, and Yale. He received the Bollingen Prize for poetry in 1967.

Washington, Booker T[aliaferro] 1856–1915 The black leader and educator was born in Hale's Ford, Virginia, the son of a slave mother and a white father. After the Civil War he worked in a salt furnace and a coal mine, at the same time attending night school in Malden, West Virginia. In 1872 he entered Hampton Normal Agricultural Institute in Virginia, earning his board as a janitor. He graduated in 1875, taught for two years in Malden, and undertook a further year of study at Wayland Seminary in Washington, DC. He returned to Hampton briefly to work on an educational program for Indians, and then founded the Tuskegee Institute in Alabama in 1881. In 1901 he organized the National Negro Business League in Boston, and soon became known as an influential thinker, educator, and public orator.

In the 1890s Washington urged a program of gradual development for American blacks, and emphasized training in the techniques of agricultural and industrial production. These policies soon brought him into conflict with **W.E.B. Du Bois** and other black leaders. Du Bois attacked him for not taking a sufficiently forceful stand on disenfranchisement in the South. He was criticized for emphasizing "formation of character" and for promoting vocational instruction at the expense of liberal education.

His publications include *The Future of the American Negro* (1899), *Sowing and Reaping* (1900), *Character Building* (1902), *Working with the Hands* (1904), *The Story of the Negro* (1909), *My Larger Education* (1911), and *The Man Farthest Down* (1912). His biography of **Frederick Douglass** (1906) is widely considered to be a pioneering work in the field. His autobiography, *Up From Slavery*, was published in 1901.

Washington Square A short novel by **Henry James** published serially in the *Cornhill Magazine* in 1880 and in volume form in 1881. The motherless daughter of a wealthy New York physician, Catherine Sloper is unappreciated and ignored by her father, and leads a lonely and bleak existence until she is courted by Morris Townsend. She accepts his proposal of marriage, but her father refuses to give his consent when he discovers Townsend to be a penniless fortune-hunter. Exasperated by Catherine's obstinate attachment, Dr Sloper takes her away to Europe for a year. This does not change her mind, but Morris, faced with the prospect of Catherine having to forfeit her inheritance if she marries him, breaks off the engagement. Seventeen years later, after the death of her father has made Catherine a rich woman, Morris returns and proposes again. She rejects him absolutely and settles down to the life of a spinster in the family house in Washington Square.

Waste Land, The   A long poem by **T. S. Eliot**, published in 1922, and perhaps the best-known poetic expression of the anarchy and ennui of the modern world. It has a fragmentary structure, each of its five sections dramatizing an aspect of life in the waste land – a dry and desolate country that symbolizes in part the sterility of post-war Europe. The unconventional form of the poem, with its lack of traditional narrative sequence, was as influential as its version of the decay of Western civilization.

The original manuscript was considerably longer than the published version; **Ezra Pound** was responsible for many of the cuts and revisions, and in gratitude for his assistance Eliot dedicated the poem to him. *The Waste Land* first appeared in October 1922 in *The Criterion* (London), and then a month later in *The Dial* (New York). When published as a book, also in 1922, it included 52 footnotes by Eliot. In 1971 a facsimile of the original manuscript appeared, showing Pound's suggested revisions, with an introduction by the poet's widow, Valerie Eliot.

Week on the Concord and Merrimack Rivers, A   An account by **Henry David Thoreau**, published in 1849, of a boat trip to the White Mountains of New Hampshire, taken in 1839 with his brother John. Written during the period described in **Walden**, it resembles that better-known work in its thoughtful digressions on poetry, philosophy, and religion. It was Thoreau's first major publication.

Weems, Parson (Mason Locke) 1759–1825   Weems was an Episcopal clergyman who for a time served the parish at Mount Vernon, where he may have come into contact with George Washington. For 30 years he was a book peddler and sometime author of chapbooks and edifying biographies. He is remembered for his *The Life and Memorable Actions of George Washington*, which in its fifth edition (1806) includes what is apparently the first written account of the cherry-tree myth demonstrating Washington's honesty.

Weill, Kurt 1900–50   Composer. Born in Germany, by 1925 Weill had composed two symphonies and a variety of other orchestral pieces. His first theatrical work was a three-year collaboration with Bertolt Brecht which resulted in three successful works: *The Three Penny Opera* (1928), *Happy End* (1929), and *The Rise and Fall of the City of Mahagonny* (1930). In 1933 Weill was forced to flee Germany with his wife, the actress Lotte Lenya, to avoid Nazi persecution. He emigrated to the US in 1935, and his first American score appeared in the 1936 play *Johnny Johnson*. He adapted to the American popular stage rapidly, and especially valued American jazz and folk music. His scores include *The Eternal Road* (1937), *Knickerbocker Holiday* (1938), *Lady in the Dark* (1941), *One Touch of Venus* (1943), **Street Scene** (1947), *Down in the Valley* (1948), and *Lost in the Stars* (1949). At the time of his sudden death in 1950, he was collaborating on an adaptation of **Huckleberry Finn** with **Maxwell Anderson**.

Welch, James 1940–   Born in Browning, Montana, Welch is Blackfoot Indian on his father's side and Gros Ventre on his mother's. He was educated at schools on the Blackfoot and Fort Belknap reservations, and then at the universities of Minnesota and Montana. He has worked as a laborer, a firefighter, a counselor for Upward Bound, a member of the literature panel of the National Endowment of the Arts, and an official on the Montana State Board of Pardons. His first publication, *Riding the Earthboy 40: Poems*, appeared in 1971. His first novel, *Winter in the Blood* (1974), is about a young Indian trying to make sense of his heritage in the modern world. A second novel, *The Death of Jim Loney* (1979), though set in contemporary midwestern society, is concerned with the traditional codes of behavior found in the mythic stories of the Gros Ventres.

Welty, Eudora 1909–   Born in Jackson, Mississippi, Welty attended Mississippi State College for Women (1925–7), received her

BA from the University of Wisconsin in 1929, and then studied advertising at Columbia University (1930–1). Her first collection, *A Curtain of Green, and Other Stories*, appeared in 1941, with an introduction by **Katherine Anne Porter**; such stories as "Petrified Man," "Death of a Travelling Salesman," "A Worn Path," and "Why I Live at the P.O." established her as a major Southern writer, with a powerful sense of place. Her second collection, *The Wide Net, and Other Stories* (1943), was less well received. *The Golden Apples* (1949) contains seven related stories about three generations of the MacLain, Morrison, Stark, Rainey, and Carmichael families in the fictitious small town of Morgana, Mississippi. *The Bride of the Innisfallen, and Other Stories* (1955) includes stories set in London, Italy, and Greece, as well as in the South.

Welty has also written a number of novels in the Southern Gothic tradition, among them *The Robber Bridegroom* (1942), *Delta Wedding* (1946), *The Ponder Heart* (1954), *Losing Battles* (1970), and *The Optimist's Daughter* (1972, Pulitzer Prize). She has published several volumes of critical essays, including *The Eye of the Story: Selected Essays and Reviews* (1979). *The Collected Stories of Eudora Welty* appeared in 1980. Her literary autobiography, *One Writer's Beginnings*, was published in 1984.

Wescott, Glenway 1901–   Wescott was born and raised in Wisconsin, and much of his work draws heavily on his time there. His first publication was a book of **Imagist**-influenced verse, *The Bitterns* (1920). His best-known works were published while he lived as an expatriate in France in the 1920s. These include *The Apple of the Eye* (1924) and his most successful novel, *The Grandmothers* (1926, winner of a Harper Prize). Both are stories of frontier life in Wisconsin, and in both Wescott fashions a lyrical evocation of the past, a rich and deeply felt assessment of his heritage. These two novels, along with *Good-Bye Wisconsin* (1928), a collection of stories, established him as one of the most promising American expatriate novelists. He was friendly with **Gertrude Stein** and her literary circle; **Ernest Hemingway** based his character Robert Prentiss, in *The Sun Also Rises*, on him. After his return to the US in 1933 his work grew more infrequent; his last publication of note, *The Pilgrim Hawk*,

appeared in 1940. He has, however, remained active in the literary community, and served as the president of the National Institute of Arts and Letters from 1959 to 1962. He has published several collections of essays, among them *Fear and Trembling* (1932) and *Images of Truth: Remembrances and Criticism* (1962). He has also edited *The Maugham Reader* (1950) and *Short Novels of Colette* (1951).

West, Nathanael 1903–40 The pseudonym of Nathan Wallenstein Weinstein; born in New York City, he studied at Brown University and then lived in Paris for two years. There he completed his first novel, *The Dream Life of Balso Snell* (1931), a garish and self-consciously *avant-garde* satire on the inner life of the intellectual introvert of the title. West's preoccupation with the barrenness of contemporary life was given further expression in *Miss Lonelyhearts* (1933), the story of a newspaperman who writes an advice-to-the-lovelorn column and who becomes obsessed with the need to be more than a phony savior. His initial professional detachment from his suffering correspondents turns into a tragic involvement which ends in his murder. The mockery of his sadistic editor accompanies his downfall.

A Cool Million: The Dismantling of Lemuel Pitkin (1934) is a satire of the American Dream itself: Lemuel is naive to the point of idiocy but this is no obstacle to his becoming a runner in the lethal race for riches and eminence. After he is murdered he is proclaimed a hero. West, who was earning his living as a journalist at the time, went to Hollywood in 1935 to write scripts for a minor studio. *The Day of the Locust* (1939) exposes the squalid hidden world of Hollywood – that apotheosis of the American Dream – of which the hypnotized public knows nothing. West was killed in a car crash at the age of 37.

Wharton, Edith (Newbold) 1862–1937 Born into a wealthy New York family, in 1885 Edith Jones married Edward Wharton, a man some years her senior. Her first book, written with Ogden Codman, Jr, was a work of non-fiction, *The Decoration of Houses* (1897), in which she criticized the standards of taste exhibited by the wealthy of her parents' generation, and analyzed old New York society and the effects of social snobbery based on economic status (concerns that were to dominate much of her fiction). A collection of short stories, *The Greater Inclination*, appeared in 1899 and a short novel, *The Touchstone*, in 1900. Her first full-length novel, *The Valley of Decision*, set in 18th-century Italy, was published in 1902. This was followed by two collections of essays on Italy, and in 1905 by *The House of Mirth*, which was her first popular success.

The influence of her long-time friend, **Henry James**, is evident in *Madame de Treymes* (1907), the story of an American confronting the social customs of the French. Another novel, *The Fruit of the Tree*, appeared in the same year. In 1911 she published the popular novel **Ethan Frome**, which was uncharacteristically about the lower-middle class of New England. Prior to this she had moved to Paris and joined a group of expatriate friends that included Henry James. In 1913 she was divorced from Edward Wharton. Two further novels appeared before the outbreak of World War I: *The Reef* (1912) and *The Custom of the Country* (1913). Both continued her attack on the hypocrisies of New York society. During the war she established American hostels and started an employment agency and day nursery for refugees. She was appointed a Chevalier of the Legion of Honour in 1916 for her wartime relief work. Experience of the war provided the material for two novels, *The Marne* (1918) and *A Son at the Front* (1923). Following a trip to North Africa in 1917, she produced a travel narrative, *In Morocco* (1920), and in the same year published **The Age of Innocence**, a novella, which earned her a Pulitzer Prize (making her the first woman to receive this honor). A series of four novelettes entitled *Old New York* appeared in 1924. Over the next few years she wrote three novels which deal with inter-generational differences in families: *The Mother's Recompense* (1925), *Twilight Sleep* (1927), and *The Children* (1928). Her next novels, *Hudson River Bracketed* (1929) and *The Gods Arrive* (1932), examine the artistic temperament through the character of Vance Western, a struggling novelist.

In addition to her many novels Wharton also produced eleven collections of short stories, of which the best known is probably *Xingu and Other Stories* (1916). In 1925 she published *The Writing of Fiction*, in which she discusses literary aesthetics and acknowledges her debt to Henry James. Her autobiography, *A Backward Glance*, appeared in 1934. At the time of her death she was working on another novel, *The Buccaneers* (1938), set in Saratoga in the 1860s. Her collected stories appeared in two volumes in 1968.

What Maisie Knew A novel by **Henry James**, first published in *The Chap Book* from January to August, 1897. Later that same year it was serialized in revised form in the *New Review* and also published as a volume.

The story is set in England. Maisie's parents, Beale and Ida Farange, are divorced when she is 6 years old. She is to spend half of each year with her mother and half with her father. Both parents remarry. Beale marries Miss Overmore, who had been Maisie's governess until she and Maisie's mother quarreled; Ida marries Sir Claude, but still has a succession of lovers. Maisie, now under the care of Mrs Wix, Miss Overmore's replacement, is shuttled back and forth between two households. Her two new step-parents become attracted to one another and, when their marriages to her real parents dissolve, they marry. Abandoned to Mrs Wix's care by Ida and Beale, Maisie is invited by Sir Claude, who is fond of her, to make her home with him and the former Miss Overmore. Unfortunately, the former Miss Overmore cannot abide Mrs Wix, the one "safe" adult whom Maisie absolutely refuses to give up. The final scene, which takes place in Boulogne, ends with Maisie's refusing to live with Sir Claude and his new wife: she departs for England with Mrs Wix, her means of subsistence guaranteed by Sir Claude.

It is ambiguous what sort of "knowledge" Maisie has achieved at the novel's end, and debatable whether or not she has acquired a sense of morality (or an ability to recognize immorality), whether or not she has remained innocent in spite of the sordid worldliness that surrounds her. The entire story, though written in the third person, is told from the point of view of the perceptive but somewhat naive Maisie.

Wheatley, Phillis C. 1753–84 A black American poet, born in Africa and sold as a slave in Boston at the age of 8 to a tailor, John Wheatley, who educated her with his family. She studied English, Latin, and Greek, and began to write poetry in her teens. She traveled to London when she was 18 and there published *Poems on Various Subjects, Religious and Moral* in 1773. When she returned to the US she married John Peters, a free black, and died in poverty at a young age. Her poetry encompasses the standard devices of 18th-century verse, with its use of the heroic couplet, frequent allusion to classical mythology, and intermixture of topical or contemporary matter with religious and moral subjects. Her topics include tributes to friends and famous people; discourses on Imagination, Recollection, Friendship, and Morals; and occasionally references to incidents in her own life. *Memoirs and Poems of Phillis Wheatley* was published in 1834 and a volume of her letters in 1864.

Wheelwright, John Brooks 1897–1940 Born in a wealthy suburb of Boston, he was descended from the Calvinist minister, John Wheelwright, who was banished from the Massachusetts colony by Governor Winthrop, and from John Brooks, governor of Massachusetts from 1817 to 1822. He was educated at Harvard and then studied architecture at the Massachusetts Institute of Technology. He was well known in Boston for his radicalism and was a proponent of socialist thought. His poetry emphasizes his regional interests by focusing on Boston and its environs. It is frequently accompanied by prose "arguments" which serve as interpretations rather than reiterations of the poems themselves. His first collection, *Rock and Shell*, was published in 1933. Like all the volumes published during his life, it was privately printed. The second, *Mirrors of Venus*, appeared in 1938, and a third, *Political Self-Portrait*, in 1940. While working on *Dusk to Dusk* Wheelwright was killed in an automobile accident. This fourth volume was published posthumously in *The Collected Poems of John Wheelwright* in 1972.

When Lilacs Last in the Dooryard Bloom'd See **Whitman, Walt**

White, Edmund 1940– One of America's foremost homosexual authors, White's fiction includes *Forgetting Elena* (1973), *Nocturnes for the King of Naples* (1978), and *A Boy's Own Story* (1982), a novel which treats the coming of age of an adolescent who realizes his homosexuality and must find a place for himself in contemporary society. White has also published works of non-fiction dealing with issues of sociological and cultural interest. *States of Desire: Travels in Gay America* (1980) investigates the gay communities of several major American cities. With Dr Charles Silverstein he co-wrote *The Joy of Gay Sex* (1977).

White, E[lwyn] B[rooks] 1899–1985 Born in Mount Vernon, New York, White graduated from Cornell in 1921. After a period in Seattle as a reporter, he moved to New York City where he became a writer and contributing editor for *The New Yorker* in 1926. As a regular contributor of essays to that magazine and others, he quickly gained recognition as an accomplished humorist, critic, and literary journalist. His long-term friendship with **James Thurber** included a collaboration, *Is Sex Necessary?*, in 1929. His other works include *Alice Through the Cellophane* (1933), *Quo Vadimus? Or the Case for the Bicycle* (1938), *One Man's Meat* (1942), *The Second Tree from the Corner* (1954), and *The Points of My Compass* (1962). He also revised *The Elements of Style* in 1959, a manual for writers originally written by William Strunk Jr. He wrote several children's works, including *Stuart Little* (1945) and *Charlotte's Web* (1952).

White-Jacket; or The World in a Man-of-War A novel by **Herman Melville**, published in 1850, and based on the author's experience of service on the man-of-war *United States* in 1844.

The narrative covers the homeward voyage of the frigate *Neversink* from Peru eastward round the Horn to Virginia. From scraps of cloth the narrator makes himself the white jacket that earns him his nickname and throughout the journey causes him grief, alienating him from his fellows, providing him with no protection against the elements, appalling and frightening him with its ghastly color, and indeed nearly causing his death when the wind wraps it around his head so that he falls from the yardarm into the sea. In this last incident, which occurs as they near home, he finally cuts himself free from the jacket, thus saving himself from drowning.

Most of the book, though, is devoted to describing life on board the man-of-war, emphasizing the degrading conditions the men live in, the tyrannies of the captain and officers over them, and especially the practice of flogging, which Melville criticizes on several occasions. The hierarchical organization of the navy, he argues, is dehumanizing to all involved and contradicts the spirit of American democracy. The issue of flogging was a timely one; copies of Melville's book were sent to Congress during its debate over the issue, and coincidentally the practice was abolished that year.

Whitfield, James M. 1823–78 A black Abolitionist poet born in Exeter, New Hampshire. He lived briefly in Boston, then settled in Buffalo, where he worked as a barber and began to write verse. His first volume, *Poems*, appeared in 1846, but it was not until the publication of *America, and Other Poems* in 1853 that he left off barbering and devoted his time to writing. In the following year he co-sponsored the National Emigration Convention of Colored Men with Martin Delaney, and then entered into an extended debate with **Frederick Douglass** about the benefits of colonization. In 1858 he founded the pro-colonization journal *African-American Repository*. His later poetry appeared primarily in journals such as the *Liberator* and *Frederick Douglass' Paper*. He died in California, en route to Central America to examine the possibilities of establishing a colony of free blacks in the region.

Whitman, Walt[er] 1819–92 Whitman was born in West Hills on Long Island. In 1823 his family moved to Brooklyn. He attended school there, and on his own initiative read widely in Shakespeare, the Bible, Homer, Dante, Ossian, and Scott. In 1830 he left school to become a printer's apprentice and then an itinerant teacher. He returned to Long Island in 1838 as a schoolteacher and printer, and in the same year started the newspaper *The Long Islander*, which he delivered personally to subscribers. In 1842 he went back to Brooklyn and became editor of The New York *Aurora*. Four years later he assumed editorship of the Brooklyn *Eagle*, but because of the radical tone of his editorials (which have been collected in *The Gathering of Forces*, 1920) he did not keep the post for very long. While working for these various newspapers he also began to write poetry and short stories. His early works include a

temperance tract, *Franklin Evans* (1842), written in the form of a novel. (It is included in *The Uncollected Poetry and Prose of Walt Whitman*, 1921. His other early stories are collected in *The Half-Breed and Other Stories*, 1927.)

In 1848 he traveled south to work on the New Orleans *Crescent*. The experience of the vastness of the American landscape and the variety of its people made a deep impression on him. He returned to New York later that year and turned his attention increasingly toward poetry. In 1855 he borrowed a press from some friends and set up the 12 poems (including an early version of *Song of Myself*) which made up the first edition of *Leaves of Grass*. Although he himself published an anonymous laudatory review, the book received little attention. It did, however, elicit a letter of praise from **Ralph Waldo Emerson**, which Whitman printed in the second edition (1856). This edition also included 20 new poems, among them "Crossing Brooklyn Ferry." In 1857 he became editor of the Brooklyn *Times*, his contributions to which were subsequently published in *I Sit and Look Out* (1932). In 1860 he found a publisher (Thayer and Eldridge) for a new edition of *Leaves of Grass* which contained 124 new poems, including those of the "Calamus" and "Children of Adam" sections.

Whitman's verse, with its frequent use of colloquial language and everyday events, represents a turning point in the history of American poetry – a poetic form fashioned out of specifically American experience in a distinctively American idiom. Some of his finest poems grew out of his personal experience of the horrors of the Civil War (during which he served as a volunteer nurse in army hospitals and as a correspondent for *The New York Times*), and out of his attempt to reconcile the destruction of the war with his visionary idea of America. *Drum Taps* was published in 1865, and with its companion volume, *Sequel*, appeared in the 1867 edition of *Leaves of Grass*. *Sequel* was written in the aftermath of Abraham Lincoln's assassination and includes Whitman's elegies for the dead president: "When Lilacs Last in the Dooryard Bloom'd" and "O Captain! My Captain!"

After the war Whitman worked briefly as a clerk in the Department of the Interior, but was dismissed when the Secretary learned that he was the author of the sensual and shocking *Leaves of Grass*. He continued to hold minor posts in Washington, however, and his prose work **Democratic Vistas** (1871) is a passionate reaffirmation of democratic principles in the face of the widespread corruption of the Reconstruction era. In 1873 he suffered the first of a series of paralytic strokes. The 1871 edition of *Leaves of Grass* (which included the *Passage to India* group of poems) was reprinted in 1876 as the "Author's" or "Centennial" edition. In 1876 he also published a volume of prose pieces entitled *Two Rivulets*. In 1881 a newly augmented edition of *Leaves of Grass* appeared, then comprising 293 poems in all. The following year he published another volume of prose, *Specimen Days and Collect*. A collection of his newspaper pieces, *November Boughs*, appeared in 1888. His final volume was the "Deathbed" edition of *Leaves of Grass*, which he prepared in 1891–2. It includes two annexes, the "Sands at Seventy" and "Good-bye My Fancy" groups of poems, and concludes with the prose piece "A Backward Glance O'er Travel'd Roads," in which he attempts to explain his life and work.

Whittier, John Greenleaf *c*.1807–92 The son of a Quaker family, Whittier was born and raised on his father's farm at East Haverhill, Massachusetts. His first poems were published by the Abolitionist **William Lloyd Garrison** in his paper *The Liberator*. Garrison became his friend and helped him obtain an editorial job on a Boston newspaper in 1829. His first book was *Legends of New-England in Prose and Verse* (1831). Early New England life also provided the subject for two long poems, *Moll Pitcher* (1832) and *Mogg Megone* (1836).

A career in journalism and letters seemed set, but Whittier's Quaker conscience and the influence of Garrison brought him into politics. He became involved in the anti-slavery cause and was elected to the Massachusetts legislature in 1835. He edited the *Pennsylvania Freeman* from 1838 to 1840, and published *Poems Written During the Progress of the Abolition Question* in 1838. He then became increasingly uncomfortable with Garrison's politics and founded the Liberty party, to which he contributed his skills as a journalist. *Lays of My Home and Other Poems* appeared in 1843, and further anti-slavery poems in *Voices of Freedom* in 1846. His first collected *Poems* (1849) testifies eloquently to his hatred of tyranny and his unshakable concern for the suffering of others, as does *Songs of Labor* (1850).

He continued to write in support of Abolition throughout the Civil War, but also found time for creative efforts as a poet of the countryside with *The Chapel of the Hermits* (1853), *The Panorama and Other Poems* (1856), and *Home Ballads and Poems* (1860). The Civil War was the impulse for *In War Time and Other Poems* (1864). When the struggle was over, he turned back to New England and the countryside for his inspiration and produced what is probably his best work: *Snowbound* (1866), *The Tent on the Beach* (1867), *Among the Hills* (1869), *Miriam and Other Poems* (1871), *Hazel-Blossoms* (1875), *The Vision of Echard* (1878), *Saint Gregory's Guest* (1886), and *At Sundown* (1890).

Who's Afraid of Virginia Woolf? A play by **Edward Albee**, first performed in New York City in 1962. The first of his three-act dramas, it is also the most admired of Albee's plays.

George is a history professor at a small New England college. His wife Martha is the daughter of the college president. The play depicts the events of a single night, when George and Martha bring a young colleague and his nervous wife back from a party. The elder couple involve Nick and Honey in the verbal abuse that seems to be a nightly ritual with them. Honey drinks too much and becomes ill. Martha tries to seduce Nick. The sexuality of all four characters is impugned. Albee calls the second act a "Walpurgisnacht," a night of conflict and purgation. The final purgative comes in Act Three, titled "Exorcism," when George and Martha's imaginary son, created by them as some kind of sustenance, is declared dead by Martha, thereby acknowledging their illusions and allowing compassionate feelings to surface.

Wieland; or The Transformation A gothic romance by **Charles Brockden Brown**, published in 1798, and generally recognized as one of America's first major novels. Cast in the form of a letter from Clara, the only surviving member of the Wieland family, to an unnamed friend, the story begins with a brief biography of Wieland senior, a mystic who emigrated from Germany to Pennsylvania and built a large estate which included a strange temple. While engaged one evening in an unidentified spiritual enterprise, he dies of spontaneous combustion. Following his wife's death, their children, Clara and Wieland Jr, are cared for by Catherine Pleyel, whom Wieland eventually marries. When Catherine's brother Henry arrives from Germany, Clara falls in love with him and the four enjoy each other's company insulated from the outside world.

The sense of spiritual and physical harmony is destroyed, however, following the intrusion of the mysterious Carwin. Shortly after his first appearance, disembodied voices issue various announcements and warnings. On one occasion they tell of the death of Henry Pleyel's fiancée, and this encourages him to fall in love with Clara. Later, when the voices suggest that Clara and Carwin are having an affair, Henry returns to Germany and, finding his fiancée alive, marries her. Back at the estate in Pennsylvania, the voices eventually drive Wieland insane; he murders his wife and children and is incarcerated in an asylum.

He escapes, however, and returns on the very evening that Carwin confesses to Clara that he himself had created the voices by ventriloquism. Wieland's intention is to kill his sister, but when ordered not to by the concealed Carwin's voices, he commits suicide instead. Carwin disappears, and in time Clara marries Henry, when he returns to the estate after the death of his wife.

Wigglesworth, Michael 1631–1705 A Puritan minister, poet, and physician, Wigglesworth was born in Yorkshire, England, the son of a non-conformist and successful businessman. His family emigrated to New England in 1638 and settled in Quinnipiac (later named New Haven), Connecticut. Having been tutored in Latin by Ezekiel Cheever, Wigglesworth enrolled at Harvard, where he prepared for a career in medicine, graduated first in his class in 1651, and remained to complete an MA and to teach undergraduates. In 1656 he was ordained minister of the congregation at Malden, Massachusetts. He officially held this post until his death, despite the fact that by 1663 his medical practice and his own ill health forced the congregation to commission assistants to help fulfill his ministerial responsibilities.

Wigglesworth's writing not only states the most fundamental tenets of Puritan belief, but shows American Puritanism as it was lived by the individual and the community. His most widely read poems were written either to present the articles of faith in a form which allowed for easy memorization, or to prescribe behavior fitting for a Christian: *The Day of Doom* (1662); *Meat Out of the Eater* (1670), a discourse on the uses the virtuous can find in the experience of ill health; and "God's Controversy with New England," a jeremiad in verse, first published in the 19th century by the Massachusetts Historical Society, which interprets the drought of 1662 as a Providential warning to reform. His *Diary* articulates the psychological struggle inherent in spiritual growth.

Wilbur, Richard (Purdy) 1921–   Born in New York City and educated at Amherst College and at Harvard, Wilbur served in the US Army during World War II and then returned to Harvard for further study. His first volume of poetry, *The Beautiful Changes* (1947), was written in response to the personal and public dislocation he perceived in the war and its aftermath. He was awarded the Harriet Monroe Memorial Prize in 1948 and published his second collection, *Ceremony and Other Poems*, in 1950. Following the publication of *Things of This World* (1956), he received the Pulitzer Prize and the National Book Award in 1957. *Advice to a Prophet and Other Poems* appeared in 1961 and *The Poems of Richard Wilbur* in 1963. Subsequent volumes are *Complaint* (1968), *Walking to Sleep: New Poems and Translations* (1969), *Seed Leaves* (1974), and *The Mind-Reader* (1976). His verse is characterized by its formal strictness, its urbane wit, and its oblique quality: "Poems," he argues, "are not addressed to anybody in particular . . . they are conflicts with disorder, not messages from one person to another."

Wilbur has translated three plays by Molière: *The Misanthrope* (1955), *Tartuffe* (1963), and *The School for Wives* (1971); he received the Bollingen Prize for translation in 1963. He has also published children's verse in *Loudmouse* (1963) and *Opposites* (1973); a collection of essays, *Responses: Prose Pieces 1953–*

1976 (1976); and an edition of *The Complete Poems of Poe* (1959).

Wilder, Thornton (Niven) 1897–1975 The playwright and novelist was born in Madison, Wisconsin, the son of Calvinist parents. He attended missionary schools from 1905 to 1909, while his father served as consul general in Shanghai and Hong Kong. He completed high school in California, then studied classics for two years at Oberlin College and at Yale. He studied archaeology and art in Rome for a year, and then became a teacher at Lawrenceville School in New Jersey (1921–8). He received an MA from Princeton in 1925, and later taught at the University of Chicago (1930–6 and 1941). From 1942 to 1949 he served in Air Force Intelligence in the US, North Africa, and Italy.

His early writing included a series of "three-minute" plays, 16 of which he later published in *The Angel That Troubled the Waters* (1928). His first publication, however, was the full-length play *The Trumpet Shall Sound*, which appeared serially in *The Yale Literary Magazine* in 1919. His first novel, *The Cabala*, was published in 1926. Two years later he won a Pulitzer Prize for the novel *The Bridge of San Luis Rey* (1927), a complex study of the role of destiny, or providence, in the death of five travelers when the bridge near Lima, Peru collapses in 1714. The story is supposedly taken from a manuscript written by a Franciscan monk, Brother Juniper. A third novel, *The Woman of Andros* (1930), set in ancient Greece, provoked an attack by critics who felt that Wilder was ignoring the bitter realities of contemporary American life. His other novels are *Heaven's My Destination* (1934), which concerns the fortunes of a good and simple man during the Depression; a historical novel of the last days of Julius Caesar, *The Ides of March* (1948); and two late works, *The Eighth Day* (1967) and *Theophilus North* (1973).

During the 1930s Wilder chose to concentrate most of his energies on the theatre. Stating that he wished to use the stage to capture "not verisimilitude but reality," he spent some time studying the experimentalist drama which was flourishing in Europe at the time, and eventually resolved to "shake up" the realistic theatre of the US. *The Long Christmas Dinner and Other Plays* (1931) consists of six one-act sketches, three of which are written in the realistic mode he hoped to alter, and three in a radically experimental style. He received his second Pulitzer Prize for *Our Town* (1938), a drama set in the small town of Grover's Corners, New Hampshire, and played without scenery. *The Skin of Our Teeth* (1942) was also awarded the Pulitzer, and is an expressionistic play about mankind's precarious survival. *The Matchmaker* (1955) was a revision of an earlier play called *The Merchant of Yonkers* (1939), and in turn became another success as the musical comedy *Hello Dolly!* (1963). Several of Wilder's essays on the theatre are included in *American Characteristics and Other Essays* (1979); two scenes from his uncompleted play, "The Emporium," have been published in *The Journals of Thornton Wilder, 1939–1961* (1985).

Williams, John (Alfred) 1925– A black novelist, born in Jackson, Mississippi. He served in the US Navy from 1943 to 1946, and graduated from Syracuse University in 1950. He has worked for various publishers, an advertising agency, and the American Committee on Africa in New York.

His first novel, *The Angry Ones* (1960), tells the story of Steve Hill, an artist who fights his own personal war against American racism. The protagonist of *Night Song* (1961) is a jazz musician who uses his art to combat discrimination. Williams's early work has often been compared to that of **Richard Wright**, but in his biography of Wright, *The Most Native of Sons* (1970), Williams himself criticized Wright's characterization of the black man as an individual who lacked racial and cultural consciousness. In *Sissie* (1963), *The Man Who Cried I Am* (1967), *Sons of Darkness, Sons of Light* (1969), and *Captain Blackman* (1972), Williams's voice is increasingly militant. *Mothersill and the Foxes* (1975), *The Junior Bachelor Society* (1976), and *!Click Song* (1982) are politically less radical, but remain firm in their emphasis on black unity. His non-fiction includes *Africa: Her History, Lands and People* (1962), *This Is My Country, Too* (1965), and *The King God Didn't Save* (1970). He also has edited the two collections of essays on black history and culture, *Amistad I* (1970) and *Amistad II* (1971).

Williams, Roger 1603–83 Born into a family of merchants in London, Williams was patronized in his youth by the jurist Sir Edward Coke, who arranged for his education at Charterhouse school and his admission to Pembroke College, Cambridge. He received his BA in 1627 and left Cambridge in 1629 to become household chaplain to Sir William Masham. During the course of this service, Williams grew into a radical Puritan; he embraced Congregational theology and repudiated the Church of England.

He and his wife, Mary Barnard, emigrated to Massachusetts Bay in 1631, but he did not easily find a home for his separatist views. On his arrival in Boston he refused a temporary appointment to replace John Wilson as teacher of the Boston Church because of its commitment to "non-separating congregationalism." After rejecting another offer from the church at Salem, he finally settled in Plymouth, a colony committed to a separatism which promised strict division between church and state. By 1633, however, he had found Plymouth disappointing; the magistrates too often intervened in ecclesiastical affairs and the ministers preached only a moderate separatism. In the fall of 1633 he moved to Salem and, along with Samuel Skelton, immediately became engaged in several debates both with the General Court and with the ministers of "non-separating" congregations. Intent on molding New England churches after the Apostolic model, Williams and Skelton opposed the colony's attempt to establish synods at which representatives from each congregation would arrive at uniform answers to doctrinal and ecclesiastical questions. From 1633 to 1635 Williams repeatedly angered the General Court, and was finally banished from the colony in 1635 for refusing to correct doctrinal errors such as his conviction that an absolute division between church and state must be maintained.

Over the next year Williams made his way to Rhode Island, where he founded its first settlement at Providence among the Narragansett Indians. By 1643 the Providence Plantations had expanded and Williams journeyed to England to secure a charter. En route, he wrote *A Key Into the Language of America* (London, 1643). Of interest today as a study of the habits, religion, and language of the Narragansett Indians, the treatise was used by Williams at the time to bolster his request for a charter, arguing that the Indians were in need of and prepared for conversion to Christianity. He remained in England for much of 1644 and during that time wrote some of his most frequently read works. *Mr Cotton's Letter Lately Printed, Examined, and Answered* contains his own version of the events which led to his banishment and severely criticizes the General Court's action. *The Bloudy Tenent of Persecution* presents his most fully developed defense of the freedom of conscience and the separation of church and state. *Christenings Make Not Christians*, published in 1645 after he had left England, examines the process of conversion and argues that the administration of the sacrament of baptism alone does not make one a Christian.

Following the death of King Charles in 1649 the charter was threatened, and in 1651 Williams traveled to England again to renegotiate it. While there he wrote numerous tracts. When he returned at the end of the year he assumed an unofficial, yet highly influential, role in determining the policies of the Providence Plantations. For example, because of his conviction that citizenship should be granted irrespective of religious orientation, the colony admitted Jews and Quakers, two groups who could not otherwise find a home in the New World. In 1672, however, he wrote *George Fox Digg'd Out of his Burrows*, a critique of the Quaker reliance on the "inner light." During King Philip's War (1675–6) he performed his final public function when he unsuccessfully negotiated on behalf of the Narragansett Indians.

Williams, Tennessee 1911–83 Born Thomas Lanier Williams in Columbus, Mississippi, and raised there and in St Louis, Missouri. He received a BA from the University of Iowa in 1938. His first plays were one-act pieces given in amateur and student performances between 1936 and 1940. They are partially collected in the volume *27 Wagons Full of Cotton and Other One-Act Plays* (1946, augmented 1953) and *Dragon Country: A Book of Plays* (1970).

His reputation was established by *The Glass Menagerie* (1944) and further enhanced by *A Streetcar Named Desire* (1947). Both plays show Williams's sympathy for the lost and self-punishing individual, a characteristic of many of his subsequent dramas, such as *Summer and Smoke* (1947, revised as *The Eccentricities of a Nightingale* in 1964). His gift for comedy, often an undercurrent of his more serious dramas, is evident in *The Rose Tattoo* (1951). After the experimental *Camino Real* (1953), which was poorly received by the critics, he returned to the more familiar themes of the intricacies of Southern families and Southern culture with **Cat on a Hot Tin Roof** (1955), *Sweet Bird of Youth* (1956), and *The Night of the Iguana* (1959, revised 1961). Other plays include *Suddenly Last Summer* (1958); *The Milk Train Doesn't Stop Here Anymore* (1962); *In The Bar of A Tokyo Hotel* (1969); *Small Craft Warnings* (1974); *Vieux Carré* (1977); and *Clothes For a Summer Hotel* (1980).

Williams also published two volumes of poetry, *In the Winter of Cities* (1956) and *Androgyne, Mon Amour* (1977); several collections of prose; and the novel *The Roman Spring of Mrs Stone* (1950). His *Memoirs*, published in 1975, present an account of a life consumed with guilt, anger, and a sense of failure, themes which are frequently associated with the major characters in his dramas. A volume of *Collected Stories* was issued in 1985.

Williams, William Carlos 1883–1963 Williams was born in Rutherford, New Jersey, the son of an English father and a Puerto Rican mother. He attended Swiss and French schools before studying medicine at the University of Pennsylvania, where he met **H.D.** and **Ezra Pound**. After further medical study in New York and Leipzig, and a visit to London where he met William Butler Yeats, Williams settled down to practice medicine in Rutherford in 1909.

Recognized as one of the most original and influential poets of the 20th century, his poetry is in fact deceptively simple. As critics have often noted, no object or occasion was "unpoetic" to him. "No ideas but in things," Williams declared, and he found his subjects in such homely items as refrigerated plums and wheelbarrows. His early work shows the influence of **Imagism** in its objective, precise manner of description; his later poems, however, went beyond the interests of that movement, and became more personal. They also display his metrical invention, the "vari-able foot," which he felt approximated colloquial American speech more closely than did traditional meters.

His first book, *Poems*, was privately printed in 1900. It was followed by *The Tempers* (1913), *Al Que Quiere!* (1917), *Kora in Hell: Improvisations* (1920), *Sour Grapes* (1921), and *Spring and All* (1923). Numerous other volumes followed. Among his last books were *The Desert Music and Other Poems* (1954), *Journey to Love* (1955), and *Pictures from Brueghel and Other Poems* (1962), for which he received the Pulitzer Prize posthumously in 1963. The poems also appeared in several collections, including *Selected Poems* (1949) and *Collected Later Poems* (1950). A volume entitled *Collected Earlier Poems* was published in 1951. Between 1946 and 1958 he published five books of the epic-length poem, **Paterson**, the work for which he is best known. Set in Paterson, New Jersey, the poem deals with the history and people of the town from its origins to modern times. Fragments of a sixth book were published posthumously in 1963.

Williams also published a number of prose works, both fiction and non-fiction, beginning with two collections of essays: *The Great American Novel* (1923) and *In the American Grain* (1925). *Selected Essays of William Carlos Williams* appeared in 1954. His short stories were collected in *The Farmer's Daughter: The Collected Stories* (1961); earlier volumes include *The Knife of the Times* (1932), *Life Along the Passaic River* (1938), and *Make Light of It: Collected Stories* (1950). His novels are *A Voyage to Pagany* (1928), *White Mule* (1937), *In the Money* (1940), and *The Build-Up* (1952). *The Autobiography of William Carlos Williams* was published in 1951; a collection of plays, *Many Lives and Other Plays*, appeared in 1961.

Will to Believe, The, and Other *Essays in Popular Psychology* A book by **William James**, published in 1897, setting out his philosophy of "radical empiricism." James's career as a psychologist led him to emphasize the importance of instinct and to find a belief in absolute truth philosophically untenable. The essays in the volume all elucidate aspects of his objective position in regard to scientific and religious issues.

Wilson, Edmund 1895–1972 Born in Red Bank, New Jersey, Wilson received his BA from Princeton in 1916. During World War I he served in the US Army, first as a hospital aide, then with the Intelligence Corps. Having worked briefy as a reporter before the war (for the *New York Evening Sun*, 1916–17), he became managing editor of *Vanity Fair* for one year in 1920. From 1926 to 1931 he was associate editor of *The New Republic*. He also reviewed books for *The New Yorker* – steadily from 1944 to 1948, occasionally thereafter. But Wilson was not simply a journalist; he was widely recognized as a learned and incisive critic, and in addition to critical and political essays, he wrote poetry, plays, novels, and short stories. He was a close friend of several literary figures, among them **John Dos Passos**, **F. Scott Fitzgerald**, and **Edna St Vincent Millay**. The third of his four wives was **Mary McCarthy**, to whom he was married from 1938 to 1946.

Among his works of non-fiction are: *Axel's Castle: A Study in the Imaginative Literature of 1870–1930* (1931), a standard work on Symbolist literature; *Travels in Two Democracies* (1936), a Marxist critique of life in the US and Russia; *To the Finland Station: A Study in the Writing and Acting of History* (1940), which describes the origins of the Russian Revolution, beginning with the feeling of betrayal after the French Revolution and ending with Lenin's arrival in Russia in 1917; *The Boys in the Back Room: Notes on California Novelists* (1941); *The Wound and the Bow: Seven Studies in Literature* (1941); and *Patriotic Gore: Studies in the Literature of the American Civil War* (1962).

He also edited several volumes, including an anthology of American literary criticism, *The Shock of Recognition: The Development of Literature in the United States Recorded by the Men Who Made It* (1943, enlarged in 1955), and a volume of his friend F. Scott Fitzgerald's uncollected pieces, *The Crack-up: With Other Uncollected Pieces, Note-Books and Unpublished Letters* (1945). His own fiction consists of two novels, *I Thought of Daisy* (1929) and *Galahad* (1957), and a collection of short stories, *Memoirs of Hecate County* (1946, revised in 1958). He published two autobiographies, *A Piece of My Mind: Reflections at Sixty* (1956) and *A Prelude: Landscapes, Characters and Conversations From the Earlier Years of My Life* (1967). Since his death, three volumes of his memoirs have been published, all edited by Leon Edel, and prepared from his diaries and notebooks:

The Twenties (1975), *The Thirties* (1980), and *The Forties* (1983). An edition of his letters, *Letters on Literature and Politics* appeared in 1977.

Winesburg, Ohio A collection of 23 thematically related stories by **Sherwood Anderson**, published in 1919, which explores the nature of small-town life in the fictional town of the title. The stories gain further unity through the character of George Willard, a reporter for the local newspaper who has literary ambitions and to whom all the other characters gravitate in the course of the book. The stories can be related to Anderson's own life and to his experiences in his hometown in Ohio. Their style and thematic focus reflect his naturalistic approach to American life as well as his interest in the unusual or unfamiliar aspects of human existence. The various characters in the collection, referred to as "grotesques," are portrayed in a manner which stresses both their alienation and their desperate attempts to communicate with others in their daily lives.

Wings of the Dove, The A novel by **Henry James**, published in 1902. Kate Croy, the daughter of a discredited social adventurer, is secretly engaged to Merton Densher, a journalist. While Merton is in America, Kate becomes friends with the wealthy Milly Theale, who confides to her that she is suffering from a mysterious illness, and that her doctor has told her that only happiness can postpone her death. When Merton returns to London, Kate encourages him to take an interest in Milly, hoping that they will get married, thus soon making him a rich widower whom she herself can marry. The plot appears to be working until the fortune-hunting Lord Mark, rejected by Milly, reveals to her the true relationship between Kate and Merton. Milly's health deteriorates, and soon afterwards she dies in Venice. After her death Merton receives a letter from her: she has made him rich enough to marry Kate. In an agony of shame he confronts Kate and offers to marry her only if she agrees not to accept the wealth bestowed on him by Milly. Kate declines, and the novel closes as they separate forever.

Winters, (Arthur) Yvor 1900–68 Winters was born in Chicago and educated at the universities of Chicago, Colorado, and Stanford. His verse, which is severely restrained and meticulously patterned, is among the first notable poetry of the American West. His first volume, *Poetry: The Immobile Wind*, was published in 1921. This was followed by *The Magpie's Shadow* (1922), *The Bare Hills* (1927), and *The Proof* (1930). During the 1930s and 1940s he published several more volumes, the last of which, *To the Holy Spirit*, appeared in 1947. *Collected Poems* was published in 1952. His works of criticism include *In Defense of Reason* (1947), *The Function of Criticism* (1957), and *Forms of Discovery* (1967). He was one of the first literary critics to give serious attention to American literature.

Winterset   See **Anderson, Maxwell**

Winthrop, John   1588–1649   Born in Edwardstone, Suffolk, to parents of wealth and social prestige, Winthrop matriculated at Trinity College, Cambridge in 1603 but withdrew to marry in 1605 before earning a degree. He was admitted to the Bar in 1613, then set up a legal practice in London, and eventually accepted an appointment to His Majesty's Court of Wards in 1627. During this service he resolved to join the Puritan emigration to Massachusetts, and in appreciation for his aid in negotiating the charter, the Massachusetts Bay Company elected him governor in 1629.

Winthrop sailed aboard the *Arbella* in 1630 and during the voyage wrote and delivered "A Modell of Christian Charity," a lay sermon which defined the social hierarchy he deemed necessary in order to preserve the commonwealth. He wrote a number of pamphlets while serving, until his death, as governor or deputy governor, though none proved as influential as "A Modell." *A Defence of an Order of Court Made in the Yeare 1637* supports the legislation passed by the General Court after the trial of **Anne Hutchinson**, which denied citizenship to "dissenters." His account of the Hutchinson trial was incorporated into Thomas Welde's *A Short History of the Rise, Reign and Ruine of the Antinomians* (1644). His many comments on the political affairs of Puritan New England are collected in his journal, which was published in part in 1790 and complete in 1826, entitled *The History of New England 1630–1649*. The Massachusetts Historical

Society has since collected and printed his papers.

Winthrop, Theodore 1826–61   A native of Connecticut, Winthrop attended Yale and was trained as a lawyer. He traveled extensively, both in Europe and throughout the US. He wrote fiction and travel narratives, though none of his books was published until after he was killed while serving in the Union Army during the Civil War. His best-known work is *John Brent* (1862), a novel which exploits its Western setting to produce an exciting, melodramatic plot involving kidnappings and unscrupulous Mormons. His other works include two other novels, *Cecil Dreeme* (1861) and *Edwin Brothertoft* (1862); and *Life in the Open Air* (1863) and *The Canoe and the Saddle* (1863), both travel books.

Wise, John *c.*1652–1725   A Puritan minister and theologian, Wise was the son of an indentured servant in Roxbury, Massachusetts. He graduated from Harvard in 1673, and in 1680 began preaching at the Second Church of Ipswich, where he was ordained minister in 1682. From that pulpit and until his death, he vented what scholars have called a "democratic" temper.

In 1687 he incited a vehement protest against paying taxes that violated the colony's charter rights, an act for which he was imprisoned briefly by Royal Governor Andros. Signing a petition to vindicate those accused of witchcraft in 1703, he helped the colony recover from the social damage done by the trials of 1692. He opposed the attempt to centralize church government, and his advocacy of autonomous congregations produced his two most important and popular publications: *The Churches Quarrel Espoused* (1710), a systematic refutation of the proposal for ecclesiastical centralization presented in *Questions and Proposals* by **Cotton Mather** and **Increase Mather**; and *A Vindication of the Government of New-England Churches* (1717), a definition and defense of Congregationalism. That both works advance egalitarian principles explains their subsequent appeal to American revolutionaries and Abolitionists in the 18th and 19th centuries, when they were reprinted in large quantities. Not long before his death he promoted innoculation for smallpox and published his last remembered work,

A Word of Comfort to a Melancholy Country (1721), a defense of paper money.

Wise Blood A novel by **Flannery O'Connor**, published in 1952. A highly disturbing book, it attempts to analyze the effects of religious belief and the nature of such belief in the "fallen" world of the post-bellum South.

It concerns the spiritual quest of Hazel Motes, a Southerner recently returned from World War II. He is obsessed by the idea that redemption is impossible and that the whole notion of Jesus as savior is suspect. As he sets himself up as a preacher of non-belief, he meets a variety of outcasts and social misfits. In particular, it is his encounter with the false preacher Asa Hawkes (who has supposedly blinded himself out of religious fervor) and his daughter Sabbath Lily that precipitates his downfall. Though apparently a non-believer, Hazel is devastated when he discovers that Asa is only pretending to be blind, having been too cowardly to carry out the act. Eventually, after Asa leaves town, Hazel murders another phony preacher, who has been parodying Hazel's own "Church of Christ Without Christ." He then blinds himself and performs various acts of self-torture in atonement – although he cannot say for what. Finally, after being exposed to freezing wind and rain for two days, he is picked up by the police and clubbed into silence. He dies on the trip back to his landlady's house.

Wister, Owen 1860–1938 A novelist and short-story writer, known primarily for Western fiction. Born in Pennsylvania and educated at Harvard, he first traveled west (to Wyoming) in order to improve his health, and this experience became the basis for his early writings. *Red Man and White* (1896), *Lin McLean* (1896), and *The Jimmyjohn Boss* (1900) are all collections of stories set in the Western cattle country. His best-known work, **The Virginian** (1902), was a popular novel of legendary proportions. Its heroic cowpuncher, unassumingly masterful, crude but innately gentle, became the standard for the Western hero in countless novels and movies. Having become famous for his Westerns, Wister decided to turn to the East for his subjects. *Philosophy Four* (1903) is a story about undergraduate life at Harvard. *Lady Baltimore* (1906) is a romantic novel set in Charleston. He also wrote a biography of

Grant (1900), and in 1930 published *Roosevelt, The Story of a Friendship, 1880–1919* from his own reminiscences of Theodore Roosevelt, the boyhood friend to whom he had dedicated *The Virginian*.

With the Procession A novel by **Henry Blake Fuller**, published in 1895. Set in Fuller's native Chicago, it tells the story of a family of social climbers, focusing on the bourgeois convention that a man should amass as much money as possible and then put it at the disposal of his wife and children, who squander it. This is the situation in which David Marshall finds himself: his eldest daughter, Jane, has social ambitions for the family which change all their lives; his son Truesdale spends four years abroad at his father's expense; the youngest daughter, Rosey, a social butterfly, continually demands money from her father. Exhausted by the demands made upon him – to build a new house, to be a philanthropist, to cut a public figure – David Marshall dies, sacrificed to his family's ambition to march "with the procession."

Wolfe, Thomas (Clayton) 1900–38 The son of a stonecutter, Wolfe was born in Asheville, North Carolina, where his mother ran a boarding house. He graduated in 1920 from the University of North Carolina, where he developed an interest in the theatre, and received his MA from Harvard in 1922. His first works were plays: *Welcome to Our City* (1923), which is set in his home town of Asheville, and *The Return of Buck Gavin* (1923). From 1924 to 1930 he taught English at New York University, where he wrote the play *Mannerhouse*, about the decay of a Southern family. (The play was not published until 1945.)

Wolfe decided to become a full-time writer after the publication in 1929 of his first novel, *Look Homeward, Angel*. This strongly autobiographical work follows the life of Eugene Gant, the son of a stonecutter and a boarding-house matron, as he grows from a child in Altamont, Catawba, into the young adult who breaks with his family at the end of the novel. Wolfe's next book, a short novel entitled *A Portrait of Bascom Hawke* (1932), was later incorporated into *Of Time and the River* (1935), which continues the story of Eugene Gant, now at Harvard, and ends with his departure for Europe after a disappointing love affair. *From Death to Morning* (1935) is a collection of stories; *The Story of a Novel* (1936), his last book to be published during his lifetime, is a critical examination of his own work.

Wolfe died at the age of 38 after two operations for a brain infection following pneumonia. He left a considerable amount of material, from which Edward C. Aswell edited the semi-autobiographical novel *The Web and the Rock* (1939) and its sequel, *You Can't Go Home Again* (1940). Wolfe's *Letters to His Mother* appeared in 1943, followed by *Letters* in 1956. A volume of short stories, *The Lost Boy*, was published in 1965.

Wonder-Working Providence of Sion's Saviour in New-England, The Subtitled "A History of New-England, from the English planting in the Yeere 1628 until the Yeere 1652," **Edward Johnson**'s *Wonder-Working Providence* was published anonymously by Nathaniel Brooke in 1653 (actually dated 1654) and circulated in book form and as a manuscript in New England throughout the 17th century. Motivated by the critique of Congregational practice and principle made both by disaffected Puritans in New England and Presbyterians hoping to influence the Westminster Assembly's reformation of the Church of England, the work divides into three books and catalogues instances of divine intervention in New England's history which, Johnson argues, indicate God's approval of the New England Way. Book I (1628–37) considers the conditions in England which compelled removal to America, the journey across the Atlantic, and the settlement of towns and congregations. Book II (1637–45) and Book III (1645–51) portray the Puritans coping with those incidents – the Antinomian affair and the Pequot War, for example – which most seriously threatened the colony's existence. Although scholars have questioned the accuracy of some of Johnson's facts, *Wonder-Working Providence* offers the perceptions of a common, albeit zealous, faithful, and wealthy Puritan.

Woodworth, Samuel 1785–1842 Born in Massachusetts, Woodworth began working in 1809 as a journalist in New York City, and later edited the *New York Mirror* and other papers. He is best remembered for poems such as "The Old Oaken Bucket" (1818), which was reprinted in the collection *Melodies, Duets, Songs, and Ballads* (1826). He published one novel, *The Champions of Freedom* (2 vols., 1816), a romance set during the War of 1812. His plays include a melodrama, *Lafayette* (1824); a domestic tragedy of the Revolutionary period entitled *The Widow's Son* (1825); and a comedy, *The Forest Rose; or, American Farmers*, which is known for its presentation of the typical Yankee character, Jonathan Ploughboy.

Woolson, Constance (Fenimore) 1840–94 Born in Claremont, New Hampshire, Woolson spent much of her youth in Ohio. She lived in various parts of the US and used her knowledge of the country as background material when she became a novelist. *Castle Nowhere: Lake-Country Sketches* (1875) tells of the French settlers in the Great Lakes region. Her residence in Florida and the Carolinas gave rise to *Rodman the Keeper: Southern Sketches* (1880), which contrasts the life of the Old South with the South during Reconstruction.

She also lived in Italy, which provides the setting for *The Front Yard: and Other Italian Stories* (1895). While abroad, however, she wrote several novels with an American setting. *Anna* (1882) tells of a Mackinac Island (Michigan) girl in New York City. *For the Major* (1883) is the story of a North Carolina woman helping to preserve her husband's illusions about the South. *East Angels* (1886) is set in Florida; *Jupiter Lights* (1889) portrays two sisters-in-law in conflict, one representing the North and the other the South. Her last novel, *Horace Chase* (1894), is a domestic drama about a woman who despises her self-made husband but discovers, almost too late, his sterling character. *Dorothy, and Other Italian Stories* (1896), her last book, concerns Americans in Europe. **Henry James** became a friend of Woolson, and portrayed her in his story ***The Aspern Papers***.

Wright, James 1927–80 Wright attended Kenyon College, then served in the army during World War II, subsequently receiving an MS and PhD from the University of Washington. He taught at Hunter College in New York City from 1966 until his death. Whether writing about nature, politics, social outcasts, or his home town of Martin's Ferry,

Ohio, Wright emphasizes the common human element in the subjects of his poems. His language is colloquial and unadorned, and his tone compassionate. He himself said that he wanted his poems to "say something humanly important instead of just showing off with language."

His first volume, *The Green Wall*, was published in 1957; it was followed by *Saint Judas* (1959), *The Lion's Tail and Eyes* (1962), *This Branch Will Not Break* (1963), *Shall We Gather at the River?* (1968), *Collected Poems* (1971, Pulitzer Prize), *Two Citizens* (1973), *Moments of the Italian Summer* (1976), and *To a Blossoming Pear Tree* (1977). His translations include *Twenty Poems of Caesar Vellejo* (1963, with **Robert Bly** and John Knoepfle), *The Rider of the White Horse: Selected Short Fiction of Theodore Storm* (1964), and *Twenty Poems of Pablo Neruda* (1967, with Robert Bly). A final volume of verse, *This Journey*, was published posthumously in 1982.

Wright, Richard 1908–60 Novelist and social critic, born near Natchez, Mississippi. Wright's childhood and youth were spent in impoverished conditions, and his formal education ended with graduation from junior high school. In 1925 he moved to Memphis, Tennessee, and survived by working at odd jobs. It was at this time that his interest in literature developed. He began reading **H. L. Mencken**, **Theodore Dreiser**, **Sinclair Lewis**, and **Sherwood Anderson**. After two years, he moved north to Chicago, where he soon started writing fiction. He began attending meetings of the John Reed club in 1933, and joined the Communist party in

1936, remaining a member until 1944 when he became disillusioned with the movement.

Before moving to New York City in 1937 he had written most of the novel *Lawd Today*, which was published posthumously in 1963. His first published volume was a collection of short stories about Southern racism, ironically entitled *Uncle Tom's Children* (1938, enlarged edition 1940). Noted for its naturalistic style, the book won the *Story* magazine prize, and its financial success enabled Wright to stop working on the New York Writers Project and the journal *Daily Worker*, and to begin another novel. **Native Son** was published in 1940 and, with its memorable portrait of the rebellious Bigger Thomas, brought Wright widespread recognition.

In 1940 he left the US to live in Mexico, and then in 1946 moved to Paris, where he remained for the rest of his life. His other novels are *The Outsider* (1953), which chronicles a black intellectual's search for identity; *Savage Holiday* (1954); and *The Long Dream* (1958). *Eight Men*, published posthumously in 1961, is a collection of short stories, radio plays, a novella, and an autobiography. Wright's non-fictional work includes *Twelve Million Black Voices* (1941), an illustrated folk history of American blacks; and the acclaimed autobiography *Black Boy* (1945). *American Hunger*, a continuation of *Black Boy*, was published posthumously in 1977. He also published three books of social criticism inspired by his travels: *Black Power* (1954), about Africa; *The Color Curtain* (1956), about Asia; and *Pagan Spain* (1957). A collection of lectures on racial injustice, *White Man, Listen!*, appeared in 1957.

Y

Yemassee, The: *A Romance of Carolina* A novel by **William Gilmore Simms**, published in 1835 and reissued with minor revisions in 1853. Set in South Carolina, it is based on the 1715 uprising of the Yemassee Indians against the English colonists – although Simms takes some artistic license in his presentation of the affair.

Sanutee, the Yemassee chief, perceives the threat the expanding colonies pose to his tribe. Urged on by the Spaniards, and aided by a renegade English officer named Chorley, he prepares to attack the white settlements. His son Occonestoga, who has been corrupted by white men's ways (and by alcohol in particular), sides with the whites against his tribe. Gabriel Harrison leads the defense of the settlement. Both he and Hugh Grayson, a young man who comes to emulate the naturally noble Harrison, are in love with Bess Matthews, who embodies the Southern ideal of womanhood. The Indians attack, led by Chorley, and kill many settlers. Harrison sends Occonestoga to spy on his tribe, but he is captured and formally expelled from the tribe. To be thus stripped of identity is a sentence more severe than death, and his mother kills him to save him from the disgrace. She also helps his friend Harrison to escape when he is captured by the Yemassee. Bess and her father are taken by Chorley, but Harrison saves them and kills Chorley. Matthews agrees to the union of Bess and Harrison, who then reveals his true identity: he is in fact Charles Craven, the governor of Carolina. He leaves Hugh Grayson in charge of the local forces and travels to Charleston to organize the force which finally destroys the Yemassee. The book ends with the death of Sanutee.

Yerby, Frank 1916–   Black novelist, born in Augusta, Georgia. He attended Paine College in Augusta and received an MA from Fisk University in Tennessee in 1938. Writing about racial injustice, he won early recognition (he received the O. Henry Award in 1944) for his stories "Health Card" (1944) and "The Homecoming" (1946). He then turned to historical novels, the first of which, *The Foxes of Harrow* (1947), won immediate success and sold over one million copies. He has since written some 30 melodramatic costume novels, most of them revolving around his favorite theme of the "eternal warfare of the sexes." The first six are set in the 19th century; he moves back in time to the 18th century in *The Devil's Laughter* (1953) and *Bride of Liberty* (1954), to the 17th century in *The Golden Hawk* (1948), and to biblical times in *Judas My Brother* (1968). *The Dahomean* (1971) is his only novel dealing primarily with blacks. Yerby currently lives in Madrid, Spain.

Yezierska, Anzia c.1885–1970   A Russian-American novelist and short-story writer, Yezierska was born at Plinsk, in Russian Poland, and emigrated with her family to the US in the 1890s. They settled in the ghetto of New York City's Lower East Side. She attended night school to improve her English, won a scholarship which enabled her to become a domestic science teacher, and taught cooking from 1905 to 1913. During this time she also became a US citizen (1912) and had two brief marriages. She was involved romantically with the noted philosopher and educator **John Dewey**, then dean at Columbia Teachers College (1917–18).

Yezierska's stories and novels deal realistically with the lives of struggling immigrants living in the ghetto. Her protagonists are usually women. She published her first story in 1915. *Hungry Hearts*, a collection of ten short stories, appeared in 1920. Hollywood bought the screen rights to the volume, and Yezierska was hired as a writer there. She published her first novel, *Salome of the Tenements*, in 1922. It is the story of Sonya Vrunsky, a Russian Jewish immigrant who marries wealthy, American-born John Manning but then renounces her marriage to make a life of her own. Subsequent works include another collection of short stories, *Children of Loneliness* (1923); *Bread Givers: A Novel: A Struggle Between a Father of the Old World and a Daughter of the New* (1925); *Arrogant Beggar* (1927), another novel; *All I Could Never Be* (1932), a semi-autobiographical novel; and her autobiography, *Red Ribbon on a White Horse* (1950). She also wrote articles and book reviews. She died in poverty in Ontario, California.

You Can't Go Home Again　See **Wolfe, Thomas**

Z

Zaturenska, Marya 1902–82 Born in Kiev, Russia, Zaturenska emigrated to the US in 1910 and was naturalized in 1912. She attended Valparaiso University (1922–3) and the University of Wisconsin (1923–5), before marrying the poet **Horace Gregory** in 1925. With him she edited numerous anthologies and wrote *A History of American Poetry 1900–1940* (1946). *Threshold and Hearth* (1934) was her first volume of poetry. *Cold Morning Sky*, published in 1937, brought her critical acclaim and the Pulitzer Prize in 1938. Other collections of her poetry include *The Listening Landscape* (1941), *Golden Mirror* (1943), *Terraces of Light* (1960), and *The Hidden Waterfalls* (1974). *Christina Rossetti* (1949) was a biography of the English poet.

Zoo Story, The A long one-act play by **Edward Albee**. The first of his plays to be performed professionally, it opened in Berlin in 1959 and in New York City in 1960. It concerns the confrontation in New York's Central Park between Jerry, an alienated and unhappy homosexual, and Peter, a middle-aged and distinctly ordinary man. Jerry frustrates all of Peter's attempts to leave with harangues about his alienated condition, and finally tricks Peter into helping him kill himself.

Zukofsky, Louis 1904–78 Zukofsky was born in New York City and educated at Columbia University. He was associated with the **Objectivist** school and his poetry was first published in *An "Objectivists" Anthology* (1932), which he edited. His work was admired by fellow poets such as **William Carlos Williams** and **Ezra Pound**, but until recently it has lacked more general critical acclaim. His second publication, *First Half of "A,"* appeared in 1940. Further sections of the long poem *"A"* were published over the next 38 years as Zukofsky kept expanding the poem, which eventually comprised 24 separate sections. It was published in complete form in 1978. In it he explores the interrelationship of poetry and music, and treats questions of aesthetics, philosophy, and history. The concluding section has been set to music based on Handel by his wife, Celia Zukofsky.

Zukofsky also published several volumes of shorter poems, including *55 Poems* (1941), *Anew* (1946), *Some Time* (1956), *Barely and Widely* (1958), *I's* (1963), *After I's* (1964), and *I Sent Thee Late* (1965). *All: The Collected Shorter Poems, 1923–1964* appeared in 1966. *A Test of Poetry* (1948) and *Prepositions* (1967) are collections of essays on modern poets and poetry. He also wrote a play, *Arise, Arise* (1965), and a novel, *Little: A Fragment for Careenagers* (1970).

Chronology of American history

Chronology of American literature

1607	Colonists land at Jamestown
1619	African blacks brought to Jamestown – beginning of slavery in Virginia colony
1620	Mayflower Compact signed, Pilgrims disembark in Plymouth
1626	Peter Minuet purchases Manhattan Island; establishment of New Amsterdam – later New York
1630	John Winthrop and Puritans arrive aboard the *Arbella* at Salem
1636	Harvard College founded, first university in colonies
1637	Anne Hutchinson tried and convicted of religious heresy in Massachusetts
1644	Roger Williams secures Royal Charter for Providence, Rhode Island, haven of religious toleration
1662	Halfway Covenant, Puritan arrangement to assimilate new generations into church membership
1676	Bacon's Rebellion in Virginia
1692	Salem witchcraft trials
1734	Jonathan Edwards preaches, Great Awakening begins
1735	John Peter Zenger tried for seditious libel of New York's governor and acquitted – important precedent for freedom of the press
1754–63	French and Indian Wars
1754	Albany Congress outlines plan for union of colonies
1760	George III ascends the throne of England
1764	Sugar Act (American Revenue Act) passed in Parliament, first act to raise revenue from colonies

1630 *History of Plimmoth Plantation* by William Bradford (1590–1657); full version completed 1651, published 1856

1640 *Bay Psalm Book*
1644 *The Bloudy Tenent of Persecution* by Roger Williams (1603–83)

1650 *The Tenth Muse Lately Sprung up in America* by Anne Bradstreet (1612–72)
1662 *The Day of Doom* by Michael Wigglesworth (1631–1705)

1702 *Magnalia Christi Americana* by Cotton Mather (1663–1728)
1729 Edward Taylor (*c.*1642–1729) dies; his work remains unpublished until 1939
1732 *Poor Richard's Almanack* by Benjamin Franklin (1706–90); continues publication until 1757

1741 *Sinners in the Hands of an Angry God* by Jonathan Edwards (1703–58)
1754 *Freedom of the Will* by Jonathan Edwards

1770	Boston Massacre – British troops open fire on mob in Boston, kill five civilians		
1773	Tea Act levied on colonies, prompts Boston Tea Party in December		
1774	First Continental Congress meets in Philadelphia		
1775	Colonial militia battle British troops at Lexington and Concord, Revolutionary War begins		
1776	July 4, Declaration of Independence signed	1776	*Common Sense* by Thomas Paine (1737–1809)
1781	Articles of Confederation ratified		
		1786–7	*The Anarchiad* by the Connecticut Wits
		1787	*The Contrast* by Royall Tyler (1757–1826)
1788	Constitution ratified		
1789	First session of Congress meets, Washington inaugurated		
1791	Bill of Rights passed		
		1792–1815	*Modern Chivalry* by Hugh Henry Brackenridge (1748–1816)
1793	Eli Whitney invents the cotton gin		
		1798	*Wieland* by Charles Brockden Brown (1771–1810)
1800	Washington DC becomes capital of national government		
1803	Marbury v. Madison establishes right of Supreme Court to judicial review		
1803	Louisiana Purchase – Jefferson's acquisition of Louisiana territory doubles size of US		
1812–14	War of 1812		
		1819–20	*The Sketch Book* by Washington Irving (1783–1859)
1820	Missouri Compromise outlaws slavery north of latitude 36° 30′		
1823	Monroe Doctrine reaffirms America's diplomatic independence from Europe	1823	*The Pioneers* by James Fenimore Cooper (1789–1851), the first of the Leatherstocking Tales
1831	Nat Turner's slave insurrection	1835	*The Yemassee* by William Gilmore Simms (1806–70)
		1836	*Nature* by Ralph Waldo Emerson (1803–82)
		1837	*Twice-Told Tales* by Nathaniel Hawthorne (1804–64)
		1838	*Divinity School Address* by Ralph Waldo Emerson
		1840	*Tales of the Grotesque and Arabesque* by Edgar Allan Poe (1809–49) *The Dial*; continues publication until 1844

1846–8   Mexican War

1848   Seneca Falls Convention, women's rights convention
Gold discovered in California, Western Gold Rush begins

1857   Dred Scott Decision – Supreme Court denies blacks standing in court, rules Missouri Compromise unconstitutional, denies popular sovereignty of territories
1858   Lincoln–Douglas debates
1859   John Brown's raid on Harper's Ferry
1860   Lincoln elected president, Republican party becomes major political force
1861–5   Civil War
1863   Emancipation Proclamation, slaves freed
1865   Robert E. Lee surrenders to Ulysses S. Grant at Appomattox Courthouse
1865   Lincoln assassinated
1865–77   Reconstruction
1869   First transcontinental railroad completed
1876   Alexander Graham Bell invents the telephone

1886   American Federation of Labor (AFL) formed
1886   Haymarket Riot for eight-hour day in Chicago
1887   Dawes Act sanctions the gradual elimination of Indian tribal ownership of land

1845   *Narrative of the Life of Frederick Douglass* by Frederick Douglass (1817–95)
1846   *Typee* by Herman Melville (1819–91)
1847   *Evangeline* by Henry Wadsworth Longfellow (1807–82)

1849   *Civil Disobedience* by Henry David Thoreau (1817–62)
1850   *The Scarlet Letter* by Nathaniel Hawthorne
1851   *Moby-Dick* by Herman Melville
1852   *Uncle Tom's Cabin* by Harriet Beecher Stowe (1811–96)
1854   *Walden* by Henry David Thoreau
1855   *Leaves of Grass*, first edition, by Walt Whitman (1819–92); final edition 1891–2

1869   *Innocents Abroad* by Samuel L. Clemens [Mark Twain] (1835–1910)
1876   *Roderick Hudson* by Henry James (1843–1916)
1880   *The Grandissimes* by George Washington Cable (1844–1925)
1881   *The Portrait of a Lady* by Henry James
1884   *Adventures of Huckleberry Finn* by Mark Twain
1885   *The Rise of Silas Lapham* by William Dean Howells (1837–1920)

1889   Jane Addams establishes Hull House in Chicago

1890   Ellis Island opened as immigration depot

1892   Populists organize, nominate first candidate for president

1896   Supreme Court endorses doctrine of "Separate but Equal" in Plessy v. Ferguson

1898   USS *Maine* blown up in Havana harbor, Spanish–American War begins

1901   McKinley assassinated, Theodore Roosevelt becomes president

1903   Wright brothers' flight

1909   National Association for the Advancement of Colored People (NAACP) founded

1911   Triangle Shirtwaist factory fire in New York's East Side prompts investigation of sweatshops

1913   Federal Income Tax introduced

1913   Armory Show opens in New York

1914   World War I begins

1917   Prohibition instituted
       US enters World War I

1920   19th Amendment ratified, women get the vote

1888   *Looking Backward* by Edward Bellamy (1850–98)

1890   *Poems* by Emily Dickinson (1830–86); first published volume of her verse

1891   *Main-Travelled Roads* by Hamlin Garland (1860–1940)

1895   *The Red Badge of Courage* by Stephen Crane (1871–1900)

1896   *The Damnation of Theron Ware* by Harold Frederic (1856–98)

1899   *The Awakening* by Kate Chopin (1851–1904); *McTeague* by Frank Norris (1870–1902)

1900   *Sister Carrie* by Theodore Dreiser (1871–1945)

1903   *The Ambassadors* by Henry James; *The Call of the Wild* by Jack London (1876–1916)

1907   *The Education of Henry Adams* by Henry Adams (1838–1918)

1912   *Poetry: A Magazine of Verse* founded by Harriet Monroe (1860–1936); still in publication

1913   *A Boy's Will* by Robert Frost (1874–1963)

1917   *The Love Song of J. Alfred Prufrock* by T. S. Eliot (1888–1965; he was awarded a Nobel Prize in 1948)

1918   *My Ántonia* by Willa Cather (1873–1947)

1919   *Winesburg, Ohio* by Sherwood Anderson (1876–1941)

1921   *Collected Poems* by Edwin Arlington Robinson (1869–1935)

1923   *Cane* by Jean Toomer (1894–1967)

1924   First publication of *Billy Budd* by Herman Melville

1925   Scopes trial

1925   *Manhattan Transfer* by John Dos Passos (1896–1970); *An American Tragedy* by Theodore Dreiser (1871–1945); *In Our Time* by Ernest Hemingway (1898–1961; he was awarded a Nobel Prize in 1954); *The Great Gatsby* by F. Scott Fitzgerald (1896–1940); *The Cantos* by Ezra Pound (1885–1972), complete edition published in 1970

1926   *The Sun Also Rises* by Ernest Hemingway

1927   Charles Lindberg's trans-Atlantic flight

1927   Sacco and Vanzetti executed

1929   October 29, stock market crashes – Great Depression begins

1929   *The Sound and the Fury* by William Faulkner (1897–1962; he was awarded a Nobel Prize in 1950)

1930   *The Bridge* by Hart Crane (1899–1932); *I'll Take My Stand* by the Southern Agrarians

1931   *The Good Earth* by Pearl S. Buck (1892–1973; she was awarded a Nobel Prize in 1938)

1933   Franklin D. Roosevelt inaugurated, initiates New Deal programs

1934   *The Ways of White Folks* by Langston Hughes (1902–67)

1936   *Absalom, Absalom!* by William Faulkner

1939   World War II begins

1939   *The Grapes of Wrath* by John Steinbeck (1902–68; he was awarded a Nobel Prize in 1962)

1940   *Native Son* by Richard Wright (1908–60)

1941   Pearl Harbor bombed, US enters war

1945   Atomic bomb dropped on Hiroshima and Nagasaki

1946   *Paterson* by William Carlos Williams (1883–1963)

1947   Truman Doctrine pledges US support for "free peoples . . . resisting attempted subjugation"

1947   *A Streetcar Named Desire* by Tennessee Williams (1914–83)

1949   *Death of a Salesman* by Arthur Miller (1915–)

1950   US enters Korea in "Police Action"

1951   *The Catcher in the Rye* by J. D. Salinger (1919–)

1952   *Invisible Man* by Ralph Ellison (1914–); *Wise Blood* by Flannery O'Connor (1925–64)

1953   Julius and Ethel Rosenberg executed for espionage

1954	Supreme Court in Brown v. Board of Education rules doctrine of "Separate but Equal" unconstitutional	1954	*Collected Poems* by Wallace Stevens (1879–1955)
1955–6	Montgomery, Alabama, bus boycott – Rosa Parks refuses to give her seat to white riders	1955	*Notes of a Native Son* by James Baldwin (1924–); *The Recognitions* by William Gaddis (1922–)
		1956	*Howl* by Allen Ginsberg (1926–); *A Long Day's Journey into Night* by Eugene O'Neill (1888–1953; he was awarded a Nobel Prize in 1936)
1957	Soviet Union launches Sputnik satellite	1957	*On the Road* by Jack Kerouac (1922–69); *The Assistant* by Bernard Malamud (1914–86)
		1958	*Lolita* by Vladimir Nabokov (1899–1977)
		1959	*Life Studies* by Robert Lowell (1917–77)
1960	John F. Kennedy elected president	1960	*The Sot-Weed Factor* by John Barth (1930–)
1961	Greensboro, North Carolina, sit-ins, black students attempt to desegregate lunch counters	1961	*Catch-22* by Joseph Heller (1923–)
1962	Cuban missile crisis	1962	*Who's Afraid of Virginia Woolf?* by Edward Albee (1928–)
1963	November 22, JFK assassinated Nuclear test-ban treaty approved by US, USSR, and GB		
		1964	*Herzog* by Saul Bellow (1915–)
1965	March on Washington in support of equal rights for blacks Bombing of North Vietnam begins, combat troops sent in		
1966	National Organization for Women founded	1966	*The Crying of Lot 49* by Thomas Pynchon (1937–)
1968	Martin Luther King assassinated Robert Kennedy assassinated	1968	*Armies of the Night* by Norman Mailer (1923–)
1969	First moon landing	1969	*Portnoy's Complaint* by Philip Roth (1933–)
1970	Four students killed in anti-war demonstration at Kent State University		
1971	18-year-olds get the vote		
1972	Watergate break-in		
		1973	*Gravity's Rainbow* by Thomas Pynchon
1974	President Richard M. Nixon resigns		
		1977	*Song of Solomon* by Toni Morrison (1931–)
		1978	*The Dream of a Common Language* by Adrienne Rich (1929–)
1980	Iranian hostage crisis Ronald Reagan elected president	1980	*The Collected Stories* by Eudora Welty (1909–)
		1983	First complete edition of *The Maximus Poems* by Charles Olson (1910–70)
1984	Geraldine Ferraro becomes first woman nominated by a major political party for Executive Office	1984	*A Wave* by John Ashbery (1927–)

Select bibliography

This list comprises a selection of the most important critical and historical studies of American literature of the last 50 years. The one category of book to be omitted, for obvious reasons of space, is the study of an individual writer. The cut-off date is December 31, 1983. In all cases we have given details of the US publication only.

GENERAL SURVEYS

Brigham, Clarence S., *Journals and Journeymen: A Contribution to the History of Early American Newspapers*, Philadelphia: University of Pennsylvania Press, 1950, 114 pp.

Chase, Richard Volney, *The American Novel and its Tradition*, Garden City: Doubleday, 1957, 266 pp.

Cowie, Alexander, *The Rise of the American Novel*, New York: American Book, 1948, 877 pp.

Cunliffe, Marcus, *The Literature of the United States*, 1954; 3rd edn, Baltimore: Penguin Books, 1967, 409 pp.

Grimsted, David, *Melodrama Unveiled: American Theater and Culture 1800–1950*, Chicago: University of Chicago Press, 1968, 285 pp.

Howard, Leon, *Literature and the American Tradition*, New York: Doubleday, 1960, 354 pp.

Jones, Howard Mumford, *The Theory of American Literature*, 1948; rev. edn, Ithaca: Cornell University Press, 1965, 225 pp.

Lehmann-Haupt, Hellmut, et al., *The Book in America: A History of the Making and Selling of Books in the United States*, 1939; rev. edn, New York: R. R. Bowker, 1951, 493 pp.

Mott, Frank Luther, *American Journalism: A History, 1690–1960*, 1941; 3rd edn, New York: Macmillan, 1962, 901 pp.

A History of American Magazines, 5 vols.: I, *1741–1850*, New York: Appleton, 1930; II, *1850–1865*; III, *1865–1885*; IV, *1885–1905*; V, *Sketches of 21 Magazines, 1905–1930*, Cambridge, MA: Harvard University Press, 1938–68, 3,558 pp.

Parrington, Vernon Louis, *Main Currents in American Thought: An Interpretation of American Literature from the Beginnings to 1920*, 3 vols., New York: Harcourt, Brace & World, 1927–30, 1,335 pp.

Quinn, Arthur Hobson, *A History of the American Drama*, 2 Parts: *From the Beginning to the Civil War*, 1923; rev. edn, New York: Crofts, 1946, 530pp.

From the Civil War to the Present Day, 1927; rev. edn, New York: Appleton-Century-Crofts, 1936, 132pp.

Spiller, Robert E., et al., eds., *Literary History of the United States*, 3 vols., 1948; 4th edn, 2 vols., New York: Macmillan, 1974, 1,824 pp.

Stauffer, Donald Barlow, *A Short History of American Poetry*, New York: E. P. Dutton, 1974, 459 pp.

Stovall, Floyd, ed., *The Development of American Literary Criticism*, Chapel Hill: University of North Carolina Press, 1955, 262 pp.

Taylor, Walter Fuller, *The Story of American Letters*, Chicago: Henry Regnery, 1956, 504 pp.

Voss, Arthur, *The American Short Story: A Critical Survey*, Norman: University of Oklahoma Press, 1973, 399 pp.

Wagenknecht, Edward, *Cavalcade of the American Novel: From the Birth of the Nation to the Middle of the Twentieth Century*, New York: Henry Holt, 1952, 575 pp.

Waggoner, Hyatt H., *American Poets from the Puritans to the Present*, 1968; rev. edn, Baton Rouge: Louisiana State University Press, 1984, 735 pp.

Wilson, Edmund, ed., *The Shock of Recognition: The Development of Literature in the United States, Recorded by the Men Who Made It*, Garden City: Doubleday, Doran, 1943, 1,290 pp.

COLONIAL PERIOD

Aldridge, Alfred Owen, *Early American Literature: A Comparatist Approach*, Princeton: Princeton University Press, 1982, 322 pp.

Bercovitch, Sacvan, *The American Jeremiad*, Madison: University of Wisconsin Press, 1978, 239 pp.

The Puritan Origins of the American Self, New Haven: Yale University Press, 1975, 250 pp.

Caldwell, Patricia, *The Puritan Conversion Narrative: The Beginnings of American*

Expression, New York: Cambridge University Press, 1983, 210 pp.

Daly, Robert, *God's Altar: The World and the Flesh in Puritan Poetry*, Berkeley: University of California Press, 1978, 253 pp.

Davis, Richard Beale, *Intellectual Life in the Colonial South, 1585–1763*, 3 vols., Knoxville: University of Tennessee Press, 1978, 1,810 pp.

Elliott, Emory, *Power and the Pulpit in Puritan New England*, Princeton: Princeton University Press, 1975, 240 pp.

Revolutionary Writers: Literature and Authority in the New Republic, 1725–1810, New York: Oxford University Press, 1982, 324 pp.

Ellis, Joseph J., *After the Revolution: Profiles of Early American Culture*, New York: W. W. Norton, 1979, 256 pp.

Fliegelman, Jay, *Prodigals and Pilgrims: The American Revolution against Patriarchal Authority, 1750–1800*, New York: Cambridge University Press, 1982, 328 pp.

Gura, Philip F., *A Glimpse of Sion's Glory: Puritan Radicalism in New England, 1620–1660*, Middletown, CT: Wesleyan University Press, 1984, 398 pp.

Jones, Howard Mumford, *The Literature of Virginia in the Seventeenth Century*, Charlottesville: University Press of Virginia, 1968, 124 pp.

Leverenz, David, *The Language of Puritan Feeling: An Exploration in Literature, Psychology and Social History*, New Brunswick: Rutgers University Press, 1980, 346 pp.

Lowance, Mason I., *The Language of Canaan: Metaphor and Symbol in New England from the Puritans to the Transcendentalists*, Cambridge, MA: Harvard University Press, 1980, 335 pp.

Miller, Perry, *The New England Mind: From Colony to Province*, Cambridge, MA: Harvard University Press, 1953, 513 pp.

The New England Mind: The Seventeenth Century, New York: Macmillan, 1939, 528 pp.

Morison, Samuel Eliot, *The Intellectual Life of Colonial New England*, Ithaca: Cornell University Press, 1960, 288 pp.

Murdock, Kenneth, *Literature and Theology in Colonial New England*, Cambridge, MA: Harvard University Press, 1949, 235 pp.

Nye, Russel B., *American Literary History:* *1607–1830*, New York: Alfred A. Knopf, 1970, 271 pp.

Petter, Henri, *The Early American Novel*, Columbus: Ohio State University Press, 1971, 500 pp.

Rankin, Hugh F., *The Theater in Colonial America*, Chapel Hill: University of North Carolina Press, 1965, 239 pp.

Seelye, John, *Prophetic Waters: The River in Early American Life and Literature*, New York: Oxford University Press, 1977, 423 pp.

Shaw, Peter, *American Patriots and the Rituals of Revolution*, Cambridge, MA: Harvard University Press, 1981, 279 pp.

Shea, Daniel B., *Spiritual Autobiography in Early America*, Princeton: Princeton University Press, 1968, 280 pp.

Silverman, Kenneth, *A Cultural History of the American Revolution: Painting, Music, Literature, and the Theatre in the Colonies and the United States from the Treaty of Paris to the Inauguration of George Washington, 1763–1789*, New York: Thomas Y. Crowell, 1976, 699 pp.

Ziff, Larzer, *Puritanism in America: New Culture in a New World*, New York: Viking Press, 1973, 338 pp.

NINETEENTH CENTURY

Aaron, Daniel, *The Unwritten War: American Writers and the Civil War*, New York: Alfred A. Knopf, 1973, 385 pp.

Anderson, Quentin, *The Imperial Self: An Essay in American Literary and Cultural History*, New York: Alfred A. Knopf, 1971, 274 pp.

Baym, Nina, *Woman's Fiction: A Guide to Novels by and about Women in America, 1820–1870*, Ithaca: Cornell University Press, 1978, 320 pp.

Bell, Michael Davitt, *The Development of American Romance: The Sacrifice of Relation*, Chicago: University of Chicago Press, 1980, 291 pp.

Berthoff, Warner, *The Ferment of Realism: American Literature, 1884–1919*, New York: Free Press, 1965, 330 pp.

Bewley, Marius, *The Eccentric Design: Form in the Classic American Novel*, New York: Columbia University Press, 1959, 327 pp.

Brooks, Van Wyck, *The Times of Melville and*

Whitman, New York: E. P. Dutton, 1947, 489 pp.

Buell, Lawrence, *Literary Transcendentalism: Style and Vision in the American Renaissance*, Ithaca: Cornell University Press, 1973, 336 pp.

Cady, Edwin H., *The Light of Common Day: Realism in American Fiction*, Bloomington: Indiana University Press, 1971, 224 pp.

Callow, James T., *Kindred Spirits: Knickerbocker Writers and American Artists, 1807–1855*, Chapel Hill: University of North Carolina Press, 1967, 287 pp.

Carter, Everett, *The American Idea: The Literary Response to American Optimism*, Chapel Hill: University of North Carolina Press, 1977, 276 pp.

Charvat, William, *Literary Publishing in America 1790–1850*, Philadelphia: University of Pennsylvania Press, 1959, 94 pp.

Cooley, Thomas, *Educated Lives: The Rise of Modern Autobiography in America*, Columbus: Ohio State University Press, 1976, 190 pp.

Dormon, James H., Jr, *Theater in the Ante Bellum South, 1815–1861*, Chapel Hill: University of North Carolina Press, 1967, 322 pp.

Douglas, Ann, *The Feminization of American Culture*, New York: Alfred A. Knopf, 1977, 403 pp.

Eakin, Paul John, *The New England Girl: Cultural Ideals in Hawthorne, Stowe, Howells and James*, Athens: University of Georgia Press, 1976, 252 pp.

Franklin, H. Bruce, *Future Perfect: American Science Fiction of the Nineteenth Century*, 1966; rev. edn, New York: Oxford University Press, 1978, 404 pp.

Fryer, Judith, *The Faces of Eve: Women in the Nineteenth-Century American Novel*, New York: Oxford University Press, 1976, 294 pp.

Fussell, Edwin, *Frontier: American Literature and the American West*, Princeton: Princeton University Press, 1965, 450 pp.

Gura, Philip F., *The Wisdom of Words: Language, Theology, and Literature in the New England Renaissance*, Middletown, CT: Wesleyan University Press, 1981, 203 pp.

Havens, Daniel F., *The Columbian Muse of Comedy: The Development of a Native Tradition in Early American Social Comedy, 1787–1845*, Carbondale: Southern Illinois University Press, 1973, 181 pp.

Hoffman, Daniel G., *Form and Fable in American Fiction*, New York: Oxford University Press, 1961, 368 pp.

Kaplan, Harold, *Democratic Humanism and American Literature*, Chicago: University of Chicago Press, 1972, 298 pp.

Kaul, A. N., *The American Vision: Actual and Ideal Society in Nineteenth-Century Fiction*, New Haven: Yale University Press, 1963, 340 pp.

Knight, Grant C., *The Critical Period in American Literature*, Chapel Hill: University of North Carolina Press, 1951, 208 pp.

Kolb, Harold H., Jr, *The Illusion of Life: American Realism as a Literary Form*, Charlottesville: University Press of Virginia, 1969, 180 pp.

Levin, Harry, *The Power of Blackness: Hawthorne, Poe, Melville*, New York: Alfred A. Knopf, 1958, 263 pp.

Lewis, R. W. B., *The American Adam: Innocence, Tragedy and Tradition in the Nineteenth Century*, Chicago: University of Chicago Press, 1959, 205 pp.

Martin, Jay, *Harvest of Change: American Literature 1865–1914*, Englewood Cliffs: Prentice-Hall, 1967, 382 pp.

Matthiessen, Francis Otto, *American Renaissance: Art and Expression in the Age of Emerson and Whitman*, New York: Oxford University Press, 1941, 678 pp.

Miller, Perry, *The Raven and the Whale: The War of Words and Wits in the Era of Poe and Melville*, New York: Harcourt, Brace, 1956, 370 pp.

Mitchell, Lee Clark, *Witnesses to a Vanishing America: The Nineteenth-Century Response*, Princeton: Princeton University Press, 1981, 320 pp.

Pizer, Donald, *Realism and Naturalism in Nineteenth-Century American Literature*, Carbondale: Southern Illinois University Press, 1966, 176 pp.

Pritchard, John Paul, *Return to the Fountains: Some Classical Sources of American Criticism*, Durham: Duke University Press, 1942, 271 pp.

Reynolds, David S., *Faith in Fiction: The Emergence of Religious Literature in America*, Cambridge, MA: Harvard University Press, 1981, 269 pp.

Richardson, Robert D., Jr, *Myth and Literature*

in the American Renaissance, Bloomington: Indiana University Press, 1978, 309 pp.

Ridgely, J. V., *Nineteenth-Century Southern Literature*, Lexington: University Press of Kentucky, 1980, 128 pp.

Smith, Henry Nash, *Democracy and the Novel: Popular Resistance to Classic American Writers*, New York: Oxford University Press, 1978, 204 pp.

    Virgin Land: The American West as Symbol and Myth, Cambridge, MA: Harvard University Press, 1950, 305 pp.

Stern, Madeleine B., ed., *Publishers for Mass Entertainment in Nineteenth Century America*, Boston: G. K. Hall, 1980, 358 pp.

Sundquist, Eric J., *Home as Found: Authority and Genealogy in Nineteenth-Century American Literature*, Baltimore: The Johns Hopkins University Press, 1979, 209 pp.

    ed., *American Realism: New Essays*, Baltimore: The Johns Hopkins University Press, 1982, 298 pp.

Taylor, Gordon O., *The Passages of Thought: Psychological Representation in the American Novel 1870–1900*, New York: Oxford University Press, 1969, 172 pp.

Wilson, Edmund, *Patriotic Gore: Studies in the Literature of the American Civil War*, New York: Oxford University Press, 1962, 816 pp.

Ziff, Larzer, *The American 1890s: Life and Times of a Lost Generation*, New York: Viking Press, 1966, 376 pp.

    Literary Democracy: The Declaration of Cultural Independence in America, New York: Viking Press, 1981, 333 pp.

TWENTIETH CENTURY

Aaron, Daniel, *Writers on the Left: Episodes in American Literary Communism*, New York: Harcourt, Brace & World, 1961, 460 pp.

Abramson, Doris E., *Negro Playwrights in the American Theater 1925–1959*, New York: Columbia University Press, 1969, 335 pp.

Aldridge, John W., *In Search of Heresy: American Literature in an Age of Conformity*, New York: McGraw-Hill, 1956, 210 pp.

Alvarez, A., *Stewards of Excellence: Studies in Modern English and American Poets*, New York: Charles Scribner's Sons, 1958, 191 pp.

Bentley, Eric, *The Dramatic Event: An Ameri-can Chronicle*, New York: Horizon Press, 1954, 278 pp.

Bigsby, C. W. E., *A Critical Introduction to Twentieth-Century American Drama*, 2 vols.: I, *1900–1940*; II, *Tennessee Williams, Arthur Miller, Edward Albee*, New York: Cambridge University Press, 1982–4, 697 pp.

Blackmur, R. P., *The Double Agent: Essays in Craft and Elucidation*, New York: Arrow, 1935, 302 pp.

Blotner, Joseph, *The Modern American Political Novel, 1900–1960*, Austin: University of Texas Press, 1966, 424 pp.

Bradbury, John M., *The Fugitives: A Critical Account*, Chapel Hill: University of North Carolina Press, 1958, 300 pp.

Cambon, Glauco, *The Inclusive Flame: Studies in American Poetry*, Bloomington: Indiana University Press, 1963, 248 pp.

Clurman, Harold, *The Fervent Years: The Story of the Group Theatre and the Thirties*, New York: Alfred A. Knopf, 1945, 298 pp.

Coffman, Stanley K., Jr, *Imagism: A Chapter for the History of Modern Poetry*, Norman: University of Oklahoma Press, 1951, 235 pp.

Conn, Peter, *The Divided Mind: Ideology and Imagination in America, 1898–1917*, New York: Cambridge University Press, 1983, 358 pp.

Cook, Bruce, *The Beat Generation*, New York: Charles Scribner's Sons, 1971, 248 pp.

Cooperman, Stanley, *World War I and the American Novel*, Baltimore: The Johns Hopkins University Press, 1967, 271 pp.

Cowan, Louise, *The Fugitive Group: A Literary History*, Baton Rouge: Louisiana State University Press, 1959, 277 pp.

Cowley, Malcolm, *Exile's Return: A Literary Odyssey of the 1920s*, New York: W. W. Norton, 1934, 322 pp.

    A Second Flowering: Works and Days of the Lost Generation, New York: Viking Press, 1973, 276 pp.

    Think Back On Us: A Contemporary Chronicle of the 1930s, ed. with an introduction by Henry Dan Piper, Carbondale: Southern Illinois University Press, 1967, 400 pp.

    ed., *After the Genteel Tradition: American Writers Since 1910*, New York: W. W. Norton, 1937, 270 pp.

Dembo, L. S., *Conceptions of Reality in Modern*

American Poetry, Berkeley: University of California Press, 1966, 248 pp.

Downer, Alan S., *Fifty Years of American Drama, 1900–1950*, Chicago: Henry Regnery, 1951, 158 pp.

Earnest, Ernest, *The Single Vision: The Alienation of American Intellectuals*, New York: New York University Press, 1970, 241 pp.

Eisinger, Chester E., *Fiction of the Forties*, Chicago: University of Chicago Press, 1963, 392 pp.

Fabre, Geneviève, *Drumbeats, Masks and Metaphor: Contemporary Afro-American Theatre*, transl. by Melvin Dixon, Cambridge, MA: Harvard University Press, 1983, 274 pp.

French, Warren, *The Social Novel at the End of an Era*, Carbondale: Southern Illinois University Press, 1966, 212 pp.

Frohock, W. M., *The Novel of Violence in America*, 1950; rev. edn, Dallas: Southern Methodist University Press, 1957, 238 pp.

Geismer, Maxwell, *American Moderns: From Rebellion to Conformity*, New York: Hill and Wang, 1958, 265 pp.

The Last of the Provincials: The American Novel, 1915–1925. Boston: Houghton Mifflin, 1947, 404 pp.

Writers in Crisis: The American Novel, 1925–1940, Boston: Houghton Mifflin, 1942, 308 pp.

Girgus, Sam B., *The Law of the Heart: Individualism and the Modern Self in American Literature*, Austin: University of Texas Press, 1979, 192 pp.

Golden, Joseph, *The Death of Tinker Bell: The American Theatre in the Twentieth Century*, Syracuse: Syracuse University Press, 1967, 181 pp.

Goldstein, Malcolm, *The Political Stage: American Drama and Theater of the Great Depression*, New York: Oxford University Press, 1974, 482 pp.

Gregory, Horace and Marya Zaturenska, *A History of American Poetry, 1900–1940*, New York: Harcourt, Brace, 1946, 524 pp.

Hassan, Ihab, *Radical Innocence: Studies in the Contemporary American Novel*, Princeton: Princeton University Press, 1961, 362 pp.

Himelstein, Morgan Y., *Drama was a Weapon: The Left-Wing Theatre in New York, 1929–1941*, New Brunswick: Rutgers University Press, 1963, 300 pp.

Hoffman, Frederick J., *The Art of Southern Fiction: A Study of Some Modern Novelists*, Carbondale: Southern Illinois University Press, 1967, 198 pp.

Freudianism and the Literary Mind, 1945; rev. edn, Baton Rouge: Louisiana State University Press, 1957, 350 pp.

Hoffman, Fredrick J., Charles Allen, and Carolyn F. Ulrich, *The Little Magazine: A History and a Bibliography*, Princeton: Princeton University Press, 1947, 450 pp.

Hyman, Stanley Edgar, *The Armed Vision: A Study in the Methods of Modern Literary Criticism*, 1948; rev. edn, New York: Vintage Books, 1955, 402 pp.

Karl, Frederick, *American Fictions, 1940–1980: A Comprehensive History and Critical Evaluation*, New York: Harper & Row, 1983, 637 pp.

Kazin, Alfred, *Bright Book of Life: American Novelists & Storytellers from Hemingway to Mailer*, Boston: Little, Brown, 1973, 334 pp.

On Native Grounds: An Interpretation of Modern American Prose Literature, New York: Reynal and Hitchcock, 1942, 541 pp.

Kenner, Hugh, *A Homemade World: The American Modernist Writers*, New York: Alfred A. Knopf, 1975, 221 pp.

King, Richard H., *A Southern Renaissance: The Cultural Awakening of the American South, 1930–1955*, New York: Oxford University Press, 1980, 350 pp.

Klein, Marcus, *After Alienation: American Novels in Mid-Century*, Cleveland: World Publishing, 1962, 307 pp.

Foreigners: The Making of American Literature, 1900–1940, Chicago: University of Chicago Press, 1981, 332 pp.

Klinkowitz, Jerome, *Literary Disruptions: The Making of a Post-Contemporary American Fiction*, 1975; rev. edn, Urbana: University of Illinois Press, 1980, 296 pp.

Knight, Grant C., *The Strenuous Age in American Literature*, Chapel Hill: University of North Carolina Press, 1954, 270 pp.

Kramer, Dale, *Chicago Renaissance: The Literary Life in the Midwest, 1900–1930*, New York: Appleton-Century, 1966, 369 pp.

Krutch, Joseph Wood, *The American Drama Since 1918: An Informal History*, 1939; rev. edn, New York: Braziller, 1957, 344 pp.

Lipton, Lawrence, *The Holy Barbarians*, New York: Messner, 1959, 318 pp.

Love, Glen A., *New Americans: The Westerner and the Modern Experience in the American Novel*, Lewisburg, PA: Bucknell University Press, 1982, 265 pp.

Lynn, Kenneth S., *The Dream of Success: A Study of the Modern American Imagination*, Boston: Atlantic/Little, Brown, 1955, 269 pp.

McCormick, John, *The Middle Distance: A Comparative History of American Imaginative Literature: 1919–1932*, New York: Free Press, 1971, 256 pp.

Malin, Irving, *Jews and Americans*, Carbondale: Southern Illinois University Press, 1965, 193 pp.

Margolies, Edward, *Native Sons: A Critical Study of Twentieth-Century Negro American Authors*, Philadelphia: Lippincott, 1968, 210 pp.

Mazzaro, Jerome, *Postmodern American Poetry*, Urbana: University of Illinois Press, 1980, 203 pp.

Millgate, Michael, *American Social Fiction: James to Cozzens*, New York: Barnes and Noble, 1965, 217 pp.

Peden, William, *The American Short Story: Front Line in the National Defense of Literature*, 1964; 2nd edn, revised, enlarged, and with new title, *The American Short Story: Continuity and Change, 1940–1975*, Boston: Houghton Mifflin, 1975, 215 pp.

Rideout, Walter B., *The Radical Novel in the United States 1900–1954: Some Interrelations of Literature and Society*, Cambridge, MA: Harvard University Press, 1956, 339 pp.

Scholes, Robert, *The Fabulators*, New York: Oxford University Press, 1967, 180 pp.

Straumann, Heinrich, *American Literature in the Twentieth Century*, 1951; rev. edn, New York: Harper Torchbooks, 1965, 224 pp.

Tanner, Tony, *City of Words: American Fiction 1950–1970*, New York: Harper & Row, 1971, 463 pp.

Thorp, Willard, *American Writing in the Twentieth Century*, Cambridge, MA: Harvard University Press, 1960, 353 pp.

Vendler, Helen, *Part of Nature, Part of Us: Modern American Poets*, Cambridge, MA: Harvard University Press, 1980, 376 pp.

Waggoner, Hyatt, H., *The Heel of Elohim: Science and Values in Modern American Poetry*, Norman: University of Oklahoma Press, 1950, 235 pp.

Weales, Gerald, *American Drama Since World War II*, New York: Harcourt, Brace & World, 1962, 246 pp.

Webster, Grant, *The Republic of Letters: A History of Postwar American Literary Opinion*, Baltimore: The Johns Hopkins University Press, 1979, 38 pp.

Wickes, George, *Americans in Paris*, Garden City, NY: Doubleday, 1969, 290 pp.

Wilson, Edmund, *The American Earthquake: A Documentary of the Twenties and Thirties*, New York: Doubleday, 1958, 576 pp.

   The Bit Between My Teeth: A Literary Chronicle of 1950–1965, New York: Farrar, Straus, 1965, 694 pp.

   Classics and Commercials: A Literary Chronicle of the Forties, New York: Farrar, Straus, 1950, 534 pp.

Young, Thomas Daniel, *The Past in the Present: A Thematic Study of Modern Southern Fiction*, Baton Rouge: Louisiana State University Press, 1981, 189 pp.

THEMES

Allen, Paula Gunn, ed., *Studies in American Indian Literature: Critical Essays and Course Designs*, New York: Modern Language Association of America, 1983, 384 pp.

Baker, Houston A., Jr, *The Journey Back: Issues in Black Literature and Criticism*, Chicago: University of Chicago Press, 1980, 198 pp.

Banta, Martha, *Failure and Success in America: A Literary Debate*, Princeton: Princeton University Press, 1978, 568 pp.

Blair, Walter and Hamlin Hill, eds., *America's Humor: From Poor Richard to Doonesbury*, New York: Oxford University Press, 1978, 559 pp.

Bone, Robert, *The Negro Novel in America*, 1958; rev. edn, New Haven: Yale University Press, 1965, 289 pp.

Bowden, Edwin T., *The Dungeon of the Heart: Human Isolation and the American Novel*, New York: Macmillan, 1961, 175 pp.

Charvat, William, *The Profession of Authorship in America, 1800–1870; the Papers of William Charvat*, ed. Matthew J. Bruccoli, Columbus: Ohio State University Press, 1968, 327 pp.

Feidelson, Charles, Jr, *Symbolism and American Literature*, Chicago: University of Chicago Press, 1953, 355 pp.

Fiedler, Leslie A., *Love and Death in the Ameri-*

can Novel, 1960; rev. edn, New York: Stein and Day, 1966, 512 pp.

The Return of the Vanishing American, New York: Stein and Day, 1968, 192 pp.

Franklin, H. Bruce, *The Victim as Criminal and Artist: Literature from the American Prison*, New York: Oxford University Press, 1978, 337 pp.

Gunn, Giles, *The Interpretation of Otherness: Literature, Religion, and the American Imagination*, New York: Oxford University Press, 1979, 250 pp.

Guttman, Allen, *The Conservative Tradition in America*, New York: Oxford University Press, 1967, 214 pp.

The Jewish Writer in America: Assimilation and the Crisis of Identity, New York: Oxford University Press, 1971, 256 pp.

Hicks, Granville, *The Great Tradition: An Interpretation of American Literature since the Civil War*, 1933; rev. edn, New York: Macmillan, 1935, 341 pp.

Hubbell, Jay B., *The South in American Literature: 1607–1900*, Durham: Duke University Press, 1954, 987 pp.

Kolodny, Annette, *The Lay of the Land: Metaphor as Experience and History in American Life and Letters.* Chapel Hill: University of North Carolina Press, 1975, 185 pp.

The Land Before Then: Fantasy and Experience of the American Frontier, 1630–1860, Chapel Hill: University of North Carolina Press, 1984, 293 pp.

Krause, Sydney J., *Essays on Determinism in American Literature*, Kent, OH: Kent State University Press, 1964, 116 pp.

Lawrence, D. H., *Studies in Classic American Literature*, New York: Seltzer, 1923, 264 pp.

Lease, Benjamin, *Anglo-American Encounters: England and the Rise of American Literature*, New York: Cambridge University Press, 1981, 299 pp.

Lindberg, Gary, *The Confidence Man in American Literature*, New York: Oxford University Press, 1982, 319 pp.

Marx, Leo, *The Machine in the Garden: Technology and the Pastoral Ideal*, New York: Oxford University Press, 1964, 392 pp.

Maxwell, D. E. S., *American Fiction: The Intellectual Background*, New York: Columbia University Press, 1963, 306 pp.

Mencken, H. L., *The American Language*, 4th edn, New York: Alfred A. Knopf, 1937, 798 pp.

Mizener, Arthur, *The Sense of Life in the Modern Novel*, Boston: Houghton Mifflin, 1963, 291 pp.

Pearce, Roy Harvey, *The Continuity of American Poetry*, Princeton: Princeton University Press, 1961, 442 pp.

Persons, Stow, *The Decline of American Gentility*, New York: Columbia University Press, 1973, 336 pp.

Poirier, Richard, *The Performing Self: Compositions and Decompositions in the Languages of Contemporary Life*, New York: Oxford University Press, 1971, 203 pp.

Rahv, Philip, *Literature and the Sixth Sense*, Boston: Houghton Mifflin, 1969, 445 pp.

Rosenblatt, Roger, *Black Fiction*, Cambridge, MA: Harvard University Press, 1974, 211 pp.

Rourke, Constance, *American Humor: A Study of the National Character*, New York: Harcourt, Brace, 1931, 324 pp.

Rubin, Louis D., Jr, ed., *The Comic Imagination in American Literature*, New Brunswick: Rutgers University Press, 1973, 430 pp.

Santayana, George, *The Genteel Tradition: Nine Essays*, ed. Douglas L. Wilson, Cambridge, MA: Harvard University Press, 1967, 201 pp.

Simpson, Lewis P., *The Brazen Face of History: Studies in the Literary Consciousness in America*, Baton Rouge: Louisiana State University Press, 1980, 276 pp.

Slotkin, Richard, *Regeneration through Violence: The Mythology of the American Frontier, 1600–1860*, Middletown, CT: Wesleyan University Press, 1973, 670 pp.

Spencer, Benjamin, *The Quest for Nationality: An American Literary Campaign*, Syracuse: Syracuse University Press, 1957, 389 pp.

Spender, Stephen, *Love-Hate Relations: English and American Sensibilities*, New York: Random House, 1974, 318 pp.

Stepto, Robert, *From Behind the Veil: A Study of Afro-American Narrative*, Urbana: University of Illinois Press, 1979, 203 pp.

Stewart, Randall, *American Literature and Christian Doctrine*, Baton Rouge: Louisiana State University Press, 1958, 154 pp.

Strout, Cushing, *The Veracious Imagination: Essays on American History, Literature, and Biography*, Middletown, CT: Wesleyan University Press, 1981, 301 pp.

Tanner, Tony, *The Reign of Wonder: Naivety and Reality in American Literature*, New

York: Cambridge University Press, 1965, 388 pp.

Tichi, Cecelia, *New World, New Earth: Environmental Reform in American Literature from the Puritans Through Whitman*, New Haven: Yale University Press, 1979, 290 pp.

Trilling, Lionel, *The Liberal Imagination: Essays on Literature and Society*, New York: Viking Press, 1950, 303 pp.

Tuttleton, James W., *The Novel of Manners in America*, Chapel Hill: University of North Carolina Press, 1972, 304 pp.

Wadlington, Warwick, *The Confidence Game in American Literature*, Princeton: Princeton University Press, 1975, 321 pp.

Waggoner, Hyatt H., *American Visionary Poetry*, Baton Rouge: Louisiana State University Press, 1982, 226 pp.

Walcutt, Charles Child, *American Literary Naturalism: A Divided Stream*, Minneapolis: University of Minnesota Press, 1956, 332 pp.

Winters, Yvor, *In Defense of Reason*, Denver: Swallow, 1947, 611 pp.